FOLK PSYCHOLOGY
AND THE
PHILOSOPHY OF MIND

FOLK PSYCHOLOGY
AND THE
PHILOSOPHY OF MIND

Edited by

Scott M. Christensen
Dale R. Turner
University of California, Riverside

 LAWRENCE ERLBAUM ASSOCIATES, PUBLISHERS
1993   Hillsdale, New Jersey   Hove and London

Lawrence Erlbaum Associates, Inc., Publishers
365 Broadway
Hillsdale, New Jersey 07642

Library of Congress Cataloging-in-Publication Data

Folk psychology and the philosophy of mind/ edited by Scott M.
Christensen & Dale R. Turner.
p. cm.
Includes bibliographical references and index.
ISBN 0-8058-0931-7
1. Philosophy of mind. 2. Ethnopsychology. 3. Mind and body.
I. Christensen, Scott M. II. Turner, Dale R.
BD418.3.F65 1993
128'.2—dc20   92'19886
                                                             CIP

Books published by Lawrence Erlbaum Associates are printed on acid-free paper, and their
bindings are chosen for strength and durability.

Printed in the United States of America
10 9 8 7 6 5 4 3 2 1

For Our Folks

Contents

Contributors

A. A. Abrahamsen
Department of Psychology
Georgia State University

William P. Bechtel
Department of Philosophy
Georgia State University

Paul M. Churchland
Department of Philosophy
University of California, San Diego

Daniel C. Dennett
Department of Philosophy
Tufts University

Paul Feyerabend
Department of Philosophy
University of California, Berkeley

Jerry A. Fodor
Department of Philosophy
The Graduate Center, CUNY

Joseph Garon
Department of Philosophy
University of California, San Diego

George Graham
Department of Philosophy
University of Alabama

John Haldane
Department of Moral Philosophy
University of Saint Andrews
Scotland

Terence Horgan
Department of Philosophy
Memphis State University

Robert N. McCauley
Department of Philosophy
Emory University

Gerald J. O'Brien
Department of Philosophy
The University of Adelaide
South Australia

William Ramsey
Department of Philosophy
University of Notre Dame

Richard Rorty
University of Virginia,
   Charlottesville

Robert A. Sharpe
Department of Philosophy
Saint David's University College
University of Wales

Stephen P. Stich
Department of Philosophy
Rutgers, The State University of
   New Jersey

Kathleen V. Wilkes
Department of Philosophy
St. Hilda's College
Oxford University

James Woodward
Division of Human and
   Social Science
California Institute of Technology

Acknowledgments

To all our contributors for their courteous and speedy responses, and helpful suggestions, many of which we incorporated for the betterment of our anthology. To Deidra Price, Vicki Rickard, Gretchen Cheney, and Cindy Teagarden in the UCR Philosophy Department Office. To Allison Shalinsky, in whose seminar this anthology was originally conceived. To John Fischer for his encouragement and for imparting his experience in assembling fine anthologies. To Alex Rosenberg for his multifaceted support. To William Bechtel for recommending LEA to us, and us to them. To See's Coffee, where this anthology was conceived and gestated, for tolerating us. To Michelle Barber for help in compiling the bibliography. To Judith Amsel, Amy Peirce and Kathy Dolan at LEA for patiently guiding us in our first anthology. To Bernd Magnus and the staff of the Center for Ideas and Society for their kindness and technical support. To David Barlow, David Depew, John Fischer, Alex Rosenberg, and Larry Wright for reading and commenting on drafts of our project and for moral support. Finally, we would give a special thanks to Karen Yun and Dolores Reza for their support and encouragement.

Introduction

Scott M. Christensen and Dale R. Turner
University of California, Riverside

They can trace everything you say, do and feel to the number of molecules in a certain region.

What happens to good and evil in this system? Passion, envy and hate? Do they become a tangle of neurons? Are you telling me that a whole tradition of human failings is now at an end, that cowardice, sadism, molestation are meaningless terms? Are we being asked to regard these things nostalgically? What about murderous rage? A murderer used to have a certain fearsome size to him. His crime was large. What happens when we reduce it to cells and molecules? (p. 200)[1]

WHY THE FUSS ABOUT FOLK?

Our everyday life is infused with talk about our mental states. For example:

- Tonight I wish to go to a fine restaurant, where I believe I will be greeted by a polite host, and where I hope to eat a delicious meal.
- I am concerned that he fears going to the grocery store after school.
- When I asked my fiance to marry me, I hoped that she would say yes. Given everything that I knew about her — her attitudes about marriage and attitudes about me — I also believed that she would say "yes."

---

[1]Delillo, D. (1984). *White noise.* New York: Penguin Books.

In order to communicate with each other, we employ this kind of "talk" all the time. When we want to tell someone how we feel, what we think, and what we want, we have recourse to the concepts that constitute what some philosophers like to call *folk psychology.*

Just what is this thing called folk psychology? This is one of the questions that most of the authors in this anthology will try to answer (see especially Graham & Sharpe, this volume). It is an important question because the way one defines folk psychology influences one's views about its importance and viability. So our introduction must begin with a discussion of folk psychology in order to explain what all the fuss is about.

Briefly, folk psychology is the tag given to ordinary talk about the mind. It does not refer to talk about the biology of the brain and central nervous system; rather it refers to talk about beliefs and desires, intentions and fears, wishes and hopes. It is essentially the vocabulary we use to talk about and explain ourselves and others. It is the vocabulary of the mental.

What is at issue in the debate represented in this antholoy is the status of this vocabulary — the status of folk psychology. How could anyone question the importance of folk psychology? The terms of folk psychology provide us with what seems to be a very efficient method of understanding and predicting behavior. Consider the following example:

> One can explain why I asked my fiance to marry me by making reference to a host of beliefs and desires I have concerning her and marriage. Moreover, one can use these concepts in making predictions about future behavior. Knowing that I want to marry my fiance and that she wants to marry me allows us to predict that, other things being equal, I will say the words "I do" in a wedding ceremony sometime in the foreseeable future.

Folk psychology allows us to communicate with one another, it allows us to explain and understand ourselves as well as others, and it allows us to make fairly reliable predictions about the behavior of ourselves and others. These are impressive achievements for any vocabulary, so why all the fuss?

To understand the controversy concerning the status of folk psychology, it will be helpful to consider the origin of the name. Folk psychology, also called common sense psychology, was christened with this perhaps tendentious title by those who regard the vocabulary of the mental as belonging to an outdated, prescientific view of the world. Folk psychology has been around, almost unchanged for at least two thousand years. So, some philosophers argue that folk psychology shares the same conceptual space as other 'folk' models, such as folk physics. A brief discussion of folk physics will make it clear why some philosophers (most notably Wilkes, this volume) are appalled by the radical claim that folk psychology is no different from other folk theories.

Our naive conception of the physical world, our intuitions about physical objects, do not match up very neatly with the scientific understanding of the physical world provided by modern physics. For example, instead of using the Newtonian paradigm to understand how physical bodies move through space, most of us apply a model resembling Aristotelian physics and impetus theory. These common sense intuitions lead, not merely to misconceptions of hypothetical situations, but alterations in actual behavior. Aristotelian mechanics implies that, in order to remain in motion, a projectile must continually be caused to do so via an external force; in impetus theory, a projectile acquires an internal disposition to continue moving. Newton explained, however, that an object moving through space continues to do so until acted upon by some external force: "Every body persists in its state of rest or of uniform motion in a straight line unless it is compelled to change that state by forces impressed on it" (McCloskey, 1983). Folk physics, the name given to this "set" of naive intuitions concerning the motions of bodies through space, works relatively well as long as we do not need to be very accurate. In other words, unless you need to know how far a projectile will move through space before it hits the ground, folk physics will work just fine. However, when prediction and accuracy become important, folk physics loses ground to modern physics and science. And when "truth" becomes a paramount virtue, folk physics simply becomes antiquated superstition.

Now it should be obvious why many philosophers attack the claim that folk psychology occupies the same conceptual space as folk physics. For if this claim is true, it seems that folk psychology should share the same fate as folk physics: replacement by a mature scientific (i.e., testable) theory. Just as folk physics was replaced by Newtonian physics, so folk psychology should be replaced by a truly scientific theory of the mind. The reason: Just as the concepts of folk physics do not correspond with the physical world, the concepts of folk psychology—belief, desire, hope, fear, passion, envy, hate, and so forth—do not correspond to anything that goes on in our heads. The common sense notions of folk psychology have no bearing on the real world; therefore, they cannot play any role in a truly scientific account of the mind.

This is what is at stake. Most philosophers take the common sense talk about the mind to be folk psychology, just as they take common sense talk about moving objects to be folk physics. If folk psychology and folk physics are nothing more than outdated, pretheoretic attempts to understand the mind and the world respectively, then at best we should expect a reduction of the vocabulary of folk theories to the vocabulary of mature scientific theories, and it is more likely still that the fate of the folk is a complete replacement of the vocabulary of folk psychology with a scientific vocabulary of the brain and central nervous system.

A PHILOSOPHICAL ROADMAP

Now that we have introduced the notion of folk psychology, let us provide a brief tour of the philosophical landscape regarding the various positions philosophers can take on the status of folk psychology.

We will begin by granting, for the moment, that folk psychology is, in fact, a theory (see especially Sharpe and Wilkes, this volume, for arguments against this presupposition). If we accept this claim, it looks as though there are three possible positions one can take concerning the future of folk psychology. First, one could argue that the theory embedded in folk psychology will be reduced to a lower level neurobiological theory. If this turns out to be the case, and many philosophers in the past have thought that it will, the mind reduces to, or is identical with, the brain, and the terms of folk psychology will be defined in terms of the lower level theory it reduces to.

Second, one could argue that no such reduction is possible, or for that matter desirable; because talk about the mind explains little or nothing about the workings of the brain or even psychological processes, such as memory, the best course of action with respect to folk psychology is simply to dispense with it altogether. Those who take this position are eliminativists. *Eliminative materialism* is, hence, the position that, although folk psychology cannot be reduced to neurobiology, it should nevertheless be purged from our vocabulary because it is bereft of explanatory power. Of course the eliminativist presupposes that science provides the best, if not the only, explanation of psychological phenomena, and, therefore, if folk psychology cannot be neatly integrated into the rest of science, it has no legitimate role to play in the explanation of behavior and mental processes.

As previously mentioned, reduction and elimination spell bad news for the defenders of "folk." However, there is a view one can adopt that is not hostile to folk psychology: *functionalism*. Like the eliminative materialist, the functionalist claims that a reduction of folk psychology to some lower level theory is not likely, but the functionalist draws a very different moral from this conclusion. The functionalist holds that reduction is not likely because folk psychology forms the basis of a rigorous science of the mind that is situated at an autonomous level of discourse between the social and the biological sciences.

All three of these positions on the future of the folk result from their views on the likelihood of a reduction of folk psychology to some lower level theory. So, before spending some time discussing the virtues and vices of identity theory, eliminative materialsm, and functionalism, a word about the notion of reduction is in order.

INTERTHEORETIC RELATIONS:
"HAVE YOU LOST YOUR MIND?"

The history of science is littered with examples of what look like the reduction of one theory to another. The reduction of thermodynamics to statistical mechanics and of optics to electromagnetic theory, for example, are paradigms of reduction in science. But what is the point of reduction? How does reduction in science work?

Let us answer the first question first. The hope for reduction is fueled by the desire, on the part of scientists and philosophers alike, to provide a simple unified account of the natural world. When one theory is reduced to another, its *ontology* — the theoretical entities it postulates — reduces to, or is equated with the ontology of the reducing theory; thus, we can dispense with the ontology of the reduced theory. The result of reduction, then, is ontological housecleaning; the number of things in the universe is reduced, and the universe is simpler and more understandable because a smaller number of basic entities explains more of the natural world than before the reduction.

The traditional model of reduction (see Nagel, 1961) holds that the reduction of one theory to a lower level theory is accomplished only if both theories satisfy a strict set of constraints that insure that the reducing and reduced theories are compatible. Compatibility is the key, for if the two theories are not compatible, the proposed reduction is not possible and the ontological housekeeping is kept to a minimum. Reduction occurs when the principles, laws, and phenomena described by the to-be-reduced theory are deductively entailed by the reducing theory.

Recently Hooker (1981a, 1981b, & 1981c) and others have reformulated the notion of intertheoretic reduction. They have dropped the positivist's picture that science is a strictly accumulative endeavor and incorporated Kuhn's insights on the dynamic aspects of theory change.

Intertheoretic reduction is first and foremost a relationship between theories. Moreover, a phenomenon is said to be reduced to a lower level phenomenon by virtue of the fact that the relevant theories have been reduced. How is the new view of intertheoretic relations different from the view held by the logical positivists? The basic problem with the positivist's view is that it pictures reduction as a clean and tidy affair at the expense of the dynamic aspect of scientific change. This results in the positivist's failing to account for the fact that, even in the best cases, reduction never occurs without significant revisions in the to-be-reduced theory. Only after the to-be-reduced theory has been corrected is it in a form that allows it to be derived from the lower level theory.

Hooker injects the dynamic aspect of scientific change into an account of reduction. One theory is reduced to another theory by first correcting the to-be-reduced theory and then showing how this "new" theory is deductively entailed by the lower level theory. Of course, to-be-reduced theories all fall on a continuum according to how much they need to be corrected in order to make the reduction possible. Some theories only require relatively small corrections (e.g., theory of optics), whereas others require such large-scale and fundamental corrections that the resulting corrected theory is no longer isomorphic with the original theory (e.g., witchcraft theory of disease). In the latter cases, Hooker, following Kuhn, suggests that the old higher level theory is simply displaced by the new more powerful lower level theory. Reduction in the traditional sense is not possible. However, the fact that a higher level theory is not reducible to a lower level theory does not necessarily mean that there are two levels of reality; rather, it may just mean that the higher level theory is simply false and should be replaced by a new theory. Remember, Hooker suggests that the amount of correction needed depends on the particular theories involved and thus there is a continuum at one end of which lie theories that require little correction, and, at the other end, lie theories that need so much correction that they are incommensurable with the reducing theory and need to be replaced.

An example will make this conception of reduction clearer. The reduction of Aristotelian mechanics to Newtonian mechanics lies at the low end of the coninuum. As we have already seen, the cornerstone of Aristotle's view is that an object will stay in motion if, and only if, a force is continually applied to keep it in motion. To account for projectile motion, physicists suggested that an internal force, an impetus, was imparted to the projectile and that the projectile continued in motion until the impetus dissipated. Furthermore, impetus theory held that there was no difference between rectilinear and curvilinear motion.

Impetus theory was not neatly reduced to Newtonian mechanics. Rather, it was replaced by Newtonian mechanics. Why was it that impetus theory couldn't be corrected and then reduced to Newtonian mechanics? The biggest stumbling block for such a move is that there simply is no such thing as impetus in the Newtonian theory of motion, so there is nothing to identify impetus with and nothing to reduce it to. The Newtonian theory provides a deeper understanding of the world and allows for far greater predictive power than its predecessor. So in this case it seems perfectly reasonable to say that impetus theory is just plain false and should be replaced by, not reduced to, Newtonian mechanics.

So we have seen intertheoretic reduction in action. Of course, there are examples of smooth reductions in which the to-be-reduced theory is left fairly unscathed (e.g., the reduction of optics to electromagnetic theory). But the present example brings to the fore several points that are worth mentioning.

First, impetus theory is a folk theory. So if our mental talk constitutes a folk theory of the mind, the replacement of impetus theory by a more 'scientific' theory provides a *prima facie* reason to believe that this same fate is possible for our folk theory of the mind. Second, unlike prior conceptions of reduction, the view we are now looking at not only makes room for incommensurable theories, it uses such intertheoretic incommensurability as yet another way to clean up our ontology. We can clean the ontological house by successfully reducing one theory to another or by replacing an old theory with a new one. On this view of theory relations, unification in the sciences marches on, one way or another.

IDENTITY THEORY

The only philosophical position that holds out for the outright reduction of the mind to the brain is type *identity theory.* Crudely put, this doctrine holds that minds simply are brains. In the vocabulary of intertheoretic reduction, type identity theory holds that the corrected theory of mind will be entailed by a mature neuroscientific theory of the brain.

According to type identity theorists, kinds of sensations (mental states) correlate with kinds of states of the brain and central nervous system; and when the same or similar sensations occur in the future, they will correlate with the same or similar states of the brain and central nervous system. Mental terms and neural terms may have different intensions, but they have the same extension (just as the descriptions "lightning bolt" and "electro-magnetic discharge" have different intensions but share the same extension). In other words, they have different meanings, but refer to the same phenomena. Some identity theorists originally argued that the identity of brain and mental states held only for a few sensations. Most theorists, however, generalized the view to cover all mental experience.

In claiming that there is no ontological difference between minds and brains, the identity theorist sidesteps a serious problem for the popular view that mind and body are utterly distinct kinds of substances: providing an explanation of the interaction between mental substance and material substance. *Dualism,* the view that minds and brains are composed of essentially different stuff, has long been plagued by the problem of mind–body interaction. Obviously, there is interaction between the mind and the body. Just think of being pinched. A disturbance of the body seems to cause a sensation of pain in the mind and a volition (a mental act) seems to cause the body to exclaim "stop that!" But if the mind and body are utterly and essentially distinct substances, how could mental substance possibly be affected or affect physical substance? The answer: It cannot; thus dualism as a theory of the mind and brain fails.

Identity theory dissolves this problem by pointing out that what we once thought were two distinct things (mind and body) turn out, in fact, to be just one thing (body). The need to postulate some means of interaction between the two things thereby vanishes.

It should also be apparent that if identity theory were true, we would have the best of both worlds. The reduction of mind to brain would deepen our understanding of the world without forcing us to abandon our mental talk, or at least it would not force us to conclude that all such talk was simply false. The reduction of mind to brain would satisfy those philosophers who place a premium on the unity of science and those philosophers who want to insure a legitimate, albeit deflated, role for our mental vocabulary.

Unfortunately, difficulties vex type identity theory. One such problem stems from Leibniz's Law. Leibniz's Law maintains that given two entities (A and B) said to be identical, anything truly predicated of A must also be true of B, and vice versa. In other words, if A and B are identical, we should be able to replace any occurrence of A in any given proposition with B without changing the truth value of the proposition. For identity theory, this means that anything we say about types of mental states must also be true of types of brain states, and anything we say about types of brain states must also be true of types of mental states, if mental states and brain states are to be identical. But, as it turns out, no interesting correlations between types of brain states and types of mental states have been discovered. *Pain,* for example, is not correlated with the firing of any particular subset of neurons in the brain or central nervous system, so there isn't any type of neural state with which to identify the mental state of pain. This suggests that the vocabulary of brain and the vocabulary of the mind, and the theories in virtue of which both vocabularies have meaning, are incommensurable.

There are other problems with the identity theory (e.g., that we have seemingly direct access to our mental states but only mediated, if any at all, to our brain states). It is clear to many that identity theory is, as it stands, not a tenable position. In fact, few, if any, philosophers accept this view today. Its importance, however, for our purposes, lies not in its viability but in the fact that it is against the backdrop of identity theory that functionalism and eliminative materialism take form. So we shall proceed with our "tour" by journeying to the land of the functionalists.

FUNCTIONALISM

One response to the apparent incommensurability of psychological and neurological theories, the response taken by most psychologists, linguists and philosophers (see Fodor, for example, this volume) is to claim that all is as it should be; *psychology* is an autonomous science built by making rigorous our everyday folk theory of mental states via the use of the theory of computation and formal logic. Instead of despairing over the failure of the reductive program, functionalists rejoice in its failure and cite it as reason to believe that psychology shall forever be distinct from its lower level relations.

What is functionalism besides a reaction to the incommensurability of psychology and neuroscience? *Functionalism* holds that mental states are essentially defined by the set of causal relations between (a) input to the system from the environment, (b) other types of mental states, and (c) output, characterized by behavior. Functionalism is a marked advance over *behaviorism*, which defines mental states solely in terms of environmental input and behavioral output, because the functionalist sees mental states as causally connected to other mental states, in addition to other inputs and outputs.

Let's look at an example of functionalism. Imagine a being from a planet distant from earth. If this being is constituted in such a way that the functional economy of its mental states parallels the functional economy of the mental states of an earthling, it is said to have the same mental states that we do. In other words, if the other being's mental states were causally connected to inputs, one another, and behavior in ways that parallel our own input, internal connections, and output, the being would be said to have the same mental states that we do — pains, hopes, desires, fears — even if the being's physical and chemical composition differed radically from our own. According to functionalism, what is important for mentality is not matter, but the causal relationships that matter instantiates.

The antireductionist nature of functionalism does not stem from the fact that mental states have no material realization, but from the fact that mental states have so many material realizations that a reductive strategy is hopeless. According to reductionists, types of mental states are identical with types of brain states; but any given mental organization might be instantiated in any number of material ways, so there cannot be an easy reduction between kinds of function and kinds of structure. This is called the argument from multiple instantiability or multiple realizability: The extension of functional states is so diverse that it cannot form a natural kind (see P. S. Churchland, 1986).

But all is not well with functionalism. The first problem is the so-called "inverted spectrum thought experiment." For this thought experiment, imagine that the spectrum I see is an inversion relative to the one you see: When looking at a ripe orange, I have what is really a sensation of blue, whereas you have a normal sensation of orange. Although we may make the same discriminations between objects, my "raw feel" of blueness differs radically from your raw feel of orangeness and there is no way to compare.

Despite my spectrum being inverted relative to yours, we remain functionally identical. According to functionalism we are in an identical mental state, and yet we cannot deny that the spectrum is inverted. Functionalism seems unable to account for such a possibility.

Another problem for functionalism is the "absent qualia problem". Here we are asked to imagine a functional system characteristic of conscious intelligence radically different from a normal human: For example, a giant computer, or even all the people in China may be arranged in a complex pattern of interactions that instantiate the functional equivalence of a giant brain exchanging inputs and outputs within a single body. On a functional reading this complex system would exhibit mental states equivalent to human mental states. Intuitively, because they lack the intrinsic qualia we humans have, they would not seem to have genuine mental states (see Block, 1978).

A third problem for functionalism concerns its psychological counterpart, computational psychology. Fodor has claimed that *computational psychology* — the view that cognition is the manipulation of stored symbols according to transformation rules — is the only game in town. (For a more thorough review of computational psychology, see Bechtel & Abrahamsen, this volume.) Moreover, since computational psychology is a brand of functionalism, it too claims autonomy from lower level theories of the structure of the brain. Recently, however, this view has come under attack for not paying enough attention to how the human brain processes information. This failure has allegedly led psychologists in the computational tradition to posit models of human cognition that run counter to our understanding of how the brain works. Because we are concerned with human cognition, it is necessary to pay attention to biological constraints in the construction of psychological theories. And because computational psychology fails to give the brain its due, it is at least partially flawed.

ELIMINATIVE MATERIALISM: "REALLY, WE DON'T MIND!"

By far the most radical response to the failure of the reductionist program is the doctrine of *eliminative materialism*. The view that folk psychology should simply be eliminated originates from Rorty and Feyerabend's scepticism concerning identity theory (see Rorty, this volume; Feyerabend, this volume), but comes to fruition as a well-worked-out position on the relationship between mind talk and brain talk in the work of Paul Churchland (see Churchland, this volume). Rorty and Feyerabend's versions of eliminative materialism are called "disappearance identity theory," as opposed to the other varieties discussed and yet to be discussed, which may be called "translation identity theory." Eliminative materialism is a disappearance theory because its adherents advocate the elimination, or disappearance, of our mentalistic vocabulary instead of translating mind talk into brain talk. Eliminative materialists consider mental talk and neural talk rival theories attempting to explain the same phenomena, much like the science of meteorology competes with the ancient folk notion of gods on Mt. Olympus for explanation of changes in weather. Neuroscientific research does not uphold the close connection between mind and brain that the identity theory would require; because the mental cannot be reduced to the neural, and because the neuroscientific theory better explains what goes on in the head than does the folk-psychological theory, the folk theory should be eliminated. Like folk physics, there is nothing of interest in folk psychology that can be reduced to neurobiology. The gods cannot be reduced to meteorology, and because meteorology is more explanatorily successful, the gods have got to go! Similarly folk psychology competes with cognitive neurobiology for the best explanation of mental phenomena; similarly, cognitive neurobiology is more explanatorily successful; and because the eliminative materialist views these as competing theories, the explanatorily weaker should be disposed of, and the stronger vindicated.

The force of eliminative materialism lies in this recommendation that folk psychological notions, like intentions and their accompanying vocabulary, should be rejected. All eliminative materialists hold this view. However, Churchland radically revives the earlier versions of eliminative materialism by rejecting the view, held by both Rorty and Feyerabend, that theories and the entities they describe do not tell us, in a strict sense, what is real. Rorty and Feyerabend are antirealists and their version of eliminative materialism made no claims about the ultimate ontological status of folk psychology. Churchland, on the other hand, is a scientific realist. True theories tell us what is ultimately real. (So, for example, electrons are not just theorists' fictions, they exist, and the entities postulated in a false theory not only fail to serve a scientific purpose, they are also ontologically empty terms.) Thus Churchland hopes that the ontological bankruptcy of folk psychology will be revealed by a completed neuroscience (sometime in the next several thousand years).

Eliminative materialism suggests that the hoped-for "one-to-one match-ups" between our folk psychological framework and the concepts of theoretical neuroscience will not be found, nor will intertheoretic reduction be possible, because folk-psychological theory is false, "not to put too fine an edge on the matter". Churchland says that folk psychology is not just an incomplete representation of our internal states and activities, it is a misrepresentation; this older and outmoded framework of folk psychology "will be eliminated, as false theories are, and the familiar ontology of common sense mental states will go the way of the Stoic pneumata, the

alchemical essences, phlogiston, caloric, and the luminiferous aether."
(1979, p. 114).

Stop! Why would anyone argue for the eliminativist reponse to the
purported incompatibility of folk psychology and a completed neuroscience? Churchland suggests that we should opt for downright elimination of
folk psychology due to the fact that folk psychology fails miserably as an
explanatory theory: We have no folk psychological understanding of
memory, learning, or even sleep just to mention a few of the problem areas
for a theory that has been around for over 2,000 years. One would expect
that our theoretical understanding of these phenomena would expand,
given folk psychology's 2,000 year reign; however, Churchland argues that
folk psychology has changed little during its entire history and has made
little or no progress in explaining the recalcitrant phenomena just mentioned. (See Horgan & Woodward, this volume, for an alternative construal
of folk psychology and its successes.)

Moreover, the history of folk theories, as we mentioned before, provides
a *prima facie* reason for the acceptance of eliminative materialism. Folk
theories have, one after another, been consistently replaced by more mature
scientific theories. Why expect anything different with respect to folk
psychology? If folk physics can be replaced by Newtonian mechanics, there
is no conceptual reason to doubt that folk psychology will share a similar
fate: replacement by a mature science of the mind. So, the advantages of
eliminativism, according to Churchland, are that eliminative materialism
will point to the widespread explanatory, predictive, and manipulative
failures of folk psychology, that the vast majority — if not all — of the folk
notions in our conceptual history have been embarrassed by mature
theories, and eliminative materialism provides an a priori advantage over
identity theory and functionalism.

Churchland's brand of eliminative materialism is not, then, obviously
misguided, although it may strike us as a bit hard to swallow. One problem
that we will only touch on concerns the possibility of eliminative materialism. How is eliminative materialism possible? Simply put, the problem is
this: If eliminative materialism holds that folk psychology is false and in
need of elimination, how can the eliminative materialist assert the truth of
her or his theory without contradiction? Opponents of eliminative materialism claim that truth is a folk-psychological notion, as is meaning, and so
in saying that eliminative materialism is true, the eliminative materialist
reveals that his or her position is incoherent. Churchland's response to this
challenge is to suggest that this criticism is question-begging, presupposing
the truth of folk psychology. If eliminative materialism is true, truth and
meaningfulness must acquire their functions in some way other than the
model postulated by folk psychology. The claim that eliminative materialism is incoherent is not so easily dismissed. We want, however, to focus

on a very different problem for eliminative materialism. (Rosenberg, 1991, provides a detailed analysis of this problem and a defensible response.)

The problem we want, briefly, to discuss is raised by McCauley (this volume). McCauley grants Churchland's claim that folk psychology and neuroscience are incommensurable; however, he rejects Churchland's conclusion that neuroscience will either replace or eliminate folk psychology. McCauley argues that Churchland's account of theory relations is inadequate: Not only are there interlevel relations among theories at different levels of analysis (e.g., sociological accounts of mating and biological accounts of mating), but there are intralevel relations between theories at the same level of analysis (e.g., Ebbinghaus' "associative theory" of memory and Craik and Lockhart's "levels of processing theory" of memory).

McCauley and others (see Wimsatt, 1976) argue that incommensurability of inter-level theories does not necessitate elimination of the higher level theory. In fact, according to McCauley, "interlevel contexts, by contrast [to intralevel contexts], involve no eliminations what-so-ever. These are cross-scientific contexts where the goal is to associate theories that operate at different levels of analysis." This view of the relationship between interlevel theories is reinforced by Patricia Churchland and Terrence Sejnowski (1988):

> The ultimate goal of a unified account does not require that it be a single model that spans all the levels of organization. Instead the integration will probably consist of a chain of models linking adjacent levels. When one level is explained in terms of a lower level, this does not mean that the higher level theory is useless or that the high-level phenomena no longer exist. On the contrary, explanations will coexist at all levels . . . (p. 744)

Paul Churchland admits that folk psychology and neuroscience operate at different levels of analysis (i.e., that they are interlevel theories); if McCauley is correct, we should not expect an elimination of folk psychology by neuroscience.

But does McCauley's view imply that elimination of one theory by another is impossible? No. In fact, he embraces elimination, but only in the context of intralevel theories, that is, successor theories at the same level of analysis. Elimination occurs only within levels, not between them. So, McCauley claims that the elimination of Aristotelian physics by Newtonian physics is an intralevel elimination, not an interlevel elimination, because the latter evolved from the former through the work of Medieval physicists, Galileo, Descartes, and Kepler. At each stage of refinement, theorists hold onto as much of the old theory as possible, replacing it only when necessary.

What does this analysis of theory relations mean for the possibility of eliminative materialism? If McCauley is correct, Churchland has misplaced his hopes for eliminative materialism. Neuroscience will not eliminate folk psychology. If folk psychology is to be eliminated at all, it will have to be eliminated by a successor theory that operates at the same level of analysis as folk psychology, that is, an intralevel theory. McCauley recognizes that the hope for eliminative materialism does not lie in developments in neurobiology but in developments in cognitive psychology, but he mistakenly asserts that cognitive psychology "shows few signs of revolutionizing our psychological views, in the Kuhnian sense" (see Kuhn, 1970).

Recent developments in cognitive psychology do show signs of radically revolutionizing our understanding of cognition. The publication of Rumelhart and McClelland's volumes on parallel distributed processing (see McClelland, Rumelhart, & the PDP Research Group, 1986; Rumelhart, McClelland & the PDP Research Group, 1986) hailed the arrival of a serious intralevel threat to the future of folk psychology. Parallel distributed processing (PDP), that is, *connectionism,* contrary to the claims of Fodor and Pylyshyn (1988), and Fodor and McLaughlin (1990), is a psychological theory; therefore, if it provides a correct account of cognition, it is a successor to traditional cognitive psychology. And because some versions of PDP leave no room for the vocabulary of folk psychology, eliminative materialism may, in the end, emerge victorious.

All is not so simple. Ramsey, Stich and Garon (this volume) discuss the possibilities PDP brings for the elimination of folk psychology, suggesting the elimination of folk psychology is imminent if a particular version of PDP turns out to be true. But O'Brien (this volume) argues that PDP simply provides an accurate account of the complexities of folk psychology and thus vindicates the vocabulary of the folk. This debate has really just begun, and we leave it to the reader to decide which, if any, view is correct.

WHERE DO WE GO FROM HERE?

Now that we have provided the philosophical topology of the debate about the status of folk psychology,[2] where do we go from here? If any of the positions above leave you suspicious, we recommend a couple of metaphilosophical responses to the debate concerning the status of folk psychology.

---

[2]Of course, we have not provided an exhaustive topology of the debate; to do so would take a book in itself. However, we recommend two other anthologies on folk psychology, Greenwood, 1991a, and Bogdan, 1991c. For a substantial introduction to the philosophy of psychology, in general, we recommend Bechtel, 1988c.

THE PYRRHONIAN STANCE

We agree with McCauley that the history of science demonstrates the continual elimination of theories and the entities they postulate through the evolution of successive intralevel theories. Given that PDP has been offered as a serious intralevel rival to present-day cognitive psychology, perhaps the best advice is simply to withhold judgment concerning the future of folk psychology. The fate of folk psychology is, then, a purely empirical matter. The most beneficial position to adopt is a temporary "Pyrrhonian stance" — to wait until more evidence is in — before concluding a particular theory is correct. *Pyrrhonism,* attributed to the ancient Greek philosopher Pyrrho, recommends suspension of judgment about the nature of reality, in light of the ability to provide arguments for almost any philosophical position and because our knowledge is limited. So the Pyrrhonian stance toward folk psychology urges philosophers to go on a holiday — at least as far as folk psychology is concerned — until the time that empirical research vindicates or impugns our psychology of the mind. However, this holiday is not forced retirement, and at the appropriate time philosophers may be called to return to the task of sorting out the implications of whatever empirical theory of the mind looks promising.

THE WITTGENSTEINIAN STANCE

Although the Pyrrhonian stance has much to offer in its favor, ultimately we think it is flawed. The problem with those who adopt the Pyrrhonian stance, and of empirically minded philosophers, generally, is their adherence to the doctrine of scientific realism. It is not, as some argue (see Wilkes, this volume) that folk psychology is not a theory, but rather that it is not the kind of theory that provides scientific explanations. If folk psychology is not a scientific theory — that is, it fails to postulate easily individuated entities, and so forth — but a theory nonetheless (in that it provides an interpretive framework for understanding and communicating), it is not the kind of thing that we would expect to have a place in the scientific canon.

Those who adopt eliminative materialism or the Pyrrohonian stance both presuppose the primacy of science as the arbiter of what is real. For these scientific realists, something is "real" just in case it is the value of an existentially bound variable in a true scientific theory, as Quine put it.

We do not want to deny that what science discloses is real; to do so would make us antirealists. (See Rorty's first article in this volume; Feyerabend, this volume; and Van Fraassen, 1980.) What we do want to reject is the canonization of science, the claim that science exhaustively tells us what is real. To adopt the realist's position is to commit the fallacy of "the myth of one proper use" (Wright, 1989). The word "real," like all other words, gets its meaning from the various jobs it performs in a whole host of contexts. This "working-class theory" of meaning recommends that philosophers not forget or ignore the multifaceted work that words do. The realist position does just this by canonizing the scientific context and claiming that the word "real" is exhaustively understood by Quine's epigram.

We agree with Churchland, McCauley, and the rest of the scientific realists in thinking that neuroscience will not make reference to beliefs and desires. And in fact, if PDP is true, then cognitive psychology may not make reference to concepts of folk psychology either. But once again, the scientific context is not the only context and the vocabulary of folk psychology has a perfectly useful domain of application (see Dennett, 1991b, for a very different defense). There is little achieved by limiting the meaning of the word "real" to the scientific domain only.

So, the *Wittgensteinian stance* combines a healthy suspicion toward the use of the vocabulary of folk psychology in a complete neuroscience with an equally healthy suspicion toward the ability of any scientific theory to supplant our folk-psychological theory. The force of this position is to realize the limits and uses of our vocabularies, and that many questions about the status of the things these terms might refer to will eventually lead us to a dead end.

I | THE ELIMINATION OF FOLK PSYCHOLOGY

1 Materialism and the Mind-Body Problem*

Paul Feyerabend
University of California, Berkeley

(1) This chapter has a twofold purpose. First, it defends materialism against a certain type of attack which seems to be based upon a *truism* but which is nevertheless completely off the mark. And secondly it intends to put philosophy in its proper place. It occurs only too often that attempts to arrive at a coherent picture of the world are held up by philosophical bickering and are perhaps even given up before they can show their merits. It seems to me that those who originate such attempts ought to be a little less afraid of difficulties; that they ought to look through the arguments which are presented against them; and that they ought to recognize their irrelevance. Having disregarded irrelevant objections they ought then to proceed to the much more rewarding task of developing their point of view *in detail,* to examine its fruitfulness and thereby to get fresh insight, not only into some generalities, but into very concrete and detailed processes. To encourage such development from the abstract to the concrete, to contribute to the invention of further ideas, this is the proper task of a philosophy which aspires to be more than a hindrance to progress.

(2) The crudest form of materialism will be taken as the basis of argument. If *it* can successfully evade the objections of some philosophers, then a more refined doctrine will be even less troubled.

Materialism, as it will be discussed here, assumes that the only entities existing in the world are atoms, aggregates of atoms and that the only properties and relations are the properties of, and the relations between

---

*Reprinted from *Review of Metaphysics* 17 (1963, pp. 49–66) by permission of the author and publisher.

such aggregates. A simple atomism such as the theory of Democritus will be sufficient for our purpose. The refinements of the kinetic theory, or of the quantum theory, are outside the domain of discussion. And the question is: Will such a cosmology give a correct account of human beings?

(3) The following reason is put forth why this question must be answered in the negative: human beings, apart from being material, have *experiences;* they *think;* they *feel* pain; etc., etc. These processes cannot be analyzed in a materialistic fashion. Hence, a materialistic psychology is bound to fail.

The most decisive part of this argument consists in the assertion that experiences, thoughts, etc., are not material processes. It is customary to support this assertion in the following manner.

(4) There are statements which can be made about pains, thoughts, etc., which cannot be made about material processes; and there are other statements which can be made about material processes but which cannot be made about pains, thoughts, etc. This impossibility exists because the attempt to form such statements would lead to results which are either *false,* or else to results which are *meaningless.*

Let us consider meaninglessness first. Whether or not a statement is meaningful depends on the grammatical rules guiding the corresponding sentence. The argument appeals to such rules. It points out that the materialist, in stating his thesis, is violating them. Note that the particular *words* he uses are of no relevance here. Whatever the *words* employed by him, the resulting *system of rules* would have a structure incompatible with the structure of the idiom in which we usually describe pains and thoughts. This incompatibility is taken to refute the materialist.

It is evident that this argument is incomplete. An incompatibility between the materialistic language and the rules implicit in some other idiom will criticize the former only if the latter can be shown to possess certain advantages. Nor is it sufficient to point out that the idiom on which the comparison is based is in *common use.* This is an irrelevant historical accident. Is it really believed that a vigorous propaganda campaign which makes everyone speak the materialistic language will turn materialism into a correct doctrine? The choice of the language that is supposed to be the basis of criticism must be supported by better reasons.

(5) As far as I am aware there is only one further reason that has been offered: it is the *practical success* of ordinary English which makes it a safe basis for argument. "Our common stock of words" writes J. L. Austin ("A Plea for Excuses") "embodies all the distinctions men have found worth drawing, and the connexions they have found worth marking, in the lifetime of many generations: these surely are likely to be more numerous, more sound, since they have stood up to the long test of the survival of the fittest, and more subtle . . . than any that you or I are likely to think up. . . ."[1] This reason is very similar, and almost identical, with a certain

point of view in the philosophy of science. Ever since Newton it has been assumed that a theory which is confirmed to a very high degree is to be preferred to more tentative general ideas and it has been, and still is, believed that such general ideas must be removed in order not to hinder the course of factual discovery. "For if the possibility of hypotheses," writes Newton (reply to a letter by P. Pardies), "is to be the test of truth and reality of things, I see not how certainty can be obtained in any science; since numerous hypotheses may be devised, which shall seem to overcome new difficulties."[2] I mention this parallel in order to show that philosophical points of view which *prima facie* seem to bear the stamp of revolutionary discoveries, especially to those who are not too well acquainted with the history of ideas, may in the end turn out to be nothing but uncritical repetitions of age-old prejudices. However, it must also be emphasized, in all fairness to the scientists, that the parallel does not go very far. Scientific theories are constructed in such a way that they can be *tested*. Every application of the theory is at the same time a most sensitive investigation of its validity. This being the case there is indeed some reason to trust a theory that has been in use for a considerable time and to look with suspicion at new and vague ideas. The suspicion is mistaken, of course, as I shall try to point out presently. Still, it is not completely foolish to have such an attitude. At least *prima facie* there seems to be a grain of reason in it.

The situation is very different with "common idioms." First of all, such idioms are adapted not to *facts,* but to beliefs. If these beliefs are widely accepted; if they are intimately connected with the fears and the hopes of the community in which they occur; if they are defended, and reinforced with the help of powerful institutions; if one's whole life is somehow carried out in accordance with them – then the language representing them will be regarded as most successful. At the same time it is clear that the question of the truth of the beliefs has not been touched.

The second reason why the success of a "common" idiom is not at all on the same level as is the success of a scientific theory lies in the fact that the use of such an idiom, *even in concrete observational situations,* can hardly ever be regarded as a *test*. There is no attempt, as there is in the sciences, to conquer new fields and to try the theory in them. And even on familiar ground one can never be sure whether certain features of the descriptive statements used are *confronted* with facts, and are thereby *examined;* or whether they do not simply function as *accompanying noises.* Some more recent analyses concerning the nature of facts seem to show that the latter is the case. It is clear that the argument from success is then inapplicable.

Assume thirdly – and now I am well aware that I am arguing contrary to fact – that the idiom to which reference is made in the above argument *is* used in a testable fashion and that the parallel, alluded to above, with scientific method is a legitimate one. Is it *then* possible to reject materialism by reference to the success of a nonmaterialistic language?

The answer is NO and the reason which I have explained in detail in my "Explanation, Reduction, and Empiricism" (in Vol. III of the *Minnesota Studies in the Philosophy of Science*)[3] as well as in "Problems of Empiricism" (in Vol. II of the *Pittsburgh Studies in the Philosophy of Science*)[4] is as follows: in order to discuss the weaknesses of an all-pervasive system of thought such as is expressed by the "common" idiom, it is not sufficient to compare it with "the facts." Many such facts are formulated in terms of the idiom and therefore already prejudiced in its favor. Also there are many facts which are inaccessible, *for empirical reasons,* to a person speaking a certain idiom and which become accessible only if a different idiom is introduced. This being the case, the construction of alternative points of view and of alternative languages which radically differ from the established usage, far from precipitating confusion, *is a necessary part of the examination of this usage* and must be carried out *before* a final judgment can be made. More concretely: if you want to find out whether there *are* pains, thoughts, feelings in the sense indicated by the common usage of these words, then you must become (among other things) a materialist. Trying to eliminate materialism by reference to the common idiom, therefore, means putting the cart before the horse.

(6) The argument presented so far has some further features which are in need of criticism. Let us take it for granted that incompatibility with ordinary (or other) usage and the meaninglessness arising from it is a sufficient reason for eliminating a point of view. Then it must still be made clear that while the grammar of the *primitive terms* of the point of view may be incompatible with accepted usage, the grammar of the *defined terms* need not be so incompatible. The same applies to the "grain" of both: it has sometimes been objected that a sensation is a very simple thing, whereas a collection of atoms has a much more complex structure (it is "spotty"). This is correct. But there are still *properties* of such collections which do not participate in their "grain." The density of a fluid is an example. The fluid itself has the same "grain" as a heap of atoms. The density has not. It ceases to be applicable in domains where the fine structure of the fluid becomes apparent. There are infinitely many other properties of this kind. The defender of the customary point of view has therefore much too simple an idea of the capabilities of materialism. He overlooks that materialism might even be able to provide him with the synonyms he wants; he overlooks that the materialistic doctrine might be able to satisfy his *(irrelevant)* demand for at least partial agreement of grammar.

(7) While the argument from meaninglessness is wholly based upon language, the argument from falsity is not. That a thought cannot be a material process is, so it is believed, established *by observation.* It is by

observation that we discover the difference between the one and the other and refute materialism. We now turn to an examination of this argument.

(8) To start with we must admit that the difference does exist. Introspection does indicate, in a most decisive fashion, that my present thought of Aldebaran is not localized whereas Aldebaran is localized; that this thought has no color whereas Aldebaran has a very definite color; that this thought has no parts whereas Aldebaran consists of many parts exhibiting different physical properties. Is this character of the introspective result proof to the effect that thoughts cannot be material?

The answer is NO and the argument is the truism that what *appears to be* different does not need to *be* different. Is not the seen table very different from the felt table? Is not the heard sound very different from its mechanical manifestations (Chladni's figures; Kundt's tube, etc., etc.)? And if despite this difference of appearance we are allowed to make an identification, postulating an object in the outer world (the physical table, the physical sound), then why should the observed difference between a thought and the impression of a brain process prevent us from making another identification, postulating this time an object in the inner (material) world, viz., a brain process? It is of course quite possible that such a postulate will run into trouble and that it will be refuted by independent tests (just as the earlier identification of comets with atmospheric phenomena was refuted by independent tests). The point is that the *prima facie* observed difference between thoughts and the appearance of brain processes does *not* constitute such trouble. It is also correct that a language which is based upon the assumption that the identification has already been carried out would differ significantly from ordinary English. But this fact can be used as an argument against the identification only *after* it has been shown that the new language is *inferior* to ordinary English. And such disproof should be based upon the *fully* developed materialistic idiom and *not* on the bits and pieces of materialese which are available to the philosophers of today. It took a considerable time for ordinary English to reach its present stage of complexity and sophistication. The materialistic philosopher must be given *at least* as much time. As a matter of fact he will need more time as he intends to develop a language which is fully testable, which gives a coherent account of the most familiar facts about human beings *as well as* of thousands more recondite facts which have been unearthed by the physiologists. I also admit that there are people for whom even the reality of the external world and the identifications leading to it constitute a grave problem. My answer is that I do not address *them,* but that I presuppose a minimum of reason in my readers; I assume they are realists. And assuming this I try to point out that their realism need not be restricted to processes outside their skin — unless of course one already *presupposes* what is to be established by the argument, that things inside the skin are very different from what goes on outside. Considering all this I conclude that the argument from observation is invalid.

(9) It is quite entertaining to speculate about some results of an identification of what is observed by introspection with brain processes. Observation of microprocesses in the brain is a notoriously difficult affair. Only very rarely is it possible to investigate them in the living organism. Observation of dead tissue, on the other hand, is applied to a structure that may differ significantly from the living brain. To solve the problems arising from this apparent inaccessibility of processes in the living brain we need only realize that the living brain *is already connected with a most sensitive instrument* – the living human organism. Observation of the reactions of this organism, introspection included, may therefore be much more reliable sources of information concerning the living brain than any other "more direct" method. Using a suitable identification-hypothesis one might even be able to say that introspection leads to a *direct observation* of an otherwise quite inaccessible and very complex process *in the brain*.

(10) Against what has been said above it might, and has been, objected that in the case of thoughts, sensations, feelings, the distinction between what they *are* and what they appear to be does not apply. Mental processes are things with which we are *directly acquainted*. Unlike physical objects whose structure must be unveiled by experimental research and about whose nature we can make only more or less plausible conjectures, they can be known completely, and with certainty. Essence and appearance coincide here, and we are therefore entitled to take what they seem to be as a direct indication of what they are. This objection must now be investigated in some detail.

(11) In order to deal with all the prejudices operating in the present case, let us approach the matter at a snail's pace. What are the reasons for defending a doctrine like the one we have just outlined? If the materialist is correct, then the doctrine is false. It is then possible to test statements of introspection by physiological examination of the brain, and reject them as being based upon an introspective mistake. Is such a possibility to be denied? The doctrine we are discussing at the present moment thinks it is. And the argument is somewhat as follows.

When I am in pain, then there is no doubt, no possibility of a mistake. This certainty is not simply a psychological affair, it is not due to the fact that I am too strongly convinced to be persuaded of the opposite. It is much more related to a logical certainty: there is no possibility whatever of criticizing the statement. I might not show any physiological symptoms – but I never meant to include them into my assertion. I might not even show pain behavior – but this is not part of the content of my statement either. Now if the difference between essence and appearance was applicable in the case of pains, then such certainty could not be obtained. It *can* be obtained as has just been demonstrated. Hence, the difference does not apply and the postulation of a common object for mental processes and impressions of physiological processes cannot be carried out.

(12) The first question which arises in connection with this argument concerns the *source* of this certainty of statements concerning mental processes. The answer is very simple: it is their *lack of content* which is the source of their certainty. Statements about physical objects possess a very rich content. They are vulnerable because of the existence of this content. Thus, the statement "there is a table in front of me" leads to predictions concerning my tactual sensations; the behavior of other material objects (a glass of brandy put in a certain position will remain in this position and will not fall to the ground; a ball thrown in a certain direction will be deflected); the behavior of other people (they will walk around the table; point out objects on its surface); etc. Failure of any one of these predictions may force me to withdraw the statement. This is not the case with statements concerning thoughts, sensations, feelings; or at least there is the impression that the same kind of vulnerability does not obtain here. The reason is that their content is so much poorer. No prediction, no retrodiction can be inferred from them, and the need to withdraw them can therefore not arise. (Of course, lack of content is only a *necessary* condition of their empirical certainty; in order to have the character they possess, statements about mental events must also be such that in the appropriate circumstances their production can be achieved with complete ease; they must be *observational* statements. *This* characteristic they share with many statements concerning physical objects.)

(13) The second question is how statements about physical objects *obtain* their rich content and how it is that the content of mental statements as represented in the current argument is so much poorer.

One fairly popular answer is by reference to the "grammar" of mental statements and of physical statements respectively. We mean by pains, thoughts, etc., processes which are accessible only to one individual and which have nothing to do with the state of his body. The content of "pain," or of "thinking of Vienna" is low because "pain," "thought" are mental terms. If the content of these terms were enriched, and thereby made similar to the content of "table," they would cease to function in the peculiar way in which mental terms do as a matter of fact function, and "pain," for example, would then cease to mean what is meant by an ordinary individual who in the face of the absence of physiological symptoms, of behavioral expression, of suppressed conflicts still maintains that he is in pain. This answer may be correct, and it will be taken to be correct for the sake of argument. However, in order to defeat the materialist it must also be shown that a language structured in this way will describe the world more correctly, and more efficiently than any language the materialist could develop. No such proof is available. The argument from "common" usage and, for that matter, from any established usage is therefore irrelevant.

(14) There is only one point on which this argument may possess some force, and this point concerns the use of *words:* having shown that a materialistic pain and an "ordinary" pain would be two very different things indeed, the defender of the established usage may forbid the materialist to employ the word "pain" which for him rightfully belongs to the ordinary idiom. Now, quite apart from the fact that this would mean being very squeamish indeed, and unbearably "proper" in linguistic matters, the desired procedure *cannot be carried out.* The reason is that changes of meaning occur too frequently, and that they cannot be localized in time. Every interesting discussion, (i.e., every discussion that leads to an advance of knowledge) terminates in a situation where some decisive change of meaning has occurred. Yet it is not possible, or it is only very rarely possible, to say *when* the change took place. Moreover a distinction must be drawn between the *psychological circumstances* of the production of a sentence, and the *meaning* of the statement that is connected with that sentence. A new theory of pains will not change the pains; nor will it change the causal connection between the occurrence of pains and the production of "I am in pain," except perhaps very slightly. It *will* change the *meaning* of "I am in pain." Now it seems to me that observational terms should be correlated with causal antecedents and *not* with meanings. The causal connection between the production of a "mental" sentence and its "mental" antecedent is very strong. It has been taught in the very youth. It is the basis of all observation concerning the mind. To sever this connection is a much more laborious affair than a change of connections with meaning. The latter connections change all the time anyway. It is therefore much more sensible to establish a one-to-one connection between observational terms and their causal antecedents, than between such terms and the always variable *meanings.* This procedure has great advantages and can do no harm. An astronomer who wishes to determine the rough shape of the energy output (dependence on frequency) of a star by looking at it will hardly be seduced into thinking that the word "red" which he uses for announcing his results refers to sensations. Linguistic sensitivity may be of some value. But it should not be used to turn intelligent people into nervous wrecks.

(15) Another reply to the question of section 13 which is *prima facie* satisfactory is that we know quite a lot about physical objects and that we know much less about mental events. We use this knowledge not only on the relatively rare occasions when we answer questions involving it, but we infuse it also into the notions with which we describe material objects: a table *is* an object which deflects a ball thrown at it; which supports other objects; which is seen by other people; and so on. We let this knowledge

become part of the language we speak by allowing the laws and theories it contains to become the grammatic rules of this language. This reply would seem to be supported by the fact that objects of a relatively unknown kind always give rise to fewer predictions and that the statements concerning them are therefore relatively safe. In many such cases the only tests available are the reports of others which means that mass-hallucinations can still count as confirming evidence.

Now this reply, however plausible, does not take into account that a considerable amount is known about mental processes also; this not only by the psychologist, or the physiologist, but even by the common man, be he now British, or a native of Ancient Greece, or of Ancient Egypt. Why has *this* knowledge not been incorporated into the mental notions? Why are these notions still so poor in content?

(16) Before answering the question we must first qualify it. It is quite incorrect to assume that the relative poverty of mental notions is a common property of all languages. Quite the contrary, we find that people have at all times objectivized mental notions in a manner very similar to the manner in which we today objectivize materialistic notions. They did this mostly (but not always—the witchcraft theory of the Azande constituting a most interesting *materialistic* exception) in an objective-*idealistic* fashion and can therefore be easily criticized, or smiled about, by some progressive thinkers of today. In our present discussion such criticism is off the mark. We have *admitted,* in section 8, that the materialistic type of objectification may at some future time run into trouble. What we wanted to defend was the *initial* right to carry it out, and it was this *initial* right that was attacked by reference to "common usage." Considering this context, it is important to point out that there is hardly any interesting language, used by a historical culture, which is built in accordance with the idea of acquaintance. This idea is nothing but a philosophical invention. It is now time to reveal the motives for such an invention.

(17) We start the discussion with a still further argument intending to show that and why the knowledge we may possess about mental events must not be incorporated into the mental terms and why their content must be kept low. This argument is apparently factual and it consists in pointing out *that there is knowledge by acquaintance,* or, alternatively, that there are things which can be known by acquaintance; we *do* possess direct and full knowledge of our pains, of our thoughts, of our feelings, at least of those which are immediately present and not suppressed.

This argument is circular. If we possess knowledge by acquaintance with respect to mental states of affairs, if there seems to be something "immediately given," then this is the *result* of the low content of the statements used for expressing this knowledge. Had we enriched the notions employed in these statements in a materialistic (or an objective-idealistic) fashion *as we might well have done,* then we would not any longer be able to say that we know mental processes by acquaintance. Just as with material objects we would then be obliged to distinguish between their nature and their appearance, and each judgment concerning a mental process would be open to revision by further physiological (or behavioral) inquiry. The reference to acquaintance cannot therefore justify our reluctance to use the knowledge we possess concerning mental events, their causes, their physiological concomitants (as their physiological content will be called *before* the materialistic move) for enriching the mental notions.

(18) What has just been said deserves repetition. The argument which we attacked was as follows: there is the *fact* of knowledge by acquaintance. This fact refutes materialism which would exclude such a fact. The attack consisted in pointing out that although knowledge by acquaintance may be a fact (which was, however, doubted in section 16), this fact is the result of certain peculiarities of the language spoken *and therefore alterable.* Materialism (and, for that matter, also an objective spiritualism like the theory of the *ba* or Hegel's spiritualism) recognizes the fact and suggests that it be altered. It therefore clearly cannot be refuted by a repetition of the fact. What must be shown is that the suggestion is undesirable, and that acquaintance is desirable.

(19) We have here discovered a rather interesting feature of philosophical arguments. The argument from acquaintance presents what seems to be fact of nature, namely, our ability to acquire secure knowledge of our own states of mind. We have tried to show that this alleged fact of nature is the result of the way in which any kind of knowledge (or opinion) concerning the mind has been incorporated, or is being incorporated into the language used for describing facts: this knowledge, this opinion, is not used for *enriching* the mental concepts; it is rather used for making predictions in terms of the still unchanged and poor concepts. Or, to use terms from technical philosophy, this knowledge is interpreted instrumentalistically, and not in a realistic fashion. The alleged fact referred to above is therefore a projection, into the world, of certain peculiarities of our way of building up knowledge. Why do we (or why do philosophers who use the language described) proceed in this fashion?

(20) They proceed in this fashion because they hold a certain philosophical theory. According to this theory, which has a very long history and which influences even the most sophisticated and the most "progressive" contemporary philosophers (with the possible exception of Popper and Wittgenstein), the world consists of two domains, the domain of the outer, physical world, and the domain of the inner, or mental world. The outer world can be experienced, but only indirectly. Our knowledge of the outer world will therefore forever remain hypothetical. The inner world, the mental world, on the other hand, can be directly experienced. The

knowledge gained in this fashion is complete, and absolutely certain. This, I think, is the philosophical theory behind the method we described in the last section.

Now I am not concerned here with the question of whether this theory is correct or not. It is quite possible that it is true (though I am inclined to doubt this, especially in view of the fact that it presents what should be the result of a decision, viz., the richness or the poverty of the content of a statement and its corresponding property of being either hypothetical, or certain, *as a fact of nature* and thereby confounds the basic distinction between the *ought* and the *is*). What I *am* interested in here is the way in which the theory is *presented*. It is not presented as a hypothesis which is open to criticism and which can be rationally discussed. In a certain sense it is not even presented. It is rather incorporated into the language spoken in a fashion which makes it inaccessible to empirical criticism — whatever the empirical results, they are not used for enriching the mental concepts which will therefore forever refer to entities knowable by acquaintance.

This procedure has two results. It hides the theory and thereby removes it from criticism. And it creates what looks like a very powerful fact supporting the theory. As the theory is hidden, the philosopher can even *start* with this fact and reason from it, thereby providing a kind of inductive argument for the theory. It is only when we examine what independent support there exists for this alleged fact that we discover that it is not a fact at all but rather a reflection of the way in which empirical results are handled. We discover that "we were ignorant of our . . . activity and therefore regarded as an alien object what had been constructed by ourselves" (Kuno Fischer in his account of Kant's theory of knowledge).[5]

This is an excellent example of the circularity of philosophical argumentation even in those cases where such argumentation is based upon what seems to be an uncontrovertible fact of nature ("inner" nature, that is). This example is a warning that we should not be too impressed by empirical arguments but that we should first investigate the source of their apparent success. Such an investigation may discover a fatal circularity and thereby destroy the force of the argument. It is quite obvious that a circularity of this kind cannot be removed by considering further *empirical* evidence. But it can be removed by an examination of the *methodological* tenability of the procedure described. We now give a brief outline of such an examination.

(21) There are some philosophers who agree that the *fact* of acquaintance cannot be used as an argument against the materialist (or any other kind of "internal realist"). Their reasons are not those given above but rather the realization that none of the situations described in the ordinary idiom, in any ordinary idiom, can be known by acquaintance. Realizing this they will look for arguments which remain valid in the face of adverse facts, and they will therefore appeal to norms rather than to facts. They usually suggest the

construction of an *ideal language* containing statements of the desired property. In this they are guided by the idea that our knowledge must possess a solid, (i.e., an incorrigible foundation). The construction of such a language has sometimes been represented as a task of immense difficulty and as worthy of a great mind. I submit that this means vastly overestimating it. Of course, if this task is meant to be the discovery of *already existing* statements of the ordinary language which possess the desired property (Russell's "canoid patch of colour" indicates that he conceived his task in this fashion), then it is perhaps impossible to carry it out. It may also be impossible to give an account of complex perceptions in terms of simple sensible elements (the investigations of the *Gestalt* school of psychology most definitely indicate that such composition from psychological elements will be an extremely difficult matter). But why should the attempt to find a safe observation language be impeded by such inessential restrictions? What we want is a series of observation statements leading to knowledge by acquaintance. Such statements can be obtained *immediately* by a philosophical laboratory assistant, by taking any observation statement and eliminating its predictive and retrodictive content as well as all consequences concerning public events occurring simultaneously. The resulting string of signs will still be observational, it will be uttered on the same objective occasion as was its predecessor, but it will be incorrigible, and the object described by it will be 'known' by acquaintance. This is how acquaintance can be achieved. Now let us investigate some consequences of this procedure.

(22) Such an investigation is hardly ever carried out with due circumspection. What happens usually is this: One starts with a sentence which has a perfectly good meaning, such as "I am in pain." One interprets it as a statement concerning what can be known by acquaintance. One overlooks that such an interpretation drastically changes the original meaning of the sentence and one retains in this fashion the illusion that one is still dealing with a meaningful statement. Blinded by this illusion one cannot at all understand the objection of the opponent who takes the move towards the "given" seriously and who is incapable of getting any sense out of the result. Just investigate the matter in some detail. Being in pain I say "I am in pain" and, of course, I have some independent idea as to what pains are. They do not reside in tables and chairs; they can be eliminated by taking drugs; they concern only a single human being (hence, being in pain I shall not get alarmed about my dog); they are not contagious (hence, being in pain I shall not warn people to keep away from me). This idea is shared by everyone else and it makes people capable of understanding what I intend to convey. But now I am not supposed to let any one of these ideas contribute to the meaning of the *new* statement, expressed by the same sentence, about the immediately given; I am supposed to free this meaning of all that has just

been said; not even the idea that a dreamt pain and a pain really felt are different must now be retained. If all these elements are removed, then what do I mean by the new statement resulting from this semantical canvas cleaning? I may utter it on the occasion of pain (in the normal sense); I may also utter it in a dream with no pain present, and I may be equally convinced that this is the right thing to do. I may use it metaphorically, connecting it with a thought (in the usual sense) concerning the number two; or I may have been taught (in the usual sense of the word) to utter it when I have pleasant feelings and therefore utter it on these occasions. Clearly all these usages are now legitimate, and all of them describe the "immediately given pain." Is it not evident that using this new interpretation of the sentence I am not even in principle able to derive enlightenment from the fact that Herbert has just uttered it? Of course, I can still treat it as a *symptom* of the occurrence of an event which in the ordinary speech would be expressed in the very same fashion, viz., by saying "I am in pain." But in this case I provide my own interpretation which is very different from the interpretation we are discussing at the present moment. And we have seen that according to this interpretation the sentence cannot be taken to be the description of anything definite. It therefore means nothing; it cannot be understood by anyone (except in the sense in which a person looking at someone else's distorted face "understands" what is going on — but then he does his own interpreting); and it is completely inadequate as a "foundation of knowledge" or as a measure of factual meaning. Now if the Given were a reality, then this would mean the end of rational, objective knowledge. Not even revelation could then teach us what admittedly cannot be known in principle. Language and conversation, if they existed, would become comparable to a cat-serenade, all expression, nothing said, nothing understood. Fortunately enough, the "given" is but the reflection of our own unreason and it can be eliminated by building up language in a more sensible fashion. This finishes our discussion of the argument from acquaintance.

(23) To sum up: we have discussed three arguments against materialism. The first argument points out that materialism is not the ontology of ordinary English. We are given the reasons why this argument would be irrelevant even if ordinary English should turn out to be a highly successful testable idiom. The second argument refers to results of observation. We have pointed out that results of observation are in need of interpretation and that no reason has been given why a materialistic interpretation should be excluded. The third argument was by reference to the fact of "acquaintance." We have shown, first, that this fact is not unchangeable and, second, that if it were a fact, knowledge would be impossible. I am not aware of any other philosophical arguments against materialism (clearly all considerations of synonymy or co-extensionality belong to what we have

above called the first argument). There is, therefore, not a single reason why the attempt to give a purely physiological account of human beings should be abandoned, or why physiologists should leave the 'soul' out of their considerations.

(24) A common feature of all the discussed arguments is this: they try to criticize a theory *before* this theory has been developed in sufficient detail to be able to show its power. And they make established modes of thinking and of expression the basis of this criticism. We have pointed out that the only way of discovering the faults of established modes of thinking is by resolutely trying out a different approach. It would seem to me that the task of philosophy, or of any enterprise interested in the advance rather than the embalming of knowledge, would be to encourage the development of such new modes of approach and to participate in their improvement rather than to waste time in showing what is obvious anyway; they are different from the established ways of thinking.

FOOTNOTES

[1]*Proceedings of the Aristotelian Society,* 1956-1957. Article reprinted in *Philosophical Papers,* ed. Urmson and Warnock (Oxford, 1961), p. 130.

[2]*Isaak Newton's Papers and Letters on Natural Philosophy,* ed. I. B. Cohen (Cambridge, 1958), p. 106.

[3](Minneapolis, 1962).

[4](Pittsburgh, 1963).

[5]*Immanuel Kant und seine Lehre* (Heidelberg, 1889), p. 10.

2 Mind-Body Identity, Privacy, and Categories*

Richard Rorty
University of Virginia, Charlottesville

1. INTRODUCTORY

Current controversies about the Mind-Body Identity Theory form a case-study for the investigation of the methods practiced by linguistic philosophers. Recent criticisms of these methods question that philosophers can discern lines of demarcation between "categories" of entities, and thereby diagnose "conceptual confusions" in "reductionist" philosophical theories. Such doubts arise once we see that it is very difficult, and perhaps impossible, to draw a firm line between the "conceptual" and the "empirical," and thus to differentiate between a statement embodying a conceptual confusion and one that expresses a surprising empirical result. The proponent of the Identity Theory (by which I mean one who thinks it sensible to assert that empirical inquiry will discover that *sensations* (not thoughts) are identical with certain brain-processes[1]) holds that his opponents' arguments to the effect that empirical inquiry *could* not identify brain-processes and sensations are admirable illustrations of this difficulty. For, he argues, the classifications of linguistic expressions that are the ground of his opponents' criticism are classifications of a language which is as it is because it is the language spoken at a given stage of empirical inquiry. But the sort of empirical results that would show brain processes and sensations to be identical would also bring about changes in our ways of speaking. These changes would make these classifications out of date. To argue against the

---

*Reprinted from *Review of Metaphysics* 19 (1965, pp. 24–54) by permission of the author and publisher.

Identity Theory on the basis of the way we talk now is like arguing against an assertion that supernatural phenomena are identical with certain natural phenomena on the basis of the way in which superstitious people talk. There is simply no such thing as a method of classifying linguistic expressions that has results guaranteed to remain intact despite the results of future empirical inquiry. Thus in this area (and perhaps in all areas) there is no method which will have the sort of magisterial neutrality of which linguistic philosophers fondly dream.

In this chapter I wish to support this general line of argument. I shall begin by pressing the claims of the analogy between mental events and supernatural events. Then I shall try to rebut the objection which seems generally regarded as fatal to the claims of the Identity Theory—the objection that "privacy" is of the essence of mental events, and thus that a theory which holds that mental events might *not* be "private" is *ipso facto* confused. I shall conclude with some brief remarks on the implications of my arguments for the more general metaphilosophical issues at stake.

2. THE TWO FORMS OF THE IDENTITY THEORY

The obvious objection to the Identity Theory is that "identical" either means a relation such that

$$(x)\,(y)\,[(x = y) \supset (F)\,(Fx \equiv Fy)]$$

(the relation of "strict identity") or it does not. If it does, then we find ourselves forced into

> saying truthfully that physical processes such as brain processes are dim or fading or nagging or false, and that mental phenomena such as after-images are publicly observable or physical or spatially located or swift,[2]

and thus using meaningless expression, for

> we may say that the above expressions are meaningless in the sense that they commit a category-mistake; i.e., in forming these expressions we have predicated predicates, appropriate to one logical category, of expressions that belong to a different logical category. This is surely a conceptual mistake.[3]

But if by "identical" the Identity Theory does *not* mean a relation of strict identity, then what relation *is* intended? How does it differ from the mere relation of "correlation" which, as it is admitted on all sides, might without confusion be said to hold between sensations and brain-processes?

Given this dilemma, two forms of the identity theory may be distinguished. The first, which I shall call the *translation* form, grasps the first horn and attempts to show that the odd-sounding expressions mentioned above do not involve category-mistakes, and that this can be shown by suitable translations into "topic neutral" language of the sentences in which these terms are originally used.[4] The second, which I shall call the *disappearance* form, grasps the second horn and holds that the relation in question is in not strict identity, but rather the sort of relation which obtains between, to put it crudely, existent entities and non-existent entities when reference to the latter once served (some of) the purposes presently served by reference to the former — the sort of relation that holds, e.g., between "quantity of caloric fluid" and "mean kinetic energy of molecules." There is an obvious sense of "same" in which what used to be called "a quantity of caloric fluid" is *the same thing* as what is now called a certain mean kinetic energy of molecules, but there is no reason to think that all features truly predicated of the one may be sensibly predicated of the other.[5] The translation term of the theory holds that if we really understood what we were saying when we said things like "I am having a stabbing pain" we should see that since we are talking about "topic-neutral" matters, we might, for all we know, be talking about brain-processes. The disappearance form holds that it is unnecessary to show that suitable translations (into "topic-neutral" language) of our talk about sensations can be given — as unnecessary as to show that statements about quantities of caloric fluid, when properly understood, may be seen to be topic-neutral statements.[6]

From the point of view of this second form of the theory, it is a mistake to assume that "X's are nothing but Y's" entails "All attributes meaningfully predicable of X's are meaningfully predicated of Y's," for this assumption would forbid us ever to express the results of scientific inquiry in terms of (in Cornman's useful phrase) "cross-category identity."[7] It would seem that the verb in such statements as "Zeus's thunderbolts are discharges of static electricity" and "Demoniacal possession is a form of hallucinatory psychosis" is the "is" of identity, yet it can hardly express *strict* identity. The disappearance form of the Identity Theory suggests that we view such statements as elliptical for e.g., "What people used to call 'demoniacal possession' is a form of hallucinatory psychosis," where the relation in question *is* strict identity. Since there is no reason why "what people call 'X' " should be in the same "category" (in the Rylean sense) as "X," there is no need to claim, as the translation form of the theory must, that topic-neutral translations of statements using "X" are possible.

In what follows, I shall confine myself to a discussion and defense of the disappearance form of the theory. My first reason for this is that I believe that the analysis of "Sensations are identical with certain brain-processes" proposed by the disappearance form (viz., "What people now call 'sensations' are identical with certain brain-processes") accomplishes the same end as the translation form's program of topic-neutral translation—namely, avoiding the charge of "category-mistake," while preserving the full force of the traditional materialist position. My second reason is that I believe that an attempt to defend the translation form will inevitably get bogged down in controversy about the adequacy of proposed topic-neutral translations of statements about sensations. There is obviously a sense of "adequate translation" in which the topic-neutrality of the purported translations *ipso facto* makes them inadequate. So the proponent of the translation form of the theory will have to fall back on a weaker sense of "adequate translation." But the weaker this sense becomes, the less impressive is the claim being made, and the less difference between the Identity Theory and the non-controversial thesis that certain brain-processes may be constantly correlated with certain sensations.

3. THE ANALOGY BETWEEN DEMONS AND SENSATIONS

At first glance, there seems to be a fatal weakness in the disappearance form of the Identity Theory. For normally when we say "What people call 'X's' are nothing but Y's" we are prepared to add that "There are no X's." Thus when, e.g., we say that "What people call 'caloric fluid' is nothing but the motion of molecules" or "What people call 'witches' are nothing but psychotic women" we are prepared to say that there are no witches, and no such thing as caloric fluid. But it seems absurd to say that there might turn out to be no such things as sensations.

To see that this disanalogy is not fatal to the Identity Theory, let us consider the following situation. A certain primitive tribe holds the view that illnesses are caused by demons—a different demon for each sort of illness. When asked what more is known about these demons than that they cause illness, they reply that certain members of the tribe—the witch doctors—can see, after a meal of sacred mushrooms, various (intangible) humanoid forms on or near the bodies of patients. The witch doctors have noted, for example, that a blue demon with a long nose accompanies epileptics, a fat red one accompanies sufferers from pneumonia, etc., etc. They know such further facts as that the fat red demon dislikes a certain sort of mold which the witch doctors give people who have pneumonia. (There are various competing theories about what demons do when not causing diseases, but serious witch doctors regard such speculations as unverifiable and profitless.)

If we encountered such a tribe, we would be inclined to tell them that there are no demons. We would tell them that diseases were caused by germs, viruses, and the like. We would add that the witch doctors were not seeing demons, but merely having hallucinations. We would be quite right, but would we be right on *empirical* grounds? What empirical criteria, built into the demon-talk of the tribe, go unsatisfied? What predictions which the tribesmen make fail to come true? If there are none, a sophisticated witch doctor may reply that all modern science can do is to show (1) that the presence of demons is constantly correlated with that of germs, viruses, and the like, and (2) that eating certain mushrooms sometimes makes people think they see things that aren't really there. This is hardly sufficient to show that there are no demons. At best, it shows that if we forget about demons, then (a) a simpler account of the cause and cure of disease and (b) a simpler account of why people make the perceptual reports they do, may be given.

What do we reply to such a sophisticated witch doctor? I think that all that we would have left to say is that the simplicity of the accounts which can be offered if we forget about demons *is* an excellent reason for saying that there are no demons. Demon-discourse is one way of describing and predicting phenomena, but there are better ways. We *could* (as the witch doctor urges) tack demon-discourse on to modern science by saying, first, that diseases are caused by the compresence of demons and germs (each being a necessary, but neither a sufficient, condition) and, second, that the witch doctors (unlike drunkards and psychotics) really do see intangible beings (about whom, alas, nothing is known save their visual appearances). If we did so, we would retain all the predictive and explanatory advantages of modern science. We would know as much about the cause and cure of disease, and about hallucinations, as we did before. We would, however, be burdened with problems which we did not have before: the problem of why demons are visible only to witch doctors and the problem of why germs cannot cause diseases all by themselves. We avoid both problems by saying that demons do not exist. The witch doctor may remark that this use of Occam's Razor has the same advantage as that of theft over honest toil. To such a remark, the only reply could be an account of the practical advantages gained by the use of the Razor in the past.

Now the Identity Theorist's claim is that sensations may be to the future progress of psycho-physiology as demons are to modern science. Just as we now want to deny that there are demons, future science may want to deny that there are sensations. The only obstacle to replacing sensation-discourse with brain-discourse seems to be that sensation-statements have a reporting as well as an explanatory function. But the demon case makes clear that the discovery of a new way of explaining the phenomena previously explained by reference to a certain sort of entity, *combined with a new account of what is being reported by observation-statements about that sort of entity*, may give good reason for saying that there are no entities of that sort. The absurdity of saying "Nobody has ever felt a pain" is no greater than that of saying "Nobody has ever seen a demon," *if* we have a suitable answer to the question "What *was* I reporting when I said I felt a pain?" To this question, the science of the future may reply "You were reporting the occurrence of a certain brain-process, and it would make life simpler for us if you would, in the future, *say* 'My C-fibers are firing' instead of saying 'I'm in pain'." In so saying, he has as good a prima facie case as the scientist who answers the witch doctor's question "What *was* I reporting when I reported a demon?" by saying "You were reporting the content of your hallucination, and it would make life simpler if, in the future, you would describe your experiences in those terms."

Given this prima facie analogy between demons and sensations, we can now attend to some disanalogies. We may note, first, that there is no simple way of filling in the blank in "What people called 'demons' are nothing but _____ ." For neither "hallucinatory contents" nor "germs" will do. The observational and the explanatory roles of "demon" must be distinguished. We need to say something like "What people who reported seeing demons were reporting was simply the content of their hallucinations," and *also* something like "What people explained by reference to demons can be explained better by reference to germs, viruses, etc." Because of the need for a relatively complex account of how we are to get along without reference to demons, we cannot *identify* "What we called 'demons' " with anything. So, instead, we simply deny their existence. In the case of sensations, however, we can give a relatively simple account of how to get along in the future. Both the explanatory *and* the reporting functions of statements about sensations can be taken over by statements about brain-processes. Therefore we are prepared to identify "What we called 'sensations' " with brain-processes, and to say "What we called 'sensations' turn out to be nothing but brain-processes."

Thus this disanalogy does not have the importance which it appears to have at first. In both the demon case and the sensation case, the proposed reduction has the same pragmatic consequences: namely, that we should stop asking questions about the causal and/or spatio-temporal relationships holding between the "reduced" entities (demons, sensations) and the rest of the universe, and replace these with questions about the relationships holding between certain other entities (germs, hallucinatory experiences, brain-processes) and the rest of the universe. It happens, for the reasons just sketched, that the proposed reduction is put in the form of a denial of existence in one case, and of an identification in another case. But "There are no demons" and "What people call 'sensations' are nothing but brain processes" can both equally well be paraphrased as "Elimination of the referring use of the expression in question ('demon,' 'sensation') from our language would leave our ability to describe and predict undiminished."

Nevertheless, the claim that there might turn out to be no such thing as a "sensation" seems scandalous. The fact that a witch doctor might be scandalized by a similar claim about demons does not, in itself, do much to diminish our sense of shock. In what follows, I wish to account for this intuitive implausibility. I shall argue that it rests *solely* upon the fact that elimination of the referring use of "sensation" from our language would be in the highest degree *impractical*. If this can be shown, then I think that the Identity Theorist will be cleared of the charge of "conceptual confusion" usually leveled against him. Rather than proceeding directly to this argument, however, I shall first consider a line of argument which has often been used to show that he *is* guilty of this charge. Examining this line of argument will permit me to sketch in greater detail what the Identity Theorist is and is not saying.

4. THE ELIMINABILITY OF OBSERVATION TERMS

The usual move made by the opponents of the Identity Theory is to compare suggested reduction of sensations to brain-processes to certain other cases in which we say that "X's turn out to be nothing but Y's." There are two significantly different classes of cases and it might seem that the Identity Theorist confuses them. First, there is the sort of case in which both "X" and "Y" are used to refer to observable entities, and the claim that "What people called 'X's' are nothing but Y's" backed up by pointing out that the statement "This is an X" commits one to an empirically false proposition. For example, we say that "What people called 'unicorn horns' are nothing but narwhal horns," and urge that we cease to respond to a perceptual situation with "This is a unicorn horn." We do this because "This is a unicorn horn" commits one to the existence of unicorns, and there are, it turns out, no unicorns. Let us call this sort of case *identification of observables with other observables*. Second, there is the sort of case in which "X" is used to refer to an observable entity and "Y" is used to refer to an unobservable entity. Here we do not (typically) back up the claim that "What people called 'X's' are nothing but Y's" by citing an empirically false proposition presupposed by "This is an X." For example, the statement that "What people call 'tables' are nothing but clouds of molecules" does not suggest, or require as a ground, that people who say "This is a table" hold false beliefs. Rather, we are suggesting that something *more* has been found out about the sort of situation reported by "This is a table." Let us call this second sort of case *identification of observables with theoretical entities*.

It seems that we cannot assimilate the identification of sensations with brain-processes to either of these cases. For, unlike the typical case of identification of observables with other observables, we do not wish to say that people who have reported sensations in the past have (necessarily) any empirically disconfirmed beliefs. People are not wrong about sensations in the way in which they were wrong about "unicorn horns." Again, unlike the typical case of the identification of observables with theoretical entities, we do not want to say that brain-processes are "theoretical" or unobservable. Furthermore, in cases in which we identify an observable X with an unobservable Y, we are usually willing to accept the remark that "That does not show that there are no X's." The existence of tables is not (it would seem) impugned by their identification with clouds of electrons, as the existence of unicorn horns is impugned by their identification with narwhal horns. But a defender of the disappearance form of the Identity Theory *does* want to impugn the existence of sensations.

Because the claim that "What people call 'sensations' may turn out to be nothing but brain-processes" cannot be assimilated to either of these cases, it has been attacked as trivial or incoherent. The following dilemma is posed by those who attack it: either the Identity Theorist claims that talk about sensations presupposes some empirically disconfirmed belief (and what could it be?) or the "identity" which he has in mind is the uninteresting sort of identity which holds between tables and clouds of molecules (mere "theoretical replacability").

The point at which the Identity Theorist should attack this dilemma is the premiss invoked in stating the second horn—the premiss that the identification of tables with clouds of molecules does not permit us to infer to the nonexistence of tables. This premiss is true, but *why* is it true? That there is room for reflection here is apparent when we place the case of tables side-by-side with the case of demons. If there is any point to saying that tables are nothing but clouds of molecules it is presumably to say that, in principle, we could stop making a referring use of "table," and of any extensionally equivalent term, and still leave our ability to describe and predict undiminished. But this would seem just the point of (and the justification for) saying that there are no demons. Why does the realization that nothing would be lost by the dropping of "table" from our vocabulary still leave us with the conviction that there are tables, whereas the same realization about demons leave us with the conviction that there are no demons? I suggest that the only answer to this question which will stand examination is that although we could *in principle* drop "table," it would be monstrously inconvenient to do so, whereas it is both possible in principle and convenient in practice to drop "demon." The reason "But there still are tables" sounds so plausible is that nobody would dream of suggesting that we stop reporting our experiences in table-talk and start reporting them in molecule-talk. The reason "There are no demons" sounds so plausible is that we are quite willing to suggest that the witch-doctors stop reporting their experiences in demon-talk and start reporting them in hallucination-talk.

A conclusive argument that this practical difference is the *only* relevant difference would, obviously, canvass all the other differences which might be noted. I shall not attempt this. Instead, I shall try to make my claim plausible by sketching a general theory of the conditions under which a term may cease to have a referring use without those who made such a use being convicted of having held false beliefs.

Given the same sorts of correlations between X's and Y's, we are more likely to say "X's are nothing but Y's" when reference to X's is habitually made in non-inferential reports, and more likely to say "There are no 'X's'" when such reference is never or rarely made. (By "noninferential report" I mean a statement in response to which questions like "How did you know?" "On what evidence do you say . . . ?" and "What leads you to think . . . ?" are normally considered misplaced and unanswerable, but which is none-theless capable of empirical confirmation.) Thus we do not say that the identification of temperature with the kinetic energy of molecules shows that there is no such thing as temperature, since "temperature" originally (i.e., before the invention of thermometers) stood for something which was always reported non-inferentially, and still is frequently so reported; similarly, for all identifications of familiar macro-objects with unfamiliar micro-objects. But since in our culture-circle we do not *habitually* report non-inferentially the presence of caloric fluid, demons, etc., we do not feel unhappy at the bald suggestion that there are no such things.

Roughly speaking, then, the more accustomed we are to "X" serving as an observation-term (by which I mean a term habitually used in non-inferential reports) the more we prefer, when inquiry shows the possibility of ac-counting for the phenomena explained by reference to X's without such reference, to "identify" X's with some sort of Y's, rather than to deny existence to X's *tout court. But the more grounds we have for such identification, the more chance there is that we shall stop using "X" in non-inferential reports,* and thus the greater chance of our eventually coming to accept the claim that "there are no X's" with equanimity. This is why we find borderline cases, and gradual shifts from assimilations of X's to Y's to an assertion that X's do not exist. For example, most people do not report the presence of pink rats non-inferentially (nor inferentially, for that matter), but some do. The recognition that they are in the minority helps those who do so to admit that there are no pink rats. But suppose that the vast majority of us had always seen (intangible and uncatchable) pink rats; would it not then be likely that we should resist the bald assertion that there are no pink rats and insist on something of the form "pink rats are nothing but. . . "? It might be a very long time before we came to drop the habit of reporting pink rats and began reporting hallucinations instead.

The typical case history of an observation-term ceasing to have a referring use runs the following course: (1) X's are the subjects of both inferential and non-inferential reports;[8] (2) empirical discoveries are made which enable us to subsume X-laws under Y-laws and to produce new X-laws by studying Y's; (3) inferential reports of X's cease to be made; (4) non-inferential reports of X's are reinterpreted either (4a) as reports of Y's, *or* (4b) as reports of mental entities (thoughts that one is seeing an X, hallucinatory images, etc.); (5) non-inferential reports of X's cease to be made (because their place is taken by non-inferential reports either of Y's or of thoughts, hallucinatory images, etc.); (6) we conclude that there simply are no such things as X's.

This breakdown of stages lets us pick out two crucial conditions that must be satisfied if we are to move from "X's are nothing but Y's" (stage 2) to "there are no X's" (stage 6). These conditions are:

(A) The Y-laws must be *better* at explaining the kinds of phenomena explained by the X-laws (not just equally good). Indeed, they must be sufficiently better so that *the inconvenience of changing one's linguistic habits by ceasing to make reports about X's is less than the inconvenience of going through the routine of translating one's X-reports into Y-reports in order to get satisfactory explanations of the phenomena in question.* If this condition is not satisfied, the move from stage (2) to stage (3) will not be made, and thus no later move will be made.

(B) Either Y-reports may themselves be made non-inferentially, or X-reports may be treated as reports of mental entities. For we must be able to have some answer to the question "What *am* I reporting when I non-inferentially report about an X?," and the only answers available are "you're reporting on a Y" or "you're reporting on some merely mental entity." If neither answer is available, we can move neither to (4a) nor to (4b), nor, therefore, on to (5) and (6).

Now the reason we move from stage (2) to stage (3) in the case of demons is that (A) is obviously satisfied. The phenomena which we explained by reference to the activity of demons are so much better explained in other ways that it is simpler to stop inferring to the existence of demons altogether than to continue making such inferences, and then turning to laws about germs and the like for an explanation of the behavior of the demons. The reason why we do *not* move from (2) to (3)—much less to (6)—in the case of temperature or tables is that explanations formulated in terms of temperatures are so good, on the ground which they were originally intended to cover, that we feel no temptation to stop talking about temperatures and tables merely because we can, in some cases, get more precise predictions by going up a level to laws about molecules. The reason why we move on from (3) to (4) in the case of demons is that the alternative labeled (4b) is readily available—we can easily consign experiences of demons to that great dumping-ground of out-dated entities, the Mind. There were no experiences of demons, we say, but only experiences of mental images.

Now it seems obvious that, in the case of sensations, (A) will not be satisfied. The inconvenience of ceasing to talk about sensations would be so great that only a fanatical materialist would think it worth the trouble to cease referring to sensations. If the Identity Theorist is taken to be predicting that some day "sensation," "pain," "mental image," and the like will drop out of our vocabulary, he is almost certainly wrong. But if he is saying simply that, at no greater cost than an inconvenient linguistic reform, we *could* drop such terms, he is entirely justified. And I take this latter claim to be all that traditional materialism has ever desired.

Before leaving the analogy between demons and sensations, I wish to note one further disanalogy which an opponent of the Identity Theory might pounce upon. Even if we set aside the fact that (A) would not be satisfied in the case of sensations, such an opponent might say, we should note the difficulty in satisfying (B). It would seem that there is no satisfactory answer to the question "What *was* I non-inferentially reporting when I reported on my sensations?" For neither (4a) nor (4b) seems an available option. The first does not seem to be available because it is counter-intuitive to think of, e.g., "I am having my C-fibers stimulated," as capable of being used to make a non-inferential report. The second alternative is simply silly — there is no point in saying that when we report a sensation we are reporting some "merely mental" event. For sensations are *already* mental events. The last point is important for an understanding of the prima facie absurdity of the disappearance form of the Identity Theory. The reason why most statements of the form "there might turn out to be no X's at all" can be accepted with more or less equanimity in the context of forecasts of scientific results is that we are confident we shall always be able to "save the phenomena" by answering the question "But what about all those X's we've been accustomed to observe?" with some reference to thoughts-of X's, images-of-X's, and the like. Reference to mental entities provides non-inferential reports of X's with something to have been about. But when we want to say "There might turn out to be no mental entities at all," we cannot use this device. This result makes clear that if the analogy between the past disappearance of supernatural beings and the possible future disappearance of sensations is to be pressed, we must claim that alternative (4a) is, appearances to the contrary, still open. That is, we must hold that the question "What *was* I non-inferentially reporting when I non-inferentially reported a stabbing pain?" can be sensibly answered "You were reporting a stimulation of your C-fibers."

Now why should this *not* be a sensible answer? Let us begin by getting a bad objection to it out of the way. One can imagine someone arguing that this answer can only be given if a stimulation of C-fibers is strictly identical with a stabbing pain, and that such strict identification involves category-mistakes. But this objection presupposes that "A report of an X is a report of a Y" entails that "X's are Y's." If we grant this presupposition we shall not be able to say that the question "What was I reporting when I reported a demon?" is properly answered by "You were reporting the content of an hallucination which you were having." However, if we ask why this objection is plausible, we can see the grain of truth which it embodies and conceals. We are usually unwilling to accept "You were reporting a Y" as an answer to the question "What *was* I non-inferentially reporting when I non-inferentially reported an X?" unless (a) Y's are themselves the kind of thing we habitually report on non-inferentially, and (b) there does not exist already an habitual practice of reporting Y's non-inferentially. Thus we accept "the content of an hallucination" as a sensible answer because we know that such contents, being "mental images," are just the sort of thing which does get non-inferentially reported (once it is recognized for what it is) and because we are not accustomed to making non-inferential reports in the form "I am having an hallucinatory image of. . . ."[9] To take an example of answers to this sort of question that are *not* sensible, we reject the claim that when we report on a table we are reporting on a mass of whirling particles, for either we think we know under what circumstances we should make such a report, and know that these circumstances do not obtain, or we believe that the presence of such particles can only be inferred and never observed.

The oddity of saying that when I think I am reporting on a stabbing pain I am actually reporting on a stimulation of my C-fibers is similar to these last two cases. We either imagine a situation in which we can envisage ourselves non-inferentially reporting such stimulation (periscope hitched up to a microscope so as to give us a view of our trepanned skull, overlying fibers folded out of the way, stimulation evident by change in color, etc., etc.), or else we regard "stimulation of C-fibers" as not the sort of thing which *could* be the subject of a non-inferential report (but inherently a "theoretical" state of affairs whose existence can only be inferred, and not observed). In either case, the assertion that we have been non-inferentially reporting on a brain-process all our lives seems absurd. So the proponent of the disappearance form of the Identity Theory must show that reports of brain-processes are neither incapable of being non-inferential nor, if non-inferential, necessarily made in the way just imagined (with the periscope-microscope gadget) or in some other peculiar way. But now we must ask who bears the burden of proof. Why, after all, should we think that brain-processes are *not* a fit subject-matter for non-inferential reports? And why should it not be the case that the circumstances in which we make non-inferential reports about brain-processes are just those circumstances in which we make non-inferential reports about sensations? For this will in fact be the case if, when we were trained to say, e.g., "I'm in pain," we were in fact being trained to respond to the occurrence within ourselves of a stimulation of C-fibers. If this is the case, the situation will be perfectly parallel to the case of demons and hallucinations. We *will*, indeed, have been making non-inferential reports about brain-processes all our lives *sans le savoir.*

This latter suggestion can hardly be rejected a priori, unless we hold that we can only be taught to respond to the occurrence of A's with the utterance "A!" if we were able, prior to this teaching, to be aware, when an A was present, that it was present. But this latter claim is plausible only if we assume that there is an activity which can reasonably be called "awareness" prior to the learning of language. I do not wish to fight once again the battle which has been fought by Wittgenstein and many of his followers against such a notion of awareness. I wish rather to take it as having been won, and to take for granted that there is no a priori reason why a brain-process is inherently unsuited to be the subject of a noninferential report. The distinction between observation terms and nonobservation terms is relative to linguistic practices (practices which may change as inquiry progresses), rather than capable of being marked out once and for all by distinguishing between the "found" and the "made" elements in our experience. I think that the recognition of this relativity is the first of the steps necessary for a proper appreciation of the claims of the Identity Theory. In what follows, I want to show that this first step leads naturally to a second: the recognition that the distinction between *private* and *public* subject-matters is as relative as that between items signified by observation-terms and items not so signified.

The importance of this second step is clear. For even if we grant that reports of brain-processes may be non-inferential, we still need to get around the facts that reports of sensations have an epistemological peculiarity that leads us to call them reports of *private* entities, and that brain-processes are intrinsically *public* entities. Unless we can overcome our intuitive conviction that a report of a private matter (with its attendant infallibility) cannot be identified with a report of a public matter (with its attendant fallibility), we shall not be able to take seriously the claim of the proponents of the disappearance form of the Identity Theory that alternative (4a) is open, and hence that nothing prevents sensations from disappearing from discourse in the same manner, and for the same reasons, as supernatural beings have disappeared from discourse. So far in this paper I have deliberately avoided the problem of the "privacy" of sensations, because I wished to show that if this problem *can* be surmounted, the Identity Theorist may fairly throw the burden of proof onto his opponent by asking whether a criterion can be produced which would show that the identification of sensations and brain-processes involves a conceptual confusion, while absolving the claim that demons do not exist because of such a confusion. Since I doubt that such a criterion *can* be produced, I am inclined to say that if the problem about "privacy" is overcome, then the Identity Theorist has made out his case.

5. THE "PRIVACY" OBJECTION

The problem that the privacy of first-person sensation reports presents for the Identity Theory has recently been formulated in considerable detail by Baier.[10] In this section, I shall confine myself to a discussion of his criticism of Smart's initial reply to this argument. Smart holds that the fact that "the language of introspective reports has a different logic from the logic of material processes" is no objection to the Identity Theory, since we may expect that empirical inquiry can and will change this logic:

> It is obvious that until the brain-process theory is much improved and widely accepted there will be no *criteria* for saying 'Smith has an experience of such-and-such a sort' except Smith's introspective reports. So we have adopted a rule of language that (normally) what Smith says goes.[11]

Baier thinks that this reply "is simply a confusion of the privacy of the subject-matter and the availability of external evidence."[12] Baier's intuition is that the difference between a language-stratum in which the fact that a report is sincerely made is sufficient warrant for its truth, and one in which this situation does not obtain, seems so great as to call for an explanation — and that the only explanation is that the two strata concern different subject-matters. Indeed Baier is content to let the mental-physical distinction stand or fall with the distinction between "private" subject-matters and "public" subject-matters, and he therefore assumes that to show that "introspective reports are necessarily about something private, and that being about something private is *incompatible with being* about something public"[13] is to show, once and for all, that the Identity Theory involves a conceptual confusion. Baier, in short, is undertaking to show that "once private, always private."

He argues for his view as follows:

> To say that one day our physiological knowledge will increase to such an extent that we shall be able to make absolutely reliable encephalograph-based claims about people's experiences, is only to say that, if carefully checked, our encephalograph-based claims about 'experiences' will always be *correct,* i.e., will make the *same claims* as a *truthful* introspective reports. If correct

encephalograph-based claims about Smith's experiences contradict Smith's introspective reports, we shall be entitled to infer that he is *lying*. In that sense, what Smith says will no longer go. But we cannot of course infer that he is making a mistake, for that is nonsense. . . . *However good the evidence may be, such a physiological theory can never be used to show to the sufferer that he was mistaken in thinking that he had a pain, for such a mistake is inconceivable.* The sufferer's epistemological authority must therefore be better than the best physiological theory can ever be. Physiology can therefore never provide a person with more than *evidence* that someone else is having an experience of one sort or another. It can never lay down *criteria* for saying that someone is having an experience of a certain sort. Talk about brain-processes therefore must be about something other than talk about experiences. Hence, introspective reports and brain process talk cannot be merely different ways of talking about the same thing.[14]

Smart's own reply to this line of argument is to admit that

No physiological evidence, say from a gadget attached to my skull, could make me withdraw the statement that I have a pain when as a matter of fact I feel a pain. For example, the gadget might show no suitable similarities of cerebral processes on the various occasions on which I felt a pain. . . . I must, I think, agree with Baier that if the sort of situation which we have just envisaged did in fact come about, then I should have to reject the brain process thesis, and would perhaps espouse dualism.[15]

But this is not the interesting case. The interesting case is the one in which suitable similarities are in fact found to occur — the same similarities in all subjects — until one day (long after all empirical generalizations about sensations *qua* sensations have been subsumed under physiological laws, and long after direct manipulation of the brain has become the exclusive method of relieving pain) somebody (call him Jones) thinks he has no pain, but the encephalograph says that the brain-process correlated with pain did occur. (Let us imagine that Jones himself is observing the gadget, and that the problem about whether he might have made a mistake is a problem for Jones; this eliminates the possibility of lying.) Now in most cases in which one's observation throws doubt on a correlation which is so central to current scientific explanations, one tries to eliminate the possibility of observational error. But in Baier's view it would be absurd for Jones to do this, for "a mistake is inconceivable." Actually, however, it is fairly clear what Jones' first move would be — he will begin to suspect that he does not know what pain is — i.e., that he is not using the word "pain" in the way in which his fellows use it.[16]

So now Jones looks about for independent verification of the hypothesis that he does not use "I am in pain" incorrectly. But here he runs up against the familiar difficulty about the vocabulary used in making introspective reports—the difficulty of distinguishing between "misuse of language" and "mistake in judgment," between (a) recognizing the state of affairs which obtains for what it is, but describing it wrongly because the words used in the description are not the right words, and (b) being able to describe it rightly once it is recognized for what it is, but not in fact recognizing it for what it is (in the way in which one deceived by an illusion does not recognize the situation for what it is). If we do not have a way of determining which of these situations obtains, we do not have a genuine contrast between misnaming and misjudging. To see that there is no genuine contrast in this case, suppose that Jones was not burned prior to the time that he hitches on the encephalograph, but now he is. When he is, the encephalograph says that the brain-process constantly correlated with pain-reports occurs in Jones' brain. However, although he exhibits pain-behavior, Jones thinks that he does not feel pain. (But, now as in the past, he both exhibits pain-behavior and thinks that he feels pain when he is frozen, stuck, struck, racked, etc.) Now is it that he does not know that *pain* covers what you feel when you are burned as well as what you feel when you are stuck, struck, etc.? Or is it that he really does not feel pain when he is burned? Suppose we tell Jones that what he feels when he is burned is *also* called "pain." Suppose he then admits that he does feel *something,* but insists that what he feels is quite *different* from what he feels when he is stuck, struck, etc. Where does Jones go from here? Has he failed to learn the language properly, or is he correctly (indeed infallibly) reporting that he has different sensations than those normally had in the situation in question? (Compare the parallel question in the case of a man who uses "blue" in all the usual ways except that he refuses to grant that blue is a color—on the ground that it is so different from red, yellow, orange, violet, etc.)

The only device which would decide this question would be to establish a convention that anyone who sincerely denied that he felt a pain while exhibiting pain-behavior and being burned ipso facto did not understand how to use "pain." This denial would *prove* that he lacked such an understanding. But this would be a dangerous path to follow. For not to understand when to use the word "pain" in non-inferential reports is presumably to be unable to know which of one's sensations to call a "pain." And the denial that one felt pain in the circumstances mentioned would only prove such inability if one indeed *had* the sensation normally called a pain. So now we would have a public criterion, satisfaction of which would count as showing that the subject had such a sensation—i.e., that he felt a pain even though he did not think that he did. But if such a criterion exists, its application overrides any contradictory report that he may make—for such a report will be automatically disallowed by the fact that it constitutes a demonstration that he does not know what he is talking about. The dilemma is that either a report about one's sensations which violates a certain public criterion is a sufficient condition for saying that the reporter does not know how to use "pain" in the correct way, or there is no such criterion. If there is, the fact that one cannot be mistaken about pains does not entail that sincere reports of pain cannot be overridden. If there is not, then there is no way to answer the question formulated at the end of the last paragraph, and hence no way to eliminate the possibility that Jones may not know what pain is. Now since the a priori probability that he does not is a good deal higher than the a priori probability that the psycho-physiological theory of Jones' era is mistaken, this theory has little to fear from Jones. (Although it would have a great deal to fear from a sizable accumulation of cases like Jones'.)

To sum up this point, we may look back at the italicized sentence in the above quotation from Baier. We now see that the claim that "such a mistake is inconceivable" is an ellipsis for the claim that a mistake, made *by one who knows what pain is,* is inconceivable, for only this expanded form will entail that when Jones and the encephalograph disagree, Jones is always right. But when formulated in this way our infallibility about our pains can be seen to be empty. Being infallible about something would be useful only if we could draw the usual distinction between misnaming and misjudging, and, having ascertained that we were not misnaming, know that we were not misjudging. But where there are no criteria for misjudging (or to put it more accurately, where in the crucial cases the criteria for misjudging turn out to be the same as the criteria for misnaming) than to say that we are infallible is to pay ourselves an empty compliment. Our neighbors will not hesitate to ride roughshod over our reports of our sensations unless they are assured that we know our way around among them, and we cannot satisfy them on this point unless, up to a certain point, we tell the same sort of story about them as they do. The limits of permissible stories are flexible enough for us to be able to convince them occasionally that we have odd sensations, but not flexible enough for us to use these surprising sensations to break down, with one blow, well-confirmed scientific theories. As in the case of other infallible pronouncements, the price of retaining one's epistemological authority is a decent respect for the opinions of mankind.

Thus the common-sense remark that first-person reports always will be a better source of information about the occurrence of pains than any other source borrows its plausibility from the fact that we normally do not raise questions about a man's ability to use the word "pain" correctly. Once we *do* raise such questions seriously (as in the case of Jones), we realize that the question (1) "Does he know which sensations are called 'pains'?" and (2) "Is he a good judge of whether he is in pain or not?" are simply two ways of asking the same question: viz., "Can we fit his pain-reports into our scheme for explaining and predicting pains?" or, more bluntly, "Shall we disregard his pain-reports or not?" And once we see this we realize that if "always be a better source of information" means "will never be overridden on the sort of grounds on which presumed observational errors are overridden elsewhere in science," then our common sensical remark is probably false. If "always be a better source of information" means merely "can only be overridden on the basis of a charge of misnaming, and never on the basis of a charge of misjudging," then our common sensical remark turns out to depend upon a distinction that is not there.

This Wittgensteinian point that sensation-reports must conform to public criteria or else be disallowed may also be brought out in the following way. We determine whether to take a surprising first-person report of pain or its absence seriously (that is, whether to say that the sensation reported is something that science must try to explain) by seeing whether the reporter's overall pattern of pain-reporting is, by the usual behavioral and environmental criteria, normal. Now suppose that these public criteria (for "knowing how to use 'pain' ") change as physiology and technology progress. Suppose, in particular, that we find it convenient to speed up the learning of contrastive observation predicates (such as "painful," "tickling," etc.) by supplying children with portable encephalographs-cum-teaching-machines which, whenever the appropriate brain-process occurs, murmur the appropriate term in their ears. Now "appropriate brain-process" will start out by meaning "brain-process constantly correlated with sincere utterances of 'I'm in pain' by people taught the use of 'pain' in the old rough-and-ready way." But soon it will come to mean, "the brain-process which we have always programmed the machine to respond to with a murmur of 'pain.' " (A meter is [now, but was not always] what matches the Standard Meter; intelligence is [now, but was not always] what intelligence tests test; pains will be [but are not now] what the Standard "Pain"-Training Program calls "pain.") Given this situation, it would make sense to say things like "You say you are in pain, and I'm sure you are sincere, but you can see for yourself that your brain is not in the state to which you were trained to respond to with "Pain," so apparently the training did not work, and you do not yet understand what pain is." In such a situation, our "inability to be mistaken" about our pains would remain, but our "final epistemological authority" on the subject would be gone, for there would be a standard procedure for overriding our reports. Our inability to be mistaken is, after all, no more than our ability to have such hypothetical statements as "If you admit that I'm sincere and that I know the language, you have to accept what I say" accepted by our fellows. But this asset can only be converted into final epistemological authority if we can secure both admissions. Where a clear-cut public criterion *does* exist for "knowing the language," inability to be mistaken does not entail inability to be overridden.

Now Baier might say that if such criteria did exist, then we should no longer be talking about what we presently mean by "pains." I do not think that this needs to be conceded,[17] but suppose that it is. Would this mean that there was now a subject-matter which was not being discussed — viz., the private subject-matter the existence of which Baier's argument was intended to demonstrate? That we once had contact with such a subject-matter, but lost it? These rhetorical questions are meant to suggest that Baier's explanation of the final epistemological authority of first-person reports of pains by the fact that this "logic" is "a function of this type of subject-matter" rather than, as Smart thinks, a convention — is an explanation of the obscure by the more obscure. More precisely, it will not be an explanation of the epistemological authority in question — but only an unenlightening redescription of it — unless Baier can give a meaning to the term "private subject-matter" other than "kind of thing which is reported in reports which cannot be overridden." These considerations show the need for stepping back from Baier's argument and considering the criteria which he is using to demarcate distinct subject-matters.

6. "PRIVACY" AS A CRITERION OF CATEGOREAL DEMARCATION

The closest Baier comes to giving a definition of "private subject-matter" is to say that

> We must say that 'I have a pain' is about 'something private,' because in making this remark we report something which is (1) *necessarily owned* . . . (2) *necessarily exclusive and unsharable* . . . (3) *necessarily imperceptible by the senses* . . . (4) *necessarily asymmetrical,* for whereas it makes no sense to say 'I could see (or hear) that I had a pain,' it makes quite good sense to say 'I could see (or hear) that *he* had a pain'; (5) something about the possession of which the person who claims to possess it could not possibly examine, consider, or weigh any evidence, although other people could . . . and lastly (6) it is something about which the person whose private state it is has final epistemological authority, for it does not make sense to say 'I have a pain unless I am mistaken.'[18]

Now this definition of "something private" entails that nothing could be private except a state of a person, and is constructed to delimit all and only those states of a person which we call his "mental" states. To say that mental states are private is to say simply that mental states are described in the way in which mental states are described. But it is not hard to take *any* Rylean category of terms (call it *C*), list all the types of sentence-frames which do and do not make sense when their gaps are filled with terms belonging to this category, and say that "something C" is distinguished by the fact that it is "necessarily X," "necessarily Y," etc. where "X" and "Y" are labels for the fact that certain sentence-frames will or will not receive these terms as gap-fillers. For example, consider the thesis that:

> We must say that 'The devil is in that corner' is about 'something supernatural' because in making this report we report something which is *necessarily intangible,* since it makes no sense to ask about the texture of his skin, not *necessarily simply-located,* since it does not follow from the fact that a supernatural being is in the corner that the same supernatural being is not simultaneously at the other side of the globe, *necessarily immortal,* since it does not make sense to say that a supernatural being has died, *necessarily perceptible to exorcists,* since it would not make sense to say that a man was an exorcist and did not perceive the devil when he was present. . . .

Are devils hallucinations? No, because when one reports an hallucination one reports something which, though intangible, is simply-located, is neither mortal nor immortal, and is not always perceptible to exorcists. Are reports of devils reports of hallucinations? No, because reports of devils are reports of something supernatural and reports of hallucinations are reports of something private. Is it simply because we lack further information about devils that we take exorcists' sincere reports as the best possible source for information about them? No, for this suggestion confuses the supernatural character of the subject-matter with the availability of external evidence. Those without the supernatural powers with which the exorcist is gifted may find ways of gathering *evidence* for the presence of supernatural beings, but they can never formulate an overriding and independent *criterion* for saying that such a being is present. Their theories might become so good that we might sometimes say that a given exorcist was *lying,* but we could never say that he was *mistaken.*

If this pastiche of Baier's argument seems beside the point, it is presumably either (1) because the language-game I have described is not in fact played, or else (2) because "necessarily intangible, not necessarily simply-located, necessarily immortal, and necessarily perceptible to exorcists" does not delimit a subject-matter in the way in which "necessarily owned, exclusive, imperceptible by the senses, asymmetrical, etc., etc." does. In (1) one has to ask "what if it *had* been played?" After all, if the technique of detecting distinct subject-matters which Baier uses is a generally applicable technique, and not just constructed *ad hoc* to suit our Cartesian intuitions, then it ought to work on imaginary as well as real language games. But if it is, we ought to be able to formulate rules for applying it which would tell us *why* (2) is the case. For if we cannot, and if the language-game described once was played, then Baier's objection to the Identity Theory is an objection to the theory that reports of visible supernatural beings are reports of hallucinations.

Baier gives no more help in seeing what these rules would be. But I think that the root of Baier's conviction that "something private" is a suitable candidate for being a "distinct subject matter" is the thesis that certain terms are *intrinsically* observation predicates, and signify, so to speak, "natural explananda." When in quest of such predicates we look to the "foundations" of empirical knowledge, we tend to rapidly identify "observation predicate" with "predicate occurring in report having final epistemological authority" with "predicate occurring in report about something private." This chain of identifications leaves us with the suspicion that if there were no longer a private subject-matter to be infallible about, the whole fabric of empirical inquiry about public matters would be left up in the air, unsupported by any absolute epistemological authority. The suggestion that the distinction between items reportable in infallible reports and items not so reportable is "ultimate," or "irreducible," or "categorical," owes its intuitive force to the difficulty of imagining a stage in the progress of inquiry in which there was not *some* situation in which absolute epistemological authority about *something* would be granted to *somebody*.

There probably could *not* be such a stage, for inquiry cannot proceed if everything is to be doubted at once, and if inquiry is even to get off the ground we need to get straight about what is to be questioned and what not. These practical dictates show the kernel of truth in the notion that inquiry cannot proceed without a foundation. Where we slide from truth into error is in assuming that certain items are *naturally* reportable in infallible reports, and thus assume that the items presently so reportable always were and always will be reportable (and conversely for items not presently so reportable). A pain looks like the paradigm of such an item, with the situation described by "seems to me as if I were seeing something red" almost as well-qualified. But in both cases, we can imagine situations in which we should feel justified in overriding sincere reports using these predicates. More important, we see that the device which we should use to justify ourselves in such situations — viz., "The reporter may not know how to use the word . . ." — is one which can apply in *all* proposed cases. Because this escape-hatch is always available, and because the question of whether the reporter does know how to use the word or not is probably not itself a question which could ever be settled by recourse to any absolute epistemological authority, the situation envisaged by Baier — namely, the body of current scientific theory foundering upon the rock of a single overriding report — can probably never arise. Baier sees a difference in kind between the weight of evidence produced by such a theory and the single, authoritative, *criterion* provided by such a report. But since there can be no overriding report until the ability of the speaker to use the words used in the report is established, and since this is to be established only by the weight of the evidence and not by recourse to any single criterion, this difference in kind (even though it may indeed be "firmly embedded in the way we talk" for millennia) is always capable of being softened into a difference of degree by further empirical inquiry.

7. REDUCTIONIST PHILOSOPHICAL THEORIES AND CATEGOREAL DISTINCTIONS

In the preceding sections of this paper I have constantly invoked the fact that language changes as empirical discoveries are made, in order to argue that the thesis that "What people now call 'sensations' might be discovered to be brain-processes" is sensible and unconfused. The "deviance" of a statement of this thesis should not, I have been urging, blind us to the facts that (a) entities referred to by expressions in one Rylean category may also be referred to by expressions in another, (b) expressions in the first category may drop out of the language once this identity of reference is realized, and (c) the thesis in question is a natural way of expressing the result of this realization in the case of "sensation" and "brain-process." Now a critic might object that this strategy is subject to a *reductio ad absurdum*. For the same fact about linguistic change would seem to justify the claim that *any* statement of the form (S) "What people call 'X's' may be discovered to be 'Y's' " is *always* sensible and unconfused. Yet this seems paradoxical, for consider the result of substituting, say "neutrino" for "X" and "mushroom" for "Y." If the resulting statement is not conceptually confused, what statement is?

In answer to this objection, I should argue that it is a mistake to attribute "conceptual confusions" to *statements*. No statement can be known to express a conceptual confusion simply by virtue of an acquaintance with the meanings of its component terms. Confusion is a property of people. Deviance is a property of utterances. Deviant utterances made by using sentences of the form (S) *may* betoken confusion on the part of the speaker about the meanings of words, but it may simply indicate a vivid (but unconfused) imagination, or perhaps (as in the neutrino-mushroom case) merely idle fancy. Although the making of such statements may be prima facie evidence of conceptual confusion—i.e., of the fact that the speaker is insufficiently familiar with the language to find a nondeviant way of making his point—this evidence is only prima facie, and questioning may bring out evidence pointing the other way. Such questioning may show that the speaker actually has some detailed suggestions about possible empirical results which would point to the discovery in question, or that he has no such suggestions, but is nevertheless not inclined to use the relevant words in any *other* deviant utterances, and to cheerfully admit the deviance of his original utterance. The possibility of such evidence, pointing to imagination or to fancy rather than to confusion, shows that from the fact that certain questions are typically asked, and certain statements typically made, by victims of conceptual confusion, it does not follow that all those who use the sentences used to ask these questions or to make these statements are thus victimized.

This confusion about confusion is due to the fact that philosophers who propound "reductionist" theories (such as "There is no insensate matter," "There are no minds," "There are no physical objects," etc.) often *have* been conceptually confused. Such theories are often advocated as solutions to pseudo problems whose very formulation involves deviant uses of words — uses which in fact result from a confusion between the uses of two or more senses of the same term, or between two or more related terms (e.g., "name" and "word") or between the kind of questions appropriately asked of entities referred to by one set of terms and the kind appropriately asked of entities referred to by another. (That these deviant uses *are* the result of such confusion, it should be noticed, is only capable of being determined by questioning of those who use them — and we only feel *completely* safe in making this diagnosis when the original user has, in the light of the linguistic facts drawn to his attention, admitted that his putative "problem" has been dissolved.) Because reductionist theories may often be choked off at the source by an examination of uses of language, antireductionist philosophers have lately become prone to use "conceptual confusion" or "category-mistake" as an all-purpose diagnosis for any deviant utterance in the mouth of a philosopher. But this is a mistake. Predictions of the sort illustrated by (S) may be turned to confused purposes, and they may be made by confused people. But we could only infer with certainty from the deviance of the utterance of a sentence of the form (S) to the conceptual confusion of the speaker if we had a map of the categories which are exhibited in all possible languages, and were thus in a position to say that the cross-category identification envisaged by the statement was eternally impossible. In other words, we should only be in a position to make this inference with certainty if we knew that empirical inquiry could *never* bring about the sort of linguistic change which permits the nondeviant use of "There are no X's" in the case of the "X's" to which the statement in question refers. But philosophers are in no position to say that such change is impossible. The hunt for categoreal confusions at the source of reductionist philosophical theories is an extremely valuable enterprise. But their successes in this enterprise should not lead linguistic philosophers to think that they can do better what metaphysicians did badly — namely, prove the irreducibility of entities. Traditional materialism embodied many confusions, but at its heart was the unconfused prediction about future empirical inquiry which is the Identity Theory. The confusions may be eradicated without affecting the plausibility or interest of the prediction.[19]

FOOTNOTES

[1]A proponent of the Identity Theory is usually thought of as one who predicts that empirical inquiry *will* reach this result — but few philosophers in fact stick their necks out in this way. The issue is not the truth of the prediction, but whether such a prediction makes sense. Consequently, by "Identity Theory" I shall mean the assertion that it does make sense.

I include only sensations within the scope of the theory because the inclusion of thoughts would raise a host of separate problems (about the reducibility of intentional and semantic discourse to statements about linguistic behavior), and because the form of the Identity Theory which has been most discussed in the recent literature restricts itself to a consideration of sensations.

[2]James Cornman, "The Identity of Mind and Body," *Journal of Philosophy,* 59 (1962), p. 490.

[3]Cornman, p. 491.

[4]Cf. J. J. C. Smart, "Sensations and Brain Processes," reprinted in *The Philosophy of Mind,* ed. by V. C. Chappell (Englewood Cliffs, 1962), pp. 160–172, esp. pp. 166–68, and especially the claim that "When a person says 'I see a yellowish-orange after-image' he is saying something like this: 'There is something going on which is like what is going on when I have my eyes open, am awake, and there is an orange illuminated in good light in front of me, that is, when I really see an orange' " (p. 167). For criticisms of Smart's program of translation, see Cornman, op. cit.; Jerome Shaffer, "Could Mental States Be Brain Processes?," *Journal of Philosophy,* 58 (1961), pp. 812–822; Shaffer, "Mental Events and the Brain," *Journal of Philosophy,* 60 (1963), pp. 160–166. See also the articles cited in the first footnote to Smart's own article.

[5]No statement of the disappearance form of the theory with which I am acquainted is as clear and explicit as Smart's statement of the translation form. See, however, Feyerabend, "Mental Events and the Brain," *Journal of Philosophy,* 60 (1963b), pp. 295–296, and "Materialism and the Mind-Body Problem," *The Review of Metaphysics,* 17 (1963), pp. 49–67; this volume, pp. 3–16. See also Wilfrid Sellars, "The Identity Approach to the Mind-Body Problem," *ibid.,* 18 (1965). My indebtedness to this and other writings of Sellars will be obvious in what follows.

[6]Both forms agree, however, on the requirements which would have to be satisfied if we are to claim that the empirical discovery in question has been made. Roughly, they are (1) that one-one or one-many correlations could be established between every type of sensation and some clearly demarcated kind(s) of brain-processes; (2) that every known law which refers to sensations would be subsumed under laws about brain-processes; (3) that new laws about sensations be discovered by deduction from laws about brain-processes.

[7]Cornman, p. 492.

[8]Note that if X's are *only* referred to in inferential reports — as in the case of "neutrons" and "epicycles," no philosophically interesting reduction takes place. For in such cases there is no hope of getting rid of an explanandum; all we get rid of is a putative explanation.

[9]Note that people who *become* accustomed to making the latter sort of reports may no longer accept explanations of their erroneous non-inferential reports by reference to hallucinations. For they know what mental images are like, and they know that *this* pink rat was not an hallucinatory content. The more frequent case, fortunately, is that they just cease to report pink rats and begin reporting hallucinations, for their hallucinations no longer deceive them.

[10]Kurt Baier, "Smart on Sensations," *Australasian Journal of Philosophy,* 40 (1962), pp. 57–68.

[11]Smart, "Sensations and Brain Processes," p. 169.

[12]Baier, p. 63.

[13]Baier, p. 59.

[14]Baier, pp. 64–65; italics added.

[15]Smart, "Brain Processes and Incorrigibility—a Reply to Professor Baier," *Australasian Journal of Philosophy,* 40 (1962), p. 68.

[16]This problem will remain, of course, even if Jones merely *thinks* about whether he is in pain, but does not say anything.

[17]My reasons for thinking this concession unnecessary are the same as those presented in some recent articles by Hilary Putnam: cf. "Minds and Machines," *Dimensions of Mind,* ed. by S. Hook (New York, 1961), pp. 138–161, esp. pp. 153–160; "The Analytic and the Synthetic," *Minnesota Studies in the Philosophy of Science,* III, pp. 358–397; "Brains and Behavior," in *Analytic Philosophy,* II, ed. by R. J. Butler (Oxford, 1965).

[18]Baier, "Smart on Sensations," p. 60; the numbers in parentheses have been added.

[19]I have been greatly helped in preparing this paper by the comments of Richard Bernstein, Keith Gunderson, Amélie Rorty, and Richard Schmitt.

3 Eliminative Materialism and Propositional Attitudes*

Paul M. Churchland
University of California, San Diego

ELIMINATIVE MATERIALISM AND THE PROPOSITIONAL ATTITUDES

Eliminative materialism is the thesis that our common-sense conception of psychological phenomena constitutes a radically false theory, a theory so fundamentally defective that both the principles and the ontology of that theory will eventually be displaced, rather than smoothly reduced, by completed neuroscience. Our mutual understanding and even our introspection may then be reconstituted within the conceptual framework of completed neuroscience, a theory we may expect to be more powerful by far than the common-sense psychology it displaces, and more substantially integrated within physical science generally. My purpose in this paper is to explore these projections, especially as they bear on (1) the principal elements of common-sense psychology: the propositional attitudes (beliefs, desires, etc.), and (2) the conception of rationality in which these elements figure.

This focus represents a change in the fortunes of materialism. Twenty years ago, emotions, qualia, and "raw feels" were held to be the principal stumbling blocks for the materialist program. With these barriers dissolving,[1] the locus of opposition has shifted. Now it is the realm of the intentional, the realm of the propositional attitude, that is most commonly held up as being both irreducible to and ineliminable in favor of anything

---

*Reprinted from *Journal of Philosophy* 78 (1981, pp. 67–90) by permission of the author and publisher.

from within a materialist framework. Whether and why this is so, we must examine.

Such an examination will make little sense, however, unless it is first appreciated that the relevant network of common-sense concepts does indeed constitute an empirical theory, with all the functions, virtues, *and perils* entailed by that status. I shall therefore begin with a brief sketch of this view and a summary rehearsal of its rationale. The resistance it encounters still surprises me. After all, common sense has yielded up many theories. Recall the view that space has a preferred direction in which all things fall; that weight is an intrinsic feature of a body; that a force-free moving object will promptly return to rest; that the sphere of the heavens turns daily; and so on. These examples are clear, perhaps, but people seem willing to concede a theoretical component within common sense only if (1) the theory and the common sense involved are safely located in antiquity, and (2) the relevant theory is now so clearly false that its speculative nature is inescapable. Theories are indeed easier to discern under these circumstances. But the vision of hindsight is always 20/20. Let us aspire to some foresight for a change.

I. WHY FOLK PSYCHOLOGY IS A THEORY

Seeing our common-sense conceptual framework for mental phenomena as a theory brings a simple and unifying organization to most of the major topics in the philosophy of mind, including the explanation and prediction of behavior, the semantics of mental predicates, action theory, the other-minds problem, the intentionality of mental states, the nature of introspection, and the mind-body problem. Any view that can pull this lot together deserves careful consideration.

Let us begin with the explanation of human (and animal) behavior. The fact is that the average person is able to explain, and even predict, the behavior of other persons with a facility and success that is remarkable. Such explanations and predictions standardly make reference to the desires, beliefs, fears, intentions, perceptions, and so forth, to which the agents are presumed subject. But explanations presuppose laws — rough and ready ones, at least — that connect the explanatory conditions with the behavior explained. The same is true for the making of predictions, and for the justification of subjunctive and counterfactual conditionals concerning behavior. Reassuringly, a rich network of common-sense laws can indeed be reconstructed from this quotidian commerce of explanation and anticipation; its principles are familiar homilies; and their sundry functions are transparent. Each of us understands others, as well as we do, because we share a tacit command of an integrated body of lore concerning the law-like relations holding among external circumstances, internal states, and overt behavior. Given its nature and functions, this body of lore may quite aptly be called "folk psychology."[2]

This approach entails that the semantics of the terms in our familiar mentalistic vocabulary is to be understood in the same manner as the semantics of theoretical terms generally: the meaning of any theoretical term is fixed or constituted by the network of laws in which it figures. (This position is quite distinct from logical behaviorism. We deny that the relevant laws are analytic, and it is the lawlike connections generally that carry the semantic weight, not just the connections with overt behavior. But this view does account for what little plausibility logical behaviorism did enjoy.)

More importantly, the recognition that folk psychology is a theory provides a simple and decisive solution to an old skeptical problem, the problem of other minds. The problematic conviction that another individual is the subject of certain mental states is not inferred deductively from his behavior, nor is it inferred by inductive analogy from the perilously isolated instance of one's own case. Rather, that conviction is a singular *explanatory hypothesis* of a perfectly straightforward kind. Its function, in conjunction with the background laws of folk psychology, is to provide explanations/predictions/understanding of the individual's continuing behavior, and it is credible to the degree that it is successful in this regard over competing hypotheses. In the main, such hypotheses are successful, and so the belief that others enjoy the internal states comprehended by folk psychology is a reasonable belief.

Knowledge of other minds thus has no essential dependence on knowledge of one's own mind. Applying the principles of our folk psychology to our behavior, a Martian could justly ascribe to us the familiar run of mental states, even though his own psychology was very different from ours. He would not, therefore, be "generalizing from his own case."

As well, introspective judgments about one's own case turn out not to have any special status or integrity anyway. On the present view, an introspective judgment is just an instance of an acquired habit of conceptual response to one's internal states, and the integrity of any particular response is always contingent on the integrity of the acquired conceptual framework (theory) in which the response is framed. Accordingly, one's *introspective* certainty that one's mind is the seat of beliefs and desires may be as badly misplaced as was the classical man's *visual* certainty that the star-flecked sphere of the heavens turns daily.

Another conundrum is the intentionality of mental states. The "propositional attitudes," as Russell called them, form the systematic core of folk psychology; and their uniqueness and anomalous logical properties have inspired some to see here a fundamental contrast with anything that mere physical phenomena might conceivably display. The key to this matter lies again in the theoretical nature of folk psychology. The intentionality of mental states here emerges not as a mystery of nature, but as a structural feature of the concepts of folk psychology. Ironically, those same structural features reveal the very close affinity that folk psychology bears to theories in the physical sciences. Let me try to explain.

Consider the large variety of what might be called "numerical attitudes" appearing in the conceptual framework of physical science: '. . . has a $mass_{kg}$ of n', '. . . has a velocity of n', '. . . has a $temperature_K$ of n', and so forth. These expressions are predicate-forming expressions: when one substitutes a singular term for a number into the place held by 'n', a determinate predicate results. More interestingly, the relations between the various "numerical attitudes" that result are precisely the relations between the numbers "contained" in those attitudes. More interesting still, the argument place that takes the singular terms for numbers is open to quantification. All this permits the expression of generalizations concerning the lawlike relations that hold between the various numerical attitudes in nature. Such laws involve quantification over numbers, and they exploit the mathematical relations holding in that domain. Thus, for example,

(1) $(x)(f)(m)[((x$ has a mass of $m)$ & $(x$ suffers a net force of $f))$
$\supset (x$ accelerates at $f/m)]$

Consider now the large variety of propositional attitudes: '. . . believes that p', '. . . desires that p', '. . . fears that p', '. . . is happy that p', etc. These expressions are predicate-forming expressions also. When one substitutes a singular term for a proposition into the place held by 'p', a determinate predicate results, e.g., '. . . believes that Tom is tall.' (Sentences do not generally function as singular terms, but it is difficult to escape the idea that when a sentence occurs in the place held by 'p', it is there functioning as or like a singular term. On this, more below.) More interestingly, the relations between the resulting propositional attitudes are characteristically the relations that hold between the propositions "contained" in them, relations such as entailment, equivalence, and mutual inconsistency. More interesting still, the argument place that takes the singular terms for propositions is open to quantification. All this permits the expression of generalizations concerning the lawlike relations that hold among propositional attitudes. Such laws involve quantification over propositions, and they exploit various relations holding in that domain. Thus, for example,

(2) $(x)(p)[(x$ fears that $p) \supset (x$ desires that $\sim p)]$

(3) $(x)(p)[((x$ hopes that $p)$ & $(x$ discovers that $p))$
$\supset (x$ is pleased that $p)]$

(4) $(x)(p)(q)[((x$ believes that $p)$ & $(x$ believes that (if p then $q)))$
$\supset$ (barring confusion, distraction, etc., x believes that $q)]$

(5) $(x)(p)(q)[((x$ desires that $p)$ & $(x$ believes that (if q then $p))$
& $(x$ is able to bring it about that $q))$
$\supset$ (barring conflicting desires or preferred strategies,
x brings it about that $q)]^3$

Not only is folk psychology a theory, it is so *obviously* a theory that it must be held a major mystery why it has taken until the last half of the twentieth century for philosophers to realize it. The structural features of folk psychology parallel perfectly those of mathematical physics; the only difference lies in the respective domain of abstract entities they exploit — numbers in the case of physics, and propositions in the case of psychology.

Finally, the realization that folk psychology is a theory puts a new light on the mind-body problem. The issue becomes a matter of how the ontology of one theory (folk psychology) is, or is not, going to be related to the ontology of another theory (completed neuroscience); and the major philosophical positions on the mind-body problem emerge as so many different anticipations of what future research will reveal about the intertheoretic status and integrity of folk psychology.

The identity theorist optimistically expects that folk psychology will be smoothly *reduced* by completed neuroscience, and its ontology preserved by dint of transtheoretic identities. The dualist expects that it will prove *ir*reducible to completed neuroscience, by dint of being a nonredundant description of an autonomous, nonphysical domain of natural phenomena. The functionalist also expects that it will prove irreducible, but on the quite different grounds that the internal economy characterized by folk psychology is not, in the last analysis, a law-governed economy of natural states, but an abstract organization of functional states, an organization instantiable in a variety of quite different material substrates. It is therefore irreducible to the principles peculiar to any of them.

Finally, the eliminative materialist is also pessimistic about the prospects for reduction, but his reason is that folk psychology is a radically inadequate account of our internal activities, too confused and too defective to win survival through intertheoretic reduction. On his view it will simply be displaced by a better theory of those activities.

Which of these fates is the real destiny of folk psychology we shall attempt to divine presently. For now, the point to keep in mind is that we shall be exploring the fate of a theory, a systematic, corrigible, speculative *theory*.

II. WHY FOLK PSYCHOLOGY MIGHT (REALLY) BE FALSE

Given that folk psychology is an empirical theory, it is at least an abstract possibility that its principles are radically false and that its ontology is an illusion. With the exception of eliminative materialism, however, none of the major positions takes this possibility seriously. None of them doubts the basic integrity or truth of folk psychology (hereafter, "FP"), and all of them anticipate a future in which its laws and categories are conserved. This conservatism is not without some foundation. After all, FP does enjoy a substantial amount of explanatory and predictive success. And what better grounds than this for confidence in the integrity of its categories?

What better grounds indeed? Even so, the presumption in FP's favor is spurious, born of innocence and tunnel vision. A more searching examination reveals a different picture. First, we must reckon not only with FP's successes, but with its explanatory failures, and with their extent and seriousness. Second, we must consider the long-term history of FP, its growth, fertility, and current promise of future development. And third, we must consider what sorts of theories are *likely* to be true of the etiology of our behavior, given what else we have learned about ourselves in recent history. That is, we must evaluate FP with regard to its coherence and continuity with fertile and well-established theories in adjacent and over-lapping domains — with evolutionary theory, biology, and neuroscience, for example — because active coherence with the rest of what we presume to know is perhaps the final measure of any hypothesis.

A serious inventory of this sort reveals a very troubled situation, one which would evoke open skepticism in the case of any theory less familiar and dear to us. Let me sketch some relevant detail. When one centers one's attention not on what FP can explain, but on what it cannot explain or fails even to address, one discovers that there is a very great deal. As examples of central and important mental phenomena that remain largely or wholly mysterious within the framework of FP, consider the nature and dynamics of mental illness, the faculty of creative imagination, or the ground of intelligence differences between individuals. Consider our utter ignorance of the nature and psychological functions of sleep, that curious state in which a third of one's life is spent. Reflect on the common ability to catch an outfield fly ball on the run, or hit a moving car with a snowball. Consider the internal construction of a 3-D visual image from subtle differences in the 2-D array of stimulations in our respective retinas. Consider the rich variety of perceptual illusions, visual and otherwise. Or consider the miracle of memory, with its lightning capacity for relevant retrieval. On these and many other mental phenomena, FP sheds negligible light.

One particularly outstanding mystery is the nature of the learning process itself, especially where it involves large-scale conceptual change, and especially as it appears in its prelinguistic or entirely nonlinguistic form (as in infants and animals), which is by far the most common form in nature. FP is faced with special difficulties here, since its conception of learning as the manipulation and storage of propositional attitudes founders on the fact that how to formulate, manipulate, and store a rich fabric of propositional attitudes is itself something that is learned, and is only one among many acquired cognitive skills. FP would thus appear constitutionally incapable of even addressing this most basic of mysteries.[4]

Failures on such a large scale do not (yet) show that FP is a false theory, but they do move that prospect well into the range of real possibility, and they do show decisively that FP is *at best* a highly superficial theory, a partial and unpenetrating gloss on a deeper and more complex reality. Having reached this opinion, we may be forgiven for exploring the possibility that FP provides a positively misleading sketch of our internal kinematics and dynamics, one whose success is owed more to selective application and forced interpretation on our part than to genuine theoretical insight on FP's part.

A look at the history of FP does little to allay such fears, once raised. The story is one of retreat, infertility, and decadence. The presumed domain of FP used to be much larger than it is now. In primitive cultures, the behavior of most of the elements of nature were understood in intentional terms. The wind could know anger, the moon jealousy, the river generosity, the sea fury, and so forth. These were not metaphors. Sacrifices were made and auguries undertaken to placate or divine the changing passions of the gods. Despite its sterility, this animistic approach to nature has dominated our history, and it is only in the last two or three thousand years that we have restricted FP's literal application to the domain of the higher animals.

Even in this preferred domain, however, both the content and the success of FP have not advanced sensibly in two or three thousand years. The FP of the Greeks is essentially the FP we use today, and we are negligibly better at explaining human behavior in its terms than was Sophocles. This is a very long period of stagnation and infertility for any theory to display, especially when faced with such an enormous backlog of anomalies and mysteries in its own explanatory domain. Perfect theories, perhaps, have no need to evolve. But FP is profoundly imperfect. Its failure to develop its resources and extend its range of success is therefore darkly curious, and one must query the integrity of its basic categories. To use Imre Lakatos' terms, FP is a stagnant or degenerating research program, and has been for millennia.

Explanatory success to date is of course not the only dimension in which a theory can display virtue or promise. A troubled or stagnant theory may merit patience and solicitude on other grounds; for example, on grounds that it is the only theory or theoretical approach that fits well with other theories about adjacent subject matters, or the only one that promises to reduce to or be explained by some established background theory whose domain encompasses the domain of the theory at issue. In sum, it may rate credence because it holds promise of theoretical integration. How does FP rate in this dimension?

It is just here, perhaps, that FP fares poorest of all. If we approach *homo sapiens* from the perspective of natural history and the physical sciences, we can tell a coherent story of his constitution, development, and behavioral capacities which encompasses particle physics, atomic and molecular theory, organic chemistry, evolutionary theory, biology, physiology, and materialistic neuroscience. That story, though still radically incomplete, is already extremely powerful, outperforming FP at many points even in its own domain. And it is deliberately and self-consciously coherent with the rest of our developing world picture. In short, the greatest theoretical synthesis in the history of the human race is currently in our hands, and parts of it already provide searching descriptions and explanations of human sensory input, neural activity, and motor control.

But FP is no part of this growing synthesis. Its intentional categories stand magnificently alone, without visible prospect of reduction to that larger corpus. A successful reduction cannot be ruled out, in my view, but FP's explanatory impotence and long stagnation inspire little faith that its categories will find themselves neatly reflected in the framework of neuroscience. On the contrary, one is reminded of how alchemy must have looked as elemental chemistry was taking form, how Aristotelean cosmology must have looked as classical mechanics was being articulated, or how the vitalist conception of life must have looked as organic chemistry marched forward.

In sketching a fair summary of this situation, we must make a special effort to abstract from the fact that FP is a central part of our current *lebenswelt,* and serves as the principal vehicle of our interpersonal commerce. For these facts provide FP with a conceptual inertia that goes far beyond its purely theoretical virtues. Restricting ourselves to this latter dimension, what we must say is that FP suffers explanatory failures on an epic scale, that it has been stagnant for at least twenty-five centuries, and that its categories appear (so far) to be incommensurable with or orthogonal to the categories of the background physical science whose long-term claim to explain human behavior seems undeniable. Any theory that meets this description must be allowed a serious candidate for outright elimination.

We can of course insist on no stronger conclusion at this stage. Nor is it my concern to do so. We are here exploring a possibility, and the facts demand no more, and no less, than it be taken seriously. The distinguishing feature of the eliminative materialist is that he takes it very seriously indeed.

III. ARGUMENTS AGAINST ELIMINATION

Thus the basic rationale of eliminative materialism: FP is a theory, and quite probably a false one; let us attempt, therefore to transcend it.

The rationale is clear and simple, but many find it uncompelling. It will be objected that FP is not, strictly speaking, an *empirical* theory; that it is not false, or at least not refutable by empirical considerations; and that it ought not or cannot be transcended in the fashion of a defunct empirical theory. In what follows we shall examine these objections as they flow from the most popular and best-founded of the competing positions in the philosophy of mind: functionalism.

An antipathy toward eliminative materialism arises from two distinct threads running through contemporary functionalism. The first thread concerns the *normative* character of FP, or at least of that central core of FP which treats of the propositional attitudes. FP, some will say, is a characterization of an ideal, or at least praiseworthy mode of internal activity. It outlines not only what it is to have and process beliefs and desires, but also (and inevitably) what it is to be rational in their administration. The ideal laid down by FP may be imperfectly achieved by empirical humans, but this does not impugn FP as a normative characterization. Nor need such failures seriously impugn FP even as a descriptive characterization, for it remains true that our activities can be both usefully and accurately understood as rational *except for* the occasional lapse due to noise, interference, or other breakdown, which defects empirical research may eventually unravel. Accordingly, though neuroscience may usefully augment it, FP has no pressing need to be displaced, even as a descriptive theory; nor could it be replaced, qua normative characterization, by any descriptive theory of neural mechanisms, since rationality is defined over propositional attitudes like beliefs and desires. FP, therefore, is here to stay.

Daniel Dennett has defended a view along these lines.[5] And the view just outlined gives voice to a theme of the property dualists as well. Karl Popper and Joseph Margolis both cite the normative nature of mental and linguistic activity as a bar to their penetration or elimination by any descriptive/materialist theory.[6] I hope to deflate the appeal of such moves below.

The second thread concerns the *abstract* nature of FP. The central claim of functionalism is that the principles of FP characterize our internal states in a fashion that makes no reference to their intrinsic nature or physical constitution. Rather, they are characterized in terms of the network of causal relations they bear to one another, and to sensory circumstances and overt behavior. Given its abstract specification, that internal economy may therefore be realized in a nomically heterogeneous variety of physical systems. All of them may differ, even radically, in their physical constitution, and yet at another level, they will all share the same nature. This view, says Fodor, "is compatible with very strong claims about the ineliminability of mental language from behavioral theories."[7] Given the real possibility of multiple instantiations in heterogeneous physical substrates, we cannot eliminate the functional characterization in favor of any theory peculiar to one such substrate. That would preclude our being able to describe the (abstract) organization that any one instantiation shares with all the others. A functional characterization of our internal states is therefore here to stay.

This second theme, like the first, assigns a faintly stipulative character to FP, as if the onus were on the empirical systems to instantiate faithfully the organization that FP specifies, instead of the onus being on FP to describe faithfully the internal activities of a naturally distinct class of empirical systems. This impression is enhanced by the standard examples used to illustrate the claims of functionalism—mousetraps, valve-lifters, arithmetical calculators, computers, robots, and the like. These are artifacts, constructed to fill a preconceived bill. In such cases, a failure of fit between the physical system and the relevant functional characterization impugns only the former, not the latter. The functional characterization is thus removed from empirical criticism in a way that is most unlike the case of an empirical theory. One prominent functionalist—Hilary Putnam—has argued outright that FP is not a corrigible theory at all.[8] Plainly, if FP is construed on these models, as regularly it is, the question of its empirical integrity is unlikely ever to pose itself, let alone receive a critical answer.

Although fair to some functionalists, the preceding is not entirely fair to Fodor. On his view the aim of psychology is to find the *best* functional characterization of ourselves, and what that is remains an empirical question. As well, his argument for the ineliminability of mental vocabulary from psychology does not pick out current FP in particular as ineliminable. It need claim only that *some* abstract functional characterization must be retained, some articulation or refinement of FP perhaps.

His estimate of eliminative materialism remains low, however. First, it is plain that Fodor thinks there is nothing fundamentally or interestingly wrong with FP. On the contrary, FP's central conception of cognitive activity—as consisting in the manipulation of propositional attitudes—turns up as the central element in Fodor's own theory on the nature of thought *(The Language of Thought, op. cit.)*. And second, there remains the point that, whatever tidying up FP may or may not require, it cannot be displaced by any naturalistic theory of our physical substrate, since it is the abstract functional features of his internal states that make a person, not the chemistry of his substrate.

All of this is appealing. But almost none of it, I think, is right. Functionalism has too long enjoyed its reputation as a daring and *avant garde* position. It needs to be revealed for the short-sighted and reactionary position it is.

IV. THE CONSERVATIVE NATURE OF FUNCTIONALISM

A valuable perspective on functionalism can be gained from the following story. To begin with, recall the alchemists' theory of inanimate matter. We have here a long and variegated tradition, of course, not a single theory, but our purposes will be served by a gloss.

The alchemists conceived the "inanimate" as entirely continuous with animated matter, in that the sensible and behavioral properties of the various substances are owed to the ensoulment of baser matter by various spirits or essences. These nonmaterial aspects were held to undergo development, just as we find growth and development in the various souls of plants, animals, and humans. The alchemist's peculiar skill lay in knowing how to seed, nourish, and bring to maturity the desired spirits enmattered in the appropriate combinations.

On one orthodoxy, the four fundamental spirits (for "inanimate" matter) were named "mercury," "sulphur," "yellow arsenic," and "sal ammoniac." Each of these spirits was held responsible for a rough but characteristic syndrome of sensible, combinatorial, and causal properties. The spirit mercury, for example, was held responsible for certain features typical of metallic substances—their shininess, liquefiability, and so forth. Sulphur was held responsible for certain residual features typical of metals, and for those displayed by the ores from which running metal could be distilled. Any given metallic substance was a critical orchestration principally of these two spirits. A similar story held for the other two spirits, and among the four of them a certain domain of physical features and transformations was rendered intelligible and controllable.

The degree of control was always limited, of course. Or better, such prediction and control as the alchemists possessed was owed more to the manipulative lore acquired as an apprentice to a master, than to any genuine insight supplied by the theory. The theory followed, more than it dictated, practice. But the theory did supply some rhyme to the practice, and in the absence of a developed alternative it was sufficiently compelling to sustain a long and stubborn tradition.

The tradition had become faded and fragmented by the time the elemental chemistry of Lavoisier and Dalton arose to replace it for good. But let us suppose that it had hung on a little longer—perhaps because the four-spirit orthodoxy had become a thumb-worn part of everyman's common sense—and let us examine the nature of the conflict between the two theories and some possible avenues of resolution.

No doubt the simplest line of resolution, and the one which historically took place, is outright displacement. The dualistic interpretation of the four essences—as immaterial spirits—will appear both feckless and unnecessary given the power of the corpuscularian taxonomy of atomic chemistry. And a reduction of the old taxonomy to the new will appear impossible, given the extent to which the comparatively toothless old theory cross-classifies things relative to the new. Elimination would thus appear the only alternative—*unless* some cunning and determined defender of the alchemical vision has the wit to suggest the following defense.

Being "ensouled by mercury," or "sulphur," or either of the other two so-called spirits, is actually a *functional* state. The first, for example, is defined by the disposition to reflect light, to liquefy under heat, to unite with other matter in the same state, and so forth. And each of these four states is related to the others, in that the syndrome for each varies as a function of which of the other three states is also instantiated in the same substrate. Thus the level of description comprehended by the alchemical vocabulary is abstract: various material substances, suitably "ensouled," can display the features of a metal, for example, or even of gold specifically. For it is the total syndrome of occurrent and causal properties which matters, not the corpuscularian details of the substrate. Alchemy, it is concluded, comprehends a level of organization in reality distinct from and irreducible to the organization found at the level of corpuscularian chemistry.

This view might have had considerable appeal. After all, it spares alchemists the burden of defending immaterial souls that come and go; it frees them from having to meet the very strong demands of a naturalistic reduction; and it spares them the shock and confusion of outright elimination. Alchemical theory emerges as basically all right! Nor need they appear too obviously stubborn or dogmatic in this. Alchemy as it stands, they concede, may need substantial tidying up, and experience must be our guide. But we need not fear its naturalistic displacement, they remind us, since it is the particular orchestration of the syndromes of occurrent and causal properties which makes a piece of matter gold, not the idiosyncratic details of its corpuscularian substrate. A further circumstance would have made this claim even more plausible. For the fact is, the alchemists *did* know how to make gold, in this relevantly weakened sense of 'gold,' and they could do so in a variety of ways. Their "gold" was never as perfect, alas, as the "gold" nurtured in nature's womb, but what mortal can expect to match the skills of nature herself?

What this story shows is that it is at least possible for the constellation of moves, claims, and defenses characteristic of functionalism to constitute an outrage against reason and truth, and to do so with a plausibility that is frightening. Alchemy is a terrible theory, well-deserving of its complete elimination, and the defense of it just explored is reactionary, obfuscatory, retrograde, and wrong. But in historical context, that defense might have seemed wholly sensible, even to reasonable people.

The alchemical example is a deliberately transparent case of what might well be called "the functionalist stratagem," and other cases are easy to imagine. A cracking good defense of the phlogiston theory of combustion can also be constructed along these lines. Construe being highly phlogisticated and being dephlogisticated as functional states defined by certain syndromes of causal dispositions; point to the great variety of natural substrates capable of combustion and calcification; claim an irreducible functional integrity for what has proved to lack any natural integrity; and bury the remaining defects under a pledge to contrive improvements. A similar recipe will provide new life for the four humors of medieval medicine, for the vital essence or archeus of premodern biology, and so forth.

If its application in these other cases is any guide, the functionalist stratagem is a smokescreen for the preservation of error and confusion. Whence derives our assurance that in contemporary journals the same charade is not being played out on behalf of FP? The parallel with the case of alchemy is in all other respects distressingly complete, right down to the parallel between the search for artificial gold and the search for artificial intelligence!

Let me not be misunderstood on this last point. Both aims are worthy aims: thanks to nuclear physics, artificial (but real) gold is finally within our means, if only in submicroscopic quantities; and artificial (but real) intelligence eventually will be. But just as the careful orchestration of superficial syndromes was the wrong way to produce genuine gold, so may the careful orchestration of superficial syndromes be the wrong way to produce genuine intelligence. Just as with gold, what may be required is that our science penetrate to the underlying *natural* kind that gives rise to the total syndrome directly.

In summary, when confronted with the explanatory impotence, stagnant history, and systematic isolation of the intentional idioms of FP, it is not an adequate or responsive defense to insist that those idioms are abstract, functional, and irreducible in character. For one thing, this same defense could have been mounted with comparable plausibility no matter *what* haywire network of internal states our folklore had ascribed to us. And for another, the defense assumes essentially what is at issue: it assumes that it is the intentional idioms of FP, plus or minus a bit, that express the *important* features shared by all cognitive systems. But they may not. Certainly it is wrong to assume that they do, and then argue against the possibility of a materialistic displacement on grounds that it must describe matters at a level that is different from the important level. This just begs the question in favor of the older framework.

Finally, it is very important to point out that eliminative materialism is strictly *consistent* with the claim that the essence of a cognitive system resides in the abstract functional organization of its internal states. The eliminative materialist is not committed to the idea that the correct account of cognition *must* be a naturalistic account, though he may be forgiven for exploring the possibility. What he does hold is that the correct account of cognition, whether functionalistic or naturalistic, will bear about as much resemblance to FP as modern chemistry bears to four-spirit alchemy.

Let us now try to deal with the argument, against eliminative materialism, from the normative dimension of FP. This can be dealt with rather swiftly, I believe.

First, the fact that the regularities ascribed by the intentional core of FP are predicated on certain logical relations among propositions is not by itself grounds for claiming anything essentially normative about FP. To draw a relevant parallel, the fact that the regularities ascribed by the classical gas law are predicated on arithmetical relations between numbers does not imply anything essentially normative about the classical gas law. And logical relations between propositions are as much an objective matter of abstract fact as are arithmetical relations between numbers. In this respect, the law

(4) $(x)(p)(q)[((x$ believes that $p)$ & $(x$ believes that (if p then $q)))$
$\supset$ (barring confusion, distraction, etc., x believes that $q)]$

is entirely on a par with the classical gas law

(6) $(x)(P)(V)(\mu)[((x$ has a pressure $P)$ & $(x$ has a volume $V)$
& $(x$ has a quantity $\mu)) \supset$ (barring very high pressure or density,
x has a temperature of $PV/\mu R)]$

A normative dimension enters only because we happen to *value* most of the patterns ascribed by FP. But we do not value all of them. Consider

(7) $(x)(p)[((x$ desires with all his heart that $p)$ & $(x$ learns that $\sim p))$
$\supset$ (barring unusual strength of character, x is shattered that $\sim p)]$

Moreover, and as with normative convictions generally, fresh insight may motivate major changes in what we value.

Second, the laws of FP ascribe to us only a very minimal and truncated rationality, not an ideal rationality as some have suggested. The rationality characterized by the set of all FP laws falls well short of an ideal rationality. This is not surprising. We have no clear or finished conception of ideal rationality anyway; certainly the ordinary man does not. Accordingly, it is just not plausible to suppose that the explanatory failures from which FP suffers are owed primarily to human failure to live up to the ideal standard it provides. Quite to the contrary, the conception of rationality it provides appears limping and superficial, especially when compared with the dialectical complexity of our scientific history, or with the ratiocinative virtuosity displayed by any child.

Third, even if our current conception of rationality – and more generally, of cognitive virtue – is largely constituted within the sentential/propositional framework of FP, there is no guarantee that this framework is adequate to the deeper and more accurate account of cognitive virtue which is clearly needed. Even if we concede the categorial integrity of FP, at least as applied to language-using humans, it remains far from clear that the basic parameters of intellectual virtue are to be found at the categorial level comprehended by the propositional attitudes. After all, language use is something that is learned, by a brain already capable of vigorous cognitive activity; language use is acquired as only one among a great variety of learned manipulative skills; and it is mastered by a brain that evolution has shaped for a great many functions, language use being only the very latest and perhaps the least of them. Against the background of these facts, language use appears as an extremely peripheral activity, as a racially idiosyncratic mode of social interaction, which is mastered thanks to the versatility and power of a more basic mode of activity. Why accept then, a theory of cognitive activity that models its elements on the elements of human language? And why assume that the fundamental parameters of intellectual virtue are or can be defined over the elements at this superficial level?

A serious advance in our appreciation of cognitive virtue would thus seem to *require* that we go beyond FP, that we transcend the poverty of FP's conception of rationality by transcending its propositional kinematics entirely, by developing a deeper and more general kinematics of cognitive activity, and by distinguishing within this new framework which of the kinematically possible modes of activity are to be valued and encouraged (as more efficient, reliable, productive, or whatever). Eliminative materialism thus does not imply the end of our normative concerns. It implies only that they will have to be reconstituted at a more revealing level of understanding, the level that a matured neuroscience will provide.

What a theoretically informed future might hold in store for us, we shall now turn to explore. Not because we can foresee matters with any special clarity, but because it is important to try to break the grip on our imagination held by the propositional kinematics of FP. As far as the present section is concerned, we may summarize our conclusions as follows. FP is nothing more and nothing less than a culturally entrenched theory of how we and the higher animals work. It has no special features that make it empirically invulnerable, no unique functions that make it irreplaceable, no special status of any kind whatsoever. We shall turn a skeptical ear then, to any special pleading on its behalf.

V. BEYOND FOLK PSYCHOLOGY

What might the elimination of FP actually involve—not just the comparatively straightforward idioms for sensation, but the entire apparatus of propositional attitudes? That depends heavily on what neuroscience might discover, and on our determination to capitalize on it. Here follow three scenarios in which the operative conception of cognitive activity is progressively divorced from the forms and categories that characterize natural language. If the reader will indulge the lack of actual substance, I shall try to sketch some plausible form.

First suppose that research into the structure and activity of the brain, both fine-grained and global, finally does yield a new kinematics and correlative dynamics for what is now thought of as cognitive activity. The theory is uniform for all terrestrial brains, not just human brains, and it makes suitable conceptual contact with both evolutionary biology and nonequilibrium thermodynamics. It ascribes to us, at any given time, a set or configuration of complex states, which are specified within the theory as figurative "solids" within a four- or five-dimensional phase space. The laws of the theory govern the interaction, motion, and transformation of these "solid" states within that space, and also their relations to whatever sensory and motor transducers the system possesses. As with celestial mechanics, the exact specification of the "solids" involved and the exhaustive accounting of all dynamically relevant adjacent "solids" is not practically possible, for many reasons, but here also it turns out that the obvious approximations we fall back on yield excellent explanations/predictions of internal change and external behavior, at least in the short term. Regarding long-term activity, the theory provides powerful and unified accounts of the learning process, the nature of mental illness, and variations in character and intelligence across the animal kingdom as well as across individual humans.

Moreover, it provides a straightforward account of "knowledge," as traditionally conceived. According to the new theory, any declarative sentence to which a speaker would give confident assent is merely a one-dimensional *projection* — through the compound lens of Wernicke's and Broca's areas onto the idiosyncratic surface of the speaker's language — a one-dimensional projection of a four- or five-dimensional "solid" that is an element in his true kinematical state. (Recall the shadows on the wall of Plato's cave.) Being projections of that inner reality, such sentences do carry significant information regarding it and are thus fit to function as elements in a communication system. On the other hand, being *sub*dimensional projections, they reflect but a narrow part of the reality projected. They are therefore *un*fit to represent the deeper reality in all its kinematically, dynamically, and even normatively relevant respects. That is to say, a system of propositional attitudes, such as FP, must inevitably fail to capture what is going on here, though it may reflect just enough superficial structure to sustain an alchemylike tradition among folk who lack any better theory. From the perspective of the newer theory, however, it is plain that there simply are no law-governed states of the kind FP postulates. The real laws governing our internal activities are defined over different and much more complex kinematical states and configurations, as are the normative criteria for developmental integrity and intellectual virtue.

A theoretical outcome of the kind just described may fairly be counted as a case of elimination of one theoretical ontology in favor of another, but the success here imagined for systematic neuroscience need not have any sensible effect on common practice. Old ways die hard, and in the absence of some practical necessity, they may not die at all. Even so, it is not inconceivable that some segment of the population, or all of it, should become intimately familiar with the vocabulary required to characterize our kinematical states, learn the laws governing their interactions and behavioral projections, acquire a facility in their first-person ascription, and displace the use of FP altogether, even in the marketplace. The demise of FP's ontology would then be complete.

We may now explore a second and rather more radical possibility. Everyone is familiar with Chomsky's thesis that the human mind or brain contains innately and uniquely the abstract structures for learning and using specifically human natural languages. A competing hypothesis is that our brain does indeed contain innate structures, but that those structures have as their original and still primary function the organization of perceptual experience, the administration of linguistic categories being an acquired and additional function for which evolution has only incidentally suited them.[9] This hypothesis has the advantage of not requiring the evolutionary saltation that Chomsky's view would seem to require, and there are other advantages as well. But these matters need not concern us here. Suppose, for our purposes, that this competing view is true, and consider the following story.

Research into the neural structures that fund the organization and processing of perceptual information reveals that they are capable of administering a great variety of complex tasks, some of them showing a complexity far in excess of that shown by natural language. Natural languages, it turns out, exploit only a very elementary portion of the available machinery, the bulk of which serves far more complex activities beyond the ken of the propositional conceptions of FP. The detailed unraveling of what that machinery is and of the capacities it has makes it plain that a form of language far more sophisticated than "natural" language, though decidedly "alien" in its syntactic and semantic structures, could also be learned and used by our innate systems. Such a novel system of communication, it is quickly realized, could raise the efficiency of information exchange between brains by an order of magnitude, and would enhance epistemic evaluation by a comparable amount, since it would reflect the underlying structure of our cognitive activities in greater detail than does natural language.

Guided by our new understanding of those internal structures, we manage to construct a new system of verbal communication entirely distinct from natural language, with a new and more powerful combinatorial grammar over novel elements forming novel combinations with exotic properties. The compounded strings of this alternative system — call them "übersatzen" — are not evaluated as true or false, nor are the relations between them remotely analogous to the relations of entailment, etc., that hold between sentences. They display a different organization and manifest different virtues.

Once constructed, this "language" proves to be learnable; it has the power projected; and in two generations it has swept the planet. Everyone uses the new system. The syntactic forms and semantic categories of so-called "natural" language disappear entirely. And with them disappear the propositional attitudes of FP, displaced by a more revealing scheme in which (of course) "übersatzenal attitudes" play the leading role. FP again suffers elimination.

This second story, note, illustrates a theme with endless variations. There are possible as many different "folk psychologies" as there are possible differently structured communication systems to serve as models for them.

A third and even stranger possibility can be outlined as follows. We know that there is considerable lateralization of function between the two cerebral hemispheres, and that the two hemispheres make use of the information they get from each other by way of the great cerebral commissure — the corpus callosum — a giant cable of neurons connecting them. Patients whose commissure has been surgically severed display a variety of behavioral deficits that indicate a loss of access by one hemisphere to information it used to get from the other. However, in people with callosal agenesis (a congenital defect in which the connecting cable is simply absent), there is little or no behavioral deficit, suggesting that the two hemisphere have learned to exploit the information carried in other less direct pathways connecting them through the subcortical regions. This suggests that, even in the normal case, a developing hemisphere *learns* to make use of the information the cerebral commissure deposits at its doorstep. What we have then, in the case of a normal human, is two physically distinct cognitive systems (both capable of independent function) responding in a systematic and learned fashion to exchanged information. And what is especially interesting about this case is the sheer amount of information exchanged. The cable of the commissure consists of ≈ 200 million neurons,[10] and even if we assume that each of these fibres is capable of one of only two possible states each second (a most conservative estimate), we are looking at a channel whose information capacity is $> 2 \times 10^8$ binary bits/second. Compare this to the < 500 bits/second capacity of spoken English.

Now, if two distinct hemispheres can learn to communicate on so impressive a scale, why shouldn't two distinct brains learn to do it also? This would require an artificial "commissure" of some kind, but let us suppose that we can fashion a workable transducer for implantation at some site in the brain that research reveals to be suitable, a transducer to convert a symphony of neural activity into (say) microwaves radiated from an aerial in the forehead, and to perform the reverse function of converting received microwaves back into neural activation. Connecting it up need not be an insuperable problem. We simply trick the normal processes of dendritic arborization into growing their own myriad connections with the active microsurface of the transducer.

Once the channel is opened between two or more people, they can learn *(learn)* to exchange information and coordinate their behavior with the same intimacy and virtuosity displayed by your own cerebral hemispheres. Think what this might do for hockey teams, and ballet companies, and research teams! If the entire population were thus fitted out, spoken language of any kind might well disappear completely, a victim of the "why crawl when you can fly?" principle. Libraries become filled not with books, but with long recordings of exemplary bouts of neural activity. These constitute a growing cultural heritage, an evolving "Third World," to use Karl Popper's terms. But they do not consist of sentences or arguments.

How will such people understand and conceive of other individuals? To this question I can only answer, "In roughly the same fashion that your right hemisphere 'understands' and 'conceives of' your left hemisphere — intimately and efficiently, but not propositionally!"

These speculations, I hope, will evoke the required sense of untapped possibilities, and I shall in any case bring them to a close here. Their function is to make some inroads into the aura of inconceivability that commonly surrounds the idea that we might reject FP. The felt conceptual strain even finds expression in an argument to the effect that the thesis of eliminative materialism is incoherent since it denies the very conditions presupposed by the assumption that it is meaningful. I shall close with a brief discussion of this very popular move.

As I have received it, the reductio proceeds by pointing out that the statement of eliminative materialism is just a meaningless string of marks or noises, unless that string is the expression of a certain *belief,* and a certain *intention* to communicate, and a *knowledge* of the grammar of the language, and so forth. But if the statement of eliminative materialism is true, then there are no such states to express. The statement at issue would then be a meaningless string of marks or noises. It would therefore *not* be true. Therefore it is not true. Q.E.D.

The difficulty with any nonformal reductio is that the conclusion against the initial assumption is always no better than the material assumptions invoked to reach the incoherent conclusion. In this case the additional assumptions involve a certain theory of meaning, one that presupposes the integrity of FP. But formally speaking, one can as well infer, from the incoherent result, that this theory of meaning is what must be rejected. Given the independent critique of FP leveled earlier, this would even seem the preferred option. But in any case, one cannot simply assume that particular theory of meaning without begging the question at issue, namely, the integrity of FP.

The question-begging nature of this move is most graphically illustrated by the following analogue, which I owe to Patricia Churchland.[11] The issue here, placed in the seventeenth century, is whether there exists such a substance as *vital spirit*. At the time, this substance was held, without significant awareness of real alternatives, to be that which distinguished the animate from the inanimate. Given the monopoly enjoyed by this conception, given the degree to which it was integrated with many of our other conceptions, and given the magnitude of the revisions any serious alternative conception would require, the following refutation of any anti-vitalist claim would be found instantly plausible.

> The anti-vitalist says that there is no such thing as vital spirit. But this claim is self-refuting. The speaker can expect to be taken seriously only if his claim cannot. For if the claim is true, then the speaker does not have vital spirit and must be *dead*. But if he is dead, then his statement is a meaningless string of noises, devoid of reason and truth.

The question-begging nature of this argument does not, I assume, require elaboration. To those moved by the earlier argument, I commend the parallel for examination.

The thesis of this paper may be summarized as follows. The propositional attitudes of folk psychology do not constitute an unbreachable barrier to the advancing tide of neuroscience. On the contrary, the principled displacement of folk psychology is not only richly possible, it represents one of the most intriguing theoretical displacements we can currently imagine.

FOOTNOTES

[1]See Paul Feyerabend, "Materialism and the Mind-Body Problem," *Review of Metaphysics,* xvii.1, 65 (September 1963): 49–66; this volume, pp. 3–16; Richard Rorty, "Mind-Body Identity, Privacy, and Categories," *ibid.,* xix.1, 73 (September 1965): 24–54; this volume, pp. 17–41; and my *Scientific Realism and the Plasticity of Mind* (New York: Cambridge, 1979).

[2]We shall examine a handful of these laws presently. For a more comprehensive sampling of the laws of folk psychology, see my *Scientific Realism and Plasticity of Mind, op. cit.,* ch. 4. For a detailed examination of the folk principles that underwrite action explanations in particular, see my "The Logical Character of Action Explanations," *Philosophical Review,* lxxix, 2 (April 1970): 214–236.

[3]Staying within an objectual interpretation of the quantifiers, perhaps the simplest way to make systematic sense of expressions like ⌜x believes that p⌝ and closed sentences formed therefrom is just to construe whatever occurs in the nested position held by 'p', 'q', etc. as there having the function of a singular term. Accordingly, the standard connectives, as they occur between terms in that nested position, must be construed as there functioning as operators that form compound singular terms from other singular terms, and not as sentence operators. The compound singular terms so formed denote the appropriate compound propositions. Substitutional quantification will of course underwrite a different interpretation, and there are other approaches as well. Especially appealing is the prosentential approach of Dorothy Grover, Joseph Camp, and Nuel Belnap, "A Prosentential Theory of Truth," *Philosophical Studies,* xxvii, 2 (February 1975): 73–125. But the resolution of these issues is not vital to the present discussion.

[4]A possible response here is to insist that the cognitive activity of animals and infants is linguaformal in its elements, structures, and processing right from birth. J. A. Fodor, in *The Language of Thought* (New York: Crowell 1975), has erected a positive theory of thought on the assumption that the innate forms of cognitive activity have precisely the form here denied. For a critique of Fodor's view, see Patricia Churchland, "Fodor on Language Learning," *Synthese,* xxxviii, 1 (May 1978): 149–159.

[5]Most explicitly in "Three Kinds of Intentional Psychology," (this volume, pp. 121–143), but this theme of Dennett's goes all the way back to his "Intentional Systems," THE JOURNAL OF PHILOSOPHY, LXVIII, 4 (Feb. 25, 1971): 87–106; reprinted in his *Brainstorms* (Montgomery, Vt.: Bradford Books, 1978).

[6]Popper, *Objective Knowledge* (New York: Oxford, 1972); with J. Eccles, *The Self and Its Brain* (New York: Springer Verlag, 1978). Margolis, *Persons and Minds* (Boston: Reidel, 1978).

[7]*Psychological Explanation* (New York: Random House, 1968), p. 116.

[8]"Robots: Machines or Artificially Created Life?", THE JOURNAL OF PHILOSOPHY, LXI, 21 (Nov. 12, 1964): 668–691, pp. 675, 681 ff.

[9]Richard Gregory defends such a view in "The Grammar of Vision," *Listener,* LXXXIII, 2133 (February 1970): 242–246; reprinted in his *Concepts and Mechanisms of Perception* (London: Duckworth, 1975), pp. 622–629.

[10]M. S. Gazzaniga and J. E. LeDoux, *The Integrated Mind* (New York: Plenum Press, 1975).

[11]"Is Determinism Self-Refuting?", *Mind,* forthcoming.

4 Intertheoretic Relations and the Future of Psychology*

Robert N. McCauley
Emory University

I

Eliminative materialism has enjoyed a resurgence recently in the work of Paul Churchland (for example, 1979, 1984, this volume, pp. 42–62) who argues for that view in the course of defending both a unified model of intertheoretic relations and the minimalist metaphysics of a scientific realist. His arguments, no doubt, offer solace to many scientifically minded philosophers and philosophically minded scientists who are generally sympathetic to the eliminativist program but who have been unwilling to abide the recent antirealism of its first generation defenders, Richard Rorty and Paul Feyerabend.

Churchland, by contrast, construes the pertinent issues as empirical through and through. His eliminativism is a direct consequence of his detailed analysis of intertheoretic relations in science, a plausible projection about future neuroscientific research, and his realist interpretation of scientific theories. According to Churchland, we will rid ourselves of the mental, because neuroscience will offer physical explanations of human activity superior to and thoroughly incommensurable with mentalistic psychological theories in general and our intentional folk psychology, in particular. A neuroscientific approach will replace our psychological theories (and their ontologies) without diminishing our ability to describe, predict, and explain.

Churchland's work explores with great insight the implications of work in the philosophy of language over the past two decades for an account of

*Reprinted from *Philosophy of Science* 53 (1986, pp. 179–198) by permission of the author and publisher.

intertheoretic relations in science. It is on the basis of both this discussion and his scientific realism that Churchland argues for eliminative materialism. I will maintain, however, that although it is not at all unreasonable on at least one level to expect the eventual elimination of intentional psychology, Churchland's arguments fail to justify this expectation, because his analysis of intertheoretic relations in science is too coarse grained. Specifically, he gives insufficient attention to the combined role of considerations concerning levels of analysis and of certain temporal features of intertheoretic relations.

Churchland's emphasis is on the incommensurability of scientific theories as the grounds for an ontic housecleaning. This emphasis is in marked contrast to the traditional microreductive model of intertheoretic relations (for example, Nagel 1961) which holds that ontological economizing is the result of satisfying strict formal and empirical conditions which insure the theories' commensurability. One theory microreduces another when the principles of the latter follow as deductive consequences from the principles of the former with the aid of reduction functions that identify the entities (and their properties) in one theory with those in the other on the basis of part-whole relationships (see McCauley 1981). The reducing theory explains the reduced theory and, thus, in the process demonstrates its dispensability.[1]

Eliminative materialists, on the other hand, look to Kuhn (1970) and Feyerabend (1962) who have emphasized the role of revolutionary change in science, where, because of the incommensurability of two theories, one simply *replaces* the other. That the two theories may use many of the same terms can obscure their disparity. In the history of science, shared terms typically prove more troublesome than those each theory employs uniquely, since in the different theories they often differ both intensionally and extensionally. This sort of condition often proves sufficient to short-circuit both the formal and empirical requirements of traditional microreduction. Thus, although both of these accounts of intertheoretic relations seek ontological deflation, they rely on analyses that are opposed on many important counts.

When two theories are so irreconcilable, sooner or later scientists simply abandon one or the other. The upheaval that follows this sort of theory replacement is comprehensive, often overthrowing the entire research tradition associated with the older theory—including its accompanying problems, methods, and ontology. Attending the new theory is a new research program whose specifics emerge as the theory develops—generating in its turn new problems, new research projects, and even new facts. (See Feyerabend 1962, pp. 28-29, 1975, pp. 67, 176-77.) Phlogiston theory is no longer with us, *not* because of its deductive and identity relations with the principles and ontology of modern chemical theory respectively, but rather because it proved incommensurable with the development of that superior theory. For the scientific realist, phlogiston theory is false and modern chemistry is true, so it is *impossible* for the former to follow from the latter deductively. (See Wimsatt 1976a, p. 218.)

Eliminative materialists construe the relationship of psychology and neuroscience along precisely these lines. Churchland is especially clear on this matter:

> The eliminative materialist holds that the P-theory [psychological theory], not to put too fine an edge on the matter, is a *false* theory. Accordingly, when we finally manage to construct an adequate theory of our neurophysiological activity, that theory will simply displace its primitive precursor. The P-theory will be eliminated, as false theories are, and the familiar ontology of common-sense mental states will go the way of the Stoic pneumata, the alchemical essences, phlogiston, caloric, and the luminiferous aether. (1979, p. 114)

Among other things, this analysis defuses certain defenses of psychology which seek to demonstrate the impossibility of its microreduction (for example, Fodor 1975, pp. 1–26, 1981, pp. 146–74). It defuses them, because it both embraces their premises concerning the incommensurability of the theories in question *and* offers an alternative model of intertheoretic relations on which those premises suffice to justify the sort of full scale elimination of psychology from which its defenders hoped to protect it! Hence, arguments against the microreduction of psychological theories are superfluous, if theories in neuroscience can simply replace them.

A realist revival of eliminative materialism is particularly welcome on a number of counts, since eliminativism, in any of its forms, has enjoyed a number of advantages over other materialist accounts of mind and over the various forms of the identity theory in particular. For example, the identification of entities across theories is not at issue when one theory *replaces* another. Eliminative materialism avoids all of the difficulties surrounding hypothetical identities in science (McCauley 1981). If neuroscience eliminates psychological theories and their accompanying ontological commitments, nothing will remain in the ontology of science to identify neural events with. (See Rorty 1970, p. 424.) These considerations motivate Rorty's characterization of eliminative materialism as the "disappearance form" of the identity theory (Rorty this volume, pp. 17–41). Nothing, however, *really* disappears, because, in Rorty's earlier view, there was nothing there to disappear in the first place and, in his more recent antirealistic view, these and other questions which scientific realists pose simply reflect metaphysical confusions. (For example, see Rorty 1979, p. 239 or Rorty 1982, chapters 1, 3, and 5.)

Eliminative materialism also eludes objections to materialism based on the notion of a category mistake. (See, for example, Cornman 1962.) Our conceptual arsenal changes as science progresses. Old categories go the way of the unsuccessful theories that contain them. The category problems those old categories inspire should fall out of sight as quickly as those categories do, which for the scientific realist will be just as quickly as the theories do in which they are embedded. No conceptual consideration should preclude, a priori, the ability of neuroscientific talk to assume both the explanatory and reporting functions of psychological idioms.

Furthermore, these considerations also release the eliminative materialist from both "the ideology of common sense" (Feyerabend 1975, p. 164) and the additional conceptual objections it motivates (such as any of the recent forms of essentialism). Many scientific breakthroughs have come at the expense of common sense. In the face of theoretical progress in science no category is immune to revision. The popularity (or commonality) of common sense is no ground for according epistemic privilege to its categories,[2] despite the considerable conceptual inertia that the categories of common sense enjoy. "As well as reflecting the wisdom of our ancestors, language also reflects their muddles and mistakes" (Sutherland 1970, p. 104). Experimental work indicates that categories and theories that science has overthrown long ago, nonetheless, often retain a firm foothold in common sense. (See McCloskey 1983.) Typical subjects' mechanical intuitions, for example, often seem to be consistent with accounts unique to physical theories prominent in the late Middle Ages. The eliminative materialist holds that the exact same sort of confusions prevail in our common-sense understanding of persons (Churchland 1979, p. 5).

Of course, the persistence of both the ideology and its idioms in psychology (and in mechanics as well) would seem a source of potential embarrassment for eliminativists. Not only do we still employ the language of intention in psychology, but we still use the classical notions of space, time, and mass in our everyday dealings with the world. Rorty and Feyerabend (willingly) and Churchland (grudgingly) (this volume, pp. 57–58) admit that mentalistic *talk* may be *so* socially entrenched that it may persist even after neuroscience can supersede it. Feyerabend suggests that we will eventually attribute physical connotations to mental terms (1962, p. 90). Rorty argues that if practicality is the only issue, then the eliminativist has already won the day. For once we admit that "at no greater cost than an inconvenient linguistic reform, we *could* drop such terms . . ." and that in this case ". . . ontological issues boil down to matters of talk," we can justifiably conclude that "they cease to be ontological issues" (this volume, p. 27; see also Rorty 1970, p. 424).

More recently, Rorty has adopted a more explicitly pragmatic form of eliminativism. He now advocates abandoning all "metaphysical comforts"

(1982, p. 166), so that the sense in which "matters of talk" cease to concern ontological issues cuts *both* ways now. Neither common sense *nor neuro-science* have epistemic privilege. Rather they offer solutions to various problems human beings face—each of which they handle with greater or lesser effectiveness. Thus "vocabularies are useful or useless . . . they are not 'more objective' or 'less objective' nor more or less 'scientific' " (1982, p. 203).[3] For Rorty the mind-body distinction is merely a pragmatic response to the extraordinary complexity of our neural hardware. We would have abandoned it long ago (or, perhaps, never even have formulated it), if that hardware had only been more perspicuous. (See Rorty 1979, pp. 242–43.) The issue now for Rorty is exclusively a "matter of talk." Rorty's eliminative materialism in its present form is a rather bland consequence of his new (and much more controversial) brand of pragmatism, which "regards all vocabularies," including that of science, "as tools for accomplishing purposes and *none* as representations of how things really are" (1982, p. xlvi). Thus the first generation eliminativists (Rorty, in particular) have, to a considerable extent, abandoned their scientific and realistic moorings in favor of arguments more "pragmatic" in character.

II

It is Rorty's (and Feyerabend's) apparent lack of sympathy for scientific realism (see Rorty 1979, pp. 274–84) which has alienated scientifically minded physicalists otherwise attracted to eliminative materialism. It is *that* audience, no doubt, that is most pleased to find Churchland's defense of eliminative materialism firmly grounded in his scientific realism.

Churchland's arguments for eliminative materialism differ on some counts from those of his predecessors. The first difference concerns the status of common sense and of common sense psychology, in particular. Churchland emphasizes that common sense is theoretical to the core and neither merely the repository of past wisdom, heterogeneous intuitions, and the surviving categories of debunked theories, nor the source of epistemically transparent insight. Consequently, he asserts that "the profound complacency most philosophers display concerning the status and/or the staying power of the common-sense conception of reality appears to me to be ill founded in the extreme" (1979, p. 43). With respect to human behavior specifically, Churchland claims that it is a *serious mistake* to construe the categorical framework of common sense psychology "as something *manifest* rather than as something conjectural." Theories in psychology (common sensical or otherwise) are no better than the solutions they offer for our empirical problems concerning human behavior. Churchland insists, therefore, that psychology[4] ". . . has no special features that make it empirically invulnerable, no unique functions that make it irreplaceable, no special status of any kind whatsoever" (this volume, p. 56). In fact, Churchland is convinced that all mentalistic or intentional psychology is just plain false.

The crucial point for now, though, is that once we recognize the theoretical character of intentional psychology, we should bring all of the criteria by which we evaluate theories to bear on this theory as well. Two considerations are particularly important, namely, the theory's relations with our best theories in contiguous and overlapping fields and the theory's overall ability to solve empirical problems in its own field. Generally speaking, a successful theory should organize a body of phenomena, provide insight into the causal and functional relationships which unify the domain, and, as a result, offer some empirical projections about similar events at other points in time. In addition, it should minimally cohere with what we know generally and, ideally, reinforce what we know about conceptually proximal areas in particular. (See Churchland this volume, pp. 46-47).

Churchland's assessment of the relevant theories is unequivocal. He argues that our psychological theories (and our folk psychological theories in particular) are woefully deficient in their treatment of phenomena which are *paradigmatic on their own account* of things! According to Churchland, they offer unconvincing and superficial tales about many aspects of reasoning, emotion, perception, pathology, and (perhaps most importantly) learning (1979, pp. 114-15, 127-37). Such psychological theorizing has neither conquered new territory nor suggested new research. It is sprawling, imprecise, sterile, and even inconsistent at times. In short, "the story is one of retreat, infertility, and decadence" (this volume, p. 48). Churchland implies that intentional psychology is the last surviving manifestation of an animistic view of nature inherited from our primitive ancestors and which we have, for the most part, abandoned over time. He holds, therefore, that its days, too, are numbered.

It comes as no surprise that Churchland is comparably pessimistic about the probability of successfully integrating common sense psychology with fertile theories in adjoining sciences. He does, however, think that the story is more complex than the one his predecessors told. The major concern of the eliminative materialist is "how the ontology of one theory (folk psychology) is, or is not, going to be related to the ontology of another (completed neuroscience)" (Churchland this volume, p. 46). Like Rorty and Feyerabend, Churchland thinks: (1) that all forms of intentional psychology will prove particularly recalcitrant to a smooth mapping onto theories in neuroscience, (2) that mapping theories onto one another is basically a special case of translating languages into one another, and (3) that the failure of neat translation in this case reveals a radical incommensurability between the two theories involved. Specifically for Churchland, it is a function of our inability to map those propositions of psychology which are semantically and systemically most important onto the claims of neuroscience. What Churchland denies, however, is that cases of radical incommensurability pose any serious threat to either scientific rationality or scientific realism — a denial based on his detailed analysis of intertheoretic relations.

Churchland argues that although intertheoretic relations in science span a wide variety of cases, they do fall on an identifiable continuum. Theoretical relations stretch from the radically incommensurable to the thoroughly continuous, with numerous positions in between. The point, quite simply, is that some intertheoretic relations are considerably more straightforward than others. Consequently, "we must be prepared to count reducibility as a matter of degree. Like translation, which may be faithful or lame, reduction may be smooth, or bumpy, or anywhere in between" (1979, p. 84). The degree of reducibility is a direct function of (1) the number of the reduced theory's propositions that are important both semantically and systemically that we can map onto the propositions of the reducing theory and (2) the ease with which they can be mapped.

On this account of intertheoretic reduction a true theory may even be able to reduce a false one, if it maps the latter sufficiently well (for example, Churchland argues that relativity theory offers a sufficiently clean mapping of classical mechanics). The emphasis is on the preservation of a reasonably faithful image of the central claims of the reduced theory in the conceptual structure of the reducing theory, and this requires neither establishing deductive relations between the two, nor preserving either the truth of most of the reduced theory's claims or the truth of the reduced theory's most (observationally) basic claims. (See 1979, pp. 84–85.) Thus "a successful reduction is a fell-swoop proof of displaceability; and it succeeds by showing that the new theory contains as a substructure an equipotent image of the old" (1979, p. 82). Because the reducing theory does offer an account of the pertinent domain that is generally continuous with that of the reduced theory, and because we can straightforwardly ascertain the superiority of one theory over the other on the basis of traditional criteria for theory choice, such reductions require few, if any, revisions in our general background knowledge (see 1979, p. 82) and, thus, pose little threat to accounts of scientific rationality. Generally, the reducing theory not only does most, if not all, of the work of the reduced theory, but more as well. In addition, it is capable of outlining where and why the reduced theory's limitations appear. Here, the process of theory change is apparently more evolutionary, and it is not too difficult to trace the adaptations which inform the reducing theory's success. The adjustments are sufficiently small that the ontology of the old theory is reduced and, thereby approximately preserved, in the ontology of the new. (Although in the remainder of this paper I will occasionally employ evolutionary notions in the explication of intertheoretic relations, that should not be construed as an endorsement of any of the versions of evolutionary epistemology. The claims are *only* analogical and like all analogies do not carry over in all respects. It is not the tradition of evolutionary epistemology which inspires this talk, but rather the fact that evolutionary talk offers the most natural contrast to the well-entrenched tradition of *revolutionary* talk. It is in this contrastive sense that I mean to employ it.)

Typically, translations are least convincing where the belief systems of cultures radically differ. Analogously, when theories in science are radically incommensurable, they seem to describe different worlds. (See Kuhn 1970, chapter 10.) In such revolutionary contexts we are able to map very few of a theory's important propositions onto those of its (eventual) successor, for example, in an attempt to map late medieval celestial mechanics onto a Keplerian (or Newtonian) view. The two theories are so disparate that all translations are bad translations to the extent that they fail to reproduce many of the most crucial claims of either theory in terms of the other. In periods of rapid change, partisans for competing views seem to talk past one another — not because they deal with different worlds, but because they employ widely divergent conceptual frameworks to describe the world with which we all must deal. In these contexts the two theories find little ground for agreement. They need not concur about the relative importance of problems, the boundaries between disciplines, the appropriateness of methods, the relevance of various observations, or even the range or interpretation of the facts to be explained. Thus, the standard criteria for theory choice are less helpful here because initially, at least, neither theory has the resources to encompass those of its competitor. When this happens whole theories and their ontologies replace one another. Decisions between the theories must rely on more considerations than just empirical tests, since the competing theories may profoundly disagree about the status of the empirical evidence.

Although Churchland is not particularly forthcoming at this point, he would, presumably, argue that revolutionary changes in science, also, need not impugn its rationality. (See Churchland 1979, sections 4 and 6.) Two or more scientific theories compete as accounts of some domain. Inevitably, over time they will differentially cohere with the rest of what we know and, thereby, garner more or less empirical support.[5]

Whether they result from evolutionary or revolutionary changes in science, our currently best theories deserve our ontological allegiances. Scientific realism for Churchland can be summarized as adherence to the tenet that "excellence in theory is the measure of ontology" (1979, p. 43). What our best science takes to be real is what *should* be taken to be real (because of all that stands behind the notion of "our best science"). Indeed, for Churchland, science provides the criteria of what *is* real. Churchland's eliminative materialism follows immediately: "the empirical virtues of the P-theory are sufficiently meagre that it is unreasonable to expect that it will reduce with sufficient smoothness to float an ontological reduction, and more reasonably to expect that it will simply be dropped, forsaken, as it were, for a prettier face" (1979, p. 115), namely, that of neuroscience. All the evidence indicates that neuroscience will *not* offer a very faithful translation of intentional psychology, which is to say that we will not ask it to provide any translation at all. We will not reinterpret our psychological claims in the light of new neuroscientific findings; rather, we will eliminate them in favor of those neuroscientific findings.

III

Churchland's model of intertheoretic relations (to some extent anticipated in Schaffner 1967) offers a unified account of the two traditional strategies for ontological deflation in the philosophy of science. Rather than taking microreduction and revolutionary science as contradictory and mutually exclusive accounts of intertheoretic relations, he construes each as extreme points on a continuum of possible semantic relations between theories. He characterizes neither of these positions in such extreme terms as their champions have. Our best intertheoretic mappings are not as rigorous as the traditional microreductionists claimed, nor are our worst as completely discontinuous as Kuhn and Feyerabend seem to imply. Churchland's temperance enables him to develop a model of intertheoretic relations which is both more generally applicable and more detailed than theirs. In addition, he provides a relatively clear strategy for assessing particular cases in terms of our ability to plausibly map theoretically important sentences from one theory onto the other.

Churchland's model of intertheoretic relations suffices so far as it goes, but it does not go far enough. The basic story is even more complex than the one Churchland tells. Although I too anticipate the replacement of common sense psychology, I disagree with Churchland about how that will be accomplished.

All eliminative materialists achieve their stark results on the basis of three assumptions. The first is virtually uncontroversial; namely, that the exploration of at least some intertheoretic contexts involves the comparison of substantially incommensurable theories. The second is that such contexts invariably require a nearly complete elimination of one theory or the other. (The successes of the superior theory entitle it to stake its conceptual claim on the disputed ontological territory.) Finally, the eliminativists' third assumption is that the relation of psychology and neuroscience is just such a context.

A more detailed account of intertheoretic contexts, however, offers grounds for denying the eliminativists' second and third assumptions. Although common sense psychology and contemporary neuroscience *are* thoroughly discontinuous, that need not (and *in this case does not*) necessitate the elimination or replacement of one by the other. Although Churchland has properly emphasized the relative conceptual continuity of theories, he and most other writers on intertheoretic relations[6] have focused almost exclusively on the structural relations between both theories and their domains. This general trend is, certainly in part, the result of philosophers' traditional preoccupations with the logical structure of theories generally, the deductive relations that hold between theoretical principles, in particular, and the part-whole relations which hold between entities in theories' respective domains. An examination of the functional dimensions of intertheoretic relations, however, proves equally revealing. A discussion of these functional relations, though, awaits the examination of two important preliminaries, the notion of levels of analysis and the role of temporal considerations in theory comparison.

At some point virtually every discussion of intertheoretic relations presupposes distinctions between levels of analysis. It is certainly implicit in all microreduction talk, where the view is that a lower-level theory and its ontology reduce a higher-level theory and its ontology. Microreductionists hold that if we can exhaustively describe and predict upper-level (or macro-) entities, properties, and principles in terms of lower-level (or micro-) entities, properties, and principles, then we can reduce the former to the latter (and dispense with the upper-level analysis). The key to the notion of levels of analysis is a view (arguably necessary for doing science) of nature as organized into parts and wholes, at least, and, hence, that to some extent all entities are subject to componential analysis. (See Bechtel 1984.) Crucially, however, this does not mean that we must necessarily describe components structurally. Functional accounts not only suffice for many theoretical purposes in such fields as ecology and physiology, they are typically preferable when dealing with systems of substantial complexity. Corresponding to the simple hierarchy of levels of organization in nature is a similar, roughly hierarchical, arrangement of levels of analysis in science.

Broadly speaking, chemistry is a higher level of analysis than subatomic physics, since it concerns larger units and events which stand in causal relationships most economically described in chemical terms and to some extent susceptible to systematic analysis without reference to subatomic particles or principles. Again, broadly speaking, biology is an even higher level, and psychology higher than that. The altitude of a level of analysis is inversely proportional to the size of the domain of events with which it is concerned, so cell biology, for example, proceeds at a higher level of analysis than does biochemistry, since it deals with only a subset of the phenomena that the latter addresses. The altitude of a level of analysis is also directly proportional to the complexity of the systems with which it deals. Thus, higher-level sciences deal with increasingly restricted ranges of events having to do with increasingly organized physical systems. Consequently, purely structural considerations less perspicuously distinguish levels the higher in the hierarchy we go. The higher levels generally deal with more complex systems and a wider range of variables. The behavior of such systems is more diverse. Different parts are functionally equivalent and the same part can serve more than one function. In such contexts functional ascriptions assume greater importance. Frequently, however, we can usefully idealize (in physiology, for example) many processes as the products of relatively closed, self-regulating functional systems operating at a particular level.

It is also worthwhile to distinguish between diachronic and synchronic features of intertheoretic relations. At times Churchland's treatment reflects his sensitivity on this point (1979, p. 81), at other times it does not (1979, p. 107). Most specifically, it is important to distinguish the relations that hold between successive theories at a single level of analysis over time as opposed to those between theories at different levels of analysis at the same time. The former, following Wimsatt (1976a), I will call intralevel or successional contexts, the latter, interlevel or microreductive[7] contexts. Intralevel contexts include Kuhnian revolutionary situations (such as the relation of Chomsky's theories of language to his structuralist and behaviorist predecessors). On the other hand, the relation of genetics and biochemistry in the early 1950s is a particularly revealing illustration of the importance of interlevel relationships. These two sorts of contexts involve relations between theories that differ considerably on both functional *and structural* grounds. Consequently, unified models of reduction (like Nagel's [1961] or Schaffner's [1967]) and even unidimensional models (like Churchland's) oversimplify and therefore obscure the diversity of actual relationships between theories in science. (See Wimsatt 1976a, pp. 214–15.)

Churchland's model is helpful on a number of counts. It is not, however, a reliable guide concerning the sufficient conditions for theory replacement in science and it is, of course, precisely that goal of Churchland's model on which his and most other versions of eliminative materialism rest.

Churchland's continuum of theory commensurability captures an important dimension of intralevel relations. His model (in contrast to Feyerabend's [1962], for example) preserves a systematic account of the conceptual and empirical proximity of classical and relativistic mechanics, since it allows superior theories to reduce their predecessors at least some of the time, the falsity and mild incommensurability of these older theories notwithstanding. By eschewing the strong deductive and empirical requirements the microreductionists defended and to which others overreacted, Churchland offers a more subtle reading of the range of relevant cases. There is, however, more.

In intralevel contexts where the mapping between theories is reasonably good, the new theory typically *corrects* the old. It *explains the older theory* in the sense that it offers a principled account of when and why it fails. Kepler's laws enabled him to explain and predict the successes and failures of Copernican astronomical calculations that assumed that the heavenly bodies moved in circles. The new theory typically possesses greater precision, a wider domain, or both. It includes the accomplishments of its predecessor as special cases where certain parametric values fall within some range which does not confine the new theory. Within that restricted domain the old theory constitutes an approximation of the new and serves as an effective *heuristic of calculation,* sufficient, at least, for the purposes of engineers. (See Wimsatt 1976a, p. 174 and McCauley 1986.)

In *these* intralevel contexts where succeeding theories are, for the most part, continuous, we rarely, if ever, claim to have eliminated the older theory's ontology. Rather, terms and propositions undergo reinterpretations in light of their new positions in the conceptual framework of the new theory. These reinterpretations can have both intensional and extensional consequences. The continuity of the theories, though, is precisely a function of intensional and extensional overlap between the old and new. Generally, new theories retain old terms when possible. We have retained terms such as "planet," "evolution," and "gravity" and propositions about rectilinear inertial motion through numerous reinterpretations, because the effects of these reinterpretations taken individually were not especially severe. Most of the bodies that the ancients called "planets," for example, still are. (See Brown 1979, p. 118.) We can take some successive theories to be talking about at least some of the same things, to be making some of the same claims about those things, and to be offering explanations about some common explananda. So long as the relevant changes have reasonably local effects that do not destroy larger conceptual patterns, to claim that incommensurability seriously threatens theory comparison is to overstate the case.

Intralevel relations at the other end of Churchland's continuum— genuine, unanticipated (philosophically provocative) scientific revolutions—are more rare than the literature of the past two decades indicates. When substantial meaning changes and wholly new theoretical elements yield fundamental incompatibilities between theories, their conceptual patterns fail to coincide. Whether these difficulties arise as the result of revolutionary developments *or* accumulate over a series of successive theories, they *do* undermine efforts to map some theories onto some of their successors. Where serious incommensurability arises in a single step, we may be unable to translate an old theory into its *immediate* successor. During such crises scientists decide to replace (and eliminate) one of the theories. Since they offer thoroughly incompatible accounts of at least much of the "same" phenomena, science cannot abide both for too long. If the challenger succeeds, it *explains the old theory away*. Here the superior theory eliminates its competitor (and its ontology) when it replaces it (see, for example, Brewer 1974). Whereas in intralevel contexts with little conceptual friction (and relatively straightforward mapping between theories) although new theories replace old theories, features of the older theory persist, and it can still serve as a calculating heuristic. In addition, a reasonably faithful image of much of its ontology endures in that of its successor.

All intralevel contexts *eventually* result in the total elimination of some theories. Over time in intralevel contexts incommensurability *increases* (and the goodness of mapping between older theories, separated by generations of successors, and the present reigning theory, therefore, inevitably *decreases*). Scientific revolutions block intertheoretic translation within a particular level of analysis, but so does scientific evolution, given enough time. (See Laudan 1977, p. 139).

A simple illustration of this sort of evolutionary change may help. Arguably, part of Galilean dynamics is continuous with contemporary mechanics in the sense that the latter makes predictions which coincide reasonably well with Galileo's law of free fall, so long as the fall is not too long and so long as it occurs relatively near to the surface of the earth. Galileo's notion of natural circular motion, though, is of a piece with the mechanics of his neo-Aristotelian predecessors. At least one aspect of Galilean dynamics, then, maps onto contemporary theory while another maps at least as well on to late medieval theory, but little, if any, of late medieval dynamics maps continuously beyond the seventeenth century and much, if not most, does not survive Galilean innovations. (See Brown 1979, pp. 111–21.) The point, though, is that the revolutionary character of Galileo's work was not *all* encompassing. When he could, he used traditional concepts as consistently as his new system would allow. It is not too difficult to locate the radical changes Galileo proposed and to trace their consequences. By the time Kepler had undermined the sanctity of circular motion, Descartes had suggested rectilinear inertial motion, and Newton had economically consolidated terrestrial and celestial mechanics and had completely *eliminated* the notion of natural motions, late medieval mechanics had not only been replaced, it had been eliminated.

Whether scientific revolutions (for example, the Copernican) or the cumulative effects of successive theories in a science (for example, in seventeenth- and eighteenth-century mechanics) preclude felicitous theoretical translations, such barriers inevitably arise as the sciences change and develop. With time, theoretical generations inevitably accumulate incongruencies in the mappings of successive theories at a level of analysis, until we can safely say that we have not only replaced some ancestral theories, but that we have eliminated all traces of some as well. Although this is surely not a principled consequence of scientific change, it is a real one.

Interlevel contexts, by contrast, involve no eliminations whatsoever. These are cross-scientific contexts where the goal is to associate theories that operate at different levels of analysis. Scientists explore whether their theories cohere with (and they hope are reinforced by) what is known at contiguous and overlapping levels.

The componential assumptions which underlie levels in science also inform scientists' interlevel concerns. Scientists look to other levels of analysis to gain new explanatory and problem solving angles on what is assumed to be the same phenomena under different descriptions. (See McCauley 1986.) Interlevel explorations establish ties between the concepts of different theories in the continuing process (1) of justifying the assumption that the theories share a common explanandum and (2) of stimulating further research.

Once theories at adjacent levels of analysis are sufficiently developed to address issues on the borders between the two sciences directly, they tend to *constrain one another's form.* The whole of science creates selection pressures on theories at any particular level. (See Wimsatt 1976a, pp. 231–36.) Nearly always, the reigning theories at immediately adjoining levels exert the most profound forces in the local conceptual space. They help to define one another's research problems. Here theories typically do not correct one another so much as they attempt to accommodate one another's demands. The constraints that physical chemistry and biochemistry exert upon one another with respect to accounting for the transfer of sodium ions across cell membranes offers a fitting illustration (see Robinson 1982).

The strongest sense of replacement appropriate in interlevel contexts, where theories map relatively neatly (along lines *approximating* those outlined in traditional microreductive models), is, *at best,* partial replaceability. A theory at one level, well integrated with theories at adjacent levels, can (ideally) do some of their work under certain special circumstances. Generally speaking, when relevant variables at upper levels are held constant, well-integrated lower-level theories ideally offer sufficient accounts of the phenomena for most of our explanatory and predictive purposes (although, typically, at tremendous calculating expense), for example, in the relation of statistical mechanics and thermodynamics. Upper-level theories, on the other hand, provide the rationale for organizing what is, for all appearances, otherwise disparate lower level phenomena, for example, when physiological concerns inform extremely complex biochemical research.

The borders between levels populated by relatively immature theories and/or those between levels that, for intralevel reasons, have undergone substantial change, represent the other extreme on Churchland's continuum of theoretical continuity applied to interlevel cases. As the relata change within their own levels — a process, incidentally, which interlevel forces constrain, but which intralevel dynamics drive — they *may* become increasingly discontinuous with one another. In the absence of a plausible competing theory, interlevel forces are neither necessary nor sufficient to provoke changes in (let alone overthrow) an established theory at any given level. Consider, for example, the persistence of transformational grammars in linguistics in the face of important counterevidence in experimental psycholinguistics (see McCauley 1984). Interlevel forces only help to define what will count as a plausible alternative; on their own they are incapable of dethroning a reigning theory at some level.

As the translations between theories at different levels become more and more difficult, talk even of replaceability (let alone replacement) becomes less and less justified: "in interlevel reduction, the more difficult the translation becomes, the more *irreplaceable* the upper level theory is! It becomes the only practical way of handling the regularities it describes" (Wimsatt 1976a, p. 222). Interlevel contexts with considerable intertheoretic discontinuity, that is, high incommensurability, should be the least likely (of the four cases considered here) to involve either the replacement or elimination of theories and their ontologies. (See Fig. 4.1.) Radical incommensurability in some intertheoretic contexts, namely, interlevel ones, neither requires the elimination of theories on principled grounds nor provokes such eliminations, in fact.

What lower-level theories (like upper-level theories) attempt to explain in interlevel contexts are the phenomena in question, *not* the upper-level theory. It is the phenomena, not the theories, which are (re)explained. The lower- and upper-level theories share an explanandum for which, in this case, they offer substantially incompatible accounts. They bring different conceptual resources to bear and, consequently, highlight different aspects of the phenomena in question. Nonetheless, intertheoretic excursions in interlevel contexts inevitably tend, over time, to *reduce* the incommensurability of neighboring, incompatible theories. Such interlevel moves are important *heuristics of discovery*. (See McCauley, 1986 and Bechtel, 1986.)

Scientists search for logically related consequences of theories from contiguous levels. Logical conflicts suggest new tests which offer, for the winner, new sources of empirical support, and for the loser, direction for further research and possible adjustments. Specifically, scientists attempt to exploit the componential assumptions underlying the levels

Degree of intertheo-retic continuity (Churchland's continuum) / Type of intertheo-retic context	High (extensive inter-theoretic mapping)	Low (little, if any, intertheoretic mapping)
Intralevel (same level over time) theories replace one another	scientific evolution 1. new theory explains (and corrects) immediate predecessor 2. eventual elimination of some earlier predecessors 3. recent predecessors as calculating heuristics	scientific revolutions 1. new theory explains immediate predecessor away 2. rapid elimination of predecessors 3. new paradigm
Interlevel (different levels at the same time) theories accomodate one another	microreductive contexts 1. increasingly unified explanation of phenomena where adjacent theories sharply constrain one anothers' form 2. partial replaceability of theories at adjacent levels 3. possible interlevel theories	explanatory pluralism 1. multiple, disparate explanations of phenomena 2. no replaceability of theories at adjacent levels 3. interlevel excursions as heuristic of discovery

FIG. 4.1.

framework by postulating hypothetical identities between collections of parts (the entities of the lower level theories) and wholes (the entities of the upper level theories). These identity claims are hypothetical claims which suggest important avenues for empirical research (see McCauley 1981). These hypothetical identities are an important source of interlevel explorations' heuristic power as engines of discovery.[8]

Note that in these interlevel contexts the influences of theories on one another are not unidirectional (the pervasive reductionist biases of many philosophers and scientists notwithstanding). (See Allen 1983 for a discussion of some of cognitive psychology's influence on neuroscience.) Failures of translation ". . . carry with them no automatic presumption of upper-level guilt" (Wimsatt 1976a, p. 222). Whatever priority any theory deserves should not be grounded in our ontological prejudices, but rather in superior empirical performance. The absence of tidy interlevel translations does not constitute, a priori, a reason to accord explanatory and/or ontological priority to lower-level theories or their ontologies. As Laudan (1977, p. 56) has observed, ". . . noting . . . a logical inconsistency or a relation of nonreinforcement between two theories need *not* force scientists to abandon one, or the other, or both." (See also pp. 50–54.)

Considerable conceptual discontinuity between theories at adjoining levels usually inspires empirical research. If each theory is modified to accommodate the new results, the theories will tend to become increasingly continuous conceptually. Interlevel situations in which theories at proximal levels, whose conceptual structures conflict only mildly, may occasion interlevel theories (Maull 1977). An interlevel theory exploits the descriptive and explanatory resources of theories from more than one level of analysis, for example, in molecular genetics. It incorporates information about causal relations and concepts from various theories in its hypotheses in order to provide a more integrated, informed, and comprehensive account of phenomena. These enhanced descriptive capabilities enable an interlevel theory to explore problems that lower-level theories alone cannot address. The theoretical resources of biochemistry, for example, are not sufficient to generate an account of the mechanisms of inheritance and development. They require guidance and supplementation from cytology and genetics. Molecular genetics has become the focus for such research.

None of these points preclude Churchland's realism; they only undermine *his* (and his predecessors') eliminativism. The relation of psychology (intentional, common sense, mentalistic, and/or cognitive) and neuroscience is one (as Churchland has emphasized) between *theories*. The crucial point is that *these theories operate at different levels of analysis.* Psychology and neuroscience offer fundamentally different accounts of a range of human activities. Psychological systems certainly depend upon neural systems (just as neural systems depend upon biochemical systems). The phenomena that neuroscience discusses are to some extent constitutive of the phenomena which psychology discusses, though as Fodor and others have noted, not in any simple way. Hence, like physiological systems, we typically approach the descriptions of the components of psychological systems functionally. Psychology and neuroscience employ different concepts and principles, and each highlights different aspects of the object of study. Each offers accounts that are more or less effective with different problems. Scientific researchers in both fields (and in philosophy) have eagerly endorsed hypothetical identity relations between components of their ontologies, which, at least in neuroscience, has stimulated some empirical research. Neuroscience is concerned with a wider class of events than psychology, but that is to be expected since it operates at a lower level. Present, then, are all the earmarks of *interlevel* theoretic relations.

The mistake *all* versions of eliminative materialism have made is to draw their eliminativist conclusions about the *inter*level relationship between psychology and neuroscience on the basis of an analysis appropriate to *intra*level contexts. The eliminativists *correctly* claim that theories at the two levels have many important conceptual discontinuities, but they incorrectly conclude (spurred on, no doubt, by strident Kuhnians) that such incommensurability requires the elimination of one or the other. In *intra*level contexts during scientific revolutions such crises *do* require that sort of radical surgery, but in interlevel contexts such a measure would eliminate potentially important stimuli for scientific discovery. *The history* *of science reveals no precedent for theory replacement or elimination in interlevel contexts.* The only way it might is in those interlevel situations at the completely opposite end of Churchland's spectrum. That is a case where all the principles of the upper-level theory follow as *deductive consequences* from those of the lower-level theory and where all the upper-level entities and all of their properties could be *strictly identified* with aggregates of lower-level entities and their properties[9]—which is to say, the case of a classical microreduction. Even this, though, would not constitute a logical warrant for the elimination of the upper-level theory, since it would necessarily employ a set of reduction functions which are not themselves reducible to the lower-level theory.[10]

I wish to conclude, however, by endorsing Churchland's defense of scientific realism from skeptical onslaughts, his insistence on the fundamentally theoretical dimension of all common sense, and his prediction that future science will not abide common sense psychology. The replacement of theories, though, is an *intralevel* phenomenon. Therefore, defenders of the ideology of common sense psychology ought to be *most* wary, not of developments in neuroscience, but rather of those in experimental cognitive psychology. Although that field shows few signs of revolutionizing our psychological views, in the Kuhnian sense, it does not follow that it is, therefore, incapable of *eventually* replacing (and, perhaps, even completely eliminating) common sense psychology.[11] As in the case of Galileo's law of free fall, though, common sense psychology handles the majority of situations we face from day to day reasonably well for many of our explanatory and predictive purposes. But also like Galileo's law, this suggests nothing more than that a faint image of some of our common sense psychological views *may* persist in some future psychology.

FOOTNOTES

[1]Robert Causey (1977) has offered the most comprehensive account of the complexities involved here.

[2]Feyerabend (1962) argues:

> No number of examples of usefulness of an idiom is ever sufficient to show that the idiom will have to be retained forever . . . conceptual changes may occur anywhere in the system that is employed at a certain time for the explanation of the properties of the world we live in. (p. 89)

[3]More recently, Feyerabend has argued for similar views concerning the status of science (1978). I confine my comments here to the evolution of Rorty's views, because he has been the more outspoken defender of eliminativism.

[4]Although Churchland directs his arguments primarily against what he calls, in this volume, pp. 42–62, "folk psychology," it is clear that he takes his arguments to cut with equal force against theories in cognitive psychology as well. In his (1979) Churchland explicitly targets any

theory which does not readily lend itself to traditional microreduction. Arguably, this includes virtually all psychological theories (including most forms of behaviorism). For Churchland, so far as science is concerned, both mentalism and intentionality are vicious. There are no benign forms.

[5]Whether political, social, and/or psychological biases underlie the emergence of one theory over another is the subject for students of particular historical episodes (see Maull, 1977, p. 151, note 19). Rarely, if ever, are the victories so abrupt *and* the incommensurabilities so radical that in the long run they overshadow a story told in terms of empirical considerations and scientific problem solving effectiveness.

[6]Two important exceptions are Wimsatt (1976a, 1976b) and Nickles (1973). I am particularly indebted to the work of the former.

[7]Describing these contexts as microreductive is simply to aid in their identification. I will ultimately endorse few, if any, of the microreductionists' conclusions. (See notes 9 and 10 below.)

[8]See Darden and Maull (1977) on the identification of genes and chromosomes by Mendelian geneticists and cytologists in the early decades of this century.

[9]This is a simplified account of what Causey (1977) calls a uniform microreduction. I have discussed elsewhere (1981) the substantial skepticism as to whether such a situation has ever held at any time between two theories from different levels. The reduction of thermodynamics to statistical mechanics is the most plausible candidate that comes to mind, but even here the concepts and ontology of classical thermodynamics have proven sufficiently robust in other sciences that no one has suggested eliminating or denying the reality of gases, pressures, temperatures, etc.

[10]As I argued in my 1981, Causey's strategies for avoiding this problem are ineffective.

[11]Hence, although I am generally sympathetic to Kitcher's discussion (1984, especially pp. 102–6) of intertheoretic relations so far as it goes, I do not agree that her argument offers an ultimately compelling "defense of intentional psychology."

5 Will the Concepts of Folk Psychology Find a Place in Cognitive Science?*

Stephen P. Stich
Rutgers University, New Brunswick

Two conceptions of cognitive science have been proposed which promise an affirmative answer [to the question of whether the folk psychological notion of belief was likely to find a comfortable place in cognitive science, viz . . .], namely, the Strong and the Weak Representational Theories of the Mind. But I have argued in previous work (Stich, 1983) that neither of these views is tenable. To replace them, I have urged the adoption of the Syntactic Theory of the Mind (STM), which construes cognitive mental states as relations to purely formal or syntactic mental sentences. If as I have argued, cognitive science is and should be adhering to the STM paradigm, then it would appear that there is no place for the folk concept of belief in cognitive science. This conclusion follows from three related observations. First, the mental state tokens postulated by cognitive theories in the STM mold need not and often will not admit of any comfortable ascription of content. Second, an STM theory may view mental state tokens to which content *can* be ascribed as type identical to tokens with quite a different content. Thus, third, it will generally not be possible to correlate the state types postulated by STM theories with any truth condition or content sentence. But it is of the essence of folk psychological belief state types that they have content or truth conditions. Folk psychology individuates beliefs and specifies the causal relations among them in terms of their content. Thus we cannot identify folk psychological belief state types with mental state types as they are conceived in STM theories. The folk psychological

*Reprinted from *From Folk Psychology to Cognitive Science: The Case Against Belief* (Cambridge: The MIT Press, 1983) by permission of the author and publisher.

property of *believing that snow is white* cannot be identified with any property recognized by an STM cognitive theory.

To the best of my knowledge, this strategy of arguing against the scientific utility of folk psychological concepts is quite new in the literature. Not so the conclusion it supports. A number of other writers have argued that folk psychology and serious science are ill suited to one another, and this chapter will be devoted to a survey of their arguments. I am inclined to think that each of the arguments I recount lends some further support to the conclusion, though none of them is free from problems.

1. FOLK PSYCHOLOGY IS A DEGENERATING RESEARCH PROGRAM

In a number of places[1] Patricia and Paul Churchland have argued that folk psychology "is a stagnant or degenerating research program, and has been for millennia."[2] Underlying this claim is the view that folk psychology constitutes "an empirical theory, with all the functions, virtues, *and perils* entailed by that status."[3] The function of folk psychology, qua theory, is to explain behavior, and its most conspicuous virtue is that it enables us to "explain, and even predict, the behavior of other persons with a facility and success that is remarkable."[4] The peril alluded to is that folk psychology might "constitute a radically false theory, a theory so fundamentally defective that both the principles and the ontology of that theory will eventually be displaced."[5] On the Churchlands' view, it is at least a good bet that the concepts and ontology of folk psychology will not find any place in the scientific canon of the future.

The argument for this conjecture consists of three observations. First, for all its workaday utility, folk psychology has some very notable shortcomings.

> Its comprehension both of practical and of factual reasoning is sketchy at best; the kinematics and dynamics of emotions it provides is vague and superficial; the vicissitudes of perception and perceptual illusion are, in its terms, largely mysterious; its comprehension of the learning process is extraordinarily thin; and its grasp on the nature and causes of mental illness is almost nil.[6]

> Consider our utter ignorance of the nature and psychological functions of sleep, that curious state in which a third of one's life is spent. Reflect on the common ability to catch an outfield fly ball on the run, or hit a moving car with a snowball. Consider the internal construction of a 3-D visual image from subtle differences in the 2-D array of stimulations in our respective retinas. . . . Or consider the miracle of memory, with its lightning capacity

for relevant retrieval. On these and many other mental phenomena, [folk psychology] sheds negligible light.[7]

From all of this Churchland would have us conclude that folk psychology is "*at best* a highly superficial theory, a partial and unpenetrating gloss on a deeper and more complex reality. Having reached this opinion," he writes, "we may be forgiven for exploring the possibility that [folk psychology] provides a positively misleading sketch of our internal kinematics and dynamics, one whose success is owed more to selective application and forced interpretation on our part than to genuine theoretical insight on [folk psychology's] part.[8]

The second observation is historical. The story of folk psychology is "one of retreat, infertility, and decadence."[9]

> The [folk psychology] of the Greeks is essentially the [folk psychology] we use today, and we are negligibly better at explaining human behavior in its terms than was Sophocles. This is a very long period of stagnation and infertility for any theory to display, especially when faced with such an enormous backlog of anomalies and mysteries in its own explanatory domain. . . . [Folk psychology's] failure to develop its resources and extend its range of success is therefore darkly curious, and one must query the integrity of its basic categories.[10]

The Churchlands' third observation is that folk psychology comports poorly with those other, better developed sciences whose explanatory domains overlap to a greater or lesser extent with that of folk psychology. The point is an important one since it bears on the degree of tolerance we should extend in the face of folk psychology's failings. "A troubled or stagnant theory may merit patience and solicitude on other grounds; for example, on grounds that it is the only theory or theoretical approach that fits well with other theories about adjacent subject matters, or the only one that promises to reduce or to be explained by some established background theory whose domain encompasses the domain of the theory at issue."[11] But, Churchland argues, "it is just here, perhaps, that [folk psychology] fares poorest of all."[12]

> If we approach *homo sapiens* from the perspective of natural history and the physical sciences, we can tell a coherent story of his constitution, development, and behavioral capacities which encompasses particle physics, atomic and molecular theory, organic chemistry, evolutionary theory, biology, physiology, and materialistic neuro-science. That story, though still radically incomplete, is already extremely powerful, outperforming [folk psychology] at many points even in its own domain. And it is deliberately and self-consciously coherent with the rest of our developing world picture. In short,

the greatest theoretical synthesis in the history of the human race is currently in our hands, and parts of it already provide searching descriptions and explanations of human sensory input, neural activity and motor control.

But [folk psychology] is no part of this growing synthesis. Its intentional categories stand magnificently alone, without visible prospect of reduction to that larger corpus.[13]

Churchland offers the following eloquent summary of his argument:

What we must say is that [folk psychology] suffers explanatory failures on a epic scale, that it has been stagnant for at least twenty-five centuries, and that its categories appear (so far) to be incommensurable with or orthogonal to the categories of the background physical science whose long-term claim to explain human behavior seems undeniable. Any theory that meets this description must be allowed a serious candidate for outright elimination.[14]

Although I have considerable sympathy for some of the claims the Churchlands are urging, I am inclined to think that this is the weakest of the arguments to be considered in this chapter. It is clear that folk psychology leaves a great deal to be desired as a science, and that it has not made much progress since the time of Sophocles.[15] Still, there are at least three objections to the Churchland argument which undercut a fair amount of its persuasive power.

The first is the observation, lately stressed by Wilkes[16] that folk psychology is not properly viewed *merely* as a crude explanatory, scientific theory, since the terms of folk psychology have more work to do than do scientific terms.

Although they share with the latter the tasks of describing, explaining and predicting, they have countless other roles as well: to warn, threaten, assess, applaud, praise, blame, discourage, urge, wheedle, sneer, hint, imply, insult . . . and so on. The conceptual apparatus of common-sense psychology stands to that of scientific psychology as a multi-purpose tool stands to a spanner.[17]

Wilkes actually argues for a much stronger thesis, viz., that "there is no useful sense of the term 'theory' whereby everyday psychological explanation suggests or contains a theory of the mind."[18] But this seems to me to overstate the case quite seriously. Our everyday use of folk psychological concepts to explain and predict the behavior of our fellows clearly presupposes some rough and ready laws which detail the dynamics of belief and desire formation and connect these states to behavior. These presupposed laws can with a bit of effort be teased out and made explicit.[19] Collectively they surely count as a common sense theory. But to make the point against the Churchlands' argument we need only the weaker, and hardly controversial, observation that common sense psychological notions are pressed into service in many ways besides explaining and predicting behavior. Given the many and varied uses of folk psychological notions, the failure of folk psychological theory to make any serious progress in the last two millennia seems less surprising. Since folk concepts served well in their non-protoscientific roles, and since (as Churchland concedes) folk assumptions were not recognized as protoscientific theories, there was little pressure for them to evolve into better theories.

A second objection to the Churchlands' argument is that it exaggerates the importance of the stagnation in the history of folk psychology. True enough, our common sense psychology has changed but little since Sophocles. But during most of the intervening millennia the very idea of doing empirical science and evolving and elaborating concepts to meet the needs of a developing science was quite unknown. If folk psychology scored no major gains in the two thousand years after Aristotle, the same must be said for biology, chemistry, and economics. Those latter disciplines, or at least the first two, have fared rather better in the last few centuries. But this progress can be traced in substantial measure to the fact that their domains have become the subject matter of increasingly professionalized experimental sciences. Psychology, by contrast, has barely a century of history as an experimental discipline. What is more, though the earliest experimental psychologists — Wundt, James, and others — often attempted to exploit the conceptual apparatus of folk psychology, this strategy was largely extinguished in experimental psychology during the decades when behaviorism dominated the scene. It is only with the flourishing of the cognitive paradigm during the last decade or two that the idea of exploiting folk psychological notions in experimental psychology has regained respectability. So those who would defend the conceptual apparatus of folk psychology might plausibly protest that the program of exploiting these notions in serious science has barely begun. The charge of stagnation is thus, perhaps, premature.

A final objection to the Churchlands' argument focuses on the prospects for integration with other sciences. Though the Churchlands are surely correct in their contention that the conceptual apparatus of folk psychology comports poorly with the growing body of theory in the physical sciences, just the opposite is true if we look to the social sciences. Economics, political science, sociology, and anthropology are up to their ears in the intentional idiom that is the hallmark of folk psychology. If all talk of beliefs, desires, expectations, preferences, fears, suspicions, plans, and the like were banished from the social sciences, those disciplines as we know them today would disappear. We simply have no way of recounting our knowledge of social, political, and economic processes without invoking the intentional language of folk psychology. Of course, this observation might be viewed as a two-edged sword, indicating not that folk psychology is more respectable than the Churchlands maintain, but rather that the social sciences which share its conceptual apparatus are themselves targets for elimination from the growing canon of science. But, absent further argument, it is tempting to dismiss this move as no more than a crass physicalist prejudice. If, as Laudan urges, we choose between theories largely on the basis of the problems they solve, then for all their evident difficulties, the social sciences will be around for the foreseeable future.[20] For there are simply no serious competing theories which address problems in the social domain and which do not invoke the intentional concepts of folk psychology.

2. THE INFRALINGUISTIC CATASTROPHE

A second argument due to Patricia and Paul Churchland turns on the fact that many creatures, including very young members of our own species, are not plausibly described as having beliefs at all.[21] There are no content sentences which are serious candidates to characterize the mental states of these creatures. Still, there is reason to suppose that the cognitive processes operative in ourselves are not fundamentally different from those in young children and nonlinguistic animals. Thus if the cognitive processes in infralinguistic creatures are not appropriately characterized in folk psychological terms, there is reason to think that the best theory characterizing our own cognitive activity will not characterize it in folk psychological terms either.

Here is how Paul Churchland elaborates the argument. The first premise is that

> the behavior of an infant during the first several months after birth invites description/explanation in terms of specific perceptions, beliefs and reasonings no more than does the (more leisurely) behavior of many plants, or the (more frantic) behavior of many microscopic protozoa. The apparently chaotic economy of an infant's behavior — and there is plenty of behavior if one looks closely — is not rendered transparent or coherent by any such projection of familiar categories. The relevant organization in its behavioral economy has yet to develop. Were it not for the fact that infants resemble and eventually develop into thinking adults, whereas plants and protozoa do not, we would not even be much tempted to ascribe propositional attitudes and our usual cognitive concepts to them.[22]

As Churchland notes, an opponent might insist that despite appearances very young children do have propositional attitudes, though "the particular propositions that would express the infant's attitudes are inexpressible in our language, the infant's ideas or concepts being primitive ones quite different from our own."[23] But he rightly dismisses this move as "a near paradigm of an untestable hypothesis."[24] Indeed without some better account of just what sort of entities propositions are supposed to be and what it is for a psychological state to "express" a proposition or to "have" one as its content, I am inclined to think that the "inexpressible propositions" move is worse than untestable; it is incomprehensible.

The second premise in Paul Churchland's version of the argument is that

> the basic parameters of rational intellectual activity are the same whatever its stage of development, notwithstanding the increasing degree to which that activity becomes "comprehensible" in terms of propositional attitudes as we consider the later stages of its development.[25]

More particularly Churchland claims that there are conspicuous continuities between infants and older, language-using children along "three dimensions of human development: the behavioural, the structural, and the functional."[26] Under the first heading, there is a "steady articulation of the infant's behavioural repertoire—from the stage where our usual cognitive concepts simply fail to find adequate purchase to a stage where they find paradigmatic application. . . . If there is any basic change or shift in the infant's mode of intellectual activity during that first year, it does not show itself in any characteristic change in the development of its behaviour."[27] Under the heading of "physiological or structural considerations, the situation with respect to continuity appears, at least at a gross level, much the same."

> The major brain cells or neurons are already formed some months before birth. Development from there consists most noticeably in such things as the branching growth of dendrites, the lengthening of axons, and the progressive myelinization of these interconnective impulse-carrying fibres. . . . All of these processes begin very early (prenatally, in fact), develop continuously, and continue to develop through infancy, childhood, and well into adult life. This apparent continuity of structural development speaks in favour of [the second premise].[28]

Finally, under the heading of functional continuity, what little we do know again speaks in favor of the second premise:

> We know that the network of neurons/axons/dendrites generates and conducts nervous impulses, and that the conductive/generative dispositions of that network can be modified by the successive impulses to which it is subject. We know that the gross structure of that network is of a kind that fits it for

the processing of information, and for evolving in the manner in which it does so. . . . And we know that the structural development that the brain undergoes fits it for processing information in more and more complex ways. But nervous activity in a network of this kind is a characteristic of the brain at *all* stages of its development, even to some degree of its immature, prenatal stage. The brain, in short, is a self-modifying information processor from its inception to its death.[29]

The conclusion that Churchland would draw from these two premises is as follows:

As a general approach to what rational intellectual development consists in, the [folk psychological] approach is pursuing what must be superficial parameters. That is, sentential parameters cannot be among the primitive parameters comprehended by a truly adequate theory of rational intellectual development, and the relevance of sentential parameters must be superficial or at best derivative even in the case of fully mature language-using adults.[30]

In contrast with the previous "degenerating research program" argument, this argument is one I am inclined to endorse with little reservation. Indeed, it is very similar in spirit, if not in detail, to an argument I developed in previous work (see Stich, 1983a, chap. 7). Among my basic themes there was that in opting for a cognitive psychology built from folk notions we are likely to lose important generalizations, since folk psychology cannot characterize the mental states of young children or "exotic" folk. So if there are generalizations which apply equally to their cognitive processes and to our own, a cognitive theory couched in the language of folk psychology will be unable to articulate them. Churchland has given us some positive reasons to suspect that there are generalizations which encompass the cognitive processes of both infants and familiar adults. And he agrees with my contention that folk psychological descriptions have no comfortable purchase on the cognitive states of infants. The theory about our common sense notion of belief . . . that I have . . . developed (see Stich, 1983a, chap. 5) might in fact be a welcome supplement to Churchland's argument, since it explains why it is that the behavior of infants does not invite "description/ explanation in terms of specific perceptions, beliefs and reasonings." Note, though, that Churchland's fulminations against "superficial sentential parameters" are justified only when they are directed toward theories which take cognitive states to be contentful or semantically interpreted mental sentences. Nothing Churchland says casts any suspicion on the purely syntactic theories that I have been urging. Churchland gives us no reason to think that the cognitive processes of infants cannot be characterized in purely syntactic terms. Thus if we attempt to extend his argument against "sentential parameters" to mental states conceived as they are in the STM paradigm, the first premise of the argument will go without support.

3. THE MULTIPLICITY OF MENTAL STATES

For all its length and complexity, there is one important respect in which the account of our folk psychological notion of belief developed in Stich, 1983a, chap. 5, was oversimplified. As I portrayed it, folk psychology deals with only a *pair* of basic mental categories — *beliefs,* which represent the world as we take it to be, and *desires,* which represent the world as we wish it would be. But this does not begin to capture the actual diversity of mental states recognized by common sense. In addition to *believing* that p, a person may *suspect* that p, *think* that p, *feel* that p, *assume* that p, *remember* that p, *recall* that p, *anticipate* that p, or *take* p *for granted.* With a modicum of effort this list of belief-like states would be easy to extend. And, of course, there is a parallel list for desire-like states. It was Wittgenstein who first focused philosophical attention on the diversity of mental state concepts expressible in ordinary language, and Wittgenstein too who first stressed the many and complex ways in which these concepts interrelate with one another as well as with various social and linguistic practices. Without an appropriate background of practices, we quickly lose our grip on the subtle distinctions embedded in our common sense conceptual framework. In extreme cases the whole folk psychological conceptual network can seem awkward or inapplicable. Thus as Hacking notes, enthnographers often find themselves quite unable to locate familiar mental states in alien cultures.

> As soon as you get to interesting concepts, things go poorly. You may find that hoping or expressions of anger or joy don't have a place in that culture, thanks to a lack of the same array of practices that we have in ours. Likewise for *their* important concepts. Moreover, having grasped "hope," the other people needn't by analogy grasp our "joy" or "anger," for each is embedded in its own web. This may even be true for speech acts, like promising or even stating, that are sometimes held out as neutral between cultures.[31]

What Hacking reports about joy, anger, and hope is also apparently true of belief and its conceptual cousins. Needham gives a painstaking analysis of various more or less belief-like mental states recognized by a variety of societies and concludes that in many cases there just is nothing that matches up with our own notion of belief.[32] The practices of stating, reporting, avowing, accepting, defending, and so on, which form the backdrop for our own notion of belief, are unrecognizable in those societies. Thus to the extent that these practices constitute a necessary prerequisite for belief, persons in these societies simply do not have any beliefs.

All of this poses some obvious difficulties for the cognitive scientist who tries to press the folk notion of belief into service in his theory. The nuance and subtlety built into our folk notions serve a host of practical purposes in facilitating communication, analysis, and social relations. But they are unlikely to be of much interest to the cognitive scientist. What he needs is a broad cover term which embraces indifferently a wide range of subtly different folk notions in the belief family. The presupposed background of practices built into our folk notion of belief is problematic in another way for the cognitive scientist, since it threatens him with Needham's problem: in many societies the background practices are sufficiently different that there just isn't anything looking all that much like prototypical cases of belief.

Confronted with this difficulty, the obvious move for the theorist to make is to patch and trim the folk notion of belief, blotting out the fine distinctions that divide believing that p from thinking that p, remembering that p, feeling that p, suspecting that p, etc., and ignoring many of the conceptual ties that bind the folk notion of belief to various background practices or "language games." But once this conceptual surgery is complete, we might well wonder whether the resulting notion has much more than a label in common with the folk notion of belief. On Wilkes's view, the modifications needed to eliminate the "riotous overlap, alluring vagueness, categorial ambiguity, and rich shades of nuance"[33] in our folk notions are so drastic that we are left with a quite new concept.

> Once ordinary-language concepts have been adopted, they then have to be adapted — modified, tidied up, extended or restricted — in short, denaturalized: baked in the theoretical kiln until they bear as little resemblance to their parent concepts as do the physicists' notions of force, mass and energy.[34]

The curious thing about these conceptual contortions is that people making them do not take themselves to be twisting common concepts beyond recognition. Psychologists who adopt terms like 'belief' or 'memory' occasionally note that their technical usage departs a bit from ordinary language, but they clearly do not think they are doing violence to ordinary notions. A possible explanation of this fact is simply a lack of sensitivity to the richness and complexity of common sense notions. But an alternative and equally plausible explanation is that in ordinary language the term 'belief' already serves as a broad general purpose cover term. Pursuing this idea Morton argues that while we sometimes use 'believes' in such a way that it contrasts with 'think,' 'conjecture,' and the rest, "we also use 'believes' as a particularly neutral member of the list." It is almost, though not quite "a neutral core for an accretion of further specifications."[35] If Morton is right, then the modifications mandated by the cognitive scientist's "theoretical kiln" might be viewed as relatively modest ones along lines already partly anticipated by everyday usage.

I do not propose to take sides in this dispute, for I suspect that the truth lies somewhere in the middle. The sort of broad nuance-neglecting use of 'believes' that would be required in a psychological theory would probably leaven distinctions to a greater extent than does the neutral use that Morton recounts. Whether these changes would be substantial enough to qualify as a change in the underlying concept is a question without an answer. Perhaps the best place to leave this issue is with the observation that if the arguments of the previous three chapters are correct, then the question is moot. The best strategy for cognitive science is the one advocated by the Syntactic Theory of the Mind, and by the time folk concepts have been modified *that* drastically, there can be little question that they no longer merit their ancestral titles.

FOOTNOTES

[1] P. M. Churchland (1979, this volume, pp. 42–62), P. M. Churchland and P. S. Churchland (1981).

[2] P. M. Churchland (this volume, p. 48).

[3] Ibid., p. 43.

[4] Ibid.

[5] Ibid., p. 42.

[6] P. M. Churchland (1979, p. 114).

[7] P. M. Churchland (this volume, p. 47).

[8] Ibid., p. 48.

[9] Ibid.

[10] Ibid., p. 48.

[11] Ibid.

[12] Ibid.

[13] Ibid.

[14] Ibid., p. 49.

[15] For a fascinating, occasionally far-fetched reconstruction of the prehistory during which folk psychology was evolving and developing, see Jaynes (1976).

[16] See Wilkes (1978, 1981).

[17] Wilkes (1981, pp. 149–150).

[18] Ibid., p. 149.

[19] See P. M. Churchland (1970).

[20] See Laudan (1977).

[21] See P. S. Churchland (1980) and P. M. Churchland (1979, sec. 19).

[22] P. M. Churchland (1979, p. 129).

[23] Ibid.

[24] Ibid., p. 130.

[25] Ibid., p. 133.

[26] Ibid.

[27] Ibid., p. 134.

[28] Ibid., p. 136.

[29] Ibid.

[30] Ibid., p. 128.

[31] Hacking (1982, p. 44).

[32] See Needham (1972).

[33] Wilkes (1981, p. 152).

[34] Ibid., p. 155.

[35] Morton (1980, p. 95).

6 The Future of Folk Psychology*

Stephen P. Stich
Rutgers University, New Brunswick

If the more virulent strains of behaviorism had proved to be viable, then our common sense world view, the "manifest image" of what we are like, would be in serious trouble. For Watson and others, the mental states postulated by common sense — beliefs among them — are the superstitious posits of our savage past. In the sober light of science we can see that there *are* no such things, just as there are no gods to throw thunderbolts, nor witches to poison wells. Now, though the ghost still rattles its chains here and there, virulent behaviorism is a dead issue in psychology. It was done in by the cognitivist revolution whose partisans currently dominate the scientific study of mental states and processes. But if I am right in my contention that contemporary cognitivism makes no use of the folk psychological notion of belief and its intentional kin, then the status of the manifest image of mind is once again a live issue. For if the best science of the mind we now have does not mention the contentful states of folk psychology, is that not ample reason to conclude that the states posited by common sense do not exist and that statements of the form 'S believes that p' are uniformly false? Have we not perhaps shown that the behaviorists were *right* about the status of common sense psychological posits, albeit for the wrong reason?

It is possible to be encouraged along this line of thought by a naive reading of Quine's doctrine on what there is.[1] For Quine the entities we are committed to are simply those quantified over in our best scientific theories. Thus if our best theories fail to quantify over putative entities of a certain

---

*Reprinted from *From Folk Psychology to Cognitive Science: The Case Against Belief* (Cambridge: The MIT Press, 1983) by permission of the author and publisher.

sort, we should conclude that there are no such things. And since (ex-hypothesis) cognitive science does not invoke the language or concepts of folk psychology, the states of folk psychology are not among the entities over which it quantifies. So these putative states do not exist.

I am quite sure that it is possible to be tempted by this argument, since I was so tempted, and for rather longer than I would like to admit. But I am now convinced that the temptation is one which must be resisted. For even if we accept the view that science alone is the arbiter of what exists and what does not,* we cannot infer from the fact that a term does not occur in the vocabulary of a theory to the conclusion that the theory does not quantify over the putative entities in the extension of the term.[2] So it is plainly mistaken to infer from the fact that a term occurs nowhere in science to the conclusion that the entities putatively denoted by the term do not exist. Consider, for example, such terms as 'favored by Elizabeth I,' 'slept in by George Washington,' or 'looks like Winston Churchill.' Surely none of these terms occurs in any currently received scientific theory. Nor is it likely that they will find a place in the scientific canon of the future. But it would be simply perverse to deny, on these grounds, that there are any beds slept in by George Washington or any men (or statues) that look like Winston Churchill. It would be comparably perverse to deny the existence of people who believe that p on the grounds that 'believes that p' is not invoked in cognitive science, or to deny the existence of beliefs that p because '(is a) belief that p' is ill suited to cognitive theory building.

Let us pursue this analogy a bit further. What we want to say, in the 'looks like Churchill' case is that our science does quantify over *human beings;* men and women are among the values of the variables of anthropology, physiology, etc. And, as it happens, some of those human beings look like Churchill; that is, they are entities which satisfy the predicate 'looks like Churchill.' Before attempting to tell an analogous story about beliefs, let me introduce an assumption that will substantially simplify our discussion. The assumption is that the correct cognitive theory is a Syntactic Theory of Mind which cleaves reasonably closely to the general pattern presupposed by folk psychology. Such a theory will postulate belief-like states which interact with desire-like states, with perception, and so on.[3] The tokens of these states are particulars, which may have all sorts of properties in addition to those in virtue of which they count as syntactic states of a certain type. And it would seem perfectly plausible to say that certain of these syntactic state tokens are, as it happens, beliefs that p — that a certain current syntactic state token of mine, for example, happens to be a belief that Ouagadougou is the capital of Upper Volta. The analogy with

---

*In fairness to Quine, it is far from clear that he ever held such a view. The argument of the previous paragraph was billed as being inspired by a *naive* reading of Quine.

'looks like Churchill' is in some respects quite a good one, since if the analysis (Stich, 1983a, chap. 5) is on the right track, then for a syntactic state token to count as a belief that Ouagadougou is the capital of Upper Volta, it must be *similar* to the state that typically underlies our own normal utterance of the content sentence. And it is certainly plausible to think that there are such belief-like state tokens, just as there are men and statues which look like Churchill, despite the fact that neither 'looks like Churchill' nor 'is a belief that Ouagadougou is the capital of Upper Volta' is a predicate to be taken seriously by science.

One way of construing the view I have been sketching is as a sort of token identity theory for beliefs: Each token of a belief that p is identical with some syntactic state token. I am not entirely happy about this way of putting the matter, however, because it suggests that 'token of the belief that p' specifies some well-defined class or category. But of course this is not the case. Since belief ascriptions behave like similarity judgments, whether or not a person can appropriately be said to believe that p, and thus whether or not one of his syntactic states can appropriately be described as the belief that p, will depend on the context in which the description is offered. So rather than talking of belief tokens being identical with syntactic state tokens, it would be less misleading, though more long-winded, to say that anything which, in a given context, may be appropriately described as a belief that p is identical with some belief-like syntactic state token. We will shortly see another reason for resisting talk of belief tokens.

It is important to note that while anything which can be described as a belief that p is identical with some syntactic state token, the converse of this identity claim is false. It is not the case that every belief-like syntactic state token can be described as a belief that p. For to count as a belief that p, a state must suitably resemble the state which typically underlies the production of some content sentence in our language. And if the correct cognitive theory does indeed posit a category of belief-like states, then almost certainly there are some belief-like state tokens among the very young, the very ill, or among exotic folk which do not much resemble the belief-like states giving rise to any of our own utterances.

This chapter began with the worry that our manifest image of the mind might be in conflict with the scientific image urged by cognitive science. But now it is beginning to look as though a much more optimistic conclusion is in order. It is not quite the Panglossian picture sketched (Stich, 1983a, chap. 2), which portrayed cognitive science as adopting the language and concepts of folk psychology. Rather, the picture that is emerging is of a cognitive science that does not invoke the concepts of commonsense psychology but nonetheless postulates states many of whose tokens turn out to be describable as the belief that p, the desire that p, and so on. If this view can be sustained, then perhaps we need not worry about our scientific psychology undermining the humanities, the social sciences, and the many social institutions which are so intimately interwoven with the conceptual framework of folk psychology. To borrow a phrase from Fodor, such a conclusion would surely justify at least "modified rapture."[4] In the remaining pages of this section, I want to examine this cheerful view more carefully, looking first at what it has to say about the belief state *types* of folk psychology, second at what it entails about the generalizations of folk psychology, and finally at the account it suggests about the relation between cognitive science and the social sciences. Lest the reader be overcome by modified rapture, I should warn that like most silver linings, this one has its cloud. It will appear in the following section.

On the view we have been considering, my belief that Ouagadougou is the capital of Upper Volta is identical to some belief-like syntactic state token. But what about *believing that Ouagadougou is the capital of Upper Volta,* the property or state type which I share with other geographically knowledgeable people? What, if anything, is the property of believing that p to be identified with? The obvious suggestion is to identify folk psychological belief types with syntactic state types. But this simply won't do, since the proposed identification would entail what we earlier called the correlation thesis, and the correlation thesis is false.[5] Because of the role of reference and ideological similarity in determining whether a given state token counts as a belief that p, it is possible for a pair of syntactic state tokens to share the same syntactic state type even though one of those tokens would be a belief that p while the other would not. Conversely it is possible for a pair of belief-like syntactic state tokens both to count as beliefs that p in a given context even though the syntactic state tokens in question are different in syntactic type. This would be the case, for example, if the context emphasizes ideological or reference similarity, while requiring no more than a very rough causal-pattern similarity. It would also be the case in those contexts which require only a rough similarity in all dimensions. I am inclined to think that most of our attributions of beliefs to animals illustrate this sort of misfit between folk psychological and syntactic taxonomies. It would be quite remarkable if cats turned out to have cognitive states which are syntactically type identical with any of ours. But despite the fact that Tabby and I share no syntactically type identical states, it is often quite appropriate to describe one of her belief-like states as "the belief that her food is in the dish." Since the property of believing that p is not in general coextensive with any syntactic state type, the property of believing that p cannot be identified with a syntactic state type.

But now if common sense belief properties cannot be identified with syntactic state properties, just where do they fit into the ontological scheme of things? One proposal that seems to be suggested by our analysis of belief sentences is that the property of being a belief that p is simply the property of being similar to the syntactic state which typically underlies our normal utterance of 'p'. But I am inclined to think that this answer will not do either, since on any reasonable account of what a property is, it will turn out that there is no such thing as the property of being similar to the syntactic state . . . etc. The problem is that properties are the sorts of things which either are or are not possessed by an entity in a given possible world. But because of the context sensitivity of similarity, it is not the case that a syntactic state either is or is not similar to the one underlying our normal utterance of 'p'. In one conversational context it may be perfectly appropriate to describe a syntactic state in this way, while in another context the description may be utterly inappropriate. It is simply a mistake to assume that every meaningful predicate or open sentence corresponds to or expresses a property.

All of this still leaves us with no account of the property of believing that p. But, on reflection, perhaps that is just where we want to be. [As I have argued previously (Stich 1983, chap. 5),] a predicate of the form 'is a belief that p' can be analyzed as a predicate making a similarity claim. And, as we have just seen, such predicates typically do not express properties at all. What this suggests is that *there is no such thing as the property of believing that p.* The predicate 'is a belief that p' does not express or correspond to a property. If this is right, then we have yet another reason for not thinking of folk psychological beliefs as state tokens, since a state token is the instantiation of a property by an individual during a time interval, and if there is no property, then there can be no state token. It is important to realize, however, that the nonexistence of belief *properties* and belief *state tokens* does not entail that *predicates* of the form 'is a belief that p' are meaningless or never apply to anything, just as the nonexistence of the property of being similar to the USSR does not entail that 'is similar to the USSR' is meaningless or that it never applies to anything. In both cases the predicates in question apply to things quite unproblematically, though in different contexts they may apply to quite different things. A question I have often encountered in setting out my views about belief is whether I think there are any such things as beliefs. But the question is less than clear. If it means: Are statements of the form 'S believes that p' or 'x is a belief that p' ever true, the answer is plainly *yes,* at least on the modified Panglossian view we are currently exploring. However, if the question is construed as asking whether there are belief state tokens or belief state types (i.e., properties), then the answer is negative.

As Dennett has rightly noted, much recent work in the philosophy of mind can be construed as attempting to say what a pair of organisms or systems have in common when the same folk psychological predicate is true of each.[6] Often this question turns into a quest for some *property* that subjects share when they are thinking of Vienna or when they believe that

Ouagadougou is the capital of Upper Volta. What our recent reflections make plain is that this quest is bound to end in failure. It is not in virtue of sharing some property that subjects both believe that p. So there is a sense in which Needham's painstaking Wittgensteinian survey of belief in various cultures came to just the right conclusion: There is no such thing as believing that p.[7] But putting the point in this way suggests a paradox which is not there. In denying that believing that p is a property, we need not deny that statements of the form 'x is a belief that p' are often unproblematically true.

Let us turn our attention, now, to the generalizations of folk psychology. What status do they have on the modified Panglossian view I am elaborating? I have already argued at length that such generalizations have no role to play in a serious cognitive science (Stich, 1983a, chapter 7). But nothing in those arguments nor anything in the arguments of the current section suffices to show that these generalizations might not turn out to be *true*. They are, to be sure, *vague* claims, since they inherit all the intrinsic vagueness of the folk psychological language of content. But no matter; vagueness is not incompatible with truth. Even if the generalizations turn out to be empirically false, it is reasonable to think that they can be hedged into truths by adding some folk psychological qualifications and making clear that the regularities they aver, although they generally obtain, are not without exception. These generalizations might be thought of as analogous to rule-of-thumb generalizations in cooking. Consider, for example, the generalization that separated mayonnaise can usually be repaired by beating a bit of it into dry mustard, then gradually beating in the rest.[8] This generalization, like the generalizations of folk psychology, suffers from a certain vagueness. It is not clear just what counts as separated mayonnaise, nor is it clear where mixing gives way to beating and beating to whipping. Another point of analogy between the generalizations of cooking and those of folk psychology is that neither sort of generalization will find a place in a serious explanatory science. But nonetheless many of the generalizations known to good cooks are *true,* and wonderfully useful. A final analogy between folk psychological and culinary generalizations is that in both cases it is plausible to suppose that serious science will be able to explain why the rough-and-ready folk generalizations are generally true, and perhaps even explain why they are sometimes false. In the case of mayonnaise, I would guess that the explanation will come from the physical chemistry of colloids along with some detailed investigation of what, from the physical chemist's point of view, a separated mayonnaise actually is. And in the case of belief, the explanation will come from an STM cognitive theory along with some detailed investigation of what syntactic state or states are generally describable as beliefs that p. I am not at all clear about what is required to *reduce* one science or set of generalizations to another. But I suppose that if the term is used in some suitably loose sense, the prospect we are envisioning could be described as the reduction of folk psychology to STM cognitive theory.

To conclude our discussion of the modified Panglossian prospect, let us consider how the humanities and social sciences would fare if the view we are considering should prevail. If the posits of folk psychology should turn out not to exist, then the descriptive claims of historians, literary critics, and others would turn out to be false. If the notion of believing that p is no more scientifically respectable than the notion of being bewitched, then any account of what Henry VIII believed Pope Clement would do is bound to be false. But on the modified Panglossian view, the historian's pronouncements are perfectly respectable and have a fair shot at being true. To say 'Henry VIII believed that Pope Clement would allow the annulment' is to claim that Henry was in a belief-like state similar to the one that would underlie our own normal utterance of the content sentence. And that may well be true. Even the vagueness of belief sentences need not be much of a problem to the historian, since it is generally reduced by context. And historians have context to spare. Of course historians often use the language of folk psychology to make *causal* claims in addition to purely descriptive ones. Thus for example it might be claimed that Henry decided to remarry *because* he believed that Catherine would not produce an heir to the throne. These causal claims, too, may well turn out to be true. If Henry's belief is some syntactic state token and if the facts turn out right, then this state could well be among the causes of his decision and his subsequent actions.

The social sciences often do more than make singular causal claims invoking the language of folk psychology; they try to formulate generalizations or laws. These attempts are a bit more problematic for the modified Panglossian, since economic or sociological generalizations cast in the language of folk psychology will suffer from the same vagueness and the same limitations that afflict the attempt to state psychological generalizations in folk psychological language. But I think the Panglossian might well persevere in his upbeat outlook by viewing these generalizations as rough-and-ready, rule-of-thumb generalizations, rather like those invoked by the experienced cook. When suitably hedged, the economist's or the sociologist's generalizations may be both true and useful, just as the chef's are. When (or if) a social science matures to the point where the vagueness and limitations of folk psychology become problematic, social scientists can begin to recast their theories about the relation between mental states and social processes in the content free language forged by the STM cognitive theorist. The modified Panglossian can take much the same line about philosophical theories cast in folk psychological terms. If the vagueness and limitations of folk language are problematic at a given stage of inquiry and if cognitive science has forged a less troublesome vocabulary, then by all means the philosopher should use it.[9]

1. COULD IT TURN OUT THAT THERE ARE NO SUCH THINGS AS BELIEFS?

The modified Panglossian prospect that I have been sketching is a thoroughly attractive vision. It promises the best of both worlds: a serious cognitive science and a respectable folk psychology whose vocabulary can be invoked in good conscience to write history, literary criticism, and even social science. The optimist in me very much hopes that this vision can be sustained. But in more pessimistic moods I am inclined to think that the future will be rather less cheerful. Underlying my pessimism is the fact that the modified Panglossian story makes essential use of a pair of empirical assumptions. And the truth of these assumptions is very much an open question. If either of them should turn out to be mistaken, the proposed reconciliation between cognitive science and folk psychology would collapse. Let me focus on these assumptions one at a time.

The first was made quite explicitly in the previous section. In order to tell the story we did, we had to assume that "the correct cognitive theory is an STM theory *which cleaves reasonably closely to the pattern presupposed by folk psychology.* Such a theory will postulate belief-like states which interact with desire-like states, with perceptions, etc." But now suppose that this assumption should turn out to be false. Suppose that the best theory of the mind we can come up with is not an STM theory at all. Or, rather more plausibly, suppose that it *is* an STM theory, but one whose general organization or gross functional architecture is *significantly* different from the functional architecture presupposed by folk psychology. If this should turn out to be the case, then we could no longer say that belief sentences stand a good shot at being true. For in saying 'S believes that p' we are saying that S is in a belief-like state similar to the one that would underlie our own ordinary utterance of the content sentence. And if it turns out that the overall structure of the human cognitive system is significantly different from the structure postulated by folk psychology, then this claim will be false. There will *be no* belief-like states, and thus S will be in none. (Nor, of course, will there be one underlying our own normal utterance of 'p'.) If folk psychology turns out to be seriously mistaken about the overall organization of our cognitive economy, then there will be nothing to which the predicate 'is a belief that p' applies.

Is there any reason to take this possibility seriously, any reason to think that folk psychology *might* turn out to be quite radically wrong about the general organization of our cognitive system? I want to propose two rather different lines of argument suggesting that the answer is yes, there is a real possibility that folk psychology might turn out to be quite radically wrong.

The first argument, the less serious of the pair, is an inductive generalization from the sorry history of folk theories in general.[10] It starts with the observation that folk psychology really is a *folk* theory, a cultural inheritance whose origin and evolution are largely lost in prehistory. The very fact that it is a folk theory should make us suspicious. For in just about every other domain one can think of, the ancient shepherds and camel drivers whose speculations were woven into folk theory have a notoriously bad track record. Folk astronomy was false astronomy and not just in detail. The general conception of the cosmos embedded in the folk wisdom of the West was utterly and thoroughly mistaken. Much the same could be said for folk biology, folk chemistry, and folk physics. However wonderful and imaginative folk theorizing and speculation has been, it has turned out to be screamingly false in every domain where we now have a reasonably sophisticated science. Nor is there any reason to think that ancient camel drivers would have greater insight or better luck when the subject at hand was the structure of their own minds rather than the structure of matter or of the cosmos. None of this constitutes an argument for the *falsity* of the folk theory about the general structure of the mind. But that is not the question at hand. The issue before us is whether we should view the possibility of folk psychology being false as anything more than a mere logical possibility. And I think the general failure of folk theories is reason enough to think that folk psychology might suffer the same fate.

At this point it might well be protested that casting aspersions on the origins and family history of a theory carries little weight once the theory has been fleshed out and pressed into service as a serious empirical hypothesis. If the functional architecture posited by folk psychology is useful in explaining the results of psychological experiments, then we should take the posit seriously no matter how disreputable its origins. And if some other account of the functional architecture of the mind does a better job, then we have reason enough to be skeptical of the folk story without insulting its parentage. The protest is one with which I have considerable sympathy. Ultimately questions about the general organization of the mind will have to be settled by building and testing theories embodying different organizational assumptions. What is more, optimists who think that the gross architecture of folk psychology will stand up to scientific scrutiny have plenty of ammunition in their arsenal. A great deal of the recent work in cognitive science has, tacitly or explicitly, assumed very much the picture of mental organization that folk psychology proposes. There are other straws in the wind, however. There are findings and theories suggesting that something is seriously wrong with the simple belief-desire structure implicit in common sense wisdom. It would be out of place here to attempt any general census of the literature, tallying up those studies that presuppose folk structures and those that do not. Nor do I think there would be much point in the exercise, since the field is too new and too much in flux. But I do want to argue that the tenability of the folk conception of mental organization is very much an open empirical question. And to that end I will briefly review some work which seems to suggest that our cognitive system is organized along lines quite different from those posited by folk psychology.

The work I wish to review is drawn from the experimental social psychology literature on dissonance and self-attribution. Before considering this work, however, I want to focus attention on the fundamental feature of folk psychology which, I think, the work to be reviewed calls into question. For folk psychology, a belief is a state which can interact in many ways with many other states and which can be implicated in the etiology of many different sorts of behavior. A pattern of interaction which looms large in our common sense scheme of things is the one linking beliefs to their normal, sincere linguistic expression. It is via this link that folk psychology describes belief. A belief *that p* is a belief-like state similar to one which we would *normally express by uttering 'p'*. But, of course, the belief that p does much more than merely contribute to the causation of its own linguistic expression. It may interact with desires in many ways, some of which will ultimately issue in nonverbal behavior. It is a fundamental tenet of folk psychology that *the very same* state which underlies the sincere assertion of 'p' also may lead to a variety of nonverbal behaviors. There is, however, nothing necessary or a priori about the claim that the states underlying assertions also underlie nonverbal behavior. There are other ways to organize a cognitive system. There might, for example, be a cognitive system which, so to speak, keeps two sets of books, or two subsystems of vaguely belief-like states. One of these subsystems would interact with those parts of the system responsible for verbal reporting, while the other interacted with those parts of the system responsible for nonverbal behavior. Of course it might be the case that the two belief-like subsystems frequently agreed with each other. But it might also be the case that from time to time they did not agree on some point. When this situation arose, there would be a disparity between what the subject said and what he did. What is striking about the results I shall sketch is that they strongly suggest that *our* cognitive system keeps two sets of books in this way. And this is a finding for which folk psychology is radically unprepared. If it is true, then states similar to the one underlying our own ordinary utterance of 'p' do *not* also participate in the production of our nonverbal behavior. In those cases when our verbal subsystem leads us to say 'p' and our nonverbal subsystem leads us to behave as though we believed some incompatible proposition, there will simply be no saying which we believe. Even in the (presumably more common) case where the two subsystems agree, there is no saying which state is the belief that p. If we really do have separate verbal and nonverbal cognitive storage systems, then the functional economy of the mind postulated by folk theory is quite radically mistaken. And under those circumstances I am strongly inclined to think that the right thing to say is that *there are no such things as beliefs.*

With this by way of stage setting, let me turn to a quick review of the salient studies from the attribution and dissonance literature. The central idea of attribution theory is that people attempt to explain their own physical, emotional, and behavioral responses by invoking relatively crude theories or rules of thumb. As the jargon would have it, they "attribute" their responses to the hypothesized causes suggested by their theory about how they work. What is more, this attribution itself has a host of further mental and behavioral effects.[11] A typical attribution experiment will attempt to focus on the attributional processes by leading a subject to make the *wrong* inference about the cause of his response. The subject will then be led to behave as though this mistaken attribution were correct. An example will serve to give the flavor of this work. Storms and Nisbett[12] asked insomniac subjects to record the time they went to bed and the time they finally fell asleep. After several days of record keeping, one group of subjects (the "arousal" group) was given a placebo pill to take fifteen minutes before going to bed. They were told that the pill would produce rapid heart rate, breathing irregularities, bodily warmth, and alertness, which are just the typical symptoms of insomnia. A second group of subjects (the "relaxation" group) was told that the pills would produce the opposite symptoms: lowered heart rate, breathing rate, body temperature, and alertness. Attribution theory predicts that the arousal group subjects would get to sleep *faster* on the nights they took the pills, because they would attribute their symptoms to the pills rather than to the emotionally laden thoughts that were running through their minds. It also predicts that subjects in the relaxation group will take *longer* to get to sleep. Since their symptoms persist despite having taken a pill intended to relieve the symptoms, they will infer that their emotionally laden thoughts must be particularly disturbing to them, and this belief will upset them further, making it all that much harder to get to sleep. Remarkably enough, both of these predictions were borne out. Arousal group subjects got to sleep 28 percent faster on the nights they took the pill, while relaxation subjects took 42 percent longer to get to sleep.

The core idea of dissonance research is that if subjects are led to behave in ways they find uncomfortable or unappealing and if they do not have what they take to be an adequate reason for enduring the effects of this behavior, then they will come to view the behavior or its effects as more attractive. Conversely if subjects are given some special reward for engaging in behavior they take to be intrinsically attractive, they will come to view the behavior as less attractive than if they had not received the special reward. The explanation offered for the "inadequate justification" phenomenon is that subjects note they have done something they thought to be unpleasant without any adequate reason and explain this prima facie anomalous behavior with the hypothesis that the behavior or its consequences are not so unpleasant as they had thought. The "overjustification" phenomenon is explained by supposing that subjects note they were rewarded to engage in the behavior, and they infer that, since they were motivated by the reward, the behavior itself must have played less of a role in motivating them. From this they infer that it must not be quite so intrinsically attractive. Once again an example will give the flavor of the work in this area. In a classic study, Zimbardo et al. asked subjects to endure a series of electric shocks while performing a learning task.[13] When the learning task was completed, they asked the subjects to repeat it. Some subjects were given adequate justification for repeating the task (the research was important, and nothing of value could be learned from the experiment unless the task was repeated). Other subjects were given insufficient justification (the experimenter was just curious about what would happen if they did it again). The prediction was that subjects in the inadequate justification group would come to think that the shocks were not all that unpleasant. This prediction was borne out in a startling way. Subjects in the insufficient justification group performed better in the second round of the learning task than did subjects in the adequate justification group. They also exhibited significantly lower galvanic skin responses to the shocks than did the subjects in the adequate justification group.

So far the work I have been recounting does not bear directly on the hypothesis that verbal and nonverbal behavior are subserved by different belief-like cognitive subsystems. To join that issue we must look at the work of Nisbett and Wilson. These investigators noted that the experimentally manipulated effect (or "dependent variable") in attribution and dissonance studies was generally some nonverbal indicator belief or attitude. However, when the nonverbal behavior of subjects under different experimental conditions seemed clearly to indicate that they differed in belief or attitude, their verbal behavior often did not indicate any difference in belief or attitude. Moreover when subjects' attention was drawn to the fact that their behavior indicated some change had taken place, they denied that the experimentally manipulated cause (or "independent variable") had been at all relevant to the change. Rather, they constructed some explanation of the change in their behavior in line with socially shared views about what sorts of causes are likely to produce the behavior in question. The picture this suggests is that subjects' verbal reporting systems have no access to the processes actually underlying their nonverbal behavioral changes. What the verbal reporting system does is to hypothesize explanations of the behavioral changes that have been noted, invoking relatively crude socially shared theories about how such behavior is to be explained. To use Nisbett's and Wilson's apt phrase, when we are called upon to explain why we acted in a certain way, we often respond by "telling more than we can know."

To see in a bit more detail what led Nisbett and Wilson to this view, let us return to our two illustrative studies. After the completion of the insomnia studies it was pointed out to arousal group subjects that they had gotten to sleep more quickly after taking the pill and to relaxation group subjects that they had taken longer to fall asleep. Subjects were asked why this had happened.

> Arousal subjects typically replied that they usually found it easier to get to sleep later in the week, or that they had taken an exam that had worried them but had done well on it and could now relax, or that problems with a roommate or girlfriend seemed on their way to resolution. Relaxation subjects were able to find similar sorts of reasons to explain their increased sleeplessness. When subjects were asked if they had thought about the pills at all before getting to sleep, they almost uniformly insisted that after taking the pills they had completely forgotten about them. When asked if it had occurred to them that the pill might be producing (or counteracting) their arousal symptoms, they reiterated their insistence that they had not thought about the pills at all after taking them. Finally, the experimental hypothesis and the postulated attribution process were described in detail. Subjects showed no recognition of the hypothesized process and . . . made little pretense of believing that *any* subjects could have gone through such processes.[14]

Analogous results were reported in the shock experiment.

> We pointed out to experimental subjects that they had learned more quickly the second time. A typical response would have been, "I guess maybe you turned the shock down."

> I don't remember any subject who ever described anything like the process of dissonance reduction that we knew to have occurred.[15]

In the Nisbett and Wilson paper the focus was on cognitive *processes*. Their central thesis was that subjects' reports about their own cognitive processes were not accurate introspective reports from an internal font of knowledge. Instead they proposed that

> when people are asked to report how a particular stimulus influenced a particular response, they do not do so by consulting a memory of the mediating process, but by applying or generating causal theories about the

effects of that type of stimulus or that type of response. They simply make judgments, in other words, about how plausible it is that the stimulus would have influenced the response. These plausibility judgments exist prior to, or at least independently of, any actual contact with the particular stimulus embedded in a particular complex stimulus configuration.[16]

In support of their contention that verbal reports about underlying cognitive processes are often grounded in socially shared theories, Nisbett and Wilson cite numerous studies which indicate that a subject's verbal reports about the stimuli affecting his behavior and his reports about the processes mediating between stimulus and response correlate well with the predictions offered by nonparticipant "observer" subjects who were simply read verbal descriptions of the experiments and asked to predict what stimuli would affect the subject's behavior and what the processes would be. The most plausible explanation for this correlation is that both participant and observer subjects are basing their verbal reports on a shared set of theories about the processes underlying behavior.

Nisbett and Wilson are less clear on the status of verbal reports about mental *states*. Indeed in the final section of their paper they go out of their way to acknowledge that, while verbal reports about our own mental processes are typically rooted in common sense theory rather than in accurate introspective access, verbal expressions of beliefs, emotions, evaluations, and plans probably do reflect access to "a great storehouse of private knowledge." As a number of critics have noted, however, it is extremely implausible to suppose that verbal reports of states are generally accurate if verbal reports of processes are not, since in many instances the inferential processes which the investigators attribute to the subjects involve the generation of new states from previously existing ones, from stimuli, etc.[17] And it would be anomalous indeed for subjects with no verbalizable access to their cognitive processes to be able to verbalize the various states invoked or produced in the intermediate stages of these processes. Quite apart from such a priori considerations, it is often clear from the evidence that subjects are not able to report on the various states invoked in attribution and dissonance processes. Consider, for example, the subjects in the Storms and Nisbett insomnia experiment. The attribution theory explanation requires that subjects undergo a reasoning process something like the following:

I am alert, warm, breathing irregularly, and have a rapid heart rate; I have just taken a pill which should alleviate all of these symptoms; since the symptoms are as severe as ever, the troubled thoughts or emotions which cause the symptoms must be even more severe than usual tonight.

However, subjects resolutely deny that they had any such thoughts and they find it thoroughly implausible that anyone could have gone through such a thought process.

In a recent paper Wilson acknowledges that when the issue at hand is the accessibility to verbal reports, the distinction between states and processes is untenable.[18] Instead he proposes a model which hypothesizes two relatively independent cognitive systems. One of these systems "mediates behavior (especially unregulated behavior), is largely unconscious, and is, perhaps, the older of the two systems in evolutionary terms. The other, perhaps newer, system is largely conscious, and its function is to attempt to verbalize, explain, and communicate what is occurring in the unconscious system."[19] This second system, which Wilson calls the "verbal explanatory system," does not generally tap into the system mediating behavior. Rather, it proceeds by "making inferences based on theories about the self and the situation."[20]

In support of this hypothesis Wilson describes a number of experiments aimed at showing that the behavior controlling system and the verbal explanatory system can be manipulated independently. An example will illustrate how these experiments work. Wilson, Hull, and Johnson induced subjects to agree to visit senior citizens in a nursing home.[21] For one group of subjects overt pressure from the experimenter was made salient as a reason for agreeing to make the visit. For a second group of subjects pressure from the experimenter was not made salient. It was hypothesized that in subjects in the second (no pressure) group the behavior controlling system would infer that the subject had agreed because he or she was a helpful person; no such inference was expected in the first (pressure) group. A behavioral test of this hypothesis was included in the experiment. A second experimenter, as part of what was supposedly a second study, asked subjects if they would volunteer to help former mental patients. As expected, subjects in the no-pressure group were significantly more likely to volunteer to help former mental patients.

Crosscutting this manipulation of the hypothesized behavior controlling system was an attempt to manipulate the verbal explanatory system. Immediately after agreeing to visit the nursing home, half of the subjects in each group were asked to list all of the reasons they could think of that might explain why they agreed to go, and to rate the relative importance of the reasons. (This group of subjects will be referred to as the "reasons analysis" group.) Some time later all subjects were given a questionnaire, again administered by a second experimenter and supposedly as part of a second study. In the questionnaire, subjects were asked to rate themselves on various traits relevant to helpfulness. The hypothesis was that the reasons analysis manipulation would not affect the subjects' nonverbal behavior, i.e., that it would not affect their willingness to volunteer to help the former mental patients. It was further hypothesized that the reason analysis manipulation would prime the verbal explanatory system and thus that it would affect subjects' reports about how helpful they were. Both predictions were borne out. When induced to think about reasons, subjects in the no-pressure group rated themselves as significantly more helpful than did subjects in the pressure group. These results are just what we would expect if there are indeed separate behavior controlling and verbal explanatory systems which can be manipulated independently. Thus the results provide some intriguing evidence in favor of the model which postulates two more-or-less independent cognitive systems.*

Wilson is careful to stress the tentative and rather speculative status of the dual systems hypothesis. He urges that we view the model "more as a heuristic for generating research than as a theory with firm empirical underpinnings."[22] Given the fragmentary nature of the evidence and the rather rudimentary state of the model, his caution is certainly appropriate. But for our current purposes, even a tentative model suffices to establish the point. My thesis is not that the presuppositions of folk psychology have been shown to be false. My claim is only that the jury is still out. Much important work is being done in a framework compatible with the folk psychological picture of the structure of the mind. However, as Wilson's model illustrates, there is also much serious work which does not comport comfortably with that folk psychological picture.

The modified Panglossian story of the previous section makes a pair of empirical assumptions. Thus far we have been focusing on the assumption about the general organization or "gross architecture" of our cognitive system. I want to turn, now, to the second assumption. This one, unlike the first, will require some effort to tease out of the story we have told about folk psychology. To simplify matters, I will begin by assuming that the folk psychological account of our cognitive architecture is correct, though this assumption too is often challenged by the models which cast doubt on the second assumption.

When we invoke a content sentence to attribute a belief to someone, we are characterizing that person's belief by comparing it with a potential belief of our own. We are saying that the subject has a belief state similar to the one which would play the central causal role if our utterance of the content sentence had had a typical causal history. This assumes a certain degree of

---

*For another line of argument in support of a dual system model, see Wason and Evans 1975. To forestall a possible objection, it might be worth noting that neither of the dual systems postulated by Wilson would count was a "module" as Fodor (1983) uses that term. What Wilson is proposing is a quite radical cleavage in what folk psychology encourages us to think of as the central store of beliefs. Neither of the two resulting subsystems of states can comfortably be regarded as a system of beliefs.

what I shall call *modularity* in the organization of our belief or memory store.[23] A belief or memory storage system is *modular* to the extent that *there is some more or less isolatable part of the system which plays (or would play) the central role in a typical causal history leading to the utterance of a sentence.* There is no a priori guarantee that our belief store is organized in this way. It might be the case that there is no natural or segregatable part of the belief store which *can* be isolated as playing a special role in the production of individual speech acts. If this turns out to be the case, however, typical belief attributions will misfire in a quite radical way. They assume that there is some isolable belief state which plays a central role in the production of speech acts, and they assert that the subject has a state similar to the one which would play this role were the content sentence uttered in earnest. If the assumption turns out to be false, belief ascriptions will typically lack a truth value. They will in effect be invoking definite descriptions ('similar to *the belief state which would play the central causal role . . .*') which fail to denote.

Perhaps the best way of seeing what is involved in the modularity assumption is to look at some mental models which are plainly compatible with it. Many workers in cognitive psychology and artificial intelligence are interested in the structure or organization of human memory. Some models of memory organization postulate a distinct sentence or sentence-like structure for each memory. On these models, memory may be viewed as a list of sentence-like structures, with each one corresponding to a separate belief. The best known advocate of these sentential models of memory is John McCarthy.[24] If the memory or belief store is organized in this way, then it is a relatively straightforward matter to locate the belief state underlying an utterance. It will be a separate sentence or formula, one of many on the memory list. The modularity assumption is clearly satisfied. Note that the sentential theorist need not and should not claim that to believe that p is *merely* to have a certain formula on the memory list. To count as a belief that p, a formula must be embedded in a suitable doxastic neighborhood; there must be many other related beliefs on the memory list in addition to the formula that leads to the utterance of 'p'. This after all is the lesson to be learned from our discussion of holism and ideological similarity. Still a McCarthy-style sentential model of memory is a paradigm case of what I am calling a modular organization. Given a suitable background, there is a straightforward way to say which part or element of the memory store would underlie a sincere assertion of the content sentence.

From the point of view of the memory-model builder, sentential models have a number of advantages. Perhaps the most conspicuous is that they are easy to modify. If we assume an appropriately rich set of background beliefs, then to add a new belief requires only the addition of a single new formula. Thus, for example, if we have a model of my current memory and if tomorrow I come to believe that my son will star in his school play, we can add this belief to the model by adding the appropriate formula. But sentential models also have some much discussed disadvantages. The most notorious is that their relatively unstructured format makes it difficult to locate information which is *relevant* to the task at hand. If the model is supposed to explain how subjects recover information from memory in, say, answering questions, then as the size of the memory increases, the task of locating the answer gets harder. The problem is compounded if the answer is not explicitly represented in the memory but is entailed by formulae which are explicitly represented. For in that case no simplistic matching search will suffice, and complicated heuristics are required to locate premises which may be relevant to answering the question.

In an effort to deal with these problems, a number of different proposals have been explored. One idea is to model memory as a complex network of nodes and labeled links, where the nodes represent concepts and the links represent various sorts of relations among concepts.[25] The network structure provides a systematic way to search through the memory when hunting for information relevant to a certain concept or set of concepts. Network models are still quite far over to the modular end of the spectrum, however. For in a network model it is generally unproblematic to isolate the part of the network which would play a central role in a normal utterance of a given content sentence. There will be a distinct fragment of the network which represents the belief that the hippie touched the debutante. The belief that the policeman touched the hippie will be represented by another fragment sharing various nodes with the first.

In recent years a number of theorists have expressed considerable skepticism about highly modular models. Part of their skepticism can be traced to the suspicion that sentential and network models cannot explain our ability to locate relevant information in memory quickly and efficiently. But added to this is a growing concern about modeling non-deductive inference. It has grown increasingly clear that language use and comprehension require enormous amounts of nondeductive inference.[26] Information relevant to the subject matter of the discourse, the intentions of the speaker, the setting of the conversation, and more must all be brought into play in reaching an interpretation of simple, everyday discourse. And much of the needed information is not logically entailed by anything the hearer believes. It is at best plausibly suggested by the information he has stored in memory, plus the information conveyed by the utterances to be interpreted. Thus models which aim at explaining our ability to interpret a discourse must propose a memory structure which will facilitate the efficient use of memory in nondeductive inference. Similar problems confront theorists concerned to model thinking, problem solving, or creative thought.

There is certainly no consensus on how these problems are best attacked.

What is important for our purposes, however, is that a number of leading theorists have urged that the best way to tackle them is to build models in which no single component or naturally isolatable part can be said to underlie the expression of a belief or a desire. Winograd for example notes that in early artificial intelligence models of language use and memory structure, it was typically assumed that "there is a systematic way of correlating sentences in natural language with the structure in the representation system that corresponds to the same facts about the world."[27] He adds, quite rightly, that a model incorporating this assumption "corresponds quite closely to the model of language and meaning developed by philosophers of language like Frege, drawing on ideas back to Aristotle and beyond."[28] It is in short an assumption that early models borrowed from folk psychology. Winograd, however, describes his work as a progressive departure from this assumption. He cites with approval Maturana's observation that many phenomena which *for an observer* can be described in terms of representation" may nonetheless be understood as "the activity of a structure-determined system with no mechanism corresponding to a representation. As a simple example," Winograd continues,

> we might watch a baby successfully getting milk from its mother's nipple and argue that it has a "representation" of the relevant anatomy, or of the activity of feeding. On the other hand, we might note that there is a reflex that causes it to react to a touch on the cheek by turning its head in that direction, and another that triggers sucking when something touches its mouth. From the viewpoint of effective behavior, it has a "correct representation," but it would be fruitless to look for neurophysiological mechanisms that correspond to reasoning that uses facts about breasts or milk.[29]

Winograd suggests that we should explore the same idea in modeling higher cognitive functions. We would be modeling the cognitive processes of subjects whose behavior tempts us to describe them in terms of beliefs and desires, representations, and so on, though the models themselves would have nothing "either physical or functional" which correlates in any straightforward way with the beliefs, desires or representations. Comparing the situation to programming in a rather different domain, Winograd notes:

> If I say of a program, "It has the goal of minimizing the number of jobs on the waiting queue," there is unlikely to be a "goal structure" somewhere in memory or a "problem solving" mechanism that uses strategies to achieve specified goals. *There may be dozens or even hundreds of places throughout the code where specific actions are taken, the net effect of which is being described.*[30]

It is interesting to note that the philosopher D. C. Dennett has used a very similar illustration in arguing that beliefs and desires need not correspond in any systematic way to distinct functional states.

In a recent conversation with the designer of a chess-playing program I heard the following criticism of a rival program: "It thinks it should get its queen out early." This assigns a propositional attitude to the program in a very useful and predictive way, for as the designer went on to say, one can usually count on chasing that queen around the board. But for all the many levels of explicit representation to be found in that program, nowhere is anything roughly synonymous with "I should get my queen out early." explicitly tokened. The level of analysis to which the designer's remark belongs describes features of the program that are, in an entirely innocent way, emergent properties of the computational processes that have "engineering reality." I see no reason to believe that the relation between belief-talk and psychological-process talk will be any more direct.[31]

Another major figure in artificial intelligence who has long been urging nonmodular approaches to memory storage is Marvin Minsky. In his widely discussed "Frames" paper he urges that we move away from theories which try "to represent knowledge as collections of separate, simple fragments."[32] On Minsky's view, "the strategy of complete separation of specific knowledge from general rules of inference is much too radical. We need more direct ways for linking fragments of knowledge to advice about how they are to be used."[33] In a more recent paper Minsky elaborates what he calls a "Society of Mind" view in which the mechanisms of thought are divided into many separate "specialists that intercommunicate only sparsely."[34] On the picture Minsky suggests, none of the distinct units or parts of the mental model "have meanings in themselves"[35] and thus none can be identified with individual beliefs, desires, etc. Modularity—I borrow the term from Minsky—is violated in a radical way since meaning or content emerges only from "great webs of structure" and no natural part of the system can be correlated with "explicit" or verbally expressible beliefs.[36]

At this point the optimal strategy would be to supplement the programmatic and often rather metaphorical views I have been reporting with the description of a few up-and-running nonmodular models of memory and language use. Unfortunately the optimal strategy is not one I can follow, since to the best of my knowledge there are no such up-and-running models. The absence of well-developed nonmodular alternatives would be a real deficit in my argument if my goal were to show that modular theories of memory structure are *false*. But my goal has been the more modest one of establishing that the falsity of modular models is a possibility to be taken seriously. And to show this, I think it suffices to demonstrate that serious theorists take the prospect very seriously indeed.

Let me summarize the argument of this section. We began by asking whether it might turn out that there are no such things as beliefs. Might it be the case that ordinary folk-psychological belief ascriptions will turn out, quite generally, not to be true? The answer I have been urging is that this is indeed a serious possibility, since ordinary belief ascription makes a pair of empirical assumptions, both of which might turn out to be false. On my view, then, it is too early to say whether folk psychology has a future. The modified Panglossian prospect sketched in the previous section promises a welcome reconciliation between the scientific and the manifest images of the mind. But if it turns out that either the modularity or the gross architecture presupposed by folk psychology is mistaken, the proposed reconciliation will crumble.

2. THE INSTRUMENTALIST VIEW OF FOLK PSYCHOLOGY

I think it would be appropriate to bring this chapter to a close with some brief reflections on the views of a philosopher who has struggled, perhaps more persistently than anyone else, to come to grips with the possibility that folk psychology may turn out to be false psychology. The philosopher is D. C. Dennett, and from his earliest work to his most recent he has sought some way to insulate our common sense attributions of belief and desire from the possibility that scientific advances may show them all to be mistaken. Underlying Dennett's concern is a pair of convictions with which I have considerable sympathy. The first is that folk psychology is intimately interwoven with our view of ourselves as persons and as moral agents. If we had to renounce folk psychology, we should probably have to reject the notions of personhood and moral agency as well. But to do this is to plunge into the abyss, since the concept of personhood stands at the very center of our conception of ourselves and our place in the universe. Dennett's second conviction is that folk psychology is almost certainly not going to mesh very well with a mature cognitive science. Though he is prepared to admit that the issue is an empirical one, and still far from settled, he is not optimistic about the Panglossian vision of cognitive science, in either its original or its modified form. Thus as Dennett sees it, some other way must be found to protect our conception of ourselves from the ravages of science.

The central doctrine in Dennett's effort to insulate folk psychology from potential scientific falsification maintains that folk notions like belief and desire either are or can be reinterpreted as *instrumentalistic* concepts. On this view, attributions of belief and desire are to be construed as part of an idealized predictive calculus, and the states attributed are not taken to correspond to any actual physical or functional state within the organism or system. As Dennett puts it, "the beliefs and other intentions of an intentional system need [not] be *represented* 'within' the system in any way for us to get a purchase on predicting its behavior by ascribing such intentions to it."[37] Rather, these "putative . . . states" can be relegated "to the role of idealized fictions in an action-predicting, action-explaining calculus."[38] Beliefs and desires are not what Reichenbach calls "illata—posited theoretical entities." Instead, as he sees it, they are "abstracta—calculation bound entities or logical constructs."[39] Their status is analogous to the lines in a parallelogram of forces.[40] The virtue of this view is that it shields ascriptions of belief and desire from most sorts of scientific falsification. Since beliefs and desires are explicitly relegated to the status of instrumentalistic fictions, they are compatible with *anything* we might discover about the physiological or functional organization of the human cognitive system, so long as the instrumentalistic calculus does indeed provide a useful predictive device.

Dennett tends to waffle a bit on whether he views our *actual* folk psychological concepts as instrumentalistic or whether he is proposing that these concepts might be *replaced* by instrumentalistic substitutes.[41] In what follows, I will attend to these alternatives in turn. First let us consider the suggestion that the folk psychological notions we actually use are instrumentalistic and thus make no substantive commitments about underlying internal mechanisms. Is this true? Two lines of argument point toward a negative answer.

The first begins with the fact that we often talk about beliefs and desires as though they had *causal* properties. Suppose for example that you have been accused of giving false information to the police. They asked you where Harry was on the day of the crime, and you reported that he was in Chicago. Later evidence has made it clear that he could not possibly have been in Chicago on that day, and the false report has landed you in considerable trouble. On hearing of your plight, I ask with some puzzlement, "Whatever caused you to say that to the police?" And you reply, "I really believed Harry was in Chicago." For a second example suppose that Otto, a notorious stick-in-the-mud, has recently quit his job and is now spending most of his time planning an extended trip around the world. On hearing of this, I ask you, "What caused the radical change in Otto's behavior?" and you reply, "Oh, he has always had a strong desire to travel, though he could never afford it. But recently an uncle died leaving him almost a million dollars." Now there are two things to note about these little dialogues. The first is that they are perfectly natural; we say things like that all the time. The second is that they appear to be ascribing causal properties to beliefs and desires. It may of course be that these surface appearances are deceptive and that the remarks must be analyzed in some way which does not ascribe causal properties to folk psychological states. But without a persuasive argument to this effect, I am inclined to take common sense discourse about beliefs and desires at face value. Beliefs and desires, as they are conceived by folk psychology, do have both causes and effects. If this is right, however, it is a problem for the instrumentalist view, since only real entities, "illata," can have causes and effects. "Abstracta" or calculational fictions cannot. It makes no sense to ask about the causes or effects of a line in a parallelogram of forces.

A second argument against the view that folk psychology conceives of beliefs and desires instrumentally rests on our intuitions about various cases in which the innards of an apparent intentional system turn out not to be what we expected. If Dennett is right, there is nothing we *could* find out about the inner workings of a person which would convince us that he did not have beliefs and desires, so long as he behaved in a way which was compatible with the instrumentalistic belief-desire calculus. But surely there are things we might find out which would convince us that a "person" who behaved normally enough did not really have beliefs. Ned Block has conjured the case of a chess-playing computer which, though it plays a decent game of chess, has no internal representation of rules or goals or strategy. Rather, this computer's memory contains an *enormous* multiple branching tree representation of every possible chess game up to, say, 100 moves in length. At each point in the game, the computer simply plays the appropriate prerecorded move. Watching the play of such a machine, we might be tempted at some point to say, "It believes I am going to attack with my queen." But on learning just how the machine works we are much less inclined to say this. Analogously, if we were to run across (what appeared to be) a person whose conversations, chess playing, and other behaviors were controlled by an enormous, preprogrammed branching list of what to do when, I think our intuition would rebel at saying that the "person" believed that I was about to attack with my queen — or indeed that he believed anything else! Entities with innards like that don't have beliefs.

In one of his papers Dennett in effect concedes the point that the inner workings of an organism which behaves like an intentional system *are* relevant in determining whether it has beliefs and desires. "In a science fiction mood," he writes, "we can imagine startling discoveries (e.g., some 'people' are organic puppets remotely controlled by Martians) that would upset any home truths about believers and moral agenthood you like."[42] But once this has been granted, it can no longer seriously be maintained that our folk-psychological notions of belief and desire are instrumentalistic. If belief and desire ascriptions were simply elements of a predictive calculus, then the transceivers inside these organic puppets should be quite irrelevant to the truth or falsity of such ascriptions.

As I mentioned earlier, it is not clear whether Dennett really thinks that ordinary folk-psychological ascriptions of belief and desire are intended instrumentalistically. As often as not, he appears to be arguing that our notions of personhood, moral agency, and the like can be preserved by *replacing* folk notions with suitably similar concepts, reconstructed explicitly to avoid any possible clash with scientific psychology. Dennett and I have made something of a sport out of debating whether the ersatz notions he proposes would sustain our view of ourselves as rational, free, moral agents.[43] I do not propose to launch another volley in that game here. For it seems to me that even if his proposed instrumentalistic substitutes would protect the notion of personhood from the threat of being undermined by science, there is something patently disreputable about the move. In a clever and insightful paper. Paul Churchland points out that the strategy Dennett recommends for saving folk psychology from falsification could have been marshaled, mutatis mutandis, by an alchemist seeking to protect his doctrine of "immaterial spirits" from the challenge posed by the materialistic elemental chemistry of Lavoisier and Dalton.[44] By construing his fundamental notions of "spirit" and "ensoulment" instrumentally, an alchemist could insist that atomic theory leaves alchemy unscathed. "Spirit" and "ensoulment" are "abstracta—calculation bound entities or logical constructs;" their role is that of "idealized fictions" in a reaction predicting calculus. A similar instrumentalistic defense could be mounted for the phlogiston theory of combustion. But, as Churchland properly notes, these defenses are "an outrage against reason and truth. . . . Alchemy is a terrible theory, well-deserving of its complete elimination, and the defense of it just explored is reactionary, obfuscatory, retrograde, and wrong."[45]

The instrumentalistic strategy Dennett recommends is reminiscent of Osiander's notorious though well-meaning attempt to take the sting out of Copernican theory by treating it as no more than a calculating tool—"sky geometry, without reference to physical reality."[46] In both cases we see an attempt to protect some cherished part of our world view by reconstruing a realistic theory as an instrumentalistic one. There is, however, no reason to think that Dennett's ploy will be any more successful than Osiander's. If the empirical presuppositions of folk psychology turn out to be false, as well they might, then we are in for hard times. Deprived of its empirical underpinnings, our age-old conception of the universe within will crumble just as certainly as the venerable conception of the external universe crumbled during the Renaissance. But that analogy ultimately suggests an optimistic conclusion. The picture of the external universe that has emerged from the rubble of the geocentric view is more beautiful, more powerful, and more satisfying than anything Aristotle or Dante could imagine. Moreover, the path from Copernicus to the present has been full of high intellectual adventure. The thrust of my argument is that we may be poised to begin a similar adventure. And that, surely, is an exciting place to be.

FOOTNOTES

[1]See Quine (1948).
[2]See Chomsky and Scheffler (1958).
[3]See Stich, 1983a, chapter 5, section 1.

[4]Fodor (1983).

[5]See Stich, 1983a, chapter 9, section 2.

[6]Dennett (1978d).

[7]Needham (1972).

[8]See Child, Bertholle, and Beck (1967, p. 88).

[9]See Goldman (1978a, 1978b).

[10]I have discussed this argument, on several occasions, with Paul and Patricia Churchland, though I have quite forgotten whether they suggested it to me or I suggested it to them. I also seem to recall Daniel Dennett suggesting or endorsing a similar argument in conversation.

[11]See Bem (1972).

[12]Storms and Nisbett (1970).

[13]Zimbardo, Cohen, Weisenberg, Dworkin, and Firestone (1969).

[14]Nisbett and Wilson (1977, p. 238).

[15]Ibid. In this passage Nisbett and Wilson are quoting from a letter from Zimbardo.

[16]Ibid., p. 248.

[17]See, for example, Ericsson and Simon (1980).

[18]Wilson (forthcoming).

[19]Ibid., ms. pp. 21–22.

[20]Ibid., ms. p. 1.

[21]Wilson, Hull, and Johnson (1981).

[22]Wilson (forthcoming, ms. p. 20).

[23]I use this term with some reluctance, since it has recently been pressed into service by Jerry Fodor with a very different meaning. See Fodor (1983). Readers familiar with Fodor's essay are urged to keep the difference in mind.

[24]See McCarthy (1959, 1977).

[25]There are many variations on this theme. Among the more sophisticated are Anderson and Bower (1973) and Anderson (1976). See also Kintsch (1974), Norman and Rumelhart (1975), and Collins and Quillian (1972).

[26]See Schank and Abelson (1977), Schank (1981), and Winograd (1981).

[27]Winograd (1981, p. 233).

[28]Ibid.

[29]Ibid., p. 249.

[30]Ibid., p. 250, emphasis added.

[31]Dennett (1977, p. 107). For an important recent discussion of the use of explicit representations in psychological theories, see Stabler (1983).

[32]Minsky (1981a, p. 95). See also Minsky (1975).

[33]Minsky (1981a, p. 127).

[34]Minsky (1981b, p. 95).

[35]Ibid., p. 100.

[36]Ibid.

[37]Dennett (1976, p. 277).

[38]Dennett (1978a, p. 30).

[39]Dennett (this volume).

[40]Ibid.

[41]See Stich (1981, pp. 58 ff).

[42]Dennett (1980, p. 73).

[43]See Stich (1980a), Dennett (1980), Stich (1981), Dennett (1981a).

[44]P. M. Churchland (this volume, pp. 42–62).

[45]Ibid., p. 53.

[46]See Koestler (1959, part 3). The quote is from p. 194.

II THE CASE AGAINST THE CASE AGAINST BELIEF

7 Three Kinds of Intentional Psychology*

Daniel C. Dennett
Tufts University

FOLK PSYCHOLOGY AS A SOURCE OF THEORY

Suppose you and I both believe that cats eat fish. Exactly what feature must we share for this to be true of us? More generally, recalling Socrates' favorite style of question, what must be in common between things truly ascribed an *intentional* predicate—such as "wants to visit China" or "expects noodles for supper"? As Socrates points out, in the *Meno* and elsewhere, such questions are ambiguous or vague in their intent. One can be asking on the one hand for something rather like a definition, or on the other hand for something rather like a theory. (Socrates of course preferred the former sort of answer.) What do all magnets have in common? First answer: they all attract iron. Second answer: they all have such-and-such a microphysical property (a property that explains their capacity to attract iron). In one sense people knew what magnets were—they were things that attracted iron—long before science told them what magnets were. A child learns what the word "magnet" means not, typically, by learning an explicit definition, but by learning the "folk physics" of magnets, in which the ordinary term "magnet" is embedded or implicitly defined as a theoretical term.

Sometimes terms are embedded in more powerful theories, and sometimes they are embedded by explicit definition. What do all chemical elements with the same valence have in common? First answer: they are

---

*Reprinted from R. Healey (Ed.), *Reduction, Time and Reality* (New York: Cambridge University Press, 1981, pp. 37–61) by permission of the author and publisher.

disposed to combine with other elements in the same integral ratios. Second answer: they all have such-and-such a microphysical property (a property which explains their capacity so to combine). The theory of valences in chemistry was well in hand before its microphysical explanation was known. In one sense chemists knew what valences were before physicists told them.

So what appears in Plato to be a contrast between giving a definition and giving a theory can be viewed as just a special case of the contrast between giving one theoretical answer and giving another, more "reductive" theoretical answer. Fodor (1975) draws the same contrast between "conceptual" and "causal" answers to such questions and argues that Ryle (1949) champions conceptual answers at the expense of causal answers, wrongly supposing them to be in conflict. There is justice in Fodor's charge against Ryle, for there are certainly many passages in which Ryle seems to propose his conceptual answers as a bulwark against the possibility of *any* causal, scientific, psychological answers, but there is a better view of Ryle's (or perhaps at best a view he ought to have held) that deserves rehabilitation. Ryle's "logical behaviorism" is composed of his steadfastly conceptual answers to the Socratic questions about matters mental. If Ryle thought these answers ruled out psychology, ruled out causal (or reductive) answers to the Socratic questions, he was wrong, but if he thought only that the conceptual answers to the questions were not to be given by a microreductive psychology, he was on firmer ground. It is one thing to give a causal explanation of some phenomenon and quite another to cite the cause of a phenomenon in the analysis of the concept of it.

Some concepts have what might be called an essential causal element (see Fodor 1975, p. 7, n6). For instance, the concept of a genuine Winston Churchill *autograph* has it that how the trail of ink was in fact caused is essential to its status as an autograph. Photocopies, forgeries, inadvertently indistinguishable signatures — but perhaps not carbon copies — are ruled out. These considerations are part of the *conceptual* answer to the Socratic question about autographs.

Now some, including Fodor, have held that such concepts as the concept of intelligent action also have an essential causal element; behavior that appeared to be intelligent might be shown not to be by being shown to have the wrong sort of cause. Against such positions Ryle can argue that even if it is true that every instance of intelligent behavior is caused (and hence has a causal explanation), exactly *how* it is caused is inessential to its being intelligent — something that could be true even if all intelligent behavior exhibited in fact some common pattern of causation. That is, Ryle can plausibly claim that no account in causal terms could capture the class of intelligent actions except *per accidens*. In aid of such a position — for which there is much to be said in spite of the current infatuation with causal theories — Ryle can make claims of the sort Fodor disparages ("it's not the mental activity that makes the clowning clever because what makes the clowning clever is such facts as that it took place out where the children can see it") without committing the error of supposing causal and conceptual answers are incompatible.[1]

Ryle's logical behaviorism was in fact tainted by a groundless anti-scientific bias, but it need not have been. Note that the introduction of the concept of valence in chemistry was a bit of *logical chemical behaviorism:* to have valence n was "by definition" to be disposed to behave in such-and-such ways under such-and-such conditions, *however* that disposition to behave might someday be explained by physics. In this particular instance the relation between the chemical theory and the physical theory is now well charted and understood — even if in the throes of ideology people sometimes misdescribe it — and the explanation of those dispositional combinatorial properties by physics is a prime example of the sort of success in science that inspires reductionist doctrines. Chemistry has been shown to reduce, in some sense, to physics, and this is clearly a Good Thing, the sort of thing we should try for more of.

Such progress invites the prospect of a parallel development in psychology. First we will answer the question "What do all believers-that-p have in common?" the first way, the "conceptual" way, and then see if we can go on to "reduce" the theory that emerges in our first answer to something else — neurophysiology most likely. Many theorists seem to take it for granted that *some* such reduction is both possible and desirable, and perhaps even inevitable, even while recent critics of reductionism, such as Putnam and Fodor, have warned us of the excesses of "classical" reductionist creeds. No one today hopes to conduct the psychology of the future in the vocabulary of the neurophysiologist, let alone that of the physicist, and principled ways of relaxing the classical "rules" of reduction have been proposed. The issue, then, is *what kind* of theoretical bonds can we expect — or ought we to hope — to find uniting psychological claims about beliefs, desires, and so forth with the claims of neurophysiologists, biologists, and other physical scientists?

Since the terms "belief" and "desire" and their kin are parts of ordinary language, like "magnet," rather than technical terms like "valence," we must first look to "folk psychology" to see what kind of things we are being asked to explain. What do we learn beliefs are when we learn how to use the words "believe" and "belief"? The first point to make is that we do not really learn what beliefs are when we learn how to use these words.[2] Certainly no one *tells us* what beliefs are, or if someone does, or if we happen to speculate on the topic on our own, the answer we come to, wise or foolish, will figure only weakly in our habits of thought about what people believe. We learn to *use* folk psychology as a vernacular social technology, a craft; but we don't learn it self-consciously as a theory — we learn no metatheory with the theory — and in this regard our knowledge of folk psychology is like our knowledge of the grammar of our native tongue. This fact does not make our knowledge of folk psychology entirely unlike human knowledge of explicit academic theories, however; one could probably be a good practicing chemist and yet find it embarrassingly difficult to produce a satisfactory textbook definition of a metal or an ion.

There are no introductory textbooks on folk psychology (although Ryle's *The Concept of Mind* might be pressed into service), but many explorations of the field have been undertaken by ordinary language philosophers (under slightly different intentions) and more recently by more theoretically minded philosophers of mind, and from all this work an account of folk psychology — part truism and the rest controversy — can be gleaned. What are beliefs? Very roughly, folk psychology has it that *beliefs* are information-bearing states of people that arise from perceptions and that, together with appropriately related *desires,* lead to intelligent *action.* That much is relatively uncontroversial, but does folk psychology also have it that nonhuman animals have beliefs? If so, what is the role of language in belief? Are beliefs constructed of parts? If so, what are the parts? Ideas? Concepts? Words? Pictures? Are beliefs like speech acts or maps or instruction manuals or sentences? Is it implicit in folk psychology that beliefs enter into causal relations, or that they don't? How do decisions and intentions intervene between belief-desire complexes and actions? Are beliefs introspectible, and if so, what authority do the believer's pronouncements have?

All these questions deserve answers, but one must bear in mind that there are different reasons for being interested in the details of folk psychology. One reason is that it exists as a phenomenon, like a religion or a language or a dress code, to be studied with the techniques and attitudes of anthropology. It may be a myth, but it is a myth we live in, so it is an "important" phenomenon in nature. A different reason is that it seems to be a *true* theory, by and large, and hence is a candidate — like the folk physics of magnets and unlike the folk science of astrology — for incorporation into science. These different reasons generate different but overlapping investigations. The anthropological question should include in its account of folk psychology whatever folk actually include in their theory, however misguided, incoherent, gratuitous some of it may be. (When the anthropologist marks part of the catalogue of folk theory as false, he may speak of *false consciousness* or *ideology,* but the role of such false theory *qua* anthropological phenomenon is not thereby diminished.) The proto-scientific quest, on the other hand, as an attempt to prepare folk theory for subsequent incorporation into, or reduction to, the rest of science, should be critical and should eliminate all that is false or ill founded, however well entrenched in popular doctrine. (Thales thought that lodestones had souls, we are told. Even if most people agreed, this would be something to eliminate from the folk physics of magnets prior to "reduction.") One way of distinguishing the good from the bad, the essential from the gratuitous, in folk theory is to see what must be included in the theory to account for whatever predictive or explanatory success it seems to have in ordinary use. In this way we can criticize as we analyze, and it is even open to us in the end to discard folk psychology if it turns out to be a bad theory, and with it the presumed theoretical entities named therein. If we discard folk psychology as a theory, we would have to replace it with another theory, which, while it did violence to many ordinary intuitions, would explain the predictive power of the residual folk craft.

We use folk psychology all the time, to explain and predict each other's behavior; we attribute beliefs and desires to each other with confidence — and quite unself-consciously — and spend a substantial portion of our waking lives formulating the world — not excluding ourselves — in these terms. Folk psychology is about as pervasive a part of our second nature as is our folk physics of middle-sized objects. How good is folk psychology? If we concentrate on its weaknesses we will notice that we often are unable to make sense of particular bits of human behavior (our own included) in terms of belief and desire, even in retrospect; we often cannot predict accurately or reliably what a person will do or when; we often can find no resources within the theory for settling disagreements about particular attributions of belief or desire. If we concentrate on its strengths we find first that there are large areas in which it is extraordinarily reliable in its predictive power. Every time we venture out on a highway, for example, we stake our lives on the reliability of our general expectations about the perceptual beliefs, normal desires, and decision proclivities of the other motorists. Second, we find that it is a theory of great generative power and efficiency. For instance, watching a film with a highly original and unstereotypical plot, we see the hero smile at the villain and we all swiftly and effortlessly arrive at the same complex theoretical diagnosis: "Aha!" we conclude (but perhaps not consciously), "he wants her to think he doesn't know she intends to defraud his brother!" Third, we find that even small children pick up facility with the theory at a time when they have a very limited experience of human activity from which to induce a theory. Fourth, we find that we all use folk psychology knowing next to nothing about what actually happens inside people's skulls. "Use your head," we are told, and we know some people are brainier than others, but our capacity to use folk psychology is quite unaffected by ignorance about brain processes — or even by large-scale misinformation about brain processes.

As many philosophers have observed, a feature of folk psychology that sets it apart from both folk physics and the academic physical sciences is that explanations of actions citing beliefs and desires normally not only describe the provenance of the actions, but at the same time defend them as reasonable under the circumstances. They are reason-giving explanations, which make an ineliminable allusion to the rationality of the agent. Primarily for this reason, but also because of the pattern of strengths and weaknesses just described, I suggest that folk psychology might best be viewed as a rationalistic calculus of interpretation and prediction—an idealizing, abstract, instrumentalistic interpretation method that has evolved because it works and works because we have evolved. We approach each other as *intentional systems* (Dennett 1971), that is, as entities whose behavior can be predicted by the method of attributing beliefs, desires, and rational acumen according to the following rough and ready principles:

(1) A system's beliefs are those it *ought to have,* given its perceptual capacities, its epistemic needs, and its biography. Thus, in general, its beliefs are both true and relevant to its life, and when false beliefs are attributed, special stories must be told to explain how the error resulted from the presence of features in the environment that are deceptive relative to the perceptual capacities of the system.

(2) A system's desires are those it *ought to have,* given its biological needs and the most practicable means of satisfying them. Thus intentional systems desire survival and procreation, and hence desire food, security, health, sex, wealth, power, influence, and so forth, and also whatever local arrangements tend (in their eyes—given their beliefs) to further these ends in appropriate measure. Again, "abnormal" desires are attributable if special stories can be told.

(3) A system's behavior will consist of those acts that *it would be rational* for an agent with those beliefs and desires to perform.

In (1) and (2) "ought to have" means "would have if it were *ideally* ensconced in its environmental niche." Thus all dangers and vicissitudes in its environment it will *recognize as such* (i.e., *believe* to be dangers) and all the benefits—relative to its needs, of course—it will *desire.* When a fact about its surroundings is particularly relevant to its current projects (which themselves will be the projects such a being ought to have in order to get ahead in its world), it will *know* that fact and act accordingly. And so forth and so on. This gives us the notion of an ideal epistemic and conative operator or agent, relativized to a set of needs for survival and procreation and to the environment(s) in which its ancestors have evolved and to which it is adapted. But this notion is still too crude and overstated. For instance, a being may come to have an epistemic need that its perceptual apparatus cannot provide for (suddenly all the green food is poisonous, but alas it is colorblind), hence the relativity to perceptual capacities. Moreover, it may or may not have had the occasion to learn from experience about something, so its beliefs are also relative to its biography in this way: it will have learned what it ought to have learned, viz., what it had been given evidence for in a form compatible with its cognitive apparatus—providing the evidence was "relevant" to its project then.

But this is still too crude, for evolution does not give us a best of all possible worlds, but only a passable jury-rig, so we should look for design shortcuts that in specifiably abnormal circumstances yield false perceptual beliefs, etc. (We are not immune to illusions—which we would be if our perceptual systems were *perfect*.) To offset the design shortcuts we should also expect design bonuses: circumstances in which the "cheap" way for nature to design a cognitive system has the side benefit of giving good, reliable results even outside the environment in which the system evolved. Our eyes are well adapted for giving us true beliefs on Mars as well as on Earth, because the cheap solution for our Earth-evolving eyes happens to be a more general solution (cf. Sober 1981).

I propose that we can continue the mode of thinking just illustrated *all the way in*—not just for eye design, but for deliberation design and belief design and strategy-concocter design. In using this optimistic set of assumptions (nature has built us to do things right; look for systems to believe the truth and love the good), we impute no occult powers to epistemic needs, perceptual capacities, and biography but only the powers common sense already imputes to evolution and learning.

In short, we treat each other as if we were rational agents, and this myth—for surely we are not all that rational—works very well because we are *pretty* rational. This single assumption, in combination with home truths about our needs, capacities and typical circumstances, generates both an intentional interpretation of us as believers and desirers and actual predictions of behavior in great profusion. I am claiming, then, that folk psychology can best be viewed as a sort of logical behaviorism: *what it means* to say that someone believes that *p,* is that that person is disposed to behave in certain ways under certain conditions. What ways under what conditions? The ways it would be rational to behave, given the person's other beliefs and desires. The answer looks in danger of being circular, but consider: an account of what it is for an element to have a particular valence will similarly make ineliminable reference to the valences of other elements. What one is given with valence talk is a whole system of interlocking attributions, which is saved from vacuity by yielding independently testable predictions.

I have just described in outline a method of predicting and explaining the behavior of people and other intelligent creatures. Let me distinguish two questions about it: is it something we could do, and is it something we in fact do? I think the answer to the first is obviously yes, which is not to say the method will always yield good results. That much one can ascertain by reflection and thought experiment. Moreover, one can recognize that the method is familiar. Although we don't usually use the method self-consciously, we do use it self-consciously on those occasions when we are perplexed by a person's behavior, and then it often yields satisfactory results. Moreover, the ease and naturalness with which we resort to this self-conscious and deliberate form of problem-solving provide some support for the claim that what we are doing on those occasions is not switching methods but simply becoming self-conscious and explicit about what we ordinarily accomplish tacitly or unconsciously.

No other view of folk psychology, I think, can explain the fact that we do so well predicting each other's behavior on such slender and peripheral evidence; treating each other as intentional systems works (to the extent that it does) because we really are well designed by evolution and hence we *approximate* to the ideal version of ourselves exploited to yield the predictions. But not only does evolution not guarantee that we will always do what is rational; it guarantees that we won't. If we are designed by evolution, then we are almost certainly nothing more than a bag of tricks, patched together by a *satisficing* Nature — Herbert Simon's term (1957) — and no better than our ancestors had to be to get by. Moreover, the demands of nature and the demands of a logic course are not the same. Sometimes — even *normally* in certain circumstances — it pays to jump to conclusions swiftly (and even to forget that you've done so), so by most philosophical measures of rationality (logical consistency, refraining from invalid inference) there has probably been some positive evolutionary pressure in favor of "irrational" methods.[3]

How rational are we? Recent research in social and cognitive psychology (e.g., Tversky and Kahneman 1974; Nisbett and Ross 1978) suggests we are only minimally rational, appallingly ready to leap to conclusions or be swayed by logically irrelevant features of situations, but this jaundiced view is an illusion engendered by the fact that these psychologists are deliberately trying to produce situations that provoke irrational responses — inducing pathology in a system by putting strain on it — and succeeding, being good psychologists. No one would hire a psychologist to prove that people will choose a paid vacation to a week in jail if offered an informed choice. At least not in the better psychology departments. A more optimistic impression of our rationality is engendered by a review of the difficulties encountered in artificial intelligence research. Even the most sophisticated AI programs stumble blindly into misinterpretations and misunderstandings that even small children reliably evade without a second thought (see, e.g., Schank 1976; Schank and Abelson 1977). From this vantage point we seem marvelously rational.

However rational we are, it is the myth of our rational agenthood that structures and organizes our attributions of belief and desire to others and that regulates our own deliberations and investigations. We aspire to rationality, and without the myth of our rationality the concepts of belief and desire would be uprooted. Folk psychology, then, is *idealized* in that it produces its predictions and explanations by calculating in a normative system; it predicts what we will believe, desire, and do, by determining what we ought to believe, desire, and do.[4]

Folk psychology is *abstract* in that the beliefs and desires it attributes are not—or need not be—presumed to be intervening distinguishable states of an internal behavior-causing system. (The point will be enlarged upon later.) The role of the concept of belief is like the role of the concept of a center of gravity, and the calculations that yield the predictions are more like the calculations one performs with a parallelogram of forces than like the calculations one performs with a blueprint of internal levers and cogs.

Folk psychology is thus *instrumentalistic* in a way the most ardent realist should permit: people really do have beliefs and desires, on my version of folk psychology, just the way they really have centers of gravity and the earth has an Equator.[5] Reichenbach distinguished between two sorts of referents for theoretical terms: *illata*—posited theoretical entities—and *abstracta*—calculation-bound entities or logical constructs.[6] Beliefs and desires of folk psychology (but not all mental events and states) are *abstracta*.

This view of folk psychology emerges more clearly when contrasted to a diametrically opposed view, each of whose tenets has been held by some philosopher, and at least most of which have been espoused by Fodor:

> Beliefs and desires, just like pains, thoughts, sensations and other episodes, are taken by folk psychology to be real, intervening, internal states or events, in causal interaction, subsumed under covering laws of causal stripe. Folk psychology is not an idealized, rationalistic calculus but a naturalistic, empirical, descriptive theory, imputing causal regularities discovered by extensive induction over experience. To suppose two people share a belief is to suppose them to be ultimately in some structurally similar internal condition, e.g. for them to have the same words of Mentalese written in the functionally relevant places in their brains.

I want to deflect this head-on collision of analyses by taking two steps. First, I am prepared to grant a measure of the claims made by the opposition. Of course we don't all sit in the dark in our studies like mad Leibnizians rationalistically excogitating behavioral predictions from pure, idealized concepts of our neighbors, nor do we derive all our readiness to attribute desires from a careful generation of them from the ultimate goal of survival. We may observe that some folks seem to desire cigarettes, or pain, or notoriety (we observe this by hearing them tell us, seeing what they choose, etc.) and without any conviction that these people, given their circumstances, ought to have these desires, we attribute them anyway. So rationalistic generation of attributions is augmented and even corrected on occasion by empirical generalizations about belief and desire that guide our attributions and are learned more or less inductively. For instance, small children believe in Santa Claus, people are inclined to believe the more self-serving of two interpretations of an event in which they are involved (unless they are depressed), and people can be made to want things they don't need by making them believe that glamorous people like those things. And so forth in familiar profusion. This folklore does not consist in *laws*— even probabilistic laws—but some of it is being turned into science of a sort, for example theories of "hot cognition" and cognitive dissonance. I grant the existence of all this naturalistic generalization, and its role in the normal calculations of folk psychologists—that is, all of us. People do rely on their own parochial group of neighbors when framing intentional interpretations. That is why people have so much difficulty understanding foreigners—their behavior, to say nothing of their languages. They impute more of their own beliefs and desires, and those of their neighbors, than they would if they followed my principles of attribution slavishly. Of course this is a perfectly reasonable shortcut for people to take, even when it often leads to bad results. We are in this matter, as in most, satisficers, not optimizers, when it comes to information gathering and theory construction. I would insist, however, that all this empirically obtained lore is laid over a fundamental generative and normative framework that has the features I have described.

My second step away from the conflict I have set up is to recall that the issue is not what folk psychology as found in the field truly is, but what it is at its best, what deserves to be taken seriously and incorporated into science. It is not particularly to the point to argue against me that folk psychology is *in fact* committed to beliefs and desires as distinguishable, causally interacting *illata;* what must be shown is that it ought to be. The latter claim I will deal with in due course. The former claim I *could* concede without embarrassment to my overall project, but I do not concede it, for it seems to me that the evidence is quite strong that our ordinary notion of belief has next to nothing of the concrete in it. Jacques shoots his uncle dead in Trafalgar Square and is apprehended on the spot by Sherlock; Tom reads about it in the *Guardian* and Boris learns of it in *Pravda.* Now Jacques, Sherlock, Tom, and Boris have had remarkably different experiences—to say nothing of their earlier biographies and future prospects—but there is one thing they share: they all believe that a Frenchman has committed murder in Trafalgar Square. They did not all *say* this, not even "to themselves"; *that proposition* did not, we can suppose, "occur to" any of them, and even if it had, it would have had entirely different import for Jacques, Sherlock, Tom, and Boris. Yet they all believe that a Frenchman committed murder in Trafalgar Square. This is a shared property that is visible, as it were, only from one very limited point of view—the point of view of folk psychology. Ordinary folk psychologists have no difficulty imputing such useful but elusive commonalities to people. If they then insist that in doing so they are postulating a similarly structured object in each head, this is a gratuitous bit of misplaced concreteness, a regrettable lapse in ideology.

But in any case there is no doubt that folk psychology is a mixed bag, like folk productions generally, and there is no reason in the end not to grant that it is much more complex, variegated (and in danger of incoherence) than my sketch has made it out to be. The *ordinary* notion of belief no doubt does place beliefs somewhere midway between being *illata* and being *abstracta*. What this suggests to me is that the concept of belief found in ordinary understanding, that is, in folk psychology, is unappealing as a scientific concept. I am reminded of Anaxagoras's strange precursor to atomism: the theory of seeds. There is a portion of everything in everything, he is reputed to have claimed. Every object consists of an infinity of seeds, of all possible varieties. How do you make bread out of flour, yeast, and water? Flour contains bread seeds in abundance (but flour seeds predominate—that's what makes it flour), and so do yeast and water, and when these ingredients are mixed together, the bread seeds form a new majority, so bread is what you get. Bread nourishes by containing flesh and blood and bone seeds in addition to its majority of bread seeds. Not good theoretical entities, these seeds, for as a sort of bastardized cross between properties and proper parts they have a penchant for generating vicious regresses, and their identity conditions are problematic to say the least.

Beliefs are rather like that. There seems no comfortable way of avoiding the claim that we have an infinity of beliefs, and common intuition does not give us a stable answer to such puzzles as whether the belief that 3 is greater than 2 is none other than the belief that 2 is less than 3. The obvious response to the challenge of an infinity of beliefs with slippery identity conditions is to suppose these beliefs are not all "stored separately"; many—in fact *most* if we are really talking about infinity—will be stored *implicitly* in virtue of the *explicit* storage of a few (or a few million)—the *core beliefs* (see Dennett 1975; also Fodor 1975 and Field 1978). The core beliefs will be "stored separately," and they look like promising *illata* in contrast to the virtual or implicit beliefs which look like paradigmatic *abstracta*. But although this might turn out to be the way our brains are organized, I suspect things will be more complicated than this: there is no reason to suppose the core *elements,* the concrete, salient, separately stored representation tokens (and there must be some such elements in any complex information processing system), will explicitly represent (or *be*) a subset of our *beliefs* at all. That is, if you were to sit down and write out a list of a thousand or so of your paradigmatic beliefs, *all* of them could turn out to be virtual, only implicitly stored or represented, and what was explicitly stored would be information (e.g. about memory addresses, procedures for problem-solving, or recognition, etc.) that was entirely unfamiliar. It would be folly to prejudge this empirical issue by insisting that our core representations of information (whichever they turn out to be) are beliefs *par excellence,* for when the facts are in, our intuitions may instead support the contrary view: the least controversial self-attributions of belief may pick out beliefs that from the vantage point of developed cognitive theory are invariably virtual.[7]

In such an eventuality what could we say about the causal roles we assign ordinarily to beliefs (e.g. "Her belief that John knew her secret caused her to blush")? We could say that whatever the core elements were in virtue of which she virtually believed that John knew her secret, they, the core elements, played a direct causal role (somehow) in triggering the blushing response. We would be wise, as this example shows, not to tamper with our *ordinary* catalogue of beliefs (virtual though they might all turn out to be), for these are predictable, readily understandable, manipulable regularities in psychological phenomena in spite of their apparent neutrality with regard to the explicit/implicit (or core/virtual) distinction. What Jacques, Sherlock, Boris, and Tom have in common is probably only a virtual belief "derived" from largely different explicit stores of information in each of them, but virtual or not, it is their sharing of *this* belief that would explain (or permit us to predict) in some imagined circumstances their all taking the same action when given the same new information. ("And now for one million dollars, Tom [Jacques, Sherlock, Boris], answer our jackpot question correctly: has a French citizen ever committed a major crime in London?")

At the same time we want to cling to the equally ordinary notion that beliefs can cause not only actions, but blushes, verbal slips, heart attacks, and the like. Much of the debate over whether or not intentional explanations are causal explanations can be bypassed by noting how the core elements, *whatever they may be,* can be cited as playing the causal role, while belief remains virtual. "Had Tom not believed that p and wanted that q, he would not have done A." Is this a causal explanation? It is tantamount to this: Tom was in some one of an indefinitely large number of structurally different states of type B that have in common just that each one of them licenses attribution of belief that p and desire that q in virtue of its normal relations with many other states of Tom, and this state, whichever one it was, was causally sufficient, given the "background conditions" of course, to initiate the intention to perform A, and thereupon A was performed, and had he not been in one of those indefinitely many type B states, he would not have done A. One can call this a causal explanation because it talks about causes, but it is surely as unspecific and unhelpful as a causal explanation can get. It commits itself to there being some causal explanation or other falling within a very broad area (i.e., the intentional interpretation is held to be supervenient on Tom's bodily condition), but its true informativeness and utility in actual prediction lie, not surprisingly, in its assertion that Tom, however his body is currently structured, has a particular set of these elusive intentional properties, beliefs, and desires.

The ordinary notion of belief is pulled in two directions. If we want to have good theoretical entities, good *illata,* or good logical constructs, good *abstracta,* we will have to jettison some of the ordinary freight of the concepts of belief and desire. So I propose a divorce. Since we seem to have both notions wedded in folk psychology, let's split them apart and create two new theories: one strictly abstract, idealizing, holistic, instrumentalistic — pure intentional system theory — and the other a concrete, microtheoretical science of the actual realization of those intentional systems — what I will call subpersonal cognitive psychology. By exploring their differences and interrelations, we should be able to tell whether any plausible "reductions" are in the offing.

INTENTIONAL SYSTEM THEORY AS A COMPETENCE THEORY

The first new theory, intentional system theory, is envisaged as a close kin of, and overlapping with, such already existing disciplines as decision theory and game theory, which are similarly abstract, normative, and couched in intentional language. It borrows the ordinary terms "belief" and "desire" but gives them a technical meaning within the theory. It is a sort of holistic logical behaviorism because it deals with the prediction and explanation from belief-desire profiles of the actions of whole systems (either alone in environments or in interaction with other intentional systems), but it treats the individual realizations of the systems as black boxes. The *subject* of all the intentional attributions is the whole system (the person, the animal, or even the corporation or nation [see Dennett 1976]) rather than any of its parts, and individual beliefs and desires are not attributable in isolation, independently of other belief and desire attributions. The latter point distinguishes intentional system theory most clearly from Ryle's logical behaviorism, which took on the impossible burden of characterizing individual beliefs (and other mental states) as particular individual dispositions to outward behavior.

The theory deals with the "production" of new beliefs and desires from old, via an interaction among old beliefs and desires, features in the environment, and the system's actions; and this creates the illusion that the theory contains naturalistic descriptions of internal processing in the systems the theory is about, when in fact the processing is all in the manipulation of the theory and consists in updating the intentional characterization of the whole system according to the rules of attribution. An analogous illusion of process would befall a naive student who, when confronted with a parallelogram of forces, supposed that it pictured a mechanical linkage of rods and pivots of some kind instead of being simply a graphic way of representing and plotting the effect of several simultaneously acting forces.

Richard Jeffrey (1970), in developing his concept of probability kinematics, has usefully drawn attention to an analogy with the distinction in physics between kinematics and dynamics. In kinematics,

> you talk about the propagation of motions through a system in terms of such constraints as rigidity and manner of linkage. It is the physics of position and time, in terms of which you can talk about velocity and acceleration, but not about force and mass. When you talk about forces — *causes* of accelerations — you are in the realm of dynamics. (p. 172)

Kinematics provides a simplified and idealized level of abstraction appropriate for many purposes — for example, for the *initial* design development of a gearbox — but when one must deal with more concrete details of systems — when the gearbox designer must worry about friction, bending, energetic efficiency, and the like — one must switch to dynamics for more detailed and reliable predictions, at the cost of increased complexity and diminished generality. Similarly, one can approach the study of belief (and desire and so forth) at a highly abstract level, ignoring problems of realization and simply setting out what the normative demands on the design of a believer are. For instance, one can ask such questions as "What must a system's epistemic capabilities and propensities be for it to survive in environment *A?*" (cf. Campbell 1973, 1977) or "What must this system already know in order for it to be able to learn *B?*" or "What intentions must this system have in order to mean something by saying something?"

Intentional system theory deals just with the performance specifications of believers while remaining silent on how the systems are to be implemented. In fact this neutrality with regard to implementation is the most useful feature of intentional characterizations. Consider, for instance, the role of intentional characterizations in evolutionary biology. If we are to explain the evolution of complex behavioral capabilities or cognitive talents by natural selection, we must note that it is the intentionally characterized capacity (e.g., the capacity to acquire a belief, a desire, to perform an intentional action) that has survival value, however it happens to be realized as a result of mutation. If a particularly noxious insect makes its appearance in an environment, the birds and bats with a survival advantage will be those that come to believe this insect is not good to eat. In view of the vast differences in neural structure, genetic background, and perceptual capacity between birds and bats, it is highly unlikely that this useful trait they may come to share has a common description at any level more concrete or less abstract than intentional system theory. It is not only that the intentional predicate is a projectible predicate in evolutionary theory; since it is more general than its species-specific counterpart predicates (which characterize the successful mutation just in birds, or just in bats), it is preferable. So from the point of view of evolutionary biology, we would not want to "reduce" all intentional characterizations even if we knew in particular instances what the physiological implementation was.

This level of generality is essential if we want a theory to have anything meaningful and defensible to say about such topics as intelligence in general (as opposed, say, to just human or even terrestrial or natural intelligence) or such grand topics as meaning or reference or representation. Suppose, to pursue a familiar philosophical theme, we are invaded by Martians, and the question arises: do they have beliefs and desires? Are they that much *like us?* According to intentional system theory, if these Martians are smart enough to get here, then they most certainly have beliefs and desires — in the technical sense proprietary to the theory — no matter what their internal structure, and no matter how our folk-psychological intuitions rebel at the thought.

This principled blindness of intentional system theory to internal structure seems to invite the retort: but there has to be *some* explanation of the *success* of intentional prediction of the behavior of systems (e.g., Fodor, 1985, p. 79). It isn't just magic. It isn't a mere coincidence that one can generate all these *abstracta,* manipulate them via some version of practical reasoning, and come up with an action prediction that has a good chance of being true. There must be some way in which the internal processes of the system mirror the complexities of the intentional interpretation, or its success would be a miracle.

Of course. This is all quite true and important. Nothing without a great deal of structural and processing complexity could conceivably realize an intentional system of any interest, and the complexity of the realization will surely bear a striking resemblance to the complexity of the instrumentalistic interpretation. Similarly, the success of valence theory in chemistry is no coincidence, and people were entirely right to expect that deep microphysical similarities would be discovered between elements with the same valence and that the structural similarities found would explain the dispositional similarities. But since people and animals are unlike atoms and molecules not only in being the products of a complex evolutionary history, but also in being the products of their individual learning histories, there is no reason to suppose that individual (human) believers that p—like individual (carbon) atoms with valence 4—regulate their dispositions with *exactly* the same machinery. Discovering the constraints on design and implementation variation, and demonstrating how particular species and individuals in fact succeed in realizing intentional systems, is the job for the third theory: subpersonal cognitive psychology.

SUBPERSONAL COGNITIVE PSYCHOLOGY AS A PERFORMANCE THEORY

The task of subpersonal cognitive psychology is to explain something that at first glance seems utterly mysterious and inexplicable. The brain, as intentional system theory and evolutionary biology show us, is a *semantic engine;* its task is to discover what its multifarious inputs *mean,* to discriminate them by their significance and "act accordingly."[8] That's what brains *are for.* But the brain, as physiology or plain common sense shows us, is just a *syntactic engine;* all it can do is discriminate its inputs by their structural, temporal, and physical features and let its entirely mechanical activities be governed by these "syntactic" features of its inputs. That's all brains *can do.* Now how does the brain manage to get semantics from syntax? How could *any* entity (how could a genius or an angel or God) get the semantics of a system from nothing but its syntax? It couldn't. The syntax of a system doesn't determine its semantics. By what alchemy, then, does the brain extract semantically reliable results from syntactically driven operations? It cannot be designed to do an impossible task, but it could be designed to *approximate* the impossible task, to *mimic* the behavior of the impossible object (the semantic engine) by capitalizing on close (close enough) fortuitous correspondences between structural regularities—of the environment and of its own internal states and operations—and semantic types.

The basic idea is familiar. An animal needs to know when it has satisfied the goal of finding and ingesting food, but it settles for a friction-in-the-throat-followed-by-stretched-stomach detector, a mechanical switch turned on by a relatively simple mechanical condition that normally co-occurs with the satisfaction of the animals "real" goal. It's not fancy and can easily be exploited to trick the animal into either eating when it shouldn't or leaving off eating when it shouldn't, but it does well enough by the animal in its normal environment. Or suppose I am monitoring telegraph transmissions and have been asked to intercept all *death threats* (but only death threats in English—to make it "easy"). I'd like to build a machine to save me the trouble of interpreting semantically every message sent, but how could this be done? No machine could be designed to do the job perfectly, for that would require defining the semantic category *death threat in English* as some tremendously complex feature of strings of alphabetic symbols, and there is utterly no reason to suppose this could be done in a principled way. (If somehow by brute-force inspection and subsequent enumeration we could list all and only the English death threats of, say, less than a thousand characters, we could easily enough build a filter to detect them, but we are looking for a principled, projectible, extendable method.) A really crude device could be made to discriminate all messages containing the symbol strings

. . . I will kill you . . .

or

. . . you . . . die . . . unless . . .

or

. . . (for some finite disjunction of likely patterns to be found in English death threats).

This device would have some utility, and further refinements could screen the material that passed this first filter, and so on. An unpromising beginning for constructing a sentence understander, but if you want to get semantics out of syntax (whether the syntax of messages in a natural language or the syntax of afferent neuron impulses), variations on this basic strategy are your only hope.[9] You must put together a bag of tricks and hope nature will be kind enough to let your device get by. Of course some tricks are elegant and appeal to deep principles of organization, but in the end all one can hope to produce (all natural selection can have produced) are systems that *seem* to discriminate meanings by actually discriminating things (tokens of no doubt wildly disjunctive types) that co-vary reliably with meanings.[10] Evolution has designed our brains not only to do this but to evolve and follow strategies of self-improvement in this activity during their individual lifetimes (see Dennett 1974b).

It is the task of subpersonal cognitive psychology to propose and test models of such activity—of pattern recognition or stimulus generalization, concept learning, expectation, learning, goal-directed behavior, problem-solving—that not only produce a simulacrum of genuine content-sensitivity, but that do this in ways demonstrably like the way people's brains do it, exhibiting the same powers and the same vulnerabilities to deception, overload, and confusion. It is here that we will find our good theoretical entities, our useful *illata,* and while some of them may well resemble the familiar entities of folk psychology—beliefs, desires, judgments, decisions—many will certainly not (see, e.g., the subdoxastic states proposed by Stich 1978b). The only *similarity* we can be sure of discovering in the *illata* of subpersonal cognitive psychology is the intentionality of their labels (see *Brainstorms,* pp. 23–38). They will be characterized as events with content, bearing information, signaling this and ordering that.

In order to give the *illata* these labels, in order to maintain any intentional interpretation of their operation at all, the theorist must always keep glancing outside the system, to see what normally produces the configuration he is describing, what effects the system's responses normally have on the environment, and what benefit normally accrues to the whole system from this activity. In other words the cognitive psychologist cannot ignore the fact that it is the realization of an intentional system he is studying on pain of abandoning semantic interpretation and hence psychology. On the other hand, progress in subpersonal cognitive psychology will blur the boundaries between it and intentional system theory, knitting them together much as chemistry and physics have been knit together.

The alternative of ignoring the external world and its relations to the internal machinery (what Putnam has called psychology in the narrow sense, or methodological solipsism, and Gunderson has lampooned as black world glass box perspectivalism) is not really psychology at all, but just at best abstract neurophysiology—pure internal syntax with no hope of a semantic interpretation. Psychology "reduced" to neurophysiology in this fashion would not be psychology, for it would not be able to provide an explanation of the regularities it is psychology's particular job to explain: the reliability with which "intelligent" organisms can cope with their environments and thus prolong their lives. Psychology can, and should,

Black Box Behaviorism   Black World Glass Box Perspectivalism

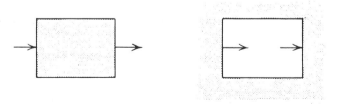

FIG. 7.1.

work toward an account of the physiological foundations of psychological processes, not by eliminating psychological or intentional characterizations of those processes, but by exhibiting how the brain implements the intentionally characterized performance specifications of subpersonal theories.

Friedman, discussing the current perplexity in cognitive psychology, suggests that the problem

> is the direction of reduction. Contemporary psychology tries to explain *individual* cognitive activity independently from *social* cognitive activity, and then tries to give a *micro* reduction of social cognitive activity — that is, the use of a public language — in terms of a prior theory of individual cognitive activity. The opposing suggestion is that we first look for a theory of social activity, and then try to give a *macro* reduction of individual cognitive activity — the activity of applying concepts, making judgments, and so forth — in terms of our prior social theory. (1981, pp. 15–16)

With the idea of macroreduction in psychology I largely agree, except that Friedman's identification of the macro level as explicitly social is only part of the story. The cognitive capacities of non-language-using animals (and Robinson Crusoes, if there are any) must also be accounted for, and not just in terms of an analogy with the practices of us language users. The macro level *up* to which we should relate microprocesses in the brain in order to understand them as psychological is more broadly the level of organism-environment interaction, development, and evolution. That level includes social interaction as a particularly important part (see Burge 1979), but still a proper part.

There is no way to capture the semantic properties of things (word tokens, diagrams, nerve impulses, brain states) by a microreduction. Semantic properties are not just relational but, you might say, superrelational, for the relation a particular vehicle of content, or token, must bear in order to have content is not just a relation it bears to other similar things (e.g., other tokens, or parts of tokens, or sets of tokens, or causes of tokens) but a relation between the token and the whole life — and counterfactual life[11] — of the organism it "serves" *and* that organism's requirements for survival *and* its evolutionary ancestry.

THE PROSPECTS OF REDUCTION

Of our three psychologies — folk psychology, intentional system theory, and sub-personal cognitive psychology — what then might reduce to what? Certainly the one-step microreduction of folk psychology to physiology alluded to in the slogans of the early identity theorists will never be found – and should never be missed, even by staunch friends of materialism and scientific unity. A prospect worth exploring, though, is that folk psychology (more precisely, the part of folk psychology worth caring about) reduces – conceptually – to intentional system theory. What this would amount to can best be brought out by contrasting this proposed conceptual reduction with more familiar alternatives: "type-type identity theory" and "Turing machine functionalism." According to type-type identity theory, for every mentalistic term or predicate *"M"*, there is some predicate *"P" expressible in the vocabulary of the physical sciences* such that a creature is *M* if and only if it is *P*. In symbols:

(1) $(x) (Mx \equiv Px)$

This is reductionism with a vengeance, taking on the burden of replacing, in principle, all mentalistic predicates with co-extensive predicates composed truth-functionally from the predicates of physics. It is now widely agreed to be hopelessly too strong a demand. Believing that cats eat fish is, intuitively, a *functional* state that might be variously implemented physically, so there is no reason to suppose the commonality referred to on the left-hand side of (1) can be reliably picked out by any predicate, however complex, of physics. What is needed to express the predicate on the right-hand side is, it seems, a physically neutral language for speaking of functions and functional states, and the obvious candidates are the languages used to describe automata – for instance, Turing machine language.

The Turing machine functionalist then proposes

(2) $(x) (Mx \equiv x$ realizes some Turing machine k in logical state $A)$

In other words, for two things both to believe that cats eat fish they need not be physically similar in any specifiable way, but they must both be in a "functional" condition specifiable in principle in the most general functional language; they must share a Turing machine description according to which they are both in some particular logical state. This is still a reductionist doctrine, for it proposes to identify each mental type with a functional type picked out in the language of automata theory. But this is still too strong, for there is no more reason to suppose Jacques, Sherlock, Boris, and Tom "have the same program" in *any* relaxed and abstract sense, considering the differences in their nature and nurture, than that their brains have some crucially identical physico-chemical feature. We must weaken the requirements for the right-hand side of our formula still further.

Consider

(3) $(x) (x$ believes that $p \equiv x$ can be predictively attributed the belief that $p)$

This appears to be blatantly circular and uninformative, with the language on the right simply mirroring the language on the left. But all we need to make an informative answer of this formula is a systematic way of making the attributions alluded to on the right-hand side. Consider the parallel case of Turing machines. What do two different realizations or embodiments of a Turing machine have in common when they are in the same logical state? Just this: there is a system of description such that according to it both are described as being realizations of some particular Turing machine, and according to this description, which is predictive of the operation of both entities, both are in the same state of that Turing machine's machine table. One doesn't *reduce* Turing machine talk to some more fundamental idiom; one *legitimizes* Turing machine talk by providing it with rules of attribution and exhibiting its predictive powers. If we can similarly legitimize "mentalistic" talk, we will have no need of a reduction, and that is the point of the concept of an intentional system. Intentional systems are supposed to play a role in the legitimization of mentalistic predicates parallel to the role played by the abstract notion of a Turing machine in setting down rules for the interpretation of artifacts as computational automata. I fear my concept is woefully informal and unsystematic compared with Turing's, but then the domain it attempts to systematize — our everyday attributions in mentalistic or intentional language — is itself something of a mess, at least compared with the clearly defined field of recursive function theory, the domain of Turing machines.

The analogy between the theoretical roles of Turing machines and intentional systems is more than superficial. Consider that warhorse in the philosophy of mind, Brentano's Thesis that intentionality is the mark of the mental: all mental phenomena exhibit intentionality and no physical phenomena exhibit intentionality. This has been traditionally taken to be an *irreducibility* thesis: the mental, in virtue of its intentionality, cannot be reduced to the physical. But given the concept of an intentional system, we can construe the first half of Brentano's Thesis — all mental phenomena are intentional — as a *reductionist* thesis of sorts, parallel to Church's Thesis in the foundations of mathematics.

According to Church's Thesis, every "effective" procedure in mathematics is recursive, that is, Turing-computable. Church's Thesis is not provable, since it hinges on the intuitive and informal notion of an effective procedure, but it is generally accepted, and it provides a very useful reduction of a fuzzy-but-useful mathematical notion to a crisply defined notion of apparently equal scope and greater power. Analogously, the claim that every mental phenomenon alluded to in folk psychology is *intentional-system-characterizable* would, if true, provide a reduction of the mental as ordinarily understood — a domain whose boundaries are at best fixed by mutual acknowledgment and shared intuition — to a clearly defined domain of entities whose principles of organization are familiar, relatively formal and systematic, and entirely general.[12]

This reduction claim, like Church's Thesis, cannot be proven but could be made compelling by piecemeal progress on particular (and particularly difficult) cases—a project I set myself elsewhere (in *Brainstorms*). The final reductive task would be to show not how the terms of intentional system theory are eliminable in favor of physiological terms via subpersonal cognitive psychology, but almost the reverse: to show how a system described in physiological terms could warrant an interpretation as a realized intentional system.

FOOTNOTES

[1]This paragraph corrects a misrepresentation of both Fodor's and Ryle's positions in my critical notice of Fodor's book in *Mind* (1977) reprinted in *Brainstorms*, pp. 90–108.

[2]I think it is just worth noting that philosophers' use of "believe" as the standard and general ordinary language term is a considerable distortion. We seldom talk about what people *believe;* we talk about what they *think* and what they *know.*

[3]While in general true beliefs have to be more useful than false beliefs (and hence a system ought to have true beliefs), in special circumstances it may be better to have a few false beliefs. For instance it might be better for beast *B* to have some false beliefs about whom *B* can beat up and whom *B* can't. Ranking *B*'s likely antagonists from ferocious to pushover, we certainly want *B* to believe it can't beat up all the ferocious ones and can beat up all the obvious pushovers, but it is better (because it "costs less" in discrimination tasks and protects against random perturbations such as bad days and lucky blows) for *B* to extend "I can't beat up *x*" to cover even some beasts it can in fact beat up. *Erring on the side of prudence* is a well-recognized good strategy, and so Nature can be expected to have valued it on occasions when it came up. An alternative strategy in this instance would be to abide by the rule: avoid conflict with penumbral cases. But one might have to "pay more" to implement that strategy than to implement the strategy designed to produce, and rely on, some false beliefs.

[4]It tests its predictions in two ways: action predictions it tests directly by looking to see what the agent does; belief and desire predictions are tested indirectly by employing the predicted attributions in further predictions of eventual action. As usual, the Duhemian thesis holds: belief and desire attributions are underdetermined by the available data.

[5]Michael Friedman's "Theoretical Explanation" (1981) provides an excellent analysis of the role of instrumentalistic thinking within realistic science. Scheffler (1963) provides a useful distinction between *instrumentalism* and *fictionalism.* In his terms I am characterizing folk psychology as instrumentalistic, not fictionalistic.

[6]"Our observations of concrete things confer a certain probability on the existence of *illata*-nothing more. . . . Second, there are inferences to *abstracta*. These inferences are . . . equivalences, not probability inferences. Consequently, the existence of abstracta is reducible to the existence of concreta. There is, therefore, no problem of their objective existence; their status depends on a convention." (Reichenbach 1938, pp. 211–12).

[7]See Field 1978, p. 55, n. 12 on "minor concessions" to such instrumentalistic treatments of belief.

[8]More accurately if less picturesquely, the brain's task is to come to produce internal mediating responses that reliably vary in concert with variation in the actual environmental significance (the natural and nonnatural meanings, in Grice's (1957) sense) of their distal causes

and independently of meaning-irrelevant variations in their proximal causes, and moreover to respond to its own mediating responses in ways that systematically tend to improve the creature's prospects in its environment if the mediating responses are varying as they ought to vary.

[9]One might think that while in principle one cannot derive the semantics of a system from nothing but its syntax, in practice one might be able to cheat a little and exploit syntactic features that don't imply a semantical interpretation but strongly suggest one. For instance, faced with the task of deciphering isolated documents in an entirely unknown and alien language, one might note that while the symbol that looks like a duck doesn't have to mean "duck," there is a good chance that it does, especially if the symbol that looks like a wolf seems to be eating the symbol that looks like a duck, and not vice versa. Call this *hoping for hieroglyphics* and note the form it has taken in psychological theories from Locke to the present: we will be able to tell which mental representations are which (which idea is the idea of *dog* and which of *cat*) because the former will look like a dog and the latter like a cat. This is all very well as a crutch for us observers on the outside, trying to assign content to the events in some brain, but it is of no use to the brain . . . because brains don't know what dogs look like! Or better, this cannot be the brain's fundamental method of eking semantic classes out of raw syntax, for any brain (or brain part) that could be said — in an extended sense — to know what dogs look like would be a brain (or brain part) that had already solved its problem, that was already (a simulacrum of) a semantic engine. But this is still misleading, for brains in any event do not *assign* content to their own events in the way observers might: brains *fix* the content of their internal events in the act of reacting as they do. There are good reasons for positing *mental images* of one sort or another in cognitive theories (see "Two Approaches to Mental Images" in *Brainstorms*, pp. 174–89) but hoping for hieroglyphics isn't one of them, though I suspect it is covertly influential.

[10]I take this point to be closely related to Davidson's reasons for claiming there can be no psycho-physical laws, but I am unsure that Davidson wants to draw the same conclusions from it that I do. See Davidson 1970b.

[11]What I mean is this: counterfactuals enter because content is in part a matter of the *normal* or *designed* role of a vehicle whether or not it ever gets to play that role. Cf. Sober 1981 and Millikan 1984.

[12]Ned Block (1978) presents arguments supposed to show how the various possible functionalist theories of mind all slide into the sins of "chauvinism" (improperly excluding Martians from the class of possible mind-havers) or "liberalism" (improperly including various contraptions, human puppets, and so forth among the mind-havers). My view embraces the broadest liberalism, gladly paying the price of a few recalcitrant intuitions for the generality gained.

8 Folk Psychology is Here to Stay*

Terence Horgan
Memphis State University

James Woodward
California Institute of Technology

Folk psychology is a network of principles which constitutes a sort of common-sense theory about how to explain human behavior. These principles provide a central role to certain propositional attitudes, particularly beliefs and desires. The theory asserts, for example, that if someone desires that p, and this desire is not overridden by other desires, and he believes that an action of kind K will bring it about that p, and he believes that such an action is within his power, and he does not believe that some other kind of action is within his power and is a preferable way to bring it about that p, then *ceteris paribus,* the desire and the beliefs will cause him to perform an action of kind K. The theory is largely functional, in that the states it postulates are characterized primarily in terms of their causal relations to each other, to perception and other environmental stimuli, and to behavior.

Folk psychology (henceforth FP) is deeply ingrained in our common-sense conception of ourselves as persons. Whatever else a person is, he is supposed to be a rational (at least largely rational) *agent* – that is, a creature whose behavior is systematically caused by, and explainable in terms of, his beliefs, desires, and related propositional attitudes. The wholesale rejection of FP, therefore, would entail a drastic revision of our conceptual scheme. This fact seems to us to constitute a good *prima facie* reason for not discarding FP too quickly in the face of apparent difficulties.

Recently, however, FP has come under fire from two quarters. Paul Churchland (this volume, pp. 42–62) has argued that since FP has been with

---

*Reprinted from *The Philosophical Review* 94 (1985, pp. 197–226) by permission of the authors and publisher.

us for at least twenty-five centuries, and thus is not the product of any deliberate and self-conscious attempt to develop a psychological theory which coheres with the account of *homo sapiens* that the natural sciences provide, there is little reason to suppose that FP is true, or that humans undergo beliefs, desires, and the like. And Stephen Stich (1983a) has argued that current work in cognitive science suggests that no events or states posited by a mature cognitive psychology will be identifiable as the events and states posited by FP; Stich maintains that if this turns out to be the case, then it will show that FP is radically false, and that humans simply do not undergo such mental states as beliefs and desires.

In this paper we shall argue that neither Churchland nor Stich has provided convincing reasons for doubting the integrity of FP. Much of our discussion will be devoted to showing that they each employ an implausibly stringent conception of how FP would have to mesh with lower-level theories in order to be compatible with them. We do not deny the possibility that FP will fail to be compatible with more comprehensive theories; this would happen, for instance, if the correct theoretical psychology turned out to be a version of radical Skinnerian behaviorism. But we maintain that there is no good reason to suppose that it will *actually* happen.

Before proceeding, several preliminaries. First, we shall use the rubric 'event' in a broad sense, to include not only token changes, but also token states and token processes. Thus, nonmomentary folk-psychological token states will count as mental events, in our terminology.

Second, we shall take FP to consist of two components: a set of *theoretical principles,* and an *existential thesis.* Many or all of the theoretical principles may be expected to have the general form exemplified by the example in our opening paragraph; that is, they are universal closures of conditional formulas.[1] As such they do not carry any existential import, since they might all be vacuously true. The existential thesis of FP, on the other hand, is the assertion that generally our everyday folk-psychological descriptions of people are true, and that humans generally do undergo the folk-psychological events that we commonly attribute to them. We take it that Churchland and Stich are arguing primarily against the existential thesis of FP; i.e., they are claiming that our everyday folk-psychological ascriptions are radically false, and that there simply do not exist such things as beliefs, desires, and the rest. Thus their argument, as we understand it, leaves open the possibility that the theoretical principles of FP are true but merely vacuously so.

Third, we are not necessarily claiming that FP is fully correct in every respect, or that there is no room to correct or improve FP on the basis of new developments in cognitive science or neuroscience. Rather, we are claiming that FP's theoretical principles are *by and large* correct, and that everyday folk-psychological ascriptions are often true.

Fourth, we want to dissociate ourselves from one currently influential strategy for insulating FP from potential scientific falsification—viz., the instrumentalism of Daniel Dennett (1978a, 1981, this volume). He says, of beliefs and desires, that these "putative . . . states" can be relegated "to the role of idealized fictions in an action-predicting, action-explaining calculus" (1978a, p. 30). They are not what Reichenbach calls "illata—posited theoretical entities"; instead, he maintains, they are "abstracta—calculation-bound entities or logical constructs" (1981, this volume), whose status is analogous to components in a parallelogram of forces (1981, this volume). In short, he evidently holds that they are instrumentalistic fictions, and hence that they are compatible with virtually anything we might discover in cognitive science or neuroscience. We reject Dennett's instrumentalism. We maintain that FP, in addition to providing a useful framework for prediction, also provides genuine *causal explanations*. Although an instrumentalistic attitude toward the intentional idioms of FP is compatible with the mere predictive use of these idioms, it simply is not compatible with their explanatory use, or with talk of beliefs and desires as causes. Accordingly, FP requires a defense more vigorous than Dennett's instrumentalism.

Churchland's (this volume, pp. 42–62) argument against the compatibility of FP and neuroscience rests on three considerations. First, "FP suffers explanatory failures on an epic scale" (p. 49). Second, "it has been stagnant for at least twenty-five centuries" (p. 49). And third, "its intentional categories stand magnificently alone, without any visible prospect of reduction" to neuroscience (p. 49). Irreducibility is the main consideration, and it is allegedly reinforced by the other two points: "A successful reduction cannot be ruled out, in my view, but FP's explanatory impotence and long stagnation inspire little faith that its categories will find themselves neatly reflected in the framework of neuroscience" (p. 49).

Let us consider each of Churchland's three points in turn. In elaboration of the first point, he writes:

> As examples of central and important mental phenomena that remain largely or wholly mysterious within the framework of FP, consider the nature and dynamics of mental illness, the faculty of creative imagination . . . the nature and psychological functions of sleep . . . the common ability to catch an outfield fly ball on the run . . . the internal construction of a 3-D visual image . . . the rich variety of perceptual illusions . . . the miracle of memory . . . the nature of the learning process itself . . . (p. 47).

There are at least two important respects in which this passage is misleading. First, while FP itself may have little to say about the matters

Churchland mentions, theories based on concepts deriving from FP have a good deal to say about them. For example, cognitive psychologists have developed extensive and detailed theories about visual perception, memory, and learning that employ concepts recognizably like the folk-psychological concepts of belief, desire, judgment, etc.[2] The versions of attribution theory and cognitive dissonance theory considered below in connection with Stich are important cases of theories of this kind. That all such theories are unexplanatory is most implausible, and in any case requires detailed empirical argument of a sort Churchland does not provide.

Secondly, Churchland's argument seems to impose the *a priori* demand that any successful psychological theory account for a certain pre-established range of phenomena, and do so in a unified way. Arguments of this general type deserve to be treated with skepticism and caution. The history of science is full of examples in which our pretheoretical expectations about which phenomena it is reasonable to expect a theory to account for or group together have turned out to be quite misleading. For example, the demand was frequently imposed on early optical theories that they account for facts which we would now recognize as having to do with the physiology or psychology of vision; this had a deleterious effect on early optical theorizing. Similar examples can readily be found in the history of chemistry.[3]

The general point is that reasonable judgments about which phenomena a theory of some general type should be expected to account for require considerable theoretical knowledge; when our theoretical knowledge is relatively primitive, as it is with regard to many psychological phenomena, such judgments can go seriously astray. There is no good reason, *a priori,* to expect that a theory like FP, designed primarily to explain common human actions in terms of beliefs, desires, and the like, should also account for phenomena having to do with visual perception, sleep, or complicated muscular coordination. The truth about the latter phenomena may simply be very different from the truth about the former.

What about Churchland's second argument, viz., that FP has remained stagnant for centuries? To begin with, it seems to us at least arguable that FP has indeed changed in significant and empirically progressive ways over the centuries, rather than stagnating. For example, it is a plausible conjecture that Europeans in the 18th or 19th centuries were much more likely to explain human behavior in terms of character types with enduring personality traits than 20th century Europeans, who often appeal instead to "situational" factors. (Certainly this difference is dramatically evident in 18th and 20th century literature; contrast, say, Jane Austen and John Barth.)[4] Another example of empirically progressive change, perhaps, is the greater willingness, in contemporary culture, to appeal to unconscious beliefs and motivations.

Another reason to question the "empirical unprogressiveness" argument is that cognitive psychological theories employing belief-like and desire-like events have led to a number of novel and surprising predictions, which have borne out by experiment. (We discuss some pertinent examples below. For other striking cases the reader is referred to Nisbett and Ross (1980).) Yet Churchland seems to argue as though the (alleged) empirical unprogressiveness of FP is a good reason for taking any theory modelled on FP to be false.[5] This is rather like arguing that any sophisticated physical theory employing central forces must be false on the grounds that the ordinary person's notions of pushing and pulling have been empirically unprogressive.

Furthermore, the standard of "empirical progressiveness" is not very useful in assessing a theory like FP anyway. The typical user of FP is interested in applying a pre-existing theory to make particular causal judgments about particular instances of human behavior, not in formulating new causal generalizations. He is a consumer of causal generalizations, not an inventor of them. In this respect he resembles the historian, the detective, or the person who makes ordinary singular causal judgments about inanimate objects. It is not appropriate, we submit, to assess these activities using a standard explicitly designed to assess theories that aim at formulating novel causal generalizations.

This point emerges clearly when one realizes that much of the implicit theory behind many ordinary (but nonpsychological) particular causal judgments has presumably changed very slowly, if at all, over the past thousand years. Both we and our ancestors judge that the impact of the rock caused the shattering of the pot, that the lack of water caused the camel to die, that a very sharp blow on the head caused A's death, that heat causes water to boil, etc. None of these judgments are part of a (swiftly) empirically progressive theory, yet it seems ludicrous to conclude (on those grounds alone) that they are probably false. A similar point can be made about much (although by no means all) of the implicit causal theory employed by historians. These examples serve to remind us that not all folk theorizing is now regarded as radically false.

This brings us to Churchland's third, and most fundamental, argument for the alleged incommensurability of FP with neuroscience: viz., the likely irreducibility of the former to the latter. An ideal intertheoretic reduction, as he describes it, has two main features:

First, it provides us with a set of rules—"correspondence rules" or "bridge laws," as the standard vernacular has it—which effect a mapping of the terms of the old theory (T_o) onto a subset of the expressions of the new or reducing theory (T_n). These rules guide the application of those selected expressions of T_n in the following way: we are free to make singular applications of those expressions in all those cases where we normally make singular applications of their correspondence-rule doppelgangers in T_o. . . .

Second, and equally important, a successful reduction ideally has the outcome that, under the term mapping effected by the correspondence rules, the central principles of T_o (those of semantic and systematic importance) are mapped onto general sentences of T_n that are *theorems* of T_n (1979, p. 81).

We certainly agree that an ideal, or approximately ideal, reduction of FP to natural science would be *one* way of salvaging FP. And we also agree that such a reduction — indeed, even a species-specific reduction — is an unlikely prospect, given that FP is at least twenty-five centuries old and hence obviously was not formulated with an eye toward smooth term-by-term absorption into 20th century science. (A non-species-specific reduction is even less likely, because if FP is true of humans then it can equally well be true of Martians whose physico-chemical composition is vastly different from our own — so different that there are no theoretically interesting physical descriptions that can subsume both the physico-chemical properties which "realize" FP in humans and the corresponding physico-chemical properties in Martians.)

But even if FP cannot be reduced to lower-level theories, and even if lower-level theories can themselves provide a marvelous account of the nature and behavior of *homo sapiens,* it simply does not follow that FP is radically false, or that humans do not undergo the intentional events it posits. Churchland's eliminative materialism is not the only viable naturalistic alternative to reductive materialism. Another important alternative is the nonreductive, noneliminative materialism of Donald Davidson (1970b, 1973, 1974).

Davidson advocates a thesis which asserts that every concrete mental event is identical to some concrete neurological event, but which does not assert (indeed, denies) that there are systematic bridge laws linking mental event-*types,* or properties, with neurological event-types. He calls this view *anomalous monism;* it is a form of monism because it posits psychophysical identities, and it is "anomalous" because it rejects reductive bridge laws (or reductive type-type identities).[6]

The availability of anomalous monism as an alternative to reductive materialism makes it clear that even if FP is not reducible to neuroscience, nevertheless the token mental events posited by FP might well exist, and might well bear all the causal relations to each other, to sensation, and to behavior which FP says they do.

Churchland never mentions Davidson's version of the identity theory — a very odd fact, given its enormous influence and its obvious relevance to his argument. Instead he argues directly from the premise that FP probably is not reducible to neuroscience to the conclusion that FP probably is false. So his argument is fallacious, in light of token-token identity theory as an alternative possible account of the relation between FP and neuroscience. He is just mistaken to assume that FP must be reducible to neuroscience in order to be compatible with it.

II

Let us now consider Stich's reasons for claiming that FP probably will not prove compatible with a developed cognitive science (henceforth CS). Unlike Churchland, Stich does not assume that FP must be reducible to more comprehensive lower-level theories in order to be compatible with them. We shall say more presently about the way he thinks FP must fit with these theories.

Stich offers two arguments against the compatibility of FP and CS; we shall examine these in this section and the next. The first argument purports to show that the overall causal organization of the cognitive system probably does not conform with the causal organization which FP ascribes to it. The argument runs as follows. Events which satisfy a given sortal predicate of the form ". . . is a belief that p" are supposed to have typical behavioral effects of both verbal and nonverbal kinds. On the verbal side, the events in this class are ones which typically cause the subject, under appropriate elicitation conditions, to utter an assertion that p. On the nonverbal side, these events are ones which, in combination with a subject's other beliefs, desires, and the like, typically cause the subject to perform those actions which FP says are appropriate to the combination of that belief with those other propositional attitudes. But recent experimental evidence suggests, according to Stich, that the psychological events which control nonverbal behavior are essentially independent of those which control verbal behavior—and hence that the cognitive system simply does not contain events which, taken singly, occupy the causal role which FP assigns to beliefs. If these experimental results prove generalizable, and if CS subsequently develops in the direction of positing separate, largely independent, cognitive subsystems for the control of verbal and nonverbal behavior respectively, then we will be forced to conclude, argues Stich, that there are no such things as beliefs.

One of his central empirical examples is a study in attribution theory, performed by Storms and Nisbett (1970). He describes its first phase this way:

> Storms and Nisbett . . . asked insomniac subjects to record the time they went to bed and the time they finally fell asleep. After several days of record keeping, one group of subjects (the "arousal" group) was given a placebo pill

to take fifteen minutes before going to bed. They were told that the pill would produce rapid heart rate, breathing irregularities, bodily warmth and alertness, which are just the typical symptoms of insomnia. A second group of subjects (the "relaxation" group) was told that the pills would produce the opposite symptoms: lowered heart rate, breathing rate, body temperature and alertness. Attribution theory predicts that the arousal group subjects would get to sleep *faster* on the nights they took the pills, because they would attribute their symptoms to the pills rather than to the emotionally laden thoughts that were running through their minds. It also predicts that subjects in the relaxation group will take *longer* to get to sleep. Since their symptoms persist despite having taken a pill intended to relieve the symptoms, they will infer that their emotionally laden thoughts must be particularly disturbing to them. And this belief will upset them further, making it all that much harder to get to sleep. Remarkably enough, both of these predictions were borne out. Arousal group subjects got to sleep 28 percent faster on the nights they took the pill, while relaxation subjects took 42 percent longer to get to sleep (Stich, 1983a, p. 232; this volume, p. 103).

What Stich finds particularly significant is the second phase of this study. After the completion of the initial insomnia experiments, the members of the arousal group were informed that they had gotten to sleep more quickly after taking the pill, and the members of the relaxation group were informed that they had taken longer to fall asleep. They were asked *why* this happened, and Nisbett and Wilson report the following pattern of responses:

> Arousal subjects typically replied that they usually found it easier to get to sleep later in the week, or that they had taken an exam that had worried them but had done well on it and could now relax, or that problems with a roommate or girlfriend seemed on their way to resolution. Relaxation subjects were able to find similar sorts of reasons to explain their increased sleeplessness. When subjects were asked if they had thought about the pills at all before getting to sleep, they almost uniformly insisted that after taking the pills they had completely forgotten about them. When asked if it had occurred to them that the pill might be producing (or counteracting) the arousal symptoms, they reiterated their insistence that they had not thought about the pills at all after taking them. Finally, the experimental hypothesis and the postulated attribution process were described in detail. Subjects showed no recognition of the hypothesized process and . . . made little pretense of believing that *any* of the subjects could have gone through such processes (Nisbett and Wilson, 1977, p. 238).

It is very likely, given the data from the first phase of the study, that the cognitive mechanisms which controlled the subjects' verbal responses in the second phase were largely distinct from the cognitive mechanisms which influenced their actual sleep patterns. And in numerous other studies in the literature of attribution theory and cognitive dissonance theory, the data support a similar conclusion: the mechanisms which control an initial piece of nonverbal behavior are largely distinct from the mechanisms which control the subject's subsequent verbal accounts of the reasons for that behavior.[7]

Stich, if we understand his argument correctly, draws three further conclusions. (1) In cases of the sort described, there is no cogent and consistent way to ascribe beliefs and desires; for FP typically attributes both verbal and nonverbal behavioral effects to particular beliefs and desires, but in these cases the cognitive causes of the nonverbal behavior are distinct from the cognitive causes of the verbal behavior, and hence neither kind of cause can comfortably be identified with a belief or desire. (2) It is likely that *in general* our verbal behavior is controlled by cognitive mechanisms different from those that control our nonverbal behavior; for the Storms-Nisbett pattern emerges in a broad range of studies in attribution theory and dissonance theory. From (1) and (2) he concludes: (3) It is likely that FP is radically false, that is, that humans do not undergo beliefs and desires.

We do not dispute the contention that in a surprising number of cases, as revealed by studies in attribution theory and dissonance theory, the mental states and processes which cause an initial item of nonverbal behavior are distinct from the states and processes which cause a subject's subsequent remarks about the etiology of that behavior. But we deny that either (1) or (2) is warranted by this contention. And without (1) or (2), of course the argument for (3) collapses.

Consider (1). Is there really a problem in consistently ascribing beliefs, desires, and other folk-psychological states in light of the phenomena described in the Storms-Nisbett study, for instance? No. For we can appeal to *unconscious* beliefs, desires, and inferences. Although FP asserts that beliefs and desires *normally* give rise to their own verbal expression under appropriate elicitation conditions, it does not assert this about unconscious beliefs and desires. On the contrary, part of what it means to say that a mental event is unconscious is that it lacks the usual sorts of direct causal influence over verbal behavior. Thus we have available the following natural and plausible folk-psychological account of the subjects' behavior in the Storms-Nisbett study: their initial non-verbal behavior was caused by unconscious beliefs and inferences, whereas their subsequent verbal behavior was caused by distinct, conscious, beliefs about the likely causes of their initial nonverbal behavior. In short, FP does not break down in such cases, because one has the option—the natural and plausible option—of positing unconscious folk-psychological causes.

There is a temptation, we realize, to identify FP with "what common sense would say," and to take the fact that the Storms/Nisbett results confute our common-sense expectations as automatically falsifying some component of FP. But this temptation should be resisted. Common sense would not postulate the relevant unconscious beliefs and desires. But once we *do* postulate them, perhaps on the basis of rather subtle nonverbal behavioral evidence, FP seems to yield the *correct* predictions about how the subjects will perform in Storms and Nisbett's study.

Indeed, as we understand the views of psychologists like Storms, Nisbett, and Wilson who cite such studies as evidence that verbal and nonverbal behavior often are under separate cognitive controls, this appeal to unconscious folk-psychological causes is precisely the theoretical move *they* are making concerning such cases. Attribution theory and cognitive dissonance theory give center stage to folk-psychological notions like desire and belief. Accordingly, the dual control thesis is nothing other than the folk-psychological thesis just stated: it is the claim that unconscious beliefs and inferences cause the subjects' initial nonverbal behavior, whereas distinct conscious beliefs (which constitute hypotheses about the causes of their original behavior) cause their subsequent verbal behavior.[8] Notice how Stich himself, in the above quoted passage, describes the first phase of the Storms-Nisbett study. "Attribution theory," he says, "predicts that subjects in the relaxation group will *infer* that their emotionally laden thoughts must be particularly disturbing to them. And this *belief* will upset them further . . ." (emphasis ours). Now Stich may have in mind a way of reinterpreting these claims so that the notions of belief and inference they employ are very different from the FP-notions, but in the absence of such a reinterpretation, his contention that beliefs and belief-generating mechanisms cannot be cogently ascribed to subjects like those of Storms and Nisbett is quite unfounded.

Our construal of the dual-control thesis assumes, of course, that it makes sense to speak of beliefs and other mental events as unconscious. But Storms, Nisbett, and Wilson claim quite explicitly that there can be nonverbal behavioral criteria which warrant the ascription of beliefs and other mental events even when a subject's verbal behavior appears inconsistent with the existence of such events.[9]

It may well be that the appeal to these criteria — and to unconscious beliefs and inferences generally — constitutes an extension and partial modification of traditional FP; but even if it does, this is hardly a wholesale rejection of folk-psychological notions. On the contrary, the very naturalness of the appeal to unconscious folk-psychological causes reflects the fact that the overall causal architecture posited by FP remains largely intact even when we introduce the conscious/unconscious distinction.

So conclusion (1) should be rejected. This means that even if (2) were accepted, FP would not necessarily be undermined. But conclusion (2) should be rejected in any case. From the fact that unconscious mental mechanisms control our nonverbal behavior in a surprising number of cases, one may not reasonably infer that *in general* our verbal and nonverbal behavior are under separate cognitive control. The findings of attribution theory and dissonance theory, although they do caution us against excessive confidence in our ability to know ourselves, fall far short of establishing such a sweeping conclusion. In this connection it is useful to examine the remarks of Timothy Wilson (1985), a leading advocate of the idea of "dual cognitive control" over verbal and nonverbal behavior respectively. Stich makes much of Wilson's position, which he construes as the radical thesis that our own statements concerning the mental events that cause our nonverbal behavior are virtually *never* caused by those mental events themselves. But this is a mistaken interpretation, in our judgment. Wilson articulates his proposal this way:

> In essence the argument is that there are two mental systems: One which mediates behavior (especially unregulated behavior), is largely nonconscious, and is perhaps, the older of the two systems in evolutionary terms. The other, perhaps newer system, is largely conscious, and its function is to attempt to verbalize, explain, and communicate mental states. As argued earlier, people often have direct access to their mental states, and in these cases the verbal system can make direct and accurate reports. When there is limited access, however, the verbal system makes inferences about what these processes and states might be.

It seems clear from this passage that Wilson is not suggesting that *in general* our utterances about our mental events are generated by cognitive events other than those mental events themselves. Rather, he is acknowledging that people often have direct conscious access to the mental causes of their behavior, and that at such times these states typically cause accurate reports about themselves. Only where access is limited, where the events are not conscious, are our subsequent utterances caused by inferences about likely mental causes rather than by the mental events themselves.[10]

Wilson goes on to suggest that it will typically be events that are results of considerable processing which will be relatively inaccessible to the agent, and that "more immediate states" (such as precognitive states) may be much more accessible. Moreover, there are many cases which do seem to involve complex processing in which people exhibit integrated verbal and nonverbal behavior in a way that seems difficult to understand if the systems controlling verbal and nonverbal behavior are entirely independent. Consider engaging in some complicated task while explaining to someone else what you are doing—as in working logic problems on the blackboard as one lectures. It is hard to see how such an integrated performance is possible performance is possible if the actor has no access to the beliefs which cause the nonverbal portion of his behavior (other than via after-the-fact inferences).

We conclude, then, that neither conclusion (1) nor conclusion (2) is warranted by the kinds of psychological studies Stich cites, and hence that his "dual-control" argument against FP is not successful.

III

The "dual-control" argument does not presuppose any particular conception of how FP must be related to CS in order for the two theories to be compatible. Stich's second argument for the incompatibility of FP and CS, however, does rest upon such a conception. In particular, he requires that beliefs, desires, and the like should be identical with "naturally isolable" parts of the cognitive system; he calls this the *modularity* principle.

Stich does not attempt to make this principle precise, but instead leaves the notion of natural isolability at the intuitive level. Accordingly, we too shall use this notion without explication; we think the points we shall make are applicable under any reasonable construal.

Stich argues that FP probably fails to satisfy the modularity principle *vis-à-vis* CS, and hence that there probably are no such events as beliefs, desires, and the like. He focuses on recent trends within CS concerning the modeling of human memory. Some early models of memory organization, he points out, postulate a distinct sentence or sentence-like structure for each memory. These models are clearly modular, he says, because the distinct sentence-like structures can be identified with separate beliefs. Another sort of model, motivated largely by the desire to explain how people are able to locate information relevant to a given task at hand, treats memory as a complex network of nodes and labeled links, with the nodes representing concepts and the links representing various sorts of relations among concepts. Stich regards network models as "still quite far over to the modular end of the spectrum," however, because in a network model it is generally unproblematic to isolate the part of the network which would play the causal role characteristic of a given belief (1983, p. 239; this volume, p. 110).

But in recent years, he points out, several leading theorists have become quite skeptical about highly modular models, largely because such models do not seem capable of handling the enormous amount of nondeductive inference which is involved in language use and comprehension. Citing Minsky (1981) as an example, Stich writes:

> In a . . . recent paper Minsky elaborates what he calls a "Society of Mind"
> view in which the mechanisms of thought are divided into many separate

"specialists that communicate only sparsely" (p. 95). On the picture Minsky suggests, none of the distinct units or parts of the mental model "have meanings in themselves" (p. 100) and thus none can be identified with individual beliefs, desires, etc. Modularity—I borrow the term from Minsky—is violated in a radical way since meaning or content emerges only from "great webs of structure" (p. 100) and no natural part of the system can be correlated with "explicit" or verbally expressible beliefs (1983a, p. 241; this volume, p. 112).

If Minsky's "Society of Mind" view is the direction that CS will take in the future, then presumably modularity will indeed be violated in a radical way.

We are quite prepared to acknowledge that CS may well become dramatically nonmodular, and hence that the modularity principle may well end up being refuted empirically.[11] Indeed, if one considers the relation between FP and neuroscience—or even the relation between CS and neuroscience, for that matter—one would expect modularity to be violated in an even more dramatic way. There are tens of billions of neurons in the human central nervous system, and thousands of billions of synaptic junctures; so if the "naturally isolable" events of neuroscience are events like neuron-firings and intersynaptic transfers of electrical energy, then it is entirely likely that the naturally-isolable events of both FP and CS will involve "great webs of structure" neurally—that is, great conglomerations of naturally-isolable neural events.

So if modularity is really needed in order for FP-events to exist and to enter into causal relations, then the failure of modularity would indeed spell big trouble for the proffered compatibility of FP with lower-level theories. In fact, it also would spell big trouble for the proffered compatibility of *cognitive science* with lower-level theories like neuroscience; thus Stich's style of argument appears to prove more than he, as an advocate of CS, would like it to prove! And indeed, the demand for modularity even spells big trouble for the compatibility of *neuroscience* with physics-chemistry; for, if the natural-kind predicates of physics-chemistry are predicates like ". . . is an electron" and ". . . is a hydrogen atom," then it is most unlikely that entities falling under neuroscientific natural-kind terms like ". . . is a neuron" will also fall under physico-chemical natural kind terms. Rather, neurons and neuron-firings are entities which, from the physico-chemical point of view, involve "great webs of structure."

We point out these generalizations of Stich's argument because we think they make clear the enormous implausibility of the modularity principle as an intertheoretic compatibility condition. Surely objects like neurons, or events like neuron-firings, don't have to be "naturally isolable" from the perspective of fundamental physics-chemistry in order to be compatible with it; rather, it is enough that they be fully decomposable into naturally-isolable *parts*. Similarly, cognitive-psychological events don't have to be naturally isolable from the perspective of neuroscience in order to be compatible with it; again, it is enough that these events are decomposable into naturally-isolable parts.[12]

The situation is exactly the same, we submit, for folk-psychological events in relation to the events of CS. Perhaps Minsky is right, and the role of a belief (say) is typically played by a vast, highly gerrymandered, conglomeration of CS-events. This doesn't show that the belief doesn't exist. On the contrary, all it shows is that the belief is an enormously *complex* event, consisting of numerous CS-events as parts.[13] After all, we expect those CS-events, in turn, to consist of numerous neurological events as parts; and we expect those neurological events, in their turn, to consist of numerous physico-chemical events as parts.

Stich never attempts to justify the modularity principle as a compatibility condition, just as Churchland never attempts to justify the demand for reducibility. Thus Stich's modularity argument suffers the same defect as Churchland's reducibility argument: viz., it rests upon an unsubstantiated, and implausibly strong, conception of how FP must mesh with more comprehensive lower-level theories in order to be compatible with them. (It is important to note, incidentally, that even though Stich does not demand reducibility, still in a certain way his notion of intertheoretic fit is actually *stronger* than Churchland's notion. For, even a reductionist need not require that entities falling under higher-level natural-kind sortals should be naturally isolable from the lower-level perspective. A reductionist does require that there should be biconditional bridge laws correlating the higher-level sortals with open sentences of the lower-level theory, but these lower-level open sentences can be quite complex, rather than being (say) simple natural-kind sortal predicates.)

Although Stich offers no explicit rationale for the modularity principle, perhaps he is influenced by the following line of thought:

> The propositional attitudes of FP involve a relation between a cognizer and a sentence-like "internal representation" (Fodor 1975, 1978; Field 1978; Lycan 1982). If FP is true, then part of the task of CS is to explain the nature of these internal representations. But CS cannot do this unless internal representations fall under its natural-kind predicates, or at any rate are *somehow* "naturally isolable" within the cognitive system. And if Minsky's "Society of Mind" approach is the direction CS will take in the future, then this requirement will not be met. Hence if the events of FP do not obey the modularity principle vis-à-vis CS, then FP must be radically false.

One reason we have for rejecting this line of reasoning is that we doubt whether propositional attitudes really involve internal representations – or whether they have "objects" at all. (Cf. footnote 1 above.) Furthermore, if Minsky's approach did become the general trend in CS, then presumably this fact too would tend to undermine the claim that sentence-like representations are involved in the propositional attitudes — just as his approach already tends to undermine the claim that such representations are involved in the non-deductive inference that underlies the use and comprehension of language.

Moreover, even if the internal-representation view is correct, and even if part of the task of CS is to give an account of these representations, approaches like Minsky's would not necessarily render CS incapable of accomplishing this task. For it might turn out that the "atoms" of CS are the components of Minsky's Society of Minds, and that CS also posits complex, sentence-like "molecules" constructed from these "atoms." The molecules might be *very* complex, and highly gerrymandered. If so, then they won't count as naturally isolable components of the cognitive system when that system is viewed from the atomic perspective; however, they *will* count as naturally isolable from the higher, molecular perspective. (We think it more likely, however, that if the "Society of Minds" approach proves generalizable within CS, then the result will be a widespread rejection of the mental-representation view of propositional attitudes — a view which, as we said, we think is mistaken anyway.)

Another way one might try to defend the modularity principle is by appeal to Davidsonian considerations involving the role of laws in causality. One might argue (i) that FP contains no strict laws, but only so-called "heteronomic" generalizations (Davidson 1970b, 1974); (ii) that two events are related as cause and effect only if they have descriptions which instantiate a strict law (Davidson 1967); and (iii) that event-descriptions which instantiate a strict law of a given theory must pick out events that are naturally isolable from the perspective of that theory. From these three claims, plus the assumption that folk-psychological events enter into causal relations, the modularity principle seems to follow.[14]

But suppose an event c causes an event e, where c and e both are naturally isolable from the perspective of FP. Suppose that c is fully decomposable into events which respectively satisfy the sortal predicates $F_1 \ldots F_m$ of an underlying homonomic theory T, and hence that these component-events all are naturally isolable from the perspective of T; suppose also that these events jointly satisfy a (possibly quite complex) description D_1 of T which specifies their structural interconnection. Likewise, suppose that e is fully decomposable into events which respectively satisfy the sortal predicates $G_1 \ldots G_n$ of T, and hence that these components events all are naturally isolable from the perspective of T; suppose also that these component events jointly satisfy a description D_2 of T which specifies their structural interconnection. Now even if c and e do not have natural-kind descriptions under which they themselves instantiate a strict law of T, nevertheless the strict laws of T might jointly entail an assertion of the following form:

For any event x, if x is fully decomposable into events $x_1 \ldots x_m$ such that $D_1(x_1 \ldots x_m)$ and $F_1(x_1)$, $F_2(x_2)$, and $\ldots$ and $F_m(x_m)$, then x will be followed by an event y that is fully decomposable into events $y_1 \ldots y_n$ such that $D_2(y_1 \ldots y_n)$ and $G_1(y_1)$, $G_2(y_2)$, and $\ldots G_n(y_n)$.

We see no reason why the causal relation between c and e cannot rest upon a regularity of this form. One either can call such regularities strict laws, in which case claim (iii) above will be false; or else one can reserve the term 'strict law' for the relatively simple nomic postulates of a homonomic theory, rather than the set of logical consequences of those postulates — in which case claim (ii) above will be false. Either way, the Davidson-inspired argument for the modularity principle has a false premise. (Incidentally, we do not mean to attribute the argument to Davidson himself, since we doubt whether he would accept claim (iii).)

IV

We have been arguing that FP-events might well be identical with arbitrarily complex, highly gerrymandered, CS-events which themselves are not naturally-isolable relative to CS, but instead are fully decomposable into *parts* which have this feature. Of course, if FP-events really do exist, then they will have to accord with the causal architecture of FP; that is, they will have to be causally related to each other, to sensation, and to behavior in the ways that FP says they are. Indeed, as functionalists in philosophy of mind have so often stressed, the causal or functional principles of FP are crucial to the very individuation of FP-events; what makes a given event count (say) as a token belief-that-p is, to a considerable extent, the fact that it occupies the causal role which FP assigns to tokens of that belief-type.[15]

So if our nonmodular picture of the relation between FP and CS is to be plausible, it is essential that complex, gerrymandered events can properly be considered causes, even if they involve "great webs of structure" relative to lower-level theory. While a detailed discussion must be beyond the scope of this paper, a brief consideration of the causal status of complex events will help to clarify our argument.

Let us say that an event e *minimally* causes an event f just in case e causes f and no proper part of e causes f. We want to advance two claims about minimal causation, each of which will receive some support below. First, even if an event e is a genuine cause of an event f, nevertheless f also might be caused by some event which is a proper part of e; thus e might be a genuine cause of f without being a minimal cause of f. Second, if e causes not only f but also some other event g, then it might be that the part of e which minimally causes f is different from the part of e which minimally causes g.[16]

These two facts are important because they make it relatively easy for events to exist which satisfy the causal principles of FP. If FP attributes both the event f and the event g to a single cause e at time t, and in fact there are distinct (though perhaps partially overlapping) events e_1 and e_2 such that e_1 minimally causes f (at t) and e_2 minimally causes g (at t), this does not necessarily falsify FP. For, e might well have both e_1 and e_2 as *parts;* indeed, it might well have as parts all those events which minimally cause (at t) one or another of the various events which FP says are effects (at t) of e. As long as this complex event is itself the effect of whatever prior events FP says are e's causes, the event will be (identical with) e.

The upshot is that FP could very easily turn out to be true, even if modularity is dramatically violated. Not only can FP-events be complex and highly gerrymandered, with numerous naturally-isolable CS-events as parts, but any given FP-event e can cause its effects in a conglomerative manner, with different effects having different parts of e as their respective minimal causes.[17]

V

Perhaps it will be objected that our analysis is too permissive; that unless we adopt Stich's modularity condition, over and above the requirement that FP-events conform to the causal architecture which FP assigns to them, we impose no non-trivial constraints on the truth conditions of upper-level causal claims; that is, we allow such claims to come out true regardless of the character of the theory that underlies them. We shall conclude by considering this objection.

It is clear that some underlying theories are inconsistent with the truth of some upper-level causal claims. For example, if the world is anything like the way our current chemistry and physics describe it, then possession by the devil cannot be a cause of any psychological disorders, and loss of phlogiston cannot be a cause of the chemical changes undergone by metals when they oxidize. To consider a case which is closer to home, it seems clear that if we are Skinnerian creatures—that is, creatures whose behavior is fully described and explained by the basic principles of Skinnerian psychology—then folk-psychological claims postulating beliefs, desires, and the like as among the causes of our behavior cannot be true.

The worry under consideration is that our nonmodular approach to intertheoretic compatibility is so liberal that it would allow claims of the above sort to come out true even though they seem clearly inconsistent with underlying theory. We shall argue that this worry is ill-founded.

It will be helpful to distinguish two different conceptions or expectations regarding the epistemic role of a radical failure of fit or integration between an upper-level theory and an underlying theory. On the first conception one thinks of this failure of fit as an important epistemic route to the falsity of the upper-level theory, where that falsity may not be obvious otherwise. The idea is that even if direct evidence at the upper level does not clearly point to the falsity of an upper-level theory (and indeed may even seem to support this theory), nonetheless we can detect the falsity of the upper-level theory by noting its failure to fit in some appropriate way with some underlying theory which we have strong reason to believe is true. Clearly, both Stich and Churchland argue in accordance with this conception.

We find more plausible an importantly different conception of the epistemic significance of failure of fit between an upper-level and a lower-level theory. We do not deny, of course, that lower-level theories can be incompatible with upper-level theories. We do doubt, however, whether it is common or typical that one can know that an upper-level theory is false only by noting its failure to fit with a true underlying theory. More typically, when an upper-level theory is false there is direct evidence for this fact, independently of the failure of fit. The incompatibility arises not because of a failure of modularity, but rather because there simply are no events — either simple or complex — which have all the features which the upper-level theory attributes to the events it posits. Crudely put, the idea is that while various theories of juvenile delinquency or learning behavior can be inconsistent with neurophysiological theories or with physical theories, the former are *likely* to be confirmable or disconfirmable by the sorts of evidence available to sociologists and psychologists. It will be rare for a theory to be supported by a very wide range of evidence available to the sociologist or the psychologist and yet turn out to be radically false (because its ontology fails to mesh properly with that of some underlying theory). So our conception suggests a greater epistemological autonomy for upper-level disciplines like psychology than does a conception of intertheoretic compatibility which incorporates a modularity condition.

We have emphasized this epistemological point because it bears directly on worries about the permissiveness of our nonmodular conception. While our approach is by no means trivial in the sense that it allows every upper-level theory to be compatible with every underlying theory, it is permissive and deflationary in that, at least for a wide variety of cases, considerations of fit will not play the sort of independent normative role which they would play under a modularity requirement.

With this in mind, let us return to the examples with which we began this section. Consider first the case of possession by the devil. Like other causally explanatory notions, the notion of possession by the devil is to be understood, in large measure, in terms of the role it plays in a network of causal relations. Possession by the devil causes or may cause various kinds of pathological behavior. Such effects may be diminished or eliminated by the use of appropriate religious ceremonies (e.g., prayers or exorcism). When behavior is due to possession by the devil, there is no reason to suppose that it will be affected by other forms of treatment (drugs, nutritional changes, psychotherapy, etc.). The state of possession is itself the effect of the activities of a being who has many other extraordinary powers.

Now if an event of possession by the devil (call it d) is to be a cause of a certain bit of behavior (e.g., jabbering incoherently), then d must, on our analysis, be identifiable with some event (call it e) describable in terms of the predicates of our underlying theory; and it must be the case that, given this identification, at least most of the other causal generalizations in which d is held to figure, according to the theory of devil-possession, should come out true. (Although our conception of intertheoretic fit countenances failures of modularity, it does insist that the identifications we make preserve the "causal architecture" of the upper-level theory.) We submit that no matter how large and complex one makes the event e with which one proposes to identify d, and no matter how willing one may be to regard proper parts of e as causally efficacious, there is simply *no* plausible candidate for e which, given our present physical and chemical theory, will make the network of causal claims associated with possession by the devil come out mainly true. That is, there is simply no event e, however complex, which is linked by law to various forms of behavior associated with possession, which is inefficacious in producing such behavior when exorcism is used, which is shown by law to be produced by an agency having the properties of the devil, and so forth.

This example illustrates the general epistemological claim made above. In effect, we have argued that causal claims about possession by the devil are false not because of sophisticated considerations having to do with modularity (or with "smoothness of reduction"), but because the causal architecture associated with possession by the devil is radically mistaken; nothing stands in the network of causal relations with various other events in the way that possession by the devil is supposed to. We can see this immediately by noting that the falsity of claims attributing causal efficacy to devil-possession is, so to speak, directly discoverable without considerations having to do with chemistry, physics, or biology. If one were to run suitably controlled experiments, then presumably one would quickly discover that exorcism does not affect devil-possession type behavior, that certain other therapies do, and so forth.[18]

A similar set of observations seems relevant in connection with the allegation that our approach would permit causal claims about beliefs to be true even if we are Skinnerian creatures. FP asserts that beliefs, desires, and other propositional attitudes are related to one another in many and various ways, over and above their causal relations to sensation and behavior. Skinnerian theory, on the other hand, denies that we need to postulate such richly-interacting internal events in order to explain behavior, and it also denies that such events exist at all. Rather, the Skinnerian claims that the causal chains leading from environmental "stimulus" to behavioral "response" are largely isolated from one another, rather like the various parallel noninteracting communication-channels in a fiber-optics communications line; thus, whatever internal events are involved in any particular stimulus-response pairing will not bear very many significant causal relations to the internal events that are involved in other stimulus-response pairings; that is, the Skinnerian claims that as a matter of empirical fact, the generalizations linking stimuli and behavior are so simple and straightforward that they are incompatible with the existence of internal events which interact in the rich way which folk-psychological events are supposed to interact with one another. So if the Skinnerian is right, then there simply are no internal events, in humans or in other organisms, which bear all the causal relations to sensation, to behavior, and to one another which FP assigns to beliefs, desires, and the like. Thus our non-modular conception of intertheoretic fit would indeed by violated if humans should turn out to be mere Skinnerian creatures. Accordingly, this conception is not unduly permissive after all.

This example also illustrates the epistemological claims made above. It is satisfaction of the "causal architecture" of FP, by some set of (possibly complex) events in the central nervous system, which is crucial to the truth of FP. Hence if we are Skinnerian creatures, so that the causal architecture assumed by FP is not instantiated in us by any events either simple or complex, then presumably this fact will show up at the level of a relatively coarse-grained analysis of our molar behavior. Stimulus-response laws that are incompatible with the causal architecture of FP will be discoverable, and will be usable to explain and predict the full range of human behavior. Hence it will not be the case that FP seems to be largely true, according to the best available coarse-grained evidence, and yet turns out to be false merely because of failure to fit properly with some underlying theory.

The upshot, then, is that our approach seems exactly as permissive as it should be, and this fact speaks in its favor; by contrast, a modular conception of intertheoretic fit seems excessively strict, since it is unmotivated and it denies higher-level theories an adequate degree of epistemological autonomy. So, given (i) the notable failure, to date, of behaviorist-inspired psychology's efforts to unearth stimulus-response laws which are applicable to human behavior generally and which undercut the causal architecture of FP, (ii) the fact that folk-psychological notions seem to lie at the very heart of cognitivist theories like attribution theory and cognitive dissonance theory, and (iii) the fact that FP serves us very well in the everyday explanation and prediction of behavior, it seems very hard to deny that in all probability, folk psychology is here to stay.[19,20,21]

FOOTNOTES

[1]Actually, we regard the example in the first paragraph as a schema which yields a whole range of instances when various sentences are substituted for the letter 'p' and various sortal predicates are substituted for the dummy phrase 'of kind K'. (The word 'someone,' though, functions as a quantificational term; under appropriate regimentation, it would go over into a universal quantifier whose scope is the whole schema.) We prefer to think of predicates of the form ". . . believes that p" as what Quine (1970) calls *attitudinatives* — i.e., complex one-place predicates constructed by appending a predicate-forming operator ('believes that') to a sentence. On this view, propositional attitudes have no "objects," since they are not relational states. For further discussion see Horgan (1988).

[2]For visual perception, see, e.g. Gregory (1970).

[3]For example, eighteenth century chemical theories attempted to explain such properties of metals as their shininess and ductility by appeal to the same factors which were also thought to explain the compound-forming behavior of metals. Chemical theories such as Lavosier's focused just on compounds, and originally were criticized for their failure to provide also a unified explanation of metallic shininess and ductility.

[4]For some striking evidence that situational theories are more empirically adequate, and hence that this change has been a progressive one, see Nisbett and Ross (1980).

[5]Thus his critical remarks on Fodor (1975), and in general on cognitive psychological theories that take information to be stored in sentential form; cf. Churchland (this volume, pp. 51 ff.).

[6]In order to elevate anomalous monism into a full-fledged version of materialism, one must add to it an account of the metaphysical status of mental state-types (properties) *vis à vis* physico-chemical state-types. The appropriate doctrine, we think, is one also propounded by Davidson (1970b, 1974): viz., that mental properties are *supervenient* upon physical ones. Several philosophers recently have developed this idea, arguing that materialism should incorporate some sort of supervenience thesis. Cf. Kim (1978, 1982); Haugeland (1982); Horgan (1981b, 1982b); and Lewis (1983). Also see the papers collected in the Spindel issue of *The Southern Journal of Philosophy,* 22, 1984.

[7]For surveys of the relevant literature, see Nisbett and Wilson (1977), and Wilson (1985).

[8]At any rate, this is what the dual-control thesis amounts to as regards the Storms/Nisbett study. Other kinds of mental events besides beliefs and inferences might sometimes be involved too.

[9]See, for instance, Wilson (unpublished), pp. 7 ff.

[10]Still, one can understand why Stich would be led to attribute the radical dual-control thesis to Wilson, even though Wilson evidently does not actually hold this view. Stich quotes from what evidently was an earlier version of the above-quoted passage, wherein Wilson said that the function of the verbal system "is to attempt to verbalize, explain and communicate what is occurring in the unconscious system." Admittedly, this earlier wording suggests that in verbalizing our mental states we *never* have conscious access to those states. But the present passage, with its explicit acknowledgment of frequent conscious access, evidently cancels this suggestion, along with any implicit commitment to the radical dual-control thesis.

[11]Although we think it quite possible that CS will become non-modular at its most fundamental levels, we also believe that certain higher-level branches of theoretical psychology probably not only will remain modular, but will continue to employ the concepts of FP itself. Attribution theory is a case in point. (By a "higher-level" psychological theory we mean one which posits events that are wholes whose parts are the events posited by "lower-level" psychological theories. More on this below.)

[12]It is worth noting another respect in which Stich's (and Churchland's) arguments seem to lead to sweeping and implausibly strong conclusions. Much formal theory in the social sciences

involves ascribing to individual actors states which are recognizably like, or recognizably descended from, the FP notions of belief and desire. Within economic and game theory, for example, individual actors are thought of as having indifference curves, utility schedules, or preference orderings over various possible outcomes, and beliefs about the subjective probabilities of these outcomes. Within economic theories of voting or political party behavior, similar assumptions are made. Even among theorists of voting behavior who reject the "economic" approach, typically there are appeals to voters' beliefs and attitudes to explain behavior. (See, for example, Campbell *et al.* (1960).) Clearly, if Stich's modularity requirement and Churchland's smoothness of reduction requirement are not satisfied by the FP notions of belief and desire, then they are unlikely to be satisfied by the notions of utility, degree of belief, and so forth employed by such theories. Thus Stich and Churchland seem to have produced general arguments which, if cogent, would show—quite independently of any detailed empirical investigation of the actual behavior of markets, voters, etc.—that all these theories must be false, at least on their most natural interpretation.

[13]A complex event of the relevant kind might be a mereological sum, or *fusion,* of simpler events; alternatively, it might be an entity distinct from this event-fusion. We shall take no stand on this matter here. (The issue is closely related to the question whether an entity like a ship is identical with the fusion of its physical parts, or is instead an entity distinct from this fusion, with different intraworld and transworld identity conditions.) To our knowledge, the most explicit and well-developed theory of parts and wholes for events is that of Thomson (1977); event-fusions are the only kinds of complex events she explicitly countenances.

[14]This Davidsonian argument was suggested to us by Stich himself, in conversation.

[15]But as the famous case of Twin Earth (Putnam, 1975a) seems to show, an event's causal role is not the only factor relevant to its folk-psychological individuation. Our *doppelgangers* on Twin Earth don't undergo tokens of the type *believing that water is good to drink,* even though they do undergo events that are functionally indistinguishable from our own token beliefs that water is good to drink. The trouble is that the stuff they call "water" isn't water at all. Cf. Burge (1979).

[16]While a full defense of these claims must be beyond the scope of this paper, we think they are required for the truth of many causal statements in contexts where highly developed and precise formal theories are not available. Consider the claims (a) that application of a certain fertilizer causes plants to increase in mean height, and also causes them to increase in leaf width; (b) that following a certain study routine R causes an increase in SAT verbal scores, and also causes an increase in SAT mathematical scores; or (c) that certain child-rearing practices cause an increase in the incidence of juvenile delinquency in certain populations. There is an enormous literature detailing complex and ingenious statistical techniques for testing such claims. (Fischer (1935) is an early classic, inspired largely by problems connected with testing claims like (a); and many books on "causal modeling," like Blalock (1971), discuss procedures that are relevant to (b) and (c).) These techniques might well establish that the three claims are true. Yet the cases described in (a), (b), and (c) can easily fail to be minimal causes: the fertilizer will commonly be a mixture, containing compounds which are inert, or which have other effects on the plant besides those mentioned in (a); and it seems implausible to suppose that every feature or detail of study routine R or child rearing practice C is causally necessary for the above effects. (Typically, we have no practical way of determining what the minimal causes in such cases are.) Thus (a) can be true even though the fertilizer is a mixture of several distinct compounds, one of which causes increase in height (but not increase in leaf width) while the other causes increase in leaf width (but not height). Similarly, (b) can be true even though different aspects of study routine R are responsible for the increases in math and in verbal scores. (See Thomson (1977) for further defense of the claim that genuine causes don't have to be minimal causes.)

[17]The point about conglomerative causation is also relevant to Stich's dual-control argument against FP. Even if verbal and nonverbal behavior should turn out to have largely separate

minimal causes, FP could be true anyway; for, FP-events might be complexes of the minimal causes, and these complex events might be genuine causes (albeit nonminimal causes) of both the verbal and the nonverbal behavior. (We should stress, however, that we are *not* claiming that if the dual-control thesis is true, then whenever a subject is in some state B of his nonverbal behavioral system and some state V of his verbal system, it will always be possible, consistently with FP, to ascribe to him some single folk-psychological cause of both his verbal and nonverbal behavior. Whether this will be possible depends upon the specific states V and B and upon the behavior they cause. In the Storms-Wilson insomnia experiment, for example, the state B (subjects' attribution of their symptoms to pills) which causes the arousal group to fall asleep is not merely distinct from the state V which causes their verbal behavior (denial that the above attribution had anything to do with their falling asleep); but in addition, these two states cannot, consistently with the causal principles embodied in FP, be treated as components of some single belief.)

[18]Of course, it might be that some cases of exorcism appear to be efficacious, but this is only because they involve certain features which are also cited by other, more secular, theories (e.g., reassuring the "possessed" person, giving him attention, etc.). Establishing this can require ingenuity in experimental design, but poses no problem in principle. It is just false that we could never obtain direct experimental evidence (distinct from considerations of modularity or failure of fit) that would make it rational to reject the claim that exorcism is efficacious in itself, by virtue of dislodging the devil.

[19]Although we have assumed throughout that folk-psychological events are complex events consisting of lower-level events as their parts, we want to acknowledge that it may be possible to defend the compatibility of FP and CS without this assumption. Jaegwon Kim (1966, 1969, 1973) holds that an event is an entity consisting in the instantiation of a property by an object at a time, and that mental events consist in the instantiation of mental properties by individuals at times. Under this approach, it is unclear whether lower-level events can sensibly be treated as parts of FP-events. Nevertheless, an advocate of Kim's theory of events still might be able to argue that FP-events exist and bear all the causal relations to one another that FP says they do. For he might be able to argue that these events are supervenient upon groups of lower-level events, and that supervenience transmits causal efficacy. Cf. Kim (1979, 1982, 1984).

[20]Throughout this paper we have assumed, as is usual, that if everyday folk-psychological statements are indeed true, then there really exist folk-psychological mental events—that is, token desires, token beliefs, and so forth. In fact, however, one of us (Horgan) thinks there are good reasons for denying the existence of events in general; cf. Horgan (1978, 1981a, 1982a). Horgan also thinks that if physico-chemical events exist, then normally there will be numerous classes of physico-chemical events from within someone's head which jointly meet all the causal conditions which would qualify a given class for identification with the class consisting of that person's folk-psychological mental events; and he takes this to indicate that even if physico-chemical events exist, and even if garden-variety folk-psychological statements (including statements about mental causation) are often true, nevertheless there really are no such entities as mental events; cf. Horgan and Tye (1985). We believe that the essential points of the present paper can be reformulated in a way which does not require the existence of mental events (even if physico-chemical events are assumed to exist), and also in a way which does not require the existence of any events at all. But our objective here has been the more limited one of defending FP within the framework of the ontology of events which is widely taken for granted in contemporary philosophy of mind.

[21]We thank Stephen Stich, William Tolhurst, and Michael Tye for helpful comments on an earlier version of this chapter.

9 The Relationship Between Scientific Psychology and Common Sense Psychology*

Kathleen V. Wilkes
Oxford University, England

INTRODUCTION

Fashions in philosophy are curious things. Only a few years ago few people talked in terms of 'common sense' (or 'folk') psychology; instead they talked of 'the mind', 'the mental', 'the psychological'. But, suddenly, it has assumed center stage. This is primarily because of the recent interest in it *qua* scientific theory. Some (e.g. P. M. Churchland [this volume], P. S. Churchland [1986a], Stich [1983a]) see it as a would-be scientific theory, but a very inadequate and stagnating one which needs to be 'eliminated' and supplanted by something quite different. Others, for example Davidson [1970b, 1974], think that we are stuck with common sense psychology, but that it can never be tightened up into a genuine science, and that *therefore* psychology is not a science. (Revealingly, the title of his 1974 paper is 'Psychology as Philosophy'.) A third numerous group — in particular, many of those whose work is described sometimes as 'cognitive science,' and sometimes as 'philosophical psychology' (Fodor [1975, 1978], Field [1978], and Lycan [1981] are good examples) — think that it is basically all right as a fledgling science: 'We have no reason to doubt that it is possible to have a scientific psychology that vindicates common sense belief/desire explanation' (Fodor [1987], p. 16; this volume, p. 235). Such people expect that common sense psychological concepts will provide the conceptual framework within which 'theories' of action, of perception, and of thought will flourish.

I think that almost all these eminent characters miss the heart of the

*Reprinted from *Synthese* 89 (1991, pp. 15–39) by permission of the author and Kluwer Academic Publishers.

matter by a long chalk. I am 'for' common sense psychology; but not for the reasons that any of the above would wish to offer.

A note on the terminology. *Not* 'Folk Psychology'! This is too 'folksy'; once it is so baptised, it inevitably finds it hard to live down its folksiness. There is an inbuilt temptation to see it as twee, a bit primitive. And that is a very substantial mistake. So 'Common Sense Psychology,' hence 'CSP'. *Scientific* Psychology will be 'SP'.

In this chapter I try to do two things. First, to distinguish CSP from SP. Second, to draw out some implications of these claims; for instance, that the 'theories of action/perception' dreamed-up by philosophers in arm-chairs are and will be going nowhere; put more generally, the point is that the new and recently-fashionable label 'philosophical psychology' has no content — any more than 'philosophical physics,' or 'philosophical chemistry' would have any content, were anyone silly enough to invent them. There *is* room for an enterprise called 'the philosophy of mind'; there is also much room for the philosophy *of* psychology as one branch of the philosophy of science. But that's all: 'philosophical psychology' should have been aborted. So I shall offer *first:* the distinction between CSP and SP; *second,* some implications.

CSP *VERSUS* (?) SP

Ebbinghaus: 'Psychology has a long past and a short history.' What he meant was clear. I shall begin with the 'long past'; but as will quickly become apparent, description of CSP will entail discussion of SP too.

Long before we had written records humans had a language, they developed tools, and lived in a complex social environment. Social animals with a massive cranial capacity and high encephalization quotient,[1] living in a *complex* society — that is, I am not talking about sheep, which are gregarious/social, but which are also rather bird-brained, animals — have many problems. They have the problem of surviving in an environment that contains many possibilities and many dangers; but equally they must be able to coexist with their peers, to persuade them to undertake sometimes unpleasant tasks, to mollify, encourage, or support them, to find out when it is necessary to kill them off, to woo and win them in the face of rivals . . . and et cetera *ad indefinitum*. This requires a sophisticated ability to predict the actions of their conspecifics; to read expressions, interpret linguistic and nonlinguistic behaviour; to invent and use artifacts. The fact that we are still here suggests that we got much of it right.

Then came written records. The earliest such records we possess show how sophisticated common sense psychology was. Very early records, though, are somewhat scrappy; so I shall turn to the more familiar ground of the earliest Greek writings of major importance, Homer in particular. The descriptions of character and behaviour given by Homer—in the *Odyssey* especially, but also in the *Iliad*—are instantly recognisable today. Much surprises us, true: we find that in order to explain irrational behaviour, Homer pulls in the gods (whereas we, perhaps, pull in Freud). But Homer's understanding of the human psyche is as recognisable in 1990 as is Chaucer's, or Proust's. Plus ca. change. . . .

Moving on from Homer: why do we still stage the plays of Sophocles, Euripides, Aristophanes, Menander? (These are the more 'psychological' ancient Greek dramatists, especially Euripides.) Precisely because the chords struck by these writers still echo today; because the playwrights concerned had identified common strands, threads, preoccupations, concerns. Strawson: '[t]here is a massive central core of human thinking which has no history . . . there are categories and concepts which, in their most fundamental character, change not at all' ([1959], p. 10). However we need not stick just to the cerebral productions of playwrights and philosophers. How do generals win battles? By coming up with secure and well-founded predictions about what the opposing commander is planning, about the endurance, morale, and enthusiasm of his own forces, with ideas about how best to motivate them, and so forth—and this was as true when the Greeks were defeating Xerxes as it is when the Americans are confronting Saddam Hussein. The general point is that from the very start of human history, we have needed to be able to produce well-backed, sophisticated, and penetrating analyses of human behaviour and motivation . . . and that we did and do. The proper study of mankind not only is, but has to be, man. It will soon be clearer why I am spending so much time on this point; meanwhile I shall quote a telling passage from Dennett, which I can use to support the claim above. We do not need to cite Proust, or Dostoievsky, or Henry James, to illustrate the depth and detail of common sense psychology, because:

> watching a film with a highly original and unstereotypical plot, we see the hero smile at the villain and we all swiftly and effortlessly arrive at the same complex theoretical diagnosis: 'Aha!' we conclude (but perhaps not consciously), 'he wants her to think he doesn't know she intends to defraud his brother!' (this volume, p. 125).

The brute fact is that we all do this sort of thing rather well; and that our analyses, as Dennett's example illustrates, are quite extraordinary in their penetration, accuracy, and predictive/explanatory power. Greek audiences, though, were no less capable of interpreting a piece of body language from one of Aristophanes' characters on stage.[2]

This seems to me most patently *obvious* as soon as we reflect on our most mundane and routine social activities, let alone when we reflect on the diagnoses we make when the behaviour of friends or colleagues seem initially out of character, or puzzling: we employ unthinkingly, and largely successfully, a rich, intricate, and sophisticated framework of CSP. Thus I shall not argue for this at length — the claim, as exemplified in the quotation from Dennett, speaks for itself.

SP could not provide such an explanation of why the hero smiled at the villain. But this is not a criticism of SP: it is not trying to. No more (and for the same reasons) does contemporary physics take on as an *explanandum* the following sequence of events: John was ironing his shirt; the iron slipped off the board on to his bare feet; his little toe was fractured, and his second toe mildly burned. My argument will be that CSP and SP are not *in competition*. In other words, there is no 'mind-mind' *problem*.

They are not in competition for several reasons. I have argued this elsewhere[3], and so my summary will be brief. It all stems from the basic idea that the claim, made most strongly perhaps by P. M. Churchland, is wholly false. Churchland asserts:

> Not only is folk psychology a theory, it is so *obviously* a theory that it must be held a major mystery why it has taken until the last half of the twentieth century for philosophers to realise it. The structural features of folk psychology parallel perfectly those of mathematical physics; the only difference lies in the respect domains of abstract entities they exploit — numbers in the case of physics, and propositions in the case of psychology (this volume, p. 46).

But, contrary both to this view and to the weaker claim that common sense psychology is a *quasi*-scientific theory, and that an elaboration of it is both needed and would make it a genuine theory, CSP is not a 'theory' in any substantial sense of that term; and hence *neither* is it interested in the same phenomena as is SP, *nor* is it subject to the same criteria for assessment as is SP.

To support my claim that CSP isn't a 'theory,' I shall offer a rather extended quotation from Hacking. Hacking is talking of Feyerabend's claim about 'our habit of saying the table is brown when we view it under normal circumstances,' and comments:

> Now taken literally . . . this is, to be polite, rather hastily said. For example, what is this 'habit of saying the table is brown when we view it under normal circumstances'? I doubt that ever in my life, before, have I uttered either the sentence 'the table is brown' or 'the table seems to be brown.' I am certainly not in the habit of uttering the first sentence when looking at a table in good light. I have only met one person with such a habit, a French lunatic. . . .
>
> Of course we have all sorts of expectations, prejudices, opinions, working hypotheses and habits when we say anything. . . . But when I read aloud, or

make corrections on this page I simply interact with something of interest to me, and it is wrong to speak of assumptions. In particular it is wrong to speak of theoretical assumptions. I have not the remotest idea what a theory of non-distortion by the air would be like.

Of course if you want to call every belief, proto-belief, and belief that could be invented, a theory, do so ([1983], pp. 175-6).

But *if* we do so, then theory-shmeory; everything becomes a theory, and that becomes equivalent to saying that nothing is. The term 'theory,' as Hacking comments just before the above quotation, is 'best reserved for some fairly specific body of speculation or propositions with a definite subject matter' (*ibid.* p. 175). We surely should support this: science is an activity distinct from what goes on in conversation on the street, no matter how 'continuous' they may be. Continuity holds between entities that can be far apart: bumps in my lawn, and the Himalayas. 'Mere' continuity doesn't in any way imply that there is not a very substantial difference between elements on the continuum.

The continuum holds in the following respect: CSP and SP are both concerned to explain and predict the behaviour of humans and of other animals. But after that anodyne point, the similarities end. SP attempts to explain and predict *generally*. CSP however is interested in explaining the *particular*. George wants to know why his daughter Georgina has become a skinhead, a mathematics professor, or a born-again Christian, rather than why teenagers are tempted to become skinheads, to take up mathematics, or to get waylaid by fundamentalism. Certainly he would have a much better chance of finding a satisfactory explanation if he looks to the specificities of Georgina's individual history — which as her father he probably knows rather well — than if he resorted to his local university collection in psychology (which is not to say that he would not find indirect help there for his researches: more of that anon). CSP wants to know, roughly, why *this* X did exactly *that* action O at exactly *that* time and in *this* manner. (Compare here Dennett's audience at the film where the hero smiles at the villain.) SP wants to know how it is that people do the sorts of things that people characteristically do.

This immediately has an obvious implication. While both CSP and SP purport to explain and predict, SP unlike CSP wants to do this *systematically*. That means that SP must search for a description (a) of behaviours, and (b) of psychological states, which could be described as 'natural kind' explanations. Talk of 'natural kinds' has recently come in for attack — indicted as being vague and handwaving. Although there is some justice to this, I think the assault is wrong-headed. In any case, all I need here is assent to another anodyne point: science (all science) needs to find a description of its *explananda* and *explanantia* under which the former can be SYSTEM-

ATICALLY explained by the latter. Arguably the primary reason for the fragmented state of SP at present is its inability to get an agreed taxonomy of its *explananda* and *explanantia*.[4] But surely it would not and should not take on board: 'applying for a mathematics chair at Oslo'; but maybe it might need to take on board: 'talent or interest in mathematics.' Compare: we do not ask physics to give us the microstructure of *ashtrays,* but might ask for the microstructure of glass — and many ashtrays are made of glass. CSP is no more interested in natural kinds than a cook or a churchgoer are interested in the close species-relationship between garlic and lilies, which undoubtedly engages the interest of biologists. (This is Dupré's example, and I shall be borrowing arguments and examples from his excellent article [1981] in the next paragraph or two, since I agree with him almost without reservation.) Cooks don't want lilies in the soup; and churchgoers have vested interests in putting lilies, but not cloves of garlic, in churches. Putnam is wrong: the man in the street does not always defer to experts. Even if the experts tell him that lilies and garlic are only marginally distinguishable, the layman knows — from his soup and from his church — that the expert is not answering his needs.

The layman is indeed often concerned with 'natural kinds,' whether such kinds are psychological or physical. We — and here I speak as a layman — are interested in gold, in oxygen, in water, in redwoods, in trapdoor spiders, in tigers, all of which are good candidates for being natural kinds. But the reason that common sense often coincides in its categorization with the categories offered by science is *not* because common sense is interested in systematic explanation. Quite the reverse: we have all sorts of different, and often highly prudential, reasons. Gold is a valuable and decorative commodity; oxygen is essential to life, as is water; redwoods are enormous, and so are enormously striking; trapdoor spiders are fascinating; and tigers are not only impressive animals, but are also highly dangerous. More mundanely, common sense is just as fully concerned with categories that by no stretch of the imagination are 'natural kinds': farmers have to think about fences, policemen about riot-shields, painters and art-historians about paint-covered canvasses. We would not, I think, dream of asking the physical sciences to give us an account of fences, riot shields, or paint-covered canvasses. *CSP is, or ought to be, in the same position.* In other words, why should CSP — unlike common sense in every other domain — be expected to supply the categories appropriate for systematic science? As in any other domain, common sense terms can be and are adopted by science — consider the 'spin' of an electron, or 'energy' — but then are invariably adapted: baked in a theoretical kiln, refined and defined to suit the (different) goals of the systematic study.[5]

Part of the problem here is of course that CSP is, and has been for millennia, very sophisticated and successful within its own domain; whereas

SP has only recently celebrated its centenary.[6] (That is because after Descartes we neglected Aristotle's theory of mind, incidentally. Aristotle did indeed pursue SP.) The 'long past' has distorted the 'short history.' This is less true of the relationship between common sense physics and scientific physics. Even so: even if we accept (as we should accept) that common sense provides in all sciences *one* springboard from which science dives, diving-boards are not swimming pools. That is: common sense can note regularities (water boils at about 100° C, and freezes at about 0° C; many octogenarians have poor short-term memory; there are far more earthquakes in Yugoslavia than there are in Britain). Science takes these observations (*inter,* of course, much *alia*) on board, and then tries to work out to what extent they are true; and, insofar as they are true, why this might be (up a mountain the boiling and freezing points of water change substantially; many octogenarians have a better short-term memory than some teenagers; possibly Yugoslavia may have a decade with no earthquakes while in that same period Britain suffers two or three). CSP needs such rough and handy rules of thumb, but does not need or desire to make them more precise — simply because it is not in the business of explaining systematically. What the man in the street needs is to be able to exploit his hearer's understanding of the fact that elderly people frequently have poor short-term memory, when what he wants to do is to explain why, when he was visiting his great-aunt Henrietta, she locked him out of her house the preceding night.

'Exploit his hearer's understanding' . . . but *not* through any grip, implicit or explicit, of *laws.* Just as the apparatus of CSP is not rightly seen as a theory, so equally our command of it is not a command of laws. Or, to borrow again from Hacking's argument above, call them laws if you want to, but then the notion of a law gets devalued. All the weight in the so-called 'laws' of CSP found in the literature is taken, inevitably, by the capacious and indeterminate *'ceteris paribus'* (sometimes *'ceteris absentibus'*) conditions that make them true, but trivial: so platitudinous as to be vacuous. 'Out of sight, out of mind': true, *ceteris paribus.* 'Absence makes the heart grow fonder': true, if a different set of *ceteris* are *paribus.* The grip that we indeed have, which explains our sophisticated mastery of this network of concepts, is the grip we have on our own language, and our training in the links and implications between the elements of it: know-how. Some links are very strong: if someone is afraid of some event, he is likely also to want it not to happen. Some are much weaker: if someone is watching something, he is fairly likely to be interested in it. We know the sorts of things that generous people *typically* do. The so-called 'holism of the mental,' or such a bland form of it as this, is or should be undisputed; but our success at CSP lies in finding our feet within it, and not in mastering laws. Whether someone who is watching an event is or is not 'interested' in it depends on what else—idiosyncratically—is true of his psychological make-up, as well as on the specific circumstances in which he finds himself.

One reason for the success of CSP is the riotous richness of the framework. We can exploit overlapping shades of meaning, nuances, ambiguities, to convey accurately and precisely whatever we want. Explaining behaviour by citing wanting, wishing, desiring, craving, hoping, lusting after, longing for—all in context may convey quite different implications. And, as we have already seen, since CSP explanations are typically of specific actions of specific agents at specific times, they all belong to an equally specific and individual context. Consider the size of Roget's *Thesaurus,* and then consider what proportion of it is given over to 'mental' terms—a colossal proportion. Consider too how few of these terms have *sharp* definitions; it is precisely because they are free of such, are in fact amorphous and nuance-ridden, that they enjoy the flexibility and richness that allows us to wield them to such effect in a given context. The richness of the context ensures that what is conveyed is precise, accurate, and economical.

SP gets its precision from diametrically opposed sources. We have already seen that unlike CSP it searches for 'natural kind' *explananda* and *explanantia,* so seeks a systematic taxonomy. But this goes along with the ambition, shared by all scientific theories, to devise a sparse, nonredundant, and economical vocabulary, from which ambiguities, contextually-based nuances, and overlapping shades of meaning, are to be banished, and where the ambition at least is to provide terms with *sharp* definitions.[7] Further, such precision as SP has rests on the fact that the 'context' is *not* unique or individual. This should not be a contentious fact. There is an ambition in science that experiments and observations should be *repeatable.* This is a remark that of course needs heavy qualification; as Hacking, again, has stressed, some experiments are just too expensive—because of the size of the research team, or because chimpanzees cost so much—to be repeated; and many experiments are not simply 'repeated,' but are repeated with variations that may with luck serve the function both of testing the original findings, and of taking them one step further. Moreover, that part of SP which involves the study of animals in the wild may produce reports of behaviour that are not observed again.[8] Given such qualifications, though, 'repeat*ability*' is a goal, particularly for a science such as SP which is still struggling after 'scientific respectability.' But then, if experiments are to be repeated, with or without variations, then the parameters must be fixed and stable, so that psychologists in Oxford can assess the findings of their colleagues in Ottawa. Put bluntly, it is because the context is so rich and unique that explanations in CSP are so precise; it is to the extent that the context of experiments in SP is so sparse and repeatable (nonunique) that findings in SP win agreement. We could even say that observations and experiments in SP aim to be context-*transcendent.*

Related to this is the intended audience for explanations in CSP and SP. Just as the context for the former is unique to that explanatory occasion, so also is the hearer. Discussions of behaviour usually take place between people who know each other, who know what feature of the behaviour the other finds puzzling, who know and can guess how much the other is aware and unaware of features of the agent, of the circumstances of his action, etc. Thus massive amounts of relevant details can often simply be presupposed. The explanation of the same behaviour may need to be framed quite differently for another audience, who may not only have a different degree of familiarity with the agent and the circumstances, but may also be puzzled by a quite different aspect of the event in question. Of course explanations in SP also make presuppositions—we do not need to be told that the experimenter was sober as he ran his rats through the T-maze. But because of the public and (in principle) repeatable nature of scientific experimentation, publication of findings in SP must ensure that all relevant details of the experiment must either be such as anyone can take for granted, like the sobriety of the experimenter, or spelled out, like the species of the rats chosen or the nature of the equipment used; and the description under which the problem to which the experiment is addressed must be unambiguous. To adapt and correct a claim of van Fraassen's ([1980], p. 127): it is precisely because 'why did Adam eat the apple?' is a question of common sense and *not* of science that it allows for so many diverse explanations (why Adam rather than Eve; why did he eat it rather than throw it; why an apple and not a kiwi fruit); it is precisely because 'Why did the sample burn green?' *is* a question within science that it does not.

An implication of all this is that there is a huge *methodological* difference between CSP and SP. Or, to put the point another way, CSP has and needs nothing deserving the name 'methodology.' SP has traditionally tried to aspire to the methodological rigour of the natural sciences; in part, I suppose, because so many of the German founding-fathers of the discipline trained as physiologists (cf. for instance the two greatest figures—albeit working in very different SP fields—Wundt and Freud[9]) . . . and physiology leant very heavily on physics. But we can see this very clearly as far back as Hume, who aspired to be 'the Newton of the moral sciences'; and cf. J. S. Mill: '[t]he backward state of the moral sciences can only be remedied by applying to them the methods of Physical Sciences, duly extended and generalized' ([1862]; [1906], p. xv). It perhaps sometimes goes, or has gone, too far in this direction, binding itself into a straitjacket of unattainable methodological purity:

The rejected child of drab philosophy and lowborn physiology, [psychology] has sometimes persuaded itself that actually it was the child of highborn physics. It identified with the aspirations of the physical sciences, and, consequently, acquired an idealized version of the parental image as a super-ego, especially concerning scientific morality, i.e., the 'right' way for a scientist to behave (R. I. Watson [1973], p. 20).

Moreover, many—Ebbinghaus is an early example—criticized the dominance of physics as a methodological superego; more recently, Lipsey has complained that when psychology emulates the physical sciences, it 'resembles the duck that has imprinted on the football' ([1974], p. 409). Nonetheless, large chunks of our current SP have achieved what they have achieved because of a *deliberate* attempt to emulate the methodological standards of better-established sciences; and CSP neither wants to, nor should, do this.

To conclude this part of the discussion of the separation between CSP and SP: so far I have been accepting that CSP describes and explains (but not systematically). It is time to qualify that. It does; but it has countless other things to do besides description and explanation. Any attempt at a list would be inordinately long, and anyone could add to it, so I'll simply remind the reader of a few: joking, jeering, exhorting, discouraging, blaming, praising, warning, insulting, evaluating, advertising, hinting. The framework of CSP is a multipurpose tool. The ambitions of science in general and SP in particular are to describe and explain systematically (where 'explain' should be taken, often at least, to include 'predict'). It has no other obligations: it is a single-purpose tool. This means that not only *is* CSP not a theory; it could never become one, and nobody should wish it to.

There is a further difference, which is more profound and more contentious than what I have said so far (what I have said so far strikes me as obvious, but I must be wrong about that since so many disagree). And that is the different relationships that CSP and SP have to the neurosciences. CSP, bluntly, has no relationship whatsoever. The layman has a vague belief that the brain, somehow, underpins psychological competence; but he can equally read Euripides' plays without being handicapped by the fact that Euripides probably had a vague belief that the heart, somehow, underpinned psychological competence. We have no difficulties when reading science-fictional stories about HAL in '2001,' or fairy stories about talking rabbits, ice-maidens, Galatea, or Pinocchio. It is hard to think of any neurophysiological fact that could alter a comment made in CSP. (There is an interesting contrast here with common sense medicine: the discoveries of scientists have indeed quite seriously affected people's attitudes to their bodies, their diet, and their exercise. Even though I do smoke, I think I shouldn't—because of what medical science has discovered.)

Of course, *since* CSP and SP are on a continuum, there are places in between. Consider for instance depression. CSP, without science, finds this puzzling, frustrating, something to try to talk the patient through. But after the discovery that some forms of depression are closely correlated with a deficiency of catecholamine in the limbic system, these types of depression are less often regarded as something which falls into CSP, and are instead treated by drugs. We shall return to this. The general point nevertheless holds: CSP is 'autonomous' to a massive degree from the physiological.

SP, I maintain, is not. This of course suggests an allegiance to some form of physicalism, and I am (independently) a physicalist. The burden of this point is best illustrated as follows: even if we take an hypothesis of SP that is currently being pursued independently, or largely independently, of neuroscience (such as, for instance, the development of transitive reasoning in the young child), it is accepted that in principle neuroscientific discoveries could support or falsify the conjectures and explanations. Or take a branch of psychology that is and will remain for a long time substantially 'independent' of neurophysiology, Freudian psychoanalysis. This may or may not count as a 'scientific' theory. Right now I don't need to come down on one side or the other of that debate. But *if* it is, then — as is very clear from Freud himself — two things follow. First: neuroscience will one day help to confirm, or maybe to refute, it. The early 'Project' ([1895]) shows this. Of course Freud later disavowed the 'Project.' However we find him writing as late as 1920 that it is possible that '[b]iology . . . will blow away the whole of our artificial structure of hypotheses' ([1920]; [1963], p. 60). Second, for the present psychoanalysis must carry on without reference to neuroscience; both sciences need much more development before one could be brought into kilter with the other. Developmental psychology and psychoanalysis, although at present needing to pursue most of their research independently of the neurosciences, are nonetheless tied to them in the long run. Then at the other extreme, of course, the study of such competences as visual perception have from the very start been conducted by psychology hand-in-hand with neuropsychology, which is in turn hand-in-hand with neurophysiology. But more about this very soon.

As I have mentioned already, Freud studied biology, anatomy, neuroanatomy, medicine; and Wundt, the father of SP, studied physiology for seventeen years — part of the time under von Helmholtz — before creating the 'New Science' of SP. These are only the two most conspicuous of the figures who, I suggest, have been and are working in SP and who simply take physicalism for granted. There are hundreds more. Later we shall see why SP must take it for granted. Whatever the contemporary 'reconstruction' of SP by philosophers — which is coloured through and through by their Cartesian inheritance — those in laboratories and white coats have — unless they unwisely listen to the philosophers — regarded SP as an intrinsic and continuous part of the brain and behavioural sciences more generally.

Right now, because this socio-historical claim is a separate subject and needs a separate paper, I am simply stating this. But I submit that the history of the science would fully bear out this contention.

CSP, then, unlike SP, is not threatened or heartened by any advances in neuropsychology or neuroscience, because it is cheerfully independent of them. This means that—in its eclectic manner—it can pick up whatever it wants from scientific theories, and generally of course (because it is the psychology of the layman) prefers to pick up terms and ideas that are trendy enough to get discussed in glossy magazines. So someone can be described as 'having an Oedipal complex'—a once-trendy way of saying that he's fond of his mother. Strident feminists can be insulted by accusing them of 'penis envy.' Needless to say, terms such as 'Oedipal complex' and 'penis envy' are used in CSP very loosely, in a manner that infuriates psychoanalysts concerned with the scientific status of their discipline; but, for the reasons given above, CSP does not want to use terms with 'strict' definitions, and instead 'woolifies' them to give them the flexibility needed if they are to be, say, adequately insulting for the purpose in hand. Such terms and phrases will persist for just as long as they are thought to serve some function, and will be dropped when or if they fall out of fashion. At the same time CSP has a melange of terms that derive from ancient views about the heart ('I believe it with all my heart'), from the dominance of the 'theatre model' of mind ('introspection', 'in my mind's eye'), from the idea of the mind as a spatial entity ('weighing on my mind', 'at the back of my mind'), from phrenology ('I have no bump of direction'); no doubt some terms from computer technology will soon join the brew. There is no more point in indicting some claims drawn from this unholy mix as being *false* than there is any point in criticising someone who says that he is 'in two minds' on the grounds that he has not undergone commissurotomy, or who says that 'my heart went out to him' on the grounds that he has had no heart transplant.

This brings this section to a head, and to a close. Since CSP is not a 'theory,' and since it has no evidential tie to what goes on in the brain, or in the heart, questions of truth or falsity (or at least truth *by correspondence;* the all-pervading holism of the mental would allow us to affirm or deny truth by coherence of individual ascriptions) rarely arise. Indeed, the debate between realism and instrumentalism doesn't really arise. Since it isn't a theory, bits of it might need to be construed realistically (I *really* have an agonising pain in my toe) and other bits instrumentalistically ('I gave him a piece of my mind'); but with the vast majority the issue is not clear enough to be posed ('I stumbled at the top because I thought there was another step'; 'that idiot dog thinks the cat is still up that tree').[10] Since it is not a theory . . . none of this matters a ha'porth. Any more than it matters a ha'porth for that cliche that there are no ha'porths left.

IMPLICATIONS

I Want to Highlight Four Implications of All This (a) First, the mind-body problem. There is no such *problem* for CSP. Those using CSP probably, mostly, think that the mind is realised by the brain; most sensible laymen are not dualists. Sometimes, too, individual mental events (such as occurrent pains, thoughts that run through the head) need a realist construal—after all, they have temporal parameters, and pains are also usually located; and then one might idly speculate that there may be some token-token identity with, or instantiation by, neural events 'going on in there'. This is strictly parallel to looking at a fountain pen, and wondering idly just what exact structure its atomic lattice has. It has some such structure, sure. Other thoughts might not tempt even so idle a speculation; ascription of some thoughts to people might be more like the familiar ascription to a chess-playing computer, 'it wants to get its queen out early.'—'Really?'—'Yes and no: depends what you mean by "really" '. Then there is in the middle a third category, where terms in CSP do, as a matter of fact coincide closely or roughly with terms that are in fact 'natural kind' terms (in the sense sketched above). For example, let us suppose, 'headaches,' or certain forms of depression. Here CSP might be referring to phenomena that do indeed correlate systematically with states and processes identified by neuropsychologists or neurophysiologists— more of a type-type relation. But if so, then by accident; just as it is an accident (as far as the layman is concerned) that although both fences, and gold, interest us on occasion, the latter but not the former also happens to be an object of systematic scientific scrutiny. The point here is that absorbability-into-science is not a prerequisite for CSP to be valid, and valuable.

But SP doesn't genuinely have a mind-body problem either. This is because it begs the question from the start, by assuming physicalism. The object is to identify and describe the competences characteristic of humans, or of other animals; and to try to discover how the brain and CNS are organised to explain these competences. Not 'and *then* to try,' note: there is no preferred direction-of-explanation here. In other words I am not, and most of those in laboratories and white coats are not, enrolled among the 'top down' theorists. Research can enter the game at any one of the *numerous* levels that characterise the brain and behavioural sciences. That is, one can work exclusively at the 'top'—for instance, studying the development of transitive reasoning. Or one can take on board the question of the differences in psychological competence between the two hemispheres of the human brain. Or one can consider the hippocampus as a cognitive map. Or the amygdala, as the 'comparator,' which compares incoming with expected stimuli. Or the role of the network of neurons in the cerebellum. Or cell-columns in the visual cortex that react to input from vertical lines. Or of course to the dynamics and biochemistry of individual nerve cells. Work at all levels is required, and is undertaken. Just as in other sciences, the explanation at one level of a phenomenon at a slightly 'higher' level — explaining, for instance, what it is about the amygdala that allows it to compare incoming with expected stimuli — may refine and redefine the original *explanandum*. Or, to take a more 'macro' example, it was primarily neuropsychological and neurosurgical work that showed conclusively that it is a mistake to consider 'memory' as a *single* competence at the 'psychological' level.

So we can see how inevitable it is that SP must beg the question against dualism. *Explananda* are proposed by a 'higher' level; this gives the next level down its marching-orders, a target. *Explananda* propose, but the *explanantia* dispose, by (perhaps) forcing a redescription of the target *explanandum*. Conversely: those working at 'lower' levels find patterns, regularities, networks, which demand to be pulled in to a higher-level account. Example of both: those studying 'pure alexia' found among other things a surprising disjunction: pure alexics can write, but cannot read. Implications for the higher level — maybe reading and writing competences are not as closely interlocked as might have been thought; maybe the description of the holism of psychological competences such as these needs rewriting. Implications for neurophysiology — how can this be? Just how, and why, do these two capacities become disengaged?

If the 'next level down' can't handle the *explanandum* proposed by a higher level at all, then the suspicion is eventually bound to arise that the target *explanandum* is the psychological equivalent of a fence, rather than gold: not a genuine phenomenon for systematic study. Put very bluntly, if it cannot be handled within the driving presupposition of systematic physicalism, then it is not a genuine part of SP; the question is most thoroughly begged. This interlocking relationship has been described by P. S. Churchland as a 'coevolution' of psychology and neuroscience. I agree, but with the hefty reservation that it isn't a coevolution of *two theories;* it is a coevolution of *numerous* levels of description within the mind/brain. It simply does not matter, except for bureaucratic purposes, what bits of it are called — psychology, neuropsychology, psychophysics, physiological psychology, psychophysiology, neurophysiology — just so long as the scientists know in what building they can find their offices.

So That's the End of the Mind-Body Problem! (b) CSP is superb, I have claimed; but now we must assess its most resounding weakness. Simply put: it cannot handle irrational, abnormal, aberrant behaviour. It has never been able to. But the reason is simple; it succeeds as it does because it aims to show how the behaviour to be explained is, given the background, the circumstances, the rest of the agent's holistic web of psychological states, rationally intelligible after all. We have to approach the explanation of behaviour and the ascription of psychological states with what has been called a 'principle of rationality,' or a 'principle of humanity'; what *counts* as an explanation is something which shows how despite appearances it is after all rational for this agent to behave so oddly. I will not run through these arguments, which are adequately familiar.

Unsurprisingly, then, weakness of will, and self-deception, have throughout the history of the philosophy of mind remained as unsolved problems. (i.c.: in my judgcment Davidson's discussion of *akrasia* [1970a] is more technically sophisticated than Aristotle's in the *Nicomachean Ethics;* but I don't find it any *better.*) Just as unsurprisingly, Homer's account of why his heroes behaved irrationally fails to satisfy us now, because abnormal behaviour was explained by the gods temporarily clouding the judgment of one warrior, or putting inexplicable terror into another; and today we reject the Homeric pantheon. But consider how we understand the gods' behaviour: they took sides in the battle, and had favourites, and so *they* were being thoroughly rational when clouding Agamemnon's judgement. (He stole Achilles' slave girl; so Achilles sulked in his tent; which removed the world heavyweight from the scene, so the Trojans temporarily triumphed over the Greeks.) In other words human irrationality was explained *via* a higher, indeed divine, rationality. In the Middle Ages inexplicable behaviour was often explained by the malign or benign, but again rationally-intelligible, purposes of demons, witches, warlocks. Now we have Freud. But his enterprise is to show how, *given* the genesis of ideas in the 'System Ucs,' then we can see how *if* an agent thought this, feared that, longed for the other . . . then *of course* he would wash his hands 2,000 times a day. Perfectly sensible, really, given the circumstances in which the ego finds itself. The anthropomorphism, at least in the more popularising works, given to what Asher has nicely called 'those shady Middle European refugees—the Ego, the Super Ego and the Id' ([1972], p. 36) reminds one irresistibly of the battle of the gods that distorted the behaviour of the Iliadic heroes.

The reason why CSP is so penetrating, then—because it can show how *prima facie* puzzling actions are rationally intelligible after all—is equally the explanation of its failure to explain the irrational. Can SP do any better?

Yes, at least in principle; because of its connections with the neuro-sciences. I am not of course suggesting that SP has explained weakness of will, or self deception. But two examples, both briefly mentioned already, will illustrate the sort of thing I have in mind. One is very straightforward.

Pure alexia must trouble CSP. It does not make sense that someone who can write, recognise almost all everyday objects (often including written *numbers*), sort and match colour chips, tell you the colours of blood or the sky or grass, nevertheless cannot recognise letters or words, or tell you what colour a painted colour chip is. This is not rationally intelligible. But there is a wholly satisfactory explanation. Very crudely: there is a brain lesion which destroys the left visual cortex, and a part of the great cerebral commissure called the splenium which provides the *direct* link from the right visual regions to the language centres in the left hemisphere.[11] So visual input, if it is to get to the language centres (and so get identified verbally) must travel by indirect routes. Something like a hammer has connections with the motor cortex and the auditory cortex (we pick up, and bang, hammers). So a seen hammer will arouse associations in auditory and motor regions of the right hemisphere. From there, from those connections, the information can travel by intact commissural paths—i.e., *not* via the splenium—to the language centres. Colours, though, and letters, rarely have nonvisual associations; and so if the direct (splenium) route to the language centres is cut, there is no other one. Numbers are often learned, initially, by counting on one's fingers; so they may get recognised, because the information can travel indirectly, via the motor cortex's intact

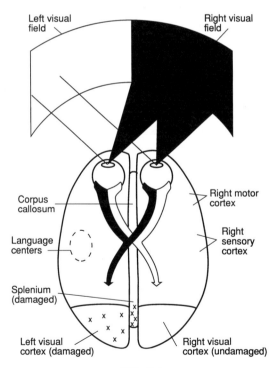

FIG. 9.1.

commissural links with the left hemisphere's language centres. QED. This fully explains.[12] It is not a rational explanation; but it has removed the need to provide one. Pure alexia is no longer puzzling for CSP, any more than the failure of a favorite to win a race is puzzling when we hear that it had a hairline fracture in a hoof.

Now consider depression. It is hard for CSP to understand depression if the patient seems to have nothing special to be depressed about. But at least some forms of depression are systematically correlated with a deficiency of catecholamine in the limbic system. However there are 'higher level' *SP* theories, such as Seligman's account [1975] in terms of 'learned helplessness.' Between these two we certainly find a looming gap. Seligman's account tries to make rational sense of depression—to show how the phenomenon is intelligible, given a specific type of history. The biochemical account is far lower down the hierarchy, and makes no reference to *rational* intelligibility. My optimistic proposal is that when or if we find out more about the role of the limbic system, and of catecholamine, and the sorts of effects the system and the substance have upon other functions of the brain, then we would be getting closer to a mixed psycho-physiological account which would both answer the demand on SP to show how behaviour can be rationally understood; and provide a partial explanation of it in non-rational (not *ir*rational, note) terms.

I agree that at present this is optimistic handwaving. But it shows the sort of direction along which SP can in principle proceed, when confronted with what CSP just cannot explain at all, abnormal or irrational behaviour.

(c) The third implication I want to mention briefly is unlikely to convince. This concerns my rejection, right at the beginning, of so-called 'philosophical psychology.' By this I mean the sorts of *theories*—whether of action, or of perception, or whatever—dreamed up by philosophers in armchairs rather than by scientists in laboratories: theoretical elaborations of CSP. Sometimes they are not so much dreamed-up as attacked; P. M. Churchland, for example, believes that CSP gives us 'theories of action,' which are well entrenched but false; P. S. Churchland believes that we operate in CSP with a 'sentential paradigm' that is 'dinky,' misleading, and again false. I am sure that many philosophers have produced theories which fall to both these sorts of criticism. But CSP itself does not.

Such theories respect the constraints of 'real' theorising to the extent that they come up with a stripped-down vocabulary; consider for instance Davidson [1963] talking about *two* sources of action: beliefs, and proattitudes. Others constructing, or reconstructing, or criticising, such 'theories' produce alleged 'laws' of CSP, such as 'If *X* fears that p, and discovers that not-p, then X is pleased' (or more sophisticated versions, each with its essential protective shield of *ceteris paribus/absentibus* conditions).

All such theories make several hefty presuppositions. They assume that the *explananda* provided by CSP are amenable to systematic explanation (which I do not believe for a moment). But further: they assume that actions are caused (I believe this); that beliefs and desires explain actions (I believe that too, at least to some extent); and that beliefs and desires explain actions *by* causing them (this needs but never gets defence, and I myself do not believe it). Hence their need to devise theories which have law-like relations between beliefs and desires, and behaviour.

It should already be clear, from the first section, why I think that such armchair theories cannot get off the ground, and so I shall not go over that again; the root cause is simple, in that CSP simply isn't a theory at all. Right now I want only to pose a question to those either propounding, or assuming and then attacking, such theories: *they* have my 'mind-mind' problem. Just what is their relationship meant to be with the theories produced by empirical work? More specifically, what connection does a CSP term like 'belief' have to the terms postulated by scientists to account for the processing — different forms of processing for different kinds of input — of information, its storage, retrieval, etc? Why, too, is there no parallel in other domains — why, that is, are there no common sense theories (in a full-blooded sense of 'theory') in physics or chemistry? In the older and better-established sciences, nobody dreams of inventing 'philosophical theories,' such as 'philosophical chemistry.' I am very confused about what the theories *of philosophers* are trying to do: to bring some order into the chaotic and intricate web of CSP? But CSP, to borrow from a remark of Hampshire's, is like a plate of spaghetti. What makes something a good pasta meal is the intricacy of the interlocking of numerous strands, and the way the sauce weaves in and out. The philosophical theorists, to my mind, seem to be trying to burrow-down into the plate and to pull out a few 'crucial' strands, then to lay them side by side and wipe the sauce off them, and describe the result. Whatever else that is, it would be a bad meal; and it is not a systematisation of CSP. Insofar as it is a theory, it is a bad one because its empirical base is inadequate. What the spaghetti of CSP allows and invites is a description of the plate as it is; and that, I take it, is the task of the philosophy of mind. These theories, then, lose what is interesting about CSP, while failing to attain what works (at least to some extent) in SP.

(d) The final implication concerns the last, because it involves what I see as the inaccuracy of the 'reconstructions' of SP produced by 'philosophical psychologists'. 'The psychological' is heterogeneous; so heterogeneous, indeed, that as we have seen what counts as psychology, as neuropsychology, and as neurophysiology is no more than a trivially verbal question. The 'theories' devised or attacked by philosophers ignore this heterogeneity, and attempt to impose a single model on CSP and SP alike (which in general they conflate), or else to assume that they have one. Thus we have P. S.

Churchland saying that CSP is driven by an alleged 'sentential model'; I suspect that she has been reading too much Fodor, a CSP 'theorist.'[13] Such models are, as she insists, feeble because they drive dramatic divisions between 'cognitive' tasks (which can occasionally be modelled on digital computers) and all else, which mostly can't—PDP modelling looks much more promising here. As she rightly insists, this is too narrow: it is essential to the understanding of most so-called 'cognitive' tasks that we take on board such competences as sensorimotor control. Equally it is part of the task of psychology to examine pain; emotions; sexual desire; face-recognition; the way baby birds learn their song; why dunnocks and reed-warblers in particular fail to kick parasitic cuckoo eggs from their nests, in contrast to more sensible birds; the mobbing behaviour of chaffinches; Korsakoff's syndrome; alcoholism. P. S. Churchland would not disagree with this—indeed, she wants to emphasise it; and no doubt all of these phenomena will need to incorporate some strands from what is now called 'cognitive psychology.' My quarrel with her is that she is not talking about the nitty-gritty, nose-to-the-grindstone, work of SP; and equally what she says does not hold for CSP. The scientists and the laymen alike have always, and routinely, been talking of a far richer and more diverse field than has the relatively recent AI, or 'cognitive science,' community.

I hinted earlier, and was only exaggerating mildly, that sensible psychologists get on with their job better if they don't heed the reconstructions of the philosophers. Fortunately, by and large, they do not. But they can be made uneasy for two reasons. First there are the philosophers, pestering them to impose a single 'model' (whether it is Descartes' exclusion of all nonconscious mentality, and hence Hume's theatre model of mind; or Watson's telephone exchange model of mind; or the computer model—serial or parallel as the case may be). Second, there is the prestige of physics combined with SP's desire for scientific respectability. Physics, as R. I. Watson put it, is a sort of superego of the other sciences; and, unless you are a practising physicist, you will distort the superego exactly as Freud describes, and come up with a wholly unrealistic set of norms to which psychology should try to subscribe. Given a distorted impression of the 'purity' of physics, impressionable psychologists have thought that they should have a 'single' model, a 'single' methodology; that (perhaps) the 'top down' strategy of computational AI is indeed, as Fodor says somewhere, 'the only ball game in town.'

If however physics were to be seen in its true colors—as an extremely impressive and successful, but also highly heterogeneous, mess; with literally hundreds of models, methodologies, strategies; with *explananda* drawn from all levels of description[14]—then it could indeed serve as a *benign* superego for contemporary SP. For instance, psychology need not worry that few of its 'laws' are as strict and exceptionless as are *some* laws of physics, when it reflects on (say) qualitative mechanics. It should firmly abjure the search for 'single' models and 'single' methodologies when it looks at virtually any part of physics. Above all, though, it could and should take a more detached view of its relationship to CSP. SP and CSP are not unrelated, any more than the cook's concern when creating a new recipe is unrelated to what chemistry has to say; contemporary physics and mechanics are heavily exploited when new buildings are put up (tell that, though, to the Greeks, Romans, and medievals, whose buildings have a rather more impressive track-record than ours). SP has the particular problem that CSP, in *its* domain, is vastly more sophisticated than SP has so far been in its (different) domain. But we have seen some of the reasons for that.[15]

FOOTNOTES

[1]The 'encephalization quotient' (EQ) juggles brain weight and body weight in an ill-disguised attempt to find a formula that brings man out ahead of the other animals. $EQ = E_t/kP^a$; where E_t is the real brain size, P is body weight, and k and a are designer-constants.

[2]Greek plays were performed with the players wearing masks, and so Dennett's example of a smile won't work there. But *mutatis mutandis* the point still holds, since any gesture, or intonation, would serve my purposes as well as a smile.

[3]The two places where I have argued for this most explicitly are in *Inquiry* 1984 and 1986.

[4]The problem, for contemporary SP, can scarcely be exaggerated. Few agree—to take just *one* example—how best to describe memory. The preferred taxonomies ranges from 2 to 22 'types' of memory; and the categories are very various: short term, medium term, long term; 'scratch-pad'; working; procedural; declarative; semantic; episodic; iconic; non-cognitive; somatic; habit; . . . and so on. The diversity of 'memory' is emphasized by the corresponding diversity in types of memory-*loss:* different ailments (e.g. Korsakoff's, Huntington's, Alzheimer's, various head injuries) produce characteristically variant disturbances of memory. Unfortunately very many more examples of highly central SP concepts could be cited—one of the trendiest, and most disputed, is that of a 'representation.'

Nestle [1982] has a study in which eleven prominent psychologists failed to agree on what work in psychology counted as 'important.'

[5]This point is forcefully made in a widely-neglected book (or at least neglected by philosophers) by Mandler and Kessen [1959].

[6]I join the majority in dating the beginning of SP to Wilhelm Wundt, with his 'new science,' and the world's first laboratory of psychology in Leipzig.

[7]This needs to be qualified. On the 'moving frontier of science,' we frequently find concepts that are vague and unclear when first introduced; 'field' and 'spacetime' are two examples which, as Newton-Smith [1981] has pointed out, were attacked for their obscurity initially, but which then allowed for—indeed, made possible—just those experiments by means of which they were, or are being, refined and clarified. My point is merely that science *aims* at precise and well-defined concepts.

[8]Even so, such observations often attract charges (sometimes fair charges) of being 'merely anecdotal.'

[9]I am not (here) committing myself to a judgment on the question of whether Freudian theory should count as a 'science.' Probably not; but Freud knew well what genuine science required, and struggled hard to make his theory fit the pattern.

[10]Here my version of CSP instrumentalism differs from that of Dennett. At least I think so; but I find his instrumentalism hard to follow — as I think does Stich: see his [1983a], ch. 11, this volume, pp. 93-117.

[11]Most but not all people (including left-handers) have language capacity primarily in the left hemisphere. Pure alexia would take the converse form in that small percentage who have it specialised in the right hemisphere: the damage to the visual cortex would have to be to the left side. A very few have hemispheres equipotent for language; if the hypothesis is correct, it should be impossible to find pure alexia with them.

[12]Note that this hypothesis is also *testable*. Pure alexics should be unable to name other 'purely visual' objects, such as clouds, on sight alone; conversely, patients who had learned their letters in childhood by playing manually with letter-shapes should be able to recognise letters, even if not words.

[13]And see the earlier quotation from P.M. Churchland (this volume, pp. 45-46), comparing the role of numbers in physics to 'propositions' in psychology.

[14]Nancy Cartwright [1983] has decisively shown the extent to which much successful physics is a 'guess-and-by-golly', 'muddle-through' matter whereby *numerous* models, often technically incompatible with each other, have their own roles to play within parts of the science; and in which 'strict' laws often play a far less significant explanatory role than do what she calls 'phenomenal' laws, and variously-fudged approximations.

[15]An earlier version of this paper ran the gamut of presentation at universities in Ontario, the university of Warwick, the Institute of Philosophy of the Academy of Sciences in Moscow, and the 8th Inter-Nordic Philosophical Symposium in Oslo. I am very grateful for the comments and criticisms it received on these occasions.

10 The Very Idea of a Folk Psychology*

Robert A. Sharpe
University of Wales, United Kingdom

Philosophers with a yen for conceptual reform are nowadays prone to describe our ordinary, common sense, Rylean description of the mind as 'folk psychology,' the implication being that when we ascribe intentions, beliefs, motives, and emotions to others we are offering explanations of those persons' behaviour, explanations which belong to a sort of pre-scientific theory. Though the term is in vogue, the philosophers whose belief in folk psychology make their writings very acceptable clay pigeons are Paul and Patricia Churchland and Stephen Stich.[1] All three contrast folk psychology with a pukka theory about the mind and its workings which is either broadly materialist or more specifically based on the computer model. For all three, folk psychology is thought of as a stone-age relative of more respectable scientific theories. For all three, folk psychology is as theoretical an enterprise as the explanation of the reflex contraction of the pupil in the face of a bright light in terms of a neural network. The origin of these ideas seems to lie in Wilfrid Sellars's work of a couple of decades ago;[2] I shall argue that our policy should be 'caveat emptor.'

The philosophical connections of this issue are considerable. Philosophers who believe that explanation in the physical sciences is the model for understanding in general tend to regard common-sense explanations as successful to the extent that they converge on the scientific model. There is then a motive for thinking of common-sense explanations as rivals to more creditable scientific theories. My view is that our understanding of persons, of their behaviour, and of their creations is different from our knowledge

---

*Reprinted from *Inquiry* 30 (1987, pp. 381–393) by permission of the author and publisher.

of physical processes and events, though the degree of the difference is variable. But certainly I view our knowledge of the human personality as being nearly as far from our knowledge of natural processes as it is possible to get — only the arts lie further along the hermeneutic spectrum — and the arts provide a sort of idealized paradigm of our knowledge of persons.

The recent debate in *Inquiry*[3] revealed a number of telling arguments against the claim that ordinary ascriptions of mental terms belong to a sort of primitive science, particularly by Madell, whose style of argument is close to that found in this paper. Of the three arguments I shall offer against the idea that there is a folk-psychological theory, the ideas contained in at least two are familiar enough, namely 'intentionality' and 'privileged access,' though I propose to make a rather distinctive use of them. So, all in all, it seemed worth adding a pennorth to the debate, though without much hope of converting the principals; Churchland's response to Madell showed how much the battle positions are now drawn up at ideological boundaries.

What is somewhat surprising is that those philosophers who have used the idea have not stopped to ask whether the attribution of beliefs, etc., shows the characteristics of theory explanation. I shall argue that in some respects 'mental statements' have the characteristics of theoretical explanations whilst in other ways they are not theory-like. I find myself then midway between Churchland, on the one hand, who thinks that common-sense ascription of mental predicates is unambiguously theoretical and Kathy Wilkes,[4] on the other, who denies that we have a prescientific theory of the mind. But I shall also try to show that the way in which mental statements are theory-like is of no use to those philosophers like Stich and the Churchlands who either wish to replace folk psychology with a more respectable scientific alternative or think that this is an option for us. Quite the reverse. The theoretical form of statements about the mind actually places insuperable obstacles in the way of a replacement of folk psychology by a computational or neurological alternative.

The Churchlands take our attribution of beliefs to persons to posit causal relationships between psychological states or events and the behaviour which these explain. Thus when I use the practical syllogism to explain why a man is signing his name I point out that it is a cheque which he is signing and that he believes that if he signs this bit of paper he thereby purchases the book he desires. So the action is explained by postulating a desire and a belief. The theory can be generalized to give a set of universal statements which give a theory of the inner dynamics of human beings and contain detailed hypotheses about the determinants of human behaviour, hypotheses which enable us to explain and predict.

Paul Churchland also thinks that this theory is deficient in many ways. First, it gives very inadequate accounts of the dynamics of emotions, creativity, perceptual illusion, differences in intelligence or of mental illness. Second, and perhaps more significantly, it has shown no improvement in millennia. Third, it assumes a discontinuity between the mental life of infants, animals, and ourselves which is obviously false. For a fourth and final charge against folk psychology I turn again to Stich. Phenomena like cognitive dissonance show the unsatisfactory nature of folk psychology.[5]

Some of these charges can be quickly dismissed. Common sense makes attributions of emotions and beliefs to animals and infants without any great difficulty. Irrationality of the sort displayed in akrasia, cognitive dissonance, or self-deception is hardly to be laid at the door of the common-sense theory of the mind. We would need some general grounds for supposing that the failings are to be placed at the feet of the theory rather than at those of the individual concerned. Behind this may be the suspicion that if self-deception is so widespread as to be endemic then the conclusion ought to be that we have our theory wrong. But, of course, these forms of irrationality are not so widespread as to be excluded on the basis of Davidsonian arguments. In any case, like the blunderbuss use of the principle of charity or humanity, this ignores what is peculiarly human about inconsistency, the desire not to hurt or be hurt, to deal gently with other people as well as to present yourself, to yourself and others, in the best light.

We need to start by considering, however briefly and inadequately, what it is for something to be a theory. The paradigms of theories for our age are, of course, those to be found in the physical sciences, the kinetic theory of gases, Newtonian mechanics, the general theory of relativity, or the chemical theory of valency are examples. In old-fashioned textbooks on the philosophy of science we find them presented as though they are hypotheses from which the phenomena they explain may be deduced. Of course, theories do not have to take this form. A theory which does not entail what it purports to explain or whose laws are not really 'laws' may still be a theory and, though flawed, may, through these very flaws, prove highly fertile as the subject develops. It is interesting to note, however, that the deductive paradigm for theoretical explanation has at least one parallel in action, and that is in practical inference; here we connect belief and desire with action through the practical syllogism. Looking away from natural science, consider Moore's theory of ethics. Again we describe it as a theory even though its disparate ingredients, the non-natural theory of the good, its consequentialism, and its enumeration of the paramount goods are not deductively integrated, nor is there anything remotely resembling a law of nature.

What these cases have in common is that they explain in a generalizable way. A theory does not have to be general; a historian may have a specific hypothesis about a specific event or action. But scientific explanations, and these are the model for Stich and the Churchlands, are general. For these writers, the model of physical theory is the paradigm of what a scientific theory will be like. So in what ensues it must be remembered that folk psychology is thought to explain in the way that atomic theory explains. The idea is that of an internal mechanism which accounts for behavioural phenomena through its nature and structure. They offer 'hidden mechanism' forms of explanation. To summarize, then, we explain discrete bits of behaviour by postulating desires, wants, beliefs, etc., on the part of the agent. But in order to do this we require generalizations of a rather vague sort. Paul Churchland lists such banalities as 'Persons who are angry tend to frown,' 'Persons who are angry tend to be impatient,' and 'Persons who are deprived of fluids tend to feel thirst.' Patricia Churchland suggests 'barring a stronger impulse, hunger causes eating' and 'barring stimulants or desperate purposes, weariness causes sleep.' We are then able to explain behaviour so that we can say of a person that he or she wants a drink not for the sake of sociability but because he or she is thirsty.

Now one very important question which has a bearing on the criticisms I shall make later is whether all our talk of mind is folk psychological in this way or whether only some of it is. Stich is unclear;[6] he describes folk psychology as evolving as an aid to our dealings one with another. Paul Churchland is unequivocal.[7] Since folk psychology is simultaneously a solution to the problem of other minds it seems clear that all mental ascriptions are folk psychological and that consequently all our accounts of other minds are theory facilitated. (Hereafter 'Churchland' unqualified refers to Paul though the two Churchlands appear to agree on this matter.) The general idea, astounding when presented this way, seems to be that I ask myself why it is that bits of the world keep bumping uncomfortably against me. Is it perhaps because I keep treading on parts of the world? I then formulate the hypothesis that treading on bits of the world makes those bits angry and the anger results in reprisals against me. By a process of refinement we eventually reach the explanation that Smith hits me because I annoy him by standing on his toe. In what follows I shall assume the stronger version, that all mental ascriptions are folk psychological, not just because Churchland subscribes to it, but also because the weaker theory is neither interesting nor controversial. It would, after all, hardly surprise us to learn that people sometimes formulate theories about other people in terms of ordinary talk about the mind, nor that some of the concepts we use originate in theorizing. Indeed I shall say more about the latter towards the end of this essay.

Now to the first of the three criticisms which I propose to make of folk psychology theory. I have privileged access to some of my mental states and of these I can offer direct self-revelation. There is an antique flavour to this claim; nevertheless I think it is, fortunately, true. I sometimes have thoughts, even during a philosophy seminar, which I am relieved to know are not transparent. I am making no claim to the incorrigibility which is usually associated with the idea of privileged access, incidentally. Of course, I may postulate a belief on the part of an agent as a means of explaining what he does, but he may also tell me. He can explain his behaviour to me, and he can do so because, in many cases, he knows straight off what he believes and the role his belief plays in his action. He has privileged access to his belief and I learn of it through his direct self-revelation. Certainly there are cases where I do not know why I do something, but cases of self-deception or illusion are a minority. It is easy, in the interests of stressing the similarity between mental and physical explanations, to do what Churchland does, and exaggerate the number and importance of these quasi-pathological cases. If the reader feels as uncomfortable as I about the idea of privileged access then he is welcome to translate the discussion into terms less immediately perspicuous but less burdened with Cartesianism. We need only remark that many attributions to ourselves are not explanations.

This is an issue much discussed by believers in folk psychology. But its real force has not been appreciated. For the point about these cases of privileged access as far as the folk-psychological thesis is concerned is the following. Amongst the mental states to which I have privileged access are mental states which apparently play no role in the explanation of behaviour and which are certainly not postulated in the way that Churchland and other advocates of the existence of a folk psychology suggest. For example, I find, when playing the piano, that all sorts of fragmentary memories of places flit across my mind in a way I cannot account for. All of us probably have this experience of suddenly recalling people or places apparently *ex nihilo*. Though there may be an explanation as to why I recall in this way, there does not have to be and I may not know what it is. However this may be, it does seem that nothing is explained by these memories even if there is in turn an explanation of why I have them. What folk-psychological theorists have to assume is that their existence is required to explain behaviour. I suppose that their existence explains the criticism I am currently making of Churchland and Stich, but it is somewhat preposterous to suggest that their existence is postulated to make possible a criticism of the professors in question. Normally they are simply unconnected intrusions into the stream of my mental life. They are, in truth, more like brute facts than bits of theory, and this is something that the other side does not seem to recognize. For believers in a folk-psychological theory the facts are bits of behaviour and what explains these facts are the hypothesized mental states.

An objection which has much the same force and structure uses the case of qualia. Phenomenologically my experience of blue is different from my experience of red, though if there was a reversal of the spectrum, so that what looks blue looks red and vice versa, there need be no behavioural consequences. This is disputed and so, for this reason and also because of the size of the literature it has generated, I do not propose to place much emphasis on it here. Madell is eloquent on its behalf in the aforementioned symposium. But if you think that there is a case for taking qualia to be unconnected with behaviour then their existence is a counterexample for believers in the existence of a folk psychology inasmuch as the existence of qualia cannot explain behaviour; only the distinction between them does that. Again even though the existence of qualia has at least one behavioural consequence, namely the writing of philosophical articles about them, it would be ludicrous to say that their existence was postulated to explain that chunk of behaviour.

Needless to say, the concept of behaviour is not itself a demotic one. It is worth pointing out just how much philosophical sophistication is presumed in the hypothesis of a folk psychology. In order to set up the explanation of behaviour by recourse to inner mental states, we need a Cartesian distinction between behaviour and the mind. Normally, scientific theories do not require such philosophically loaded points of origin. We may assume that ordinary scientific theories can be expressed in any one of a number of ontologies. For example, it is always assumed that Newtonian theory can be expressed in a realist or in a phenomenalist metaphysics. It is, indeed, difficult to think of a case of a scientific theory which not only originates in a discredited philosophy theory, many do that, but could not get off the ground without the philosophical assumptions. The philosophy is never essential to the framing of the scientific theory though it may be, contingently, its point of origin. Science is invariant with respect to philosophical presuppositions. That this is not the case with respect to an imagined folk psychology is a strong reason for suspecting its scientific credentials.

Having seen one way in which some mental statements are unlike theoretical postulates and more like statements of observation, let us look at a way in which they are more like bits of theory. It is a commonplace that much mental talk is intentional. Motives, desires, emotions, wishes, and intentions have objects. If I am afraid, there is something of which I am afraid; if I have an intention, then it is an intention to do something specific; there is something which I intend to accomplish; if I remember, then there is something which I remember, and so on. There is a further feature which might be marked by speaking of contents rather than objects. Mental states incorporate contents in the sense that we speak of beliefs as having 'contents'. 'Incorporate' covers a multitude of sins here; I shall try to do something to redeem it later on. For the moment allow that if I desire something then I believe that that thing has properties which make it desirable. If I fear something then that object has properties which, in my belief, make it dangerous. All this, of course, must be qualified by the observation that my beliefs about them may be mistaken. I can be afraid of a perfectly inoffensive dog.

Next we need to note that the identity of these mental states will involve component objects. We discriminate hopes, fears, beliefs, and intentions in terms of their objects; this desire is different from that desire in virtue of what it is a desire for. So although I have a multiplicity of desires at any one time, their discrimination is possible because of their different objects; I both want to get this argument straight and want a cup of coffee. Some of my desires are short term and some long term. Now, there are no phenomenological features of the desire which enable me to pick it out; they do not feel different; they differ in their objects and in the strength which I feel them to have. But their mode of existence is that they have objects; change the object and you change the desire. Consequently, the scope for describing the same desire in different terms is extremely limited. Although it would be rather imprecise to say that if you change the description you change the desire which is thereby designated, it is not far from the truth. The point about desires is that they are identified and individuated by us under specific descriptions and that is their mode of existence.

When we act we typically act in the belief that something or other will be brought about; there are exceptions but for the sake of this argument they do not matter, since we are essentially interested in constructing counter-examples. Actions are defined in terms of what, to borrow a term from another area of philosophy, may be called their history of production; the difference between sticking my arm out of the window to stretch and sticking it out to acknowledge a friend lies in the intention with which I do it. But intentions have objects and without this feature I cannot distinguish them. *Qua* movements they may be indistinguishable. *Qua* actions they are distinguished in terms of my intention in doing them. In the case of actions the history of production is part of the way in which we individuate that action. Without it we may be unable to distinguish one action from another. More seriously, and this is the crucial consideration, viewed as behaviour alone, we have no reason to discriminate them. Not until we distinguish them have we any reason to explain one differently from the other. In order to distinguish them, and to offer different explanations, we have to regard them as actions and not as mere bodily movements. What this shows, of course, is that we have to presume the concepts of intention, purpose, etc., themselves mental concepts, in order to individuate the objects of explanation.

So an important interim conclusion is this.

1. Folk psychology is thought to postulate mental states such as intentions to explain behaviour.
2. But behaviour once thus explained is action.
3. Action incorporates intentions and is individuated on that basis.
4. Consequently the account offered would make the folk-psychological enterprise question-begging. We need 'mental' states in order to distinguish the things which they are introduced to explain.

I want to develop this objection a little further. I have argued that two bits of behaviour may be indistinguishable without drawing on the apparatus of 'mental concepts' which we require for their explanation. But moreover, the boundaries we draw between one bit of behaviour and another we draw on the basis of that mental content which is embodied in these bits when viewed as action. To put it more crudely, how do we chop up behaviour into explanation-sized bites? We take a whole sentence and not a sentence-and-a-half as the locus of explanation; if our interest was purely in the phenomena *qua* neurological occurrence, then there is no reason why we should draw the bounds where we do. The criteria for taking a group of neural events together need not be the same. We do so on the unacknowledged assumption that we are dealing with actions. We are again left with the objection that folk-psychological theory requires us to assume the theory in order to discriminate the objects which it has been introduced to explain.

In order to ease the passage of the next stage in my argument, I assume further that many actions are performed in the belief that they are actions of a type. They incorporate beliefs much as they incorporate intentions. Consequently, if what folk psychology is explaining is human action then part of what is explained will be content. It is characteristic of many actions that, when doing them, I believe that that is what I am doing when I am doing it. This is particularly evident when the action involves a process like driving to work. If I intended to drive to work but did not believe that I was on the right road, I would alter my action accordingly. My belief, as well as my intention, distinguishes my taking a car for a test drive as opposed to a pleasure trip, for instance. Beliefs, in many cases, 'track' actions. This is not simply a contingency. It is necessary, not just that I have the intention to drive to work, but also that I believe that that I am doing so in order that it count as driving to work. There would be an inconsistency in the idea that I intend that I now be driving to work whilst believing that I am not doing so. How I individuate my action depends upon the accompanying belief just as it depends upon the related intention.

These considerations may seem grist to the mill of those who think of beliefs as theoretical entities. 'This falling body is under gravitational attraction' is not the same as 'This body is seeking its natural location,' even though, at least for realists, both describe the same phenomenon, one description couched in Newtonian theory and the other in Aristotelian. The difference between them seems analogous to the difference in content between distinct beliefs for, again, identity depends upon content.

However, beliefs present special problems for the advocate of eliminative materialism. As we have seen, where replacement by another theory is possible the same entity has to be described in terms of a fresh theory. But if the identity conditions for beliefs are as I have said, then virtually no other description is possible which individuates the same entity. What I believe must be expressed in the terms which register the content of the belief. If it is expressed in other terms we have another possible or actual belief, or perhaps no belief at all. So the theoretical form of beliefs presents insuperable obstacles in the way of replacement. Another way of putting the same point is to say that there is an essentialist description of thought. Their content is such that only one way of understanding them is possible. So when, for instance, Freud tells us that a thought of the Queen is really a thought of one's mother he has not said anything intelligible. Of course, there may be ways of teasing out the significance of this idea but taken *in sensu stricto,* one cannot make anything of it.

Note that there is no exit here via any fancy ideas about incommensurability. Those who think they see a folk psychology are adamant that it makes sense to ask whether computational psychology or neurological theory are improvements on folk psychology, so they cannot accept that these alternatives are not rivals between themselves and with folk psychology. An improved theory must, amongst its conditions, explain the same phenomena as the old theory even if its scope overlaps with the previous incumbent rather than being coextensive with it. So we are then required to identify the facts that folk psychology explains. Churchland seems to have no doubt that these facts are bits of human behaviour. So although Churchland thinks that he accepts a form of incommensurability, it is hard to see how he can and certainly the form he offers is so weak as hardly to deserve the name.

The point is, I think, that Stich and Churchland are in the grip of a realist theory here. The temptation is to think of a layer of mental facts which are represented by our beliefs and then to imagine further that these facts could be represented in quite a different way, as an array of neurones and synapses, for example. What I argue is that beliefs are already like theory-encoded facts precisely because of their intensionality. So any rival theory must give us the same understanding of these as our present untutored 'folk psychological' theory. But this effectively excludes replacement. Either we have replaced it with something which is not the same belief, as in my Freudian example, or we replace it with something which is not a belief at all, an arrangement of neurones or an internalized VDU. Here the minimum continuity required for it to be proper to speak of improvement or replacement seems to be missing. After all, if you think, like Stich, that irrationality is inadequately explained in terms of folk psychology, then one can only say that it is not explained at all in our grand new computational or neurobiological theory, because nothing remotely resembling the concept is going to appear.

So the finale of this second argument runs like this: actions incorporate beliefs inasmuch as they are required to individuate actions. But the identity conditions for beliefs so intimately incorporate content as to render implausible the replacement of 'mental concepts' by alternatives. Given that those philosophers most anxious to classify common-sense talk of the mind as folk psychology are also keen on its replacement by neurological or computational theory this objection is very telling.

The third and most general of the objections I shall make has to do with the idea that human behaviour can be explained in such a general way. Theoretical explanation, it has to be remembered, is an activity with a history. Somebody formulates or some group of people formulate a theory in order to explain certain puzzling phenomena; the theory is then communicated to others and it may come to enjoy wide currency so that it becomes the accepted explanation of phenomena previously found problematic. If we think of folk psychology in this way then we speculate that at some point in our distant past, one or more of our ancestors, seeing a neighbour hurl a woolly rhinoceros bone at the wall with a howl, suddenly thought to himself, 'By Jove he's angry; he has certain attitudes, beliefs, and wishes with respect to the situation which in conjunction cause that behaviour.' Now the idea that anybody should have formulated such an hypothesis in such a way is as implausible as Russell's derisive hypothesis about the origins of language, that a group of hitherto speechless elders met and decided to call a wolf a 'wolf.' On the absurdity of this Patricia Churchland and myself agree. But what alternative is there? Explanatory theories do not arise *ex nihilo*. For folk psychology to be an explanatory theory it is necessary that somebody should have designed it that way. But who could think this?

When I use the words 'He is angry,' I may do so because I see straight off that the man is angry. I do not infer this from his behaviour. I am not hypothesizing an inner state to explain his behaviour. Indeed for such 'mental predicates' to get off the ground it is necessary that some should be transparent. In the same way I know that I am in my study and not seated on Concorde. It is the Wittgensteinian move which I think is the point here. Statements like 'He is angry' may or may not be explanations, depending on context, for theorizing can take place in whatever terms we choose. The idea that there is a fixed language of theorizing involving a vocabulary of specifically theoretical terms, an idea which consumed so many man-hours a few decades ago, is so much eyewash; of course, in making a statement like 'he is angry' I have further commitments; I expect the man to act in certain ways and if he does not so react I will have second thoughts. What does seem wrong is to suggest that the original introduction of such terms was an explanatory move, or that we postulate the existence of inner states. This arbitrarily invests ordinary talk about the mind with philosophical dualism. Churchland can easily allow that they can now be used straight off inasmuch as we have absorbed their theoretical function into our descriptive repertoire, but if their initial use was explanatory it becomes unclear how we could have learnt or taught the relevant concepts in the first place. 'Anger' must already be given some sense in order to occur in an explanation, and for this to be the case some concepts in this group must have been introduced in a descriptive mode.

Theorizing is a form of explaining, often, though not invariably, a form where the explaining is less certain or confident. In order for theorizing to take place, something must be explained or an attempt be made at explaining it. This explanans might itself be a piece of theorizing at some point or another, but it does not have to be and it will not be at the point at which explanation takes place. In this way descriptions are prior to explanation. Now the fact that when we describe we bring what we describe under concepts should not be confused, as it often is, with the process of explanation. From the fact that there are no descriptions without concepts, it does not follow that every description is a sort of truncated explanation. To speak for the moment in vulgar Kantianism, to place a sensation under a concept is not *ipso facto* to record or to postulate an explanation. For explanations essentially involve relationships of dependence and such a relationship is not necessarily involved here. At the heart of the Churchlands' argument here may be an equivocation on 'theory.' For the move from the premise that every description involves concepts and is theoretical in that sense to the conclusion that all such descriptions are scientific explanations *manqués* is the crucial error.

Certainly an observation may be regarded as true while being couched in a theoretical vocabulary which is now *passé* because the theory is false, so there can be no objection in principle to the idea that our modes of describing the mind are replete with outmoded theory. It does not follow that everything we say commits us to any theory which the language incorporates. When I speak of seeing the sunrise for example, I do not thereby commit myself to Ptolemaic theory. No doubt talk of sunrises invites some theoretical extrapolation, and this may be true when we speak of human behaviour in terms which betray their metaphorical origin. If we describe somebody as defensive then certain moves towards a theory look more likely than others. But if all descriptions of the mind entailed an explanatory theory, the explanations would become tautological. The generalizations about human behaviour cited by the Churchlands may be trivial but they are not tautological. So there is an important distinction here between the idea that talk of the mind comes trailing bits of theory and the idea that talk of the minds is explanatory of behaviour. The first is true in the sense that the application of concepts invariably has implications which take us beyond the here and now. The second is only sometimes true, as I have shown in this paper.

These considerations do not suggest that folk psychology is not a possible theory. It is a way of explaining the complex and resourceful behaviour of

Homo sapiens which might occur to Martians. However, its advocates do not claim that it is a possible theory but that it actually is a theory. For it to be an actual theory it is necessary that somebody offer it as such. Whatever it may be for Venusians, Martians, the Churchlands or Stich (who after all may be evidence that we are not alone), it is not a possible theory for us.

There is a large and interesting class of ideas about human beings which reflect beliefs which are specific to a culture. States such as anomie, alienation, accidie, and angst go with a whole galaxy of attitudes and theories about people which may percolate into the general consciousness. At one time, perhaps, the theory of humours had the status now accorded to talk about 'defensive reactions.' We speak so generally nowadays about complexes and about the unconscious that it is quite allowable to speak of such theories as part of the ordinary commerce of thought and discussion. If by 'folk psychology' is meant such an eclectic *ad hoc* assemblage of bits of half-digested Adler and Freud, then there is no harm in the idea and I would be the first to agree that common-sense explanation of human behaviour is imbued with such theorizing. The problem is that believers in folk psychology have wished to classify all our mental ascriptions as theory. The verdict is inescapable. This is utterly implausible.[8]

FOOTNOTES

[1]Main source material is in Paul M. Churchland, 'Eliminative Materialism and the Propositional Attitudes,' this volume, esp. pp. 43–46, though I have also used his *Scientific Realism and the Plasticity of Mind* (Cambridge: Cambridge University Press, 1979) and *Matter and Consciousness* (Cambridge, Mass.: M.I.T. Press, 1984), and Patricia Smith Churchland, 'Replies to Comments,' *Inquiry* 29 (1986), pp. 241–72, part of a symposium on her *Neurophilosophy* (Cambridge, Mass.: M.I.T. Press, 1986) which together with Stephen Stich, *From Folk Psychology to Cognitive Science: the Case against Belief* (Cambridge, Mass.: M.I.T. Press, 1983), esp. ch. 10 (this volume, pp. 82–92), is also a major source.

[2]Wilfrid Sellars, 'Empiricism and the Philosophy of Mind,' in Sellars, *Science, Perception, and Reality* (London: Routledge & Kegan Paul, 1963), see sect. xv.

[3]Symposium on Patricia Smith Churchland's *Neurophilosophy, Inquiry,* op. cit., esp. Geoffrey Madell's 'Neurophilosophy: A Principled Sceptic's Response,' and K. V. Wilkes, 'Nemo Psychologus nisi Physiologus.'

[4]K. V. Wilkes, 'Pragmatics in Science and Theory in Common Sense,' *Inquiry* 27 (1984), pp. 339–61, and the cited contribution to the symposium, *Inquiry,* op. cit.

[5]Stich, op. cit., p. 230, this volume, p. 102.

[6]Stich, op. cit., p. 101.

[7]'Eliminative Materialism,' op. cit., p. 44.

[8]Earlier versions of this paper have been the rounds and I am indebted to philosophers at St. Andrews, Lampeter, Stirling, Dundee, Glasgow, Bangor, Swansea, and Aberystwyth. Jack Smart and David Cockburn were kind enough to read and comment upon earlier versions.

11 The Origins of Folk Psychology*

George Graham
University of Alabama, Birmingham

Call the concept of mind the concept of that which thinks, or is capable of thinking, in a broad sense of 'thinking' that includes not just episodes of conscious deliberation but also believing, desiring, sensing, perceiving, purposively moving and acting. I shall use the expression 'concept of mind' in this way. Such, for example, is the manner in which Armstrong (1981) and Moore (1953) deploy the concept. I shall suppose the mind to be that which thinks, in the broad sense. Thus understood we may say that creatures deploying the concept possess (to use the current term of philosophic art) a *folk psychology*. In conceiving of themselves as thinkers they are able to explain and predict behavior – to represent behavior as the product of thought. A typical putative example of use of the concept to explain or predict is the case where someone ascribes thought to another to understand the motivation behind the person's behavior. For example, someone pictures another person as thinking it would be best to walk to the river; his walking is anticipated and explained by appeal to his being moved by thought.

I shall not attempt any discussion of the concept of mind – or folk psychology – in general. I shall consider the entrenchment of folk psychology in evolutionary history. I shall bring out some characteristics of folk psychology, or the concept of mind, that I take to have bearing on methodological and epistemological questions about the deployment of the concept or psychology. My remarks will center on origins of the concept and certain claims about its adaptive biological utility: very briefly, that the

*Reprinted from *Inquiry* 30 (1987, pp. 357–379) by permission of the author and publisher.

concept became part of human conceptual equipment because it helped us to survive and proliferate. Such a view I call 'Adaptationalism.' I shall defend a modified form of adaptationalism, made sensitive to the question of how our folk grandparents competently deployed the concept.

Questioning the origins of the mind concept, or folk psychology, should be of interest, I believe, to philosophers with widely different ontological orientations in the philosophy of mind. Those like Keith Campbell (1986) who believe that the concept or psychology is ineliminable should find the question of interest because its answer may explain or help to explain why the concept is ineliminable; and thus they may find below a study in the entrenchment of the concept. But even those who prefer an eliminativist attitude (e.g. P. S. Churchland [1986a]) may find some explanation in the following study for why others believe that the concept is ineliminable.

I. THE ADAPTATIONALIST ANSWER

An important theme of nineteenth- and twentieth-century science is that men and animals are natural creatures and products of biological evolution. Also men's and animal's minds are products of biological evolution. If we think, it must be because such a capacity historically performed a service which helped us to survive and proliferate. Recently a number of philosophers and psychologists have added that our having a conception of what it means to have a mind, to think, is also the product of biological evolution. It is said that the concept of mind, or folk psychology, historically performed a service which helped us to survive and proliferate. Having the concept, or conceiving of mind, is something that man does in the world, and has adapted him to the world, by contrast with which not conceiving of it, or being stripped of the concept, is something objectively different and less biologically advantageous.

It will be difficult to give an account of the view which says that the concept of mind is the product of evolution; it requires that we reconstruct arguments from different sources and press alternative terms and terminologies into single-minded service. But it will be worthwhile to get into the logic of the argument, since it provides an answer to the question of why folk may have thought of themselves as thinkers in the first place.

No doubt possessing a mind (being able to think) protects a creature from dissolution and decomposition, and thus plays a role in individual survival. An important pre-Darwinian story of the mind's contribution to individual survival can be extracted from the De Anima of Aristotle. On his view the mind is responsible for locomotion; having a mind enables an animal to move on its own without being pushed or pulled, and, as a concomitant, to survive without being dependent on the solicitude of the immediate environment. When a creature thinks of something as eatworthy or chew-worthy, for example, it might move toward and ingest it; the creature does not have to wait for food to come to it. Or when a creature believes that something is harmful, for example, it might avoid it; it might move to safety and not have to wait for a hole to open up underneath it or to be blown into security. Individuals without the ability to think, mindless creatures, would not do well 'in a world of changes in what brought them (access to the) necessities of life' (Nozick [1981, p. 703]). Minded creatures can and do adapt to such changes.

With Darwin (1871 and 1872) and thereafter in both the nineteenth- (Romanes [1884] and [1888]; James [1890]; Morgan [1896]) and twentieth- (Griffin [1976] and [1984]; Sagan [1977]) centuries, the story suggested by Aristotle of minds being instrumental in individual survival has been supplemented by the related idea that minds are products of natural selection, and contribute to the survival of whole populations or species. On this view, the mind is responsible for certain animals' success at replication and reproduction, at locating mates and mating as well as, for example, securing food and avoiding injury. When a creature possesses a mind it can mate with others in thinking of them as breed worthy or mate worthy. It moves to mates, or to attract mates, and copulates without being dependent on the environment to scatter its seeds or fertilize its eggs. It is not rooted like a plant.

Some, agreeing with Darwin, hold that in addition the *concept* of mind is instrumental in promoting survival, for certain species (Dennett [1983] and [1984]; Humphrey [1983]; Levin [1984]). The idea is that species whose members possess the concept are better suited to their environment than similar species shorn of the concept. They are better able to approach benefits, avoid harms, and replicate. On this view, the concept of mind is the concept of that which thinks (believes, desires, etc.) and moves or locomotes because it thinks. Such a concept occurs only in creatures in whom the concept has been instilled by the forces of natural selection; or at least, the concept occurs in certain creatures such as human beings *because it has been instilled by the forces of natural selection.*

To be able to assess the view that the concept of mind is instrumental in survival and adaptive, for human beings, it will be worthwhile to modify a Just So Story or Myth of Wilfrid Sellars (1963, pp. 186–96). Imagine a village of prehistoric human beings endowed with minds, in that they move of their own accord, or think, but are unable to think that they think. They are capable of behavior of considerable complexity, even able to hear and vocalize, but are stripped of the ability to recognize that they think. There is eating, avoiding of trauma, mating, building of shelters, and so forth. But there is no concept of minds or thinkers operative in those activities.

The following example might help to illuminate the condition of the villagers. I drive home after work, too tired to concentrate. However, I brake at the red lights, negotiate difficult turns, avoid pedestrians, and so forth, and pull into the driveway safe and sound. Now my behavior was no doubt guided by thought. I thought of certain turns or I would not have turned. I thought of certain pedestrians or I would not have avoided them; and so on. But no doubt I also did not *think* of myself as thinking in guiding the drive. I was on a kind of 'automatic pilot.' Such is the condition of the villagers, though they move automatically, as it were, not from fatigue but because they do not think of themselves as thinkers. They don't have the concept of mind.

Now the question is, Is the village impoverished because of this? Would it be a good thing, or adaptive, for someone to discover or invent the concept of mind — the concept of oneself and others as moved by thought? The question is not whether someone could discover or invent the concept, but whether once discovered or invented it would help the village survive. To answer this question, let us introduce a strain of biological mutants, the Joneses. The Joneses are the first villagers to think of themselves and others as moved by thought. So now the question is, What advantage does this bring? Why cherish the emergence of the Joneses? After all, the non-Joneses survive — was their survival precarious in some way as a result? Did they lack the means for dealing with certain aspects of their environment? Among them behavior was controlled by thought of the injurious, mate-worthy, and chew-worthy, but not in terms of thought of thought.

Sellars says that in possessing the concept of mind Joneses have something useful which non-Joneses do not have. He calls this 'the germ of a theory,' by which he means that in the concept the Joneses have a kind of theoretical tool with which they can explain and predict the behavior of themselves and their ecological fellows (conspecifics and animals in the same niche) (1963, p. 187). Non-Joneses do not have this tool or piece of conceptual equipment, and thus are unable, or less able, to explain and predict behavior. Joneses detect certain sources of thought-directed movement, and thereby anticipate what their fellows are going to do, or appreciate why they behave as they do.

Consider examples. Fred Jones sees a lion approaching. What will the creature do? If Fred believes the lion regards him as attack worthy, he might predict that the lion will attack. Or suppose Sam Jones is walking through the village and spots Edna Jones in the middle distance. What will Edna do? If Sam thinks that Edna thinks of him as mate worthy, he might predict she will try to lead him into the mating hut. Or again, suppose Edna is hungry, and Sam hands her a piece of fruit. She might explain his behavior to herself thus: 'Sam gives me fruit because he believes I am hungry.'

Are one's conspecifics or others going to attack, mate, or offer fruit? That depends on whether they are moved by thought of the attack worthy, the mate worthy, or by the desire to relieve hunger. Attuned to such mind-impregnated possibilities, Joneses would be able to predict and explain behavior, but ignorant non-Joneses would not. Or if this judgment sounds too harsh, they would be significantly less able to predict and explain than Joneses. Supposing Sellars' surmise, there are then predictive and explanatory capacities involved in having the concept of mind. Primitives blessed with the concept have a predictive and explanatory theory or germ of a theory. They have a rudimentary folk psychology.

In such a case the question arises, Are the Joneses better off because they have the germ of a theory, and can predict and explain, or do this better than non-Joneses? Are there certain aspects of human survival and well-being (for example, freedom from predators) in which non-Joneses would not be able to keep up with the Joneses?

Levin remarks:

> Creatures who can detect the thoughts . . . of human and non-human fellow creatures have an evolutionary advantage over those who cannot, because they can . . . predict what their fellow creatures are going to do. (1984, p. 347)

In general it seems to certain theorists that the ability to predict and explain afforded by the capacity to think of oneself and others as moved by thought yields an adaptive advantage. The theme is as follows: There are certain aspects of human survival and well-being (for example, freedom from predators) that are important and peculiarly vulnerable. Due in large part to people's inability to predict or explain the thought-directed behavior of others, persons would on the whole be better off if those aspects of survival and well-being were protected by ensuring that people had the ability to predict and explain. This can be done in one or more of three ways—in terms of the neurophysiological origins of behavior; in terms of correlations between external circumstances, movements, and individual learning (reward/punishment) histories; and/or in terms of the concept of mind. Now there are various reasons, according to these theorists, for preferring instillation of predictive and explanatory ability in terms of the concept of mind.

II. ADVANTAGES ON THE ADAPTATIONALIST VIEW

One such reason is connected with what might be called *the brain ignorance problem*. Consider the problem. The concept of mind was born of a period, presumably, in which people were ignorant of neurophysiology—and, in which behavior could not be predicted (or explained) (hereafter I shall focus on prediction) under description of its neurophysiological origins. The germ of theory provided by the concept of mind is 'quite unaffected by ignorance about brain processes—or even by large-scale misinformation about brain processes' (Dennett, this volume, p. 125). It can thus be applied without regard to ignorance concerning the neurophysiological origins of behavior. Sam, using the concept, might predict Edna will mate, or move to mate, because she thinks of him as mate worthy. Sam might predict this while being massively ignorant of the neurophysiological origins of behavior, or sexual impulses in Edna. The concept of mind thus provides a way of realizing, among anatomically ignorant people, the desired ability. There is yet another, related reason for preferring the concept of mind. A behavioral psychologist might be able to predict the behavior of certain creatures in terms of external stimuli and the creatures' learning history, or trajectory of reward and punishment. When Edna kicks Sam, will Sam shout? Pick up a club? Or run to the mating hut? Reliable behavioral conditionals like

If x has been kicked, and negatively reinforced on a variable ratio schedule for picking up a club after having been kicked, then x will pick up a club.

might be available to the psychologist, but for creatures without records of individual learning histories, or unfamiliar—explicitly—with reinforcement schedules, the concept of mind is a handy crutch. What nature would want in such circumstances is one easy to use germ of a theory 'that will do the predictive job of . . . purely behavioral conditionals' (Levin, pp. 349–50). Once the concept of mind is in place, the crutch is in hand. In thinking of themselves as moved by thought, Joneses acquire a predictive power they can get in no other way.

Advocates of the adaptationalist argument are not clear as to what aspects of human survival and well-being are protected by the concept of mind. But examples are easy to supply. Consider social cooperation. Certainly social cooperation is advantageous, and in a primitive village would be required for certain biologically essential activities, such as hunting and/or food production. But social cooperation raises a *coordination problem*. A coordination problem is any problem in which what is best (adaptive) for a person to do depends on what others are going to do. It might be best for Fred to do A if Sam is going to do B, but to do C if Sam is going to do D. And the problem is that the outcome that is best is not likely to be reached if each person must act without predicting what others will do. Instilling the concept of mind provides the needed result. Fred will think that Sam is planning on doing B, and himself do A. Or if he believes Sam intends to do D, he will do C. Without the concept, villagers might not be able to 'reap the rewards of cooperative enterprise' (Humphrey [1983, p. 52]). Another example is freedom from predators. If it is a question of being approached by a predator, villagers who can predict the creature's behavior will gain the advantage. Instilling the concept again provides the needed result. Fred will think of the lion as finding him attack worthy, and flee. More obtuse strains, in Levin's words, 'are likely to have been selected out, if they ever existed' (Levin, p. 349).

What we see then is that there are situations in which being able to predict or explain is essential to appropriate response. Certain aspects of human survival and well-being can depend on having the ability. This then remains a powerful argument for the adaptivity of the concept of mind. There was a unique contribution made by the concept in the survival and proliferation of Joneses or primitive folk.

III. THE COMPETENCY PROBLEM

We have been sketching an argument in support of the biological utility of the concept of mind. The argument, however, is not complete. There is a problem.

One might say: Well, at least the concept is important as a predictive and explanatory tool. Intuitively, however, this does not seem to produce an advantage. The concept looks as if it could be fallible equipment, e.g. possibly misrepresenting what others are thinking or going to do. Thus, one needs to demonstrate that Joneses would be *competent* detectors or predictors. Proper ascription of thought to others is essential in bestowing an evolutionary advantage on those who have the concept of mind, unless other reasons can be found for saying the concept is adaptive. Cases of predation provide excellent examples. When the lion approaches Fred, does Fred flee? Suppose Fred attributes the wrong thought to the lion, and gets eaten as a result. There are such thoughts which Fred might attribute, and they would produce a survival disadvantage that would have to be compensated for by more adept users of the concept than Fred.

Though advocates of the adaptationalist thesis agree that the concept of mind must be deployed competently, there are differences about how exactly competent use might become entrenched, and consequently about whether the mere possession of the concept is adaptive, or needs to be supplemented by other concepts, perhaps proper parts of the concept.

Levin's remark about obtuse strains, quoted above, contains one suggestion. The theme is as follows: If certain primitives did not deploy the concept of mind competently and with sufficient accuracy, and were in competition with strains who were intelligent attributers, after an extended period of natural selection we would expect the strain of competent deployers to outcompete their incompetent conspecifics. The latter's proportion of faulty predictions would be higher; more of them, e.g., would be killed by predators, fewer would be able to participate in cooperative social enterprises.

Undoubtedly this argument has plausibility. Faulty predictions involve costs. Shall we conclude, then, that adaptationalists should embrace this argument for competent deployment? That is difficult to decide, for we would first have to decide upon the likelihood of the concept of mind's being uncovered or invented if people did not deploy it competently from the start. If it is likely that they did so deploy it, then we will have no need of the idea that competent deployers outcompeted incompetent deployers.

Let us focus, then, on versions of the argument for competent deployment which find this embedded in the concept of mind, or the conditions of its invention at the start.[1] Thus, if Joneses attribute thought to others, and predict their behavior, or deploy the concept as the germ of a theory, then they must do so competently.

(1) The Concept of Similar Mind

One possibility is a line of thought suggested by Humphrey (1983), also Levin (1984), and in another context Stich (1982). We might say as a first approximation that the concept of mind applicable to a Jonesean is the concept of a mind similar to one's own, or the Concept of Similar Mind. If one attributes thoughts to another, these will be thoughts one has oneself, or would have, in those circumstances. And the other has, or is likely to have, such thoughts in those circumstances because the other's mind is similar to one's own. There is a kind of pre-established harmony between what people attribute and what others think. If Joneses attribute thought at all, that is, if they think of other fellows as moved by thought, then they do so by picturing them in cognitive uniformity at the level of particular thought with themselves. As Humphrey says:

> [A villager's] picture of the inner reasons for his own behaviour is one which he will immediately and naturally project on other people. He can and will use his own experience to get inside other people's skins . . . [and] since the chances are he himself is not in reality untypical of human beings [in the village] . . . this kind of imaginative projection gives him an explanatory scheme of remarkable generality and power. (1983, pp. 53–54)

So the hypothesis is that when Fred thinks of Sam being moved by certain thoughts, these are likely to be Sam's thoughts, and Sam is likely to do just what Fred believes he is going to do.

Now despite the neat and nimble way in which the idea of similar mind would ensure competent deployment, something in this line of reasoning does not ring true. For one thing it assumes that people think alike — that however dissimilar or unfamiliar their circumstances, it is somehow possible *in principle* to take them to be thinking similarly. But an interesting if speculative possibility is suggested by Julian Jaynes.

> In the forced . . . intermingling of peoples from different nations, different
> gods, the observation that strangers, even though looking like oneself, spoke
> differently . . . and behaved differently might lead to the supposition of
> something inside them that was different. . . . It is thus a possibility that
> [man] first posited [mind] in strangers, as the thing that causes their different
> and bewildering behavior. (1976, p. 217)

In that case, of course, a uniformist would have to abjure his claim to derive
competent deployment from the concept of similar mind—unless, that is,
there are cognitive similarities which Jaynes and we have overlooked. The
worry is this. A Jonesean properly uses the concept of similar mind when,
but only when, he deploys it for creatures with similar minds or thought.
And the theoretical utility gained in the package deal of concept and
competent deployment is outweighed by the *disutility* of being unable to
deploy the concept in a situation where there are grounds for doubting the
presence of similarity.

The idea of similar mind, at least in the extreme form I have presented it,
faces another obvious problem. The crucial notion of people having similar
thoughts is unclear. Fred and Edna have active sexual impulses, and thus
are inclined to think that everyone is preoccupied with thoughts of The
Mate worthy. Yet Fred is, while Edna is not, interested in the animal hunt.
For them at least, though Edna might accompany Fred on the hunt, she has
no accurate idea what he thinks in those circumstances. Minds are minds,
and if people have similar minds at all, it is likely that they have them only
in certain respects, or at certain times, or in a certain range of cases—a
presumption which means there is no reason to attribute thoughts to others
which are similar to one's own unless one is shown that another's thoughts
are likely to be similar, not because another's mind is similar, but for
independent reasons, e.g., that another's learning history or neurophysiological condition is similar.

(2) The Concept of Rational Mind

As a first approximation to a second package deal we might say
(following a lead suggested by Dennett [e.g. (1983)]) that the concept of
mind applicable to a Jonesean is the concept of a mind rationally adjusted
to or tracked into its circumstances, or the Concept of Rational Mind. This
means that if one attributes thoughts to another these are going to be
thoughts a creature *ought* to have in those circumstances. Further, another
does have, or in all likelihood has, such thoughts in those circumstances
because another's mind is rationally adjusted to its circumstances. Again,
imagine Fred attributing thought to Sam in circumstances C. Fred attributes
thoughts to Sam which Sam should have in C. Second, Sam, being a
rational creature, has such thoughts in C. Again, this means that there is a

kind of pre-established harmony between what people attribute and what others think.

The 'rationality model' of attribution can yield competent deployment; but, and this is an important qualification, only if an assumption is built into the model, namely that the range of rational thought in circumstances in which thought is attributed is limited. Thus, the thought Fred attributes to Sam in *C* must be *the thought* a person ought to have in *C*. If there are other thoughts a rational creature might have, the constraint that one attributes what is rational does not by itself determine what Sam thinks. A person might think, or attribute, any number of thoughts, each rational, or equally tracked into *C*.

Some critics would object to the model because it presupposes that people are rationally adjusted to their circumstances or situations (Stich [1982] and [1985]). If folk are not rational, taking them to think what they ought will not produce competent deployment. Fred might take Sam to think of *A* as do-worthy, when Sam thinks of *Z* as do-worthy, which might be completely inappropriate in the circumstances. But I am not sure this is a satisfactory objection. It is open to an advocate of the rationality model of competent deployment to insist that the model be meant to apply in primitive, prehistorical circumstances. In such circumstances it is likely that unless people think what they ought they would not be afoot in a Jonesean village. For example, in his discussion of animal learning and adaptation, J. E. R. Staddon (1983) makes the point that certain behavior (for example, eating) is essential to life, and failure to engage in such behavior, and allocate time to it, at least over the long term, does not favor a large posterity. If we are talking about evolutionary adaptation, the same point can be made about thought-directed movement in Joneses. Certain thoughts, and thought-directed behavior, are essential to life, and failure over the long term to engage in such behavior does not favor a large posterity. Joneses are thus likely to think and be moved by thoughts which, at least over the long term, are adjusted to their circumstances. They are unlikely to be moved by thoughts which do not favor a large posterity. (But see Stich [1985] for objections to the assumption of human rationality even in primitive circumstances.)

Now while the assumption of (primitive) rationality might be true, should there not at least be good reasons for saying that the range of rational thought is limited? Rationality is obviously a relative concept. Whether a given thought — or piece of behavior — is rational will depend on other thoughts the person has and other things he does, and certainly there can be more than one thought which it is rational to have in certain circumstances. Generally, a person is rational if what he thinks meets certain very general restrictions on thought and behavior. In specifying thought, rationality is an open-ended constraint. Suppose Edna, who is childless, observes Ethel, who has just given birth, and one asks 'What thought should Edna ascribe to Ethel?' That she had better tell her husband? That she should start breastfeeding? That the baby looks like Uncle Sam? That Edna is a busybody? The problem is not just the practical one of ascertaining another's thought in a given case, but the conceptual one of what is to be understood by *rational thought,* and what kind of limitations rationality places on the range of states of mind of which people, and creatures with minds, are capable.

Let me try to emphasize this point by reference again to Sam in circumstances *C.* Suppose Sam is rational. When this assumption is added, does the question 'What does Sam think in *C?*' take on a limited, specific answer? This seems clearly a necessary condition for the concept of rational mind's producing competent deployment of the concept of mind for the rationality model. But to justify this condition, we clearly need to restrict what one ought to believe in *C,* so that the attributer has some definite thought to attribute to Sam. We clearly need an attribution rule like the following: 'Sam is in situation *C;* and in a situation of that type, or in that situation, the thought to think is *x.*' But what in many circumstances a person ought to think includes not necessarily just *x,* but any of a range of thoughts. Although Sam might think all of these, the rationality assumption would be satisfied if he thought just one of them. Sam would believe what he ought, and the attributer correctly take Sam to be thinking as he ought, but the attribution could be incorrect and lead to faulty predictions.

In thus dissenting from the rationality model of competent deployment, I do not wish to deny that people are rational. I maintain only that whether primitives think as they ought, and so ascribe thought, is insufficient to produce competent deployment of the concept of mind. Rationality and the concept of rational mind alone do not explain how Joneses could competently ascribe thoughts.

(3) The Rich Concept Theory

I have argued that two varieties of package deal between the concept of mind and its competent deployment do not in fact ensure competent deployment. Perhaps these deals can be modified in certain respects, or melded together, or perhaps other package deals are possible. One such possibility is to endow (perhaps as some sort of mutation) Joneses with a rich or complex concept—i.e., with thought of different types and roles in the production of movement. Then one can argue that Joneses would not persist in the use of such a concept unless, in general, they accurately represented the thoughts of others. For example, suppose Sam attributes, or has the capacity to attribute, all sorts of thoughts to his fellows—beliefs, desires, cravings, wishings, and so forth. Now if Nature endows Sam with the rich concept, the best explanation of his persisting in deploying the concept might be that he uses it competently. Perhaps the concept is too complex to be used incompetently. The point is that there would be no reason for Sam to persist in using the rich concept, or to have it, if he was incompetent or a faulty predictor. The richness of the concept secures the package deal, or more precisely, establishes a presumption of competent deployment.

Now I am inclined to regard this proposal as not worth pursuing. It should be a condition of historical plausibility, or reasoned imaginability, for a Myth of Jones that richness is not part of the concept of mind possessed by primitives. The concept *developed in richness* historically. Inasmuch as a Jonesean has the concept, it is on the whole more plausible to think of him as equipped at first with a limited or relatively impoverished battery of thoughts and types to attribute to others.

I will not here attempt to make the idea of a rich concept of mind precise, but leave it at an intuitive level. I suppose the point I have just made about the concept (that it fits ill with a Jonesean myth) applies under any reasonable construal. However, poverty too has limits. What Joneses must think if they are to be moved by thought, or to predict by ascribing thought, must be made explicit, or more determinate. For one thing, thinking is not always (or just) a source of behavior or movement. I might think of crossing a frozen pond, but not cross. Also, it is possible for someone to ascribe thought, to believe I am pondering crossing, but not predict I am going to cross. It is therefore essential to understand the Joneses as having, and attributing, thought in types sufficient for movement or behavior. We must explicitly recognize some richness (or functional detail) in the Joneses' concept of mind.

Consider in a rough and informal manner the bare minimum Joneses require in their psychological make-up if they are to be moved by thought, or engage in thought-directed behavior. An important insight can be extracted from a homely but revealing passage in James's *Principles,* which identifies the necessity. I quote the passage in full.

> We know what it is to get out of bed on a freezing morning in a room without a fire, and how the very vital principle within us protests against the ordeal. Probably most persons have lain on certain mornings for an hour at a time unable to brace themselves to the resolve. . . . Now how do we ever get up under such circumstances? If I may generalize from my own experience, we more often than not get up without any struggle or decision at all. We suddenly find that we *have* got up. A fortunate lapse of consciousness occurs; we forget both the warmth and the cold; we fall into some revery connected with the day's life, in the course of which the idea flashes across us, 'Hollo! I must lie here no longer' — an idea which at that lucky instant awakens no contradictory or paralyzing suggestions, and consequently produces immedi-

ately its appropriate motor effects. It was our acute consciousness of both the warmth and the cold during the period of struggle, which paralyzed our activity then and kept our idea of rising in the condition of *wish* and not of *will*. The moment these inhibitory ideas ceased the original idea exerted its effects. (1890, II, pp. 524–25, orig. emph.)

Underlying James's story is the notion that *motivation* is needed to produce thought-directed movement. If someone in bed was to think of getting up but did not purpose to get up, he would not get up without being pushed or pulled. This notion identifies the Joneses' necessity. When thinking motivates, thought produces behavior but otherwise not. Brand (1984) makes the same point when he writes: 'Without conative features, action could not begin. . . . The proximate cause of action involves . . . the motivation to undertake that course' (1984, pp. 45–46). If James and Brand are right, the minimum Joneses need in order to be moved by thought is purpose or motivation to move. They require something to 'energize' behavior, not merely to represent either it or its upshot as a possibility.

The exact nature of motivation is a puzzle of considerable complexity, as listing the various sorts of notions which philosophers use to identify the phenomenon testifies: desire (Davidson [1963]), intention (Brand [1984]; Searle [1983]), volition (Goldman [1976]), and intended practition (Castañeda [1980]).

It is tempting to try to be more exact, or formal, about the Jonesean need and concept of motivation. But then one has to judge how much complexity to pack into their mind and self-understanding. Should Joneses be said to deliberate? Should their motivations be said to vary in intensity? Should their movement or behavior be said to be represented by them as mere bodily motion (e.g., moving a leg) or as the upshots or effects of such motion (e.g., crossing a pond) or, depending on the circumstances, as both? It is likely that Joneses must think of *some* behavior in terms of the effects of bodily motions; and here I have been classifying their behavior, and movement-directing thought, in such terms. One Jones mates, another escapes, and still another crosses a pond. Such behavior is adaptive, not merely bodily motion. But answers to these and related questions are not obvious. There are possible differences in emphasis, of detail, and points of importance in the philosophy of action and mind, which would have to be weighed or settled in attempting a more exact specification of the character of Jonesean motivation. For the present, I shall restrict myself to the rough essence of Jonesean motivation. We should be able to get by with a 'simple,' not too fine-grained account of the character of Joneses' motivating thought.

Regarding the various identifications mentioned above of the motivational element in thought, I prefer an idea which is neutral as between several notions: that of thinking of something as 'do-worthy.' Thinking something to be do-worthy is believing it worthwhile for one to do. One is therein energized or motivated to do it. Now there are any number of reasons, or causes, why one might believe something is do-worthy, e.g., protection, pleasure, fulfillment. However, the central point is that in thinking something do-worthy one is already motivated. Sam thinks of Edna not just as someone with whom he might mate, but as mate worthy, or of mating with her as do-worthy. The desire to mate with her washes over him. Meanwhile, Fred conceives of Sam as thinking to mate with Edna. He is therefore not surprised when he observes them entering the mating hut.

Reference to being motivated accounts for a certain thought's producing behavior. I shall continue to use 'thought of the do-worthy' to refer to motivating thought.

Note that the conception of mind which I have been using thus far, while broad, is also relatively weak phenomenologically. I have not addressed, for instance, the question of whether Joneses must, or would, possess 'intro-spective access' to their thoughts, or the degree to which Joneses are self-conscious or self-aware. Some such conception of introspective access lies at the heart of the ordinary notion of thought. We can accept this, I think, while remaining agnostic about whether, or to what extent, Joneses enjoy introspective access to their thoughts. I am concerned here only with the *practice* of ascribing thoughts to others, as a means of prediction (and explanation). My aim is to show in what manner such a practice is adaptive. One might, however, reasonably continue to worry about attempts to discover one's own thoughts in the original position — behind the veil of neurobehavioral ignorance which covers the Village of Jones.

(4) The Concept of Similar Rational Mind

Is there a package deal which can be built on the recognition, or explicit acknowledgement, of motivation in thought? One suggestion — derived loosely from David Lewis (1974, 1983b) — is to introduce the Concept of Similar Rational Mind.

The Concept of Similar Rational Mind has a mixed character. On the one hand, it is the concept of a rational creature whose thought and behavior are appropriately tracked into its environment. On the other hand, it is the concept of a similar creature whose thought is similar to the thought of those who ascribe thought to it.

From a strictly conceptual standpoint, it seems to me, we can distinguish two advantages that the concept of similar rational mind has over concepts of (simply) rational or (simply) similar minds. Given the concept of rational mind, as the second proposal construed it, there is the problem of too many thoughts to attribute and the impossibility of using rationality alone to select from among them. Where determinate ascription, in this sense, cannot be achieved, there is the possibility of another person's being said to think things he does not think even though he is rightly assumed to be rational. It is preferable therefore to constrain the assumption of rationality, to introduce an added assumption which might select from rational thoughts one which, on a given occasion, or in a given circumstance, moves another. The assumption of similarity is one such constraint. If another is similar, he does not think *everything* he ought; he thinks only what he should, given that he thinks like oneself or others. In the words of David Lewis, another 'should be represented as believing what he ought to believe, and desiring what he ought to desire. And what is that? [H]e ought to believe what we believe . . . and he ought to desire what we desire' (1983b, p. 112). The supposition of similarity offers a way of selecting, from among various rational thoughts, those which can make ascription determinate. It precludes certain thoughts, though rational, from moving or motivating another.

Furthermore, given the assumption of similar mind, as the first proposal construed it, there is the problem of the impossibility of ascribing thought to another when that other's situation or circumstance is unfamiliar or foreign. It is preferable, therefore, to enhance the assumption of similarity and embolden it, to introduce an assumption which might make thought available for ascription in unfamiliar or novel circumstances. An assumption of rationality is such an enhancement. Another person does not think exactly like oneself. He thinks as one does, given he is also rational, and thinks what he ought. Again in the words of Lewis, another 'should be represented as a rational agent' (Lewis, p. 113). His thought should be 'coherent' (p. 114) and give him 'good reasons' (p. 113) for his behavior. The invocation of the notion of rationality is a way of refraining, in the assumption of similarity, from thinking another thoughtless just because one might oneself be thoughtless in those circumstances. It allows certain thoughts, though untypical of the attributer, to move another.

The Concept of Similar Rational Mind is the concept of a creature rational enough to be motivated by thought in novel circumstances, but similar enough to the ascriber (or to a Jones) not to be packed with every conceivable rational thought in any circumstance. His thought and behavior is *somehow similarly* tracked into the environment. Meanwhile his thought is similar *somehow rationally* to the thought of the attributer.

The fourth proposal might be clarified by means of an example. Suppose Ethel has just had a baby. Edna observes Ethel with the newborn child. Edna has never had a baby. In fact, Edna has never nurtured children, though she is often motivated to feed other hungry people in the village. Now were she equipped only with the concept of rational mind, Edna could not (except by happenstance) deploy such a concept to detect Ethel's thought. There would be too many possibilities. A number of thoughts might be tracked into Ethel's environment—that the baby is feedworthy, that he resembles Sam, and so forth. Presumably Ethel would or could not be moved by them all. Likewise, if Edna was equipped with only the concept of similar mind, she might not ascribe any thought to Ethel. She has never been in Ethel's shoes. She has never had a baby. She has never nurtured children. But the question of what thought to ascribe might be a manageable problem if Edna was equipped with a concept of similar rational mind. Its rationality component might give her *some* thought to attribute, despite unfamiliar circumstances. Its added similarity component might give her some *single* thought to attribute, despite Ethel's being assumed to think what she ought.

In assuming rationality, Edna might represent Ethel as thinking that the child is feed worthy or as believing that he resembles Sam, and so on. In assuming similarity, she might represent Ethel as being motivated to feed the hungry. In assuming similar rationality, with these two assumptions melded together, each working with the other, she might represent Ethel as thinking the child feed worthy. The baby is hungry. Edna is often motivated to feed hungry villagers.

The fourth proposal, or package deal, seems to me a genuine possibility. Some theorists say the standard assumption people make in deciding what others think is that they think pretty much like oneself, and this is, somehow, appropriate or expresses an underlying rationality. As Swinburne puts it, we assume that 'people's beliefs change when presented with stimuli in regular ways,' and we assume that 'other people have purposes of a kind which we also have ourselves' (1981, p. 13). We suppose common and reasonable motivations propel people. The 'standard' assumption may not be one which folk conceptualize to themselves in any direct or obvious way (unless they are philosophers!). It might govern ascriptions without people being aware of this. A person thinks of others through a process of projection with the tacit assumption that everyone is rather like oneself, and in most matters is neither much more nor much less rational than oneself.[2]

But the foregoing proposal has of course its difficulties. The main problem is to find some justification other than wishful thinking for adopting it. Whether others are rational or moved by thoughts like one's own must be established. Another problem is how to apply standards of motivational similarity; the notion of similar purposes has to be refined to deal with questions of whether two people are actually propelled for the same reasons. For instance, Dennett (1984a) establishes the assumption of similar motivation by supposing that people's biological drives are the same; that everyone wants to avoid pain, eat, achieve some measure of sexual pleasure, stay warm, and so forth. It might be argued that motivations divide into subclasses supported by fundamental biological impulses. This doesn't mean that everyone wants the same particulars (corn, not toma-toes); it means that people's intentions reflect the same general interests (food, not starvation). We could perhaps see more fully what these interests are by adding further relevant components of a situation. We might find that there is a low likelihood of Ethel thinking of Uncle Sam, whereas it is highly likely she thinks to feed the child, for exactly the reason that an intention to feed the hungry is an expression of a fundamental drive or interest which we share with Ethel. Given that the baby is hungry, and that we would think to feed the hungry, we can expect her to think of feeding and be motivated to feed the child.

Quite clearly the idea of a similar rational mind presents another package deal. But, as we saw in the discussion of the first two, although it may be convenient to pack rationality or similarity into the concept of mind, it is difficult to specify exactly what this might involve. There is considerable room for maneuver over notions of similar motivation and rationality. We must take as a consequence of the fourth proposal some explanation of how Jonesean or pre-historic circumstances could give rise to similar motivations and rationality.

IV. COMPETENCY AND COMPETITION

Despite being tempted by the fourth proposal, I shall stop considering whether a *package deal* will serve the adaptationalist thesis. However, it is important to note that the failure of the first three deals does not spell the end of package deals; a fourth waits to be examined. Rather than proceed with that examination, however, it will be more expedient here to return to the thesis that the concept of mind and its proper deployment do *not* form a package deal. Competent deployment itself evolved due to the *contingencies of relative advantage*. Competent deployers outcompeted their incompetent conspecifics.

There are a number of ways in which this idea is satisfying. First, it is consistent with this idea that the Concept of Similar Rational Mind is an element in competent deployment. It is just that this concept could not be universal Jonesean equipment. It would have had to be part of the evolved ability of competent deployers to defeat incompetent deployers. Imagine two Jonesean strains, the Sams and Hams. The Sams suppose others to be moved by similar and appropriate intentions; the Hams, unfortunately, do not. *Supposing* others are moved by Sam-similar appropriate intentions, the Sams should defeat the Hams. The Sams should enjoy greater predictive success. The concept of a similar rational mind would be behind their evolutionary victory.

Second, the idea of outcompeting provides an explanation for the entrenchment of the concept of mind. We seem almost involuntarily to think of ourselves as moved by thought. There must exist some explanation of this, some reason why picturing ourselves as motivated by thoughtful states seems unavoidable, natural, inescapable. Perhaps the answer is that the concept is inherited spoil of our ancestral victory over incompetent conspecifics (whether the concept of a similar rational mind is the spoil is irrelevant to this second reason, as also to the third below). We survived by proper use of the germ of a theory, and are unable to switch to alternative conceptions, or to think of ourselves as anything less or other than thinkers. Against this evolutionary background, it must be idle to deny that we think: the concept of mind is not some artifact that we can scorn. As we have evolved, the concept occupies a position of utility which we underestimate at our ecological peril.

Finally, the idea has the merit of attempting to do full justice to the notion that faulty predictions have costs. Imagine two Jonesean strains, the Freds and Jeds. Suppose the Freds and Jeds enter the hunt. The Freds ascribe the right thought to prey, anticipate prey behavior and bring home food for supper. The Jeds do not. They mispredict because they ascribe thought to prey which prey do not have; they cannot anticipate prey behavior and return hungry. Such incompetence, over the long haul, and if ramified in a number of sorts of crucial circumstances, and barring such compensations as altruistic Freds, should get defeated. The Freds' competence should get 'selected for,' or somehow get programmed into the practice of hunting for food (etc.).

Of course neither of the above considerations amounts to a demonstrative case for the relative-advantage idea. Either might be challenged. But together they are a rather strong set of reasons for finding it attractive. So, let us note some conclusions which can be drawn from our reconstruction of the adaptationalist argument and formulate some observations.

V. CONCLUSION AND OBSERVATIONS

The adaptationalist thesis is that possessing the concept of a mind is adaptive and in particular is the product of natural selection. There seems reason for endorsing the thesis. There is still room to question the exact genesis of competent deployment. One might wonder whether the concept and its proper deployment formed a package deal or were shaped through competition. But a promising line is that assuming the concept of mind figures as the germ of a competently deployed theory, it is adaptive and the product of biological evolution. People properly equipped with the concept would be better off than non-equipped or incompetently deploying conspecifics.

Having sketched the adaptationalist argument and suggested why one might endorse it, I shall close with four observations, including responses to two criticisms.

(1) Recall that the adaptationalist argument rests on the premise that the concept of mind is handy for people ignorant of brain function and reinforcement principles. Actually, of course, the premise can be made more general. The concept is handy for otherwise ignorant people, viz., folk unassisted by God or Nature in the prediction, or explanation, of behavior free of the push and pull of the local environment. So, it is a constraint on the Joneses that other, or better, tools for prediction and explanation are not available. This is an empirically controversial constraint. Perhaps, contrary to our earlier assumption, a behaviorist theory might be available to Joneses to predict and explain behavior. If so, villagers might not need or even be helped by a concept of mind. In truth a good deal more may need to be said to assess the behaviorist option. So, the premise in question must be understood to be just that, a premise. *If* Joneses were otherwise ignorant and did not deploy some notion of reinforcement, possessing the concept of mind would have been useful and given them a biological advantage.

(2) There might be ways to demonstrate that the concept of mind is adaptive which are not exhausted by its being used theoretically to predict or explain. For example, the concept — or folk psychology — might be a proper part of introspective self-awareness, something like a primitive's direct, first-person access to his own thoughts, which might mean that the concept is adaptive for reasons unconnected with prediction or explanation. Certainly respect for this possibility is not precluded by anything I or others to my knowledge have said about the utility of the concept of mind. In fact, such a thesis might complement the adaptationalist case here outlined.

(3) I have focused on the case of using the concept of mind to predict. It should be noted that a concept can be predictively useful without being explanatorily successful (e.g., Salmon [1984]). Now not every fan of the adaptationalist thesis assumes that the concept of mind — or folk psychology — explains. Some say it merely predicts (see Dennett [1983] and compare [1978a]). But I assume it predicts because it explains, and so do most adaptationalists about the concept of mind. So, I assume that establishing its *predictive* adaptive utility secures also its *explanatory* adaptive utility. A defense of the assumption would take another paper entirely.

(4) Finally, two objections. I have said the concept is a product of biological evolution. I defended this thesis by considering a race of pre-historic humans. Perhaps, it will be objected, the concept has outlived its biological utility (e.g., Skinner [1971], P. M. Churchland [this volume, pp. 42–62]). It now must yield to anti-cognitive advances in behavioral and neuroscience. Although such claims are compatible with anything I have

said here, they are not, I believe, compatible with the truth. The success of folk in daily life depends on continued functioning of the concept of mind. As descendants of Mother Jones, we are still basically unaware of any comprehensive method for predicting and explaining behavior which does not involve reference to mind or thought. Even psychological science uses the concept or variants of the concept. (See Brand [1984]; compare Horgan and Woodward [this volume] with Stich [1983a].) Of course, there is significant information about the brain, or central nervous system, and about reinforcement and conditioning which is predictive, and perhaps explanatory. Certainly this information is useful in the description of certain behavior. But wholesale application of such models has thus far proven impossible. We seem bound to conceive of ourselves as moved by thought. It is not appropriate, therefore, to say that the concept of mind has lost its adaptive utility. Perhaps we shall not survive with it, but we cannot cope without it.

A second objection is potentially more forceful. The adaptive value of the concept of mind may, for all we know, not prove that our having the concept is the result of *biological* evolution. There are biologically useful traits for which there has been social rather than natural selection (e.g., Gould [1977] on cultural transmission vs. biological evolution).[3] It does not follow, therefore, that if the concept is adaptive it must have been biologically selected for. Joneses able and prone to think of themselves and others as moved by thought were better able to escape from predators than their conceptless conspecifics, and they gained some increased efficiency in leaving great-grand-progeny. But this could have been because the concept was socially transmitted.

Actually, much of the argumentation of this paper can be translated without loss into an argument that the concept of mind is the product of evolution, *simpliciter,* leaving it open whether the evolution is biological or social. I have focused on its adaptive utility, and this can be expressed biologically or culturally. However, I am strongly disinclined to concede that the concept evolved socially, at least without evolving biologically first. In order to show that the concept is a product of social or cultural evolution one must construct a reasonable scenario, some means by which social transmission could have taken place among the first folk to deploy the concept. I, for one, have not been able to conceive of such a scenario. Remember the task is not to imagine cultural evolution simply, but cultural evolution at its first conception in our primitive ancestors. No doubt the concept has evolved socially from Homer to Stich. But what is wanted is a script for its social evolution in the Adams and Cains of Jones. To appreciate the difficulty in constructing such a scenario, let us ask what it would be for the concept to be socially transmitted from the first Jones to other potential Joneses. The process of transmission strikes me as an impossible one. For example, what does the first Jones do, *tell* his people that he thinks? He must do this without presupposing that others believe that he thinks. However, in fact, others must believe that he thinks if they are to interpret his noise as speech, as message or communication. So, he cannot succeed in informing them, 'I'm a thinker,' without their already believing this. (I am equally stymied when I ponder other scripts.) By contrast, in natural evolution, patterned along Darwinian lines, the Joneses had something in their biological or neuro-organizational make-up which produced in them the recognition of thought or the concept of mind—the potential germ of theory, folk psychology. Deployers of the concept were then tested and selected through interaction with the natural and social environment. Non-Joneses were eliminated. Social evolution was no doubt responsible for later developments in the concept, as the germ of theory became Theory, but initial folk psychologists were mutations for whom the concept was a Natural Selection.[4]

FOOTNOTES

[1]Some of these versions come from outside the literature explicitly on adaptive utility and inside the literature on propositional attitude ascription.

[2]See Vendler (1984) for an interesting discussion of the logic of projection.

[3]There are also biologically useful traits for which there has been neither natural nor social selection, traits which have been selected but not selected for. A complete and systematic defense of the adaptationalist thesis—which this paper is not—would have to show that the mind concept is not such a trait. It would also have to indicate how the concept of mind genetically supervenes, e.g., on whatever codes for a certain sort of brain or neurological organization. Such tasks are difficult. My method in this paper has been to focus on certain aspects of adaptationalism.

[4]An earlier version of this paper was presented at the University of South Carolina at Columbia, South Carolina, where I profited from audience discussion. I thank Harold Kincaid, James Rachels, Chris Maloney, and Bob Mulvaney for help.

12 The Persistence of the Attitudes*

Jerry A. Fodor
The Graduate Center, CUNY

A Midsummer Night's Dream, act 3, scene 2.
Enter Demetrius and Hermia.

Dem.   O, why rebuke you him that loves you so?
Lay breath so bitter on your bitter foe.

Herm. Now I but chide, but I should use thee worse;
For thou, I fear, hast given me cause to curse.
If thou hast slain Lysander in his sleep,
Being o'er shoes in blood, plunge in the deep,
And kill me too.
The sun was not so true unto the day
As he to me: would he have stol'n away
From sleeping Hermia? I'll believe as soon
This whole earth may be bor'd; and that the moon
May through the centre creep, and so displease
Her brother's noontide with the antipodes.
It cannot be but thou hast murder'd him;
So should a murderer look; so dead, so grim.

Very nice. And also very *plausible;* a convincing (though informal) piece of implicit, nondemonstrative, theoretical inference.

Here, leaving out a lot of lemmas, is how the inference must have gone: Hermia has reason to believe herself beloved of Lysander. (Lysander has told her that he loves her—repeatedly and in elegant iambics—and inferences

---

*Reprinted from *Psychosemantics* (Cambridge: The MIT Press, 1987, pp. 1–26) by permission of the author and publisher.

from how people say they feel to how they do feel are reliable, *ceteris paribus*.) But if Lysander does indeed love Hermia, then, *a fortiori*, Lysander wishes Hermia well. But if Lysander wishes Hermia well, then Lysander does not voluntarily desert Hermia at night in a darkling wood. (There may be lions. "There is not a more fearful wild-fowl than your lion living.") But Hermia was, in fact, so deserted by Lysander. Therefore not voluntarily. Therefore *in*voluntarily. Therefore it is plausible that Lysander has come to harm. At whose hands? Plausibly at Demetrius's hands. For Demetrius is Lysander's rival for the love of Hermia, and the presumption is that rivals in love do *not* wish one another well. Specifically, Hermia believes that Demetrius believes that a live Lysander is an impediment to the success of his (Demetrius's) wooing of her (Hermia). Moreover, Hermia believes (correctly) that if x wants that P, and x believes that not-P unless Q, and x believes that x can bring it about that Q, then (*ceteris paribus*) x tries to bring it about that Q. Moreover, Hermia believes (again correctly) that, by and large, people succeed in bringing about what they try to bring about. *So:* Knowing and believing all this, Hermia infers that perhaps Demetrius has killed Lysander. And we, the audience, who know what Hermia knows and believes and who share, more or less, her views about the psychology of lovers and rivals, understand how she has come to draw this inference. We sympathize.

In fact, Hermia has it all wrong. Demetrius is innocent and Lysander lives. The intricate theory that connects beliefs, desires, and actions—the implicit theory that Hermia relies on to make sense of what Lysander did and what Demetrius may have done; and that *we* rely on to make sense of Hermia's inferring what she does; and that Shakespeare relies on to predict and manipulate our sympathies (*'deconstruction' my foot,* by the way)—this theory makes no provision for nocturnal interventions by mischievous fairies. Unbeknownst to Hermia, a peripatetic sprite has sprung the *ceteris paribus* clause and made her plausible inference go awry. "Reason and love keep little company together nowadays: the more the pity that some honest neighbours will not make them friends."

Granting, however, that the theory fails from time to time—and not just when fairies intervene—I nevertheless want to emphasize *(1) how often it goes right, (2) how deep it is, and (3) how much we do depend upon it.* Common sense belief/desire psychology has recently come under a lot of philosophical pressure, and it's possible to doubt whether it can be saved in face of the sorts of problems that its critics have raised. There is, however, a prior question: whether it's worth the effort of trying to save it. That's the issue I propose to start with.

1. HOW OFTEN IT WORKS

Hermia got it wrong; her lover was less constant than she had supposed. Applications of common sense psychology mediate our relations with one another, and when its predictions fail these relations break down. The resulting disarray is likely to happen in public and to be highly noticeable.

> *Herm.* Since night you lov'd me; yet since night you left me;
> Why, then, you left me, — O, the gods forbid! —
> In earnest, shall I say?

> *Lys.* Ay, by my life;
> And never did desire to see thee more.
> Therefore be out of hope. . . .

This sort of thing makes excellent theater; the *successes* of common sense psychology, by contrast, are ubiquitous and — for that very reason — practically invisible.

Common sense psychology works so well it disappears. It's like those mythical Rolls Royce cars whose engines are sealed when they leave the factory; only it's better because it isn't mythical. Someone I don't know phones me at my office in New York from — as it might be — Arizona. 'Would you like to lecture here next Tuesday?' are the words that he utters. 'Yes, thank you. I'll be at your airport on the 3 p.m. flight' are the words that I reply. That's *all* that happens, but it's more than enough; the rest of the burden of predicting behavior — of bridging the gap between utterances and actions — is routinely taken up by theory. And the theory works so well that several days later (or weeks later, or months later, or years later; you can vary the example to taste) and several thousand miles away, there I am at the airport, and there he is to meet me. Or if I *don't* turn up, it's less likely that the theory has failed than that something went wrong with the airline. It's not possible to say, in quantitative terms, just how successfully common sense psychology allows us to coordinate our behaviors. But I have the impression that we manage pretty well with one another; often rather better than we cope with less complex machines.

The point — to repeat — is that the theory from which we get this extraordinary predictive power is just good old common sense belief/desire psychology. That's what tells us, for example, how to infer people's intentions from the sounds they make (if someone utters the form of words 'I'll be at your airport on the 3 p.m. flight,' then, *ceteris paribus*, he intends to be at your airport on the 3 p.m. flight) and how to infer people's behavior from their intentions (if someone intends to be at your airport on the 3 p.m. flight, then, *ceteris paribus*, he will produce behavior of a sort which will eventuate in his arriving at that place at that time, barring mechanical failures and acts of God). And all this works not just with people whose psychology you know intimately: your closest friends, say, or the spouse of your bosom. It works with *absolute strangers;* people you wouldn't know if you bumped into them. And it works not just in laboratory conditions —

where you can control the interacting variables – but also, indeed preeminently, in field conditions where all you know about the sources of variance is what common sense psychology tells you about them. Remarkable. If we could do that well with predicting the weather, no one would ever get his feet wet; and yet the etiology of the weather must surely be child's play compared with the causes of behavior.

Yes, but what about all those *ceteris paribuses*? I commence to digress:

Philosophers sometimes argue that the appearance of predictive adequacy that accrues to the generalizations of common sense psychology is spurious. For, they say, as soon as you try to make these generalizations explicit, you see that they have to be hedged about with *ceteris paribus* clauses; hedged about in ways that make them *trivially* incapable of disconfirmation. "False or vacuous" is the charge.

Consider the defeasibility of 'if someone utters the form of words "I'll be at your airport on the 3 p.m. flight," then he intends to be at your airport on the 3 p.m. flight.' This generalization does *not* hold if, for example, the speaker is lying; or if the speaker is using the utterance as an example (of a false sentence, say); or if he is a monolingual speaker of Urdu who happens to have uttered the sentence by accident; or if the speaker is talking in his sleep; or . . . whatever. You can, of course, defend the generalization in the usual way; you can say that '*all else being equal,* if someone utters the form of words "I'll be at your airport on the 3 p.m. flight," then he intends to be at your airport on the 3 p.m. flight.' But perhaps this last means nothing more than: 'if someone says that he intends to be there, then he does intend to be there – unless he doesn't.' That, of course, is predictively adequate for sure; nothing that happens will disconfirm it; nothing that happens could.

A lot of philosophers seem to be moved by this sort of argument; yet, even at first blush, it would be surprising if it were any good. After all, we do use common sense psychological generalizations to predict one another's behavior; and the predictions do – very often – come out true. But how could that be so if the generalizations that we base the predictions on are *empty*?

I'm inclined to think that what is alleged about the implicit reliance of commonsense psychology on uncashed *ceteris paribus* clauses is in fact a perfectly general property of the *explicit* generalizations in *all* the special sciences; in all empirical explanatory schemes, that is to say, other than basic physics. Consider the following modest truth of geology: A meandering river erodes its outside bank. "False or vacuous"; so a philosopher might argue. "Take it straight – as a strictly universal generalization – and it is surely false. Think of the case where the weather changes and the river freezes; or the world comes to an end; or somebody builds a dam; or somebody builds a concrete wall on the outside bank; or the rains stop and the river dries up . . . or whatever. You can, of course, defend the generalization in the usual way – by appending a *ceteris paribus* clause: '*All else being equal,* a meandering river erodes its outside bank.' But perhaps this last means nothing more than: 'A meandering river erodes its outside bank—unless it doesn't.' That, of course, is predictively adequate for sure. Nothing that happens will disconfirm it; nothing that happens could."

Patently, something has gone wrong. For 'All else being equal, a meandering river erodes its outside bank' is neither false nor vacuous, and it doesn't mean 'A meandering river erodes its outside bank—unless it doesn't.' It is, I expect, a long story how the generalizations of the special sciences manage to be both hedged and informative (or, if you like, how they manage to support counterfactuals even though they have exceptions). Telling that story is part of making clear why we have special sciences at all; why we don't just have basic physics (see Fodor, 1974). It is also part of making clear how idealization works in science. For surely *'Ceteris paribus,* a meandering river erodes its outside bank' means something like 'A meandering river erodes its outside bank in any nomologically possible world where the operative idealizations of geology are satisfied.' That this is, in general, stronger than *'P* in any world where not not-*P'* is certain. So if, as it would appear, commonsense psychology relies upon its *ceteris paribus* clauses, so too does geology.

There is, then, a face similarity between the way implicit generalizations work in common sense psychology and the way explicit generalizations work in the special sciences. But maybe this similarity is *merely* superficial. Donald Davidson is famous for having argued that the generalizations of real science, unlike those that underlie common sense belief/desire explanations, are "perfectible." In the real, but not the intentional, sciences we can (in principle, anyhow) get rid of the *ceteris paribus* clauses by actually enumerating the conditions under which the generalizations are supposed to hold.

By this criterion, however, the only real science is basic physics. For it simply isn't true that we can, even in principle, specify the conditions under which—say—geological generalizations hold *so long as we stick to the vocabulary of geology.* Or, to put it less in the formal mode, the causes of exceptions to geological generalizations are, quite typically, not themselves *geological* events. Try it and see: 'A meandering river erodes its outer banks unless, for example, the weather changes and the river dries up.' But 'weather' isn't a term in *geology;* nor are 'the world comes to an end,' 'somebody builds a dam,' and indefinitely many other descriptors required to specify the sorts of things that can go wrong. All you can say that's any use is: If the generalization failed to hold, then the operative idealizations must somehow have failed to be satisfied. But so, too, in common sense psychology: If he didn't turn up when he intended to, then something must have gone wrong.

Exceptions to the generalizations of a special science are typically *inexplicable* from the point of view of (that is, in the vocabulary of) that science. That's one of the things that makes it a *special* science. But, of course, it may nevertheless be perfectly possible to explain the exceptions *in the vocabulary of some other science.* In the most familiar case, you go 'down' one or more levels and use the vocabulary of a more 'basic' science. (The current failed to run through the circuit because the terminals were oxidized; he no longer recognizes familiar objects because of a cerebral accident. And so forth.) The availability of this strategy is one of the things that the hierarchical arrangement of our sciences buys for us. Anyhow, to put the point succinctly, the same pattern that holds for the special sciences seems to hold for common sense psychology as well. On the one hand, its *ceteris paribus* clauses are ineliminable from the point of view of its proprietary conceptual resources. But, on the other hand, we have – so far at least – no reason to doubt that they can be discharged in the vocabulary of some lower-level science (neurology, say, or biochemistry; at worst, physics).

If the world is describable as a closed causal system at all, it is so only in the vocabulary of our most basic science. From this nothing follows that a psychologist (or a geologist) needs to worry about.

I cease to digress. The moral so far is that the predictive adequacy of common sense psychology is beyond rational dispute; nor is there any reason to suppose that it's obtained by cheating. If you want to know where my physical body will be next Thursday, mechanics – our best science of middle-sized objects after all, and reputed to be pretty good in its field – is *no use to you at all.* Far the best way to find out (usually, in practice, the *only* way to find out) is: *ask me!*

2. THE DEPTH OF THE THEORY

It's tempting to think of common sense psychology as merely a budget of such truisms as one learns at Granny's knee: that the burnt child fears the fire, that all the world loves a lover, that money can't buy happiness, that reinforcement affects response rate, and that the way to a man's heart is through his stomach. None of these, I agree, is worth saving. However, as even the simple example sketched above serves to make clear, subsumption under platitudes is *not* the typical form of common sense psychological explanation. Rather, when such explanations are made explicit, they are frequently seen to exhibit the 'deductive structure' that is so characteristic of explanation in real science. There are two parts to this: the theory's underlying generalizations are defined over unobservables, and they lead to its predictions by iterating and interacting rather than by being directly instantiated.

Hermia, for example, is no fool and no behaviorist; she is perfectly aware both that Demetrius's behavior is caused by his mental states and that the pattern of such causation is typically intricate. There are, in particular, no plausible and counterfactual-supporting generalizations of the form *(x) (y) (x is a rival of y)* → *(x kills y)*. Nothing like that is remotely true; not even *ceteris paribus*. Rather, the generalization Hermia takes to be operative — the one that *is* true and counterfactual-supporting — must be something like *If x is y's rival, then x prefers y's discomfiture, all else being equal.* This principle, however, doesn't so much as mention behavior; it leads to behavioral predictions, but only via a lot of further assumptions about how people's preferences may affect their actions in given situations. Or rather, since there probably are no generalizations which connect preferences to actions irrespective of beliefs, what Hermia must be relying on is an implicit theory of how beliefs, preferences, and behaviors interact; an implicit decision theory, no less.

It is a deep fact about the world that the most powerful etiological generalizations hold of unobservable causes. Such facts shape our science (they'd better!). It is thus a test of the depth of a theory that many of its generalizations subsume interactions among unobservables. By this test, our implicit, common sense *meteorology* is presumably *not* a deep theory, since it consists largely of rule-of-thumb generalizations of the "red at night, sailor's delight" variety. Correspondingly, the reasoning that mediates applications of common sense meteorology probably involves not a lot more than instantiation and *modus ponens*. (All this being so, it is perhaps not surprising that common sense meteorology doesn't work very well.) Common sense psychology, by contrast, passes the test. It takes for granted that overt behavior comes at the end of a causal chain whose links are mental events — hence unobservable — and which may be arbitratily long (and arbitrarily kinky). Like Hermia, we are all — quite literally, I expect — born mentalists and realists; and we stay that way until common sense is driven out by bad philosophy.

3. ITS INDISPENSABILITY

We have, in practice, no alternative to the vocabulary of common sense psychological explanation; we have no other way of describing our behaviors and their causes if we want our behaviors and their causes to be subsumed by any counterfactual-supporting generalizations that we know about. This is, again, hard to see because it's so close.

For example, a few paragraphs back, I spoke of the common sense psychological generalization *people generally do what they say that they will do* as bridging the gap between an exchange of utterances ("Will you come and lecture . . . ," "I'll be at your airport on Thursday . . .") and the consequent behaviors of the speakers (my arriving at the airport, his being there to meet me). But this understates the case for the indispensability of common sense psychology, since without it we can't even describe the utterances as forms of words (to say nothing of describing the ensuing behaviors as kinds of acts). *Word* is a *psychological* category. (It is, indeed, *irreducibly* psychological, so far as anybody knows; there are, for example, no acoustic properties that all and only tokens of the same word type must share. In fact, surprisingly, there are no acoustic properties that all and only *fully intelligible* tokens of the same word type must share. Which is why our best technology is currently unable to build a typewriter that you can dictate to.)

As things now stand—to spell it out—we have *no* vocabulary for specifying event types that meets the following four conditions:

1. My behavior in uttering 'I'll be there on Thursday . . .' counts as an event of type T_i.
2. My arriving there on Thursday counts as an event of Type T_j.
3. 'Events of type T_j are consequent upon events of type T_i' is even roughly true and counterfactual supporting.
4. Categories T_i and T_j are other than irreducibly psychological.

For the only known taxonomies that meet conditions 1–3 acknowledge such event types as uttering the *form of words* 'I'll be there on Thursday,' or *saying that* one will be there on Thursday, or *performing the act* of meeting someone at the airport; so they fail condition 4.

Philosophers and psychologists used to dream of an alternative conceptual apparatus, one in which the common sense inventory of types of *behavior* is replaced by an inventory of types of *movements;* the counterfactual-supporting generalizations of psychology would then exhibit the contingency of these movements upon environmental and/or organic variables. That behavior is indeed contingent upon environmental and organic variables is, I suppose, not to be denied; yet the generalizations were not forthcoming. Why? There's a standard answer: It's because behavior consists of actions, and actions cross-classify movements. The generalization is that the burnt child avoids the fire; but what movement constitutes avoidance depends on where the child is, where the fire is . . . and so, drearily, forth. If you want to know what generalizations subsume a behavioral event, you have to know what *action type* it belongs to; knowing what *motion type* it belongs to usually doesn't buy anything. I take all that to be Gospel.

Yet it is generally assumed that this situation *must* be remediable, at least in principle. After all, the generalizations of a completed physics would presumably subsume every motion of every thing, hence the motions of organisms *inter alia.* So, if we wait long enough, we will after all have counterfactual-supporting generalizations that subsume the motions of organisms *under that description.* Presumably, God has them already.

This is, however, a little misleading. For, the (putative) generalizations of the (putative) completed physics would apply to the motions of organisms qua motions, but not qua organismic. Physics presumably has as little use for the categories of macrobiology as it does for the categories of common-sense psychology; it dissolves the behav*er* as well as the behav*ior*. What's left is atoms in the void. The subsumption of the motions of organisms – and of everything else – by the counterfactual-supporting generalizations of physics does not therefore guarantee that there is any science whose ontology recognizes organisms and their motions. That is: The subsumption of the motions of organisms – and of everything else – by the laws of physics does not guarantee that there are any laws about the motions of organisms qua motions of organisms. So far as anybody knows – barring, perhaps, a little bit of the psychology of classical reflexes – there are no such laws; and there is no metaphysical reason to expect any.[1]

Anyhow, this is all poppycock. Even if psychology were dispensable *in principle,* that would be no argument for dispensing with it. (Perhaps geology is dispensable in principle; every river is a physical object after all. Would that be a reason for supposing that rivers aren't a natural kind? Or that 'meandering rivers erode their outside banks' is untrue?) What's relevant to whether common sense psychology is worth defending is its dispensability *in fact.* And here the situation is absolutely clear. We have no idea of how to explain ourselves to ourselves except in a vocabulary which is *saturated* with belief/desire psychology. One is tempted to transcendental argument: What Kant said to Hume about physical objects holds, *mutatis mutandis,* for the propositional attitudes; we can't give them up *because we don't know how to.*[2]

So maybe we had better try to hold onto them. Holding onto the attitudes – vindicating common sense psychology – means showing how you could have (or, at a minimum, showing *that* you could have) a respectable science whose ontology explicitly acknowledges states that exhibit the sorts of properties that common sense attributes to the attitudes. That is what the rest of this book is about. This undertaking presupposes, however, some consensus about what sorts of properties common sense does attribute to the attitudes. That is what the next bit of this chapter is about.

The Essence of the Attitudes

How do we tell whether a psychology *is* a belief/desire psychology? How, in general, do we know if propositional attitudes are among the entities that the ontology of a theory acknowledges? These sorts of questions raise familiar and perplexing issues of intertheoretic identification. How do you distinguish elimination from reduction and reconstruction? Is the right story that there's no such thing as dephlogistinated matter, or is 'dephlogistinizing' just a word for oxidizing? Even behaviorists had trouble deciding whether they wanted to deny the existence of the mental or to assert its identity with the behavioral. (Sometimes they did both, in successive sentences. Ah, they really knew about insouciance in those days.)

I propose to stipulate. I will view a psychology as being commonsensical about the attitudes — in fact, as endorsing them — just in case it postulates states (entities, events, whatever) satisfying the following conditions:

(i) They are semantically evaluable.
(ii) They have causal powers.
(iii) The implicit generalizations of common sense belief/desire psychology are largely true of them.

In effect, I'm assuming that (i)-(iii) are the essential properties of the attitudes. This seems to me intuitively plausible; if it doesn't seem intuitively plausible to you, so be it. Squabbling about intuitions strikes me as vulgar.

A word about each of these conditions.

(i) Semantic Evaluation

Beliefs are the kinds of things that are true or false; desires are the kinds of things that get frustrated or fulfilled; hunches are the kinds of things that turn out to be right or wrong; so it goes. I will assume that what makes a belief true (/false) is something about its relation to the nonpsychological world (and not — e.g. — something about its relation to other beliefs; unless it happens to be a belief about beliefs). Hence, to say of a belief that it is true (/false) is to evaluate that belief in terms of its relation to the world. I will call such evaluations 'semantic.' Similarly, *mutatis mutandis*, with desires, hunches, and so forth.

It is, as I remarked in the preface, a puzzle about beliefs, desires, and the like that they are semantically evaluable; almost nothing else is. (Trees aren't; numbers aren't; people aren't. Propositions *are* [assuming that there are such things], but that's hardly surprising; propositions exist to be what beliefs and desires are attitudes *toward*.) We will see, later in this book, that it is primarily the semantic evaluability of beliefs and desires that gets them into philosophical trouble — and that a defense of belief/desire psychology needs to be a defense of.

Sometimes I'll talk of the *content* of a psychological state rather than its semantic evaluability. These two ideas are intimately interconnected. Consider — for a change of plays — Hamlet's belief that his uncle killed his father. That belief has a certain semantic value; in particular, it's a *true* belief. Why true? Well, because it corresponds to a certain fact. Which fact? Well, the fact that Hamlet's uncle killed Hamlet's father. But why is it *that* fact that determines the semantic evaluation of Hamlet's belief? Why not the fact that two is a prime number, or the fact that Demetrius didn't kill Lysander? Well, because the *content* of Hamlet's belief is *that* his uncle killed his father. (If you like, the belief 'expresses the proposition' that Hamlet's uncle killed his father.) *If you know what the content of a belief is, then you know what it is about the world that determines the semantic evaluation of the belief;* that, at a minimum, is how the notions of content and semantic evaluation connect.

I propose to say almost nothing more about content at this stage; its time will come. Suffice it just to add that propositional attitudes have their contents essentially: the canonical way of picking out an attitude is to say (a) what sort of attitude it is (a belief, a desire, a hunch, or whatever); and (b) what the content of the attitude is (that Hamlet's uncle killed his father; that 2 is a prime number; that Hermia believes that Demetrius dislikes Lysander; or whatever). In what follows, nothing will count as a propositional-attitude psychology — as a reduction or reconstruction or vindication of common sense belief/desire explanation — that does not acknowledge states that can be individuated in this sort of way.

(ii) Causal Powers

Common sense psychological explanation is deeply committed to mental causation of at least three sorts: the causation of behavior by mental states; the causation of mental states by impinging environmental events (by 'proximal stimulation,' as psychologists sometimes say); and — in some ways the most interesting common sense psychological etiologies — the causation of mental states by one another. As an example of the last sort, common sense acknowledges *chains of thought* as species of complex mental events. A chain of thought is presumably a *causal* chain in which one semantically evaluable mental state gives rise to another; a process that often terminates in the fixation of belief. (That, as you will remember, was the sort of thing Sherlock Holmes was supposed to be very good at.)

Every psychology that is realist about the mental ipso facto acknowledges its causal powers.[3] Philosophers of 'functionalist' persuasion even hold that the causal powers of a mental state determine its identity (that for a mental state to be, as it might be, the state of believing that Demetrius killed Lysander is just for it to have a characteristic galaxy of potential and actual causal relations). This is a position of some interest to us, since if it is true — and if it is also true that propositional attitudes have their contents essentially—it follows that the causal powers of a mental state somehow determine its content. I do not, however, believe that it is true. More of this later.

What's important for now is this: It is characteristic of common sense belief/desire psychology—and hence of any explicit theory that I'm prepared to view as vindicating common sense belief/desire psychology—that it attributes contents and causal powers *to the very same mental things that it takes to be semantically evaluable.* It is Hamlet's belief that Claudius killed his father—the very same belief which is true or false in virtue of the facts about his father's death—that causes him to behave in such a beastly way to Gertrude.[4]

In fact, there's a deeper point to make. It's not just that, in a psychology of propositional attitudes, content and causal powers are attributed to the same things. It's also that causal relations among propositional attitudes somehow typically contrive to respect their relations of content, and belief/desire explanations often turn on this. Hamlet believed that somebody had killed his father because he believed that Claudius had killed his father. His having the second belief explains his having the first. How? Well, presumably via some such causal generalization as 'if someone believes *Fa,* then *ceteris paribus* he believes $\exists x(Fx)$.' This generalization specifies a causal relation between two kinds of mental states picked out by reference to (the logical form of) the propositions they express; so we have the usual pattern of a simultaneous attribution of content and causal powers. The present point, however, is that the contents of the mental states that the causal generalization subsumes are themselves semantically related; *Fa entails $\exists x(Fx)$,* so, of course, the semantic value of the latter belief is not independent of the semantic value of the former.

Or, compare the pattern of implicit reasoning attributed to Hermia at the beginning of this chapter. I suggested that she must be relying crucially on some such causal generalization as: 'If x wants that P, and x believes that—P unless Q, and x believes that it is within his power to bring it about that Q, then *ceteris paribus* x tries to bring it about that Q.' Common sense seems pretty clearly to hold that something like that is true and counter-factual supporting; hence that one has explained x's attempt to bring it about that Q if one shows that x had beliefs and desires of the sort that the generalization specifies. What is absolutely typical is (a) the appeal to causal relations among semantically evaluable mental states as part and parcel of the explanation; and (b) the existence of content relations among the mental states thus appealed to.

Witness the recurrent schematic letters; they function precisely to constrain the content relations among the mental states that the generalization subsumes. Thus, unless, in a given case, what x wants is the same as what x believes that he can't have without Q, and unless what x believes to be required for *P* is the same as what he tries to bring about, the generalization isn't satisfied and the explanation fails. It is self-evident that the explanatory principles of common sense psychology achieve generality by quantifying over agents (the 'practical syllogism' purports to apply, *ceteris paribus*, to all the *x*'s). But it bears emphasis that they also achieve generality by abstracting over *contents* ('If you want *P* and you believe not-*P* unless *Q* . . . you try to bring it about that *Q*,' whatever the *P* and *Q* may be). The latter strategy works only because, very often, the same *P*'s and *Q*'s — the same contents — recur in causally related mental states; viz., only because causal relations very often respect semantic ones.

This parallelism between causal powers and contents engenders what is, surely, one of the most striking facts about the cognitive mind as common-sense belief/desire psychology conceives it: the frequent similarity between trains of thought and *arguments*. Here, for example, is Sherlock Holmes doing his thing at the end of "The Speckled Band":

> I instantly reconsidered my position when . . . it became clear to me that whatever danger threatened an occupant of the room couldn't come either from the window or the door. My attention was speedily drawn, as I have already remarked to you, to this ventilator, and to the bell-rope which hung down to the bed. The discovery that this was a dummy, and that the bed was clamped to the floor, instantly gave rise to the suspicion that the rope was there as a bridge for something passing through the hole, and coming to the bed. The idea of a snake instantly occurred to me, and when I coupled it with my knowledge that the Doctor was furnished with a supply of the creatures from India I felt that I was probably on the right track.

The passage purports to be a bit of reconstructive psychology: a capsule history of the sequence of mental states which brought Holmes first to suspect, then to believe, that the doctor did it with his pet snake. What is therefore interesting, for our purposes, is that Holmes's story isn't *just* reconstructive psychology. It does double duty, since it also serves to assemble *premises* for a plausible inference to the *conclusion* that the doctor did it with the snake. Because his train of thought is like an argument, Holmes expects Watson to be *convinced* by the considerations which, when they occurred to Holmes, caused his own conviction. What connects the causal-history aspect of Holmes's story with its plausible-inference aspect is the fact that the thoughts that fix the belief that *P* provide, often enough, reasonable *grounds* for believing that *P*. Were this not the case — were there not this general harmony between the semantical and the causal properties of thoughts, so that, as Holmes puts it in another story, "one true inference invariably suggests others" — there wouldn't, after all, be much profit in thinking.

All this raises a budget of philosophical issues; just *what sorts* of content relations are preserved in the generalizations that subsume typical cases of belief/desire causation? And — in many ways a harder question — how could the mind be so constructed that such generalizations are true of it? What sort of mechanism could have states that are both semantically and causally connected, and such that the causal connections respect the semantic ones? It is the intractability of such questions that causes many philosophers to despair of common sense psychology. But, of course, the argument cuts both ways: if the parallelism between content and causal relations is, as it seems to be, a deep fact about the cognitive mind, then unless we can save the notion of content, there is a deep fact about the cognitive mind that our psychology is going to miss.

(iii) Generalizations Preserved

What I've said so far amounts largely to this: An explicit psychology that vindicates common sense belief/desire explanations must permit the assignment of content to causally efficacious mental states and must recognize behavioral explanations in which covering generalizations refer to (or quantify over) the contents of the mental states that they subsume. I now add that the generalizations that are recognized by the vindicating theory mustn't be *crazy* from the point of view of common sense; the causal powers of the attitudes must be, more or less, what common sense supposes that they are. After all, common sense psychology won't be vindicated unless it turns out to be at least approximately true.

I don't, however, have a shopping list of common sense generalizations that must be honored by a theory if it wants to be ontologically committed to bona fide propositional attitudes. A lot of what common sense believes about the attitudes must surely be false (a lot of what common sense believes about *anything* must surely be false). Indeed, one rather hopes that there will prove to be many more — and much odder — things in the mind than common sense had dreamed of; or else what's the fun of doing psychology? The indications are, and have been since Freud, that this hope will be abundantly gratified. For example, contrary to common sense, it looks as though much of what's in the mind is unconscious; and, contrary to common sense, it looks as though much of what's in the mind is unlearned. I retain my countenance, I remain self-possessed.

On the other hand, there is a lot of common sense psychology that we have — so far at least — no reason to doubt, and that friends of the attitudes would hate to abandon. So, it's hard to imagine a psychology of action that is committed to the attitudes but doesn't acknowledge some such causal relations among beliefs, desires, and behavioral intentions (the 'maxims' of acts) as decision theories explicate. Similarly, it's hard to imagine a psycholinguistics (for English) which attributes beliefs, desires, communicative intentions, and such to speaker/hearers but fails to entail an infinity of theorems recognizably similar to these:

- 'Demetrius killed Lysander' is the form of words standardly used to communicate the belief that Demetrius killed Lysander.
- 'The cat is on the mat' is the form of words standardly used to communicate the belief that the cat is on the mat.
- 'Demetrius killed Lysander or the cat is on the mat' is the form of words standardly used to communicate the belief that Demetrius killed Lysander or the cat is on the mat.

And so on indefinitely. Indeed, it's hard to imagine a psycholinguistics that appeals to the propositional attitudes of speaker/hearers of English to explain their verbal behavior but that doesn't entail that they *know* at least one such theorem for each sentence of their language. So there's an infinite amount of common sense for psychology to vindicate already.

Self-confident essentialism is philosophically fashionable this week. There are people around who have Very Strong Views ('modal intuitions,' these views are called) about whether there could be cats in a world in which all the domestic felines are Martian robots, and whether there could be Homer in a world where nobody wrote the *Odyssey* or the *Iliad*. Ducky for them; their epistemic condition is enviable, but I don't myself aspire to it. I just don't know how much common sense psychology would have to be true for there to be beliefs and desires. Let's say, some of it at a minimum; lots of it by preference. Since I have no doubt at all but that lots of it *is* true, this is an issue about which I do not stay up nights worrying.

RTM

The main thesis of this book (Fodor [1987]) can now be put as follows: *We have no reason to doubt — indeed, we have substantial reason to believe — that it is possible to have a scientific psychology that vindicates common sense belief/desire explanation.* But though that is my thesis, I don't propose to argue the case in quite so abstract a form. For there is already in the field a (more or less) empirical theory that is, in my view, reasonably construed as ontologically committed to the attitudes and that — again, in my view — is quite probably approximately true. If I'm right about this theory, it *is* a vindication of the attitudes. Since, moreover, it's the only thing of its kind around (it's the *only* proposal for a scientific belief/desire psychology that's in the field), defending the common sense assumptions about the attitudes and defending this theory turn out to be much the same enterprise; extensionally, as one might say.

That, in any event, is the strategy that I'll pursue: I'll argue that the sorts of objections philosophers have recently raised against belief/desire explanation are (to put it mildly) not conclusive against the best vindicating theory currently available. The rest of this chapter is therefore devoted to a sketch of how this theory treats the attitudes and why its treatment of the attitudes seems so promising. Since this story is now pretty well known in both philosophical and psychological circles, I propose to be quick.

What I'm selling is the Representational Theory of Mind (hence RTM; for discussion see, among other sources, Fodor, [1978]; Fodor, [1975]; Field, [1978]). At the heart of the theory is the postulation of a language of thought: an infinite set of 'mental representations' which function both as the immediate objects of propositional attitudes and as the domains of mental processes. More precisely, RTM is the conjunction of the following two claims:

Claim 1 (the nature of propositional attitudes):

For any organism *O,* and any attitude *A* toward the proposition *P,* there is a ('computational'/'functional') relation *R* and a mental representation *MP* such that

MP means that *P,* and

O has *A* if *O* bears *R* to *MP.*

(We'll see presently that the biconditional needs to be watered down a little; but not in a way that much affects the spirit of the proposal.)

It's a thin line between clarity and pomposity. A cruder but more intelligible way of putting claim 1 would be this: To believe that such and such is to have a mental symbol that means that such and such tokened in your head in a certain way; it's to have such a token 'in your belief box,' as I'll sometimes say. Correspondingly, to hope that such and such is to have a token of that same mental symbol tokened in your head, but in a rather different way; it's to have it tokened 'in your hope box.' (The difference between having the token in one box or the other corresponds to the difference between the causal roles of beliefs and desires. Talking about belief boxes and such as a shorthand for representing the attitudes as *functional* states is an idea due to Steve Schiffer. For more on this, see the Appendix, Fodor [1987].) And so on for every attitude that you can bear toward a proposition; and so on for every proposition toward which you can bear an attitude.

Claim 2 (the nature of mental processes):

Mental processes are causal sequences of tokenings of mental representations.

A train of thoughts, for example, is a causal sequence of tokenings of mental representations which express the propositions that are the objects of the thoughts. To a first approximation, to think 'It's going to rain; so I'll go indoors' is to have a tokening of a mental representation that means *I'll go indoors* caused, in a certain way, by a tokening of a mental representation that means *It's going to rain.*

So much for formulating RTM.

There are, I think, a number of reasons for believing that RTM may be more or less true. The best reason is that some version or other of RTM underlies practically all current psychological research on mentation, and our best science is ipso facto our best estimate of what there is and what it's made of. There are those of my colleagues in philosophy who do not find this sort of argument persuasive. I blush for them. (For a lengthy discussion of how RTM shapes current work on cognition, see Fodor, [1975], especially chapter 1. For a discussion of the connection between RTM and commonsense Intentional Realism — and some arguments that, given the latter, the former is practically mandatory — see the Appendix, Fodor [1987].)

But we have a reason for suspecting that RTM may be true even aside from the details of its empirical success. I remarked above that there is a striking parallelism between the causal relations among mental states, on the one hand, and the semantic relations that hold among their propositional objects, on the other; and that very deep properties of the mental — as, for example, that trains of thought are largely truth preserving — turn on this symmetry. RTM suggests a plausible mechanism for this relation, and that is something that no previous account of mentation has been able to do. I propose to spell this out a bit; it helps make clear just *why* RTM has such a central place in the way that psychologists now think about the mind.

The trick is to combine the postulation of mental representations with the 'computer metaphor.' Computers show us how to connect semantical with causal properties for *symbols.* So, if having a propositional attitude involves tokening a symbol, then we can get some leverage on connecting semantical properties with causal ones for *thoughts.* In this respect, I think there really has been something like an intellectual breakthrough. Technical details to one side, this is — in my view — the only aspect of contemporary cognitive science that represents a major advance over the versions of mentalism that were its eighteenth- and nineteenth-century predecessors. Exactly what was wrong with Associationism, for example, was that there proved to be no way to get a *rational* mental life to emerge from the sorts of causal relations among thoughts that the 'laws of association' recognized. (See the concluding pages of Joyce's *Ulysses* for a — presumably inadvertent — parody of the contrary view.)

Here, in barest outline, is how the new story is supposed to go: You connect the causal properties of a symbol with its semantic properties *via its syntax.* The syntax of a symbol is one of its higher-order physical properties. To a metaphorical first approximation, we can think of the syntactic structure of a symbol as an abstract feature of its shape.[5] Because, to all intents and purposes, syntax reduces to shape, and because the shape of a symbol is a potential determinant of its causal role, it is fairly easy to see how there could be environments in which the causal role of a symbol correlates with its syntax. It's easy, that is to say, to imagine symbol tokens interacting causally *in virtue of* their syntactic structures. The syntax of a symbol might determine the causes and effects of its tokenings in much the way that the geometry of a key determines which locks it will open.

But, now, we know from modern logic that certain of the semantic relations among symbols can be, as it were, 'mimicked' by their syntactic relations; that, when seen from a very great distance, is what proof-theory is about. So, within certain famous limits, the semantic relation that holds between two symbols when the proposition expressed by the one is entailed by the proposition expressed by the other can be mimicked by syntactic relations in virtue of which one of the symbols is derivable from the other. We can therefore build machines which have, again within famous limits, the following property:

> The operations of the machine consist entirely of transformations of symbols;

> in the course of performing these operations, the machine is sensitive solely to syntactic properties of the symbols;

> and the operations that the machine performs on the symbols are entirely confined to altering their shapes.

Yet the machine is so devised that it will transform one symbol into another if and only if the propositions expressed by the symbols that are so transformed stand in certain *semantic* relations — e.g., the relation that the premises bear to the conclusion in a valid argument. Such machines — computers, of course — just *are* environments in which the syntax of a symbol determines its causal role in a way that respects its content. This is, I think, a perfectly terrific idea; not least because it works.

I expect it's clear how this is supposed to connect with RTM and ontological commitment to mental representations. Computers are a solution to the problem of mediating between the causal properties of symbols and their semantic properties. So *if* the mind is a sort of computer, we begin to see how you can have a theory of mental processes that succeeds where — literally — all previous attempts had abjectly failed; a theory which explains how there could be nonarbitrary content relations among causally related thoughts. But, patently, there are going to have to be mental representations if this proposal is going to work. In computer design, causal role is brought into phase with content by exploiting parallelisms between the syntax of a symbol and its semantics. But that idea won't do the theory of *mind* any good unless there are *mental* symbols: mental particulars possessed of both semantical and syntactic properties. There must be mental symbols because, in a nutshell, only symbols have syntax, and our best available theory of mental processes — indeed, the *only* available theory of mental processes that isn't *known* to be false — needs the picture of the mind as a syntax-driven machine.

It is sometimes alleged against common sense belief/desire psychology, by those who admire it less than I do (see especially Churchland, this volume, pp. 42–62; Stich [1983a]), that it is a "sterile" theory; one that arguably hasn't progressed much since Homer and hasn't progressed at all since Jane Austen. There is, no doubt, a sense in which this charge is warranted; common sense psychology may be implicit science, but it isn't, on anybody's story, implicit *research* science. (What novelists and poets do doesn't count as research by the present austere criteria.) If, in short, you want to evaluate progress, you need to look not at the implicit common sense theory but at the best candidate for its explicit vindication. And here the progress has been enormous. It's not just that we now know a little about memory and perception (qua means to the fixation of belief), and a little about language (qua means to the communication of belief); see any standard psychology text. The real achievement is that we are (maybe) on the verge of solving a great mystery about the mind: *How could its causal processes be semantically coherent?* Or, if you like yours with drums and trumpets: *How is rationality mechanically possible?*[6] Notice that this sort of problem can't even be stated, let alone solved, unless we suppose — just as common sense belief/desire psychology wants us to — that there are mental states with both semantic contents and causal roles. A good theory is one that leads you to ask questions that have answers. And vice versa, *ceteris paribus*.

Still, RTM won't do in quite the raw form set forth above. I propose to end this chapter with a little polishing.

According to claim 1, RTM requires both of the following:

> For each tokening of a propositional attitude, there is a tokening of a corresponding relation between an organism and a mental representation;

and

> For each tokening of that relation, there is a corresponding tokening of a propositional attitude.[7]

This is, however, much too strong; the equivalence fails in both directions.

As, indeed, we should expect it to, given our experience in other cases where explicit science co-opts the conceptual apparatus of common sense. For example, as everybody points out, it is simply not true that chemistry identifies each sample of water with a sample of H_2O; not, at least, if the operative notion of water is the common sense one according to which what we drink, sail on, and fill our bathtubs with all qualifies. What chemistry does is reconstruct the common sense categories *in what the theory itself identifies as core cases: chemically pure* water is H_2O. The ecological infrequency of such core cases is, of course, no argument against the claim that chemical science vindicates the common sense taxonomy: Common sense was right about there being such stuff as water, right about there being water in the Charles River, and right again that it's the water in what we drink that quenches our thirst. It never said that the water in the Charles is chemically pure; 'chemically pure' isn't a phrase in the common sense vocabulary.

Exactly similarly, RTM vindicates common sense psychology for what RTM identifies as the core cases; in those cases, what common sense takes to be tokenings of propositional attitudes are indeed tokenings of a relation between an organism and a mental representation. The other cases — where you get either attitude tokenings without the relation or relation tokenings without the attitudes — the theory treats as derivative. This is all, I repeat, *exactly* what you'd expect from scientific precedent. Nevertheless, philosophers have made an awful fuss about it in discussing the vindication of the attitudes (see the controversy over the 'explicit representation' — or otherwise — of grammars recently conducted by, among others, Stabler [1983] and Demopoulos and Matthews [1983]). So let's consider the details awhile. Doing so will lead to a sharpening of claim 1, which is all to the good.

Case 1. Attitudes without Mental Representations

Here's a case from Dennett:

> In a recent conversation with the designer of a chess-playing program I heard the following criticism of a rival program: "It thinks it should get its queen out early." This ascribes a propositional attitude to the program in a very useful and predictive way, for as the designer went on to say, one can usually count on chasing that queen around the board. But for all the many levels of explicit representation to be found in that program, nowhere is anything roughly synonymous with "I should get my queen out early" explicitly tokened. The level of analysis to which the designer's remark belongs describes features of the program that are, in an entirely innocent way, emergent properties of the computational processes that have "engineering reality." I see no reason to believe that the relation between belief-talk and psychological-process talk will be any more direct ([1978a], p. 107; see also Matthews, [1984])

Notice that the problem Dennett raises isn't just that some of what common sense takes to be one's propositional attitudes are *dispositional*. It's not like the worry that I might now be said to believe some abstruse consequence of number theory—one that I have, commonsensically speaking, never even thought of—because I *would* accept the proof of the theorem *if* I were shown it. It's true, of course, that merely dispositional beliefs couldn't correspond to *occurrent* tokenings of relations to mental representations, and claim 1 must therefore be reformulated. But the problem is superficial, since the relevant revision of claim 1 would be pretty obvious; viz., that for each *occurrent* belief there is a corresponding *occurrent* tokening of a mental representation; and for each *dispositional* belief there is a corresponding *disposition* to token a mental representation.

This would leave open a question that arises independent of one's views about RTM: viz., when are attributions of dispositional beliefs *true?* I suppose that one's dispositional beliefs could reasonably be identified with the closure of one's occurrent beliefs under principles of inference that one explicitly accepts. And, if it's a little vague just what beliefs belong to such a closure, RTM could live with that. *Qua dispositional,* attitudes play no causal role in *actual* mental processes; only occurrent attitudes—for that matter, only occurrent *anythings*—are actual causes. So RTM can afford to be a little operationalist about merely dispositional beliefs (see Lycan, [forthcoming]) so long as it takes a hard line about occurrent ones.

However, to repeat, the problem raised in Dennett's text is not of this sort. It's not that the program believes 'get your queen out early' *potentially.* Dennett's point is that the program actually operates on this principle; but not in virtue of any tokening of any symbol that expresses it. And chess isn't, of course, the only sort of case. Behavioral commitment to modus ponens, or to the syntactic rule of 'wh'-movement, *might* betoken that these are inscribed in brain writing. But it needn't, since these rules might be—as philosophers sometimes say—complied with but not literally followed.

In Dennett's example, you have an attitude being, as it were, an emergent out of its own implementation. This way of putting it might seem to suggest a way of saving claim 1: The machine doesn't explicitly represent 'get your queen out early,' but at least we may suppose that it *does* represent, explicitly, some more detailed rules of play (the ones that Dennett says have "engineering reality"). For these rules, at least, a strong form of claim 1 would thus be satisfied. But that suggestion won't work either. *None* of the principles in accordance with which a computational system operates need be explicitly represented by a formula tokened in the device; there is no guarantee that the program of a machine will be explicitly represented in the machine whose program it is. (See Cummins, [1982]; roughly, the point is that for any machine that computes a function by executing an explicit algorithm, there exists another machine—one that's 'hard-wired'—that computes the same function but *not* by executing an explicit algorithm.) So what, you might wonder, does the 'computer metaphor' buy for RTM after all?

There is even a point of principle here — one that is sometimes read in (or into) Lewis Carroll's dialogue between Achilles and the Tortoise: Not all the rules of inference that a computational system runs on *can* be represented *just* explicitly in the system; some of them have to be, as one says, 'realized in the hardware.' Otherwise the machine won't run at all. A computer in which the principles of operation are *only* explicitly represented is just like a blackboard on which the principles have been written down. It has Hamlet's problem: When you turn the thing on, nothing happens.

Since this is all clearly correct and arguably important, the question arises how to state RTM so that these cases where programs are hardwired don't count as disconfirmations of claim 1. We'll return to this momentarily; first let's consider:

Case 2. Mental Representations without Attitudes

What RTM borrows from computers is, in the first instance, the recipe for mechanizing rationality: Use a syntactically driven machine to exploit parallelisms between the syntactic and semantic properties of symbols. Some — but not all — versions of RTM borrow more than this; not just a theory of rationality but a theory of intelligence too. According to this story, intelligent behavior typically exploits a 'cognitive architecture' constituted of *hierarchies* of symbol processors. At the top of such a hierarchy might be a quite complex capacity: solving a problem, making a plan, uttering a sentence. At the bottom, however, are only the sorts of unintelligent operations that Turing machines can perform: deleting symbols, storing symbols, copying symbols, and the rest. Filling in the middle levels is tantamount to reducing — analyzing — an intelligent capacity into a complex of dumb ones; hence to a kind of explanation of the former.

Here's a typical example of a kind of representational theory that runs along these lines:

> This is the way we tie our shoes: There is a little man who lives in one's head. The little man keeps a library. When one acts upon the intention to tie one's shoes, the little man fetches down a volume entitled *Tying One's Shoes*. The volume says such things as: "Take the left free end of the shoelace in the left hand. Cross the left free end of the shoelace over the right free end of the shoelace . . . ," etc. . . . When the little man reads "take the left free end of the shoelace in the left hand," we imagine him ringing up the shop foreman in charge of grasping shoelaces. The shop foreman goes about supervising that activity in a way that is, in essence, a microcosm of tying one's shoe. Indeed, the shop foreman might be imagined to superintend a detail of wage slaves, whose functions include: searching representations of visual inputs for traces

of shoelace, dispatching orders to flex and contract fingers on the left hand, etc. (Fodor, [1968], 63–65, slightly revised)

At the very top are states which may well correspond to propositional attitudes that common sense is prepared to acknowledge (knowing how to tie one's shoes, thinking about shoe tying). But at the bottom and middle levels there are bound to be lots of symbol-processing operations that correspond to nothing that *people* — as opposed to their nervous systems — ever do. These are the operations of what Dennett has called "sub-personal" computational systems; and though they satisfy the present formulation of claim 1 (in that they involve causally efficacious tokenings of mental representations), yet it's unclear that they correspond to anything that common sense would count as the tokening of an attitude. But then how are we to formulate claim 1 so as to avoid disconfirmation by subpersonal information processes?

Vindication Vindicated

There is a sense in which these sorts of objections to claim 1 strike me as not very serious. As I remarked above, the vindication of belief/desire explanation by RTM does *not* require that every case common sense counts as the tokening of an attitude should correspond to the tokening of a mental representation, or vice versa. All that's required is that such correspondences should obtain in what the vindicating theory itself takes to be the core cases. On the other hand, RTM had better be able to say which cases it does count as core. Chemistry is allowed to hold the Charles River largely irrelevant to the confirmation of 'water is H_2O,' but only because it provides independent grounds for denying that what's in the Charles is a chemically pure sample. Of anything!

So, what are the core cases for RTM? The answer should be clear from claim 2. According to claim 2, mental processes are causal sequences of transformations of mental representations. It follows that tokenings of attitudes *must* correspond to tokenings of mental representations when they — the attitude tokenings — are episodes in mental processes. If the intentional objects of such causally efficacious attitude tokenings are *not* explicitly represented, then RTM is simply false. I repeat for emphasis: If the occurrence of a thought is an episode in a mental process, then RTM is committed to the explicit representation of its content. The motto is therefore No Intentional Causation without Explicit Representation.

Notice that this way of choosing core cases squares us with the alleged counterexamples. RTM says that the contents of a sequence of attitudes that constitutes a mental process must be expressed by explicit tokenings of mental representations. But the rules that determine the course of the transformation of these representations — *modus ponens*, 'wh'-movement, 'get the queen out early,' or whatever — need not themselves ever be explicit. They can be emergents out of explicitly represented procedures of implementation, or out of hardware structures, or both. Roughly: According to RTM, programs — corresponding to the 'laws of thought' — *may* be explicitly represented; but 'data structures' — corresponding to the contents of thoughts — *have to be*.

Thus, in Dennett's chess case, the rule 'get it out early' may or may not be expressed by a 'mental' (/program language) symbol. That depends on just how the machine works; specifically, on whether *consulting* the rule is a step in the machine's operations. I take it that in the machine that Dennett has in mind, it isn't; *entertaining the thought 'Better get the queen out early' never constitutes an episode in the mental life of that machine.*[8] But then, the intentional content of this thought need *not* be explicitly represented consonant with 'no intentional causation without explicit representation' being true. By contrast, the representations of the board — of actual or possible states of play — over which the machine's computations are defined *must* be explicit, precisely *because* the machine's computations *are* defined over them. These computations constitute the machine's 'mental processes,' so either they are causal sequences of explicit representations, or the representational theory of chess playing is simply false of the machine. To put the matter in a nutshell: Restricting one's attention to the status of rules and programs can make it seem that the computer metaphor is neutral with respect to RTM. But when one thinks about the constitution of mental processes, the connection between the idea that they are computational and the idea that there is a language of thought becomes immediately apparent.[9]

What about the subpersonal examples, where you have mental representation tokenings without attitude tokenings? Common sense belief/desire explanations are vindicated if scientific psychology is ontologically committed to beliefs and desires. But it's *not* also required that the folk-psychological inventory of propositional attitudes should turn out to exhaust a natural kind. It would be astounding if it did; how could common sense know all that? What's important about RTM — what makes RTM a vindication of intuitive belief/desire psychology — isn't that it picks out a kind that is precisely coextensive with the propositional attitudes. It's that RTM shows how intentional states could have causal powers; precisely the aspect of common sense intentional realism that seemed most perplexing from a metaphysical point of view.

Molecular physics vindicates the intuitive taxonomy of middle-sized objects into liquids and solids. But the nearest kind to the liquids that molecular physics acknowledges includes some of what common sense would not; glass, for example. So what?

So much for RTM; so much for this chapter, too. There is a strong *prima facie* case for common sense belief/desire explanation. Common sense would be vindicated if some good theory of the mind proved to be committed to entities which—like the attitudes—are both semantically evaluable and etiologically involved. RTM looks like being a good theory of the mind that is so committed; so if RTM is true, common sense is vindicated. It goes without saying that RTM needs to make an empirical case; we need good accounts, independently confirmed, of mental processes as causal sequences of transformations of mental representations. Modern cognitive psychology is devoted, practically in its entirety, to devising and confirming such accounts. For present purposes, I shall take all that as read. What the rest of this book is about is doubts about RTM that turn on its *semantic* assumptions. This is home ground for philosophers, and increasingly the natives are restless.

FOOTNOTES

[1]Perhaps there are laws that relate the *brain states* of organisms to their motions. But then again, perhaps there aren't, since it seems entirely possible that the lawful connections should hold between brain states and *actions* where, as usual, actions cross-classify movements. This is, perhaps, what you would predict upon reflection. Would you really expect the same brain state that causes the utterance of 'dog' in tokens of 'dog' to be the one that causes it in tokens of 'dogmatic'? How about utterances of (the phonetic sequence) [empedokliz lipt] when you're talking English and when you're talking German?

[2]The trouble with transcendental arguments being, however, that it's not obvious why a theory couldn't be both indispensable and *false*. I wouldn't want to buy a transcendental deduction of the attitudes if operationalism were the price I had to pay for it.

[3]Denying the etiological involvement of mental states was really what behaviorism was about; it's what 'logical' behaviorists and 'eliminativists' had in common. Thus, for example, to hold—as Ryle did, more or less—that mental states are species of dispositions is to refuse to certify as literally causal such psychological explanations as "He did it with the intention of pleasing her," or, for that matter, "His headache made him groan," to say nothing of "The mere thought of giving a lecture makes him ill." (For discussion, see Fodor, [1981c].).

[4]Some philosophers feel very strongly about enforcing an object/state (or maybe object/event) distinction here, so that what have *causal powers* are tokenings of mental state types (e.g., Hamlet's *believing* that Claudius killed his father), but what have *semantic values* are *propositions* (e.g., the proposition that Claudius killed Hamlet's father). The point is that it sounds odd to say that Hamlet's *believing* that *P* is true but all right to say that Hamlet's *belief* that *P* is.

I'm not convinced that this distinction is one that I will care about in the long run, since sounding odd is the least of my problems and in the long run I expect I want to do without propositions altogether. However, if you are squeamish about ontology, that's all right with me. In that case, the point in the text should be: Belief/desire psychology attributes causal properties to the very same things (viz., tokenings of certain mental state types) to which it attributes propositional objects. It is thus true of Hamlet's believing that Claudius killed his father both that it is implicated in the etiology of his behavior Gertrudeward and that it has as its object a certain belief, viz., the proposition that Claudius killed his father. If we then speak of Hamlet's *state* of believing that Claudius killed his father (or of the event which consists of the tokening of that state) as semantically evaluable, we can take that as an abbreviation for a more precise way of talking: The state S has the semantic value V if S has as its object a proposition whose value is V.

It goes without saying that none of this ontological fooling around makes the slightest progress toward removing the puzzles about intentionality. If (on my way of talking) it's metaphysically worrying that beliefs and desires are semantically evaluable though trees, rocks, and prime numbers aren't, it's equally metaphysically worrying (on the orthodox way of talking) that believings have propositional objects though trees, rocks, and prime numbers don't.

[5]*Any* nomic property of symbol tokens, however — any property in virtue of the possession of which they satisfy causal laws — would, in principle, do just as well. (So, for example, syntactic structure could be realized by relations among electromagnetic states rather than relations among shapes; as, indeed, it is in real computers.) This is the point of the Functionalist doctrine that, in principle, you can make a mind out of almost anything.

[6]Which is not to deny that there are (ahem!) certain residual technical difficulties. (See, for example, part 4 of Fodor, [1983].) A theory of rationality (i.e., a theory of *our* rationality) has to account not merely for the 'semantic coherence' of thought processes in the abstract but for our ability to pull off the very sorts of rational inferences that we do. (It has to account for our ability to make science, for example.) No such theory will be available by this time next week.

[7]Because I don't want to worry about the ontology of mind, I've avoided stating RTM as an identity thesis. But you could do if you were so inclined.

[8]Like Dennett, I'm assuming for purposes of argument that the machine *has* thoughts and mental processes; nothing hangs on this, since we could, of course, have had the same discussion about people.

[9]We can now see what to say about the philosophical chestnut about Kepler's Law. The allegation is that intentionalist methodology permits the inference from 'x's behavior complies with rule R' to 'R is a rule that x explicitly represents.' The embarrassment is supposed to be that this allows the inference from 'The movements of the planets comply with Kepler's Law' to some astronomical version of LOT.

But in fact no such principle of inference is assumed. What warrants the hypothesis that R is explicitly represented is not mere behavior in compliance with R; it's an etiology according to which R figures as the content of one of the intentional states whose tokenings are causally responsible for x's behavior. And, of course, it's *not* part of the etiological story about the motions of the planets that Kepler's Law occurs to them as they proceed upon their occasions.

13 Folk Psychology and the Explanation of Human Behavior*

Paul M. Churchland
University of California, San Diego

Folk psychology, insist some, is just like folk mechanics, folk thermodynamics, folk meteorology, folk chemistry, and folk biology. It is a framework of concepts, roughly adequate to the demands of everyday life, with which the humble adept comprehends, explains, predicts, and manipulates a certain domain of phenomena. It is, in short, a folk *theory*. As with any theory, it may be evaluated for its virtues or vices in all of the dimensions listed. And as with any theory, it may be rejected in its entirety if it fails the measure of such evaluation. Call this the "theoretical view" of our self-understanding.

Folk psychology, insist others, is radically unlike the examples cited. It does not consist of laws. It does not support causal explanations. It does not evolve over time. Its central purpose is normative rather than descriptive. And thus, it is not the sort of framework that might be shown to be radically defective by sheerly empirical findings. Its assimilation to theories is just a mistake. It has nothing to fear, therefore, from advances in cognitive theory or the neurosciences. Call this the "antitheoretical view" of our self-understanding.

Somebody here is deeply mistaken. The first burden of this paper is to argue that it is the antitheoretical view that harbors most, though not all, of those mistakes. In the thirty years since the theoretical view was introduced (see especially Sellars 1956; Feyerabend this volume, p. 3–16; Rorty this volume, pp. 17–41; P. M. Churchland 1970, 1979; and 1989b, chapter 1), a

---

*Reprinted from *A Neurocomputational Perspective* (Cambridge: The MIT Press, 1989, pp. 111–127) by permission of the author and publisher.

variety of objections have been leveled against it. The more interesting of those will be addressed shortly. My current view is that these objections motivate no changes whatever in the theoretical view.

The second and more important burden of this paper, however, is to outline and repair a serious failing in the traditional expressions of the theoretical view, my own expressions included. The failing, as I see it, lies in representing one's common sense understanding of human nature as consisting of *an internally stored set of general sentences,* and in representing one's predictive and explanatory activities as being a matter of *deductive inference* from those sentences plus occasional premises about the case at hand.

This certainly sounds like a major concession to the antitheoretical view, but in fact it is not. For what motivates this reappraisal of the character of our self-understanding is the gathering conviction that little or *none* of human understanding consists of stored sentences, not even the prototypically *scientific* understanding embodied in a practicing physicist, chemist, or astronomer. The familiar conception of knowledge as a set of propositional attitudes is itself a central aspect of the framework of folk psychology, according to the reappraisal at hand, and it is an aspect that needs badly to be replaced. Our self-understanding, I continue to maintain, is no different in character from our understanding of any other empirical domain. It is speculative, systematic, corrigible, and in principle replaceable. It is just not so specifically *linguistic* as we have chronically assumed.

The speculative and replaceable character of folk psychology is now somewhat easier to defend than it was in the sixties and seventies, because recent advances in connectionist AI and computational neuroscience have provided us with a fertile new framework with which to understand the perception, cognition, and behavior of intelligent creatures. Whether it will eventually prove adequate to the task of replacing folk psychology remains to be seen, but the mere possibility of systematic alternative conceptions of cognitive activity and intelligent behavior should no longer be a matter of dispute. Alternatives are already in the making. Later in the chapter I shall outline the main features of this novel framework and explore its significance for the issues here at stake. For now, let me acquiesce in the folk-psychological conception of knowledge as a system of beliefs or similar propositional attitudes, and try to meet the objections to the theoretical view already outstanding.

1 OBJECTIONS TO THE THEORETICAL VIEW

As illustrated in my 1970, 1979, and 1984, a thorough perusal of the explanatory factors that typically appear in our common sense explanations of our internal states and our overt behavior sustains the quick "reconstruction" of a large number of universally quantified conditional statements, conditionals with the conjunction of the relevant explanatory factors as the antecedent and the relevant explanandum as the consequent. It is these universal statements that are supposed to constitute the "laws" of folk psychology.

A perennial objection is that these generalizations do not have the character of genuine causal/explanatory laws; rather, they have some other, less empirical status (e.g., that of normative principles or rules of language or analytic truths). Without confronting each of the many alternatives in turn, I think we can make serious difficulties for any objection of this sort.

Note first that the concepts of folk psychology divide into two broad classes. On the one hand, there are those fully intentional concepts expressing the various propositional attitudes, such as belief and desire. And on the other hand, there are those nonintentional or quasi-intentional concepts expressing all of the other mental states, such as grief, fear, pain, hunger, and the full range of emotions and bodily sensations. Where states of the latter kind are concerned, I think it is hardly a matter for dispute that the common homilies in which they figure are causal/explanatory laws. Consider the following.

- A person who suffers severe bodily damage will feel pain.
- A person who suffers a sudden sharp pain will wince.
- A person denied food for any length will feel hunger.
- A hungry person's mouth will water at the smell of food.
- A person who feels overall warmth will tend to relax.
- A person who tastes a lemon will have a puckering sensation.
- A person who is angry will tend to be impatient.

Clearly these humble generalizations, and thousands more like them, are causal/explanatory in character. They will and regularly do support simple explanations, sustain subjunctive and counterfactual conditionals, and underwrite predictions in the standard fashion. Moreover, concepts of this simple sort carry perhaps the major part of the folk-psychological burden. The comparatively complex explanations involving the propositional attitudes are of central importance, but they are surrounded by a quotidean whirl of simple explanations like these, all quite evidently of a causal/explanatory cast.

It won't do, then, to insist that the generalizations of folk psychology are on the whole nonempirical or noncausal in character. The bulk of them, and I mean thousands upon thousands of them, are transparently causal or nomological. The best one can hope to argue is that there is a central core of folk-psychological concepts whose explanatory role is somehow *discon-*

tinuous with that of their fellows. The propositional attitudes, especially belief and desire, are the perennial candidates for such a nonempirical role, for explanations in their terms typically display the explanandum event as "rational." What shall we say of explanations in terms of beliefs and desires?

We should tell essentially the same causal/explanatory story, and for the following reason. Whatever else humans do with the concepts for the propositional attitudes, they do use them successfully to predict the future behavior of others. This means that, on the basis of presumed information about the current cognitive states of the relevant individuals, one can nonaccidentally predict at least some of their future behavior some of the time. But any principle that allows us to do this—that is, to predict one empirical state or event on the basis of another, logically distinct, empirical state or event—*has* to be empirical in character. And I assume it is clear that the event of my ducking my head is logically distinct both from the event of my perceiving an incoming snowball, and from the states of my desiring to avoid a collision and my belief that ducking is the best way to achieve this.

Indeed, one can do more than merely predict: one can control and manipulate the behavior of others by controlling the information available to them. Here one is bringing about certain behaviors by steering the cognitive states of the subject, by relating opportunities, dangers, or obligations relevant to that subject. How this is possible without an understanding of the objective empirical regularities that connect the internal states and the overt behaviors of normal people is something that the antitheoretical position needs to explain.

The confused temptation to find something special about the case of intentional action derives primarily from the fact that the central element in a full-blooded action explanation is a configuration of propositional attitudes in the light of which the explanandum behavior can be seen as sensible or rational, at least from the agent's narrow point of view. In this rational-in-the-light-of relation we seem to have some sort of supercausal *logical* relation between the explanans and the explanandum, which is an invitation to see a distinct and novel type of explanation at work.

Yet while the premise is true—there is indeed a logical relation between the explanandum and certain elements in the explanans—the conclusion does not begin to follow. Students of the subject are still regularly misled on this point, for they fail to appreciate that a circumstance of this general sort is *typical* of theoretical explanations. Far from being a sign of the nonempirical and hence nontheoretical character of the generalizations and explanations at issue, it is one of the surest signs available that we are here dealing with a high-grade theoretical framework. Let me explain.

The electric current I in a wire or any conductor is causally determined by two factors: it tends to increase with the electromotive force or voltage V

that moves the electrons down the wire, and it tends to be reduced according to the resistance R the wire offers against their motion. Briefly, $I = V/R$. Less cryptically and more revealingly,

(x)(V)(R)[(x is subject to a voltage of (V)) & (x offers a resistance of (R)) $\supset$ ($\exists$ I)((x has a current of (I)) & (I = V/R))]

The first point to notice here is that the crucial predicates — *has a resistance of (R), is subject to a voltage of (V),* and *has a current of (I)* — are what might be called "numerical attitudes": they are predicate-forming functors that take singular terms for numbers in the variable position. A complete predicate is formed only when a specific numeral appears in the relevant position. The second point to notice is that this electrodynamical law exploits a relation holding on the domain of numbers in order to express an important empirical regularity. The current I is the *quotient* of the voltage V and the resistance R, whose values will be cited in explanation of the current. And the third point to notice is that this law and the explanations it sustains are typical of laws and explanations throughout science. Most of our scientific predicates express numerical attitudes of the sort displayed, and most of our laws exploit and display relations that hold primarily on the abstract domain of numbers. Nor are they limited to numbers. Other laws exploit the abstract relations holding on the abstract domain of vectors, or on the domain of sets, or groups, or matrices. But none of this means they are nonempirical, or noncausal, or nonnomic.

Action explanations, and intentional explanations in general, follow the same pattern. The only difference is that here the domain of abstract objects being exploited is the domain of propositions, and the relations displayed are logical relations. And like the numerical and vectorial attitudes typical of theories, the expressions for the propositional attitudes are predicate-forming functors. *Believes that P,* for example, forms a complete predicate only when a specific sentence appears in the variable position P. The principles that comprehend these predicates have the same abstract and highly sophisticated structure displayed by our most typical theories. They just exploit the relations holding on a different domain of abstract objects in order to express the important empirical regularities comprehending the states and activities of cognitive creatures. That makes folk psychology a very interesting theory, perhaps, but it is hardly a sign of its being *nontheoretical.* Quite the reverse is true. (This matter is discussed at greater length in Churchland 1979, section 14, and this volume, pp. 54–56).

In sum, the simpler parts of folk psychology are transparently causal or nomic in character, and the more complex parts have the same sophisticated logical structure typical of our most powerful theories.

But we are not yet done with objections. A recurrent complaint is that in many cases the reconstructed conditionals that purport to be sample "laws" of folk psychology are either, strictly speaking, false, or they border on the trivial by reason of being qualified by various *ceteris paribus* clauses. A first reply is to point out that my position does not claim that the laws of folk psychology are either true or complete. I agree that they are a motley lot. My hope is to see them replaced entirely, and their ontology of states with them. But this reply is not wholly responsive, for the point of the objection is that it is implausible to claim the status of an entrenched theoretical framework for a bunch of "laws" that are as vague, as loose, and as festooned with *ceteris paribus* clauses as are the examples typically given.

I will make no attempt here to defend the ultimate integrity of the laws of folk psychology, for I have little confidence in them myself. But this is not what is required to meet the objection. What needs pointing out is that the "laws" of folk theories are *in general* sloppy, vague, and festooned with qualifications and *ceteris paribus* clauses. What the objectors need to do, in order to remove the relevant system of generalizations from the class of empirical theories, is to show that folk psychology is significantly *worse* in all of these respects than are the principles of folk mechanics, or folk thermodynamics, or folk biology, and so forth. In this they are sure to be disappointed, for these other folk theories are even worse than folk psychology (see McCloskey 1983). In all, folk psychology may be a fairly ramshackle theory, but a theory it remains. Nor is it a point against this that folk psychology has changed little or none since ancient times. The same is true of other theories near and dear to us. The folk physics of the twentieth century, I regret to say, is essentially the same as the folk physics of the ancient Greeks (McCloskey 1983). Our conceptual inertia on such matters may be enormous, but a theory remains a theory, however many centuries it may possess us.

A quite different objection directs our attention to the great many things beyond explanation and prediction for which we use the vocabulary and concepts of folk psychology. Their primary function, runs the objection, is not the function served by explanatory theories, but rather the myriad social functions that constitute human culture and commerce. We use the resources of folk psychology to promise, to entreat, to congratulate, to tease, to joke, to intimate, to threaten, and so on. (See Wilkes 1981, 1984).

The list of functions is clearly both long and genuine. But most of these functions surely come under the heading of control or manipulation, which is just as typical and central a function of theories as is either explanation or prediction, but which is not mentioned in the list of theoretical functions supplied by the objectors. Though the image may be popular, the idle musings of an impotent stargazer provide a poor example of what theories are and what theories do. More typically, theories are the conceptual vehicles with which we literally come to grips with the world. The fact that folk psychology serves a wealth of practical purposes is no evidence of its being nontheoretical. Quite the reverse.

Manipulation aside, we should not underestimate the importance for social commerce of the explanations and predictions that folk psychology makes possible. If one cannot predict or anticipate the behavior of one's fellows at all, then one can engage in no useful commerce with them whatever. And finding the right explanations for their past behavior is often the key to finding the appropriate premises from which to anticipate their future behavior. The objection's attempt to paint the functions of folk psychology in an exclusively nontheoretical light is simply a distortion born of tunnel vision.

In any case, it is irrelevant. For there is no inconsistency in saying that a theoretical framework should also serve a great many nontheoretical purposes. To use an example I have used before (1986b), the theory of *witches, demonic possession, exorcism,* and *trial by ordeal,* was also used for a variety of social purposes beyond strict explanation and prediction. For example, its vocabulary was used to warn, to censure, to abjure, to accuse, to badger, to sentence, and so forth. But none of this meant that demons and witches were anything other than theoretical entities, and none of this saved the ontology of demon theory from elimination when its empirical failings became acute and different conceptions of human pathology arose to replace it. Beliefs, desires, and the rest of the folk-psychological ontology all are in the same position. Their integrity, to the extent that they have any, derives from the explanatory, predictive, and manipulative prowess they display.

It is on the topic of explanation and prediction that a further objection finds fault with the theoretical view. Precisely what, begins the objection, is the observable behavior that the ontology of folk psychology is postulated to explain? Is it bodily behavior as *kinematically* described? In some cases, perhaps, but not in general, certainly, because many quite different kinematical sequences could count as the same intentional action, and it is generally the *action* that is properly the object of folk-psychological explanations of behavior. In general, the descriptions of human behavior that figure in folk-psychological explanations and predictions are descriptions that *already* imply perception, intelligence, and personhood on the part of the agent. Thus, it must be wrong to see the relation between one's psychological states and one's behavior on the model of theoretical states postulated to explain the behavior of some conceptually independent domain of phenomena (Haldane, this volume).

The premise of this objection is fairly clearly true: a large class of behavior descriptions are not conceptually independent of the concepts of folk psychology. But this affords no grounds for denying theoretical status to the ontology of folk psychology. The assumption that it does reflects a naive view of the relation between theories and the domains they explain and predict. The naive assumption is that the concepts used to describe the domain to be explained must always be conceptually independent of the theory used to explain the phenomena within that domain. That assumption is known to be false, and we need look no farther than the special theory of relativity (STR) for a living counterexample.

The introduction of STR brought with it a systematic reconfiguration of all of the basic observational concepts of mechanics: spatial length, temporal duration, velocity, mass, momentum, etc. These are all one-place predicates within classical mechanics, but they are all replaced by two-place predicates within STR. Each ostensible "property" has turned out to be a *relation,* and each has a definite value only relative to a chosen reference frame. If STR is true, and since the early years of this century it has seemed to be, then one cannot legitimately describe the observational facts of mechanics save in terms that are drawn from STR itself.

Modern chemistry provides a second example. It is a rare chemist who does not use the taxonomy of the periodic table and the combinatorial lexicon of chemical compounds to describe both the observable facts and their theoretical underpinnings alike. For starters, one can just smell hydrogen sulphide, taste sodium chloride, feel any base, and identify copper, aluminum, iron, and gold by sight.

These cases are not unusual. Our theoretical convictions typically reshape the way we describe the facts to be explained. Sometimes it happens immediately, as with STR, but more often it happens after long familiarity with the successful theory, as is evidenced by the idioms casually employed in any working laboratory. The premise of the objection is true. But it is no point at all against the theoretical view. Given the great age of folk psychology, such conceptual invasion of the explanandum domain is only to be expected.

A different critique of the theoretical view proposes an alternative account of our understanding of human behavior. According to this view, one's capacity for anticipating and understanding the behavior of others resides not in a system of nomically embedded concepts, but rather in the fact that one is a normal person oneself, and can draw on one's own reactions, to real or to imagined circumstances, in order to gain insight into the internal states and the overt behavior of others. The key idea is that of empathy. One uses oneself as a simulation (usually imagined) of the situation of another and then extrapolates the results of that simulation to the person in question (see Gordon 1986; Goldman 1989).

My first response to this line is simply to agree that an enormous amount of one's appreciation of the internal states and overt behavior of other humans derives from one's ability to examine and to extrapolate from the facts of one's own case. All of this is quite consistent with the theoretical view, and there is no reason that one should attempt to deny it. One learns from every example of humanity one encounters, and one encounters oneself on a systematic basis. What we must resist is the suggestion that extrapolating from the particulars of one's own case is the fundamental ground of one's understanding of others, a ground that renders possession of a nomic framework unnecessary. Problems for this stronger position begin to appear immediately.

For one thing, if *all* of one's understanding of others is closed under extrapolation from one's own case, then the modest contents of one's own case must form an absolute limit on what one can expect or explain in the inner life and external behavior of others. But in fact we are not so limited. People who are congenitally deaf or blind know quite well that normal people have perceptual capacities beyond what they themselves possess, and they know in some detail what those capacities entail in the way of knowledge and behavior. People who have never felt profound grief, say, or love, or rejection, can nonetheless provide appropriate predictions and explanations of the behavior of people so afflicted. And so on. In general, one's immediately available understanding of human psychology and behavior goes substantially beyond what one has experienced in one's own case, either in real life or in pointed simulations. First-person experience or simulation is plainly not *necessary* for understanding the behavior of others.

Nor is it *sufficient*. The problem is that simulations, even if they motivate predictions about others, do not by themselves provide any explanatory understanding of the behavior of others. To see this, consider the following analogy. Suppose I were to possess a marvelous miniature of the physical universe, a miniature I could manipulate in order to simulate real situations and thus predict and retrodict the behavior of the real universe. Even if my miniature unfailingly provided accurate simulations of the outcomes of real physical processes, I would still be no further ahead on the business of *explaining* the behavior of the real world. In fact, I would then have two universes, both in need of explanation.

The lesson is the same for first-person and third-person situations. A simulation itself, even a successful one, provides no explanation. What explanatory understanding requires is an appreciation of the *general patterns* that comprehend the individual events in both cases. And that brings us back to the idea of a moderately general *theory*.

We should have come to that idea directly, since the empathetic account of our understanding of others depends crucially on one's having an initial understanding of oneself. To extrapolate one's own cognitive, affective, and behavioral intricacies to others requires that one be able to conceptualize and spontaneously to recognize those intricacies in oneself. But one's ability to do this is left an unaddressed mystery by the empathetic account. Self-understanding is not seen as a problem; it is other-understanding that is held up as the problem.

But the former is no less problematic than the latter. If one is to be able to apprehend even the *first-person* intricacies at issue, then one must possess a conceptual framework that draws all of the necessary distinctions, a framework that organizes the relevant categories into the appropriate structure, a framework whose taxonomy reflects at least the more obvious of the rough nomic regularities holding across its elements, even in the first-person case. Such a framework is already a theory.

The fact is, the categories into which any important domain gets divided by a learning creature emerge jointly with an appreciation of the rough nomic regularities that connect them. A nascent taxonomy that supports the expression of no useful regularities is a taxonomy that is soon replaced by a more insightful one. The divination of useful regularities is the single most dominant force shaping the taxonomies developed by any learning creature in any domain. And it is an essential force, even in perceptual domains, since our observational taxonomies are always radically underdetermined by our untrained perceptual mechanisms. To suppose that one's conception of one's *own* mental life is innocent of a network of systematic expectations is just naive. But such a network is already a theory, even before one addresses the issue of others.

This is the cash value, I think, of P. F. Strawson's insightful claim, now thirty years old, that to be in a position to pose any question about other minds, and to be in a position to try to construct arguments from analogy with one's own case, is already to possess at least the rudiments of what is sought after, namely, a general conception of mental phenomena, of their general connections with each other and with behavior (Strawson 1958). What Strawson missed was the further insight that such a framework is nothing other than an empirical theory, one justified not by the quasi-logical character of its principles, as he attempted unsuccessfully to show, but by its impersonal success in explaining and predicting human behavior at large. There is no special justificational story to be told here. Folk psychology is justified by what standardly justifies *any* conceptual framework: namely, its explanatory, predictive, and manipulative success.

This concludes my survey of the outstanding objections to the theoretical view outlined in the opening paragraph of the present chapter. But in defending this view there is a major difference between my strategy in earlier writings and my strategy here. In my 1970 paper, for example, the question was framed as follows: "Are action explanations *deductive-nomological* explanations?" I would now prefer to frame the question thus: "Are action explanations of the same general type as the explanations typically found in the sciences?" I continue to think that the answer to this second question is pretty clearly yes. My reasons are given above. But I am no longer confident that the deductive-nomological (D-N) model itself is an adequate account of explanation in the sciences or anywhere else.

The difficulties with the D-N model are detailed elsewhere in the literature, so I shall not pause to summarize them here. My diagnosis of its failings, however, locates the basic problem in its attempt to represent knowledge and understanding by sets of sentences or propositional attitudes. In this, the framers of the D-N model were resting on the basic assumptions of folk psychology. Let me close this chapter by briefly exploring how we might conceive of knowledge, and of explanatory understanding, in a systematically different way. This is an important undertaking relative to the concerns of this chapter, for there is an objection to the theoretical view, as traditionally expressed, that seems to me to have some real bite. It is as follows.

If one's capacity for understanding and predicting the behavior of others derives from one's internal storage of thousands of laws or nomic generalizations, how is it that one is so poor at enunciating the laws on which one's explanatory and predictive prowess depends? It seems to take a trained philosopher to reconstruct them! How is it that children are so skilled at understanding and anticipating the behavior of humans in advance of ever acquiring the complex linguistic skills necessary to express those laws? How is it that social hunters such as wolves and lions can comprehend and anticipate each other's behavior in great detail when they presumably store no internal sentences at all?

We must resist the temptation to see in these questions a renewed motivation for counting folk psychology as special, for the very same problems arise with respect to any other folk theory you might care to mention: folk physics, folk biology, whatever. It even arises for theories in the highly developed sciences, since, as Kuhn has pointed out, very little of a scientist's understanding of a theory consists in his ability to state a list of laws. It consists, rather, in the ability to apply the conceptual resources of the theory to new cases, and thus to anticipate and perhaps manipulate the behavior of the relevant empirical domain. This means that our problem here concerns the character of knowledge and understanding in general. Let us finally address that problem.

2 AN ALTERNATIVE FORM OF KNOWLEDGE REPRESENTATION

One alternative to the notion of a universal generalization about F is the notion of a *prototype* of F, a central or typical example of F which all other examples of F resemble, more or less closely, in certain relevant respects.

Prototypes have certain obvious advantages over universal generalizations. Just as a picture can be worth a thousand words, so a single complex prototype can embody the same breadth of information concerning the organization of co-occurrent features that would be contained in a long list of complex generalizations. Furthermore, prototypes allow us a welcome degree of looseness that is precluded by the strict logic of a universal quantifier: not *all* Fs need be Gs, but the standard or normal ones are, and the nonstandard ones must be related by a relevant similarity relation to those that properly are G. Various theorists have independently found motive to introduce such a notion in a number of cognitive fields: they have been called 'paradigms' and 'exemplars' in the philosophy of science (Kuhn 1962), 'stereotypes' in semantics (Putnam 1970, 1975), 'frames' (Minsky 1981) and 'scripts' (Schank 1977) in AI research, and finally 'prototypes' in psychology (Rosch 1981) and linguistics (Lakoff 1987).

Their advantages aside, prototypes also have certain familiar problems. The first problem is how to determine just what clutch of elements or properties should constitute a given prototype, and the second problem is how to determine the metric of similarity along which closeness to the central prototype is to be measured. Though they pose a problem for notions at all levels, these problems are especially keen in the case of the so-called "basic" or "simple" properties, because common sense there is unable even to articulate any deeper constituting elements (for example, what elements "make up" a purple color, a sour taste, a floral smell, or the phoneme /ā/?). A final problem concerning prototypes is a familiar one: how might prototypes be effectively represented in a real cognitive creature?

This last question brings me to a possible answer, and to a path that leads to further answers. The relevant research concerns the operations of artificial neural networks, networks that mimic some of the more obvious organizational features of the brain. It concerns how they learn to recognize certain types of complex stimuli, and how they represent what they have learned. Upon repeated presentation of various real examples of the several features to be learned (*F, G, H,* etc.), and under the steady pressure of a learning algorithm that makes small adjustments in the network's synaptic connections, the network slowly but spontaneously generates a set of internal representations, one for each of the several features it is required to recognize. Collectively, those representations take the form of a set or system of similarity spaces, and the central point or volume of such a space constitutes the network's representation of a *prototypical F, G,* or *H*. After learning is completed, the system responds to any *F*-like stimulus with an internal pattern of neuronal activity that is *close to* the prototypical pattern in the relevant similarity space.

The network consists of an initial "sensory" layer of neurons, which is massively connected to a second layer of neurons. The sizes or "weights" of the many connections determine how the neurons at the second layer collectively respond to activity across the input layer. The neurons at the second layer are connected in turn to a third layer (and perhaps a fourth layer, etc., but I shall limit the discussion here to three-layer networks). During learning, what the system is searching for is a configuration of weights that will turn the neurons at the second layer into a set of *complex feature detectors*. We then want the neurons at the third or "output" layer to respond in turn to the second layer, given any *F*-like stimuli at the input layer, with a characteristic pattern of activity. All of this is achieved by presenting the network with diverse examples of *F*s, and slowly adjusting its connection weights in the light of its initially chaotic responses.

Such networks can indeed learn to recognize a wide variety of surprisingly subtle features: phonemes from voiced speech, the shapes of objects from grey-scale photos, the correct pronunciation of printed English text, the presence of metallic mines from sonar returns, and grammatical categories in novel sentences. Given a successfully trained network, if we examine the behavior of the neurons at the second or intermediate layer during the process of recognition, we discover that each neuron has come to represent, by its level of activity, some distinct aspect or dimension of the input stimulus. Taken together, their joint activity constitutes a multidimensional analysis of the stimuli at the input layer. The trained network has succeeded in finding a set of dimensions, an *abstract space,* such that all more-or-less typical *F*s produce a characteristic profile of neuronal activity across those particular dimensions, while deviant or degraded *F*s produce profiles that are variously *close* to that central prototype. The job of the third and final layer is then the relatively simple one of distinguishing that profile-region from other regions in the larger space of possible activation patterns. In this way do artificial neural networks generate and exploit prototypes. It is now more than a suggestion that real neural networks do the same thing. (For a summary of these results and how they bear on the question of theoretical knowledge, see Churchland 1989a. For a parade case of successful learning, see Rosenberg and Sejnowski 1987. For the *locus classicus* concerning the general technique, see Rumelhart et al. 1986.)

Notice that this picture contains answers to all three of the problems about prototypes noted earlier. What dimensions go into a prototype of *F*? Those that allow the system to respond to diverse examples of *F* in a distinctive and uniform way, a way that reduces the error messages from the learning algorithm to a minimum. How is similarity to a prototype measured? By geometrical proximity in the relevant parameter space. How are prototypes represented in real cognitive creatures? By canonical activity patterns across an appropriate population of neurons.

Note also that the objective features recognized by the network can also have a temporal component: a network can just as well be trained to recognize typical *sequences* and *processes* as to recognize atemporal patterns. Which brings me to my final suggestion. A normal human's understanding of the springs of human action may reside not in a set of stored generalizations about the hidden elements of mind and how they conspire to produce behavior, but rather in one or more prototypes of the deliberative or purposeful process. To understand or explain someone's behavior may be less a matter of deduction from implicit laws, and more a matter of recognitional subsumption of the case at issue under a relevant prototype. (For a more detailed treatment of this view of explanation, the *prototype activation model*, see Churchland 1989b.)

Such prototypes are no doubt at least modestly complex, and presumably they depict typical configurations of desires, beliefs, preferences, and so forth, roughly the same configurations that I have earlier attempted to express in the form of universally quantified sentences. Beyond this, I am able to say little about them, at least on this occasion. But I hope I have succeeded in making intelligible to you a novel approach to the problem of explanatory understanding in humans. This is an approach that is grounded at last in what we know about the brain. And it is an approach that ascribes to us neither reams of universally quantified premises, nor deductive activity on a heroic scale. Explanatory understanding turns out to be not quite what we thought it was, because cognition in general gets characterized in a new way. And yet explanatory understanding remains the same *sort* of process in the case of human behavior as in the case of natural phenomena generally. And the question of the *adequacy* of our commonsense understanding remains as live as ever.

3 ADDENDUM: COMMENTARY ON DENNETT[1]

I focus here on one of the relatively few issues that still divide Dennett and me: the ontological status of intentional states. We both accept the premise that neuroscience is unlikely to find "sentences in the head," or anything else that answers to the structure of individual beliefs and desires. On the strength of this shared assumption, I am willing to infer that folk psychology is false, and that its ontology is chimerical. Beliefs and desires are of a piece with phlogiston, caloric, and the alchemical essences. We therefore need an entirely new kinematics and dynamics with which to comprehend human cognitive activity, one drawn, perhaps, from computational neuroscience and connectionist AI. Folk psychology could then be put aside in favor of this descriptively more accurate and explanatorily more powerful portrayal of the reality within. Certainly, it will be put aside in the lab and in the clinic, and eventually, perhaps, in the marketplace as well.

But Dennett declines to draw this eliminativist conclusion, despite his firm acceptance of the premise cited, and despite his willingness to contemplate unorthodox forms of cognitive theory. He prefers to claim a special status for the various intentional states, a status that will permit us to be "realists" about beliefs and desires despite their projected absence from our strict scientific ontology.

This impulse in Dennett continues to strike me as arbitrary protectionism, as ill motivated special pleading on behalf of the old and familiar. His initial rationale for exempting folk psychology from the usual scientific standards involved assigning it a purely instrumental status, but this swiftly brought him all kinds of grief, as he himself explains (1987, pp. 71–72). Instrumentalism is first and foremost an *anti*realist position, hardly a welcome port given Dennett's aims, a fact Dennett now appreciates in more detail. Accordingly, his current rationale draws a much more narrowly focused analogy between intentional states and geometrical *abstracta*, such as the centers of gravity, axes of rotation, equators, etc., that are postulated to such good effect in mechanics. As Dennett sees it, these latter are not real in the same sense that *concreta* like bricks and trees are real (you can't trip over them, for example), but they can reasonably be said to be real even so. Intentional states are real in this same sense, claims Dennett.

The reality of equators, centers, and rotational axes I am happy to grant. They are all places or loci of some sort that are decisively specifiable by reference to the shape or behavior of the relevant concrete object. But the alleged similarity of these items to beliefs, desires, and other intentional states escapes me entirely. In what respects are they similar, and why should they be grouped together in advance of the issue here at stake? That is, in advance of any hopes of finding an exculpatory status for intentional states?

Dennett is quick to point out that folk psychology has some nontrivial predictive power, especially in its central domain of normal human behavior, despite the lack of any neural *concreta* answering to the propositional attitudes. He emphasizes, quite correctly, that it is an objective fact about humans that a significant amount of their behavior is accurately predictable in intentional terms.

But I think he overvalues this fact wildly. We must not forget that all sorts of false theories, with wholly chimerical ontologies, can boast very impressive predictive power in various proprietary domains. But this buys their ontology no special status. It is an objective fact that much of the behavior of metals and ores is predictable in terms of the alchemical essences, that most of the behavior of the visible heavens is predictable in terms of nested crystal spheres, that much of the behavior of moving bodies is predictable in terms of impetus, and so forth. And yet there are no alchemical essences, nor any crystal spheres, nor any impetuses. We could, of course, set about insisting that these three "things" are real and genuine after all, though mere *abstracta* to be sure. But none of us is tempted to salvage *their* reality by such a tortured and transparent ploy. Why should we be tempted in the case of the propositional attitudes?

This disagreement between us on the status of folk psychology dates from several letters now a full decade old. However, one point on which we then agreed was that neither of us could clearly imagine a systematic alternative to folk psychology. At the time I ascribed this inability to the natural poverty of our imaginations. Dennett was inclined to suspect a deeper reason. But since then the materials available to imagination have improved dramatically. The microstructure of the brain and the recent successes of connectionist AI both suggest that our principal form of representation is the high-dimensional activation vector, and that our principal form of computation is the vector-to-vector transformation, effected by a matrix of differently weighted synapses. In place of propositional attitudes and logical inferences from one to another, therefore, we can conceive of persons as the seat of vectorial attitudes and various nonlinear transformations from one vector to another. We can already see how such a vectorial system can do many of the things that humans and other animals do swiftly and easily, such as recognize faces and other highly complex stimuli, or control a complex body with both relevance and grace. The possibility of a real alternative now seems beyond dispute: we are already building it.

What remains an issue is how our familiar folk psychology will fare in light of what the new conception will reveal. Retention through reduction remains a real possibility, though the character of the theoretical developments just cited make this seem increasingly unlikely. If we rule out reduction, then elimination emerges as the only coherent alternative, Dennett's resistance notwithstanding.

In the end, Dennett's steadfast insistence that folk psychology is not just another a false theory, but rather an "abstract stance" of some kind, one with striking predictive powers, reminds me of the shopkeeper in the Monty Python sketch about the distraught customer trying to return a recently purchased but very dead parrot. Python fans will remember the shopkeeper's deliciously shifty-eyed insistence. "Naw, naw, it's not *dead!* It's just *resting!* It's just *pining* for the fiords! . . . Lovely *plumage,* the Norwegian Blue."

FOOTNOTES

[1]This is a short commentary on Daniel C. Dennett's *Intentional Stance.* It first appeared in *Behavioral and Brain Sciences* 11 (1989), no. 3, under the title, "On the Ontological Status of Intentional States: Nailing Folk Psychology to Its Perch."

14 Understanding Folk*

John Haldane
University of Saint Andrews, Scotland

I

We may say that in certain circumstances people behave in certain ways without implying that the one is cause of the other. We might, of course, content ourselves with the programme of accounting for behaviour in terms of the capacities or dispositions from which it is derivable. This, however, is not a scientific programme but one which may be carried out by anyone with sufficient experience of human affairs.[1]

— David Hamlyn

Man is free to make decisions. Otherwise counsels, precepts, prohibitions, rewards, and punishments would be pointless. As evidence of this consider how some things act without judgment [but according to efficient causes], so a stone falls to the ground. . . . But Man, by means of his cognitive capacity, acts through judging that something is to be shunned or sought after. Because the particular conclusion follows from reasoning based in experience and not from natural instinct he acts freely—being open to different options. In contingent matters reason can go either way . . . hence in regard to [particular actions] rational judgment is open to various possibilities, not determined to one.[2]

— Thomas Aquinas

Distinguish first (as it is important to do) the ascriptions of psychological states and activities to oneself and to other persons (including ascriptions

*Reprinted from *Proceedings of the Aristotelian Society* Supplementary Volume 62 (1988, pp. 223–254) by permission of the author and publisher.

made in the context of explaining their actions by reference to beliefs, desires and intentions) from the development of philosophical accounts of the nature of thought and agency. One may then say that the views of Hamlyn and Aquinas, like that of Aristotle whom they both follow, place them among the proponents of what Professor Churchland terms 'the antitheoretical view of our self-understanding'. Churchland regards this view as 'deeply mistaken,' and sets against it an account of common-sense psychology according to which our everyday efforts at mutual interpretation and explanation are applications of a theory of human behaviour that seeks to subsume its instances under causal/explanatory laws. So conceived, 'folk psychology' is commended for its methodology (subject to later qualification) but condemned for its falsity inasmuch as it radically misdescribes the inner reality behind publicly observable events. For the former is not, as perhaps we previously supposed, a mind — a locus of qualia and intentional entities — but is instead a buzzing hive of neurophysiological activity.

In one important respect Professor Churchland is in sympathy with Descartes — though, of course, he wants nothing to do with metaphysical dualism. The point of common concern is that each conceives the subject matter of psychology to be the inner mechanisms, events and processes which stand behind, and are causally responsible for, overt behaviour. There, however, agreement ends. Besides rejecting dual-substance ontology Churchland countenances, and hopes to see, the abandonment of the economy of intentions, propositional attitudes and irreducibly phenomenal features in favour of neuronal networks and their causal roles. Cartesianism in this respect is what may be called 'psychomythology'. One might wonder, however, whether Churchland's own very different hypothesis is not open to the challenge that it likewise misrepresents the truth of which our common-sense, descriptive-cum-explanatory scheme purports to give account, and does so in such a way as to invite the tag 'neuromythology.'[3] This at any rate is a possibility I want to investigate, suggesting at a later stage that we should reject both myths of the extensive sphere of inner activity and try instead to believe, as philosophers, what our mothers and experience have long taught us: that we are living, thinking, feeling, acting subjects existing in communities of like-animated creatures; that is, to understand the characteristic behaviour of human beings in the manner of Aristotelianism — as expressing, usually for all to see, the souls of rational animals.

II

Following the initial characterisation and contrast of the two views of our self-understanding, Churchland introduces the aims of his paper as being to demonstrate the errors in the antitheoretical conception, and to reformulate the opposing view in a fashion properly free from contamination by ideas generated from within folk psychology. In short, he seeks to preserve the theoretical integrity of prescientific psychology while yet repudiating it as altogether misconceiving the real nature of cognition in general, and thus of the representation of human descriptive, predictive and explanatory activities in particular. In pursuit of the first of these aims Churchland considers and replies to three objections presented against the theoretical view, which are also intended to support the opposing interpretation: first, the claim that common-sense generalisations about mental states and bodily behaviour are not causal/explanatory laws but exhibit conceptual connections of various sorts; second, the complaint that such conditionals as advocates of the theoretical view present in evidence of their account are either clearly false or else vague and extensively qualified and so cannot reasonably be treated as serious theoretical hypotheses; and third, the objection that ordinary psychological notions are not primarily employed for purposes of explanation and prediction but belong within the multitude of forms of social intercourse. Folk psychology on this contrary view is part of human life and not a theory about it. Having addressed these objections Churchland then turns to the second task, that of presenting a new model of what having the theoretical, yet common-sense understanding of psychology consists in and of how this is represented 'in' the theorist. The central element in this model is the idea of *prototypes* of the objects of inquiry, exemplars 'depicted' by neural networks.

In what follows I wish to contest the suggestion that our common understanding is a theory, in any sense more substantial than that of an account or set of ideas. In doing so I shall be concerned with the main epistemological and methodological aspects of such understanding, both of which, I think, are misrepresented in Churchland's writings. Following discussion of these matters I shall consider very briefly the coherence of the (new?) epistemology of prototypes and then offer a diagnosis of, and remedy for, the now chronic condition that has given rise to neuromythology.

III

Why then, does Professor Churchland insist that our common understanding is a (protoscientific) theory of human behaviour? I detect at least eight reasons:

(1) the belief that all observation is theory laden;[4]
(2) the belief that concepts are interrelated so that no specification of the content of any one is available independently of those of others in the scheme;[5]

(3) the belief that the attribution of psychological states is an explanatory hypothesis involving the postulation of unobservable entities in explanation of observed behaviour;[6]

(4) the belief that the meaning of psychological terms is fixed by the set of 'folk psychological' generalisations in which they figure;[7]

(5) the belief that 'folk psychology' involves a set of causal/explanatory-cum-predictive laws;[8]

(6) the belief that the logical relations holding between the terms in folk generalisations are typical of 'high-grade' theoretical frameworks;[9]

(7) the belief that the main non-explanatory function of our pre-scientific psychology is manipulation of the social world;[10]

(8) the belief that it is conceivable and indeed likely (not to say desirable) that our current self-understanding will be abandoned and replaced by a neuropsychological framework.[11]

The last of these differs from the others inasmuch as it is not part of the argument for the thesis that our common understanding is a theory. Rather it is something that this claim renders intelligible. Only if everyday psychology is a theoretical construction does it makes sense to conceive of its replacement. Thus it is a central concern of Churchland's writings to establish the empirical theoreticity of the common-sense conception, to demonstrate that, as he puts it:

> FP is nothing more and nothing less than a culturally entrenched theory of how we and the higher animals work. It has no special features that make it empirically invulnerable, no unique functions that make it irreplaceable, no special status of any kind whatsoever.[12]

The overall argument for this conclusion can usefully be divided into two, *epistemological* and *methodological,* stages, the first drawing upon reasons (1)-(4), the second upon (4)-(7). As this division suggests, the proposed network semantics for psychological terms links the idea that everyday observations are informed by a conceptual scheme with the claim that the psychological framework is largely constituted by a set of causal/explanatory laws. In the paper printed above, Churchland addresses himself principally to the task of defending the empirical law element in the theoretical view and I shall consider this defence in the next section. At this point, however, my concern is with the prior idea implicit in his discussion, and elaborated in several places elsewhere, that psychological observations are the products of a theory and have no privileged epistemological status.

To suppose the contrary is, according to Churchland, to neglect the lessons of recent epistemology which have taught us that all perception is theoretically conditioned and hence that observations cannot be regarded as independent, theory-neutral data. Accordingly, the idea that psychological descriptions might express pre-theoretical observations of mental phenomena and thus be immune to wholesale elimination emerges as an instance of the *Myth of the Given*.[13] Moreover, in this respect there is no difference between third- and first-person perception. Looking within from within is no different from looking at others from beyond their skins. All seeing is theoretically-believing.

Here one might try to turn this post-myth epistemology against the supposed conceivability of our self-understanding's coming to be eliminated, by suggesting that if observation is theory-laden then there are no neutral data and hence nothing by reference to which one account might be judged to be better than another: different theory, different data; no competition, no elimination. Adding to this a view of psychology as a descriptive/explanatory scheme the predicates and guiding principles of which are intentionalistic and normative, the conclusion would then be that psychology is autonomous in respect of both its observational objects and its practical purposes. And so it (logically) could not be threatened with reduction or elimination by neuroscience.

This objection has some appeal but it is easy to see how it might be replied to by the sophisticated proponent of the thesis that all observation is theory-laden. Firstly, then, one should notice that Churchland is concerned with the challenge presented by neuro*psychology* to its old, poor and confused folk relative; that is to say, it is assumed that the two theories address common protopsychological phenomena, the more or less independent data, which each seeks to re-characterise and explain, being human behaviour and cognitive activity.[14] Of course, observations of these are themselves conditioned by a background folk theory (and thus are in principle eliminable) but this does not prevent them from serving as neutral relative to the higher level theories. Once brought within the scope of these latter the data are redescribed and such descriptions may be 'incommensurable'. Nonetheless the theories can be compared in respect of explanatory and predictive power by reference to data characterised in the neutral relative vocabulary, and in point of the capacity of each to harmonise with other theories of different but causally related phenomena.

One might respond to this reply in Davidsonian, conceptual-dualist fashion, arguing that redescription yields explanatory autonomy. However, that concedes an asymmetry between the rationalistic account of behaviour and its antecedents, and the neuroscientific theory of them, inasmuch as it grants causal efficacy to the features specified by the latter. And this concession is one which Churchland can be expected to exploit for it allows the possibility of accommodating the scientific theory of behaviour within a wider causal explanatory account of nature while conceding that the price of autonomous rationalistic psychology is explanatory isolation. In the next section I shall reconsider the terms of this response, but here I want to propose a more radical reply to the claim that folk psychological observations, like all perceptions, are theory-laden and thus have no special status. The response is simply that there are *givens* and that psychological phenomena are among them.

The thesis that perception differs from sensation in virtue of having a conceptual content, and thus that only the former is properly speaking cognitive, is an ancient and important insight.[15] However, it neither undermines the idea that there are privileged observations nor implies that all perception is theoretical. It might seem though, that the latter claim follows when one considers the character of conceptual content and recognises that it is, if not holistic, then at least molecular. Concepts come in clusters so that to have one is to have many. Hence if perception is conceptually informed and concepts are parts of structures or schemes does this not imply that perception is theory laden? No; because a conceptual framework is not yet a theory. What, then, is a *theory?* For present purposes the following characterisation will serve. *An empirical theory is an abstract structure containing a set of predicates P, and a set of law-like generalisations G in which the elements of P occur essentially. The members of G include both inner principles, covering the behaviour of postulated unobservables; and bridge principles, relating the latter to observable phenomena. The terms in P are largely, or wholly, defined by their roles in the principles of G.* Setting aside for the moment the question of the status of our self-understanding it is clear enough that it is a necessary but not sufficient condition of being a theory that something be a conceptual framework. Accordingly, acceptance of the claims that observation is conceptually-informed and that concepts belong in schemes is compatible with denial of the thesis that all perception is theory-laden and *ipso facto* speculative and eliminable.

To have shown this much is important given the widespread conflation of schemes and theories,[16] but it is not yet to have demonstrated how there can be a level of basic pretheoretical perceptions whose content is shaped directly (though not exclusively) by the world and which may therefore be appealed to as theory-neutral arbiters in ontological disputes. Nor has it yet been shown that psychological observations are candidates for inclusion among such perceptions. Here I can only outline an argument for both conclusions. The recognition that concepts are involved in perception was connected with the distinction between seeing and sensing. The error of classical and analytical empiricism was to suppose that the latter provides *cognitive* grounds (of a logical or evidential sort) for the former. However, if sensation is not sufficient for perception it is at any rate necessary for it. Thus if I am to perceive *a* (be it always as an *F,* or as a *G,* etc.), *a* must be sensuously presented to me. This latter kind of presentation does not involve my *seeing a. A fortiori* it has no conceptual content. I am not aware of *a as* an *F,* or *as* anything else at all. Nonetheless, there is such a thing as preperceptual awareness, or what might better be termed 'environmental sensitivity.'[17] The necessity of preperceptual discrimination is conditional upon the existence of perception given that conceptual activity is not sufficient for the latter. Thus, since there is sense-perception there must be environmental sensitivities exercised in the various sensemodalities. And we have a more familiar route to the conclusion that human beings and other animals have several common and species-specific (preconceptual) discriminative capacities, i.e., through observation of infants.

Which features in its environment a creature can respond to obviously depends upon the environment itself and the sensory apparatus of the creature. It is therefore a matter of contingency what one can sense. This determined, however, it is not then a wholly contingent matter as to what one can learn to see. The structure of one's sensory set establishes one of the conditions of concept-acquisition. This is not to say, of course, that one cannot form concepts of unobservables or that one's perceptual discriminations cannot become very rich indeed. But it does imply that a nonconceptual factor operates in determining the character of one's initial observational concepts. Crudely, perception cannot get going unless the principles of individuation provided by these concepts are largely coincident with the sensory discriminations executed in the preperceptual state. Again there is an empirical illustration of this requirement available to anyone who watches an adult trying to impart concepts to a young infant. The suggestion then is that there is, since there must be, a (species-relative) observational base composed of perceptions that reproduce (though given conceptual holism they may also transcend) one's natural, precognitional discriminations. Correspondingly, certain ostensively introduced perceptual terms are not only nontheoretical but given that they have been learnt in association with awareness of salient features of one's environment, and continue to individuate them (for they would not be the terms they are if they did not), then (some of) the observation statements in which they occur belong to a privileged class. This is not to say of course, that any perceptual judgment of this sort cannot be wrong; only that the idea that such perceptions are liable to *elimination* in the face of purely theoretical developments is unintelligible. For the former provide the data upon which theorising may operate and to which it is answerable.

None of this is to deny that theory—based on daylight perception of middle-sized objects—may filter down to the observational level. However, such penetration does not eliminate pretheoretical observation. Churchland cites examples supposedly to the contrary: observations involving such concepts as *caloric fluid, phlogiston, the heavenly sphere* and *witches;* and then adds that the concepts of folk psychology await the same fate.[18]

However, the examples cited are ones for which it is easy to formulate perceptual concepts of a more basic sort that could find application in experience before and after the change in theorists' accounts of the objects of the (theory-neutral) observations: *heat, burning or rusting, the night sky,* and *wild women,* respectively. Certainly the corresponding concepts in the previous list transcend these classifications and incorporate *explanations* of the natural phenomena. This may be evidence of the theoreticity of those notions; but it also implies the relative theory-neutrality of the members of the second list while giving absolutely no reason to suppose that the latter are in turn theoretical.

The involvement of nature in determining the content of basic observations extends to perception of one's own psychological states and to those of others. In order to recognise pain and hunger, for example, one needs to possess concepts of pain and of hunger. And one could not have concepts adequate to identify and individuate states of these sorts, i.e., ones that extend in phenomenological and behavioural dimensions, unless one had preperceptual sensitivities both to subjectively presented states (sensations) and to one's objectively discriminable bodily behaviour. This duality is a general precondition of one's acquiring from others by means of ostension concepts apt for singling out states of types which have 'inner' aspects.[19] More generally still, the epistemology of psychological description as we have it is intelligible only on the assumption that some of the observations invoked in support of such ascriptions are pretheoretical perceptions of psychological states, events and processes. Professor Churchland is rightly critical of analogical and behaviourist accounts of our knowledge of other minds but the solution he fathers on our common understanding is no less unsatisfactory. He writes:

> It is of course by observing a creature's behaviour, including its verbal behaviour, that we judge it to be a conscious thinking creature. . . . From bodily damage and moaning, we infer pain. From smiles and laughter, we infer joy. From the dodging of a snowball, we infer perception. . . . From these and other things, and above all from speech, we infer conscious intelligence. . . . This much is obvious, but . . . the problem begins to emerge when we ask what *justifies* the sorts of inferences cited. . . . The hypothesis that a specific individual has conscious intelligence is . . . an explanatory [empirical] hypothesis . . . and it is plausible to the degree that the individual's continuing behaviour is best explained and predicted in terms of desires, beliefs, perceptions, emotions and so on.[20]

The first thing that should strike one about this passage is that as it stands it conspicuously fails as a statement of the problem of other minds. If one is in a position to observe *moaning, smiles, laughter, dodging,* and *speech* then there can be no general problem of how one might pass from knowledge of these to knowledge of a conscious, intelligent . . . in short, minded creature. For these phenomena are *manifestations* of mindedness. By the same token, the intrinsic connections between, for example, *dodging* (i.e., responding evasively to attack) and *perception,* or between *speech* and *thought,* make nonsense of the proposal that the inference from the first to the second in each case is licensed by an empirical, psychobehavioural generalisation.[21] Smiling, laughing and speaking are person-involving states and activities just as melting, growing, and weighing 10 lb are physical substance-involving. If, therefore, one is able to apply the predicate '. . . is speaking,' then it is presupposed in this application that the subject in question is a person.

Perhaps, however, Churchland's formulation of the problem can be given a different reading. We might then suppose that 'smiles,' 'laughter,' 'dodging,' and 'speech' are intended to pick out bodily phenomena without prejudice to the issue of whether the bodies in question are also minded. Another possibility is that while the terms are indeed taken to be 'person'-implicating their application to bodily phenomena is part of the folk psychological hypothesis; so that the quoted passage may then be read as, somewhat misleadingly, incorporating elements of the solution in the statement of the problem. This interpretation is unhappy however, since if observable behaviour is included within the domain of conscious intelligence then nothing nonpsychological remains as the phenomena for which the hypothesis would serve as an explanation. I take it, then, that the only real alternative to the original face-value reading is that offered above which supposes that what is observed is not psychologically characterised. Setting exegesis aside the important point is that whereas the original reading deprives the 'hypothesis' solution of a problem, the alternative reinstates the issue but reveals the hopelessness of the hypothetico-deductive justification as a treatment of it.

Suppose then, that the observations with which one begins, and for which an explanation is sought, do not employ person-involving concepts but draw only upon ideas of material configurations and associated sounds. The question cannot be: what justifies regarding these as expressing conscious intelligence? — since, *ex hypothesi,* they are not (yet) so regarded. Rather it is: what justifies attributing internal mentality in explanation of observable bodily states and processes? And the proposed answer is that 'the hypothesis . . . is plausible to the degree that the individual's continuing behaviour is best explained and predicted in terms of desires, beliefs, perceptions, emotions and so on. Since that is, in fact, the best way to understand the behaviour of most humans, one is therefore justified in believing that they are 'other minds'.[22] However, this suggestion collapses when one considers the terms of explanation. For example, references to combinations of beliefs and desires, etc., may be set within generalisations which relate them to behaviour. But it is behaviour individuated under *action* types which they explain; and action *types* do not in general correlate with *types* of bodily configurations. Indefinitely many different movements may realise actions of one and the same kind. Further still, it is not difficult to conceive of performances, explicable by reference to psychological states, for which there are no candidates for mere bodily movements with which those performances are even *token* identical. I am not here concerned with omissions realised by remaining stationary. The point is rather that no principles of identity and individuation of behavioural-types, other than action-kinds, will yield configurations identical with particular movements singled out via performance concepts. Consider, for example, the action of my writing (*i.e.*, longhand inscribing) the last sentence. With which bodily movement was it identical? As I wrote, my left foot tapped, my rib-cage contracted, my eyes blinked, my head turned and so on. Of course, one knows roughly which movements are relevant, *but only because one is able to employ the discriminatory criteria associated with the concept 'writing.'*

The implication of these facts is that the hypothesis of other minds, far from being the best explanation of observed bodily movements, very largely fails to engage with them *as movements,* i.e., as something less than and not type-correlated with actions. Certainly, if one avails oneself of action concepts in the description of human beings' observable behaviour, then the ascription of mindedness to them makes sense, not as an inference warranted by an empirical generalisation, but as a logical implication of such descriptions. For *actions* are then perceived as manifestations of intelligent life.

The burden of my earlier argument in defence of pretheoretical perception was the possibility of locating at least some part of our common-sense self-understanding at the level of observational data. The recognition of gestures, actions and speech as person-involving phenomena brings many features of mindedness within public view. Thus it renders nonobligatory the assumption that the ascription of psychological states to others could at best be an empirically justified hypothesis concerning the unobservable causes of observable bodily movements. That (Cartesian) assumption, together with the conceptual character of perception and the holistic structure of content, form a large part of Churchland's positive case for the theoretical nature of everyday psychology. And it is the presumed theoreticity of the latter that makes the prospect of elimination seem abstractly intelligible, if not actually imaginable. However, once this case is examined its weakness becomes apparent. And the thought that it is in fact inconceivable that we could cease to regard ourselves and others as conscious, thinking, feeling creatures can be seen to find a rational ground in the idea that folk psychology, so called, is not a body of theory but an inherited framework of person-involving concepts and generalisations. Certainly it is contingent that there are minded animals. It does not follow, however, that it is an open question whether *we* really are such.

Earlier I observed that both the epistemological case for the theoretical view and the defence of this interpretation by appeal to the methodological character of ordinary psychology invoke the belief that the predicates of rational explanation cannot in general derive their meaning from ostension but are fixed by the law-like generalisations in which they feature. This proposal is supported in part by the familiar deficiencies of theories of private demonstration and of behavioural definition; and in part also by the inference, challenged above, from semantic structuralism to theoreticity. However, in acknowledging those deficiencies one is not forced to move towards a semantics of theoretical terms. There remains the possibility introduced earlier of conceiving the conditions for the basic form of introduction of psychological concepts as including subjectively and objectively discriminable psychological states.[23] Whatever the fate of that proposal, it is appropriate to mark the transition from this section to the next with the observation that Churchland's account of the semantics of psychological predicates is itself deficient inasmuch as the constitutive principles of a network sufficient to define such terms are simply not available. Hence this argument for the theoretical view also fails.

Common-sense psychology is inherently indeterminate in respect of both its predicates and its generalisations. Churchland concedes something to this observation but maintains that:

> thorough perusal of the explanatory factors that typically appear in our common-sense explanations of our internal states and our overt behaviour sustains the quick 'reconstruction' of a large number of universally quantified conditional statements, conditionals with the conjunction of the relevant explanatory factors as the antecedent and the relevant *explanandum* as the consequent.[24]

And later he claims that being 'vague', 'loose', and 'festooned with qualifications and *ceteris paribus* clauses' is a general feature of the laws of folk theories and so gives no reason to withhold this status from our self-understanding. He continues: 'What the objectors need to do, in order to remove the relevant system of generalisations from the class of empirical theories, is to show that folk psychology is significantly worse in all of these respects than are the principles of folk mechanics, or folk thermodynamics, or folk biology, and so forth.'

Suppressing my scepticism as to the existence of such theories as are included in Churchland's list, it is important to note that the suggested line of objection is not that which the opponent of the theoretical view is either likely, or well-advised, to take. For if, as Churchland maintains, being vague, loose and qualified by *ceteris paribus* clauses is compatible with law-like, and thus with theoretical, status then it is not at all clear why being shown to exhibit these features to a great degree should be thought to demonstrate incompatibility with regard to such characteristics. The real objection is not based on a matter of quantity but on one of kind. The point is that the indeterminacy of our inherited ways of describing and understanding one another is such that no genuine, universally quantified, psycho-behavioural conditionals are specifiable. Hence the terms of this scheme cannot derive their meaning from law-like generalisations. This objection can be presented either in the form of a challenge to produce such a generalisation or as a demonstration of the impossibility of there being any. The latter draws its inspiration from the experiential, normative and intentionalistic criteria for the application of psychological and behavioural predicates and is connected with the different conception of action explanation discussed below. For now, however, it is sufficient to press the former challenge and to expose the failure of efforts to meet it.

In several of his writings Churchland offers candidates for the 'explanatory laws of folk psychology' such as the following:

(1) $(x)(p)[(x$ fears that $p) \rightarrow (x$ desires that $\sim p)]$

and

(2) $(x)(p)(q)[((x$ believes that $p)$ & $(x$ believes that (if p then $q)))$
$\rightarrow$ (barring confusion, distraction, etc., x believes that $q)]$.

However, while (1) is an unrestricted generalization it is as such patently false and will only begin to appear credible when qualified either by a *ceteris paribus* clause or, as in the style of (2), by exclusion conditions. What should be obvious, however, is that the other things which must be equal, or the conditions which must be absent, cannot be fully specified. This impossibility is barely concealed by the insertion of 'etc.' in (2). Of course we know how one might continue the list. The trouble is we also know that we cannot complete it. Thus as it stands (2) is simply *not* a law. But unless appropriate generalisations can be produced there is no hope of showing that the predicates of everyday psychology are theoretical terms functionally defined by their roles in a framework constituted by such laws.

IV

In this section the focus of my interest is the claim that the theoretical character of our self-understanding is evidenced by the pattern of action explanation and prediction which it embodies. The idea is that rationalisation of behaviour by reference to psychological states is a species of causal explanation and that by implication it is therefore an instance of the familiar empirico-theoretical method of explanation by subsumption under causal laws. Before proceeding, two points should be noted. The first is a reminder of the interesting position in which Churchland finds himself. Drawing upon a form of description that has arisen in connection with the late John Mackie's meta-ethical views, one may describe Professor Churchland as holding an 'Error' account of Folk-Theoretical Psychology. He argues on behalf of the causal theory of mind and action while from a higher perspective regarding it as radically false. In consequence he finds it appropriate to offer an alternative account of that which folk psychology misdescribes, namely, 'human behaviour and cognitive activity' [sic] and, *ipso facto,* of what instantiating folk psychology consists in. Churchland is thus unlike most contemporary proponents of the mental-cause theory of action inasmuch as he defends it against Wittgensteinian rationalism while yet conceding its falsity. Here my concern is with the former determinant of his elevated position.

The second point is to note a further difference between Churchland and many other defenders of the present orthodoxy that belief/desire psychology explains actions as consequences of prior occurrent causes. For while it is also common doctrine between them that causation is law like, Churchland regards the implication of nomologicality as expressed within psychology by the explanatory generalisations, while it is now more generally held, following Davidson, that action explanation is anomalous and that the laws which particular psycho-behavioural interactions instantiate will only be formulable in the language of physical theory. Fortunately it is possible for me to abstract from these differences while keeping in sight the central idea common to both Churchland and the Davidsonians, namely, that action explanation is achieved by specification of Humean causes. For it is in fact this feature, less than the *nomologicality* of rationalisation, that Churchland is defending when he considers and responds to the objection made on behalf of the antitheoretical view: that explanations offered within common-sense psychology do not rest upon empirical, causal generalisations.

The strength of this defence is best tested by outlining a view of the sort which it is intended to defeat. One of the things that opponents of causal theories have wanted to deny is that reasons and the actions they explain are subsumable under psycho-behavioural laws — part of the point of this denial being the avoidance of psychological determinism. However, Davidson offers a way of evading this commitment while retaining a causal theory. Another possibility, too rarely considered, is rejection of the unwarranted assumption that causality is law like.[25] Noticing these exits from nomologicality, and noticing also that both Davidson and Churchland are happy to allow that action explanation may do more than merely causally account for behaviour,[26] the question arises: Why resist the theory of mental causation? The answer, as Churchland rightly discerns it, is the belief that the connections between reasons and actions are of *rational-cum-conceptual* sorts and hence cannot be contingent, empirical relations between wholly distinct items. Churchland then attacks this idea in two ways: first, by observing that we can often predict behaviour using psycho-behavioural generalisations and that these are clearly law like; and second, by attempting to dissolve the appearance of real nonempirical connections between the terms of such explanations. As regards the first of these responses, I have already indicated that the claim for law-like status has not been made out and further suggested that it is impossible that it should be. The matter of prediction I shall return to shortly and will consider in due course the second, eliminatory response. Before that, however, it is necessary to see how a nontheoretical, rational-connection view might be sustained in the face of additional considerations pressed by mental cause theorists.

Here two points familiar from the writings of Davidson are relevant. The first is the suggestion that causal and rational connections are compatible so long as one distinguishes between events and psychobehavioural descriptions of them and locates the connections at the appropriate levels. The second consideration is less conciliatory. It is that an agent may have had many reasons in the light of which ϕing was an intelligible thing for him to have done. Accordingly, if a rationalisation is to be fully explanatory then it must not only cite reasons he had but identify those *because of which* he acted as and when he did. This additional requirement, so it is claimed,[27] can only be met by the attribution to those reasons of causal efficacy.

Far from securing the orthodoxy, however, these considerations raise questions about its intelligibility. The force of the second point is that rationalisation only makes sense if it is simultaneously both justificatory (or interpretative) and explanatory — if it locates the origins of behaviour in *rational-causes*. But the implication of the previous point is that the features of antecedent events in virtue of which they render consequences rationally intelligible are distinct from (and not even *type*-correlated with) the features in virtue of which they bring them about. Thus *rationality* and *causality* come apart, and the cost of remarriage is either acceptance of dualistic interaction or of harmonious epiphenomenalism.[28]

The former cost is not one which, for myself, I should regard as unacceptable. But whether or not it has to be paid there is need for some better account of action than mental-cause theories offer — not least because the ascription of intentional behaviour has to be made epistemologically intelligible. Earlier I argued that everyday psychology may be largely observational. Now I want to suggest how the explanation and prediction of behaviour may likewise be nontheoretical. In their concern to defend the rationalistic and non-nomological character of action explanation some authors have been too quick in dismissing the possibility of a causal account. Before doing so it would be better to consider whether the trouble with current versions lies not in the appeal to causality but in the notion of causation that is appealed to.

Modern philosophical accounts of causation have sought to discover a universal metaphysical mechanism and, failing to find one, have tended to fall back upon invariable succession, supposing that this is the minimum condition necessary for appeals to causality to have any explanatory force. Aristotle and his scholastic followers were not so prejudiced as to the adequacy of nonlaw-like causal explanations. Aquinas, for example, observes that 'the question, why? seeks a cause' and elaborates upon the very different kinds of factors to which something may be due—only one of which corresponds to the modern idea of efficient causation and certainly does not imply invariability.[29] Elsewhere he considers the causation of action and again finds that answering the question Why? introduces various types of relevant conditions.[30] Following this lead I suggest that the analysis of action explanation might be advanced by ditching the Hume/Mill/Davidson view of causation and exploring the possibility of working with a more pluralistic ontology including properly rational causes.

On this view there is no reason to suppose that the explanation of action has a single form, or that it logically requires generality or the distinct existence of the terms of the relations involved. Consider then, the kinds of factors that might be cited in answer to questions raised in connection with someone's behaviour. A child observes for the first (and perhaps the only) time a man's ears moving rhythmically. He asks *Why?* The answer: because he is wiggling them, redescribes the movement as an action by reference to a causal factor—the man himself, exercising a power *(agent cause)*. Again the child asks *Why?* and this time the answer given is: because he is trying to amuse you. Like the last answer this explains the behaviour by redescribing it, this time by specifying its intentional content *(formal-cum-final cause)*. Once more, as children will, the child asks *Why?* and now the answer is: because he saw you were crying. Here the action is explained by mentioning a prior state to which it is a response, and this includes such factors as the child's own behaviour and the man's perception of it *(efficient causes)*. Notice that while the answers provided are genuinely explanatory none depend upon its being assumed by the child or the adult that they are implicitly general. Notice also that save for the last answer the factors are logically connected with the action.

Writing in another context Professor Churchland discusses the intentionality of propositional attitudes and cautions his readers: "this use of the term 'intentionality' has nothing to do with the term 'intentional' as meaning 'done deliberately.' "[31] However, it is important for the correct understanding of action explanation to see that this is a mistake. Actions, like thoughts, are attitudinal. They involve directing oneself *(intendere)* towards objects or goals. In considering this feature of thoughts, Meinong (and others since) assumed that it indicates a relation between distinct existents: the thinker and the object of his thought. Noticing that what one is thinking of may not exist he then introduced nonactual, subsistent referents. Similarly, in discussing intentional action some authors have observed that it is distinguished from mere bodily movement by being 'for the sake of *p*', or 'in order that *q*', where *p* and *q* stand for possible states of affairs. This has encouraged some bold spirits to suggest that action is behaviour due to as yet nonactual states; and has led others who object to this as a piece of nonsense (but who share the assumption that intentional action is move-ment related to some distinct entity) to propose that the independent causal factors are prior beliefs and desires directed upon *p,* or upon *q.* The parallel with the propositional attitudes is now helpful. Just as we should see that mention of the *intentional* object of a belief is not a direct reference to an independent entity but rather a specification of the content of the belief itself,[32] so explaining an action by saying it is being done 'for the sake of *p*', or 'in order that *q*', is a matter of describing its intentional content. This yields a form of explanation which is causal (in an Aristotelian sense) and meets the earlier requirement that 'operative' reasons be indicated, but which involves ineliminable logical connections with some less specific descriptions of the actions.

To end this section I return to Professor Churchland's rejoinders to the antitheoretical view. These were, first, that since everyday psychology is explanatory and predictive of behaviour it must be an empirical/causal theory of it; and second, that the logical-cum-conceptual relations discern-ible within its generalisations are not evidence to a contrary conclusion but in fact are typical of empirico-theoretical frameworks. Concerning the first point all that remains to be considered is the question: how, on the antitheoretical view, are we able to predict one another's behaviour? In particular cases, of course, this may not be possible and that is a feature of which this view may be able to give a better explanation than its theoretical rival. For, as the introductory quotation from Aquinas indicates, it is part of our common-sense understanding that in like circumstances the same agent may behave differently. Nonetheless, the fact remains that it is very often possible to predict future behaviour. As a general capacity this is easily enough accounted for, since it rests upon a knowledge of human character, partly inherited from those around one in childhood and partly gleaned from personal experience. *Ipso facto,* this is to some extent an empirical matter. The acquisition of an understanding of what people are like, the content of that knowledge, and the occasions of its exercise, depend upon circumstances of observation. It is also contingent in the sense that the behaviour is logically distinct from past events. But none of this threatens the normative or conceptual aspects of our intuitive psychology which express themselves in the criteria for application of psycho-behavioural terms and in the relations holding between them. Given rationality constraints there are limits to what successive states it makes sense to attribute to the same individual. Likewise, in correctly describing behaviour as *speaking* one is logically entitled to conclude that its subject is an intelligent agent and to draw further conclusions about some of the (Aristotelian) causes of this activity. Intelligent animals are cognitive agents and their self-understanding is thus both rational and empirical.

Churchland's second rejoinder is that the logical relations between the terms featuring in his reconstruction folk-psychological 'laws,' or between the premises and conclusions of pieces of practical reasoning, give no reason to doubt the nonlogical, wholly empirical character of these structures. At this stage I shall direct my comments solely to the claim that logical relations between ascribed propositional-attitude states pose no threat of nonempiricality and on the contrary are 'the surest sign that we are here dealing with a high-grade theoretical framework'. The demonstration of this claim takes the form of drawing a parallel between propositional-attitude predicates and the assignment of numerical values to physical properties when relating them via empirical laws. Thus, considering a formulation of Ohm's Law, Churchland observes that the expressions 'has a resistance of R', 'is subject to a voltage of V', and 'has a current of I', are functors which yield predicates when singular terms for numbers are entered in the variable positions. He then notes that the law $(I = V/R)$ 'exploits a relation holding on the domain of numbers in order to express an important empirical regularity.'[33] The second element in the analogy follows directly: expressions for sentential attitudes are likewise predicate-forming functors and the structures in which they feature similarly exploit connections obtaining within a realm of abstract objects. But the types of states thereby related are logically or conceptually distinct. In short, they are only empirically correlated.

This argument is hardly compelling. The idea is that proponents of the antitheoretical view are misled by the contingent employment of propositions for marking off natural properties into attributing to the latter the *a priori* relations that hold between the former. But reference to propositional contents in the identification of intentional predicates is not contingent. They are individuated precisely by content. Beliefs and so forth are intrinsically propositional. It may be a contingency that resistance, voltage and current can be assigned numerical values and that the natural relations between the former are (more or less) invariable and mirrored by those holding within the realm of numbers. But one cannot seriously suppose that it is an interesting and convenient fact that, having identified beliefs and other intentional states, we can then assign propositional values to them and be served by the further contingency that the intrinsic relations between the states so 'measured' run in parallel with those holding independently on the domain of propositions. Moreover, the point of the rational-connection argument is that the normative principles that constrain the application of psychological predicates hold quite generally in virtue of the very notions of belief, desire, intention, action, etc., and in advance of the assignment of particular contents to them. Thus, for example, the claim that one cannot intend to act in a manner, or in pursuit of a goal, which one believes to be logically impossible is, if true, *a priori* true. By Churchland's own account of it however, Ohm's Law is an empirical generalisation the truth of which is only knowable *a posteriori*. Here, I think, someone has been misled but the error is in the supposition that in the case of the propositional attitudes the noncontingency of generalisations involving them is due solely to the logical relations holding between particular contents.

One might be further puzzled by how Churchland thinks it is possible to reconcile on the one hand, admission of an abstract realm of propositions with which states of natural objects are correlated by the self-explanatory (propositional?) psychology of those objects, with, on the other, a commitment to eliminative materialism. I suspect the answer is that the appearance of the former is a systematic illusion sustained by folk psychology. My own assessment is that the illusion of reality is to be located elsewhere.

V

In my introduction I suggested that in one respect Professor Churchland might fairly be likened to Descartes. When reading his ideas about nonpropositional epistemology I was strongly reminded of an earlier dualist, Plato. For speaking now not of the ontological substance of a *res cogitans* but of the medium of its cognition, the suggestion that this consists in the employment of prototypes of objects and features in the natural world is strongly reminiscent of the Platonic account of knowledge as proceeding from low-grade sensory input *(doxasta)* to the unaided contemplation of the structural elements of reality *(noeta)*. Much in Plato's scheme remains obscure and conceptually troublesome. But if Churchland is right the nature of *episteme* may soon be disclosed:

> What we are confronting here is a possible conception of knowledge that owes nothing to the sentential categories of current common sense. A global theory, we might venture, is a specific point in a creature's synaptic weight space. It is a configuration of connection weights . . . that partitions the system's

activation-vector space(s) into useful divisions and subdivisions relative to the inputs typically fed the system.[34]

Churchland's enthusiasm for this conception of knowledge draws its strength from two sources: dissatisfaction with existing accounts, and familiarity with current work in Artificial Intelligence (in particular connectivism) and neuroscience. As regards the former, he now believes it is a mistake to conceive of our everyday understanding of one another 'as consisting of an internally stored set of general sentences.' This is a point of agreement between us. However, my reasons for objecting to the 'book in the head' story also incline me against Churchland's alternative.[35]

It has not been uncommon for philosophers concerned with the nature of cognition to posit internal representations, modelling these on words or pictures. Sometimes those who propose that thinking is like using a language will then go on to emphasise that this is, and can only be, an analogy. For as Reid long ago observed, 'if the mind is stored with ideas in the manner of a book, who then should read the text and understand it? — for signs without an interpretation signify nothing'.[36] The worry about regression is not, however, Churchland's reason for rejecting the stored sentence account of cognition. He is not troubled by the positing of internal representations and cognitive activity involving them, but only by a linguistic conception of these things drawn from the folk-psychological view. I, by contrast, share the general worries of Aquinas, Reid and Wittgenstein about the intelligibility of subpersonal epistemology. In discussing the genesis and operation of prototypes, Churchland refers to work involving artificial neural networks. He writes of the latter as 'learning,' 'searching,' 'recognising' and 'representing' and goes on to speculate about similar activities engaged in by human neurophysiology. He then concludes: 'I hope I have succeeded in making intelligible to you a novel approach to the problem of explanatory understanding in humans, an approach that is grounded at last in what we know about the brain.'[37] But this is just the problem. For notwithstanding the denial of any debt to 'the categories of current common sense,' the fact remains that such meaning as can be attached to these ways of characterising processes in the brain derives its significance from their use in everyday description of person-involving activities. So much for *sense,* what of *truth-conditions?* Either talk of neural networks 'learning to recognise features' is metaphorical, or it is not. If the former, then what features of the intra-cranial world *call for* this characterisation? — i.e., why are psycho-intentionalistic predicates deemed apt? And what becomes of the charge that folk-psychological descriptions are radically false? If, however, the claim is that parts of people are engaged in learning, searching, recognising and representing, then we have homuncularism on a communal scale. At best, this simply fails as a solution to the philosophical problem of how cognition is possible; at worst it is incoherent.[38]

VI

Finally, I turn to the proposed diagnosis of the conditions apt to lead to neuromythology. One, obvious enough, is a metaphysical prejudice in favour of physicalism. If all there really is, is the void dotted about with particles gathered and separated by forces of attraction and repulsion, then there will appear little prospect of accommodating either *psychology* or *folk* within it. This said, the current fashion for ever more nearly dualistic, non-reductive physicalisms suggests that Professor Churchland's view may not be the only coherent option available to one of physicalist persuasion. It may be, however, that he believes that if psychological properties, states and activities are admitted, then, given their presumed failure to correlate with neurophysiological entities and processes, the implied result is dualism. Thus, by contraposition, he arrives at elimination. I have some sympathy with this response insofar as it is directed at anomalous monism, since, like Churchland, I think that causal efficacy is a better qualification for ontological recognition than mere conceptual irreducibility. However, I also believe it is wrong to assume that the recognition of causally efficacious psychological entities amounts to the adoption of dualism. For those entities may be person-involving and, *ipso facto,* have a physical realisation in (whole) living human beings. They may, for example, be direct expressions of rational agency, i.e., intentional actions.

Setting the issue of fundamental ontology to one side, three other conditions apt for the generation of Churchland's preferred account now come into view. One is, again, the Cartesian assumption that the task of understanding the behaviour of human beings is begun from the outside with the inspection of nonpsychological phenomena and then proceeds by hypothesising a set of inner structures and mechanisms. I will not return to the earlier discussion of this assumption, but only observe that while there is a familiar enough sense in which the mind has an essentially 'inner' aspect, it would be a major misunderstanding of this form of internality to regard it as one might regard the information that the rhythmic motions of an engine are due to events in its interior. Yet something like this interpretation of innermindedness seems to be at work in Churchland's argument against everyday psychology when he writes:

> We cannot expect a truly adequate neuroscientific account of our inner lives to provide theoretical categories that match up nicely with the categories of our common-sense framework. Accordingly, we must expect that the older

framework will simply be eliminated, rather than be reduced, by a matured neuroscience.[39]

This passage also serves to introduce a further element in the origins of the counter-myth, the absorption with neurosciences. Informed of the physiology of the brain and of attempts to model its processes in artificial systems, Churchland concludes that it is to such scientific research that we must turn if we want an account of what lies behind the eyes and mouths of perceivers and speakers. Of course, if the original explanatory enterprise were as he characterises it there could be no argument with this conclusion. If you want to know how an engine is constructed and the pattern of its inner mechanisms then ask an engineer, not a layman. But the analogy only works if the contentious assumptions are granted.

Connected with the previous point is the last of the conditions apt for the myth of the cognitive brain. This is the judgement that common-sense psychological description and explanation is patently prescientific, non-methodical and hopelessly inadequate to the task of accounting for human cognition and behaviour. As Churchland elsewhere puts the point:

> The [Folk Psychology] of the Greeks is essentially the same FP we use today, and we are negligibly better at explaining human behaviour in its terms than was Sophocles. This is a very long period of stagnation and infertility for any theory to display, especially when faced with such an enormous backlog of anomalies and mysteries in its own explanatory domain [e.g.] . . . the nature and dynamics of mental illness . . . the nature and psychological functions of sleep . . . 3-D visual images[s] . . . perceptual illusions [etc.][40]

The adequacy of an explanation is relative to the questions it attempts to answer and to the kinds of interests presupposed in setting those questions. Thus, whether a form of explanation which persists in giving answers of the same general sort over many centuries is 'stagnant' and 'infertile' depends upon the interests it serves. It is, therefore, presumptuous to judge interpretative, intentionalistic psychology as a failure for having little if anything to say about a range of matters that extend beyond the field of common observation. Our continuing to employ a descriptive-cum-interpretative scheme first established in prehistory and developed in antiquity is not a proper target for criticism if that scheme is genuinely explanatory with regard to enduring human concerns. Indeed, the oddity of Churchland's view is apparent in the suggestion that we should find it a cause for abandoning the 'narrative' forms of understanding that we are 'negligibly better at explaining behaviour in its terms than was Sophocles.' Our interest in Sophocles is precisely on account of his capacity to illuminate life's perennial ironies and to make intelligible various reactions to them.

This consideration serves also to remind us of the inevitable losses to be borne by any trading in of propositional, humanistic psychology for a science of neural exemplars. It is not only the arts and social studies that depend upon an economy of beliefs, desires, intentions and emotions, and upon the intrinsically intelligible relations that hold between them. The transmission and interpretation of results in empirical and theoretical science are likewise dependent upon the assignment of rationality and intentional content to behaviour and its products. Indeed, it is misleading simply to say that the losses would be great, as if we might imagine our abandoning some current practices but developing others. The point is that the imagined future is one from which we and any *persons* we begat would be absent.

Paradoxically, the ineliminability of person-involving psychology is indicated by the sorts of enquiries into the role of events in the brain, which so interest Professor Churchland. In various places he has written of the need to understand the real nature of human behaviour and cognitive activity and (having made the assumptions set out above) he invites us to consider certain neural networks. But the question arises: Why these rather than some other part of the brain or elsewhere in the body? The answer is clearly that certain brain activities are directly implicated in processes the bodily boundaries of which are identified via the concepts of perception and action. These networks are ones to investigate because we can trace a route back to them from perception; those, because they feed into movements involved in action. But having reached the observable surface of human life two things should be noted and never again lost sight of: first, perception and action are (sets of) capacities of whole, rational animals; second, they are exercised in relation to the natural and social environment. To investigate the functioning of the brain we need to begin with objects and states lying beyond the body and then work inwards via common-sense psychology. Once one passes from descriptions of the contents of experience and of intentional action to those of the related physiology, however, the transition is not simply from the level of common observation to that of uncommon specialist enquiry. In addition, and perhaps more importantly, the subject-matter of the investigation has changed.

The nature of this latter transition was well understood by the old Aristotelians and was marked by use of the philosophical vocabulary of hylomorphism: physiology investigates the *matter* of perception and action; psychology attends to their *forms*. Just as a part of a painting, say, is so much stuff organised in an intelligible arrangement, so an episode of drawing involves a quantity of matter (flesh and bone) successively disposed in various ways by the intention of the agent. Finally, two important points become clear: the priority of human self-understanding over physiology — for we can only come to the latter via the discriminations afforded by the former; and the compatibility of the two forms of knowledge. These conclusions are not new. In commenting on Aristotle, Aquinas writes as follows:

> [In] some definitions of the dispositions of the soul . . . the body is omitted, as when anger is defined as a desire for revenge; and sometimes the bodily or material factor is included, as when anger is called a heating of blood around the heart. . . . To the question which of these types of definition pertains to the natural scientist, I answer that the purely formal one is not physical but logical. That which includes matter but omits the form pertains to no one but the natural scientist, because only he is concerned with matter.[41]

In terms of this vocabulary I can now summarise my case against Churchland's challenge to common-sense psychology. He has lost sight of the true subjects of its interest — rational agents — by having become absorbed in the fascinating structures of their matter.[42]

FOOTNOTES

[1]D. W. Hamlyn, 'Behaviour', *Philosophy,* Vol. 28, 1953, pp. 138-9.

[2]St. Thomas Aquinas, *Summa Theologiae* [*S.T.*] (London: Blackfriars and Eyre & Spottiswoode, 1963-1975) Ia,q76,al.

[3]The similarity between the structure of Churchland's view and that of Descartes emerges in several places. Consider, for example, the following 'language use is something that is learned, by a brain already capable of vigorous cognitive activity . . . Against [this] background . . . language use appears as an extremely peripheral activity, as a racially idiosyncratic mode of social interaction which is mastered thanks to the versatility and power of a more basic mode of activity' ('Eliminative Materialism and the Propositional Attitudes' [this volume, pp. 42-62], *The Journal of Philosophy,* Vol. 78, 1981, p. 83, this volume, p. 55). Substituting 'mind' for 'brain' in this passage yields a thesis with which Descartes is certainly in agreement; see, for example, his reply to Hobbes, Objections III, IV in *The Philosophical Works of Descartes,* translated by E. Haldane & G. Ross (Cambridge: University Press, 1934) Vol. II, p. 36. The point of ontological difference is in this respect less significant than it might otherwise appear.

[4]See *Scientific Realism and the Plasticity of Mind* [Churchland, 1979] (Cambridge: University Press, 1979) Chs. 1 & 2; and *Matter and Consciousness* [Churchland, 1984] (Cambridge, Mass.: M.I.T., 1984) pp. 44-6.

[5]See Churchland, 1979, Ch. 3; and Churchland, 1984, pp. 79-80.

[6]See Churchland, 1979, Ch. 4; this volume, p. 44; and Churchland, 1984, Ch. 4.

[7]See Churchland, 1979, Ch. 3; this volume, p. 44; and Churchland, 1984, Ch. 3.

[8]See Churchland, 1979, Ch. 4; this volume, pp. 43-44; 'Folk Psychology and the Explanation of Human Behaviour' in this volume, pp. 247-262.

[9]See Churchland, 1979, Ch. 4, Sec. 14; this volume, pp. 54-56; Churchland, 1984, Ch. 3, Sec. 4; and 'FPEHB', Sec. I.

[10]See this volume, pp. 248-257.

[11]See Churchland, 1979, Chs. 5 & 6; this volume, pp. 46-49 & 54-61; Churchland, 1984, Ch. 2, Sec. 5; Ch. 3, Sec. 3; Chs. 5-7; and this volume, pp. 247-262.

[12]See this volume, p. 56.

[13]See Churchland, 1979, Ch. 1, and 'Cognitive and Conceptual Change: A Reply to Double', *Journal for the Theory of Social Behaviour,* Vol. 16, 1986, pp. 217–221. This characterisation of the view under attack draws upon the work of Wilfred Sellars, in particular 'Empiricism and the Philosophy of Mind,' reprinted in *Science, Perception and Reality* (London: Routledge & Kegan Paul, 1963).

[14]See Churchland, 1984, p. 43.

[15]Famously Thomas Reid makes much of this distinction, and in his study of the subject David Hamlyn credits Reid with being 'perhaps the first philosopher to insist upon this rigorously' (*Sensation and Perception,* (London: Routledge & Kegan Paul, 1961) p. 125). However, the distinction is present and employed in the work of Aquinas. See, for example, his *In Libros de Anima Expositio* [*In de Anima*] translated by K. Foster & S. Humphries (London: Routledg& Kegan Paul, 1951) II, VI, pp. 396–8. Also, J. Haldane, 'Aquinas on Sense-Perception,' *The Philosophical Review,* Vol. 92, 1983. For some discussion of the implications of this thesis for physicalist accounts of cognition see J. Haldane, 'Naturalism and the Problem of Intentionality,' *Inquiry,* Vol. 32, 1989, pp. 305–22.

[16]See, for example, Churchland, 1984, p. 80. Such an unwarranted conflation is compounded with fallacious inference in the following highly influential passage from Karl Popper's *The Logic of Scientific Discovery* (London: Hutchinson, 1965) pp. 94–5: 'Every description uses universal names (or symbols, or ideas); every statement has the character of a theory, of a hypothesis. The statement 'Here is a glass of water' cannot be verified by an observational experience . . . [because] the universals which appear in it cannot be correlated with any specific sense-experience'.

[17]For further discussion of this see J. Haldane, 'Psychoanalysis, Cognitive Psychology and Self-Consciousness' in C. Wright & P. Clark (eds.) *Mind, Psychoanalysis and Science* (Oxford: Blackwell, 1988). For a similar defence of 'Givens', involving the idea of 'preconceptual perception', see T. Russman, *A Prospectus for the Triumph of Realism* (Macon, Ga: Mercer University Press, 1987). However Russman's identification of Popper as a defender of pretheoretical perception is puzzling and suggests that our views may be divergent.

[18]See Churchland, 1984, pp. 43–4.

[19]See Wittgenstein, *Philosophical Investigations* (Oxford: Blackwell, 1976) § 257: "What would it be like if human beings shewed no outward signs of pain (did not groan, grimace, etc.)? Then it would be impossible to teach a child the use of the word 'toothache.' "

[20]Churchland, 1984, pp. 67 & 71.

[21]Likewise for the suggestion made in 'FPEHB' that 'A person who suffers a sudden sharp pain will wince' states a 'causal/explanatory law.'

[22]Churchland, 1984, p. 71.

[23]Ironically, Churchland criticises Wittgenstein for not seeing the proper implications of the anti-private-language argument. But from the account given of it I conclude that he has not understood the argument. Churchland writes: "If a check on correct application is what is required for meaningfulness then all that one's understanding of 'W' need include is some connections between the occurrence of the W sensation and the occurrence of *other* phenomena . . . they can be other mental states . . . and still serve as checks on the correct application of 'W' " (Churchland, 1984, pp. 54–5). Compare this with *Investigations* §. 265.

[24]See this volume, pp. 248–257.

[25]See G. E. M. Anscombe, 'Causality and Determination,' in *Collected Philosophical Papers* (Oxford: Blackwell, 1981) Vol. II.

[26]See this volume, pp. 248–257, and D. Davidson, 'Actions, Reasons and Causes,' Sec III, in *Essays on Actions and Events* (Oxford: Clarendon Press, 1980).

[27]See Davidson, *op. cit.,* and C. McGinn, *The Character of Mind* (Oxford: University Press, 1982) pp. 100–1.

[28]For discussions relevant to this issue see F. Stoutland, 'Davidson on Intentional Behaviour' in E. Le Pore & B. McLaughlin (eds.) *Perspectives in Actions and Events* (Oxford: Blackwell,

1986); and G. & C. MacDonald, 'Mental Causes and the Explanation of Action' in L. Stevenson, R. Squires & J. Haldane (eds.) *Mind, Causation and Action* (Oxford: Blackwell, 1986).

[29]*In Duodecim Libros Metaphysicorum Expositio,* V, Lectio 2.

[30]*S. T.* Ia, q82, al.

[31]Churchland, 1984, p. 63.

[32]See J. Haldane, 'Brentano's Problem,' *Grazer Philosophische Studien,* Vol. 35, 1989, pp. 1-32.

[33]This volume, pp. 248-257; see also *MC* pp. 64-5.

[34]See 'On the Nature of Theories: A Neurocomputational Perspective' in W. Savage (ed.) *Minnesota Studies in the Philosophy of Science* (Minneapolis: University of Minnesota Press) forthcoming.

[35]Let me note in passing that it is far from obvious that one's capacity to understand and respond to the regular patterns of human life, which consist largely of a set of socially acquired *practical* abilities, is properly to be thought of as issuing from *theoretical* knowledge—in whatever form this last may be realised.

[36]See *Orations* (Aberdeen: University Press, 1930). For discussion of the issue touched upon here and the contrast between Reid (and Aquinas) and contemporary ideas about mental representation see J. Haldane, 'Reid, Scholasticism and Current Philosophy of Mind' in M. Dalgarno & E. Matthews (eds.) *The Philosophy of Thomas Reid* (Dordrecht: Reidel, 1989).

[37]This volume, pp. 257-260.

[38]For more on this issue see J. Haldane, 'Psychoanalysis, Cognitive Psychology and Self-Consciousness,' sec. 7.

[39]Churchland, 1984, p. 43.

[40]This volume, pp. 47-48.

[41]*In de Anima,* I, II, 24 & 27. See also *Philosophical Investigations,* § 63, where Wittgenstein gives expression to his own (linguistic) version of hylomorphism: 'For example; we think: If you have only the unanalysed form you miss the analysis; but if you know the analysed form that gives you everything.—But can I not say that an aspect of the matter is lost on you in the *latter* case as well as the former?'

[42]I am grateful to my colleague Mr. Christopher Bryant for helpful discussions of some of the points presented above.

15 In Defense of Southern Fundamentalism*

Terence Horgan
Memphis State University

George Graham
University of Alabama, Birmingham

> What a waste it is to lose one's mind, or not to have a mind.
> — Dan Quayle

In debate over the truth or falsity of folk psychology (henceforth FP, a notation that also will go proxy for 'folk psychological'), the most influential players tend to line up on the U.S. coasts: friends of FP, like Jerry Fodor and William Lycan, on the East; foes, like Paul Churchland, Patricia Churchland, and Stephen Stich (until recently, on the West).[1] There are important voices in other locales and periodic geographic shifts among the principals, but by and large gravity seems to pull east or west.[2] This is unfortunate, we believe, for the proper perspective lies in unexplored Southern states, and in a faith in FP that borders on the evangelical. It's time for gravitational pull to Dixie.[3] It's time, in short, for Southern Fundamentalism.

1. INTRODUCTION

This chapter defends a version of realism about FP. For reasons which will be explained in a moment, we call this version *Southern Fundamentalism* (hereafter SF).

In general terms, FP realism is the doctrine that our everyday FP descriptions of people are by and large true, and thus that humans generally

*Reprinted from *Philosophical Studies* (1990) by permission of the authors and publisher.

288

do undergo the FP events, beliefs, desires, and so forth that we normally attribute to them; i.e., realism asserts that humans are, in Daniel Dennett's apt phrase, *true believers.*[4] FP antirealism, or eliminativism, is the doctrine that people really do not undergo FP events or states, and hence that FP is (radically, categorically) false. Adopting the ecclesiastical terminology we introduced in an earlier paper, we will sometimes refer to realists about FP (believers in true belief) as *churchmen,* and to antirealists or eliminativists (antibelievers) as *secularists.*[5]

In the debate between Eastern churchmen and Western secularists, the two sides typically share certain presuppositions concerning prerequisites for the truth of FP. The most popular and most fundamental presupposition is the requirement of *scientific absorbability:*

(SA) Humans are true believers only if FP is absorbable into mature science. The main idea behind (SA) is that FP, being a theory (or proto-theory) of human behavior, cannot be true unless its central principles and generalizations are destined to be part of science. Eastern churchmen argue that the total available evidence strongly favors the claim that science will absorb FP, whereas secularists argue that the evidential scales currently tip the other way.[6]

Other shared presuppositions about prerequisites for FP's truth also sometimes figure importantly in the East/West debate. In particular, Easterners and Westerners largely agree about the requirement of a *language of thought:*

(LT) Humans are true believers only if they have internal mental representations that (i) possess language-like syntactic structure, and (ii) possess the propositional content of putatively attributable FP attitudes.

Eastern churchmen argue that current evidence points strongly toward mental representations with the syntax and semantics needed to subserve FP attitudes, whereas Western secularists maintain that it points in exactly the opposite direction.

We will refer to requirements like scientific absorbability and the existence of a language of thought as *putative true-believer conditions* (for short, PTB conditions). Another common presupposition shared by Easterners and Westerners, although generally implicit in their writings, rather than explicitly stated, is the following principle of *epistemic or evidential dynamics:*

(ED) For each PTB condition C, if there were to arise strong epistemic warrant for the thesis that humans do not satisfy C, then (i) this would thereby confer strong epistemic warrant upon the thesis that humans are not true believers, and (ii) it would not confer any significant degree of epistemic warrant upon the thesis that condition C is not really a prerequisite for being a true believer.

Thus, Easterners and Westerners alike agree that FP would be falsified under certain conceivable scenarios concerning the future course of science — for instance, scenarios in which there arises empirical evidence that FP is not scientifically absorbable, or that there is no language of thought. The main disagreement between the two sides concerns the likelihood that such scenarios will come to pass.

We wish to defend a version of FP realism that differs significantly from standard East Coast realism. As mentioned, we call it *Southern Fundamentalism*. The label is chosen for two reasons. One is lighthearted; the other serious. The light-hearted reason is that we write from the recesses of the American Deep South where True Belief is unquestioned. The serious reason is that according to SF, our ordinary epistemic standards for folk-psychological attributions are linked so closely to the truth or satisfaction conditions of such attributions that the truth of FP is beyond all serious doubt. Thus, current evidence strongly warrants us in saying that humans believe, and warrants this claim in a way that would not be appreciably affected by any evidence we might acquire against theses like (SA) or (LT). More exactly, the central and particular tenets of SF are these:

(SF.1) Humans are true believers.

(SF.2) The thesis that humans are true believers is enormously well warranted, on the basis of total current evidence.

(SF.3) For each PTB condition C, if there were to arise strong epistemic warrant for the thesis that humans do not satisfy C, then (i) this would thereby confer strong epistemic warrant upon the thesis that C is not really a prerequisite for being a true believer, and (ii) it would not confer any significant degree of epistemic warrant upon the thesis that humans are not true believers.

Theses (SF.1) and (SF.2) are held in common with our realist brethren the Eastern churchmen. The crucial schism between ourselves and the Eastern sect involves (SF.3), a principle of epistemic dynamics that is flatly incompatible with the principle (ED) which the Eastern churchmen hold in common with the Western secularists. Because both Eastern churchmen and Western secularists hold (ED), the debate between them is primarily about PTB conditions. Friends of antirealism/secularism/eliminativism would see the failure to meet PTB conditions as an exciting instance of falsification, encouraging the creation of non–folk-psychological theories. Meanwhile, Eastern realists see the defense of PTB conditions as necessary apologetics, protecting the favored creed from secular assault. To fundamentalist eyes, however, the outcome of debate over PTB conditions does not affect the evidential warrant for FP, for the epistemic dynamics is that of (SF.3).

Meanwhile, theses (SF.2) and (SF.3) together express the view that the truth of secularism/eliminativism is at most a *bare epistemic possibility*. That is, not only is the current epistemic warrant for (SF.1) overwhelmingly high, but (SF.1) would retain this same high epistemic status under any scenarios that currently might plausibly be viewed as live epistemic possibilities — scenarios like the nonabsorbability of FP into science, and/or the nonexistence of language-like mental representations. Thus, FP is not vulnerable to the kind of falsification countenanced by principle (ED), because evidence against scientific absorbability or against the language of thought would actually call into question not (SF.1), that is, not folk-psychological realism, but rather the PTB conditions expressed in principles like (SA) and (LT). Even if it should turn out that FP is not absorbable or humans do not have a language of thought, (SF.1) would remain overwhelmingly warranted anyway.

2. PRELIMINARIES

We shall defend SF momentarily. Let's begin with several preparatory ablutions to more precisely demarcate our subject matter and relevant background assumptions.

First, we shall say nothing here about why FP is a theory (or tacit or proto-theory). We assume, as do the main parties to the folk realism/anti-realism debate, that FP is a theory or proto-theory. In particular, following David Lewis and others, we shall suppose that folk psychology is usefully construed as consisting of two components.[7] These include a fundamental set of theoretical principles or nomological or law-like generalizations; and, the existential or empirical thesis that people really do undergo the states specified in the fundamental principles (that is, people really do believe, desire, etc.). The primary focus of debate between churchmen and secularists is not the principles, or whether FP contains law-like generalizations and should be classified as theory, but the truth of the existential thesis. Churchmen assert it; secularists deny it. The present paper is about debate over the existential thesis, not whether FP contains law-like generalizations or is a theory. Hence, in speaking of FP being true, we mean specifically that the existential thesis (that people really do believe, etc.) is true. Of course, there are philosophers who question the plausibility of the folk-theory assumption; but without systematic, detailed discussion we should not try to defend the assumption in the present paper.[8]

Second, some remarks about the notion of the absorption of FP by science. The general idea is this: (i) beliefs, desires, intentions, and other such state-types (properties) posited by FP — or at any rate, state types very similar to these — would be posited within mature science; and (ii) the generalizations about such state types asserted by FP — or anyway, generalizations very similar to these — would be entailed by mature science. Tersely speaking, absorption could be either *horizontal* or *vertical* (or both). Horizontal absorption would involve the emergence, within cognitive science, of mature empirical psychological theories in which FP-like state types figure as natural kinds, subject to FP-like generalizations. Vertical absorption would occur if it should turn out that (i) beliefs, desires, and the other fundamental state types of FP are identical with — or anyway are nomically coextensive with — tractably describable state types within some lower-level, nonpsychological branch of mature science, such as neurobiology; and (ii) the relevant lower-level theories, together with type-type identity statements or bridge laws, entail FP-like generalizations.[9] These characterizations of horizontal and vertical absorption could be liberalized somewhat — e.g., by allowing FP to get altered or corrected in the process of absorption. Obviously the more liberal one is about what counts as absorption, the better the odds that FP will eventually prove absorbable into mature science.[10]

Third, there are a variety of empirical conditions sometimes alleged to be prerequisites for the truth of FP. In addition to the putative absorbability requirement, and the putative requirement that a creature with propositional attitudes must have language-like mental representations with the contents of those attitudes themselves, other putative conditions sometimes put forward include these: that FP agents must be ideally rational; that there must always be a precise answer to the question "What does a person (or animal) believe?"; that people must normally have privileged or first-person access to the contents of their own beliefs; and that creatures with propositional attitudes must have neurobiological composition rather than some other kind of physical constitution (e.g., tinfoil).[11] We will remain largely neutral about which such conditions, if any, might be advanced as PTB conditions. Our subsequent discussion will be applicable, *mutatis mutandis,* to any conditions which might merit this status. Thus, if there were to arise strong epistemic warrant for the thesis, for example, that beliefs may be vague and imprecise, then the SF view of the epistemic dynamics is that this would not appreciably alter the warrant for the thesis that humans are true believers, for the thesis that humans are true believers is strongly warranted anyway. The reasonable course would be to abandon the claim that there must always be a precise answer to the question of what does a person believe.

Fourth, some clarification is needed about what falls within the scope of the expression 'folk psychology.'[12] As we shall understand this phrase, 'folk psychology' includes notions like belief, desire, intention, action, and closely cognate notions; and the most fundamental principles or generalizations which common sense takes to be true of the ways such states interact with one another. So understood, FP should not be confused with what may be called *folksy psychology*. The latter includes lots of Grandma's wisdom and poetry's delight that is not presupposed by our practice of attributing propositional attitudes and proffering FP explanations; perhaps includes much of what we commonly say and believe about, e.g., passions and character traits; and perhaps also includes much that is positively contradictory or incoherent (e.g., "Out of sight, out of mind," "Absence makes the heart grow fonder"). We will remain noncommittal about where to draw the line between folk and folksy psychology; our main point is that the FP realism we are defending concerns folk (not folksy) psychology. Not every piece of conventional wisdom is really wise, and we do not want to be read as defending everything Grandma ever said about human psychology.[13]

Finally, fifth, we will be using epistemic, actional, and semantic notions in the course of the discussion. Yet concepts like epistemic warrant certainly seem folk psychological, being tied conceptually to belief and rational belief; the concept of action is folk psychological, being tied conceptually to causation by propositional attitudes (whereof more below); and, arguably, semantic notions like meaning and truth are folk psychological.[14] So, in order not to beg the question against eliminativists, we should be understood as using these notions in a "scare-quoted" sense—i.e., without prejudging whether or not they ultimately can be, or should be, replaced by secularized successors. Connected to this last point is the dialectical fact that eliminativists themselves must engage in this scare-quoted usage, in order to communicate in the present nonsecular milieu—a point they themselves appreciate. They, too, need to allow themselves notions like action and degree of epistemic warrant, as they seek to argue that secularism is the most strongly warranted view. However, from their own perspective, of course, these notions are methodological crutches, to be righteously and gleefully cast away at the dawn of the secular millennium.

3. RESONANT INTENTIONAL SYSTEMS AND THE AUSTERE CONCEPTION OF FP

The above should suffice to demarcate our subject matter. So, it's time to defend SF. Defense proceeds in two steps. First, we wish to describe a central concept which will be used in the defense; second, in sections 4 and 5, we offer two arguments in favor of SF.

In defending SF, we will borrow from Dennett the notion of an *intentional system*.[15] For him, this is a system (organism, artifact) whose behavior can be usefully predicted and explained by ascribing to it beliefs, desires, and related attitudes. We here alter Dennett's characterization as follows: the system's behavior can be usefully predicted this way, and can be *seemingly* truly explained this way. For, note that FP attributions could be predictively and heuristically explanatorily useful even if they are radically false; however, in order to be useful for *bona fide* explanation, they must be true, or at any rate, they must at least be *approximately* true.[16] In addition, let a *resonant* intentional system (RIS) be one whose overall behavioral repertoire is sufficiently rich, environmentally intricate, and *prima facie* rational that under *ordinary, behavior-based,* epistemic standards for attribution of FP attitudes, no serious question would arise whether the system really has attitudes. Ordinary people, using FP idioms in the usual everyday manner, would readily suppose that the system has attitudes, and would readily attribute specific attitudes to it. Prototypically, RIS's are competent language users; simple nonlinguistic animals don't, or don't decisively or clearly, qualify. Quine is a RIS; the moth on his copy of *The World as Will and Idea* is not.

RIS's are common ground in the realist/secularist debate, so it is not controversial that there are RIS's.[17] Everyone admits that certain organisms or creatures, particularly humans, naturally lead or strongly tempt one to ascribe beliefs, which in turn seemingly truly explain their behavior. Instead, secularists question whether RIS's really have propositional attitudes (and really perform actions), whether they are true believers. The secularists thus presuppose that rather stringent requirements (PTB conditions) must be met, over and above being a resonant intentional system, in order for a creature to be classified as a true believer; e.g., FP must be shown to be absorbable into mature science.

The fundamentalist conception of FP, however, rejects the idea that true believerhood involves stringent additional requirements beyond being an RIS in the first place. Fundamentalism concedes that there is *some* conceptual gap between being a RIS and being a true believer; there are conceivable, if highly far-fetched, scenarios under which an entity could be the former without being the latter, e.g., a robot completely controlled remotely by Martians.[18] The subattitudinal configuration or organization of such a creature is one that prevents it from being a genuine believer (it's tethered to remote controls). It's dumb. This is merely to say, however, that the connection between a system's being a RIS and its being a true believer is abductive, rather than criterial, and thus that it is possible to be a RIS without being a true believer. Further, while admitting the presence of a gap, fundamentalism also claims that the gap is not a very wide one — that rather little is required, over and above being a RIS, to have propositional attitudes. There are, to be sure, certain restrictions on allowable sub-attitudinal organization, so that a puppet-creature like the remotely controlled robot does not count as a true believer. We will not attempt here to articulate these additional requirements precisely, or even to say how precise they are (or need to be). That is a philosophical issue we need not address directly, and about which we can maintain a certain neutrality for present purposes. The relevant claim of SF is this: *whatever* the additional requirements are for being a true believer, over and above being a RIS, they are quite modest, and hence are very likely satisfied in prototypical cases of RIS's, viz., humans.[19] A creature's being a RIS, in the absence of evidence that it is a puppet-creature, is overwhelmingly strong evidence that it is a full-fledged true believer.

The term we shall deploy for the secularist (and Eastern realist) thesis that quite stringent requirements, or PTB conditions, must be met over and above being a RIS for true believerhood is *opulent*. Secularists suppose that the very concept of a folk-psychological agent or true believer (or the very property or attribute of such believerhood or agenthood) is opulent. PTB conditions are built into true believerhood. The term we shall deploy for the fundamentalist thesis that the difference between RIShood and true believerhood is quite small or metaphysically negligible is *austere*. Fundamentalists propose that the very idea of a folk psychological agent or true believer is austere, involving mostly just what is involved in being a RIS. True believerhood is *more or less* realized by being a RIS. It should be noted that the differing epistemic dynamics of secularism and fundamentalism, (ED) as opposed to (SF.3), stem from their differing conceptions of true believerhood. Secularism would count the failure to meet PTB conditions as evidence against FP because it opulently presupposes that such conditions are necessary for true belief. By contrast, fundamentalism would count such failure as evidence that the conditions are not necessary for true belief, for fundamentalism austerely presupposes that being a non-puppet RIS suffices for being a true believer.

As an example of a concept that is empirically austere, in something like the way SF alleges true believerhood is, consider *being able to fly*. There is little doubt that the very concept of being able to fly renders it correctly applicable to ordinary, prototypical birds — that is, birds who (among other things) behave in ways that meet the behavior-based epistemic standards we employ when attributing to some creature the ability to fly. Suppose that someone advances — possibly on the basis of plausible and scientifically sophisticated reasoning — a hypothesis to the effect that any creature capable of flying must satisfy a certain condition C. (For instance, the hypothesis might posit a specific minimal ratio of body surface to body weight.) And suppose that thereafter it is discovered that some birds, although they do not satisfy condition C, nonetheless do meet all the standards we normally employ in attributing the ability to fly. (In particular, they propel themselves through the air by flapping their wings.) Should we then conclude that, appearances to the contrary, these birds really cannot fly because they do not satisfy condition C? Surely not; rather, the proper conclusion would be that condition C is not after all a genuine prerequisite for being able to fly. It is too stringent, or perhaps is an appropriate marker for some kinds of flight but not flight in general.

According to SF's austere conception of FP, the concept of true believerhood works similarly; i.e., ordinary, behavior-based evidential standards are by and large sufficient for warranting the attribution of belief. This is not to say, however, that FP concepts are *analyzable* in terms of behavior or behavioral dispositions — even though the ability to fly perhaps is so analyzable. "Analytic behaviorism," nowadays rightly regarded as highly implausible, is only one (the most extreme, the limit-case) species of the austere conception of FP.[20]

What arguments can be given for the fundamentalist view?

4. CONCEPTUAL/SEMANTIC COMPETENCE AND THE AUSTERE CONCEPTION OF FP

Southern Fundamentalism asserts that since there is very strong evidence that humans are resonant intentional systems (conceded on all sides of the debate), and since the gap between resonant intentional system and true believer is negligible, there is very strong evidence that humans are true believers. So, the defense of SF must be the defense of the assertion that the gap between RIShood and true believerhood is negligible, i.e., the austere conception of FP must be defended. In this section and the next we will argue explicitly for the austere conception of FP, and thereby for Southern Fundamentalism.

The arguments we favor presuppose that the issue of whether true believerhood should be understood austerely or opulently is broadly an empirical issue. That is, whether the gap between RIShood and true believerhood is narrow (as fundamentalists assert) or wide-with-PTB conditions (as secularists [and our Eastern brethren] suppose or assert) is an empirical question. We shall consider a number of empirical facts or data concerning FP and the attribution of FP terms and concepts; and, then, in each case we shall argue that the hypothesis of austerity provides the most plausible overall explanation of those facts.

In asking how empirical considerations can be brought to bear upon this issue, it is illuminating to consider the analogous question concerning competing theories of natural-language syntax. The empirical data for syntactic theory includes certain judgments and judgment dispositions of competent language users—in particular, judgments and dispositions concerning the grammaticality or ungrammaticality of various sentence-like strings, and concerning grammatical ambiguity or nonambiguity of various sentences. Such judgments are relevant simultaneously to psychological theories of human language processing, and also to linguistic theories about the syntax of language itself. Native speakers, after all, can be expected to have judgment dispositions about these matters that reflect a solid mastery of their own language (or their own regional dialect, at any rate). So when native speakers are both intersubjectively consistent and also uniformly confident about such syntactic judgments, then normally the best psychological explanation will be that these judgments reflect the natives' syntactic competence, their mastery of the syntactic norms or syntactic structures underlying their language. And this psychological hypothesis, in turn, has a direct implication for linguistic theory—viz., that under an adequate theory of syntax for the natives' language (or dialect), those syntactic judgments will turn out correct.

Similar observations hold with respect to hypotheses or theories concerning the meanings of terms, and concerning the concepts those terms express. Here too certain robust patterns of judgment among native speakers are plausibly explained as manifesting linguistic competence; but now the operative form of competence is not syntactic, but instead pertains both to the relevant concepts themselves and to the terms expressing them. (We shall refer to this dual mastery as *conceptual/semantic* competence.) And here too, as with grammaticality judgments, much of the relevant data is close at hand, some of it in the form of our own introspectively accessible linguistic intuitions. One instance of this phenomenon is quite familiar in analytic philosophy, viz., a proposed "conceptual analysis" is advanced, purporting to articulate conditions which are, as a matter of meaning, criterial for the truth of statements of a certain kind (e.g., statements of the form 'S knows that p'); then a counterexample is produced, consisting of a scenario for which competent speakers would judge that the analysandum-statement differs in truth value from the corresponding analysans-statement; and the hypothesized conceptual analysis is thereby refuted. Other patterns of judgment by competent language users might be plausibly explainable in a similar way, viz., as manifestations of conceptual/semantic competence. When competent speakers routinely, consistently, and uniformly think it intuitively obvious that certain kinds of descriptions are correctly applicable in various situations, normally the most plausible explanation will be that these intuitive judgments are the direct and reliable products of the speakers' conceptual/semantic competence. In such cases, these patterns among the judgments will provide empirical evidence that under an adequate account of the relevant concepts and the terms expressing them, the judgments usually will be correct. We shall refer to this kind of empirical reasoning as a *conceptual/semantic competence argument*.

Are there empirical facts that will underwrite a conceptual/semantic competence argument in favor of the austere conception of FP, over against the opulent conception? Are there facts supporting the claim that everyday ascriptions of FP states and attitudes are by and large true of humans, irrespectively of whether humans satisfy any PTB conditions? There certainly are; indeed, such facts are legion. (They are present on an epic scale, to adapt the purple prose favored by our secularist bretheren.[21]) Consider the following: people constantly find themselves assigning attitudes, and employing actional descriptions of behavior, with an enormous amount of confidence; they experience no serious doubt at all that certain specific attitudinal and actional attributions, applied to themselves and to others, are correct. This fact is a datum, requiring explanation. In addition, there is enormously wide intersubjective agreement among people, across a vast range of actual and realistically hypothetical and counterfactual situations, about appropriate attitudinal and actional attributions. This strong interpersonal robustness of epistemic standards for FP attributions also calls out for explanation.

What explains such facts? What explains why people so robustly, consistently, and uniformly ascribe FP terms and concepts? Under the austere conception of FP, a simple and natural explanation is available: people make these judgments by drawing upon their conceptual/semantic competence concerning attitudinal and actional concepts and terms; by and large, therefore, people confidently ascribe attitudes and actions when, and only when, the ascriptions are actually *true*. Under the opulent conception of FP, on the other hand, no equally simple or natural explanation is forthcoming. Rather, advocates of the opulent conception face the awkward task of explaining why it should be that competent speakers uniformly adopt a set of *mistaken* epistemic standards for attitudinal and actional ascriptions — standards that are actually far too lax, because they often assign high epistemic warrant to FP ascriptions merely on the basis of behavioral evidence, irrespective of whether or not there is any available evidence for theses like (SA) or (LT). So, while the austere conception of FP provides a natural and elegant explanation of the empirical phenomena cited in the previous paragraph, the opulent conception does not. This fact constitutes weighty evidence in favor of the austere conception, over against the opulent conception.

Conceptual/semantic competence arguments are empirical arguments, a species of the genus "inference to the best explanation." So the conceptual/semantic competence argument just set forth is defeasible, admittedly. It is possible that FP actually carries very strong and controversial empirical commitments — over and above its commitment to the uncontroversial contention that humans satisfy all requisite conditions (whatever those conditions might be) for nonpuppet RIShood. If so, then the phenomenology of attitude ascription and the intersubjective agreement among ascribers are radically misleading; people are massively misguided and overconfident about this matter. They wrongly expect to know whether people have beliefs without knowing, e.g., whether mature science will make reference to beliefs. Surely, however, the reasonable "default assumption" about FP, comparable to the analogous assumptions in linguistic theory, is that people's uniformly consistent, deeply confident, linguistic intuitions about the applicability of attitudinal and actional ascriptions are generally *correct,* and thus that ordinary behavior-based epistemic standards for attitude attribution are appropriate rather than unduly lax.[22]

The following additional facts about people's judgment dispositions further strengthen the conceptual/semantic competence argument for the austere conception. In order to describe a situation where it is intuitively quite clear that an entity fails to qualify as a true believer even though it satisfies the usual behavior-based evidential standards, we need to imagine goofball cases of a sort that humans are very unlikely to be in, involving a striking lack of autonomous behavioral control — for instance, the case of a robot-body being totally controlled from afar by Martians. Phenomenologically, envisioning less bizarre scenarios — e.g., scenarios where FP proves nonabsorbable into mature science, but nothing like Martian behind-the-scenes "puppeteering" goes on — just does not seem persuasive as a case where the non-puppet RIS's in question fail to be true believers. On the contrary, the natural way of describing such scenarios is to say, "People would come to *believe* that FP is not absorbable into mature science" — a description which presupposes that people would be true believers anyway.

The most plausible explanation, once again, is that these facts too reflect people's conceptual/semantic competence with FP terms and concepts. If our linguistic intuitions do not incline us to describe a given envisioned scenario as one in which people turn out not to be true believers, then probably this is because that description is *not correct* for the given scenario. Accordingly, we have here further empirical evidence in favor of the austere conception of FP, over against the opulent conception.

5. CONCEPTUAL CONSERVATISM AND THE AUSTERE CONCEPTION OF FP

The notion of agency plays a fundamental and ubiquitous role in the conceptual scheme we all employ. People conceive of themselves and one another as agents, beings who do not merely undergo internally caused bodily movements, but who perform *actions.*[23] A number of principles are central to our conception of human agency, including these: (1) Some, but not all, human actions are *deliberate,* i.e., performed *on purpose.* (2) Normally when someone deliberately acts in a certain way, he does so *for a reason.* (3) Linguistic behavior is actional: *asserting* is an important species of doing. And (4) certain kinds of deliberate actions, assertions among them, can be performed either *sincerely* or *insincerely.*

The ordinary notion of agency, which includes the various notions and distinctions just mentioned, and more besides, evidently is thoroughly folk psychological. The distinction between action and nonactional bodily motion is one we draw in FP terms: an action is an item of behavior involving a certain characteristic kind of causation by FP states like belief, desire, and intention.[24] Acting *because* of a reason, as opposed to merely acting and having a reason, involves possessing propositional attitudes that both (i) rationalize an action of the kind performed, and (ii) cause the action. The distinction between actions performed intentionally and those performed unintentionally is clearly folk psychological: an action, described as falling under a certain act type, is intentional (as so described) only if the agent intended to perform an act of that type. The distinction between sincere and insincere assertion comes basically to this: whether the speaker does, or does not, believe what he is asserting.

So if eliminativism is true then there are no actions, properly so called; hence there are no deliberate or unintentional actions and no sincere or insincere actions, and human behavior is not really explicable on the basis of reasons. This is not to deny that there is at least a bare epistemic possibility that the notion of action, and some or all of the key distinctions associated with this notion, might be replaceable by secularized successor notions and distinctions (although the secularists themselves have been deafeningly silent about what such putative successor notions could be like).[25] But the fact remains that if humans are not true believers, then the *ordinary* notion of action is just not applicable to human behavior.

This fact provides the basis for another argument through which to strengthen the plausibility of the austere conception of FP, in addition to the conceptual/semantic competence argument set forth above. The *conceptual conservatism argument,* as we shall call this supplemental line of reasoning, goes as follows. Human concepts and language are the product of cultural (and biological) evolution. Accordingly, our concepts and terms are likely to be closely intertwined with the cultural (and biological) purposes for which we employ them. In particular, they are not likely to be more severe or restrictive than is required by these purposes; for, such restrictiveness normally would be gratuitous, and also could tend to undermine the usefulness of our concepts and terms for serving the very kinds of purposes for which they arose in the first place.

But the attitudinal and actional concepts of FP not only are pragmatically indispensible in our *current* epistemic and cultural milieu, but also would very probably remain indispensible even if we were to acquire evidence for the nonabsorbability of FP, and/or for the nonexistence of a language of thought. Although we certainly can envision a scenario in which there arises strong empirical evidence against the absorbability of FP into mature science, or against a language of thought, we cannot even conceive of what it would be for language-using, rationality-aspiring creatures like ourselves to repudiate the notion of action (since repudiating it, or attempting to repudiate it, would itself be an action); or to sincerely assert that nobody ever sincerely asserts anything; or to find epistemically warranted the contention that epistemic warrant does not exist. Nor can we conceive how such notions could be replaced by secularized successor concepts which, despite being purged of any folk psychological presuppositions, still somehow manage successfully to take over the key roles these notions play in our everyday conceptual scheme and cultural life. Nor can we conceive how attitudinal and actional attributions could be systematically false while also being indispensible and irreplaceable; for, if there are no speech acts then how can human vocal noises and written markings express truth-bearing statements at all? There seems to be no way to understand Indispensible But False "Attitudes," which do not express allegiance to FP.[26]

These considerations do not constitute an *a priori* refutation of secularism.[27] Scenarios we cannot now conceive might be metaphysically possible anyway. (Before Freud, who could conceive of unconscious attitudes? Before Einstein, who could conceive of the relativity of simultaneity, or of curved spacetime?) Rather, the crucial point is this: since at present we cannot cogently conceive of ourselves as not being true believers, and since there exists an austere conception of FP according to which FP's integrity would not be threatened by nonabsorbability into science or by the nonexistence of a language of thought, considerations of conceptual conservatism strongly favor the hypothesis that our attitudinal and actional concepts conform to the austere conception of FP, rather than to the opulent conception. It is very unlikely that FP concepts contain commitments to strong empirical theses like (SA) or (LT); for, not only would such commitments be gratuitous, but FP concepts apparently would remain indispensible even if we should discover that (SA) or (LT) is false.

Conceptual conservatism arguments are empirical arguments, and hence are defeasible. So the argument just given is empirical and defeasible, as was our earlier conceptual/semantic competence argument. But now the burden of proof falls squarely upon the shoulders of the eliminativists; they owe us arguments for opulence and against austerity that they have not provided. In the meantime, the empirical evidence strongly favors the austere conception of FP over the opulent conception, thereby strongly supporting Southern Fundamentalism.

6. APOLOGETICS

Southern Fundamentalism is very different from existing versions of folk-psychological realism and antirealism. We suspect that for this reason the position is easily misunderstood, and so we should be careful to state clearly what it says and what it does not say. To this end, we shall conclude by briefly addressing four possible questions of the fundamentalist approach to FP.

1. Putative true-believer conditions are central topics of debate between realists and antirealists. Does SF, with its austere conception of FP, deny outright all PTB conditions like (SA) and (LT)? If not, what exactly is SF's stance toward PTB conditions, and how does this stance mesh with SF's principle of epistemic dynamics (SF.3)?

Fundamentalism does not flatly deny theses like (SA) or (LT). Rather, it *relocates* the disputes about whether FP is absorbable into mature science, whether humans have a language of thought, or whether other putative empirical commitments of FP are satisfied. Under SF's austere conception of FP, these disputes are not about what it takes, over and above being nonpuppet RIS's, to qualify as true believers. Instead, the disputes involve *what it takes to be such a RIS in the first place.* RIS's, after all, are very sophisticated creatures with very sophisticated behavioral capacities. Maybe a nonpuppet creature could have these capacities only if its inner workings are describable by a scientific account that absorbs FP; or, only if it has mental representations with compositional syntax and semantics; or, only if it is not tinfoil; etc. In general, anything required for being a nonpuppet RIS is also required, *ipso facto,* for being a true believer; and the austere conception of FP, is officially neutral about what it takes to be a nonpuppet RIS.[28]

On the other hand, if indeed nonpuppet RIShood requires having a language of thought, and/or being describable by a scientific theory that absorbs FP, then these are *de facto* prerequisites; they are not built directly into the concept of a nonpuppet RIS, or into the concept of a true believer. (An analogy: perhaps the ability to fly requires a certain minimal ratio R of body surface to body weight; but even if this is a genuine prerequisite for flying, it is a *de facto* requirement, rather than a condition dictated by the very concept of flying ability.)

As a consequence, the realism/eliminativism debate now takes on a very different dialectical structure than it has had recently. From the fundamentalist perspective, disputed empirical claims associated with FP, like (SA) and (LT), just don't threaten the fate of FP at all, because the outcome of these disputes would not significantly alter our overwhelming evidence that humans are nonpuppet RIS's. If it should turn out that FP is not absorbable into mature science, or that humans don't possess a language of thought, then the proper conclusion would be not that FP is false, but rather that the given condition is not really a *de facto* prerequisite for being a nonpuppet RIS — and hence is also not really a *de facto* prerequisite for being a true believer.

Consider, for instance, (LT). Under SF, this PTB condition is properly viewed as an "engineering hypothesis" about the *de facto* cognitive-level design requirements for being a nonpuppet RIS, and thereby for being a true believer. It is not a requirement built into the very concept of a true believer (or into the very concept of a nonpuppet RIS). Briefly, an engineering hypothesis purports to describe the requisite functional architecture of the cognitive system, the mental representational and information processing mechanisms which allegedly must subserve its rich behavioral repertoire. *Qua* engineering hypothesis, (LT) might very well be true.[29] However, suppose there were to emerge strong evidence that humans do not undergo mental representations possessing both language-like syntactic structure and the semantic content of the putative FP attitudes. Such evidence certainly would not show that humans are not nonpuppet RIS's, for the evidence for humans being such RIS's is beyond question. Rather, it would show that the proposed engineering hypothesis is just mistaken — and hence that the behavioral capacities that allegedly required language-like mental representations are actually subserved, in humans, by some other form of cognitive-level architecture. Indeed, the most convincing kind of case against the existence of a language of thought would incorporate (i) some alternative cognitive-level engineering proposal; (ii) a suitable theoretical elaboration of this proposal, including new explanations of those human capacities which supposedly cannot be adequately explained except by positing a language of thought; and (iii) a suitably rich body of empirical data favoring this novel proposal over the language-of-thought hypothesis.[30] If an alternative account with these features were to emerge, says SF, then the appropriate response would be to reject the language of thought as necessary for nonpuppet RIShood and thus also as essential for being a true believer, rather than to deny that humans are nonpuppet resonant intentional systems or true believers.

Or consider principle (SA). Suppose that the natural sciences, as they mature, turn out not to employ any theoretical concepts that correlate neatly with FP concepts; i.e., FP fails to be vertically absorbable into mature science. Perhaps the corpus of the physical sciences will develop in the manner envisioned by Paul Churchland, who says of FP that "its

intentional categories stand magnificently alone, without any visible prospect of reduction to that larger corpus."[31] Under SF this would not be
grounds for concluding that FP is radically false—that humans are not true
believers. Rather, the appropriate conclusion would be that FP need not be
vertically absorbable in order to be true; instead, the mode of interlevel "fit"
between FP and physical science is more complex than simple absorbability
by means of tractable type-type identities or tractable type-type nomic
correlations.

In fact, the demand for vertical absorbability is widely considered
implausible anyway, either as a criterion of intertheoretic fit between the
"special sciences" and physics, or as a criterion of fit between FP and the
physico-biological sciences.[32] In the case of FP, at least two reasons to
reject this demand have figured prominently in the recent philosophical
literature: first, the contention that beliefs, desires, and other FP attitudes
could in principle be physically realized in indefinitely many different ways,
especially when one considers the indefinitely large range of physically
possible creatures who all would be intelligent enough to qualify, under
ordinary behavior-based standards, as true believers; and second, the
contention that typically the content of many FP attitudes is partially
determined by social or environmental facts, rather than supervening upon
"what's in the head."[33] Vertical absorption is blocked in the first case
because there is no way to tractably delimit in the language of physico-
biology what the physico-chemical realizations of attitudes might be;
whereas it is thwarted in the second because any theory which purports to
absorb FP would essentially refer to social and other non-physico-biological
facts or attributes and these references arguably presuppose FP. While these
problems may not be insurmountable, they render suspect the demand for
vertical absorption.

However, although the demand for vertical absorbability of FP is
dubious on independent grounds, there is considerably more plausibility in
the contention that *horizontal* absorbability is a prerequisite for FP's truth.
Under SF, this contention should be viewed in the same way as principle
(LT)—viz., as an engineering hypothesis about the *de facto* cognitive-level
design requirements for being a nonpuppet RIS, and thereby for being a
true believer. If a creature is complex and sophisticated enough to be a
nonpuppet RIS, the claim goes, then its inner information-processing
capacities must be describable by an empirical cognitive-level theory that
posits natural-kind states very much like beliefs and desires, interacting with
one another and with sensation and behavior in much the way FP says
beliefs and desires do. This claim might very well be true, and thus (SA)
might very well be true.

Suppose however that cognitive science, as it matures, turns out not to
employ any theoretical concepts that are recognizably similar to FP

concepts like belief, desire, intention, and the like. Perhaps it will develop in the manner envisioned by Dennett, who claims that theories in cognitive science "are or should be theories of the subpersonal level, where beliefs and desires disappear, to be replaced by representations of other sorts on other topics."[34] Under SF, this would not be grounds for concluding that FP is radically false – that humans are not true believers. Rather, the appropriate conclusion would be that FP is linked to cognitive science not by horizontal (or vertical) absorbability but instead by a relation of vertical interlevel fit. The operative mode of fit presumably would be quite baroque, rather than being simple vertical absorption. Belief types and desire types typically would be "cognitively realized" by states whose description at the level of cognitive science is very complex; and a given FP state type might well be cognitively realized in numerous different ways on the different occasions of its instantiation by humans. (Cognitive science, in turn, might itself be linked to lower-level *physical* theories by a comparably baroque relation of interlevel fit, rather than by vertical absorption.)[35]

2. A second and related question raised by SF is whether folk-psychological explanations really are or can be true if SF is true and, particularly, if FP fails to be absorbed by science. Fans of absorption might argue as follows: FP must be absorbed because FP ascribes certain causal roles to beliefs, desires, and other FP attitudes; and it proffers causal explanations in terms of such states *qua* FP attitudes. In the very proffering of causal explanations FP poses as scientific explanation; thus, FP must be absorbed by science if its explanations are to be classified as true.

The best reply to this question or criticism, we think, is to deny that causal explanations must be scientific (absorbed by science) to be true. For, it is not obvious that reference to a state type must figure in science in order for tokens of that type to be causes, or in order for the type itself to figure in genuine causal explanations. *Prima facie,* it seems that less will do, something like figuring in a sufficiently broad-ranging pattern of counterfactual dependencies.[36] After all, there are numerous singular causal explanations involving nonscientific language – e.g., 'Sam's SAT scores improved because he took the SAT preparation course', or 'The grass turned green because Tom spread fertilizer on it,' or 'Mario won the race because his car corners so well.' Predicates like 'took the SAT preparation course,' 'spread fertilizer upon,' and 'corners well' presumably do not appear in any genuine scientific laws, and presumably would not figure in a body of mature scientific theories; but this does not show that singular causal explanations employing such predicates are somehow bogus or defective. According to SF, the same would go for the terms and concepts of FP, should FP turn out not to be scientifically absorbable. Causal/explanatory truth is one thing; absorbability into science is quite another.

We wish to stress again that SF is officially neutral about the purport of

PTB principles, such as (SA). These principles might state genuine cognitive-level engineering prerequisites for being an autonomous RIS, and hence for being a true believer. SF does not *deny* (SA), but instead claims this: if there were to emerge evidence against the thesis that FP is absorbable into mature science, then the appropriate response would be to reject (SA) as essential for true believerhood, rather than to deny that humans are true believers. This counterfactual claim might well be true even if (SA) is also true.

3. Let us turn now to a question which might be pressed by realist friends in the Eastern sect. A confident Easterner might grant that FP is very likely true but argue both that (*pace* austerity) PTB conditions must be met and therefore that such conditions very likely are met. Why should such a realist consider endorsing SF with its austere conception?

We believe that a powerful consideration should incline the true friend of FP toward SF and away from Easternism. Consider the implications, for the Eastern creed, of the possibility that empirical evidence might emerge against a favored PTB condition such as, for instance, (LT). Should this happen, only two real options would be available to the nonfundamentalist. One is to concede to secularism that the failure of (LT) undermines the truth of FP, and then seek to create or discover new psychological theories which do not presuppose FP. The other is to hope that the failure of (LT) is apparent only, and that counter-defenses of (LT) may be discovered.

Now one significant consequence of the deep entrenchment of FP's attitudinal and actional concepts in our conceptual scheme is that it decreases the perceived availability and appeal of the first option. For, to create (sic!) the new theory one must imagine (sic!) doing without FP, and engaging in such activities seems to presuppose FP. The second option, however, can be also if not equally unappealing, for the more powerful the evidence against (LT), the less reasonable the hope for effective rebuttal. By contrast, if SF is correct and FP is understood austerely, then the failure by itself of favored PTB conditions would not mean that FP is false; *a fortiori* there would be no need to cling to hope of effective rebuttal, should the empirical evidence mount against (LT), (SA), or some other PTB condition.

4. Finally, consider a fourth query. One alternative to realism and to antirealism about FP is to treat FP as pragmatically inescapable (at least by current lights) without actually believing that it is literally true. Let's call this *folk psychological quasi-realism*. According to quasi-realism, FP may be culturally entrenched, but we are not warranted in endorsing it. Dennett's "instrumentalism" may be interpreted as a version of quasi-realism.[37] The question is, then, why prefer realism to quasi-realism?

If FP presupposed PTB conditions, and these were unsatisfied, then there would be strong temptation to endorse quasi-realism. Quasi-realism would offer means of recognizing the simultaneous warrant failure and cultural inescapability of FP. But this just re-raises the same question we have raised throughout this paper: why wed FP to PTB conditions? FP is austere, not opulent. Thus, the negative fate of PTB conditions should not threaten the overall warrant for FP. Fundamentalism maintains that RIShood is ample evidence of true belief; and since there is plenty of evidence that humans are RIS's, there is ample evidence that humans are true believers. That is, there is strong warrant for folk-psychological realism.

By contrast, what warrant exists for quasi-realism? Very little, as far as we can see. The most important reasons offered by Dennett, for example, are those concerning the rationality of true believers. Dennett envisages FP presupposing idealized rational agents. This allegedly has the consequence that FP is a not falsifiable theory and cannot be empirically assessed. However, Dennett saddles the advocate of realism with a contentious PTB condition, viz., the idealized rationality of true believers. Although true believerhood probably does require at least a modicum of rational coherence among a person's beliefs, desires, and actions, the demand for idealized rationality seems entirely excessive. (It's like requiring complete sinlessness as a condition for being Born Again.) The extent of rationality in a true believer evidently can be far from ideal, and hypotheses about this matter are certainly falsifiable.

Quasi-realists are like unitarians: they wish to be realists/theists but antirealists/skeptics too. They cherish the practices of believers without cherishing belief. Our response to quasi-realism reduces to: Be ye not lukewarm in commitment to Belief. Folk Psychology is the faith of our fathers, living still, in spite of phlogiston, Churchland, and Stich.

FOOTNOTES

*The order of authorship is the reverse of the order of a previous paper by the same authors. The paper is a thoroughly collaborative project. We are grateful to a number of people for comments on earlier drafts, most especially Denny Bradshaw, Peter Clark, David Henderson, Harold Kincaid, Georges Rey, John Tienson, and an anonymous referee. The second author also wishes to thank the Centre for Philosophy and Public Affairs, Department of Moral Philosophy, University of St. Andrews, Scotland, and its award of a Tennent Caledonian Research Fellowship, which helped to fund his work on this paper.

[1]Jerry Fodor, *The Language of Thought* (Scranton, PA: Crowell, 1975); "Propositional Attitudes," *The Monist,* 61 (1978), pp. 501–523; *Psychosemantics* (Cambridge, MA: MIT, 1987); William Lycan, "Toward a Homuncular Theory of Believing," *Cognition and Brain Theory,* 4 (1981), pp. 139–59; Paul Churchland, "Eliminative Materialism and Propositional Attitudes," *Journal of Philosophy,* 78 (1981), pp. 67–90, this volume, pp. 42–62; *Matter and Consciousness* (Cambridge, MA: MIT, 1984); "Folk Psychology and the Explanation of Behavior," *Proceedings of the Aristotelian Society,* supp. vol. 62 (1988), pp. 209–21, this volume, pp. 247–262; Patricia Churchland, *Neurophilosophy: Toward a Unified Theory of Mind/Brain* (Cambridge, MA: MIT, 1981); Stephen Stich, *From Folk Psychology to Cognitive Science* (Cambridge, MA: MIT, 1983).

[2]A partial list of friends includes Frank Jackson and Philip Pettit, "In Defense of Folk

Psychology" (forthcoming); Christopher Maloney, *The Mundane Matter of the Mental Language* (Cambridge: Cambridge University Press, 1989). Classical foes include W. V. Quine (e.g. "Mental Entities," in *The Ways of Paradox* [Cambridge, MA: Harvard University Press, 1976]) and B. F. Skinner (e.g., *Beyond Freedom and Dignity* [New York: Knopf, 1971]). In the interest of avoiding national and geographic chauvinism, and of accommodating philosophers' shifts to institutions in new locales, our geographic metaphors should hereafter be understood as referring to certain philosophical positions in logical space, irrespective of the geographic locations of the various philosophers who espouse these different positions.

[3]We are not the first to use geographic metaphors for recent philosophy of mind; see Daniel Dennett, "The Logical Geography of Computational Approaches," in R. Harnish and M. Brand, eds., *The Representation of Knowledge and Belief* (Tucson: University of Arizona Press, 1986).

[4]"True Believers," in *The Intentional Stance* (Cambridge, MA: MIT, 1987).

[5]George Graham and Terence Horgan, "How to be Realistic About Folk Psychology," *Philosophical Psychology,* 1 (1988), pp. 69–81.

[6]Fodor puts it this way: "Holding onto the attitudes — vindicating common sense psychology — means showing how you could have . . . a respectable science whose ontology explicitly acknowledges states that exhibit the sorts of properties that common sense attributes to the attitudes" (*Psychosemantics*, p. 10, this volume, p. 229). It is not clear why Fodor mentions in this passage that vindicating FP means demonstrating the mere *possibility* of scientific absorption. But in any case, he also adds this: "[T]here is already in the field a (more or less) empirical theory that is, in my view, reasonably construed as ontologically committed to the attitudes and that — again, in my view, is quite probably approximately true. If I'm right about this theory, it *is* a vindication of the attitudes. . . . [D]efending the common sense assumptions about the attitudes and defending the theory turn out to be much the same enterprise" (ibid., p. 16).

[7]David Lewis, "Radical Interpretation," *Synthese,* 23 (1974), pp. 331–344; Terence Horgan and James Woodward, "Folk Psychology is Here to Stay," *Philosophical Review,* 94 (1985), pp. 197–226, this volume, pp. 144–166.

[8]Robert Gordon, "Folk Psychology as Simulation," *Mind and Language,* 1 (1986), pp. 158–171; Alvin Goldman, "Interpretation Psychologized," *Mind and Language,* (1989), pp. 161–185. For a systematic defense of the folk theory assumption, see John Preston, "Folk Psychology as Theory or Practice?," *Inquiry,* 32 (1989), pp. 277–303.

[9]Tractably describable lower-level state types are either natural-kind properties of the lower-level theory, or anyway properties that are fairly crisply and cleanly describable in lower-level terminology. An example of a property of the latter kind is *mean molecular kinetic energy,* the lower-level correlate of *temperature* in the reduction of classical thermodynamics to statistical molecular mechanics.

[10]In general, in broaching the possibility of *liberal* absorption, we mean to recognize that conceptions of absorption as well as related conceptions of scientific explanation, law, confirmation, and scientific unity do not remain at rest but change, and that certain plausible changes in this family of concepts might be compatible with claiming that FP is absorbed by mature science. In contrast, many of the standard eliminativist arguments presuppose narrow and stringent concepts from this family.

[11]These conditions have been discussed in a variety of places, such as Daniel Dennett, "Making Sense of Ourselves" and "Intentional Systems in Cognitive Ethology" in *The Intentional Stance;* Christopher Cherniak, *Minimal Rationality* (Cambridge, MA: MIT, 1986); Stephen Stich, "Do Animals Have Beliefs?," *Australasian Journal of Philosophy* 57 (1979), pp. 15–28; John Searle, *Minds, Brains, and Science* (Cambridge, MA: Harvard, 1986); William Lycan, *Consciousness* (Cambridge, MA: MIT, 1987).

[12]One does well to remember that the phrase 'folk psychology' was introduced by eliminativists into the literature to derogate the attitudes (compare with 'folk physics', 'folk biology', etc.). To make elimination seem plausible secularists try to identify relevant

similarities between folk psychology and other folk theories which have been replaced by mature science. Two points are worth making here about this argument for guilt by association. The first is that folksy psychology might deserve derogation. But, on our view, FP definitely does not. The second is that the fact that other folk theories have proven mistaken does not establish that FP should also be replaced, unless FP and those other theories are relevantly similar. But, on our view, they are not. See also Barbara Hannan, " 'Nonscientific realism' as a Response to Eliminativist Arguments," *Behaviorism* (forthcoming).

[13]We do not address the issue of how to distinguish folk from folksy psychology here, since the issue raises concern about how attitudes interact, the holism of FP, and the contextual sensitivity of FP attribution. Debate over PTB conditions is likely also implicated. Suffice it to say, our guess is that various approaches to these complex topics are consistent with the argument of this paper.

[14]See e.g. Lynne Rudder Baker, *Saving Belief* (Princeton: Princeton University Press, 1987).

[15]See e.g. "Intentional Systems," in *Brainstorms* (Cambridge, MA: MIT, 1978); "Intentional Systems in Cognitive Ethology," in *The Intentional Stance.*

[16]By the qualification 'approximately' we mean only that statements that figure in genuine explanations might only be literally true under idealized circumstances (e.g. the absence of friction).

[17]Even instrumentalists — hybrids in a sense (unitarians?), half realists, half antirealists — suppose RIS's exist. See Daniel Dennett, "Reflections: Real Patterns, Deeper Facts, and Empty Questions" in *The Intentional Stance.* See also our discussion of quasi-realism at the end of the present chapter.

[18]See Christopher Peacocke, *Sense and Content* (Oxford: Clarendon Press, 1983), pp. 205-6; Ned Block, "Psychologism and Behaviorism," *Philosophical Review* 95 (1986), pp. 5-40.

[19]Fundamentalism is neutral, however, about what it takes to be a nonpuppet RIS. Perhaps it isn't possible to be a nonpuppet RIS except by having a language of thought, or by being describable by a psychological theory that is absorbable into science. But humans are certainly nonpuppet RIS's; so whatever the prerequisites are for being one, humans satisfy them. More on this point in section 6.

[20]In casting about for a position about the austerity of FP's concepts comparable to our own, we find that Jackson and Pettit's (op. cit.) common sense functionalist conception of FP's semantics perhaps is closest; and, they point out that analytic behaviorism is also the limit case of the common sense functionalist conception. Whatever its other merits (or demerits), functionalizing FP terms and concepts, in the manner Jackson and Pettit suggest, helps to keep them close to ordinary, behavior-based evidential standards for their application.

[21]Paul Churchland writes, "FP suffers explanatory failures on an epic scale, . . . it has been stagnant for at least twenty-five centuries, and . . . its categories appear (so far) to be incommensurable with or orthogonal to the categories of the background physical science whose long-term claim to explain human behavior seems undeniable." (this volume, p. 49) For replies to these putative objections to FP, see Horgan and Woodward (op. cit.); Baker (op. cit.), chapter 7; and Colin McGinn, *Mental Content* (Oxford: Basil Blackwell, 1989) chapter 2.

[22]We emphasize that we are speaking here about a kind of confidence and interpersonal agreement that reflects speakers' *linguistic intuitions,* and therefore probably stems directly from people's conceptual/semantic competence with attitudinal and actional concepts and terms. We are *not* arguing that if a belief is commonplace, then this fact constitutes good grounds for thinking the belief is true.

[23]Even if actions themselves, as ordinarily conceived, are a species of bodily motions, people construe them as fundamentally different in kind from nonactional bodily motions.

[24]See e.g. Donald Davidson, "Actions, Reasons, and Causes," *Journal of Philosophy* 60 (1963). pp. 685-700; Alvin Goldman, *A Theory of Human Action* (Englewood Cliffs, NJ: Prentice-Hall, 1970); Myles Brand, *Intending and Acting* (Cambridge, MA: MIT, 1984).

[25]Some secularists doubt whether successor notions can be developed. Stephen Stich, for example, says that it is difficult to see how the notion of sincere assertion "could be unpacked without invoking the idea of an utterance *caused by . . . belief*" (*From Folk Psychology*, p. 79; emph. his). Others, the Churchlands, seem to hope for secularized succession for at least some folk notions and roles, though, as William Bechtel writes, "they cannot now offer detailed examples of what such discourse will look like" (*Philosophy of Science: An Overview for Cognitive Science* [Hillsdale, New Jersey: Lawrence Erlbaum Associates, 1988], p. 89).

[26]The inconceivability phenomenon just canvassed reveal a "pragmatic paradox" in the suggestion that there are no actions. Various philosophers have attempted invoked pragmatic paradoxes in arguing against eliminativist. See e.g. Peter Geach, *The Virtues* (Cambridge: Cambridge University Press, 1977), p. 49; Richard Swinburne, "Review of *Scientific Realism and Plasticity of Mind*," *Philosophy*, 55 (1980), pp. 273-75; Terence Horgan, "Cognition is Real," *Behaviorism*, 15 (1987), pp. 13-25; Graham and Horgan (op. cit.); and especially Baker (op. cit.).

[27]Not every realist who uses pragmatic paradox arguments to defend FP regards them as *a priori* or transcendental refutations of eliminativism. We employed such arguments in the paper cited in Note #5, for example, where we viewed them as burden of proof arguments, which approach is perfectly consistent with admitting the epistemic possibility that FP is false.

[28]This is an important clarification or modification in our position in the paper cited in Note #5. Although our discussion in that paper is consistent with neutrality about the prerequisites for being a true believer, the earlier paper also can be read as denying outright that scientific absorbability is a prerequisite for the truth of FP. Some critics of eliminativism do deny explicitly that the truth of FP requires a language of thought; see Andy Clark, "Thoughts, Sentences, and Cognitive Science," *Philosophical Psychology* 1 (1988), pp. 263-278.

[29]Many Eastern arguments for the language of thought lend support to (LT) as thus construed. So does the argument for language-like mental representations propounded by Terence Horgan and John Tienson, "Settling into a New Paradigm," *Southern Journal of Philosophy* 24, Spindel Conference Supplement (1988), p. 97-113; "Representations without Rules," *Philosophical Topics* 17 (1989), pp. 147-174; and *Connectionism and the Philosophy of Psychology* (Cambridge, MA: MIT, forthcoming).

[30]Colin McGinn argues that the language of thought hypothesis is best viewed as pertaining to cognitive-level engineering, op. cit., Chapter 3. He defends the alternative proposal that human mental representations are map-like, rather than language-like.

[31]Churchland, "Eliminative Materialism and Propositional Attitudes" (this volume, p. 49).

[32]See e.g. Jerry Fodor, "Special Sciences (Or: Disunity of Science as a Working Hypothesis)," *Synthese*, 28 (1974), pp. 97-115. Although Fodor ardently defends the *horizontal* absorbability of FP into mature science, he explicitly repudiates the demand that the special sciences (or FP) should be vertically absorbable by lower-level theories.

[33]See Tyler Burge, "Individualism and the Mental," in P. French, T. Uehling, and H. Wettstein, eds., *Midwest Studies in Philosophy*, 4 (Minneapolis: Minnesota); "Individualism and Psychology," *Philosophical Review*, 95 (1986), pp. 3-45.

[34]Dennett, *Brainstorms* (op. cit.), p. 105.

[35]See L. Darden and N. Maull, "Interfield Theories," *Philosophy of Science*, 43 (1977), pp. 44-64; for discussion see Bechtel (op. cit.), pp. 94-118. See also Terence Horgan, "Nonreductive Materialism and the Explanatory Autonomy of Psychology" (forthcoming).

[36]For a general approach to the causal/explanatory relevance of FP state-types that is compatible with the nonabsorbability of FP into science, see Terence Horgan, "Mental Quausation," in J. Tomberlin, ed., *Philosophical Perspectives*, Vol. 4 (forthcoming); and "Actions, Reasons, and the Explanatory Role of Content," in B. McLaughlin, ed., *The Philosophy of Fred Dretske* (Basil Blackwell, forthcoming).

[37]Dennett, "Intentional Systems" (op. cit.), and "Instrumentalism Reconsidered," in *The Intentional Stance*. In the latter paper he quotes approvingly the following remarks of Michael

Friedman (from Friedman's "Theoretical Explanation," in R. Healy, ed., *Reduction, Time, and Reality* [Cambridge: Cambridge University Press, 1981], p. 4):

> Scientists themselves distinguish between aspects of theoretical structure that are intended to be taken literally and aspects that serve a purely representational function. No one believes, for example, that the so-called "state spaces" of mechanics — phase space in classical mechanics and Hilbert space in quantum mechanics — are part of the furniture of the physical world.

Shortly after quoting this passage, Dennett writes:

> My *ism* is whatever *ism* serious realists adopt with regard to centers of gravity and the like [e.g., state spaces], since I think beliefs (and other mental items drawn from folk psychology) are *like that* — in being *abstracta* rather than part of the "furniture of the physical world" and in being attributed in statements that are *true* only if we exempt them from a certain familiar standard of literality. (p. 72)

This position stands to Southern Fundamentalism roughly as Rudolph Bultmann's "demythologized" interpretation of biblical scripture (cf. his *Kerygma and Myth* [New York: Harper and Row, 1961]) stands to *religious* fundamentalism. We Southern Fundamentalists hold that attitudinal attributions are often true even when interpreted according to "a certain familiar standard of literality"; Dennett denies this.

III CONNECTIONISM: THE DEATH OF FOLK PSYCHOLOGY?

16 Connectionism, Eliminativism, and the Future of Folk Psychology*[1]

William Ramsey
University of Notre Dame

Stephen Stich
Rutgers University, New Brunswick

Joseph Garon
La Jolla, California

1. INTRODUCTION

In the years since the publication of Thomas Kuhn's *Structure of Scientific Revolutions,* the term "scientific revolution" has been used with increasing frequency in discussions of scientific change, and the magnitude required of an innovation before someone or other is tempted to call it a revolution has diminished alarmingly. Our thesis in this paper is that if a certain family of connectionist hypotheses turn out to be right, they will surely count as revolutionary, even on stringent pre-Kuhnian standards. There is no question that connectionism has already brought about major changes in the way many cognitive scientists conceive of cognition. However, as we see it, what makes certain kinds of connectionist models genuinely revolutionary is the support they lend to a thoroughgoing eliminativism about some of the central posits of common sense (or "folk") psychology. Our focus in this paper will be on beliefs or propositional memories, though the argument generalizes straightforwardly to all the other propositional attitudes. If we are right, the consequences of this kind of connectionism extend well beyond the confines of cognitive science, since these models, if successful, will require a radical reorientation in the way we think about ourselves.

Here is a quick preview of what is to come. Section 2 gives a brief account of what eliminativism claims, and sketches a pair of premises that elimina-

*Reprinted from *Philosophical Perspectives* 4 (1990, pp. 499–533) by permission of the authors and publisher.

tivist arguments typically require. Section 3 says a bit about how we conceive of common sense psychology, and the propositional attitudes that it posits. It also illustrates one sort of psychological model that exploits and builds upon the posits of folk psychology. Section 4 is devoted to connectionism. Models that have been called "connectionist" form a fuzzy and heterogeneous set whose members often share little more than a vague family resemblance. However, our argument linking connectionism to eliminativism will work only for a restricted domain of connectionist models, interpreted in a particular way; the main job of Section 4 is to say what that domain is and how the models in the domain are to be interpreted. In Section 5 we will illustrate what a connectionist model of belief that comports with our strictures might look like, and go on to argue that if models of this sort are correct, then things look bad for common sense psychology. Section 6 assembles some objections and replies. The final section is a brief conclusion.

Before plunging in we should emphasize that the thesis we propose to defend is a *conditional* claim: *If* connectionist hypotheses of the sort we will sketch turn out to be right, so too will eliminativism about propositional attitudes. Since our goal is only to show how connectionism and eliminativism are related, we will make no effort to argue for the truth or falsity of either doctrine. In particular, we will offer no argument in favor of the version of connectionism required in the antecedent of our conditional. Indeed our view is that it is early days yet—too early to tell with any assurance how well this family of connectionist hypotheses will fare. Those who are more confident of connectionism may, of course, invoke our conditional as part of a larger argument for doing away with the propositional attitudes.[2] But, as John Haugeland once remarked, one man's ponens is another man's tollens. And those who take eliminativism about propositional attitudes to be preposterous or unthinkable may well view our arguments as part of a larger case against connectionism. Thus, we'd not be at all surprised if trenchant critics of connectionism, like Fodor and Pylyshyn, found both our conditional and the argument for it to be quite congenial.[3]

2. ELIMINATIVISM AND FOLK PSYCHOLOGY

'Eliminativism', as we shall use the term, is a fancy name for a simple thesis. It is the claim that some category of entities, processes or properties exploited in a common sense or scientific account of the world do not exist. So construed, we are all eliminativists about many sorts of things. In the domain of folk theory, witches are the standard example. Once upon a time witches were widely believed to be responsible for various local calamities.

But people gradually became convinced that there are better explanations for most of the events in which witches had been implicated. There being no explanatory work for witches to do, sensible people concluded that there were no such things. In the scientific domain, phlogiston, caloric fluid and the luminiferous ether are the parade cases for eliminativism. Each was invoked by serious scientists pursuing sophisticated research programs. But in each case the program ran aground in a major way, and the theories in which the entities were invoked were replaced by successor theories in which the entities played no role. The scientific community gradually came to recognize that phlogiston and the rest do not exist.

As these examples suggest, a central step in an eliminativist argument will typically be the demonstration that the theory in which certain putative entities or processes are invoked should be rejected and replaced by a better theory. And that raises the question of how we go about showing that one theory is better than another. Notoriously, this question is easier to ask than to answer. However, it would be pretty widely agreed that if a new theory provides more accurate predictions and better explanations than an old one, and does so over a broader range of phenomena, and if the new theory comports as well or better with well established theories in neighboring domains, then there is good reason to think that the old theory is inferior, and that the new one is to be preferred. This is hardly a complete account of the conditions under which one theory is to be preferred to another, though for our purposes it will suffice.

But merely showing that a theory in which a class of entities plays a role is inferior to a successor theory plainly is not sufficient to show that the entities do not exist. Often a more appropriate conclusion is that the rejected theory was wrong, perhaps seriously wrong, about some of the properties of the entities in its domain, or about the laws governing those entities, and that the new theory gives us a more accurate account *of those very same entities.* Thus, for example, pre-Copernican astronomy was very wrong about the nature of the planets and the laws governing their movement. But it would be something of a joke to suggest that Copernicus and Galileo showed that the planets Ptolemy spoke of do not exist.[4]

In other cases the right thing to conclude is that the posits of the old theory are reducible to those of the new. Standard examples here include the reduction of temperature to mean molecular kinetic energy, the reduction of sound to wave motion in the medium, and the reduction of genes to sequences of polynucleotide bases.[5] Given our current concerns, the lesson to be learned from these cases is that even if the common sense theory in which propositional attitudes find their home is replaced by a better theory, that would not be enough to show that the posits of the common sense theory do not exist.

What more would be needed? What is it that distinguishes cases like phlogiston and caloric, on the one hand, from cases like genes or the planets on the other? Or, to ask the question in a rather different way, what made phlogiston and caloric candidates for elimination? Why wasn't it concluded that phlogiston is oxygen, that caloric is kinetic energy, and that the earlier theories had just been rather badly mistaken about some of the properties of phlogiston and caloric?

Let us introduce a bit of terminology. We will call theory changes in which the entities and processes of the old theory are retained or reduced to those of the new one *ontologically conservative* theory changes. Theory changes that are not ontologically conservative we will call *ontologically radical*. Given this terminology, the question we are asking is how to distinguish ontologically conservative theory changes from ontologically radical ones.

Once again, this is a question that is easier to ask than to answer. There is, in the philosophy of science literature, nothing that even comes close to a plausible and fully general account of when theory change sustains an eliminativist conclusion and when it does not. In the absence of a principled way of deciding when ontological elimination is in order, the best we can do is to look at the posits of the old theory—the ones that are at risk of elimination—and ask whether there is anything in the new theory that they might be identified with or reduced to. If the posits of the new theory strike us as deeply and fundamentally different from those of the old theory, in the way that molecular motion seems deeply and fundamentally different from the "exquisitely elastic" fluid posited by caloric theory, then it will be plausible to conclude that the theory change has been a radical one, and that an eliminativist conclusion is in order. But since there is no easy measure of how "deeply and fundamentally different" a pair of posits are, the conclusion we reach is bound to be a judgment call.[6]

To argue that certain sorts of connectionist models support eliminativism about the propositional attitudes, we must make it plausible that these models are not ontologically conservative. Our strategy will be to contrast these connectionist models, models like those set out in Section 5, with ontologically conservative models like the one sketched at the end of Section 3, in an effort to underscore just how ontologically radical the connectionist models are. But here we are getting ahead of ourselves. Before trying to persuade you that connectionist models are ontologically radical, we need to take a look at the folk-psychological theory that the connectionist models threaten to replace.

3. PROPOSITIONAL ATTITUDES AND COMMON SENSE PSYCHOLOGY

For present purposes we will assume that common sense psychology can plausibly be regarded as a theory, and that beliefs, desires and the rest of the propositional attitudes are plausibly viewed as posits of that theory. Though this is not an uncontroversial assumption, the case for it has been well argued by others.[7] Once it is granted that common sense psychology is indeed a theory, we expect it will be conceded by almost everyone that the theory is a likely candidate for replacement. In saying this, we do not intend to disparage folk psychology, or to beg any questions about the status of the entities it posits. Our point is simply that folk wisdom on matters psychological is not likely to tell us all there is to know. Common sense psychology, like other folk theories, is bound to be incomplete in many ways, and very likely to be inaccurate in more than a few. If this were not the case, there would be no need for a careful, quantitative, experimental science of psychology. With the possible exception of a few die-hard Wittgensteinians, just about everyone is prepared to grant that there are many psychological facts and principles beyond those embedded in common sense. If this is right, then we have the first premise needed in an eliminativist argument aimed at beliefs, propositional memories and the rest of the propositional attitudes. The theory that posits the attitudes is indeed a prime candidate for replacement.

Though common sense psychology contains a wealth of lore about beliefs, memories, desires, hopes, fears and the other propositional attitudes, the crucial folk psychological tenets in forging the link between connectionism and eliminativism are the claims that propositional attitudes are *functionally discrete, semantically interpretable,* states that play a *causal role* in the production of other propositional attitudes, and ultimately in the production of behavior. Following the suggestion in Stich (1983a), we'll call this cluster of claims *propositional modularity*[8] (The reader is cautioned not to confuse this notion of propositional modularity with the very different notion of modularity defended in Fodor (1983).)

There is a great deal of evidence that might be cited in support of the thesis that folk psychology is committed to the tenets of propositional modularity. The fact that common sense psychology takes beliefs and other propositional attitudes to have semantic properties deserves special emphasis. According to common sense:

i) when people see a dog nearby they typically come to believe *that there is a dog nearby;*

ii) when people believe *that the train will be late if there is snow in the mountains,* and come to believe *that there is snow in the mountains,* they will typically come to believe *that the train will be late;*

iii) when people who speak English say 'There is a cat in the yard', they typically believe *that there is a cat in the yard.*

And so on, for indefinitely many further examples. Note that these generalizations of common sense psychology are couched in terms of the *semantic* properties of the attitudes. It is in virtue of being the belief *that p* that a given belief has a given effect or cause. Thus common sense psychology treats the predicates expressing these semantic properties, predicates like 'believes *that the train is late,*' as *projectable* predicates — the sort of predicates that are appropriately used in nomological or law-like generalizations.

Perhaps the most obvious way to bring out folk psychology's commitment to the thesis that propositional attitudes are *functionally discrete* states is to note that it typically makes perfectly good sense to claim that a person has acquired (or lost) a single memory or belief. Thus, for example, on a given occasion it might plausibly be claimed that when Henry awoke from his nap he had completely forgotten that the car keys were hidden in the refrigerator, though he had forgotten nothing else. In saying that folk psychology views beliefs as the sorts of things that can be acquired or lost one at a time, we do not mean to be denying that having any particular belief may presuppose a substantial network of related beliefs. The belief that the car keys are in the refrigerator is not one that could be acquired by a primitive tribesman who knew nothing about cars, keys or refrigerators. But once the relevant background is in place, as we may suppose it is for us and for Henry, it seems that folk psychology is entirely comfortable with the possibility that a person may acquire (or lose) the belief that the car keys are in the refrigerator, while the remainder of his beliefs remain unchanged. Propositional modularity does not, of course, deny that acquiring one belief often leads to the acquisition of a cluster of related beliefs. When Henry is told that the keys are in the refrigerator, he may come to believe that they haven't been left in the ignition or in his jacket pocket. But then again he may not. Indeed, on the folk-psychological conception of belief it is perfectly possible for a person to have a long standing belief that the keys are in the refrigerator, and to continue searching for them in the bedroom.[9]

To illustrate the way in which folk psychology takes propositional attitudes to be functionally discrete, *causally active* states let us sketch a pair of more elaborate examples.

i) In common sense psychology, behavior is often explained by appeal to certain of the agent's beliefs and desires. Thus, to explain why Alice went to her office, we might note that she wanted to send some e-mail messages (and, of course, she believed she could do so from her office). However, in some cases an agent will have several sets of beliefs and desires each of which *might* lead to the same behavior. Thus we may suppose that Alice also wanted to talk to her research assistant and that she believed he would be at the office. In such cases, common sense psychology assumes that Alice's going to her office might have been caused by either one of the belief/desire pairs, or by both, and that determining which of these options obtains is an empirical matter. So it is entirely possible that on *this* occasion

Alice's desire to send some e-mail played no role in producing her behavior; it was the desire to talk with her research assistant that actually caused her to go to the office. However, had she not wanted to talk with her research assistant, she might have gone to the office anyhow, because the desire to send some e-mail, which was causally inert in her actual decision making, might then have become actively involved. Note that in this case common sense psychology is prepared to recognize a pair of quite distinct semantically characterized states, one of which may be causally active while the other is not.

ii) Our second illustration is parallel to the first, but focuses on beliefs and inference, rather than desires and action. On the common sense view, it may sometimes happen that a person has a number of belief clusters, any one of which might lead him to infer some further belief. When he actually does draw the inference, folk psychology assumes that it is an empirical question what he inferred it from, and that this question typically has a determinate answer. Suppose, for example, that Inspector Clouseau believes that the butler said he spent the evening at the village hotel, and that he said he arrived back on the morning train. Suppose Clouseau also believes that the village hotel is closed for the season, and that the morning train has been taken out of service. Given these beliefs, along with some widely shared background beliefs, Clouseau might well infer that the butler is lying. If he does, folk psychology presumes that the inference might be based either on his beliefs about the hotel, or on his beliefs about the train, or both. It is entirely possible, from the perspective of common sense psychology, that although Clouseau has long known that the hotel is closed for the season, this belief played no role in his inference on this particular occasion. Once again we see common sense psychology invoking a pair of distinct propositional attitudes, one of which is causally active on a particular occasion while the other is causally inert.

In the psychological literature there is no shortage of models for human belief or memory which follow the lead of common sense psychology in supposing that propositional modularity is true. Indeed, prior to the emergence of connectionism, just about all psychological models of propositional memory, save for those urged by behaviorists, were comfortably compatible with propositional modularity. Typically, these models view a subject's store of beliefs or memories as an interconnected collection of functionally discrete, semantically interpretable states which interact in systematic ways. Some of these models represent individual beliefs as sentence-like structures — strings of symbols which can be individually activated by transferring them from long-term memory to the more limited memory of a central processing unit. Other models represent beliefs as a network of labeled nodes and labeled links through which patterns of activation may spread. Still other models represent beliefs as sets of production rules.[10] In all three sorts of models, it is generally the case that for any given cognitive episode, like performing a particular inference or answering a question, some of the memory states will be actively involved, and others will be dormant.

In Figure 16.1 we have displayed a fragment of a "semantic network" representation of memory, in the style of Collins & Quillian (1972). In this model, each distinct proposition in memory is represented by an oval node along with its labeled links to various concepts. By adding assumptions about the way in which questions or other sorts of memory probes lead to activation spreading through the network, the model enables us to make predictions about speed and accuracy in various experimental studies of memory. For our purposes there are three facts about this model that are of particular importance. First, since each proposition is encoded in a functionally discrete way, it is a straightforward matter to add or subtract a *single* proposition from memory, while leaving the rest of the network unchanged. Thus, for example, Figure 16.2 depicts the result of removing one proposition from the network in Figure 16.1. Second, the model treats predicates expressing the semantic properties of beliefs or memories as *projectable*.[11] They are treated as the sorts of predicates that pick out scientifically genuine *kinds,* rather than mere accidental conglomerates, and thus are suitable for inclusion in the statement of law-like regularities. To see this, we need only consider the way in which such models are tested against empirical data about memory acquisition and forgetting. Typically, it will be assumed that if a subject is told (for example) that the policeman arrested

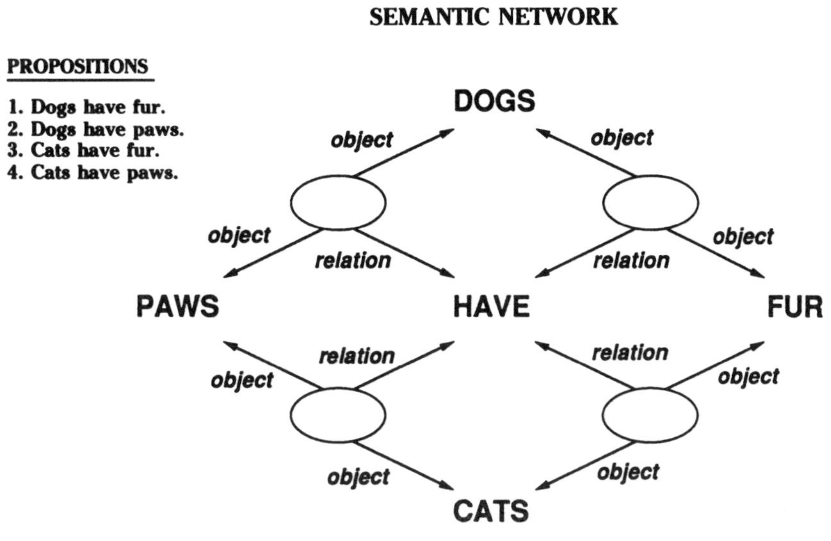

SEMANTIC NETWORK

PROPOSITIONS

1. Dogs have fur.
2. Dogs have paws.
3. Cats have fur.
4. Cats have paws.

FIG. 16.1.

SEMANTIC NETWORK

PROPOSITIONS

1. Dogs have fur.
2. Dogs have paws.
3. Cats have fur.

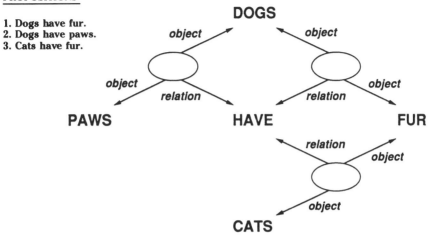

FIG. 16.2.

the hippie, then the subject will (with a certain probability) remember *that the policeman arrested the hippie.*[12] And this assumption is taken to express a nomological generalization — it captures something law-like about the way in which the cognitive system works. So while the class of people who *remember that the policeman arrested the hippie* may differ psychologically in all sorts of ways, the theory treats them as a psychologically natural kind. Third, in any given memory search or inference task exploiting a semantic network model, it makes sense to ask which propositions were activated and which were not. Thus, a search in the network of Figure 16.1 might terminate without ever activating the proposition that cats have paws.

4. A FAMILY OF CONNECTIONIST HYPOTHESES

Our theme, in the previous section, was that common sense psychology is committed to propositional modularity, and that many models of memory proposed in the cognitive psychology literature are comfortably compatible with this assumption. In the present section we want to describe a class of connectionist models which, we will argue, are *not* readily compatible with propositional modularity. The connectionist models we have in mind share three properties:

i) their encoding of information in the connection weights and in the biases on units is *widely distributed,* rather than being *localist;*

ii) individual hidden units in the network have no comfortable symbolic interpretation; they are *subsymbolic,* to use a term suggested by Paul Smolensky;

iii) the models are intended *as cognitive models,* not merely as *implementations* of cognitive models.

A bit later in this section we will elaborate further on each of these three features, and in the next section we will describe a simple example of a connectionist model that meets our three criteria. However, we are under no illusion that what we say will be sufficient to give a sharp-edged characterization of the class of connectionist models we have in mind. Nor is such a sharp-edged characterization essential for our argument. It will suffice if we can convince you that there is a significant class of connectionist models which are incompatible with the propositional modularity of folk psychology.

Before saying more about the three features on our list, we would do well to give a more general characterization of the sort of models we are calling "connectionist," and introduce some of the jargon that comes with the territory. To this end, let us quote at some length from Paul Smolensky's lucid overview.

Connectionist models are large networks of simple, parallel computing elements, each of which carries a numerical *activation value* which it computes from neighboring elements in the network, using some simple numerical formula. The network elements or *units* influence each other's values through connections that carry a numerical strength or *weight.* . . .

In a typical . . . model, input to the system is provided by imposing activation values on the *input units* of the network; these numerical values represent some encoding or *representation* of the input. The activation on the input units propagates along the connections until some set of activation values emerges on the *output units;* these activation values encode the output the system has computed from the input. In between the input and output units there may be other units, often called *hidden units,* that participate in representing neither the input nor the output.

The computation performed by the network in transforming the input pattern of activity to the output pattern depends on the set of connection strengths; *these weights are usually regarded as encoding the system's knowledge.*[13] In this sense, the connection strengths play the role of the program in a conventional computer. Much of the allure of the connectionist approach is that many connectionist networks *program themselves,* that is, they have autonomous procedures for tuning their weights to eventually perform some specific computation. Such *learning procedures* often depend on training in which the network is presented with sample input/output pairs from the function it is supposed to compute. In learning networks with hidden units, the network itself "decides" what computations the hidden units will perform; because these units represent neither inputs nor outputs, they are never "told" what their values should be, even during training. . . .[14]

One point must be added to Smolensky's portrait. In many connectionist models the hidden units and the output units are assigned a numerical "bias" which is added into the calculation determining the unit's activation level. The learning procedures for such networks typically set both the connection strengths and the biases. Thus in these networks the system's knowledge is usually regarded as encoded in *both* the connection strengths and the biases.

So much for a general overview. Let us now try to explain the three features that characterize those connectionist models we take to be incompatible with propositional modularity.

(i) In many nonconnectionist cognitive models, like the one illustrated at the end of Section 3, it is an easy matter to locate a functionally distinct part of the model encoding each proposition or state of affairs represented in the system. Indeed, according to Fodor and Pylyshyn, "conventional [computational] architecture requires that there be distinct symbolic expressions for each state of affairs that it can represent."[15] In some connectionist models an analogous sort of functional localization is possible, not only for the input and output units but for the hidden units as well. Thus, for example, in certain connectionist models, various individual units or small clusters of units are themselves intended to represent specific properties or features of the environment. When the connection strength from one such unit to another is strongly positive, this might be construed as the system's representation of the proposition that if the first feature is present, so too is the second. However, in many connectionist networks it is not possible to localize propositional representation beyond the input layer. That is, there are no particular features or states of the system which lend themselves to a straightforward semantic evaluation. This can sometimes be a real inconvenience to the connectionist model builder when the system as a whole fails to achieve its goal because it has not represented the world the way it should. When this happens, as Smolensky notes,

> [I]t is not necessarily possible to localize a failure of veridical representation. Any particular state is part of a large causal system of states, and failures of the system to meet goal conditions cannot in general be localized to any particular state or state component.[16]

It is connectionist networks of this sort, in which it is not possible to isolate the representation of particular propositions or states of affairs within the nodes, connection strengths and biases, that we have in mind when we talk about the encoding of information in the biases, weights and hidden nodes being *widely distributed* rather than *localist*.

(ii) As we've just noted, there are some connectionist models in which some or all of the units are intended to represent specific properties or features of the system's environment. These units may be viewed as the model's symbols for the properties or features in question. However, in models where the weights and biases have been tuned by learning algorithms it is often not the case that any single unit or any small collection of units will end up representing a specific feature of the environment in any straightforward way. As we shall see in the next section, it is often plausible to view such networks as collectively or holistically encoding a set of propositions, although none of the hidden units, weights or biases are comfortably viewed as *symbols*. When this is the case we will call the strategy of representation invoked in the model *subsymbolic*. Typically (perhaps always?) networks exploiting subsymbolic strategies of representation will encode information in a widely distributed way.

(iii) The third item on our list is not a feature of connectionist models themselves, but rather a point about how the models are to be interpreted. In making this point we must presuppose a notion of theoretical or explanatory level which, despite much discussion in the recent literature, is far from being a paradigm of clarity.[17] Perhaps the clearest way to introduce the notion of explanatory level is against the background of the familiar functionalist thesis that psychological theories are analogous to programs which can be implemented on a variety of very different sorts of computers.[18] If one accepts this analogy, then it makes sense to ask whether a particular connectionist model is intended as a model at the psychological level or at the level of underlying neural implementation. Because of their obvious, though in many ways very partial, similarity to real neural architectures, it is tempting to view connectionist models as models of the implementation of psychological processes. And some connectionist model builders endorse this view quite explicitly. So viewed, however, connectionist models are not *psychological* or *cognitive* models at all, any more than a story of how cognitive processes are implemented at the quantum mechanical level is a psychological story. A very different view that connectionist model builders can and often do take is that their models are at the psychological level, not at the level of implementation. So construed, the models are in competition with other psychological models of the same phenomena. Thus a connectionist model of word recognition would be an alternative to—and not simply a possible implementation of—a non-connectionist model of word recognition; a connectionist theory of memory would be a competitor to a semantic network theory, and so on. Connectionists who hold this view of their theories often illustrate the point by drawing analogies with other sciences. Smolensky, for example, suggests that connectionist models stand to traditional cognitive models (like semantic networks) in much the same way that quantum mechanics stands to classical mechanics. In each case the newer theory is deeper, more general and more accurate over a broader range of phenomena. But in each case the new theory and the old are competing at the same explanatory level. If one is right, the other must be wrong.

In light of our concerns in this chapter, there is one respect in which the analogy between connectionist models and quantum mechanics may be thought to beg an important question. For while quantum mechanics is conceded to be a *better* theory than classical mechanics, a plausible case could be made that the shift from classical to quantum mechanics was an ontologically *conservative* theory change. In any event, it is not clear that the change was ontologically *radical.* If our central thesis in this paper is correct, then the relation between connectionist models and more traditional cognitive models is more like the relation between the caloric theory of heat and the kinetic theory. The caloric and kinetic theories are at the same explanatory level, though the shift from one to the other was pretty clearly ontologically radical. In order to make the case that the caloric analogy is the more appropriate one, it will be useful to describe a concrete, though very simple, connectionist model of memory that meets the three criteria we have been trying to explicate.

5. A CONNECTIONIST MODEL OF MEMORY

Our goal in constructing the model was to produce a connectionist network that would do at least some of the tasks done by more traditional cognitive models of memory, and that would perspicuously exhibit the sort of distributed, subsymbolic encoding described in the previous section. We began by constructing a network, we'll call it Network A, that would judge the truth or falsehood of the sixteen propositions displayed above the line in Figure 16.3. The network was a typical three-tiered, feed-forward network consisting of 16 input units, four hidden units and one output unit, as shown in Figure 16.4. The input coding of each proposition is shown in the center column in Figure 16.3. Outputs close to 1 were interpreted as 'true' and outputs close to zero were interpreted as 'false'. Back propagation, a familiar connectionist learning algorithm was used to "train up" the network thereby setting the connection weights and biases. Training was terminated when the network consistently gave an output higher than .9 for each true proposition and lower than .1 for each false proposition. Figure 16.5 shows the connection weights between the input units and the left-most hidden unit in the trained up network, along with the bias on that unit. Figure 16.6 indicates the connection weights and biases further upstream.

Proposition		Input	Output	
1	Dogs have fur.	11000011 00001111	1	true
2	Dogs have paws.	11000011 00110011	1	true
3	Dogs have fleas.	11000011 00111111	1	true
4	Dogs have legs.	11000011 00111100	1	true
5	Cats have fur.	11001100 00001111	1	true
6	Cats have paws.	11001100 00110011	1	true
7	Cats have fleas.	11001100 00111111	1	true
8	Fish have scales.	11110000 00110000	1	true
9	Fish have fins.	11110000 00001100	1	true
10	Fish have gills.	11110000 00000011	1	true
11	Cats have gills.	11001100 00000011	0	false
12	Fish have legs.	11110000 00111100	0	false
13	Fish have fleas.	11110000 00111111	0	false
14	Dogs have scales.	11000011 00110000	0	false
15	Dogs have fins.	11000011 00001100	0	false
16	Cats have fins.	11001100 00001100	0	false

Added Proposition

| 17 | Fish have eggs. | 11110000 11001000 | 1 | true |

FIG. 16.3.

Figure 16.7 shows the way in which the network computes its response to the proposition *Dogs have fur* when that proposition is encoded in the input units.

There is a clear sense in which the trained up Network A may be said to have stored information about the truth or falsity of propositions (1)-(16), since when any one of these propositions is presented to the network it correctly judges whether the proposition is true or false. In this respect it is similar to various semantic network models which can be constructed to perform much the same task. However, there is a striking difference between Network A and a semantic network model like the one depicted in Figure 16.1. For, as we noted earlier, in the semantic network there is a functionally distinct subpart associated with each proposition, and thus it makes perfectly good sense to ask, for any probe of the network, whether or not the representation of a specific proposition played a causal role. In the connectionist network, by contrast, there is no distinct state or part of the network that serves to represent any particular proposition. The

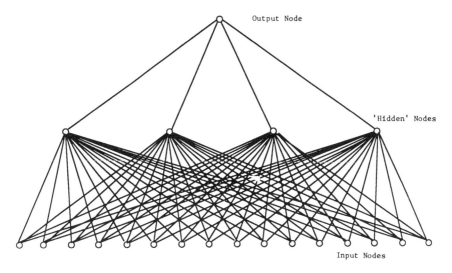

FIG. 16.4.

Network A

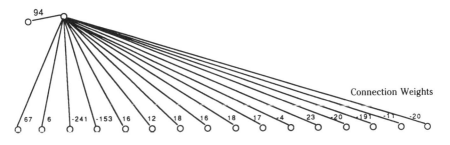

Input weights and bias to first hidden node
in network with 16 propositions.

FIG. 16.5.

information encoded in Network A is stored holistically and distributed throughout the network. Whenever information is extracted from Network A, by giving it an input string and seeing whether it computes a high or a low value for the output unit, *many* connection strengths, *many* biases and *many* hidden units play a role in the computation. And any particular weight or unit or bias will help to encode information about *many* different propositions. It simply makes no sense to ask whether or not the representation of a particular proposition plays a causal role in the network's

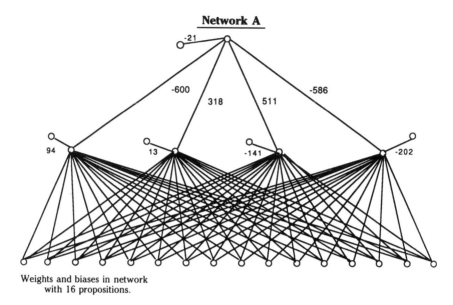

Weights and biases in network
with 16 propositions.

FIG. 16.6.

computation. It is in just this respect that our connectionist model of memory seems radically incongruent with the propositional modularity of common sense psychology. For, as we saw in Section 3, common sense psychology seems to presuppose that there is generally some answer to the question of whether a particular belief or memory played a causal role in a specific cognitive episode. But if belief and memory are subserved by a connectionist network like ours, such questions seem to have no clear meaning.

The incompatibility between propositional modularity and connectionist models like ours can be made even more vivid by contrasting Network A with a second network, we'll call it Network B, depicted in Figures 16.8 and 16.9. Network B was trained up just as the first one was, except that one additional proposition was added to the training set (coded as indicated below the line in Figure 16.3). Thus Network B encodes all the same propositions as Network A plus one more. In semantic network models, and other traditional cognitive models, it would be an easy matter to say which states or features of the system encode the added proposition, and it would be a simple task to determine whether or not the representation of the added proposition played a role in a particular episode modeled by the system. But plainly in the connectionist network those questions are quite senseless. The point is not that there are no differences between the two networks. Quite the opposite is the case; the differences are many and widespread. But these differences do not correlate in any systematic way

Network A

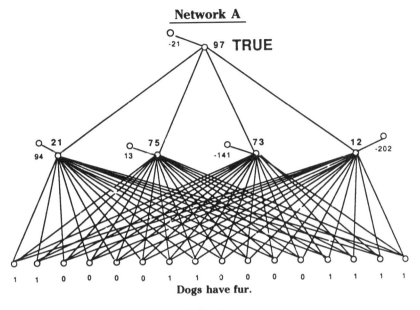

Dogs have fur.

FIG. 16.7.

Network B

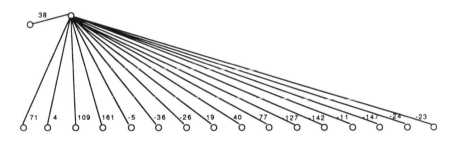

Input weights and bias to first hidden node
in network with 17 propositions.

FIG. 16.8.

with the functionally discrete, semantically interpretable states posited by folk psychology and by more traditional cognitive models. Since information is encoded in a highly distributed manner, with each connection weight and bias embodying information salient to many propositions, and information regarding any given proposition scattered throughout the network,

Network B

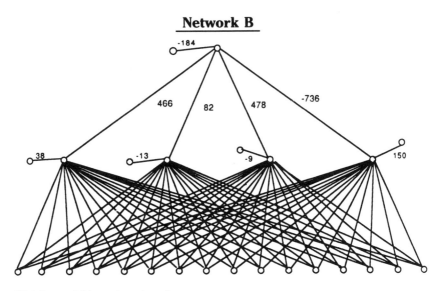

Weights and biases in network
with 17 propositions.

FIG. 16.9.

the system lacks functionally distinct, identifiable substructures that are semantically interpretable as representations of individual propositions.

The contrast between Network A and Network B enables us to make our point about the incompatibility between common sense psychology and these sorts of connectionist models in a rather different way. We noted in Section 3 that common sense psychology treats predicates expressing the semantic properties of propositional attitudes as projectable. Thus 'believes that dogs have fur' or 'remembers that dogs have fur' will be projectable predicates in common sense psychology. Now both Network A and Network B might serve as models for a cognitive agent who believes that dogs have fur; both networks store or represent the information that dogs have fur. Nor are these the only two. If we were to train up a network on the 17 propositions in Figure 16.3 plus a few (or minus a few) we would get yet another system which is as different from Networks A and B as these two are from each other. The moral here is that though there are *indefinitely* many connectionist networks that represent the information that dogs have fur just as well as Network A does, these networks have no projectable features in common that are describable in the language of connectionist theory. From the point of view of the connectionist model builder, the class of networks that might model a cognitive agent who believes that dogs have fur is not a genuine kind at all, but simply a chaotically disjunctive set. Common-sense psychology treats the class of people who believe that dogs have fur as a psychologically natural kind; connectionist psychology does not.[19]

6. OBJECTIONS AND REPLIES

The argument we've set out in the previous five sections has encountered no shortage of objections. In this section we will try to reconstruct the most interesting of these, and indicate how we would reply.

> Objection (i): Models like A and B are not serious models for human belief or propositional memory.

Of course, the models we've constructed are tiny toys that were built to illustrate the features set out in Section 4 in a perspicuous way. They were never intended to model any substantial part of human propositional memory. But various reasons have been offered for doubting that *anything like* these models could ever be taken seriously as psychological models of propositional memory. Some critics have claimed that the models simply will not scale up—that while teaching a network to recognize fifteen or twenty propositions may be easy enough, it is just not going to be possible to train up a network that can recognize a few thousand propositions, still less a few hundred thousand.[20] Others have objected that while more traditional models of memory, including those based on sentence-like storage, those using semantic networks, and those based on production systems, all provide some strategy for *inference* or *generalization* which enables the system to answer questions about propositions it was not explicitly taught, models like those we have constructed are incapable of inference and generalization. It has also been urged that these models fail as accounts of human memory because they provide no obvious way to account for the fact that suitably prepared humans can easily acquire propositional information one proposition at a time. Under ordinary circumstances, we can just *tell* Henry that the car keys are in the refrigerator, and he can readily record this fact in memory. He doesn't need anything like the sort of massive retraining that would be required to teach one of our connectionist networks a new proposition.

Reply: If this were a paper aimed at defending connectionist models of propositional memory, we would have to take on each of these putative shortcomings in some detail. And in each instance there is at least something to be said on the connectionist side. Thus, for example, it just is not true that networks like A and B don't generalize beyond the propositions on which they've been trained. In Network A, for example, the training set included:

Dogs have fur	Cats have fur.
Dogs have paws	Cats have paws.
Dogs have fleas	Cats have fleas.

It also included

Dogs have legs.

but not

Cats have legs.

When the network was given an encoding of this last proposition, however, it generalized correctly and responded affirmatively. Similarly, the network responded negatively to an encoding of

Cats have scales

though it had not previously been exposed to this proposition.

However, it is important to see that this sort of point by point response to the charge that networks like ours are inadequate models for propositional memory is not really required, given the thesis we are defending in this paper. For what we are trying to establish is a *conditional* thesis: *if* connectionist models of memory of the sort we describe in Section 4 are right, *then* propositional attitude psychology is in serious trouble. Since conditionals with false antecedents are true, we win by default if it turns out that the antecedent of our conditional is false.

> Objection (ii): Our models do not really violate the principle of propositional modularity, since the propositions the system has learned are coded in functionally discrete ways, though this may not be obvious.

We've heard this objection elaborated along three quite different lines. The first line — let's call it Objection (iia) — notes that functionally discrete coding may often be *very* hard to notice, and can not be expected to be visible on casual inspection. Consider, for example, the way in which sentences are stored in the memory of a typical von Neuman architecture computer — for concreteness we might suppose that the sentences are part of an English text and are being stored while the computer is running a word processing program. Parts of sentences may be stored at physically scattered memory addresses linked together in complex ways, and given an account of the contents of all relevant memory addresses one would be hard put to say where a particular sentence is stored. But nonetheless each sentence is stored in a *functionally discrete* way. Thus if one knew enough about the system it would be possible to erase any particular sentence it is storing by tampering with the contents of the appropriate memory addresses, while leaving the rest of the sentences the system is storing untouched. Similarly, it has been urged, connectionist networks may in fact encode propositions in functionally discrete ways, though this may not be evident from a casual inspection of the trained up network's biases and connection strengths.

Reply (iia): It is a bit difficult to come to grips with this objection, since what the critic is proposing is that in models like those we have constructed there *might* be some covert functionally discrete system of propositional encoding that has yet to be discovered. In response to this we must concede that indeed there might. We certainly have no argument that even comes close to demonstrating that the discovery of such a covert functionally discrete encoding is impossible. Moreover, we concede that if such a covert system were discovered, then our argument would be seriously undermined. However, we're inclined to think that the burden of argument is on the critic to show that such a system is not merely possible but *likely;* in the absence of any serious reason to think that networks like ours do encode propositions in functionally discrete ways, the mere logical possibility that they might is hardly a serious threat.

The second version of Objection (ii) — we'll call it Objection (iib) — makes a specific proposal about the way in which networks like A and B might be discretely, though covertly, encoding propositions. The encoding, it is urged, is to be found in the pattern of activation of the hidden nodes, when a given proposition is presented to the network. Since there are four hidden nodes in our networks, the activation pattern on presentation of any given input may be represented as an ordered 4-tuple. Thus, for example, when Network A is presented with the encoded proposition *Dogs have fur,* the relevant 4-tuple would be (21, 75, 73, 12), as shown in Figure 16.7. Equivalently, we may think of each activation pattern as a point in a four-dimensional hyperspace. Since each proposition corresponds to a unique point in the hyperspace, that point may be viewed as the encoding of the proposition. Moreover, that point represents a functionally discrete state of the system.[21]

Reply (iib): What is being proposed is that the pattern of activation of the system on presentation of an encoding of the proposition p be identified with the belief that p. But this proposal is singularly implausible. Perhaps the best way to see this is to note that in common sense psychology beliefs and propositional memories are typically of substantial duration; and they are the sorts of things that cognitive agents generally have lots of even when they are not using them. Consider an example. Are kangaroos marsupials? Surely you've believed for years that they are, though in all likelihood this is the first time today that your belief has been activated or used.[22] An activation pattern, however, is not an enduring state of a network; indeed, it is not a state of the network at all except when the network has had the relevant proposition as input. Moreover, there is an enormous number of other beliefs that you've had for years. But it makes no sense to suppose that a network could have many activation patterns continuously over a long period of time. At any given time a network exhibits at most one pattern of activation. So activation patterns are just not the sorts of things that can plausibly be identified with beliefs or their representations.

Objection (iic): At this juncture, a number of critics have suggested that long standing beliefs might be identified not with activation patterns, which are transient states of networks, but rather with *dispositions to produce activation patterns.* Thus, in network A, the belief that dogs have fur would not be identified with a location in activation hyperspace but with the network's *disposition* to end up at that location when the proposition is presented. This *dispositional state* is an enduring state of the system; it is a state the network can be in no matter what its current state of activation may be, just as a sugar cube may have a disposition to dissolve in water even when there is no water nearby.[23] Some have gone on to suggest that the familiar philosophical distinction between dispositional and occurrent beliefs might be captured, in connectionist models, as the distinction between dispositions to produce activation patterns and activation patterns themselves.

Reply (iic): Our reply to this suggestion is that while dispositions to produce activation patterns are indeed *enduring* states of the system, they are not the right sort of enduring states—they are not the discrete, independently causally active states that folk psychology requires. Recall that on the folk-psychological conception of belief and inference, there will often be a variety of quite different underlying causal patterns that may lead to the acquisition and avowal of a given belief. When Clouseau says that the butler did it, he may have just inferred this with the help of his long standing belief that the train is out of service. Or he may have inferred it by using his belief that the hotel is closed. Or both long standing beliefs may have played a role in the inference. Moreover, it is also possible that Clouseau drew this inference some time ago, and is now reporting a relatively long standing belief. But it is hard to see how anything like these distinctions can be captured by the dispositional account in question. In reacting to a given input, say p, a network takes on a specific activation value. It may also have dispositions to take on other activation values on other inputs, say q and r. But there is no obvious way to interpret the claim that these further dispositions play a causal role in the network's reaction to p—or, for that matter, that they do not play a role. Nor can we make any sense of the idea that on one occasion the encoding of q (say, the proposition that the train is out of service) played a role while the encoding of r (say, the proposition that the hotel is closed) did not, and on another occasion, things went the other way around. The propositional modularity presupposed by common sense psychology requires that belief tokens be functionally discrete states capable of causally interacting with one another in some cognitive episodes and of remaining causally inert in other cognitive episodes. However, in a distributed connectionist system like Network A, the dispositional state which produces one activation pattern is functionally inseparable from the dispositional state which produces another. Thus it is impossible to isolate some propositions as causally active in certain cognitive episodes, while others are not. We conclude that reaction pattern dispositions won't do as belief tokens. Nor, so far as we can see, are there any other states of networks like A and B that will fill the bill.

7. CONCLUSION

The thesis we have been defending in this chapter is that connectionist models of a certain sort are incompatible with the propositional modularity embedded in common sense psychology. The connectionist models in question are those which are offered as models at the *cognitive* level, and in which the encoding of information is widely distributed and subsymbolic. In such models, we have argued, there are no *discrete, semantically interpretable* states that play a *causal role* in some cognitive episodes but not others. Thus there is, in these models, nothing with which the propositional attitudes of common sense psychology can plausibly be identified. If these models turn out to offer the best accounts of human belief and memory, we will be confronting an *ontologically radical* theory change—the sort of theory change that will sustain the conclusion that propositional attitudes, like caloric and phlogiston, do not exist.

FOOTNOTES

[1]Thanks are due to Ned Block, Paul Churchland, Gary Cottrell, Adrian Cussins, Jerry Fodor, John Heil, Frank Jackson, David Kirsh, Patricia Kitcher and Philip Kitcher for useful feedback on earlier versions of this paper. Talks based on the paper have been presented at the UCSD Cognitive Science Seminar and at conferences sponsored by the Howard Hughes Medical Foundation and the University of North Carolina at Greensboro. Comments and questions from these audiences have proved helpful in many ways.

[2]See, for example, Churchland (this volume, pp. 42–62) & (1986), where explicitly

eliminativist conclusions are drawn on the basis of speculations about the success of cognitive models similar to those we shall discuss.

[3]Fodor, J. & Pylyshyn, Z. (1988).

[4]We are aware that certain philosophers and historians of science have actually entertained ideas similar to the suggestion that the planets spoken of by pre-Copernican astronomers do not exist. See, for example, Kuhn (1970), Ch. 10, and Feyerabend (1981), Ch. 4. However, we take this suggestion to be singularly implausible. Eliminativist arguments can't be that easy. Just what has gone wrong with the accounts of meaning and reference that lead to such claims is less clear. For further discussion on these matters see Kuhn (1983), and Kitcher (1978) & (1983).

[5]For some detailed discussion of scientific reduction, see Nagel (1961); Schaffner (1967); Hooker (1981); and Kitcher (1984). The genetics case is not without controversy. See Kitcher (1982) & (1984).

[6]It's worth noting that judgments on this matter can differ quite substantially. At one end of the spectrum are writers like Feyerabend (1981), and perhaps Kuhn (1962), for whom relatively small differences in theory are enough to justify the suspicion that there has been an ontologically radical change. Toward the other end are writers like Lycan, who writes:

> I am at pains to advocate a very liberal view . . . I am entirely willing to give up fairly large chunks of our commonsensical or platitudinous theory of belief or of desire (or of almost anything else) and decide that we were just wrong about a lot of things, without drawing the inference that we are no longer talking about belief or desire. . . . I think the ordinary word "belief" (qua theoretical term of folk psychology) points dimly toward a natural kind that we have not fully grasped and that only mature psychology will reveal. I expect that "belief" will turn out to refer to some kind of information bearing inner state of a sentient being. . . , but the kind of state it refers to may have only a few of the properties usually attributed to beliefs by common sense. (Lycan (1988), pp. 31–2.)

On our view, both extreme positions are implausible. As we noted earlier, the Copernican revolution did not show that the planets studied by Ptolemy do not exist. But Lavosier's chemical revolution *did* show that phlogiston does not exist. Yet on Lycan's "very liberal view" it is hard to see why we should not conclude that phlogiston really does exist after all—it's really oxygen, and prior to Lavosier "we were just very wrong about a lot of things."

[7]For an early and influential statement of the view that common sense psychology is a theory, see Sellars (1956). More recently the view has been defended by Churchland (1970) & (1979), Chs. 1 & 4; and by Fodor (1988), Ch. 1. For the opposite view, see Wilkes (1978); Madell (1986); Sharpe (1987).

[8]See Stich (1983a), pp. 237 ff, this volume, pp. 108 ff.

[9]Cherniak (1986), Ch. 3, notes that this sort of absent mindedness is commonplace in literature and in ordinary life, and sometimes leads to disastrous consequences.

[10]For sentential models, see John McCarthy (1968), (1980), & (1986); and Kintsch (1974). For semantic networks, see Quillian (1969); Collins & Quillian (1972); Rumelhart, Lindsay & Norman (1972); Anderson & Bower (1973); and Anderson (1976) & (1980), Ch. 4. For production systems, see Newell & Simon (1972); Newell (1973); Anderson (1983); and Holland, et. al. (1986).

[11]For the classic discussion of the distinction between projectable and nonprojectable predicates, see Goodman (1965).

[12]See, for example, Anderson & Bower (1973).

[13]Emphasis added.

[14]Smolensky (1988), p. 1.

[15]Fodor & Pylyshyn (1988), p. 57.

[16]Smolensky (1988), p. 15.

[17]Broadbent, D. (1985); Rumelhart & McClelland (1985); Rumelhart & McClelland (1986), Ch. 4; Smolensky (1988); Fodor & Pylyshyn (1988).

[18]The notion of program being invoked here is itself open to a pair of quite different interpretations. For the right reading, see Ramsey (1989).

[19]This way of making the point about the incompatibility between connectionist models and common sense psychology was suggested to us by Jerry Fodor.

[20]This point has been urged by Daniel Dennett, among others.

[21]Quite a number of people have suggested this move, including Gary Cottrell, & Adrian Cussins.

[22]As Lycan notes, on the common sense notion of belief, people have lots of them "even when they are asleep." (Lycan (1988), p. 57.).

[23]Something like this objection was suggested to us by Ned Block and by Frank Jackson.

17 Connectionism and the Future of Folk Psychology*[1]

William Bechtel
A. A. Abrahamsen
Georgia State University

Scientists in a variety of disciplines worry about the future viability of their disciplines: Will the subject matter on which they are currently plying their trade remain receptive to the tools of investigation of their discipline, or will it be discovered that the methods of more basic sciences are more suitable?

For example, physiologists in the early 20th century were concerned that the traditional phenomena of physiology might turn out to be best explained by, and so become the provence of, biochemistry. Biochemists routinely disrupted the organized systems of physiology (e.g., organs, tissues, cells) and attempted to study many of the activities of these systems in the remaining chemical soup. Sometimes, as in the case of understanding fermentation, this proved quite successful, although it required the discovery of a higher level of organization of chemical processes that had not previously been anticipated (see Bechtel, 1988a). In other cases, such as the case of cellular respiration, however, it did not prove as successful (see Bechtel, 1989). It turned out that physiological structures, such as membranes, were essential for respiration. But no sooner had cellular physiology been rescued from the assaults of biochemistry then a new threat emerged; this time from molecular biology, which proposed to explain the very nature of membranes at a molecular level.

Many contemporary endeavors in philosophy of psychology are directed to addressing the question of whether the job of another body of theory,

---

*Reprinted from Robert Burton (Ed.), *Minds: Natural and Artificial* (New York: SUNY Press, in press) by permission of the authors and publisher.

commonly referred to as *folk psychology,* will be usurped by the lower-level discipline of neuroscience. (For now, understand folk psychology as constituted simply by the idioms and principles used to characterize people's mental states and to explain and predict their actions. For example, we explain that a person got on a particular plane because she wanted to go to Seattle and believed that it was going there. Later, though, it will turn out that the actual characterization we give of folk psychology will be crucial.) Some philosophers have created a scenario even more threatening to the identity of folk psychology than that posed by cases such as those discussed in the previous paragraph. In the physiological cases the worry was only that the previous theorizing of one discipline might be reduced to and thus subsumed by that of a more basic science. The phenomena originally pursued by the higher level discipline of physiology are still thought to exist, but to be best investigated and explained by a discipline at a more basic level. But some philosophers of psychology have proposed that the theories of folk psychology cannot be subsumed by the theories of more basic level sciences, and therefore these theories and the phenomena they characterize are themselves destined to be banished from our maturing conception of reality (P. S. Churchland, 1986, P. M. Churchland, 1979, 1989, Stich, 1983a). This position is widely referred to as *eliminative materialism,* or just *eliminativism.*

Proposals to eliminate folk psychology first emerged in the 1960s as one approach to solving the mind-body problem. Numerous philosophers were concerned to provide a coherent account of how mental vocabulary, such as that used in folk psychology, might relate to the physical vocabulary of natural science. The first attempt to make the connection proposed that mental vocabulary did not in fact refer to particular events, but to dispositions of organisms (Ryle, 1949). To attribute a belief to a person was not to make a claim about a particular state of the person's mind, but about the disposition of the person to behave in certain ways. In many instances, however, translation of mental talk into disposition talk proved impossible, leading to two other proposals. The identity theory proposed that mental states simply corresponded to brain states (Smart, 1959). There was only one state involved, but it could be characterized in different vocabularies, including the mentalistic vocabulary and the emerging vocabulary of neuroscience. Other philosophers did not foresee such a smooth equation of mentalistically characterized states to physically characterized states, and proposed that the mentalistic vocabulary was destined to be replaced by the emerging physical vocabulary (Rorty, this volume, 17–41; and Feyerabend, this volume, pp. 3–16). The mentalistic vocabulary of beliefs and desires was a vestige of our past, and as science progressed, it would be replaced by descriptions of states of our brains. This new vocabulary would provide a far more useful characterization of us, in that we would be able to develop new understanding of our behaviors and ability to predict behavior based on the discoveries of natural science.

The eliminativists of the 1960s, however, could not produce the vocabulary that would replace mentalism, since the accounts of the operation of the brain were not yet sufficiently developed that they could sustain such a replacement and banishment of mentalistic discourse. The eliminativists of today fly much the same banner as their predecessors, but with a couple of modifications. Their attack is not directed against mentalism *per se,* but at a particular mentalistic account commonly referred to as *folk psychology.* This difference is significant. In the intervening decades a new form of mentalism has developed, which has become the basis of the contemporary cognitive sciences. The cognitive sciences are mentalistic in that they posit representational states in the head and processors that operate on these mentalistic states, without worrying too much about the physical realization of these states. But most practitioners of this new mentalism do not use the mentalistic vocabulary of *belief* and *desire* or the apparatus some philosophers have developed to analyze these states. Rather, they talk of information, and the ways in which information is processed. (This is an important point since an attack on folk psychology will not necessarily constitute an attack on the endeavors of practicing cognitive scientists.) Secondly, the new eliminativists invoke in their attack on folk psychology much more sophisticated knowledge of the workings of the brain, which has been achieved in the neurosciences over the past twenty-five years (see P. S. Churchland, 1980 and 1986 and P. M. Churchland, 1986c and 1986d). However, some of the most vigorous attacks on folk psychology (in P. S. Churchland, 1986 and in P. M. Churchland, 1989; see also Ramsey, Stich, and Garon, this volume, pp. 315–339) have not appealed to neuroscience, but rather to a new theoretical approach in cognitive science, *connectionism,* in which cognitive phenomena are modeled by means of networks that are loosely inspired by aspects of the neural system.

Our goal in this paper is to show that the eliminativists' attack on folk psychology based on connectionism is misguided. (The focus will be on connectionism, but the argument will apply equally well to eliminativist arguments based on neuroscience.) The eliminativist argument depends upon a particular conception of folk psychology which is largely a philosophical invention and which misrepresents the task for which folk psychology is needed. In developing this argument, we will not take the approach of Wilkes (1981, 1984) and Haldane (this volume, pp. 263–287), who have contended that folk psychology is not a theory and hence is not subject to elimination. Adopting a Quinean notion of a theory (Quine, 1960), it seems unproblematic to regard folk psychology as a theory. (For the classical argument that folk psychology represents a theory, see Sellars,

1963.) Rather, we will show that even construed as a theory, folk psychology is immune from attack by connectionism.

To develop this argument, we will first examine the conception of folk psychology advanced by philosophers, discuss how it is supposed to relate to scientific accounts of mind or brain, and finally how Churchland and Stich regard it as incompatible with connectionist accounts of mind and brain. After this stage setting, we will develop an alternative conception of folk psychology that is not committed to those features that figure in the eliminativists' attacks. We will argue not only that this version of folk psychology is closer to what people mean when they use folk mentalistic idioms, but that it has a quite different, yet crucial, role to play than do emerging accounts of the operation of the mind–brain. We will close with a brief discussion of how folk psychology of the sort eliminativists have criticized came into existence.

1. WHAT IS FOLK PSYCHOLOGY?

Much of the discussion of folk psychology proceeds as if the identity of folk psychology itself is unproblematic. But in fact philosophers seem to have a variety of different things in mind when they speak of folk psychology. On the one hand, the label *folk psychology* is used in the same manner as *folk physics,* where *folk physics* refers to the understanding ordinary lay people, not specifically trained in physics, have about the physical processes occurring in their environments. Not surprisingly, most people's understanding of physical processes is different from that offered by modern physics. In particular, as McCloskey (1983) has shown, people's intuitive understanding of physical processes corresponds more closely to the views of Aristotle than to those of Newton or Einstein. According to the analogy, folk psychology is the understanding ordinary lay people have of the principles underlying the behavior of themselves and other people. Ordinary people characterize each other in terms of what they know, what they believe, and what they desire. These attributions are then used to explain why someone did something or to make predictions about what someone will do. In a court of law people might be exonerated of crimes because they did not know and there was no reasonable expectation that they should have known what would be the consequences of their action. For example, if someone pushed a button with reasonable expectations that it controlled a light switch, when in fact it started the descent of an elevator which then killed someone, we would not find the person guilty of murder. Knowledge and motivation figure prominently in ethical and legal judgments; hence they provide paradigmatic cases in which we invoke folk psychology.

The claim that we do use concepts such as *know* and *desire* in such a manner in explaining and predicting people's behavior seems rather unproblematic. But philosophical discussions of folk psychology usually employ a much more detailed picture of the theoretical commitments of folk psychology, and focus on the question of whether or not this systemization of folk psychology is actually true (and therefore should be part of cognitive sciences such as psychology and philosophy of mind). We will develop this picture by tracing three stages of successively more powerful commitments. What should be noted at the outset is that these commitments of folk psychology may go beyond what ordinary users of folk psychology are committed to and, insofar as criticisms of folk psychology are directed at these features, the attack may be upon a philosophical construction, and not the psychological perspective employed by ordinary people.

Propositional Attitudes.   At the weakest level of commitment, Russell (1940) noted that our English idioms using *believe* and *desire* frequently have a particular syntactic structure. These verbs are often followed by the word *that* and a proposition. Thus, we might say "Teresa believes that her appointment is at 10:00 a.m." It thus seems plausible to view the verbs as representing attitudes people may take towards particular propositions. This decomposition into attitudes and propositions, moreover, turns out to be quite useful for many purposes. We can compare different people's beliefs by comparing and contrasting the propositions toward which they take some attitude, and by comparing and contrasting those attitudes. I might, for example, believe a proposition which you doubt. Further, the same kinds of decomposition can be used to describe the dynamics of folk psychology. If someone desires that something be the case and believes that certain actions constitute the best means for obtaining that end, and there are no competing considerations such as the belief that the actions proposed are morally wrong or will have the effect of producing yet other outcomes which one does not desire, then that person will perform the actions in question.

Propositional Modularity.   A more powerful commitment is developed by Stich (1983a) and further articulated recently by Ramsey, Stich, and Garon (this volume, pp. 315–339). They argue that folk psychology presupposes propositional modularity, that is, that it is appropriate to individuate mental states according to the propositions that provide their content. They claim, for example, that "it makes perfectly good sense to claim that a person has acquired (or lost) a single memory or belief," which would involve increasing or decreasing by one the set of beliefs toward which one adopts the attitude of belief. Similarly, they claim that folk psychology is committed to the idea that one can ascertain which propositional attitudes gave rise to a particular action. For example, it makes sense to say that the person performed an action because she wanted proposition *X* to be true, not because she wanted proposition *Y* to be true, even if she desired *Y* to be true as well, and knew that her actions would also make *Y* true. Thus, the propositions used in propositional attitude accounts have distinct identity conditions, and these conditions allow us to differentiate folk-psychological mental states.

Causally Productive Internal States.   The strongest level of commitment imputed to folk psychology is that beliefs and desires are distinct states of organisms that engage in physical interactions and so produce their behavior. Thus there is a causal, dynamic story to be told about folk-psychological states. From this, many have assumed that propositional attitudes are states located in the heads of people. Just how they are located in the heads is not taken to be particularly significant (the propositions might not be encoded in a single location in the brain), but that there are internal states constituting our beliefs and desires is taken to be necessary for these states to be able to figure in causally generating behavior. The argument contends that if there were not such entities in the head, they could not figure in causal processes so as to generate the behavior.

2. POSSIBLE FATES FOR FOLK PSYCHOLOGY

The above characterization of folk psychology in fact pushes the analogy between folk psychology and folk physics: Both concern ordinary people's theoretical accounts of a particular part of the natural world. It makes sense then to ask whether the theoretical claims made by folk psychology are in fact true. Folk physics at least turned out not to be true. Moreover, as eliminativists have argued, that has been the fate of nearly all folk theories. Theories about demonic possession, for example, have been replaced with theories about epilepsy. That observation leads to the question: Is folk psychology true? For most theorists, this question resolves into whether folk psychology will be preserved, either totally, or at least in a recognizable version, in our emerging scientific psychology. Some defenders of folk psychology contend that the basic conceptual framework employed in folk psychology will prove to be a necessary part of any future scientific psychology.

The strongest advocate of this position remains Jerry Fodor (for an overview of his position, see Fodor, 1984). Fodor's strategy is to argue that an analysis in terms of propositions is required for an adequate psychology. He maintains that in order to account for cognitive activities it is necessary to postulate internal representations which have the characteristics of the propositions used in ascribing propositional attitudes. Thus, he argues for the existence of a language of thought (Fodor, 1975). His early arguments for a language of thought depended upon the fact that he construed cognitive life as a matter of making inferences; he claimed that this requires a language in which the information upon which inference is to be made can be represented. More recently (Fodor, 1987) he has focused on what he claims are basic properties of cognition (as well as language): productivity, systematicity, and inferential coherence. To consider just the argument concerning productivity, Fodor begins by noting that there does not seem to be any limit to the set of propositional attitudes we might have; just as there is an infinite number of sentences in our language, there is an infinite number of beliefs we might hold. The question then arises as to how this is possible. Fodor's proposal is that it is only possible if we have a system of representations that can be composed according to a recursive process in which components of higher-order representations are literally parts of, or constituents of, the higher-order representations themselves.

Fodor's language of thought provides a vehicle for taking over the conceptual apparatus of folk psychology as a framework for constructing a scientific psychology. In this scheme, there actually are propositions in the head and they are manipulated according to principles of inference much like those contemplated in folk psychology. Of course, these propositions are not regarded as being encoded in the way we encode propositions linguistically, for example, by writing words sequentially on a page. Fodor's claim is that something functionally equivalent to this mode of representation is used. Given our widespread use of computers, it should be clear to us that sentences, such as the one we are now writing, can be encoded without being encoded as a linear sequence of words; they can be stored as bit patterns distributed over a number of locations in the computer's memory, for example. All that is essential is that the computer's representations enable it to perform various tasks with the sentence, such as moving it to a new location, when we give the proper commands. If we think not of sentences on which word processing is being performed, but statements in a computer program which actively determines the behavior of the computer, then we have an analogue that shows how linguistic representations can have efficacy even though they are no longer encoded in the familiar manner of sentences on a page. It is not critical to Fodor's account that the propositions of the language of thought be physically represented in any particular, recognizable manner; what is critical is that the propositions perform the functions attributed to them in the sort of account Fodor offers.

If we cannot physically find the propositions in the head that correspond to the propositions ascribed in propositional attitude statements, how do we know that they are really there? Since it is a theory that tells us that they are there in the first place, presumably we will judge whether there really are propositions in the head by the fate of the scientific theory that posits them. The critics of the language of thought defense of folk psychology propose that one of two possible futures must await this account of folk psychology in terms of a language of thought: either the language of thought account will end up being reducible to the theoretical accounts offered in the more basic sciences, or the language of thought account will be eliminated in favor of an account that is grounded in the more basic sciences (P. M. Churchland, 1989).

The reduction strategy seeks to reduce psychological theories to those at the adjacent neuroscience level. When the term *reduction* is used in this context, it refers to the philosophical model of reduction developed by the logical positivists (see Nagel, 1961). In brief, for one theory to be reduced to another it is necessary that there be translation rules for equating the terminology of the two theories (these translations need not involve one-to-one mappings, but must provide a way for equating terms in one theory in one context with terms in another theory in a particular context; see Richardson, 1979). Second, using this translation scheme, it must be possible to derive the laws of the science being reduced from the laws of the more basic science (see Bechtel, 1988b, for a more complete account and discussion of the classical theory reduction model). The eliminativist's strategy, in contrast, is to show that the prospects of a reduction, even one that allows for substantial modifications of the propositional attitude story in the course of the reduction, is not likely. The brain seems to use mechanisms of information processing quite unlike those found in the propositional attitude account, and the prospects for any reasonable mapping of the propositional attitude account onto one of neuroscience are very slim.

Such an argument for eliminitivism, appealing to the impossibility of reducing the psychological account in terms of propositional attitudes to a neuroscience account, has not disturbed defenders of propositional attitude stories like Fodor. The reason is that Fodor has long maintained that higher-level sciences, or *special sciences* as he refers to them, do not need to reduce to lower level sciences in order to be vindicated. Instead, Fodor (1974; see also Pylyshyn 1984) has argued for the autonomy of higher-level sciences. His argument is that in order for the special sciences to explain and predict the range of phenomena within their domains, it is often necessary that they develop a system of categorization that cross-cuts that of the more basic sciences. For example, it is useful to develop analyses at the economic level that use money as one of the basic concepts. But since money can be realized in an almost unlimited number of ways, a mapping of the concepts of economics onto those of more basic sciences is not to be expected. Consequently, there can be no reduction of economics to more basic sciences. This does not show, however, that we need to replace current economic theories with ones capable of being reduced. Rather, according to Fodor, we need to employ our current economic theories, or their successors, which categorize the world in ways appropriate for economic interactions. Similarly, we would not necessarily expect the categorization invoked in psychological theories to map onto those developed in more basic sciences such as neuroscience. The categorization we require in a psychological account is one that divides events in ways pertinent to explaining and predicting human actions. From the point of view of human actions, qualitatively different types of physiological events count as the same kind of action (e.g., politely greeting one's colleagues). Hence, the alternatives of reduction or elimination pose a false dichotomy for the propositional attitude theorist.

There are a variety of responses that one might take to this sort of defense of the autonomy of propositional attitude theory. One of us has argued elsewhere (Bechtel, 1988b) that the sort of autonomy Fodor defends for propositional attitude psychology is too extreme, for it cuts psychology off from the sorts of resources that higher-level sciences often procure from lower-level sciences even when a traditional reduction is not in the offing. In this context, though, it is worth noting that success or failure of reduction is not the only vehicle for evaluating propositional attitude psychology. Propositional attitude psychology purports to provide an account of operations occurring in the head, albeit an account developed at a quite abstract, functional level. This is exactly the sort of task pursued in cognitive psychology. Moreover, cognitive psychology has developed a variety of tools to test and evaluate models of internal processing against actual human performance. These include analyses of errors and processing time. The question then arises as to whether empirical research in cognitive psychology supports the sort of model Fodor advances.

The language of thought model advanced by Fodor constitutes an exemplar of the *symbolic paradigm* in cognitive science. This paradigm is modeled after the digital computer, which can store, retrieve, and manipulate formal symbols given explicit directions (encoded either in the physical architecture of the machine or stored in other symbols which are then interpreted in terms of operations provided by the physical architecture). Human cognitive performance is viewed as similarly involving operations upon formal symbols. What makes a symbol formal in this conception is that what matters is simply the "shape" of the symbol, where the shape of a word in a written natural language is its sequence of letters (which is what someone who does not know the language would use in order to look up the word in a dictionary). The shape of a symbol in a computer would be the particular bit pattern in which it is encoded. What is not included in a formal symbol is semantic information about what the word or bit pattern denotes in the world. The idea is that the operations performed on the formal symbols will result in manipulations that respect the semantics. To make the contrast with semantics, the operations which treat the symbols as purely formal are spoken of as *syntactic*. This can be misleading, however, since the formal operations are not restricted to grammar, but can also represent information about meaning through the links that are established to other formal symbols.

The model for this correspondence between syntax and semantics is found in the relation of proof theory to model theory in logic, where the goal in proof theory is to develop axiom sets which will generate new propositions from propositions already in the proof, subject to the constraint that if the original premises are judged to be true in a model, then the resulting theorems will also be true in that model. In modeling human cognition, however, the goal is not preserving truth in models, but predicting the inferences people will make from whatever propositions they begin by accepting.

The question in evaluating propositional attitude theory comes down to whether the symbolic approach is the correct approach to modeling cognition. Recently the symbolic approach within cognitive science has been challenged by an alternative known variously as *connectionist, parallel distributed processing,* or *neural network* modeling. (Here we will use the term *connectionism* as the generic term for this framework.) The challenge posed by connectionism stems from the fact that it does not treat cognitive processes as involving manipulations of symbols according to formal rules.[2] In the next section we will describe the connectionist framework for modeling cognition and discuss why it is viewed as representing such a contrast to the symbolic tradition. Before doing so, however, a clarification is in order.

There are many practitioners of cognitive science who take what they do to be in the symbolic tradition, but would not accept the characterization of the symbolic tradition provided above. When one starts to develop an account of symbol processing by drawing upon propositional attitudes and the operations of symbolic logic which are thought to operate on propositions, it is quite natural to treat the constituents of propositions (words) as atomic units and the rules specifying operations upon these propositions as deterministic. Practitioners of cognitive science who have actually engaged in the modeling of cognitive behavior, however, have not so restricted themselves. Thus, in many cognitive models numerical weights are attached to the basic symbols, indicating a degree of activation, or to the rules which operate on these symbols, making the likelihood that they will be invoked stochastic (see Anderson, 1983; Holland, Holyoak, Nisbett, and Thagard, 1986; and Newell, 1989). Furthermore, the actual symbols that are manipulated in these models are often not thought of as being at the level of words but at a much lower level, corresponding perhaps to semantic features (see Medin, 1989). Theorists who make departures such as these from the framework of traditional symbol processing have already captured a number of properties that connectionist models are designed to capture, and hence are less obviously challenged by connectionist models than are traditional symbolic models. (What they tend to retain of the more traditional symbolic approach are ordered symbol strings, whereas connectionist models lack intrinsic ordering principles and the ready capacity for sequenced and nonlocal control.) But these symbolic models are also not very congenial to the framework of propositional attitudes, since their encoding units are not propositions of the sort used in folk psychology, and they employ numerical rather than logical operations. When we are speaking of the symbolic tradition that grounds propositional attitudes and contrasting it to connectionism, therefore, we will be restricting ourselves to the more traditional symbolic models which involve logical operations on propositions.

3. THE CONNECTIONIST CHALLENGE

The connectionist framework for modeling cognition is rich and varied. It is not possible here to do more than sketch the basic outlines of that framework. (For fuller accounts, see Bechtel & Abrahamsen, 1991; McClelland, Rumelhart, and the PDP Research Group, 1986; and Rumelhart, McClelland, and the PDP Research Group, 1986.) The processing architecture for connectionism is based, more or less loosely, on the architecture of the nervous system. Corresponding to neurons are units, which are viewed as simple processing units which can take on either discrete or continuous activation values. Corresponding to axonal and dendritic processes are connections. Through these connections the activation of one unit tends to spread and to excite or inhibit other units. The degree of this excitation or inhibition is determined by the weight of the connection, which may either be fixed, or altered as a result of processing by means of *learning* procedures.

There are a variety of different architectures such networks might have. In what are known as *feed forward networks,* the units are organized in layers, including at least an input layer and an output layer. Optionally, additional layers of units (known as *hidden layers*) can be included between these *visible layers.* A pattern of activation is supplied to the input units, and activation is propagated in accordance with equations that transform and combine the initial activations to produce a new pattern of activation on the output layer. This serves as the network's answer to the problem posed on the input layer. Alternatively, a network may have an *interactive* architecture. Either units have bidirectional connections, or there are separate pathways by which a unit may receive influence back from a unit that it previously influenced. In a network of this type, activations are propagated back and forth numerous times until a stable configuration is reached. Some or all of the units may be utilized as input units to which initial activations are supplied, and some or all may be utilized as output units from which the network's solution to a problem is read once the processing in the network has stabilized.

Connectionist networks of these sorts have demonstrated impressive abilities in a variety of basic cognitive tasks. For example, they are quite adept at a number of categorization or pattern recognition tasks. A simple feed forward network without hidden units can be trained (through algorithms for changing the weights on the various connections) to respond with designated output patterns to particular inputs. Then, if supplied a new input that does not precisely match any of those on which it has been trained, it will respond with an output pattern very similar to those learned for similar input patterns. They also can perform quite well as memory retrieval devices. It is possible to develop networks, for example, that will respond with a complete pattern if just provided with a small part of the pattern. In much the same manner, interactive networks are good at soft constraint satisfaction, that is, at finding solutions to problems by treating constraints on the solutions not as rigid rules, but rather as principles to be satisfied to as great an extent as possible.

Connectionist networks have attracted a good deal of interest because they seem to be capable of performing cognitive tasks without the use of rules operating upon symbol strings. It has been suggested that traditional symbolic models are too coarse grained to model cognition adequately (see Rumelhart, 1984). Human behavior is much less rigid than that produced by such symbol systems, and degrades gradually when overloaded, rather than crashing in the manner of traditional symbolic systems. The finding that networks can more exactly replicate behavior that is only approximated by rules, and that they can acquire such behavior in a fairly natural manner has further inspired theorists to adopt the network approach and shun the use of symbols and rules in modeling cognition.

One such behavior that has been modeled in networks is past-tense formation. Children typically begin by acquiring the past tense of a few verbs, many of which are irregular. They then learn to affix -ed to regular verbs, and go through a lengthy stage of overgeneralization during which they apply this rule improperly to many irregular verbs. Finally, they reach a stage of mature performance and generate the past tenses of both regular and irregular verbs correctly. The difficulty in accounting for this behavior in terms of rules is that the stages are not sharply demarcated; during the second stage, for example, the child may sometimes form the past tense of the same irregular verb correctly and other times incorrectly. Rumelhart and McClelland (1986) have demonstrated, though, that this pattern of acquisition can be simulated in a feedforward network in which no rules operate upon symbols.

For the eliminativist, connectionism has provided a powerful tool in arguing against propositional attitude psychology: connectionist networks do not have symbols and rules as seem to be required by propositional attitude models. Ramsey, Stich, and Garon (this volume, pp. 315–339), for example, have developed a simple demonstration network to illustrate this point. They trained a feed forward network with three layers of units to supply the appropriate truth values to a number of propositions. Ramsey et al. emphasize that the memory of the truth value of a particular proposition does not reside in any one weight since the other weights are required as well, and any weight that is employed also serves in the memory of the truth value of other propositions. Thus, there is no localized storage of the propositions and their truth values in the network. Moreover, we cannot even identify the memory of a single proposition with a particular distribution of weights, since they trained another network, which learned just one more proposition, and the weights obtained in that network were quite different than in the first. There seems to be no obvious part of the network with which to identify the memory of truth values for particular propositions. They therefore conclude that a distributed network such as this does not preserve the propositional autonomy of folk psychology.

It is worth noting that defenders of the symbolic tradition such as Fodor have also recognized connectionism as a challenger and tried to answer it, whereas they have been much less concerned to answer arguments for elimination based on neuroscience. This is undoubtedly because connectionism presents itself as a competitor at just the level where symbolic theorists have postulated the existence of the symbolic engine that implements propositional attitudes. If connectionism could succeed here, it might suffice to show that mentation does not require propositions; hence, there may be no propositions toward which we have attitudes. But Fodor and Pylyshyn (1988) maintain that the challenge posed by connectionism can be repelled. They claim that connectionism is an unsuccessful competitor to the symbolic tradition precisely because it fails to capture some of the important features of cognition that the symbolic tradition was designed to capture; in particular, it cannot capture the productivity, systematicity, and inferential coherence of thought.

First, it is claimed, connectionism cannot capture productivity since it does not build larger thoughts out of a basic set of components using composition rules that can be applied recursively. Rather, each new mental structure is developed anew, in much the manner in which Ramsey et al. trained their network to respond to an additional proposition. The network accomplished this task by developing a quite different set of weights. Second, Fodor and Pylyshyn contend that connectionism fails to capture the systematicity of cognition, which they take to be an even greater failing. They contend that it would be a peculiar cognitive system that could develop an attitude toward one proposition, for example, *the florist loves Joan,* but not be able to entertain the related proposition *Joan loves the florist.* Yet, the network of Ramsey et al. faces just this problem. It was able to assign correctly a truth value to a proposition on which it had not been trained, but only because the input pattern used for that proposition was similar to that of other propositions it had learned. It could assign a truth value, therefore, according to the similarity of the encoding of the new proposition to that of ones on which it had been trained. But this is insufficient. In a natural language, there will be many different grammatical structures which will be related to a given sentence, and it is unlikely that all of these will have a sufficiently similar encoding so that responses can be based on similarities to the encodings of other propositions. Only a symbolic representation upon which rules can operate, Fodor and Pylyshyn contend, could support the needed systematicity. The argument from inferential coherence is analogous. Fodor and Pylyshyn contend that mental systems exhibit coherent *patterns* of inference. If they can infer *A* from *A and either B or C,* they will also be able to infer *A* from *A and B.* But connectionist systems must, they contend, encode each inference pattern separately since they cannot define rules to operate on symbolic representations that follow a certain pattern.

This is not the place to attempt to answer Fodor and Pylyshyn's objections. In other work, we have examined a number of research endeavors in recent connectionist research that indicate ways in which connectionists might try to account for the productivity, systematicity, and inferential coherence Fodor and Pylyshyn claim is central to cognition (Bechtel & Abrahamsen, 1991). One approach, which we labelled *compatibilist,* is followed by researchers such as Touretzky & Hinton (1988), who have developed a connectionist network that implements a limited production system (a symbolic system in which rules, some of which may include variables, operate on symbol strings). While symbol processing is realized in this network, Touretzky and Hinton argue that the connectionist implementation provides important capacities to the system that are not realized in more traditional implementations of symbol systems.

A second approach, which we called *approximationist,* construes rules as offering only a very approximate account of behavior that can be more accurately characterized by networks. This approach is exemplified in Rumelhart and McClelland's past-tense acquisition network, which was introduced above. The past-tense network simulated a variety of detailed phenomena of past-tense acquisition which would be difficult and awkward, at best, to capture in a rule system; existing rule accounts only crudely approximate the complex body of human data. Although Rumelhart and

McClelland's past-tense network does not perfectly match the data either, improved networks should provide a better fit without becoming unwieldy. Another example can be found in the work of Servan-Schreiber, Cleeremans, and McClelland (1988), who used a more complex kind of connectionist model, based on a *recurrent network,* to simulate predictions of state transitions in a finite state grammar. The grammar itself is a symbolic device, but detailed predictions concerning the strings that it generates can be obtained without any explicit representation of rules.

Closely related to the approximationist approach is a third perspective according to which formal symbols of the kind needed to exhibit productivity and systematicity are learned first as external symbols, for example words that are spoken or written, or mathematical symbols that are written. What the network learns to do is operate upon these symbols without creating internal symbolic representations. Symbols as such play a limited role: they are the external medium upon which the system performs its activities. Internally, the system propagates activations across units; it does not represent or operate upon symbols. Rumelhart, Smolensky, McClelland, and Hinton, (1986) suggest that such an approach might explicate knowledge of arithmetic, and Bechtel and Abrahamsen (1991) developed a simulation in which a network learns to evaluate formal arguments and complete enthymemes. This raises the possibility that knowledge of mathematics or logic might rest initially in the ability to work with external symbols, and that this ability might be possessed by a network which lacked any internal symbols and rules for manipulating them.

The connectionist is, therefore, not without resources in attempting to answer Fodor and Pylyshyn. The point here, however, is not to show that the symbolic account is wrong, but to see how the connectionist approach could be taken by an eliminativist as a basis for repudiating the symbolic account, and thereby folk psychology as well. In particular, P. M. Churchland (1989) has argued that connectionism provides a direct challenge to the view that cognitive systems must encode symbolic representations internally and employ rules to operate on them. In his view, this makes it far less plausible that folk psychology can be vindicated by subsuming it within a scientific psychology.

More work is needed before eliminativists can rest their case, however. One difficulty is that actually establishing that connectionism offers an adequate framework for modeling cognition will require showing that its models of cognitive activity are superior to those advanced by symbolic theorists. To date, assessments of connectionism against human data have been exploratory, rather than definitive. For examples, see Gluck & Bower (1988) for comparison of the performance of connectionist models of categorization with human data, Pinker & Prince (1988) for an argument that Rumelhart & McClelland's past-tense model fails to account for critical human data; Massaro (1989), McClelland (1991) and Massaro & Cohen (1991), for a debate over the empirical adequacy of interactive networks as models of such phenomena as the word-superiority effect; and McCloskey & Cohen (1989) and Hetherington & Seidenberg (1989) for a debate over whether connectionist models suffer catastrophic interference upon learning new information that is not exhibited by humans. As the results of more detailed performance comparisons between networks and humans become available, we will be able to make more informed judgments of the success of connectionist networks as models of human cognition.

It is worth noting again, however, that the competitors for these connectionist models are generally not symbolic models such as those discussed by Fodor and Pylyshyn, but more sophisticated symbolic models that employ numeric parameters both on the rules and on the representations. Insofar as these models employ symbolic memories, they may be able to capture productivity and systematicity more easily than connectionist models. But, by affixing numeric parameters to symbolic representations, these representations cease to act like propositions; and by including numeric parameters in rules, the calculus of rules ceases to be comparable to symbolic logic. Since the framework of propositional attitudes is closely linked to that of propositions and logical operations on propositions, these more sophisticated symbolic models may not be any more congenial to folk psychology than connectionism. Thus, the challenge to folk psychology arises not just from connectionism, but also from recent developments in the symbolic tradition itself.

4. ANOTHER PERSPECTIVE ON FOLK PSYCHOLOGY

So far we have accepted the philosophical construction of folk psychology, according to which it is committed to (a) the analysis of psychological states in terms of propositional attitudes, (b) a form of propositional modularity, and (c) a view that propositional attitudes are causally productive internal states. If folk psychology is committed to these principles, then in fact it does seem to be a candidate for elimination by psychological accounts, such as connectionist accounts, which realize a different set of philosophical commitments. In this section, however, we will argue that folk psychology is not committed to any of these principles, then try to show how it plays a role that is still required even if we accept connectionist models, and it could in fact be quite compatible with connectionism or any other nonpropositional construal of the operations in the head. We will take the three supposed commitments in reverse order:

Causally Productive Internal States.   People sometimes do attribute causal efficacy to propositional attitudes. They explain that someone did something because they had a particular belief, or because they had a particular desire. We do not intend to question the causal attributions of folk psychology as some theorists have done (see Malcolm, 1984). But it is far from clear that, in advancing such causal explanations, ordinary people are positing specific mental structures. If one asks an ordinary person, one who is not in the grip of a theory, where the belief in a particular proposition is located, he or she is most likely to find the question quite odd. Beliefs in general are associated with the head, but in other epochs they have been associated more with the heart. Moreover, in granting that beliefs are somehow associated with the brain, one is not committed to treating the beliefs as discrete entities lodged in the brain that participated in causal interactions with states constituting other mental states. If a person says "I went to the store because I thought I needed milk," that person is not committed to treating the proposition *I needed milk* as an internal structure in the brain. It is hard to imagine an ordinary person concluding, on the basis of information about what transpires in the head, that he or she lacked such a belief. What might convince a person to give up this causal analysis, however, is a demonstration that he or she had good reason for knowing that milk was not needed, and the identification of another motive that better explains the behavior of going to the store. All that person is committed to, it seems, is that *he or she* is correctly described as believing that milk was needed and the truth of the counterfactual claim that had that belief been lacking, he or she would (other things being equal) not have gone to the store. If we can provide for these commitments without positing discrete belief states then we have captured all that ordinary folk claim when using folk idioms.

Propositional Modularity.   The core notion of propositional modularity is that the propositions that figure in propositional attitudes are discretely identifiable states such that it makes sense that a person may add one belief to his or her repertoire at a time, or do something for one reason and not another. There is a weak sense in which folk theory does seem to make these claims, but that sense does not support attributing full-fledged modularity to the folk understanding. It is certainly the case that people will speak of acquiring a new belief, although more commonly they will speak of acquiring a new piece of information, or new knowledge. For example, reading that Atlanta is directly south of Detroit, a person might say "I didn't know that before; you learn something new every day." But does that entail that the person holds to a fully modular view, and would differentiate what they just learned from the proposition *Detroit is north of Atlanta* or *Atlanta is not south of Pittsburgh?* Most people do not seem to possess such a fine taxonomy of beliefs, and would find it perverse to think that these were two new beliefs that they had also acquired. They will consider quite unrelated facts, such as that Detroit is north of Windsor, to be independent, but they will not impose the sort of fine taxonomy that is suggested by the differentiation of propositions in statements of propositional attitudes. Moreover, they will not impose the fine taxonomy suggested by the attitudes either. They may not distinguish between whether they hope something will be the case, or merely desire that it be the case. How it is that folk psychology can get along without such fine distinctions is something we will need to return to later, but here it is enough to point out that ordinary folks do not seem to impose a tight propositional modularity upon folk psychology.

Propositional Attitudes.   Finally, when ordinary people make use of folk psychology, they are not committed to the propositional attitude analysis according to which they are supposedly analyzing psychological states in terms of attitudes toward propositions. This does not mean that they will not sometimes say things like "I think that he will be late to work again" or "I doubt that they will win tonight," but they need not analyze this, as Russell did, as involving an attitude adopted towards a proposition. This is simply the idiom used to characterize beliefs and other mental states. Moreover, it is not the only idiom. Many verbs of folk psychology can only be forced into the propositional attitude framework with difficulty since they are naturally completed not with propositions, but with infinitives. For example, one might say "I hope to watch the movie" which is only awkwardly cast as "I hope that I will watch the movie." Others simply take noun phrases in the accusative. "I noticed her reflection in the mirror" might be translated into the orthodox idiom as "I noticed that her reflection was in the mirror," but it is arguable whether this says the same thing. Even verbs like *believes* are not always completed with propositional expressions. We might say "I believe the sign" which could be cast as "I believe that the sign is correct," but need not be.

This contention that folk psychology is not to be equated with propositional attitude psychology will be important in the analysis that follows, so it is worth focusing on it a bit further. Some of our most basic folk psychological idioms are ones reporting what we see or otherwise are sensibly aware of. These idioms most naturally take direct objects, not propositions: *She saw the statue, he noticed the dog, I heard the birds.* Sometimes these objects are modified by adjectives *(I heard the chirping birds)* or by prepositional phrases *(he noticed the dog at the junkyard).* These are arguably the most basic uses of perceptual verbs, with propositional attitude constructions *(I saw that the car had hit the telephone pole)* being far more complex and developed locutions. On the action side, our basic psychological vocabulary specifies particular actions someone might perform: *she ran to the mailbox, he chased the dog.* Here the action is specified in the verb. We also, though, describe intentions to act, but here the primary idiom is the infinitive: *the professor wanted to publish in the National Enquirer, the wolf wished to escape the cage, the child hoped to go to the circus.* Even when we turn to more central cognitive processes and characterize an agent's knowledge, we often invoke the infinitive construction and specify what the agent knows how to do: *the cat knows how to get out through the door, the mail carrier knows how to ward off dogs.* Before we acquiesce in the philosophical characterization of folk psychology in terms of propositional attitudes, we would do well to attend to these other constructions that figure in a major way in folk characterizations of people's mental lives.

It may seem that the above challenge to philosophical interpretations of folk psychology is a prelude to dismissing folk psychology, since it suggests that the idioms of folk psychology lack the precision we would expect of a scientific theory. If the folk theory is to be saved, it may seem that we must supply the precision required for it to have a proper ontology. Our intent, however, is quite different. It is to show that folk psychology plays a much different role than has been considered in most philosophical accounts. It is not committed to providing an internal account of mental processing but is used for a much different purpose. We can appreciate this when we take seriously another part of the folk idiom. Although people can say "I have the belief that it will rain" or "she has the desire that she have a new computer," the most common locution is to say "I believe it will rain" and "she desires a new computer." What is critical here is that the folk idiom seems to be viewed most naturally as characterizing the person's mental state, not as attributing certain mental possessions. We use the idiom "I believe it will rain" to report that one is cognizant of a certain possible fact and the idiom "She desires a new computer" to report on the goals that are guiding a person's behavior. If she desires a new computer, then her goal makes it more likely than it would be otherwise that she will buy a computer that satisfies certain criteria. We can even make the distinction between active and latent states. If she is actively desiring a new computer, then she likely will engage in planning actions designed to procure a new computer (which may simply involve informing her chairperson of her desire, or may involve checking out the specifications of a number of possible computers or writing grant applications so as to secure the needed funds).

The account of folk psychology we are proposing here is similar in some respects to that advanced by philosophical behaviorists. They too insisted that mentalistic verbs did not refer to internal states. But they advanced other tenets that we are not accepting. They sought to *analyze* mentalistic states in terms of dispositions in behavior. Some (e.g., Malcolm, 1984) then argued that there was a conceptual link between mentalistic states and behaviors such that beliefs and desires could not be construed as causes of behaviors (since then it would be logically impossible to be in the appropriate mental state and not exhibit the behavior). We accept neither of these contentions. We are certainly not proposing a conceptual connection between folk psychological idioms and behavior, and moreover, we are not advocating totally severing the folk account from the internal processing account. With respect to the possibility of a conceptual connection, many critics of philosophical behaviorism have argued that it is extremely difficult to specify any conceptual connection between folk idioms and behaviors since there are simply too many nuances in the folk idiom. For example, it is perfectly possible for someone who did not previously desire a new computer to still buy one. It seems plausible to say that the person was perfectly content and had no desire for a new computer until the prospect was raised. Moreover, even at the time she bought the new computer she might not have really desired it, but felt compelled to buy one. Difficulties such as these seem to provide sufficient grounds for not trying to analyze folk-psychological idioms in terms of behavioral dispositions.

Moreover, if a folk-psychological attribution is true, other claims about internal processing must also be true. One could only believe something if there were events *of some appropriate sort* in his or her brain that could encode information and make it available in the course of behavior. But this connection between folk psychology to an internal story is far weaker than that proposed in the philosophical analysis of folk psychology. To see this it may be useful to consider one way connectionists sometimes differentiate their endeavors from those of symbolic theorists. Rumelhart and McClelland sometimes speak of rule-like behavior, that is, behavior that accords with a rule, emerging from the operation of their networks without the behavior actually being produced by a rule. For example, in Rumelhart and McClelland (1986), they describe the past-tense network as generating behavior that conforms to the rules of the past-tense in English even though it does not encode these rules. When we say that the network knows the rules for forming the past tense of English verbs we are not saying that it has those rules explicitly encoded inside, but we are saying something about its internal organization, namely, that it is so configured that it can produce verb forms that conform to those rules. Similarly, even though there is no simple or explicit encoding of propositions in Ramsey et al.'s network, when we say that it knows the truth values of certain propositions, we are committed to it having an internal configuration which is sufficient for it to produce the truth values when queried. This network had a specific configuration, but the folk characterization is compatible with a number of other internal structures which would produce the same behavior.

A similar claim might be made about folk idioms more generally. While the use of a folk idiom to describe a system does not entail any *particular* claim about the internal configuration of the system, the internal state must still conform to certain requirements if those folk attributions are correct. If we say that a system *notices the dog chasing the squirrel,* then whatever goes on in the system must enable the system to conform to the expectations we form of a system which noticed such a fact. Likewise, if we attribute a desire to a system, then the internal operations of the system must make it likely to perform some of those activities which we associate with such a desire.

What then is the folk idiom doing? In the first place, it seems to be characterizing certain kinds of systems, not directly in terms of their internal structures, but in terms of how these systems relate to their environments. When we say that "a person knew that the brakes on the car were bad," we are saying that the person was so situated as to acquire that information about the world. Moreover, we are implying that if the person were responsible, he or she would not drive the car without first having the brakes repaired. If the person did nonetheless drive the car and had an accident, we would hold him or her responsible for the accident, whereas we would not hold someone who was not privy to the information that the brakes were bad responsible, or at least as responsible. Without going inside the system to determine how it is precisely configured, the folk idiom provides a means of reporting how that system is connected to its environment.

A similar story applies on the desire side. If the person desires to go hiking, then the person may arrange her activities in the world so as to go hiking. Through the folk idiom we are reporting on the person in virtue of his or her orientation to the outside world, what information he or she has about the outside world and how he or she is inclined to behave toward that world. (Note that the claim that a system with a certain sort of desire will tend to behave in certain ways is not to be treated as analytic. We are attributing a state to a system which will only manifest itself in particular actions depending on other states of the system, and there is no prospect of being able to enumerate all of these other possible states and thus constructing a behavioral specification of what it is to be in a certain folk psychological state.) This view advocated here is close to that put forward by Dennett (1978, 1987) when he speaks of adopting *the intentional stance* toward particular systems, but it differs in two respects. First, it is not committed to an instrumentalistic attitude toward these ascriptions (see Bechtel, 1985, 1988c) and, second, it does not endorse the homuncular program according to which one can analyze the capacities to behave in certain ways into the activities of homunculi which each perform a component task that enables the system to produce the overall behavior.

The contention that the function of folk psychology is to relate organisms to their environments is supported most clearly by those idioms of folk psychology that do not employ propositional attitudes. Perceptual verbs such as *see, hear,* and *notice* specify the object from which the organism is receiving information in a particular modality. Thus, they specify an informational contact between an organism and some aspect of its environment. What is seen, of course, need not be a stationary object (Gibson, 1966). One might see, for example, a train coming toward oneself. Similarly, verbs such as *desire* specify what activities a person is striving to perform in the environment. Finally, the idiom *knowing how* typically specifies actions a person is capable of performing. (It can also be used to specify actions we are able to perform mentally without acting on the environment, such as knowing how to add numbers in our heads, but this seems to be very much a derivative ability.)

The distinction between giving an internal account of a system and an account of a system that relates it to the world around it is not unique to the case of folk psychology. It is not uncommon for a physiologist to characterize cells, or tissues, or organs in terms of the functions they perform. For example, the liver performs the function of glycogenesis and a yeast cell performs fermentation. In offering this analysis, the theorist is not giving an internal account of what makes this possible, but is simply characterizing the capacities of the system in terms of what it will do in a certain environment: in the contexts where the body needs glucose, the liver will generate glucose, and in contexts where sugar is available in the environment, the yeast cell will ferment it and generate alcohol.

Notice, by the way, that these ascriptions are, just like the idioms of folk psychology, implicitly couched in terms of *ceteris paribus* clauses. The yeast cell will ferment the sugar only if it is in an oxygen-free environment, in a medium of the right pH, at an appropriate temperature, etc. Filling in these conditions may be nearly as difficult as filling in the conditions included in the *ceteris paribus* clauses attached to folk psychology. Moreover, there are ways of disrupting the normal operation of these systems that make the physiological account useless, just as there are ways of disrupting normal humans that make folk-psychological accounts useless. P. M. Churchland suggests we should reject folk-psychology because it fails to account for the performance of neurologically disordered humans. But similar failings have not lead us to reject physiological characterizations; it is difficult to see why we should apply different standards in the case of folk psychology.

Moreover, an account that relates a system to its environment is often just as important for the development of science as the internal account. While we can construct useful divisions between systems and the environments in which they operate, and treat these systems in part as if they were unaffected by their environments, in fact we are interested most often in those activities of the system which serve to meet the demands placed on the system by its environment.[3] Without looking to the nature of the interactions a system has with its environment, it is not clear which internal properties are to be given the most attention. Some of the things we can get a system to do in a laboratory environment may turn out to be experimental artifacts which do not inform us as to the significant activities that occur in the system when it is in its natural environment. Thus, if cognitive psychology is to be informative as to the cognitive processes occurring within the person, it must determine the interactions with the environment in which the system uses its information processing capacities. Gibson (1966) made this point in the context of vision: without knowing the sorts of visual information available to the organism we cannot adequately explain visual perception (see also Marr, 1982 and Neisser, 1975). Gibson argued that organisms receive dynamically changing visual information as they move and act and that it is this kind of visual information that should be emphasized in psychological accounts. He developed ways of describing that information that were tailored to the ecological tasks of the organism. Our contention here is that folk-psychological accounts that relate cognitive systems to their environments can play much the same role with respect to information processing cognitive models as Gibsonian ecological accounts can play for visual perception models.

Furthermore, despite their differences with Gibson, it is clear that cognitive modelers do make use of just such folk-psychological characterizations of the behavior of their systems in order to design and analyze their systems. Ramsey et al. set out to design a system that would learn the truth values of sentences. The task is phrased in terms of folk psychology. We evaluate their efforts in folk-psychological idioms as well: when they succeed, we say that their system *knows these truth values*. Perhaps even more importantly, connectionists characterize the interface of their systems with the world in folk-psychological terms, for example as processing information coded in propositions or sentences. Ramsey et al.'s system receives sentences as input (albeit encoded in a bit pattern) and generates truth values as outputs. Similarly, we have designed a network that is given logical arguments as inputs and generates names of their forms and judgments of their validity as outputs (see chapter 5 in Bechtel & Abrahamsen, 1991). Other networks are designed to recognize patterns. We might present them with a sensory pattern (hence, the input is not in propositional format), but the network will be able to categorize those inputs into categories which might be labeled by English words or other symbols. Thus, we certainly use the folk-psychological idiom to characterize the activities of networks, and to characterize their inputs and outputs propositionally. And there is good reason for doing this, for what we are providing by using the folk-psychological idiom is a characterization of how the network relates to its task environment.

It should be clear now that there is a role for folk psychology according to which it is not in competition with an internal information processing story and does not need to be vindicated by a propositional account of internal processing. It serves a different function, that of specifying the relation between a cognitive system and its environment.

In finishing this story we need to return to two uncompleted parts of our challenge to the philosophical treatment of folk psychology. First, we can now make clear how folk idioms could have a causal function and yet not refer to specific internal processes. It characterizes these functions in terms of how they facilitate the system's interactions with its environment. These idioms do characterize states of the cognitive system which are achieved by internal processes. These states may be states of whole systems, not of its parts, but it is necessary that whatever account of internal processes that is developed succeed in explaining how the system behaves in accord with the characterizations given in folk psychology. But it is not necessary that it do so by positing that there are distinct internal states corresponding to those identified in folk psychology. The causal story is simply giving a job description, which some internal process must satisfy.

The second unfinished task was to explain why folk idioms had the sort of looseness that we identified in rejecting propositional modularity. This looseness, however, is no different than that found in other disciplines which are concerned to relate systems to their environment. In characterizing the adaptiveness of a species to an environment in evolutionary biology, for example, one encounters the same sort of looseness. The specification of the niche need not be precise. It is assumed that there is a range of environments, including the actual one, in which the system is well adapted, and except in rare circumstances there is no need to specify this range exactly. Moreover, preoccupation with precision could obscure interesting facts such as the evolution of multiple traits serving roughly the same biological function. Folk-psychological talk is loose for exactly the same reason: there is not a sufficiently tight fit between biological organisms and their environment that we can specify exactly the set of features in the environment with which the system is capable of dealing, either cognitively or physiologically.

As we have characterized it here, folk psychology advances a theoretical account. It therefore is subject to revision. But we need to be clear what would motivate such a revision. The account would not be replaced by one that describes internal processing but by another account at the level at which folk psychology itself operates. The internal processing story, as it develops, might tend to support or oppose such revisions, but it is simply not itself a candidate for the replacement view since it is not equipped to do the job that folk psychology or any replacement must do, namely, relate the cognitive system to its environment. (See McCauley, this volume, pp.

63–81, for an argument that theory replacement has never been driven by developments at other levels of theorizing, but only by developments at the same level as the original theory.) Such a revision could come from developments, for example, in ecological psychology which provided us with a different account of perception and action than that employed in folk psychology, or from developments in social cognition which provided us with a different account of how we operate in social contexts. The reason these are plausible candidates for forcing revision or replacement of current folk psychology is that these research endeavors are devoted to characterizing the interaction of cognitive systems with their environment. If they provide us better tools for describing these interactions, then it makes sense to employ these tools for scientific purposes. It may not happen that ordinary folk will adopt the new framework, but an endeavor such as cognitive psychology would do well to use these accounts to characterize the behavior of systems whose internal operations it seeks to explain.

The possibility that folk psychology might be improved upon or replaced shows that it is a genuine theoretical account with important work to do. If no improvements were possible, that would support the contention that folk psychological claims were analytic. A genuine scientific theory typically provides only a partially correct account of the phenomena in its domain, and future inquiries generally lead to improved theories. The critical question is whether the revisions will involve repudiation of central components of the current theory and replacement by a new one, or whether they will involve modifications within the current framework. It seems entirely too early to answer this question with certainty. But the very fact that this is a question to be considered reveals that folk psychology is filling an important role in our overall scientific account.

5. HOW DID THE PROPOSITIONAL ATTITUDE STORY ARISE?

Having fulfilled the main agenda of this paper, which is to argue that connectionist models are not only not incompatible with folk psychology, but may even require it, we will conclude with a brief discussion of how we likely came to employ the propositional attitude model that has become the focus of the eliminativist's attack. Our contention is that the propositional attitude framework is not something we simply *read off* our own internal states. Rather, we have invented and learned to use the propositional attitude framework, both culturally and as individuals, because it provided a useful way of characterizing ourselves and other people.

In order to understand how the propositional attitude framework could be a learned device we would need to turn to literature on language development. This would take us considerably beyond the scope of this chapter. But the basic idea can be sketched. In the course of language development, children generally begin with single-word utterances and gradually develop the capacity to comprehend and produce complete sentences. Presumably sentences replaced one-word utterances in cultural evolution because of the usefulness of such sentences in representing information. These sentences can provide the propositions for use in propositional attitude expressions; what we need to understand is how an organism could come to adopt an *attitude* toward these propositions. As emphasized by Bates (1976), there is a distinction even in thc carly sentences a child learns between those which represent intentions or requests, where the conditions specified are not yet satisfied, and those that specify what is already the case. Here we have prototypes of the attitudes of belief and desire. What the child requires in order to be able to express propositional attitudes is to learn that there are actually a variety of different conditions under which sentences can be uttered, that these utterances reflect a variety of different attitudes upon the part of the user of the proposition, and that there are a variety of words that designate those attitudes. Some of these attitude words, however, are already in place from the acquisition of simple propositions, in which the attitude verbs took direct objects or infinitive constructions *(See the ball, I want to go to the park)*. What the child must learn is that these attitude expressions can now be directed at propositions themselves in order to characterize someone's utterance.

There are obviously major steps in this process of acquiring the propositional attitude idiom which a full developmental account would have to specify. Even without these details of acquisition, however, we can recognize that once acquired, the propositional attitude framework provides a powerful tool for characterizing mental states. Beyond using it to characterize people who have actually made utterances, we can extend it to characterize people who have not uttered a sentence. We can characterize a person as believing, hoping, desiring, doubting, fearing various propositions that we might imagine them uttering. The usefulness of such characterizations comes as an extension of the fact that knowing what someone says helps us to predict his or her future behavior or otherwise to understand the person's relation to an environment. Projecting what people would say were they to verbalize their mental states provides a device for predicting behavior when people do not verbalize their mental states.

What is distinctive about this account is that it construes the propositional attitude idiom as a learned linguistic medium for encoding information about people. It does not assume that the person who is characterized in terms of propositional attitudes actually had a proposition in mind and adopted an attitude toward it (although neither does it rule that out). Even in the case where someone does verbalize his or her mental state propositionally, it may be that the only proposition involved is the one the person actually uttered; there may not be an additional proposition as such encoded mentally which they translated into words. In the case in which we are describing someone's unverbalized mental state, the only proposition involved may be the one we use to report the mental state. Thus, we can use the propositional attitude framework to characterize nonverbal animals, such as cats and dogs, without having to suppose that they actually have attitudes towards propositions. The fact that we do not have to assume that we are characterizing actual propositions encoded in the organism, however, does not undercut the usefulness of propositional attitude discourse. Just as language provides an extremely powerful tool for representing features of the world, propositional attitudes provide a vehicle for understanding how people or other organisms relate to features of the world.

What we have offered here is a very brief sketch of how we could have acquired the use of propositional attitude idioms as a tool for describing others, and ultimately ourselves. If we treat the grammar of propositional attitudes literally, we may be misled into thinking that they necessitate a symbolic account of information processing according to which the cognitive system encodes propositions and manipulates them in accord with the logical principles we use in describing people's reasoning. But this is a mistake. The role for which propositional attitude idioms were developed is not in any way challenged by the possibility that a nonpropositional information processing system, such as a connectionist network, is the best medium for modeling our cognitive abilities. For that role is to characterize people in terms of their relations to their environment, not in terms of internal processing.

6. CONCLUSION

In this chapter we have argued that folk psychology is not directly threatened by connectionism or by any other account of internal processing, for it is not a competitor to them. Folk psychology represents a theory at a higher level, one that characterizes what organisms know about their environment and how they seek to act in their environment. Such a perspective is needed in order for connectionism to develop its account of what goes on in the organism, for it provides connectionism with a characterization of the tasks of acquiring information about its environment and coordinating actions in that environment that the network must perform. We have argued that while propositional attitudes provide one device through which folk psychology permits us to describe such information, it is not the most basic device and that philosophers would do well to consider some of the more basic locutions where the folk idioms do not employ propositions to represent information. Finally, we have offered a speculative sketch of how humans could have developed the propositional attitude framework for characterizing mental states even if our mental life does not involve adopting attitudes towards propositions.

FOOTNOTES

[1]This paper was partly written while the first author was a member of the Mind and Brain Research Group at the Zentrum für Interdiziplinäre Forschung, Universität Bielefeld. He is most grateful for the hospitality of the Universität Bielefeld and for the discussions with other participants in the research group. Both authors also thank Robert McCauley for very helpful comments on an earlier version of this chapter.

[2]There are some connectionist models, often referred to as *localist models,* which retain some characteristics of symbolic models. In these models, an individual node is treated as a representation, and its degree of activation encodes the support for that representation. These models are similar to semantic network models, which are generally construed as implementations of propositional systems, but use unlabeled rather than labeled connections. I shall focus on a different variety of connectionist models, *distributed models,* in which semantic interpretations are only assigned to patterns of activations over numerous units and in which different patterns of activations over the same units are interpreted differently. Distributed models cannot be so directly mapped onto symbolic models.

[3]Some components of these demands can be assessed by looking inside the system. If a system requires a source of energy to perform a particular task, we might first assess whether the animal already possesses the requisite energy supply, or must secure it, by an internal examination. But typically this is not how we proceed; rather, we assess the system's needs by evaluating its success in meeting the demands placed upon it by the environment.

18 The Connectionist Vindication of Folk Psychology

Gerard J. O'Brien
The University of Adelaide, South Australia

1. INTRODUCTION: FOLK PSYCHOLOGY AND THE COMPETING COMPUTATIONAL CONCEPTIONS OF MIND

The debate between the intentional realist and the intentional eliminativist has become all too familiar. On the one hand, the eliminativist argues that folk psychology "suffers explanatory failures on an epic scale . . . has been stagnant for at least twenty-five centuries, and [has categories which] appear (so far) to be incommensurable with or orthoganal to the categories of the background physical science whose long-term claim to explain human behaviour seems undeniable," and therefore "must be allowed a serious candidate for outright elimination" (Churchland, 1981, p. 76; reprinted in this volume, p. 49). While on the other, the realist argues that "the predictive adequacy of common sense psychology is beyond rational dispute"; that folk psychology displays the same *deductive structure* that is characteristic of explanation in real science; that the vocabulary of folk psychological explanation is actually *indispensable* because "we have no other way of describing our behaviours and their causes if we want our behaviours and their causes to be subsumed by any counterfactual-supporting generalisations that we know about"; and thus that beliefs, desires and the other folk psychological entities will find a secure place in the ontology of a mature cognitive theory of mind (Fodor, 1987, pp. 2–10; reprinted in this volume, pp. 222–229).[1]

But while the debate here is all too familiar, it is fair to say that the odds have for some time been stacked in the realist's favour. This is because the realist has been able to rely on the very substantial support of what until only very recently was generally considered the best available scientific account of cognition. This, of course, is the classical computational theory of mind.[2] For as Fodor has been pointing out for years, classicism lends itself towards a vindication of folk psychology because it demonstrates how there *can* be causally efficacious, semantically interpretable states akin to beliefs and desires instantiated in a physical mechanism in the first place (Fodor, 1987, pp. 16–21; reprinted in this volume, pp. 235–240).

Suddenly, however, the situation is not so clear cut. Classicism now has a very serious rival in the form of connectionism.[3] And according to at least one very influential account of the relationship that holds between connectionism and folk psychology—that of Ramsey, Stich and Garon (1990; reprinted in this volume)—the boot is now very much on the other foot. For Ramsey, Stich and Garon argue that connectionism is actually *incompatible* with folk psychology, and thus that if connectionism turns out to characterize accurately our cognition, then it will be the intentional eliminativist who will have the final say.[4]

Now in the interests of distributive justice it might be nice to let things go this way. Realists, we might say, have had a good run with classicism, so why not let eliminativists have their turn with connectionism? Unfortunately, philosophers of mind tend not to be interested in distributive justice, they tend to be interested in the truth. And as far as I can determine, the truth is that Ramsey, Stich and Garon are mistaken: connectionism and folk psychology are not incompatible; in fact, the two of them can get along together just fine. So whether one opts for classicism or connectionism, the odds remain stacked in the realist's favour.

Having made this claim, it will be the business of the rest of this chapter to defend it. But in doing so I will not directly confront the arguments that have been presented by Ramsey, Stich and Garon.[5] Rather, my general strategy will be to show that connectionism and folk-psychology are far from being incompatible, by showing that connectionism does have the resources to capture the distinctive properties of folk psychological entities. In fact it will be my central thesis that such are the resources of connectionism, that it may have the potential to provide an even more robust vindication of folk psychology than is afforded by the classical computational theory of mind.

That, at least, is the general strategy. What I propose to do in detail has a much narrower compass. Rather than set about showing that connectionism has the wherewithal to capture the distinctive properties of all the different folk-psychological entities (i.e., not just beliefs, desires, hopes, fears and so forth, but also perceptual experiences, mental images, pains and tickles, etc.), I will concentrate my discussion on what for connectionism might be considered a "tough case." The idea here is that if it can be shown that connectionism can do well with such a case, then it can be expected to do well period. But what is an appropriate tough case?

Well, in this context it is worth noting that even among philosophers and cognitive scientists who are reasonably fond of connectionism, doubts are sometimes expressed about the capacity of the connectionist framework to deal with the "higher-level" aspects of cognition.[6] So a tough case for connectionism would be a folk-psychological entity that does its work in the higher reaches of the cognitive hierarchy. And an obvious candidate here, I suggest, is the ubiquitous *belief;* for beliefs, unlike many other folk-psychological entities (e.g., perceptual experiences, mental images, pains and tickles), are taken by most realistically inclined philosophers to be essentially higher-level cognitive states.[7] What is more, Ramsey, Stich and Garon base their own eliminativist interpretation of connectionism primarily on the folk-psychology of belief. A doubly appropriate tough case, one might think.

However, even the folk-psychological phenomenon of belief is too broad for our current purposes. As the existing literature on the subject demonstrates, it really requires a book to do it justice (and going beyond belief requires at least a very long paper!). So in an effort to keep the subject within manageable proportions, I will restrict my discussion in this paper to the *semantic properties* of beliefs.[8] This restriction will prove useful in the longrun for a second reason, as it will eventually allow us to make contact (in the final section of the paper) with another important debate in which connectionists and classicists are currently embroiled.[9]

Having given this account of the strategy of the chapter, it is now time to get down to business. And the business will proceed in the following fashion. In the section that follows I will very briefly consider the semantic properties that our folk-psychological framework ascribes to beliefs. This examination will then form the testing ground on which, in Sections 3 and 4, the classical and connectionist theories of mind will be respectively assessed. The ultimate purpose of these two sections will be to demonstrate that while classicism can do a reasonable job of capturing the semantic properties of beliefs, connectionism has the potential to do even better.

2. FOLK PSYCHOLOGY AND THE CONTENT OF BELIEF

Beliefs, according to the folk, have semantic properties. They have semantic properties, roughly speaking, because according to common sense they typically *refer to* or are *about* something. We say, for example, that Paul believes that the coffee tastes bitter, or that Patricia believes that the coffee is in the cupboard behind the muesli. And both of these beliefs, which folk psychology ascribes to Paul and Patricia respectively, are about something that has an existence independently of these two individuals — namely, coffee.

Philosophers often describe this semantic fact about beliefs by saying that beliefs are *contentful*. To a first approximation, an entity is contentful, be it a psychological state or any other physical bit of the world, if it in some way refers to or represents another bit of the world, however concrete or abstract. And the content of a belief is taken to be that bit of the world that is specified by the "that" clause in statements of belief ascription. The content of Paul's belief, for example, is that *the coffee tastes bitter,* while that of Patricia's belief is that *the coffee is in the cupboard behind the muesli.*

But notice about these two beliefs, and about beliefs more generally, that while they are about something, they are not *just* about something. Paul's belief is not just about coffee; nor is Patricia's. There is more to them than this. Each of these beliefs, for instance, attributes a certain property to the bit of the world that it is about: a bitter taste on the one hand and a physical location on the other. So we can certainly elaborate on the story we have given so far. We can say, for example, that according to our folk-psychological framework, beliefs typically ascribe properties to or describe relations between the bits of the world that they are about.

But if this is the case, then belief contents cannot be monolithic, they must be composed of parts. There must be a part of the belief content that refers to the bit of the world involved, and there must also be at least one other part of the belief content that refers to the property or relation that is ascribed or described. The upshot of all of this, of course, is that beliefs have *complex* contents: any particular belief must be composed of more simple constituents. And these more simple constituents are themselves individually contentful, as properties and relations also refer, at least in some sense, to bits of the world.

While much more can be said about the semantic properties that the folk attribute to beliefs (it will in fact be necessary to further finesse our account later in the piece), this is as far as our examination need go for the moment. For we have enough in hand already to turn to the task of assessing on this basis the relative merits of the two computational frameworks at issue. First up is the classical computational theory of mind.

3. CLASSICISM AND THE CONTENT OF BELIEF

On the typical classical account of belief, and I have in mind here Fodor's Representational Theory of Mind and its natural language variants,[10] beliefs are construed as certain computational relations that organisms bear towards mental representations. These mental representations, according to classicism, are language-like in the sense that they are taken to admit of a combinatorial syntax and semantics. This means, first, that complex mental representations are syntactic molecules that are constructed by concatenating syntactic atoms. And it means, second, that the semantic content of a complex mental representation is determined by the discrete semantic contents of the syntactic atoms from which it is composed, together with the manner in which these atoms are concatenated (i.e., together with the complex representation's "grammatical" structure).

Given this account of the content of mental representations, it is not surprising that many philosophers feel that classicism can provide a strong vindication of folk psychology. For with its commitment to combinatorial syntax and semantics, the classical framework would appear to be ideally placed to capture the folk-psychological account of belief content. Take, for example, Paul's belief that *the coffee tastes bitter*. This belief, we saw, has a certain semantic compositionality. Classicism can account for this compositionality by identifying the belief with the tokening of a complex mental symbol whose constituents include representations of the coffee, of tasting, and of bitterness. And this nicely accords with the common sense view.

Attractive though the classical account is, however, it is beset by a well-known problem. The problem arises in the following way. Compare Paul's belief above with Patricia's belief that *the coffee is in the cupboard behind the muesli*. On the classical account this belief is to be identified with the tokening of a complex mental representation whose atomic constituents include representations of the coffee, the cupboard, the muesli and the relation of behindness. And the content of this mental representation is taken to be compositionally determined by the contents of these atomic constituents. But this is where the trouble begins. For notice that both of these classical mental representations have a representation of COFFEE amongst their atomic constituents.[11] And from a classical point of view, it might be expected that these two atoms, given that they both refer to the same kind of thing in the world, are tokens of the same representation type. But they cannot be. For the semantic content of COFFEE in the representation of Paul's belief is quite distinct from the content of COFFEE in the representation of Patricia's belief. The former constituent refers to coffee-as-a-drink, while the latter refers to coffee-as-granules-in-a-container. And since these COFFEE representations have different contents, they cannot on the classical account be tokens of the same representation type. The classicist cannot say, for instance, that they are tokens of the same general representation type which attain slightly different contents as a result of the different "grammatical" roles they play in the overall constituent structure of their respective representations, because both COFFEE constituents form the subject noun of the complex representations in which they are embedded. Nor can the classicist claim, for that matter, that they are tokens of the same general representation type which attain slightly different contents merely as a result of the context in which they are embedded, because on the classical account it is the semantic content of the atoms which determines the semantic content of the molecules, not the reverse.

The classicist can respond to this problem in one of two ways. The first way is to bite the bullet and accept that the COFFEE atoms in the representations of these two beliefs do indeed each belong to a different representation type: $COFFEE_1$ and $COFFEE_2$, one might say. There are, however, real problems associated with this response. It could turn out, for example, that in order to account for subtle variations in content across different contexts, the classicist must postulate a different COFFEE representation type for every different belief that we hold about coffee. Such a position, therefore, begins to look implausible, both from a computational perspective and from a folk-psychological perspective. It is implausible from the computational perspective because as one requires an almost unlimited number of distinct representation types, the generality of these types is lost (i.e., rather than being atoms that can form a constituent part of a large number of complex molecules, these representational types only have a very limited application). And it is implausible from the folk-psychological perspective, because the obvious semantic commonality between closely related constituents, such as the two different *coffee* contents here, is similarly lost (or at least, is not *naturally* captured).

The second way the classicist might respond here is to claim that what we have been assuming is an atomic representation of the content *coffee* in each belief, is actually in and of itself a complex representation which decomposes to something like COFFEE DRINK in the one case, and COFFEE GRANULES in the other. That is, because our initial analysis was based on the verbal expression of these two belief contents, and because these verbal expressions economically suppress all the details, we failed to elicit all the atomic constituents involved. Once our analysis is properly fleshed out, we will find that the difference in the *coffee* contents across these two beliefs is actually attributable to the different complex representations with which these contents are to be identified. The advantage of this second response, of course, is that it preserves the intuition that while the *coffee* contents are certainly different across these two beliefs, there is still something that they have in common. What they have in common, according to this response, is the atomic representation type COFFEE. Where they differ is that this representation type is concatenated with the atomic representation type DRINK in one belief, and the atomic representation type GRANULES in the other.

Stronger though this second response certainly is, it does not prove entirely satisfactory. To see this, compare Paul's belief that *the coffee tastes bitter* with Steven's belief that *the coffee stained his trousers*. The *coffee* constituent in each of these beliefs refers to the drink, not to the granules. On the preceding analysis, therefore, *coffee* in each of these beliefs is to be identified with the complex representation type COFFEE DRINK. Yet, while it may not be as marked as before, the content of *coffee* across these two beliefs differs. If we were to unpack this difference, we would say that *coffee* in the first belief refers to something like coffee-as-a-drink-that-is-actually-drunk, while *coffee* in the second refers to something like coffee-as-a-dark-coloured-liquid-that-can-be-spilled, or some such.

Now, of course, the classicist may object to my analysis by claiming that the requisite decomposition of *coffee* in the second belief is not COFFEE DRINK, but something like COFFEE DARK SPILLABLE LIQUID, and it is this that explains the difference in semantic content. The idea here, of course, is that one can always finesse these decompositions in order to achieve the right result in the end. But I think this kind of response is open to the same two kinds of objections as before.

On the one hand, the position begins to look implausible from the computational perspective because in order to capture the subtle differences in the content of *coffee* across different contexts, the decompositions will need to become extremely fine-grained and long-winded. What we commonsensically verbally express as the atom 'coffee' across these different contexts will actually be identified, at the level of mental representation, with a great number of different complex molecules. And all of the individual "surface" constituents of belief contents can be expected to require this kind of decomposition; each will require its own entourage of complex mental representations. The result is a system that starts to look unwieldy and, given the computational gymnastics that would appear to be required, perhaps even unworkable.

On the other hand, and perhaps more importantly, the position begins to look implausible from the folk-psychological perspective because the whole approach seems wrong-headed. This is because our discussion to this point seems to suggest — and this is where our earlier account comes in for some finessing — that while belief contents are complex in that they are composed of contentful parts, the content of each of these parts is not entirely fixed beforehand, but seems to be partially determined by the *context* in which it is embedded. That is, in addition to the more straightforward compositional mapping of constituent contents onto particular contexts, there seems to be a reverse mapping of contexts onto constituent contents. From this common sense perspective, then, the classical approach, in attempting to capture the variations in content across different contexts by "building up" the content of the individual surface constituents "from the inside," seems to have got it backwards.

My general feeling about this, and a feeling that I think is shared by many people, is that classicism, precisely because it is wedded to the divide and conquer approach of its particular brand of combinatorial semantics, is a fairly blunt instrument with which to delineate the subtleties of mental content. For the point is that if we are to develop a computational account of mind that does real justice to the insights of folk psychology, then this computational framework must be capable of dealing with both the *compositionality* of belief contents, the fact that beliefs are composed of contentful constituents, and the *context-sensitivity* of these contentful constituents, the fact that the constituents of beliefs have contents which are partially determined by the context in which they are embedded. It must be capable, in other words, of blending a good degree of semantic discreteness with a certain amount of what we might call semantic holism. But classicism, while it is clearly capable of fulfilling the first of these requirements, is not so clearly capable of fulfilling the second.

As a consequence of this, and in spite of all the support that it has given them in recent times, the folk may in the longrun find classicism unsatisfactory. Given this possibility, the question that we must now go on to consider is whether they would be wise to jump onto the connectionist bandwagon instead.

4. CONNECTIONISM AND THE CONTENT OF BELIEF

4.1 Connectionist Mental Representations

It is open to the connectionist, I take it, to make the same general claim about beliefs as that made by the classicist. That is, the connectionist can claim that beliefs are certain relations that organisms bear towards mental representations. One difference between these two computational conceptions of mind immediately arises, however, when we come to consider the nature of connectionist mental representations.

The story to be told here, however, is complicated by the fact that we need to distinguish between what I will call *explicit* and *implicit* representations in connectionist systems. An item of information is taken to be *explicitly* represented in a connectionist system at time t if and only if a pattern of activation correlated with that item of information is generated in a network or networks of the system at time t. A pattern of activation is generated in a network whenever the network is exposed to an input array over its input units, this pattern being made up of the individual activation values of a large subset of the processing units that comprise the network. In this way, the activation pattern exists as a physically isolable state of a connectionist system, and thus even though it is distributed across a large number of individual processing units it can sustain a discrete semantic interpretation.

But these explicit activation patterns are only transient states of connectionist networks; any new input to the network can immediately bring about their obliteration. So information cannot be *stored* in connectionist systems in this explicit fashion. Associated with these activation patterns, however, are network *dispositions* which do not have this ephemerality, and thus which constitute the manner of information storage in connectionist systems. An activation pattern disposition is perhaps best described as a particular configuration of a network's connectivity matrix (i.e., the pattern of unit connectivity of the network together with the weightings on the connections between these units) which causally determines that the explicit activation pattern in question is generated in the network in response to a specific input. It is these activation pattern dispositions, as distinct from the explicit activation patterns themselves, which constitute the *implicit* representations of connectionist systems.

I do use the term *implicit* here with some trepidation, however, as this term is employed in a very different fashion in relation to the classical computational framework. On the classical account, an item of information is typically said to be implicitly represented in a cognitive system if it is entailed by the information that is explicitly represented (see, for example, Dennett, 1982, p. 216). But this is emphatically not what is meant by the implicit representation of information by activation pattern dispositions in connectionist systems. In this latter case the implicitly represented items of information, like the explicit representations, are actually *physically encoded* by the system (and, what is more, are *causally active* in the system).

But it ought perhaps be noted that the nature of the physical encodement of these implicit representations is really quite unusual. For unlike their explicit counterparts, they are not encoded in a physically isolable manner. That is, one cannot point to the "bit" of a network's connectivity matrix which stores the disposition to generate a specific activation pattern. This is because any single connectivity matrix typically stores a number of different such activation pattern dispositions (a feature of connectionist networks which is sometimes called *superpositional* storage). It is primarily for this reason that I refer to these activation patterns dispositions as *implicit* representations, as they lack the explicitness of the activation patterns themselves.[12]

When we turn to consider the content of connectionist mental representations, it is quite commonplace to hear it said that these representations are *semantically holistic*. By this it is meant that while any complex connectionist representation can be thought of as in some sense admitting of constituent parts — localised subpatterns among the global distributed pattern of activation, say — the semantic content of this representation is not compositionally determined by the discrete contents of these constituent parts. This is because in isolation the constituent parts of a connectionist representation, it is claimed, have no discrete semantic properties whatsoever. These parts, it is said, are wholly context-dependent: it is only in the context of a complex representation that they accrue any content in the first place.

Paul Smolensky is one theorist who, at least on one plausible reading of his work, would appear to hold this view. He argues, for instance, that while connectionist representations can be thought to have compositional structure, they only have this structure in an "*approximate* sense."[13] But this account of the compositionality of connectionist representations has its problems. If the constituent parts of connectionist representations have no content in isolation from their embedding context, one is entitled to question whether they can be viewed as *genuinely* contentful constituents in the first place. That is, while we might applaud the context-sensitivity that these connectionist representations obviously possess, we might wonder whether this has been achieved only at the expense of any real compositionality.

Smolensky's account of the compositionality of connectionist representations has also been roundly criticized along similar lines in a recent paper by Fodor and McLaughlin (1990). Fodor and McLaughlin point out that Smolensky's account of compositionality here is intended to be a counter to Fodor and Pylyshyn's (1988) claim that, because connectionist representations lack constituent structure, the connectionist approach to cognition cannot explain the systematicity of thought.[14] But Fodor and McLaughlin argue that Smolensky's response here is inadequate precisely because the compositionality that he delineates is merely superficial. They claim that if connectionist representations have constituents that are entirely context-dependent, then there is no way that these constituents can be thought to fill roles in a range of different structures. And according to Fodor and McLaughlin, the systematicity of thought turns on this. It requires, they think, the constituents of any particular mental representation to possess enough context-*in*dependence to be capable of participating in a number of different mental representations.

On this account of the content of connectionist mental representations, then, it would seem that connectionism suffers from exactly the reverse of the problem that we earlier diagnosed in classicism. That is, while connectionism may be able to capture the context-sensitivity of belief contents, it appears not to be capable of capturing their compositional structure. So connectionism, it might be concluded, cannot possibly fare any better than classicism in dealing with the content of belief, and, given the importance of compositionality in the folk-psychological scheme of things, quite possibly fares a lot worse. In fact, we might even go as far as suggesting that on this view of things, connectionism does indeed appear to be incompatible with folk psychology.

4.2 The Compositionality of Connectionist Representations

All is not lost, however. For as far as I can see, we have been landed with this problem simply through accepting what in truth is a needlessly simplistic account of the content of connectionist mental representations. In connectionism we surely have the resources to fashion an account which is a good deal more sophisticated than the one we have just examined.

We might begin this task by stepping back to consider why certain theorists feel compelled to claim that connectionist representations are semantically holistic in the first place. The reason, I take it, is the familiar one that the isolated activity of any individual processing unit in a connectionist network does not admit of a discrete semantic interpretation. This must be the case if the system is to operate with genuinely *distributed* representations: the representations must be distributed across a good proportion of the units in the network. This means that the smallest unit of discrete semantic value in a connectionist system is the network activation pattern.[15]

But surely we can accept this point and yet still hold that it is possible to construct *complex* representations in connectionist systems that are not globally semantically holistic in this fashion. There are a number of options that are open to us here, but one rather obvious suggestion is that these complex representations can be generated in connectionist systems by the cooperative activity of a number of *distinct* networks, each one of which contributes a constituent part. On this view of things, complex connectionist representations are decomposable into genuinely contentful constituents, because each constituent is itself the product of holistic activity across an individual connectionist network.[16]

It is important to stress that what is envisaged here is that complex connectionist representations are generated by the *cooperative* activity of these constituent networks. That is, while each network can be considered as a distinct processing facility in its own right, it is envisaged that there would be sufficient communicative connections between the networks involved such that the computational process by which the global activation pattern for the complex representation is generated is heavily *interactive*. This will have the effect of so modifying the processing activity in each of these networks, to an extent that would be determined by the weight that is placed on these internetwork communications, that the final activation pattern generated therein will show the marks of the activation patterns that are generated in the other constituent networks. In other words, the constituent parts of the complex representation are partly tailor-made on the fly, so to speak, to meet the particular exigencies of the current processing demands.

The upshot of this interactive process, then, is that while the networks that are implicated each contribute a discrete content to the complex representation that is produced, each of these constituent contents will have been shaped to suit the context in which it is embedded. Take, for example, Paul's belief that *the coffee tastes bitter*. On the connectionist account that I am putting forward, we might conjecture that this belief content is generated in the one processing episode across a number of distinct connectionist networks in Paul's brain, which at the very least contribute representations of the coffee, of tasting, and of bitterness. But because these constituent representations are generated in an interactive process, each of them will have been shaped for *this* particular context. This will mean, for example, that the COFFEE constituent in the connectionist mental representation of Paul's belief will have a different activation pattern to that of the COFFEE constituent in the connectionist representation of either Patricia's belief that *the coffee is in the cupboard behind the muesli* or Steven's belief that *the coffee stained his trousers*.

But this is not the end of the story. For while these three constituent *coffee* contents are certainly different, they are nonetheless closely related — they are more closely related, for example, than are the *coffee* and *muesli* contents in Patricia's belief. And the account of the compositionality of connectionist representations here can provide a very natural explanation of such semantic relations. As is well-known, the activation patterns of connectionist networks can be represented as n-placed vectors, where n is the number of activation values which comprise the pattern in question. This means that these activation patterns can be mapped as points in some hyperdimensional activation space. Consequently, the three COFFEE constituents in the representations of Paul's, Patricia's and Steven's beliefs respectively, can be plotted as three distinct points in this activation space. And all we need to suppose, in order to capture the semantic relatedness of these three constituents, is that these points cluster in the same *region* of this hyperdimensional space. For activation patterns which occupy the same region of activation space have similar causal powers in connectionist systems. And constituents that are identified with activation patterns which have similar causal powers, one is inclined to think, must have similar contents.[17]

The story need not end here, either. Once we consider all of the other subtlely different *coffee* contents that issue from our different coffee beliefs, we define a dense cluster in this activation hyperspace. And this might lead us to suggest that this cluster represents our *concept* of coffee. That is, our concept of coffee consists of a dense collection of subtlely different *coffee* contents each one of which is distilled from the various different beliefs that we hold about coffee. Accordingly, our concept of coffee is not identifiable with one single mental representation, but with a cluster of COFFEE representations, each of which reflects the context in which it has arisen. This, I suggest, also tallies with our own experience in this regard. If I try to think of coffee on its own, I invariably represent it to myself in a particular context – as a drink, as granules, or even, and this is significant, as a linguistic entity. What is more, the account I have sketched here has an obvious affinity with what in the cognitive psychological literature is termed the *exemplar* theory of concept possession, whereby concepts are taken to be defined not in the classical manner by a set of necessary and sufficient features, but simply by the representation of a number of exemplar instances.[18]

But this last is something of a digression. To get back to the main theme, it would seem that connectionism may after all have the wherewithal to account for the compositionality of belief contents. We need only suppose that *complex* connectionist mental representations are not semantically holistic to the extent that is commonly assumed. And crucially, the compositionality that is achieved here need not be at the expense of context-sensitivity, as we have seen. Consequently, connectionism might be capable of blending semantic discreteness and semantic holism in just the manner that folk psychology requires.

Finally, though somewhat obliquely to our purposes here, the account of the compositionality of connectionist representations that has been offered here may also form the basis of a more convincing response to the challenge that has been posed by Fodor and Pylyshyn (1988). Fodor and Pylyshyn have challenged connectionists, remember, to come up with an account of connectionist mental representations, and of the processing of these representations, which can explain the systematicity of thought. We saw earlier that Smolensky's solution appears inadequate because it fails to generate genuinely contentful constituents – constituents that are contentful independently of the context in which they occur, and thus constituents that can participate in a range of different mental representations. But it is precisely the strength of the account that I am advocating that the constituents of connectionist mental representations are context-independent to this extent. There is some reason to think, therefore, that this account may be able to do for the systematicity of thought what I have suggested it can do for the content of belief.

This mention of Fodor and Pylyshyn's challenge to connectionists, however, may bring to the minds of some readers an objection to the proposal that I have been outlining. The objection goes like this. The account of the compositionality of connectionist representations that has been offered here is unsatisfactory precisely because it is not an account of *connectionist* representation at all. Rather, it amounts to nothing more than a novel connectionist *implementation* of a classical symbol system. This is the case, it might be thought, because while the manner in which complex representations are generated owes much to the novel processing that connectionist systems can provide, the end result is nonetheless a representation whose content is a compositional function of its syntactically distinct, contentful constituents. And this, it might be concluded, is all that classicism demands.

This indeed is a serious objection. If it can be sustained then we are back to square one — back that is to the position of connectionism being unable, as a genuinely *cognitive* architecture, to account for the compositionality of belief contents. And this means, of course, that we are back with the spectre of "if connectionism (as cognitive architecture), then eliminativism."[19]

As far as I can see, however, such an objection appears persuasive only if we accept the assumption that a genuinely compositional complex representation in *any* computational model constitutes a classical symbol structure. In other words, the objection appears persuasive only if we accept the assumption that it is the *distinguishing* mark of classical computational models — the mark, that is, which distinguishes them from, for example, connectionist computational models — that their representations evince a genuine compositionality.[20] But should we accept this assumption?

I realize that to pose this question is to open a can of worms. For there are about as many different conceptions of the distinction between classicism and connectionism in the literature as there are authors willing to state their points of view.[21] But while I thus cannot hope to do this question any justice in such short compass here, I will, however, wind up the chapter by briefly defending the following claim. Connectionist systems that employ genuinely compositional representations do not merely implement classical symbol systems, because it is not the compositionality or otherwise of their representations that at the fundamental level divides these two computational frameworks. What fundamentally divides these two frameworks is that while classical models are properly characterized as *digital* computational systems, connectionist models are not. Instead, connectionist models are *analog* computational systems. And this makes all the difference.[22]

4.3 Digitality and Analogicity

A computational model is digital (or analog) if it satisfies two (complementary) conditions. First, the representational medium that the model employs must itself be digital (or analog). And second, certain specifiable aspects of model's causal operation must depend on the digital (or analog) properties of its representational medium. Let's take each of these in turn.[23]

A representational medium is digital or analog depending on the way in which representational values are mapped onto the physical magnitudes[24] that comprise the representational substrate. Baldly put, a representational medium is *analog* if the representational values are mapped onto the *primitive properties* of the physical magnitudes that comprise the representational medium, while it is *digital* if the representational values involved are mapped onto these physical magnitudes according to some *step function*.

Consider the following example adapted from David Lewis (1971, p. 323). Say our representational substrate, in a certain computer, comprises the voltages $v_0, \ldots, v_{35}$ between 36 specified pairs of wires. If we decide to map the digit 1 onto each positive voltage and the digit 0 onto each negative voltage in this substrate, we specify a digital representation medium. But note that it is not the *binary* system of representational values that is the determining factor here. The crucial point is that these binary values have been mapped onto the underlying physical magnitudes (in this case, voltages) by a step function—a function that only pays attention to arbitrarily specified, and therefore "higher-level," properties of the physical magnitudes at issue (in this case, whether the voltages have positive or negative values). In contrast, if we decide to map our representational values onto the primitive properties of these voltages—in such a fashion, that is, that any variation in the value of any one of these voltages would ipso facto be a variation in representational content—then we specify an analog representational medium. The crucial point about this latter case is that we are *directly* using the physical magnitudes themselves (in this case, voltages) as our representational medium, rather than defining some arbitrary representational medium over these physical magnitudes.

It is not enough, in order to specify a digital (or analog) computational model, to employ an a digital (or analog) representational medium, however. Zenon Pylyshyn, for example, asks us to consider "a digital computer that (perhaps by using a digital-to-analog converter to convert each newly computed number to a voltage) represents all its intermediate results in the form of voltages and displays then on a voltmeter" (1984, p. 202). Pylyshyn points out that in such a case, although the computer employs an analog representational medium, it actually operates digitally. This leads him to conclude:

> For the process, as opposed to the representation alone, to qualify as analog, the value of the property doing the representing must play the right causal role in the functioning of the system. . . . There is little point in calling something an analog process unless certain specifiable aspects of the system's operation are found to depend on its being analog, that is, on particular analog properties of the medium used for the encoding. (1984, p. 202)

Clearly, the same applies, *mutatis mutandis,* for processes to qualify as digital. So in general we can say that in order for a model to be properly characterized as a digital (or analog) computational system, not only must it employ a digital (or analog) representational medium, but certain aspects of its causal operation must depend on the digital (or analog) properties of its representational medium.

Classical models of cognition, because they derive from the computational theory that underpins the operation of general-purpose digital computers, clearly satisfy the two conditions on digitality, and are thus properly characterized as digital computational systems. But what about connectionist models? Are these digital or analog computational systems?

In coming to an answer to this question, we must first examine the manner in which connectionist systems use the physical magnitudes that comprise their representational substrate. But this is not as straightforward as it initially looks. For a quick glance at the literature might lead one to conclude that some current connectionist models employ a digital representational medium (because they employ *binary* processing units, which appear to use the physical magnitudes of their representational substrate — i.e., the activation levels of the processing units — in a digital fashion) while others employ an analog representational medium (because they employ *continuously valued* processing units, which in contrast seem to use these same physical magnitudes analogically).[25] But such a conclusion would be a mistake. When assessing the representational properties of connectionist models, one must not only consider what I have termed the *explicit* representations of these systems (i.e., activation patterns), one must also consider what I have termed the *implicit* representations of these systems (i.e., configurations of connectivity matrices). And while the former representations are mapped onto the physical magnitudes that comprise their representational substrate both digitally and analogically, the latter representations are mapped onto the physical magnitudes that comprise their representational substrate (i.e., connection weights) in a wholly analogical fashion (as connection weights, in all current connectionist models, are continuously valued). Given this, and given the primacy of implicit representations in the causal operation of connectionist networks (to be discussed shortly), it is more accurate, I suggest, to view all current connectionist models, even those that recruit binary processing units, as employing a predominantly analog representational medium.

The situation is a lot clearer when we turn to consider whether connectionist systems satisfy the second condition on analogicity — namely, whether certain specifiable aspects of the causal operation of these systems depend on the analog nature of the representational medium they employ. For connectionist systems operate by transforming patterns of activity over their network input units into patterns of activity over their network output units. And in large measure, this transformational process causally depends on the configuration of the network connection weights involved. In other words, the causal operation of connectionist networks is predominantly determined by the implicit representations that these networks encode. Given this, and given that the implicit representations of connectionist systems are analogically mapped onto their representational substrate, it follows that the causal operation of connectionist models does indeed significantly depend on the particular properties of their analog representational medium.

In short, then, connectionist models are properly characterisable as analog computational systems. And this sets them apart at a fundamental level from classical models. It is, for instance, precisely because connectionist models are analog systems that they naturally manifest many attractive cognitive properties (such as content-addressable memory, flexible generalisation, and graceful degradation) that are so difficult to realize in classical computational models. It is also because of their analogicity that connectionist models are capable of displaying the same "shadings" and "blendings" of meaning that are common in human linguistic performance.[26] And, perhaps most pertinently, it is because of their analogicity that connectionist models have the representational flexibility to naturally capture the context-sensitivity of the constituent contents of complex mental representations.

Furthermore, and to bring us back to the purpose behind our excursus here, because connectionist models are fundamentally different to classical models in this way, they cannot be viewed as merely implementing classical symbol systems when they instantiate genuinely compositional complex representations.[27] The assumption that they can, the assumption on which the earlier objection is based, is simply mistaken. And given that this assumption is mistaken, the objection which feeds off it falls away.

4.4 Conclusion

To conclude, then, we can say that connectionism, at least insofar as the content of belief is concerned, is far from being incompatible with folk psychology. In fact, if anything, connectionism has the potential to provide a more robust vindication of our folk-psychological framework than can be afforded by classicism. For we saw that classicism is a blunt tool with which to delineate the subtleties of mental content. Connectionism, with its ability to fashion representations for the contexts in which they appear, would appear to be a more appropriately delicate instrument. Thus the folk need not fear the approach of the connectionist bandwagon. Nor need they fear the possibility of overcrowding if they do decide to hitch a ride—there will be plenty of seats left vacant by alighting eliminativists.

FOOTNOTES

[1]In describing the debate between intentional realists and intentional eliminativists in terms of the existence or not of cognitive states akin to beliefs, desires, and so forth, I am clearly

opting for what Radu Bogdan has recently termed the *realist* construal of our folk psychological framework (1988). This contrasts with other construals of folk psychology (such as Dan Dennett's instrumentalist story (1981; reprinted in this volume, pp. 121–143)) which are nonempirical in the sense that they do not take folk psychological kinds to refer to real, instantiable, cognitive entities. In this I concur with Horgan and Woodward (1985, p. 199; reprinted in this volume, p. 146) when they remark, first, that folk psychology seeks to provide genuine causal explanations of our behaviour, and second, that it is only a realist construal which can explain this feature of our folk psychological framework.

[2]Generally speaking, the "classical" computational theory of mind (or just "classicism") is what until very recently was simply called the "computational theory of mind." The additional adjectival element is now employed to distinguish this computational conception of mind from the *connectionist* conception of mind. (The implication of this terminological distinction, by the way, is that there is some principled distinction *within* the general computationalist paradigm that sets connectionism apart from classicism. Exactly what this distinction amounts to, however, is something of a contentious issue in the field. I have my own go at saying how I think this distinction ought to be unpacked later in the piece – see Section 4.3.)

[3]For purposes of this chapter I will be assuming some knowledge of connectionist theory. For a comprehensive introduction to connectionism, see Rumelhart and McClelland, 1986, and McClelland and Rumelhart, 1986.

[4]In fact, Ramsey, Stich and Garon's eliminativist interpretation of connectionism is explicitly restricted to those connectionist models that employ a *distributed,* rather than *localist,* form of representation (1990, Section 4; reprinted in this volume). In all of what follows, therefore, I shall concern myself with connectionist models only insofar as they employ distributed representations. (For an account of the nature of localist representations in connectionist systems, see Feldman and Ballard, 1982.)

[5]In fact, I have directly confronted Ramsey, Stich and Garon's eliminativist interpretation of connectionism elsewhere (1990).

[6]The thought here is that while connectionist models look attractive in relation to what are sometimes seen as the more *peripheral* aspects of cognition (e.g., perceptual processing, image processing, sensorimotor coordination, and so forth), it is not immediately obvious that such models will be capable of dealing with more sophisticated cognitive tasks (such as reasoning and problem solving). This kind of sentiment can be found expressed in a number of places. For a taste, see Gardner, 1985; Derthick and Plant, 1986; and Clark, 1989.

[7]In Fodor's folk-psychologically influenced taxonomy of mind, for instance, belief-fixation is one of the primary tasks of what Fodor terms "central systems" – the systems responsible for higher cognitive processes in Fodor's scheme of things (1983).

[8]Part of the reason for this particular restriction is that while beliefs have, in addition to their semantic properties, interesting causal properties, I have examined connectionism in relation to the latter in some detail elsewhere (1990). In that paper, in something of a parallel exercise to that currently being undertaken here, I argue that connectionism has the potential to provide a more folk-psychologically realistic account of the causal dynamics of beliefs and desires than can be provided by classicism.

[9]This is the question of whether or not connectionism has the resources to deal with the so-called "systematicity of thought." See, for example, Fodor and Pylyshyn, 1988; Smolensky, 1987; and Fodor and McLaughlin, 1990.

[10]See Fodor, 1975; but also see Field, 1978; and Devitt and Sterelny, 1987.

[11]In this discussion I will follow the standard notational practice of using capitalised English words as canonical names of mental representations.

[12]For a more detailed account of the encodement of implicit representations in connectionist systems – and, for that matter, of the nature of their causal activity – see O'Brien, 1990.

[13]Smolensky, 1987, p. 147. A little later in the same paper, Smolensky makes the claim that "the constituency relation among distributed representations is one that is important for the

analysis of connectionist models . . . but it is *not* part of the causal mechanism within the model" (p. 148). His point therefore seems to be that it is really the theorist looking in at the model who *imposes* this compositionality onto connectionist representations.

[14]Very briefly, the idea that thought is *systematic* is the claim that cognitive capacities display certain structural relations as a matter of psychological law. To borrow an example from Fodor and Pylyshyn (1988), if a cognitive system can think the thought *John loves Mary* then it must also be capable of thinking the thought *Mary loves John* (and vice versa). And according to Fodor and Pylyshyn, the only way we know how to explain this cognitive systematicity is by proposing that complex mental representations exhibit a robust compositionality — the idea being that the structural relations of thoughts are captured in a uniform way by the constituent structure of these mental representations.

[15]It is perhaps worth reiterating at this point that in making these remarks I am restricting my attention to connectionist systems that employ distributed, rather than localist, representations (see footnote 4 above).

[16]For an alternative suggestion as to how genuinely compositional representations may be generated in connectionist systems, see Elman, 1989.

[17]In fact, the semantic relations that obtain between these three distinct *coffee* contents can be even more precisely characterised on this account. In addition to the fact that they tend to cluster together in activation space, and thus are semantically more similar to one another than to, say, the *muesli* content in Patricia's belief, we might suppose that their own internal semantic relations can also be captured. We might suppose, for example, that given the semantic relations that hold here, the two COFFEE constituents in the representations of Paul's and Steven's beliefs are mapped more closely together, in the region of activation space in which they cluster, than are the two COFFEE constituents in the representations of Paul's and Patricia's beliefs.

[18]For an excellent introduction to the exemplar theory of concept possession, along with other competing theories, see Smith and Medin, 1981.

[19]Ramsey, Stich and Garon point out, for example, that their eliminativist interpretation of connectionism only applies to connectionist models that are intended "*as cognitive models,* not merely as *implementations* of cognitive models" (1990, Section 4; reprinted in this volume).

[20]This assumption, by the way, does seem to be implicit in many of the remarks made by Fodor and Pylyshyn (1988) and Fodor and McLauglin (1990).

[21]The following authors, for example, all present substantially different conceptions of the difference between classical and connectionist models of cognition: Kosslyn and Hatfield, 1984; Fodor and Pylyshyn, 1988; Smolensky, 1988; Bechtel, 1988; Cummins, 1989; and Horgan and Tienson, 1989.

[22]For a more comprehensive discussion of the issues that follow here, see O'Brien, forthcoming.

[23]The account of digitality and analogicity that follows here has especially benefited from the insights of David Lewis (1971) and Zenon Pylyshyn (1984, pp. 193–223). One difference between my account and Lewis's account, however, is that while Lewis locates the analog/digital distinction in the *nature* of the representational substrate (i.e., whether or not the underlying representing dimension is a *primitive* physical magnitude), I locate it in the way that representational values are *mapped* onto the physical magnitudes that comprise the representational substrate (i.e., whether or not this mapping makes use of what I term the *primitive* properties of these physical magnitudes). In the end, however, I am not sure that this amounts to a substantive difference.

[24]As I shall use the term, a physical magnitude is a function that systematically assigns numbers to a continuously variable physical property of a physical system. Voltages, weights, lengths, and neuronal firing rates, for example, are all physical magnitudes in this sense.

[25]See, for example, the various connectionist models described in Rumelhart and McClelland, 1986, and McClelland and Rumelhart, 1986.

[26]For a nice discussion of how content-addressability, flexible generalisation, graceful degradation, and shading and blending of meaning (along with other attractive properties) arise in connectionist models, see Clark, 1989, pp. 83–126.

[27]This is not to say, by the way, that connectionist *networks* cannot in principle be used to implement classical computational models. One might, for example, be able to use connectionist networks as the representational substrate of such models—but only insofar as the computational processes defined over this substrate do not make use of (the analog properties of) the network connection weights involved. Since network connection weights are the driving force behind connectionist models, such an approach, whatever it would amount to, would not amount to a *connectionist* implementation of a classical model.

19 Consciousness, Intentionality, and Pragmatism

Richard Rorty
University of Virginia, Charlottesville

FROM DOUBTS ABOUT CONSCIOUSNESS TO DOUBTS ABOUT MENTAL REPRESENTATIONS

The term *philosophy of mind* came into currency in the English-speaking world in the 1950's, largely as a description of the debates initiated by Gilbert Ryle's pioneering book *The Concept of Mind,* published in 1949. Ryle's book was a polemic against the Cartesian idea that mental states are states of an immaterial substance. This polemic, and the ensuing discussion, turned on the question of the reducibility of mental events to behavioral dispositions. Ryle's central argument was that we had misconceived the "logic" of such words as "belief," "sensation," "conscious," etc. He thought that the traditional, Cartesian theory of mind, had "misconstrued the type-distinction between disposition and exercise into its mythical bifurcation of unwitnessable mental causes and their witnessable physical effects."[1] Ryle's attempt to do philosophy of mind as "conceptual analysis" was founded on the pre-Quinean idea that philosophical puzzles arose out of "misunderstandings of the logic of our language."

Almost as soon as Ryle's book was published, this conception of philosophy began to fall into disrepute. Quinean and Wittgensteinian doubts that there was any such thing as "the logic of our language" began to make themselves felt. Furthermore, there were doubts that Ryle had done enough to explain the plausibility of Cartesianism. He had given us too little help in understanding why anyone had ever misunderstood our language as badly as the Cartesians purportedly had — why anyone had made what Ryle called "absurd category-mistakes." Ryle thought it enough to say that

388

Descartes's admiration for Galilean mechanics committed him to viewing the mind as a quasi-mechanical process.[2] But this was hardly enough to explain how Descartes had gotten everybody to swallow the idea of nonspatial causal mechanisms, how he had gotten them to confuse a behavioral disposition with an inner event. Something had to be said about the markedly counter-intuitive character of Ryle's claim that the notion of "the mind" was simply the product of a misleading way of describing the organism's behavior.

The next stage beyond Ryle is dominated by the writings, during the '50's and '60's, of J.J.C. Smart and David Armstrong—the most prominent of the so-called "central-state materialists." These philosophers said we should just give up Ryle's counter-intuitive claim that when we thought we were talking about inner events we were "really" talking about dispositions to behave. No "conceptual analysis" could show that the "real meaning" of mentalistic discourse consisted in reference to dispositions. But that merely showed, Ryle and Armstrong thought, that philosophers should not think of themselves as concerned doing linguistic analysis. They should give up the positivistic idea that one can validate philosophical claims by an appeal to "meanings," or do philosophical work by "analyzing" meanings.

Instead, Smart and Armstrong proposed, philosophers should think of themselves as reconciling natural science and common sense by showing how various words of ordinary language can be interpreted as referring to the sorts of processes—e.g., brain states—which natural science knows how to investigate. Such interpretations were proposals, rather than discoveries—proposals dictated not by "the logic of our language" but by the state of our empirical science. In the materialists' view, the reason why Descartes went so badly wrong was that in his day brain physiology was too primitive to make a physicalistic, micro-structural, account of cognition sound like a plausible research program. So it was reasonable for Descartes to call up a "ghost in the machine." We moderns, however, are now within hailing distance of such an account. So now philosophy's task is to clear away the Cartesian debris which makes us think that psychology is more than a place-holder for biology. More specifically, its task is to persuade us that, as Armstrong put it

> The concept of a mental state is the concept of that, whatever it may turn out to be, which is brought about in a man by certain stimuli and which in turn brings about certain responses.[3]

As Armstrong noted, however, his own view and Ryle's were counter-intuitive in the same way. As he put it:

> The view that our notion of mind is nothing but that of an inner principle apt for bringing about certain sorts of behavior may be thought to share a certain

weakness with [Ryle's] Behaviorism. Modern philosophers have put the point about Behaviorism by saying that although Behaviorism may be a satisfactory account of the mind from an *other-person point of view,* it will not do as a *first-person* account. . . . We are conscious, we have experiences. Now can we say that to be conscious, to have experiences, is simply for something to go on within us apt for the causing of certain sorts of behavior?[4]

Armstrong's reply to these questions was to say that we should interpret the notion of experience, of consciousness, as that of acquisition of beliefs about our inner states. To be conscious of being in pain, for example, is a matter of acquiring a belief about our the state of our nerves. Armstrong summed up by saying:

Consciousness of our own mental state . . . may then be conceived of as an inner state or event giving a capacity for selective behavior, in this case selective behavior toward our own mental state. . . . Consciousness is a self-scanning mechanism in the central nervous system.[5]

The next stage in the development of philosophy of mind was, however, a move back from Armstrong's emphasis on physiology, in the direction of claiming a certain autonomy for the psychological. The principal motive for this antimaterialist move was Hilary Putnam's argument that many different states of a brain could cause the same behavioral disposition. Brains might be as diverse as computer hardware, but, just as the same program could run on lots of different machines (made of lots of different materials and constructed according to quite different principles), so the same mental states could occur independently of any particular physiological event.

This analogy between the study of computer hardware and physiology on the one hand, and between the study of computer software and psychology on the other, was the beginning of a transition from philosophy of mind to philosophy of psychology. Instead of the question of the '50's and '60's — "How can we refute Descartes?" — the question of the '70's became "How can we make sense of the various research programs upon which cognitive psychologists are embarked?" The answer was: by thinking of mental states as *functional* states, states which mediate between input and output in the way in which program states of computers do and which can, like program states, be viewed as symbolic representations of states of affairs — as sentential attitudes. For the next twenty years or so, "functionalism" became the dominant school of thought among Anglo-Saxon philosophers interested in the mind-body problem.

It is important to emphasize that the functionalists adopted the same attitude toward consciousness as had Ryle and the central-state materialists.

As Searle has rightly said, the entire history of philosophy of mind since Ryle is marked by a refusal to take consciousness seriously — or, more exactly, by an insistence on taking "conscious experience" to be a matter of *having beliefs*. This insistence enabled the functionalists to shrug off the question "Are computers conscious" by saying that computers can be programmed to report on their own program states,[6] to represent symbolically their own symbolic representations. Such an ability is, they said, all the notion of "conscious experience" amounts to.

The refusal to take Cartesianism seriously which was common to Ryle, Armstrong and Putnam was thus not so much a result of their inability to take the idea of a state of an immaterial entity seriously as of their inability to take the notion of "conscious experience distinct from the having of a belief" seriously. So when Thomas Nagel complained that all these philosophers had neglected the *phenomenology* of conscious experience — *what it is like* to be conscious — Daniel Dennett thought it enough to reply that "thinkings that *p* . . . exhaust our immediate awareness."[7]

Dennett's identification of experience and belief should be seen as part of the same line of thought which led philosophers away from the Lockean notion of words as names of ideas — of words as able to have meaning by naming experiences — and toward the holistic view (shared by Quine and Wittgenstein) that words have meaning by virtue of their place in a language-game. Following this line led them to become steadily more naturalistic: to accept the principle "If natural science cannot tell us more about how it works, then it does not exist." The link between a holistic philosophy of language and this naturalistic (or, if you like, "objectivistic") attitude is the view that *to understand something is to discover its law-like relations to other things*. The view that understanding *x* is a matter of finding law-like regularities which tie its behavior in with the behavior of *y, z,* and so on (rather than a matter of contemplating it in isolation, penetrating into its inner nature, finding its *intrinsic* properties, and the like) is the familiar legacy of Galileo's substitution of a law-event framework of scientific explanation for Aristotle's thing-nature framework. Galileo's example taught us to be wary of the notion of an *intrinsic* property of an entity — one which could *not* be viewed as a set of relationships between that entity and other entities.

If one shares this Galilean outlook one will distrust appeals to immediate experience, and especially the idea that certain experiences cannot be put into words and made the subject of argument. For that outlook predisposes one to think, with Wittgenstein, that if the phrase "what it is like to be conscious" has a meaning, then there must be criteria for deciding when and whether this property applies — when it merely seems to someone that she recognizes the presence of this property and when she actually does. Thus Dennett says

A defender of the subjective realm such as Nagel must grant that in general, whether or not it was like something to be *x,* whether or not the subject *experienced* being *x*—questions that *define* the subjective realm—are questions about which the subject's subsequent subjective opinion is not authoritative. But if the subject's own convictions do not settle the matter, and if, as Nagel holds, no objective considerations are conclusive either, the subjective realm floats out of ken altogether, except perhaps for the subject's convictions about the specious present.[8]

What links Ryle, Armstrong, Putnam and Dennett together, and separates them from Nagel, Kripke and Searle, is that the former philosophers are content to *let* the subjective realm float out of ken, and out of philosophy, altogether. They think that if philosophy is ever going to join hands with natural science, it must eliminate the unverifiable, not to mention the ineffable. So the claim that to talk of "conscious experience" is merely a misleading way of talking about beliefs gets its plausibility not from any particular discovery about experiences, but rather from a very general metaphilosophical outlook.

By contrast, philosophers like Nagel and Searle insist that attention to the subjective realm is just what is needed if philosophy is not to relapse into dogmatism.[9] Nagel began his seminal paper "What is it like to be a bat?" by saying "Consciousness is what makes the mind-body problem really intractable." His principal point is made in the following sentence from that article:

Certainly it *appears* unlikely that we will get closer to the real nature of human experience by leaving behind the particularity of our human point of view and striving for a description in terms accessible to beings that could not imagine what it was like to be us.[10]

Searle echoes this point when he says that the view that "mental states can be entirely defined in terms of their causal relations" has never been reached

by a close scrutiny of the phenomena in question. No one ever considered his own terrible pain or his deepest worry and concluded that they were just Turing machine states or that they could be entirely defined in terms of their causes and effects or that attributing such states to themselves was just a matter of taking a certain stance toward themselves.[11]

For Nagel's and Searle's opponents, however, all this talk of "what it is like," "real nature" and "close scrutiny" is pre-Galilean obscurantism. For them, mind is whatever psychology studies, and psychology is a discipline which finds law-like relationships between public events. No correlations of this sort are going to involve close scrutiny of what it is like to have a pain, much less of what it is like to have a belief.

***

The issue between those who think that the entire course of philosophical thought since Ryle has neglected what is most distinctive about the mind — namely, that we can take a first-person view of it — and those who think the notion of "first-person view" a misleading metaphor, is at the heart of one of the two great controversies which, at the present time, dominate this area of philosophy. This is the controversy between Dennett and Searle. The other issue which dominates philosophical discussion is a relatively new one. This is the controversy between Dennett and Fodor over whether intentionality (considered, *pace* Searle, as capable of existing *independently* of consciousness) can be intrinsic.

More precisely, it is the issue of whether we can legitimately draw a distinction between derived intentionality — the sort of intentionality (called by Searle "pseudo-intentionality") which a thermostat or a computer has, derived from the interests and purposes of those who design or employ the gadget — and *original* intentionality. Original intentionality, if it exists, is a sort of intentionality which is present in organisms rather than machines. It is present in them whether or not any third person is interested in manipulating or explaining the organism's behavior. Fodor believes in original intentionality, and Dennett does not. For Quinean, holistic reasons, Dennett does not think there is a fact of the matter about the meanings of symbols, so *a fortiori* there can be none about the attribution of intentional states. As Dennett puts it:

> We cannot begin to make sense of functional attributions until we abandon the idea that there has to be one, determinate, *right* answer to the question: what is it for? And if there is no deeper fact that could settle that question, there can be no deeper fact to settle its twin: What does it mean?[12]

Fodor, Dennett says, is attached to "meaning rationalism," the doctrine that there is a special first-person way in which organisms know what they mean (and cannot be wrong about it).[13] "How," Dennett asks:

> does Fodor establish that, in his mental idiolect, "horse" means *horse* — and not *horse-or-other-quadreped-resembling-a-horse* (or something like that)? Either Fodor must go Searle's introspective route and declare that this is something he can just tell, from the inside, or he must appeal to the very sorts of design considerations, and the "teleology/optimality" story that he wants to resist.[14]

Ten years ago, at the time of Dennett's *Brainstorms,* Dennett and Fodor were allies — fellow-proponents of what Putnam now calls, polemically,

"MIT mentalism." But now they are divided. What divides them is how far to push the holistic and contextualistic attitude which both had acquired from Quine and Wittgenstein and had invoked against Nagel and Searle. This is the attitude which says: "Forget about a first-person; immediate, subjective, view; knowledge is a matter of seeing entities in relation to other entities." Dennett wants to push this attitude all the way. Fodor wants to stop short.

The beginnings of the revolt against "MIT mentalism" — a revolt in which Dennett and Putnam are now allies against Fodor — can be found in the radically holistic and naturalistic semantics developed by Putnam and by Donald Davidson. Both these philosophers have attempted to break with the traditional picture according to which the user of a language determines what meaning his utterances have — the picture according to which, in Putnam's phrase, "meanings are in the head." The slogan "meanings are *not* in the head" has, in the last twenty years, come to summarize the view that ascription of meanings to utterances is a matter of correlating the behavior of speakers with their environment. Putnam and Davidson radicalized Quine's insistence on a behaviorist approach to meaning by dropping Quine's residual empiricism. Both have seen that, when Quine's holism is taken to its limit, "we can't in general first identify beliefs and meanings and then ask what caused them."[15]

In his recent *Representation and Realism,* Putnam now argues against his earlier, functionalist self. The starting point of his argument is that the process of determining whether you and I hold the same belief is no less complex and holistic than the process of determining that you mean by an utterance what I mean by another utterance. But that latter process involves attention to all sorts of accidents of upbringing and environment. If I have been brought up to believe that cats are divine and you have not, or if all the cats I have ever seen are Manx whereas you have seen all sorts of cats, then we are not expressing the same belief when we both say "The cat is on the mat." For that set of noises does not mean the same thing in our two idiolects. Since the only point of assigning meanings to utterances and beliefs to persons is to predict behavior, and since the difference between your background and mine will produce different behavior, we must make these differences relevant to the assignment of meaning.

The functionalist suggestion, to which Fodor still clings, had been that psychology might resolve such questions by determining whether or not we have the same "mental representations," the same "program states" (i.e., "features defined in terms of computational parameters plus relations to biologically characterized inputs and outputs"[16]). In other words: the functionalist had suggested that psychology might come up a description of mental functioning (a flow chart of the program which the brain runs, so to speak) which would give us tests for the presence or absence of beliefs —

tests less holistic than that provided by common sense. This suggestion is now condemned by Putnam as "the latest form taken by a more general tendency in the history of thought, the tendency to think of concepts as scientifically describable "psychologically real" entities in the mind or brain."[17] What is being condemned here is not the anti-immaterialist claim that a machine and human being might work in just the same way,[18] but rather the claim that post-Cartesian philosophers, or cognitive psychologists, can say something more about *what sort of thing beliefs and desires are* than can common sense. In particular, we cannot usefully treat them as "mental representations."

Putnam is joined in this anti-Fodorian polemic by Stephen Stich, who refers to beliefs and desires as "folk-psychological 'notions" which, because of what he calls their "context-sensitivity," make poor tools for the building of scientific theories.[19] So Stich concludes that if we are ever going to have anything called "cognitive science" it will not offer "analyses" or "rational reconstructions" of these common-sense notions.[20] The explanatory entities invoked by a *mature* cognitive science may turn out to have as little in common with beliefs as cells do with humors or atoms with substantial forms.

Stich tends to take for granted that we will indeed someday have "cognitive science." He takes for granted, in other words, that there is an interesting field of scientific inquiry somewhere in between brain physiology and cultural anthropology—an intervening layer in which fruitful explanations may be had, where natural kinds may be isolated and surprising nomologicals discovered.[21] But Dennett seems to be growing skeptical of this assumption—the assumption of the "psychological reality" of something reasonably like the intentional states posited by "folk psychology." As I understand Dennett's current position, he thinks that there is no guarantee that we shall ever be able to reconcile the holistic character of the attribution of beliefs with the need for relatively context-independent causal factors. So the quarrel between Dennett and Fodor over the existence of "mental representations"—entities which are belief-like enough to acquire plausibility from the success of folk psychology but context-independent enough to be the subject of fruitful empirical research—is beginning to look like a quarrel between someone who doubts that cognitive psychology has a future and someone who willing to bet everything on the claim that this discipline will eventually prove itself.[22]

More exactly put, one can say that the more the holistic line of thought about intentionality is pressed, the more unlikely it seems that a *computational* approach to cognitive psychology is going to pay off. The happy marriage between computer science and cognitive psychology celebrated in such books as Howard Gardner's *The Mind's New Science* begins to look as if it might be on the rocks. One straw in the wind which suggests this is the recent excitement, in AI circles, about connectionism — a research program which suggests that if there is anything deep to be discovered about how cognition works it is going to be discovered by going to a "sub-symbolic" level at which questions about individuation of intentional states no longer arise. If writers like Cussins are right, then we now have the prospect of a kind of cognitive science which is radically different from "MIT mentalism": one which involves "a non-syntactic notion of computation [and] a non-semantic notion of psychological content."[23] If the Dreyfuses[24] are right in suggesting that holographic projection is a more plausible model for the brain's ability to recognize similarities than computational devices which go through check lists of distinct features, then breakthroughs in this area are likely to come from attempts to construct noncomputational models of the brain. Future AI projects are likely to try to reconstruct processes which seem more physiological than psychological. Suppose that this line of speculation were correct. What moral could we then draw from the career of philosophy of mind? As I have already remarked, the sub-area of philosophy originally called, in the wake of Ryle, "the philosophy of mind," changed its name to "philosophy of psychology" in the course of the 1970's, as the project of refuting Descartes gave place to the project of defending MIT. In the course of this change questions about consciousness faded out and questions about intentionality took over. If questions about intentionality now fade out, if questions about consciousness do not come back in, and if the spotlight turns toward physiology, then it is not clear that philosophers will have any work to do in this area. The philosophy of mind may be, as Feyerabend once said about the philosophy of science, "a subject with a great past." It may be that the lines of inquiry which Ryle opened up lead us to not only to conclude that there is no entity called "the mind" but to conclude that there is nothing called "psychology" which we need to have a philosophy of. Perhaps neither "mentation" nor "cognition" nor "intentionality" is the name of a natural kind, and perhaps "cognitive science" is not the name of a discipline. It may be that psychology, when it split off from philosophy and tried to set up shop as an empirical discipline, retained too many traces of its origin. Among these traces may be the idea that words like "mind," "thought" and "knowledge" form fruitful topics of investigation. In short, it may be that psychology will only reach independence and maturity when it ceases to take its agenda either from common sense or from philosophy. It might, indeed, start taking its agenda from biology. I have no idea whether this is a realistic prospect. But it is clear that intellectual progress has often occurred by a reversal of the direction of influence from top-down to bottom-up. The least that philosophers can do, it seems to me, is to make sure that they do not block the road of inquiry by impeding such a fruitful reversal.

2. PRAGMATISM AND THE GALILEAN OUTLOOK

So far I have been telling a story about how philosophers began by replacing the notion of "conscious experience" with that of "noninferential belief" and are now replacing the notion of "mental representation" with that of "the intentional stance." In this second section, I want first to offer some general remarks about the metaphilosophical view implicit in Dennett's work. Then I shall try to relate this stance to Donald Davidson's recent suggestion that "the most promising and interesting change that is occurring in philosophy today is that these dualisms [of scheme and content, and of the objective and the subjective] are being questioned in new ways" and his further suggestion that these dualisms have their common origin in "a concept of the mind with its private states and objects."[25]

In his recent work, Dennett no longer suggests that he is clearing away the philosophical underbrush which inhibits the development of a New Science of the Mind. Rather, he presents himself merely as explaining the success of folk psychology, without committing himself to what Fodor takes to be the subject matter of that Science: causally efficacious mental representations. So Dennett now has two sets of enemies — one old and one new. The old enemies are typified by Searle, who sees both earlier and later Dennett as exemplifying the false claim that the mind can only be discussed from a third-person point of view. The new enemies are typified by Fodor, who sees Dennett as having fallen back into the view which Fodor sneeringly attributes to Ryle's logical behaviorism: the view that "rocks don't have beliefs and desires because they don't move around enough."[26] Fodor thinks that the basis of the New Science of the Mind is that "People and machines have the right sort of internal organization to satisfy belief-desire explanations; rocks and such, by contrast, don't." More generally, he thinks that his own theory of "mental representations" shows how intentional states could have causal powers, whereas Dennett's view shirks this central philosophical task.[27]

If Searle is right, we need to stop being holistic and contextualist at the very beginning. We need to block Ryle, and thereby all subsequent developments, by seeing mentality as intrinsically connected with the possibility of a first-person view: a nonrelational, phenomenological view. We must save common sense by blocking holism at the point at which it dissolves experiences into beliefs, thereby blocking the assimilation of people to computers. If Fodor is right, we can give up the notion of mentality as subjectivity and go ahead and treat people and computers as exemplifying the same natural kind, but we *cannot* give up the notion of mental representations whose powers are independent of environmental context. We must block holism at a later point: the point at which it dissolves mental representations into mere takings of the intentional stance.

Fodor and Searle are still separated by an abyss: the question of whether machines can have genuine intentionality or only pseudo-intentionality. Fodor agrees with Dennett that we can shrug off questions about whether machines are conscious, can be built to feel pain, and the like, as largely verbal. Searle does not. For Searle, as Dennett puts it, "the idea of genuine understanding, genuine 'semanticity' as he often calls it, is inextricable from the idea of consciousness. [Searle] does not so much as consider the possibility of unconscious semanticity."[28] But Fodor and Searle *agree,* against Dennett, that some intentionality is original and context-independent.[29] They agree in an attitude which I shall label "anti-pragmatist." They set their faces against the view to which I referred earlier: the Galilean outlook, which says that there is no a priori reason to assume that explanatorily useful terms like "consciousness" or "intentionality" denote properties which have intrinsic natures, or structures which empirical research can uncover.

The difference between Dennett and Searle in regard to the future progress of science in the area initially delimited by Descartes can be put as follows. Dennett thinks that if there are no nomologicals to be found in the area in which psychology has traditionally looked (no natural kinds in between anthropology and biology, to put it crudely) that will merely show that folk psychology was not a good lead for science to have followed. By contrast, Searle thinks that research *must* come up with an account of mentality. It *must* recapture common sense's distinction between people and machines by discovering the biological basis for consciousness. Biology is going to have isolate the underlying microphenomena on which consciousness is supervenient. If biology fails to find a line dividing microphenomena in a way which lets us reconstruct the conscious-nonconscious distinction, then biology has to go back to the drawing board.

By contrast, Fodor thinks that biology will only have to go back to the drawing board if it cannot find a way of dividing microphenomena which lets us reconstruct the representational-nonrepresentational distinction. Searle thinks that biology has a duty to answer the question "How is consciousness possible?," and that if it answers that one it will automatically have answered the question "How is intentionality possible?" Fodor thinks that it has a duty to answer the latter question, but that the former is a *bad* question. Dennett thinks that it has no absolute *duty* to answer *either* question, although of course it would be nice if it did. How do we go about deciding what questions science has to answer? How do we decide which are bad questions (like, for example, the Aristotelian questions "Why do all bodies above the atmosphere move in circles?" and "How can the potential intellect grasp forms without matter?") — and which are legitimate tests of scientific progress? The pragmatist view, which I assume Dennett would favor, is that we can never decide in advance. We have to wait to see what science does, and we may then have to modify our naive expectations.

Suppose future biology tell us that there are no microstructural differences with the help of which we can reconstruct the Cartesian notion of "conscious experience" (Descartes' *cogitatio*). Then we might well decide that there never was any such thing as consciousness, and that what we called "a first-person point of view" was not a point of view at all, but just a dramatization of our ability to make noninferential reports on the states of our nerves. If future science tells us that the Fodorian notion of "mental representations with causal powers" is unreconstructible in terms of supervenience upon certain distinctive physiological microprocesses, then we may decide that the mental-physical distinction is as obsolete as Aristotle's sublunary-superlunary distinction. (But, of course, that decision will no more hinder us from continuing to use folk psychology than Copernicus caused sailors to stop doing Ptolemaic navigation.)

To be an *anti*pragmatist about such matters is to say that, in some measure, philosophy *should* set the agenda for science. Anti-pragmatists think that there are some topics which scientists are not allowed to shrug off by saying that our "folk" ways of speaking have led us to ask bad, unanswerable, "merely philosophical" questions. Whereas the pragmatist will be satisfied if inquiry into microstructure gives us an ability to predict and control, the antipragmatist will not be satisfied unless microstructural descriptions explain the existence of certain supervenient macroscopic properties of a sort with which we are already familiar.

To put the matter crudely, the pragmatist is prepared to countenance the possibility that "the biology of mind" may have been as misleading a notion as "the mechanics of astrology" or "the chemistry of love potions" or "the physiology of demonic possession." He is prepared to accept Armstrong's account of the task of philosophy—sweeping away rubbish that impedes scientific progress. For all he knows, the notions of "consciousness," and "intentionality," and "mental representation" may be part of that rubbish. He agrees that giving up these notions might leave philosophers of mind and cognitive scientists without a job to do, but he thinks that this would not be the first time progress in microstructural research had killed off pseudodisciplines. From his point of view, an a priori discipline like philosophy cannot save us from getting involved with pseudodisciplines; only progress in other empirical disciplines can do that.

***

So much for the attitude which I am calling "pragmatism." I turn now to Davidson's vision of the course of recent philosophy. In an anti-Fodor passage, Davidson writes:

> it is instructive to find the effort to make psychology scientific turning into a search for internal propositional states that can be detected and identified

apart from relations to the rest of the world, much as earlier philosophers sought for something 'given in experience' which contained no necessary clue to what was going on outside. The motive is similar in the two cases: it is thought that a sound footing, whether for knowledge or for psychology, requires something inner in the sense of being nonrelational.[30]

Davidson sees recent attempts to erase the objective-subjective distinction as an extension of the Galilean outlook, of the view that nothing is to be taken as *intrinsically* nonrelational. From this Galilean point of view, anything is recontextualizable either into an context-independent substance or into a slice of an indefinitely wide web of relations, depending upon the needs of current empirical inquiry. But there is no sense in asking the question "Which is it *really,* a substance or a slice?" Just as Newton dissolved planetary orbits into balances of gravitational forces, so contemporary scientists may want to dissolve experiences and beliefs into something quite different. Philosophers cannot help in this process in the way Ryle thought they could — by "conceptual clarification." But they can help in the way in which Armstrong and Dennett try to help: by treating concepts like "consciousness" and "intentionality" pragmatically, treating them in terms of the uses to which we put them, rather than as names for entities which have an intrinsic nature.

It is a cliche of intellectual history that, when Galilean science drained the planets and the rocks and the animals of their intrinsic natures, Cartesian philosophy responded by creating "the subject" as a safe refuge for the Aristotelian notion of essence. Even after the colorfully diverse contents of Aristotelian nature were smeared together into one big swirl of corpuscles — one big substance called "matter" — there remained, here below, one other substance: the mind. The mind was its own place — in the sense that, as Davidson says, it was "an ultimate source of evidence the character of which can be wholly specified without reference to what it is evidence for."[31] It knew both its own essence (consciousness) and its own contents (the meanings of its intentional states), and it knew these things independently of its knowledge of anything else.

The cash value of the claim that the mind is its own place is that the mind is capable of swinging free of its environment — standing in relations of "aboutness" or "evidence for" to all kinds of things which have nothing to do with that environment — for example, unicorns and transfinite cardinals. This ability to swing free of the environment — the ability which Husserl thought showed what was wrong with all forms of naturalistic philosophy — is, on the view of those who think intentionality extrinsic, just as "naturalistic" as the ability to reflect light or to exert gravitational force. For although unicorns do not exist, sentences using the word "unicorn" do, and such sentence-types are no more mysterious or unnatural than numbers. To attribute a belief in unicorns to someone is to describe him as standing in a relation to a sentence-type, just as to attribute a dollar value to him is to describe him as standing in a certain relation to a slave-trader or an organ bank. The former attribution is no more "non-natural" than the latter. It is useful to talk about beliefs in unicorns, and thus about unicorns, in order to account for what we find in medieval books and tapestries, just as it is useful to talk about dollar values in order to account for the behavior of businessmen. We do not talk about the internal structure or the evolutionary niche of unicorns, because we have no need to talk about unicorns when we do biology. We do not ask about the intrinsic nature of dollar values, nor of the dollar itself, any more than about the intrinsic nature of transfinite cardinals. For values, like numbers, are *obviously* merely slices out of vast webs of relationships.[32]

To see things from Davidson's naturalistic perspective, it helps to consider the analogy between attributing states to a brain and to a mind. Nobody wants to suggest that a *brain* is its own place, or that it could lose touch with the external world. For whether a brain is hooked up to wires, computers, and photoelectric cells, or instead to the rest of a central nervous system and some protoplasmic sense organs, is irrelevant.[33] It is always hooked up to *some* external world. If it ceased to be so hooked, it would cease to be a brain. It would just be a heap of cells. Similarly, if a central processor made of metal, silicon and plastic were not hooked up to some input and output devices, it would not be a functioning central processor, but just a heap of chips. So one can imagine Davidson arguing as follows: if the mind is just the brain under another description, then both mind and brain are equally incapable of failure to hook up. The most that redescription in mentalistic rather than neural terms could do would be to describe more complicated hook-ups, not eliminate them altogether.[34]

This Davidsonian conception should, I think, be thought of as the final stage in the assault on the Cartesian idea of the mind which began with Ryle's attempt to analyze mentalistic discourse as reference to behavioral dispositions. If we follow Davidson, we shall say that it was unfortunate that the seventeenth century did not carry through on its project of recontextualizing everything by seeing the mind too as just one more slice of a vast web of relationships. If the seventeenth century had treated Descartes' *Meditations* as a symptom of an unfortunate residual Aristotelianism on the part of the author of the a great treatise on corpuscularian mechanics, we might never have had the notion of "consciousness" to worry about. If the nineteenth century had treated Kant's talk of *Vorstellungen* in the First Critique as a symptom of an unfortunate residual Wolffian Thomism on the part of the great moral philosopher who wrote the Second Critique, we might never have gotten stuck with the notion of "mental representations." But, given that our ancestors were not prudent enough to

nip these unfortunate notions in the bud, we are now in a position to prune
them away.

FOOTNOTES

[1]Gilbert Ryle, *The Concept of Mind* (London, Hutchison, 1949), p. 32.

[2]Ibid., p. 19.

[3]Armstrong, *A Materialist Theory of the Mind* (London: Routledge, 1968), p. 79.

[4]David Armstrong, "The Nature of Mind" in Ned Block, ed., *Readings in the Philosophy of Psychology,* vol. 1 (Cambridge, Mass.: Harvard University Press, 1980), p. 197.

[5]Ibid., p. 199.

[6]Putnam, in his seminal paper "Minds and Machines" of 1960—the first paper to develop the program-mind analogy in detail—uses an Armstrong-like notion of self-scanning as an analogy to introspection. See Sidney Hook, ed., *Dimensions of Mind* (New York: Collier, 1961), p. 148.

[7]Daniel Dennett, "Toward a Cognitive Theory of Consciousness" in his *Brainstorms* (Cambridge, Mass.: Bradford, 1978), p. 165.

[8]Dennett, *Brainstorms,* p. 143.

[9]See Nagel, *The View from Nowhere* (New York: Oxford University Press, 1986), p. 11: "In the name of liberation, these movements have offered us intellectual repression." See Dennett's discussion of this passage at p. 5 of *The Intentional Stance,* as well as Nagel's explanation (at p. 106) of why his position is incompatible with a Wittgensteinian conception of language.

[10]Thomas Nagel, "What is it like to be a bat?" in Block, op. cit., vol. 1, p. 164.

[11]John Searle, *Intentionality* (Cambridge: Cambridge University Press, 1983), pp. 262–263.

[12]Daniel Dennett, "Evolution, Error, and Intentionality" in his *The Intentional Stance* (Cambridge, Mass.: Bradford/MIT, 1987), p. 319. I regard this paper of Dennett's as one of his best. Together with the final paper in *The Intentional Stance,* titled "Mid-Term Examination," it forms a remarkably lucid account of the relation between Quine-Davidson holism in philosophy of language and the recent revolt against "MIT mentalism."

[13]The term "meaning rationalism" is due to Ruth Garrett Millikan. See her *Language, Thought and Other Biological Categories* (Cambridge, Mass.: Bradford/MIT, 1984), pp. 91ff. At p. 91 Millikan says that her adversary is "the view that consciousness is transparently and *infallibly* epistemic. Consciousness is or essentially involves an infallible kind of direct knowing—a knowing that is guaranteed as such from within consciousness itself." Dennett's and Millikan's positions overlap to a considerable extent.

[14]*The Intentional Stance,* p. 309. To adopt the "teleology-optimality" story would be to say that we construe organisms as believing whatever we imagine God or Evolution having designed them to believe. Dennett's point is that we can imagine quite a lot of *different* such designs. Further, something designed for one purpose in one environment might serve another purpose in a different environment (like the panda's thumb).

[15]Donald Davidson, "A Coherence Theory of Truth and Knowledge" in *Truth and Interpretation: Essays on the Philosophy of Donald Davidson,* ed. Ernest LePore (Oxford: Blackwells, 1986), p. 317.

[16]Hilary Putnam, *Representation and Realism* (Cambridge, Mass.: Bradford/MIT, 1988), p. 7.

[17]Ibid., p. 7. This is Putnam's description of what he calls "MIT mentalism."

[18]Putnam makes explicit that he is not dropping this claim. See *Representation and Realism,* p. xii.

[19]Stephen Stich, *From Folk Psychology to Cognitive Science: The Case Against Belief* (Cambridge, Mass.: Bradford/MIT, 1983), p. 139n.

[20]Actually, Stich draws the stronger conclusion (at p. 225 of his book; this volume, p. 97) that "there is no such thing as the property of believing that p." I agree with Putnam (*Representation and Realism,* p. 59) that this is overdoing things, and that, as Putnam says, Stich and the Churchlands make the odd assumption that "if the instances of X do not have something in common which is *scientifically* describable (where the paradigm science is neurobiology in the case of the Churchlands and computer science in the case of Stich), then X is a 'mythological' entity."

[21]See Stich, p. 136., where he says that people in exotic cultures "may have minds which work very much as ours do," But, of course, whether they do or not is just the wide-open question of whether there are any non-biological explanatory notions less culturally specific than those of folk psychology.

[22]See Dennett's remarks about Fodor at pp. 305-11 and 346-7 of his *The Intentional Stance* (Cambridge, Mass.: Bradford/MIT, 1987), Fodor's *Psychosemantics* (Cambridge, Mass.: Bradford, MIT/1987), and Dennett's review of that book (*Journal of Philosophy,* LXXXV [1988], pp. 384-389). *Psychosemantics* argues from the practical indispensability of folk psychology to the need to be "realist" about mental representations. Dennett is concerned to show that this is a *non sequitur.*

[23]Adrian Cussins, "The Connectionist Construction of Concepts," Ms. obtainable from the Center for the Study of Language and Information, Xerox PARC System Sciences Laboratory, 3333 Coyote Hill Road, Palo Alto CA 94304 USA. This paper replies to Fodor and Pylyshyn's "Connectionism and Cognitive Architecture" (*Cognition* 28 (1988)).

[24]See Herbert and Stuart Dreyfus, *Minds Over Machines* (Cambridge, Mass.: Bradford/ MIT, 1986), pp. 59-63 on "holistic systems" such as holographic projections. See also their article reviewing recent debates about connectionism in *Daedelus* (winter issue, 1987).

[25]Davidson, "The Myth of the Subjective," unpublished MS.

[26]*Psychosemantics,* p. 69.

[27]See *Psychosemantics,* p. 26; this volume, pp. 244-245.

[28]*The Intentional Stance,* p. 335.

[29]See *The Intentional Stance,* p. 295.

[30]Davidson, "The Myth of the Subjective."

[31]Davidson, "The Myth of the Subjective."

[32]On the analogy between assigning intentional states and assigning dollar values, see Dennett, *The Intentional Stance,* p. 208.

[33]The difference between these two alternatives creates the familiar problem of how we know that we are not brains in a vat. Davidson's solution is to say that a brain which has always been in a vat will have mostly beliefs about the vat-cum-computer environment which in fact surrounds it, no matter what input it receives from the computer. The idea that the brain in the vat has mostly false beliefs is forestalled by the fact that we have to translate most of its utterances as references to what causes these utterances.

For discussion and criticism of this Davidsonian line of argument, see Colin McGinn, "Radical Interpretation and Epistemology" in *Truth and Interpretation: Perspectives on the Philosophy of Donald Davidson,* ed. Ernest LePore (Oxford: Blackwells, 1986), pp. 369-386. It is significant that McGinn thinks that, to refute Davidson, we need to resurrect the distinction between "experience" and "belief" which Dennett tried to bury. McGinn thinks it necessary, in order to make "interpretation respect the premises on which scepticism rests," to say that "the (phenomenological) content of experience is fixed by the intrinsic condition of the brain." (p. 362) Davidson, by contrast, takes it as his aim to get rid of the premises on which scepticism rests. For him, both "the problem of the external world" and "the problem of other minds" are problems which repose on this traditional but wrong-headed distinction between "the phenomenological content of experience" and the intentional states attributed to a person on the basis of his causal interactions with his environment.

[34]For criticism of Davidson and defense of the idea of intrinsic mental states, see Mark

Johnston, "Why Having a Mind Matters" in *Truth and Interpretation* (cited in the previous footnote), pp. 422ff. Johnston is right to say that Davidson's "anomalous monism" takes "the propositional attitudes as constitutive of the mental" (p. 424). He points out that one could take the absence of law-like connections between mental and physical events, of which Davidson makes much, as showing "that the vocabulary of propositional attitudes is not made to carve out the natural mental properties which stand in law-like relations to physical properties." (p. 425) One could indeed so take them. But the point to notice is that whether biology comes up with anything which looks like the microstructural instantiation of such "natural mental properties" is an open empirical question. Davidson is assuming that it will not come up with anything like that. What Johnston calls Davidson's "interpretive view of mind" is based on this assumption.

References

Ackley, D. H., Hinton, G. E., & Sejnowski, T. J. (1985). A Learning Algorithm for Boltzmann Machines. *Cognitive Science, 9,* 147–169.

Allen, M. (1983). Models of Hemispheric Specialization. *Psychological Bulletin, 93,* 73–104.

Anderson, A. R. (Ed.). (1964). *Minds and Machines.* Englewood Cliffs, NJ: Prentice-Hall.

Anderson, J. A., & Hinton, G. E. (1981). Models of Information Processing in the Brain. In Hinton & Anderson (1981), 9–48.

Anderson, J. A., & Mozer, M. C. (1981). Categorization and Selective Neurons. In Hinton & Anderson (1981), 213–236.

Anderson, J. R. (1976). *Language, Memory and Thought.* Hillsdale, NJ: Lawrence Erlbaum Associates.

Anderson, J. R. (1980). *Cognitive Psychology and Its Implications.* San Francisco: W. H. Freeman & Co.

Anderson, J. R. (1983). *The Architecture of Cognition.* Cambridge, MA: Harvard University Press.

Anderson, J. R., & Bower, G. (1973). *Human Associative Memory.* Washington, DC: Winston.

Armstrong, D. M. (1963). Is Introspective Knowledge Incorrigible? *Philosophical Review, 72,* 417–432.

Armstrong, D. M. (1968a). The Headless Woman Illusion and the Defence of Materialism. *Analysis, 29,* 48–49.

Armstrong, D. M. (1968b). *A Materialist Theory of the Mind.* New York: Humanities Press.

Armstrong, D. M. (1981). *The Nature of Mind and Other Essays.* Ithaca, NY: Cornell University Press.

Asher, R. (1972). *Talking Sense.* London: Pitman Books, Ltd.

Atkinson, R. C., & Shiffren, R. M. (1968). Human Memory: A Proposed System and its Control Processes. In K. W. Spence & J. T. Spence (Eds.), *The Psychology of Learning and Motivation, 2.* New York: Academic Press.

Baier, K. (1962). Smart on Sensations. *Australasian Journal of Philosophy, 40,* 57–68.

Baker, L. R. (1987). *Saving Belief.* Princeton: Princeton University Press.

Ballard, D. H. (1986). Cortical Connections and Parallel Processing: Structure and Function. *Behavioral and Brain Sciences, 9,* 67–90.

Ballard, D. H., & Feldman, J. (1982). Connectionist Models and Their Properties. *Cognitive Science, 6,* 205–254.

Ballard, D. H., Hinton, G. E., & Sejnowski, T. J. (1983). Parallel Visual Computation. *Nature, 306,* 21–26.

Baron-Cohen, S., Leslie, A., & Frith, U. (1985). Does the Autistic Child Have a "Theory of Mind"? *Cognition, 21,* 37–46.

Bates, E. (1976). *Language and Context: The Acquisition of Pragmatics.* New York: Academic Press.

Bechtel, W. (1984). Autonomous Psychology: What It Should and Should Not Entail. In P. Asquith & P. Kitcher (Eds.), *PSA 1984, 1.* East Lansing, MI: Philosophy of Science Association.

Bechtel, W. (1985). Realism, Instrumentalism, and the Intentional Stance. *Cognitive Science, 9,* 265–292.

Bechtel, W. (Ed.). (1986). *Science and Psychology: Integrating Scientific Disciplines.* Dordrecht: Martinus Nijhoff.

Bechtel, W. (1988a). Guiding Assumptions and Empirical Difficulties. In A. Donovan, L. Laudan, & R. Laudan (Eds.), *Scrutinizing Science: Empirical Studies of Scientific Change* (pp. 163–180). Dordrecht, Holland: D. Reidel.

Bechtel, W. (1988b). *Philosophy of Science: An Overview for Cognitive Science.* Hillsdale, NJ: Lawrence Erlbaum Associates.

Bechtel, W. (1988c). *Philosophy of Mind: An Overview for Cognitive Science.* Hillsdale, NJ: Lawrence Erlbaum Associates.

Bechtel, W. (1988d). Connectionism and Rules and Representation Systems: Are They Compatible? *Philosophical Psychology, 1,* 5–16.

Bechtel, W. (1989). An Evolutionary Perspective on the Re-emergence of Cell Biology. In K. Halweg & C. Hooker (Eds.), *Issues in Evolutionary Epistemology* (pp. 433–457). Albany, NY: SUNY Press.

Bechtel, W., & Abrahamsen, A. A. (1991). *Connectionism and the Mind: An Introduction to Parallel Processing in Networks.* Oxford: Basil Blackwell.

Beloff, J. (1965). The Identity Hypothesis: A Critique. In Smythies (1965).

Bellugi, U., Poizner, H., & Klima, E. S. (forthcoming). *What the Hands Reveal About the Brain.* Cambridge, MA: MIT Press.

Bem, D. (1972). Self-Perception Theory. In L. Berkowitz (Ed.), *Advances in Experimental Social Psychology, 6.* New York: Academic Press.

Bennett, J. (1991a). Analysis without Noise. In Bogdan (1991c), 15–36.

Bennett, J. (1991b). Folk-Psychological Explanations. In Greenwood (1991a), 176–195.

Biro, J. I., & Shahan, R. W. (Eds.). (1982). *Mind, Brain, and Function.* Norman, OK: University of Oklahoma Press.

Blackburn, S. (1991). Losing Your Mind: Physics, Identity, and Folk Burglar Prevention. In Greenwood (1991a), 196–225.

Blakemore, C. (1977). *Mechanics of the Mind.* Cambridge: Cambridge University Press.

Blakemore, C., & Greenfield, S. (Eds.). (In Press). *Mind Matters.* Oxford: Basil Blackwell.

Blalock, H. (Ed.). (1971). *Causal Models in the Social Sciences.* New York: Aldine.

Block, N. J. (1978). Troubles With Functionalism. In C. W. Savage (Ed.), *Perception and Cognitivism: Issues in the Foundation of Psychology: Minnesota Studies in the Philosophy of Science, 9* (pp. 261–325). Minneapolis: University of Minnesota Press. Reprinted in Block (1980), 268–305.

Block, N. J. (Ed.). (1980). *Readings in the Philosophy of Psychology, 1.* Cambridge, MA: Harvard University Press.

Block, N. J. (Ed.). (1981). *Readings in the Philosophy of Psychology, 2.* Cambridge, MA: Harvard University Press.

Block, N. J. (1986). Psychologism and Behaviorism. *Philosophical Review, 95,* 5–40.
Block, N. J., & Fodor, J. (1972). What Psychological States are Not. *The Philosophical Review, 81,* 159–181.
Boden, M. (1977). *Artificial Intelligence and Natural Man.* New York: Basic Books.
Boden, M. (1984a). Animal Perception from an AI Viewpoint. In C. Hookway (Ed.). *Minds, Machines and Evolution.* Cambridge: Cambridge University Press.
Boden, M. (1984b). What is Computational Psychology? *Proceedings of the Aristotelian Society,* Suppl. Vol. 58, 17–35.
Bogdan, R. J. (1988). Mental Attitudes and Common-Sense Psychology: The Case Against Elimination. *Nous, 22,* 369–398.
Bogdan, R. J. (1991a). Common Sense Naturalized: The Practical Stance. In Bogdan (1991c), 161–206.
Bogdan, R. J. (1991b). The Folklore of the Mind. In Bogdan (1991c), 1–14.
Bogdan, R. J. (Ed.). (1991c). *Mind and Common Sense: Philosophical Essays on Common-sense Psychology.* Cambridge: Cambridge University Press.
Booth, W. (1988). Voodoo Science. *Science, 240,* 274–277.
Borger, R., & Cioffi, F. (Eds.). (1970). *Explanation in the Behavioral Sciences.* Cambridge: Cambridge University Press.
Borst, C. V. (Ed.). (1970). *The Mind/Body Identity Theory.* New York.
Bradley, M. C. (1963). Sensations, Brain-processes and Colours. *Australasian Journal of Philosophy, 41,* 385–393.
Bradley, M. C. (1964). Critical Notice of Smart's Philosophy and Scientific Realism. *Australasian Journal of Philosophy, 42,* 262–283.
Brand, M. (1984). *Intending and Acting: Toward a Naturalized Action Theory.* Cambridge, MA: MIT Press.
Brandt, R. B., & Kim, J. (1967). The Logic of the Identity Theory. *Journal of Philosophy, 64,* 515–537.
Brewer, W. (1974). There is No Convincing Evidence for Operant or Classical Conditioning in Adult Humans. In W. Weimer & D. Palermo (Eds.), *Cognition and the Symbolic Processes.* Hillsdale, NJ: Lawrence Erlbaum Associates.
Broadbent, D. E. (1958). *Perception and Communication.* Oxford: Pergamon Press.
Broadbent, D. E. (1970). Stimulus Set and Response Set. Two Kinds of Selective Attention. In D. Mostofsky (Ed.), *Attention: Contemporary Theory and Analysis,* (pp. 51–60). New York: Appleton-Century-Crofts.
Broadbent, D. E. (1985). A Question of Levels: Comment on McClelland and Rummelhart. *Journal of Experimental Psychology: General, 114,* 189–192.
Brown, H. (1979). *Perception, Theory and Commitment.* Chicago: University of Chicago Press.
Brown, S. C. (Ed.). (1974). *Philosophy of Psychology.* New York: Harper & Row.
Burge, T. (1979). Individualism and the Mental. In P. French, T. Uehling, & H. Wettstein (Eds.), *Midwest Studies in Philosophy, 5* (pp. 73–122). Minneapolis: University of Minnesota Press.
Burge, T. (1986). Individualism and Psychology. *Philosophical Review, 95,* 3–45.
Burton, R. (in press). *Minds: Natural and Artificial.* New York: SUNY Press.
Butler, R. J. (Ed.). (1965). *Analytic Philosophy, II.* Oxford: Oxford University Press.
Calabrese, R. L. (1980). Invertebrate Central Pattern Generators: Modeling and Complexity. (Commentary on Selverston 1980.) *Behavioral and Brain Sciences, 4,* 542–543.
Campbell, K. (1968). Critical Notice of The Identity of Theory. *Australasian Journal of Philosophy, 46,* 127–145.
Campbell, K. (1983). Abstract Particulars and the Philosophy of Mind. *Australasian Journal of Philosophy, 61,* 129–141.
Campbell, K. (1986). Can Intuitive Psychology Survive the Growth of Neuroscience? *Inquiry, 29,* 143–152.

Campbell, A., Converse, P., Miller, W., Stokes, D. (1960). *The American Voter*. New York: John Wiley & Sons.

Cartwright, N. (1983). *How the Laws of Physics Lie*. Oxford: Clarendon Press.

Castañeda, H. N. (Ed.). (1967). *Intentionality, Minds and Perception*. Detroit: Wayne State University Press.

Castañeda, H. N. (1980). The Doing of Thinking: Intending and Willing. In M. Bradie & M. Brand (Eds.), *Action and Responsibility* (pp. 80–93). Bowling Green: Bowling Green State University Press.

Causey, R. (1977). *Unity of Science*. Dordrecht, Holland: D. Reidel.

Chappell, V. C. (Ed.). (1962). *The Philosophy of Mind*. Englewood Cliffs, NJ: Prentice-Hall.

Charniak, E., & McDermott, D. (1985). *Introduction to Artificial Intelligence*. Reading, MA: Addison-Wesley.

Cherniak, C. (1986). *Minimal Rationality*. Cambridge, MA: MIT Press.

Chihara, C. S., & Fodor, J. (1965). Operationalism and Ordinary Language: A Critique of Wittgenstein. *American Philosophical Quarterly, 2,* 281–295.

Child, J., Bertholle, L., & Beck, S. (1967). *Mastering the Art of French Cooking*. New York: Knopf.

Chisholm, R. (1957). *Perceiving: A Philosophical Study*. Ithaca, NY: Cornell University Press.

Chisholm, R. (1967). On Some Psychological Concepts and the 'Logic' of Intentionality. In Castañeda (1967), 11–35.

Chomsky, N. (1965). *Aspects of the Theory of Syntax*. Cambridge, MA: MIT Press.

Chomsky, N., & Scheffler, I. (1958). What Is Said To Be. *Proceedings of the Aristotelian Society, 59,* 71–82.

Churchland, P. M. (1970). The Logical Character of Action Explanations. *Philosophical Review, 79,* 214–236.

Churchland, P. M. (1975). Two Grades of Evidential Bias. *Philosophy of Science, 42,* 250–259.

Churchland, P. M. (1979). *Scientific Realism and the Plasticity of Mind*. Cambridge: Cambridge University Press.

Churchland, P. M. (1980). Critical Notice: Joseph Margolis: Persons and Minds: The Prospects of Nonreductive Materialism. *Dialogue, 19,* 461–469.

Churchland, P. M. (1984). *Matter and Consciousness*. Cambridge, MA: MIT Press.

Churchland, P. M. (1985). Reduction, Qualia, and the Direct Introspection of Brain States. *Journal of Philosophy, 82,* 8–28.

Churchland, P. M. (1986a). The Continuity of Philosophy and the Sciences. *Mind and Language, 1,* 3–14.

Churchland, P. M. (1986b). Cognitive and Conceptual Change: A Reply to Double. *Journal for the Theory of Social Behavior, 16,* 217–221.

Churchland, P. M. (1986c). Some Reductive Strategies in Cognitive Neurobiology, *Mind, 95,* 279–309.

Churchland, P. M. (1986d). Cognitive Neurobiology: A Computational Hypothesis for Laminar Cortex. *Biology and Philosophy, 1,* 25–51.

Churchland, P. M. (1989a). On the Nature of Theories: A Neurocomputational Perspective. In C. W. Savage (Ed.), *The Structure and Function of Scientific Theories: Minnesota Studies in the Philosophy of Science, 14*. Minneapolis: University of Minnesota Press.

Churchland, P. M. (1989b). *The Neurocomputational Perspective*. Cambridge, MA: MIT Press.

Churchland, P. M., & Churchland, P. S. (1978). Commentary on Cognition and Consciousness in Non-human Species. *Behavioral and Brain Sciences, 4,* 565–566.

Churchland, P. M., & Churchland, P. S. (1981). Functionalism, Qualia, and Intentionality. *Philosophical Topics, 12,* 121–145. Reprinted in Biro & Shahan (1982).

Churchland, P. S. (1980a). A Perspective on Mind-Brain Research. *Journal of Philosophy, 77,* 185–207.

Churchland, P. S. (1980b). Language, Thought, and Information Processing. *Nous, 14,* 147-170.

Churchland, P. S. (1981a). On the Alleged Backwards Referral of Experiences and Its Relevance to the Mind-Body Problem. *Philosophy of Science, 48,* 165-181.

Churchland, P. S. (1981b). The Timing of Sensations: Reply to Libet. *Philosophy of Science, 48,* 492-497.

Churchland, P. S. (1981c). How Many Angels. . . ? (Commentary on Pucetti 1981). *Behavioral and Brain Sciences, 4,* 103-104.

Churchland, P. S. (1981d). Is Determinism Self-Refuting? *Mind, 90,* 99-101.

Churchland, P. S. (1982). Mind-Brain Reduction: New Light From the Philosophy of Science. *Neuroscience, 7,* 1041-1047.

Churchland, P. S. (1983). Consciousness: The Transmutation of a Concept. *Pacific Philosophical Quarterly, 64,* 80-95.

Churchland, P. S. (1986a). *Neurophilosophy: Toward a Unified Science of the Mind/Brain.* Cambridge, MA: MIT Press.

Churchland, P. S. (1986b). Replies to Comments. *Inquiry, 29,* 241-272.

Churchland, P. S., & Sejnowski, T. J. (1988). Perspectives on Cognitive Neuroscience. *Science, 242,* 741-745.

Clark, A. (1987a). From Folk-Psychology to Naive Psychology. *Cognitive Science, 11,* 139-154.

Clark, A. (1987b). Connectionism and Cognitive Science. In J. Hallam and C. Mellish (Eds.), *Advances in Artificial Intelligence* (pp. 3-15). Chichester: Wiley.

Clark, A. (1987c). The Kludge in the Machine. *Mind and Language, 2,* 277-300.

Clark, A. (1988). Thoughts, Sentences, and Cognitive Science. *Philosophical Psychology, 1,* 263-278.

Clark, A. (1989). *Microcognition: Philosophy, Cognitive Science, and Parallel Distributed Processing.* Cambridge, MA: MIT Press.

Clement, J. (1982). Students' Preconceptions in Introductory Mechanics. *American Journal of Physics, 50,* 66-71.

Cole, D. (1990). Functionalism and the Inverted Spectrum. *Synthese, 82,* 207-222.

Collins, A., & Quillian, M. (1972). Experiments on Semantic Memory and Language Comprehension. In L. Gregg (Ed.), *Cognition in Learning and Memory.* New York: Wiley.

Cornman, J. W. (1962). The Identity of Mind and Body. *Journal of Philosophy, 59,* 486-492.

Cornman, J. W. (1968). Mental Terms, Theoretical Terms, and Materialism. *Philosophy of Science, 35,* 45-63.

Cornman, J. W. (1968). On the Elimination of "Sensations" and Sensations. *Review of Metaphysics, 22,* 15-35.

Cornman, J. W. (1971). *Materialism and Sensations.* New Haven: Yale University Press.

Craik, F. I. M. (1984). Age Differences in Remembering. In L. R. Squire & N. Butters (Eds.) (1984), 3-12.

Craik, F. I. M., & Lockhart, R. S. (1972). Levels of Processing: A Framework for Memory Research. *Journal of Verbal Learning and Verbal Behavior, 11,* 671-684.

Crick, F. H. C. (1979). Thinking About the Brain. *Scientific American, 241,* 219-232.

Crick, F. H. C., & Mitchison, G. (1983). The Function of Dream Sleep. *Nature, 304,* 111-114.

Cummins, R. (1982). The Internal Manual Model of Psychological Exlanation. *Cognition and Brain Theory, 5.*

Cummins, R. (1983). *The Nature of Psychological Explanation.* Cambridge, MA: MIT Press.

Cummins, R. (1989). *Meaning and Mental Representation.* Cambridge, MA: MIT Press.

Cummins, R. (1991). Methodological Reflections on Belief. In Bogdan (1991c), 53-70.

Cupples, B. (1977). Three Types of Explanation. *Philosophy of Science, 44,* 387-408.

Darden, L., & Maull, N. (1977). Interfield Theories. *Philosophy of Science, 44,* 43-64.

Darwin, C. (1871). *The Descent of Man and Selection in Relation to Sex.* London: John Murray.

Darwin, C. (1872). *The Expression of the Emotions in Man and Animal.* London: John Murray.

Davidson, D. (1963). Actions, Reasons, and Causes. *Journal of Philosophy, 60,* 685–699.

Davidson, D. (1967). Causal Relations. *Journal of Philosophy, 64,* 691–703.

Davidson, D. (1970a). How is Weakness of the Will Possible? In J. Feinberg (Ed.), *Moral Concepts* (pp. 93–113). Oxford: Oxford University Press.

Davidson, D. (1970b). Mental Events. In L. Foster & J. W. Swanson (Eds.) *Experience and Theory* (pp. 79–101). Amherst, MA: University of Massachusetts Press.

Davidson, D. (1973). The Material Mind. In Suppes (1973). Reprinted in Haugland (1981), 339–354.

Davidson, D. (1974). Psychology as Philosophy. In Brown (1974).

Davidson, D. (1986). A Nice Derangement of Epitaphs. In LePore (1986), 433–446.

Davidson, D. (1989). The Myth of the Subjective. In M. Krausz (Ed.), Relativism: *Interpretation and Confrontation* (pp. 159–172). Notre Dame, IN: University of Notre Dame Press.

Davis, W. J. (1980). Neurophilosophical Reflections on Central Nervous Pattern Generators. *Behavioral and Brain Sciences, 3,* 543–544.

Dawkins, R., & Krebs, J. R. (1978). Animal Signals: Information or Manipulation? In J. R. Krebs & N. B. Davies (Eds.), *Behavioral Ecology: An Evolutionary Approach* (pp. 282–309). Oxford: Basil Blackwell.

Demopoulos, W., & Matthews, R. (1983). On the Hypothesis that Grammars are Mentally Represented. *Behavioral and Brain Sciences, 3,* 405–406.

Dennett, D. C. (1975). Brain Writing and Mind Reading. In K. Gunderson (Ed.), *Language, Mind and Knowledge: Minnesota Studies in the Philosophy of Science, 7.* Minneapolis: University of Minnesota Press. Reprinted in Dennett (1978).

Dennett, D. C. (1977). Critical Notice: "The Language of Thought" by Jerry Fodor. *Mind, 86,* 265–280.

Dennett, D. C. (1978a). *Brainstorms.* Cambridge, MA: MIT Press.

Dennett, D. C. (1978b). Current Issues in the Philosophy of Mind. *American Philosophical Quarterly, 15,* 249–261.

Dennett, D. C. (1979). On the Absence of Phenomenology. In D. Gustafson & B. Tapscott (Eds.), *Body, Mind, and Method: Essays in Honor of Virgil Aldrich* (pp. 93–113). Dordrecht, Holland: D. Reidel.

Dennett, D. C. (1980). Reply to Professor Stich. *Philosophical Books, 21.*

Dennett, D. C. (1981a). Making Sense of Ourselves. *Philosophical Topics, 12,* 63–82.

Dennett, D. C. (1981b). The Milk of Human Intentionality. (Commentary on Searle 1980). *Behavioral and Brain Sciences, 3,* 428–430.

Dennett, D. C. (1981c). True Believers: The Intentional Strategy and Why It Works. In Heath (1981), 53–75.

Dennett, D. C. (1982a). Beyond Belief. In Woodfield (1982), 1–95.

Dennett, D. C. (1982b). Notes on Prosthetic Imagination. *New Boston Review,* June, 3–7. Reprinted, with revision, as "The Imagination Extenders" in *Psychology Today, 16* (December), 32–39.

Dennett, D. C. (1982c). Styles of Mental Representation. *Proceedings of the Aristotelian Society, 83,* 213–226.

Dennett, D. C. (1983). Intentional Systems in Cognitive Ethology: 'The Panglossian Paradigm' Defended. *The Behavioral and Brain Sciences, 6,* 343–355. Reprinted in Dennett (1987), 237–268.

Dennett, D. C. (1984a). *Elbow Room.* Cambridge, MA: MIT Press.

Dennett, D. C. (1984b). Cognitive Wheels: The Frame Problem of Artificial Intelligence. In C. Hookway (Ed.), *Minds, Machines, and Evolution* (pp. 129–151). Cambridge: Cambridge University Press.

Dennett, D. C. (1986a). Can Machines Think? In M. Shatto (Ed.), *How We Know* (pp. 1–26). San Francisco: Harper & Row.

Dennett, D. C. (1986b). The Logical Geography of Computational Approaches. In Harnish & Brand (1986), 59–79.

Dennett, D. C. (1987). *The Intentional Stance.* Cambridge, MA: MIT Press.

Dennett, D. C. (1988). Review of Psychosemantics. *Journal of Philosophy, 85,* 384–389.

Dennett, D. C. (1988). Quining Qualia. In Marcel & Bisiach (1988), 42–77.

Dennett, D. C. (1991a). *Consciousness Explained.* Boston: Little, Brown & Co.

Dennett, D. C. (1991b). Real Patterns. *Journal of Philosophy, 89,* 27–51.

Dennett, D. C. (1991c). Two Contrasts: Folk Craft Versus Folk Science and Belief Versus Opinion. In Greenwood (1991a), 135–148.

Derthick, M., & Plant, D. C. (1986). Is Distributed Connectionism Compatible with the Physical Symbol System Hypothesis? *Proceedings of the Eighth Annual Conference of the Cognitive Science Society.* Hillsdale, NJ: Lawrence Erlbaum Associates.

Desmedt, J. E. (Ed.). (1979). *Cognitive Components in Cerebral Event-Related Potentials and Selective Attention.* New York: S. Karger.

Desmedt, J. E., Debecker, J., & Robertson, D. (1979). Serial Perceptual Processing and the Neural Basis of Changes in Event-Related Potentials Components and Slow Potential Shifts. In Desmedt (1979), 53–79.

Devitt, M., & Sterelny, K. (1987). *Language and Reality: An Introduction to the Philosophy of Language.* Cambridge, MA: MIT Press.

Dewan, E. M. (1976). Consciousness as an Emergent Causal Agent in the Context of Control System Theory. In Globus, Maxwell & Savodnik (1976), 181–198.

Donchin, E. (1975). Brain Electrical Correlates of Pattern Recognition. In G. F. Inbar (Ed.), *International Symposium on Signal Analysis and Pattern Recognition in Biomedical Engineering* (pp. 199–218). New York: Wiley.

Donchin, E., McCarthy, G., Kutas, M., & Ritter, W. (1983). Event-Related Potentials in the Study of Consciousness. In G. E. Schwartzand & D. Shapiro (Eds.), *Consciousness and Self-Regulation, 3* (pp. 81–121). New York: Plenum.

Dray, W. (1963). The Historical Explanation of Action Reconsidered. In S. Hook (Ed.), *Philosophy and History* (pp. 105–135). New York: New York University Press.

Dretske, F. I. (1981). *Knowledge and the Flow of Information.* Cambridge, MA: MIT Press.

Dretske, F. I. (1988). *Explaining Behavior: Reasons in a World of Causes.* Cambridge, MA: MIT Press.

Dreyfus, H. L. (1979). *What Computers Can't Do* (2nd ed.). New York: Harper & Row.

Dreyfus, H. L. (1981). From Micro-Worlds to Knowledge Representation: AI at an Impasse. In Haugeland (1981), 161–204.

Dreyfus, H. L., & Dreyfus, S. E. (1986). *Minds Over Machines: The Power of Human Intuition and Expertise in the Era of the Computer.* Cambridge, MA: MIT Press.

Dreyfus, H. L., & Dreyfus, S. E. (1988). Making a Mind Versus Modeling the Brain: Artificial Intelligence Back at a Branchpoint. In Graubard (1988).

Dupré, J. (1981). Natural Kinds and Biological Taxa. *Philosophical Review, 90,* 66–90.

Durham, T. (1987). Neural Brainwaves Break New Ground. *Computing, 9* (April).

Ebbinghaus, H. (1885/1913). *Memory: A Contribution to Experimental Psychology.* New York: Columbia Teacher's College.

Eccles, J. C., Ito, M., & Szentagothai, J. (1967). *The Cerebellum as a Neuronal Machine.* New York: Springer-Verlag.

Eccles, J. C., & Robinson, D. N. (1984). *The Wonder of Being Human.* New York: Free Press.

Elman, J. L. (1989). Representation and Structure in Connectionist Models. Technical Report CRL-8903, Center for Research in Language, University of California, San Diego.

Enc, B. (1983). In Defense of the Identity Theory. *Journal of Philosophy, 80,* 279–298.

Ericsson, K. A., & Simon, H. A. (1980). Verbal Reports as Data. *Psychological Review, 87,* 215–251.

Fahlman, S. (1979). *NETL: A System For Representing and Using Real-World Knowledge.* Cambridge, MA: MIT Press.

Feigl, H. (1967). *The "Mental" and the "Physical" — The Essay and a Postscript.* Minneapolis: University of Minnesota Press.

Feldman, J. A. (1985). Connectionist Models and Their Applications: Introduction. *Cognitive Science, 9,* 1–2.

Feldman, J. A., & Ballard, D. H. (1982). Connectionist Models and Their Properties. *Cognitive Science, 6,* 205–254.

Feyerabend, P. K. (1962). Explanation, Reduction, and Empiricism. In H. Feigl & G. Maxwell (Eds.), *Scientific Explanation, Space and Time: Minnesota Studies in the Philosophy of Science, 3.* Minneapolis: University of Minnesota Press. Reprinted in Feyerabend (1981), Vol. 1, pp. 44–96.

Feyerabend, P. K. (1963a). How to be a Good Empiricist: A Plea for Tolerance in Matters Epistemological. In B. Baumrin (Ed.), *Philosophy of Science: The Delaware Seminar, 2* (pp. 3–39). New York: Interscience. Reprinted in Morick (1972), 164–193.

Feyerabend, P. K. (1963b). Mental Events and the Brain. *Journal of Philosophy, 60,* 295–296.

Feyerabend, P. K. (1963c). Problems of Empiricism. *Pittsburgh Studies in the Philosophy of Science, 2.* Pittsburgh: University of Pittsburgh Press.

Feyerabend, P. K. (1975). *Against Method.* London: NLB.

Feyerabend, P. K. (1978). *Science in a Free Society.* London: NLB.

Feyerabend, P. K. (1981). *Philosophical Papers I & II.* Cambridge: Cambridge University Press.

Feyerabend, P. K., & Maxwell, G. (Eds.). (1966). *Mind, Matter, and Method: Essays in Honor of Herbert Feigl.* Minneapolis: University of Minnesota Press.

Field, H. (1977). Logic, Meaning, and Conceptual Role. *Journal of Philosophy, 74,* 379–408.

Field, H. (1978). Mental Representation. *Erkenntnis, 13,* 9–61. Reprinted in Block (1981), 78–114.

Fisher, R. (1935). *The Design of Experiments.* Edinburgh: Oliver & Boyd.

Fodor, J. A. (1968). The Appeal to Tacit Knowledge in Psychological Explanation. *Journal of Philosophy, 65,* 627–640.

Fodor, J. A. (1974). Special Sciences (Or: Disunity of Sciences as a Working Hypothesis). *Synthese, 28,* 97–115. Reprinted in Fodor (1981a).

Fodor, J. A. (1975). *The Language of Thought.* New York: Thomas Y. Crowell Company.

Fodor, J. A. (1978). Propositional Attitudes. *The Monist, 61,* 501–523. Reprinted in Fodor (1981a).

Fodor, J. A. (1980). Methodological Solipsism Considered as a Research Strategy in Cognitive Psychology. *Behavioral and Brain Sciences, 3,* 63–73. Reprinted in Haugland (1981), 307–339.

Fodor, J. A. (1981a). *Representations.* Cambridge, MA: MIT Press.

Fodor, J. A. (1981b). Some Notes on What Linguistics is About. In Block (1981), 197–207.

Fodor, J. A. (1981c). Something on the State of the Art. Introduction to Fodor (1981a).

Fodor, J. A. (1983). *The Modularity of Mind.* Cambridge, MA: MIT Press.

Fodor, J. A. (1983). Reply to Loar's "Must Beliefs Be Sentences." In P. Asquith & T. Nickles (Eds.), *Proceedings of the 1982 Biennial Meeting of the Philosophy of Science Association, 2.* East Lansing, MI: Philosophy of Science Association.

Fodor, J. A. (1985). Fodor's Guide to Mental Representation: The Intelligent Auntie's Vade-Mecum. *Mind, 94,* 76–100.

Fodor, J. A. (1987). *Psychosemantics: The Problem of Meaning in the Philosophy of Mind.* Cambridge, MA: MIT Press.

Fodor, J. A. (1990). *A Theory of Content, and Other Essays.* Cambridge, MA: MIT Press.

Fodor, J. A., & McLaughlin, B. P. (1990). Connectionism and the Problem of Systematicity: Why Smolensky's Solution Doesn't Work. *Cognition, 35,* 183-204.

Fodor, J. A., & Pylyshyn, Z. (1988). Connectionism and Cognitive Architecture: A Critical Analysis. *Cognition, 28,* 3-71.

Foss, J. (1986). Abstract Solutions versus Neurobiologically Plausible Problems. *Behavioral and Brain Sciences, 9,* 95-96.

Foster, L., & Swanson, J. W. (Eds.). (1970). *Experience and Theory.* London: Duckworth.

Freeman, W. (1979). Nonlinear Dynamics of Paleocortex Manifested in the Olfactory EEG. *Biological Cybernetics, 3,* 21-37.

Freud, S. (1895/1963). Project for a Scientific Psychology. In J. Strachey (Ed.), *The Standard Edition of the Complete Psychological Works of Sigmund Freud, 1.* London: Hogarth Press.

Freud, S. (1920/1963). Beyond the Pleasure Principle. In J. Strachey (Ed.), *The Standard Edition of the Complete Psychological Works of Sigmund Freud, 18.* London: Hogarth Press.

Friedman, M. (1981). Theoretical Explanations. In Healey (1981), 1-35.

Gardner, H. (1985). *The Mind's New Science.* New York: Basic Books.

Garnett, A. C. (1965). Body and Mind—The Identity Thesis. *Australasian Journal of Philosophy, 43,* 77-81.

Gazzaniga, M. S. (1970). *The Bisected Brain.* New York: Appleton-Century-Crofts.

Gazzaniga, M. S. (1975). Brain Mechanisms and Behavior. In M. S. Gazzaniga & C. Blakemore (Eds.), *Handbook of Psychobiology* (pp. 565-590). New York: Academic Press.

Gazzaniga, M. S. (1983). Right Hemisphere Language Following Brain Bisection: A Twenty Year Perspective. *American Psychologist, 38,* 525-537.

Gazzaniga, M. S. (1984a). Advances in Cognitive Neurosciences: The Problem of Information Storage in the Human Brain. In Lynch, McGaugh, & Weinberger (1984), 78-88.

Gazzaniga, M. S. (Ed.). (1984b). *Handbook of Cognitive Neuroscience.* New York: Plenum.

Gazzaniga, M. S. (1985). *The Social Brain: Discovering the Networks of the Mind.* New York: Basic Books.

Gazzaniga, M. S., Bogen, J. E., & Sperry, R. W. (1962). Some Functional Effects of Sectioning the Cerebral Commissures in Man. *Biological Sciences, 48,* 1765-1769.

Gazzaniga, M. S., & LeDoux, J. E. (1978). *The Integrated Mind.* New York: Plenum.

Gazzaniga, M. S., & Smylie, C. S. (1984). What Does Language Do for a Right Hemisphere? In Gazzaniga (1984b), 199-209.

Gazzaniga, M. S., & Sperry, R. W. (1967). Language After Section of the Cerebral Commissures. *Brain, 90,* 131-148.

Geschwind, N. (1974). The Alexias. In N. Geschwind (Ed.), *Collected Papers on Language and the Brain: Boston Studies in the Philosophy of Science, 16* (pp. 382-432). Dordrecht, Holland: D. Reidel.

Gibson, J. J. (1966). *The Senses Considered as Conceptual Systems.* Boston: Houghton Mifflin.

Gleitman, H. (1981). *Psychology.* New York: W. W. Norton.

Globus, G., Maxwell, G., & Savodnik, I. (Eds.). (1976). *Consciousness and the Brain.* New York: Plenum Press.

Gluck, M. A., & Bower, G. H. (1988). Evaluating an Adaptive Network Model of Human Learning. *Journal of Memory and Language, 27,* 166-195.

Gluck, M. A., & Rumelhart, D. E. (Eds.). (1990). *Neuroscience and Connectionist Theory.* Hillsdale, NJ: Lawrence Erlbaum Associates.

Goldman, A. (1970). *A Theory of Human Action.* Englewood Cliffs, NJ: Prentice-Hall.

Goldman, A. (1976). Volitional Theory Revisited. In M. Brand & D. Walton (Eds.), *Action Theory.* Dordrecht, Holland: D. Reidel.

Goldman, A. (1978a). Epistemology and the Psychology of Belief. *The Monist, 61,* 525-535.

Goldman, A. (1978b). Epistemics: The Regulative Theory of Cognition. *Journal of Philosophy, 75,* 509-523.

Goldman, A. (1989). Interpretation Psychologized. *Mind and Language, 3,* 161–185.

Goldman-Rakic, P. S. (1984). Modular Organization of the Prefrontal Cortex. *Trends in Neurosciences, 7,* 419–424.

Goodman, N. (1965). *Fact, Fiction and Forecast.* Indianapolis, IN: Bobbs-Merrill.

Gordon, R. (1986). Folk Psychology as Simulation. *Mind and Language, 1,* 158–171.

Gould, S. J. (1977). *Ever Since Darwin.* New York: W. W. Norton.

Gould, S., & Lewontin, R. (1978). The Spandrels of San Marco and the Panglossian Paradigm: A Critique of the Adaptationist Programme. In Sober (1984).

Graham, G., & Horgan, T. (1988). How to be Realistic About Folk Psychology. *Philosophical Psychology, 1,* 69–81.

Graubard, S. R. (Ed.). (1988). *The Artificial Intelligence Debate: False Starts, Real Foundations.* Cambridge, MA: MIT Press.

Greenwood, J. D. (Ed.). (1991a). *The Future of Folk Psychology: Intentionality and Cognitive Science.* Cambridge: Cambridge University Press.

Greenwood, J. D. (1991b). Reasons to Believe. In Greenwood (1991a), 70–92.

Gregory, R. (1970). *The Intelligent Eye.* New York: McGraw-Hill.

Grice, H. P. (1957). Meaning. *Philosophical Review, 66,* 377–388.

Grice, H. P. (1969). Utterer's Meaning and Intentions. *Philosophical Review, 78,* 147–177.

Griffin, D. (1976). *The Question of Animal Awareness: Evolutionary Continuity of Mental Experience.* New York: Rockefeller.

Grossberg, S. (1982). *Studies of Mind and Brain.* Dordrecht, Holland: D. Reidel.

Grover, D., Camp, J., and Belnap, N. (1975). A Propositional Theory of Truth. *Philosophical Studies, 27,* 73–125.

Gunderson, K. (1985). *Mentality and Machines.* (2nd ed.). Minneapolis: University of Minnesota Press.

Gustafson, D. F. (1963). On the Identity Theory. *Analysis, 24,* 30–32.

Hacking, I. (1982). Wittgenstein the Psychologist. *New York Review of Books, 29,* 5, April 1, 1982.

Hacking, I. (1983). *Representing and Intervening.* Cambridge: Cambridge University Press.

Haldane, J. (1983). Aquinas on Sense-Perception. *The Philosophical Review, 92,* 233–240.

Haldane, J. (1988). Understanding Folk. *Proceedings of the Aristotelian Society* Suppl. Vol. 62, 209–221.

Hallam, J., & Mellish, C. (Eds.). (1987). *Advances in Artificial Intelligence.* Chichester: Wiley and Sons.

Hamlyn, D. W. (1953). Behaviour. *Philosophy, 28,* 138–139.

Hannan, B. (1990). 'Non-scientific Realism' about Propositional Attitudes as a Response to Eliminative Arguments. Behavior and Philosophy 18, 21–31.

Hanson, N. R. (1967). Observation and Interpretation. In S. Morgenbesser (Ed.), *Philosophy of Science Today* (pp. 89–99). New York: Basic Books.

Harnish, R., & Brand, M. (Eds.). (1986). *The Representation of Knowledge and Belief.* Tucson: University of Arizona Press.

Haugeland, J. (1980). Programs, Causal Powers, and Intentionality. *Behavioral and Brain Sciences, 3,* 432–433.

Haugeland, J. (1982). Weak Supervenience. *American Philosophical Quarterly, 19,* 93–103.

Haugeland, J. (Ed.). (1981). *Mind Design.* Cambridge, MA: MIT Press.

Haugeland, J. (1985). *Artificial Intelligence: The Very Idea.* Cambridge, MA: MIT Press.

Haugeland, J. (1990). The Intentionality All-Stars. *Philosophical Perspectives, 4,* 383–427.

Hawkins, R. D., & Kandel, E. R. (1984). Steps Toward a Cell-Biological Alphabet for Elementary Forms of Learning. In Lynch, McGaugh, & Weinberger (1984), 385–404.

Hayes, P. (1979). The Naive Physics Manifesto. In D. Michie (Ed.), *Expert Systems in the Microelectronic Age.* Edinburgh: Edinburgh University Press.

Hayes, P. (1985a). The Second Naive Physics Manifesto. In Hobbs & Moore (1985), 1–36.

Hayes, P. (1985b). Naive Physics I: Ontology for Liquids. In Hobbs & Moore (1985).

Healey, R. (Ed.). (1981). *Reduction, Time and Reality*. New York: Cambridge University Press.

Heath, A. F. (Ed.). (1981). *Scientific Explanation*. New York: Oxford University Press.

Heil, J. (1991). Being Indiscrete. In Greenwood (1991a), 120–134.

Hempel, C. G. (1945). A Definition of "Degree of Confirmation." *Philosophy of Science, 12,* 98–115.

Hempel, C. G. (1958). The Theoretician's Dilemma: A Study in the Logic of Theory Construction. In H. Feigl, M. Scriven, & G. Maxwell (Eds.), *Concepts, Theories, and the Mind-Body Problem: Minnesota Studies in Philosophy, 2*. Minneapolis: University of Minnesota Press.

Hempel, C. G. (1965). *Aspects of Scientific Explanation*. New York: Free Press.

Hesse, M. (1970). Is There an Independent Observation Language? In R. Cololny (Ed.), *The Nature and Function of Scientific Theories* (pp. 36–77). Pittsburgh: University of Pittsburgh Press.

Hesse, M. (1974). *The Structure of Scientific Inference*. London: Macmillan.

Hetherington, P. A., & Seidenberg, M. S. (1989). Is There Catastrophic Interference in Connectionist Networks? *Proceedings of the Eleventh Annual Conference of the Cognitive Science Society* (pp. 26–33). Hillsdale, NJ: Lawrence Erlbaum Associates.

Hintikka, J. (1962). *Knowledge and Belief*. Ithaca, NY: Cornell University Press.

Hinton, G. E. (1981). Implementing Semantic Networks in Parallel Hardware. In Hinton & Anderson (1981), 161–187.

Hinton, G. E., & Anderson, J. A. (Eds.). (1981). *Parallel Models of Associative Memory*. Hillsdale, NJ: Lawrence Erlbaum Associates.

Hinton, G. E., & Sejnowski, T. J. (1983a). Optimal Perceptual Inference. In *Proceedings of the IEEE Conference on Computer Vision and Pattern Recognition* (pp. 448–453). Silver Spring, MD: IEEE Computer Society Press.

Hinton, G. E., & Sejnowski, T. J. (1983b). Analyzing Cooperative Computation. *Proceedings of the Fifth Annual Conference of the Cognitive Science Society*. Hillsdale, NJ: Lawrence Erlbaum Associates.

Hinton, G. E. (1984). Parallel Computations for Controlling an Arm. *Journal of Motor Behavior, 16,* 171–194.

Hinton, G. E., & Sejnowski, T. J. (1986). Learning and Relearning in Boltzmann Machines. In Remelhart, McClelland, & the PDP Research Group (1986), 282–317.

Hirst, R. J. (1968). Mind and Brain: The Identity Hypothesis. In *The Human Agent, Royal Institute of Philosophy Lectures, I,* 1966–67. New York: St. Martin's Press.

Hobbs, J., & Moore, R. (Eds.). (1985). *Formal Theories of the Commonsense World*. Norwood, NJ: Ablex.

Hockutt, M. (1967). In Defence of Materialism. *Philosophy and Phenomenological Research, 27,* 366–385.

Hoffman, R. (1967). Malcolm and Smart on Brain-Mind Identity. *Philosophy, 42,* 128–136.

Holland, J. H., Holyoak, K. J., Nisbett, R. E., & Thagard, P. R. (1986). *Induction: Processes of Inference, Learning, and Discovery*. Cambridge, MA: MIT Press.

Hook, S. (Ed.). (1960). *Dimensions of Mind*. New York: New York University Press.

Hooker, C. A. (1975). Systematic Philosophy and Meta-Philosophy of Science: Empiricism, Popperianism, and Realism. *Synthese, 32,* 177–231.

Hooker, C. A. (1981a). Towards a General Theory of Reduction – Part I: Historical and Scientific Setting. *Dialogue, 20,* 38–59.

Hooker, C. A. (1981b). Towards a General Theory of Reduction – Part II: Identity in Reduction. *Dialogue, 20,* 201–236.

Hooker, C. A. (1981c). Towards a General Theory of Reduction – Part III: Cross-Categorical Reduction. *Dialogue, 20,* 496–529.

Hookway, C. (Ed.). (1984). *Minds, Machines, and Evolution*. Cambridge: Cambridge University Press.

Horgan, T. (1978). The Case Against Events. *The Philosophical Review, 87*, 28–47.

Horgan, T. (1981a). Action Theory Without Actions. *Mind, 90*, 406–414.

Horgan, T. (1981b). Token Physicalism, Supervenience, and the Generality of Physics. *Synthese, 34*, 395–414.

Horgan, T. (1982a). Substitutivity and the Causal Connective. *Philosophical Studies, 42*, 47–52.

Horgan, T. (1982b). Supervenience and Microphysics. *Pacific Philosophical Quarterly, 63*, 29–43.

Horgan, T. (1987). Cognition is Real. *Behaviorism, 15*, 13–25.

Horgan, T. (1988). Attitudinatives. *Linguistics and Philosophy, 12*, 133–165.

Horgan, T. (1992). From Cognitive Science to Folk Psychology: Computation, Mental Representation, and Belief. *Philosophy and Phenomenological Research, 52*, 449–484.

Horgan, T. (Forthcoming). Nonreductive Materialism and the Explanatory Autonomy of Psychology.

Horgan, T. (Forthcoming). Actions, Reasons, and the Explanatory Role of Content. In McLaughlin (Forthcoming).

Horgan, T., & Tienson, J. (1988). Settling into a New Paradigm. *Southern Journal of Philosophy, 24*, 97–113.

Horgan, T., & Tienson, J. (1989). Representation without Rules. *Philosophical Topics, 17*, 147–174.

Horgan, T., & Tienson, J. (1991). *Connectionism and the Philosophy of Mind*. Dordrecht: Kluner Academic Publishers.

Horgan, T., & Tye, M. (1985). Against the Token Identity Theory. In LePore & McLaughlin (1985).

Horgan, T., & Woodward, J. (1985). Folk Psychology is Here to Stay. *Philosophical Review, 94*, 197–226.

Hornsby, J. (1986). Physicalist Thinking and Behavior. In Pettit & McDowell (1986), 95–115.

Hoyle, G. (1984). The Scope of Neuroethology. *Behavioral and Brain Sciences, 7*, 367–412.

Humphrey, N. (1983). *Consciousness Regained*. New York: Oxford University Press.

Humphrey, N. (1992). *A History of the Mind*. London: Chatto and Windus.

Israel, D. (1985). A Short Companion to the Naive Physics Manifesto. In Hobbs & Moore (1985), 427–447.

Jackendoff, R. (1987). *Consciousness and the Computational Mind*. Cambridge, MA: MIT Press.

Jackson, F. (1982). Epiphemonenal Qualia. *Philosophical Quarterly, 32*, 127–136.

Jackson, F., & Pettit, P. (1988). Functionalism and Broad Content. *Mind, 97*, 381–400.

Jackson, F., & Pettit, P. (1990). In Defense of Folk Psychology. *Philosophical Studies, 59*, 31–54.

James, W. (1890). *Principles of Psychology*. New York: Holt.

Jaynes, J. (1976). *The Origin of Consciousness and the Breakdown of the Bicameral Mind*. Boston: Houghton Mifflin.

Johnson-Laird, P., & Wason, P. (Eds.). (1977). *Thinking: Readings in Cognitive Science*. Cambridge: Cambridge University Press.

Joseph, G. (1980). The Many Sciences and the One World. *Journal of Philosophy, 77*, 773–791.

Joske, W. D. (1960). Sensations and Brain Processes: A Reply to Professor Smart. *Australasian Journal of Philosophy, 38*, 157–160.

Kaas, J. H., Nelson, R. J., Sur, M., & Merzenich, M. M. (1979). Multiple Representations of the Body Within the Primary Somatosensory Cortex of Primates. *Science, 204*, 521–523.

Kahneman, D., Slovic, P., & Tversky, A. (Eds.). (1982). *Judgement Under Uncertainty: Heuristics and Biases*. Cambridge: Cambridge University Press.

Katz, J. (1964). Mentalism in Linguistics. *Language, 40,* 124–137.

Keifer, H., & Munitz, M. (Eds.). (1970). *Languages, Belief, and Metaphysics.* Albany: State University of New York Press.

Kemeny, J. G., & Oppenheim, O. (1956). On Reduction. *Philosophical Studies, 7,* 6–17.

Kenny, A. (1963). *Action, Emotion, and Will.* London: Routledge & Kegan Paul.

Kenny, A. (1984). *The Legacy of Wittgenstein.* Oxford: Basil Blackwell.

Kim, J. (1966). On the Psycho-Physical Identity Theory. *American Philosophical Quarterly, 3,* 227–235.

Kim, J. (1969). Events and Their Descriptions: Some Considerations. In Rescher (1969).

Kim, J. (1973). Causation, Nomic Subsumption, and the Concept of Event. *Journal of Philosophy, 70,* 217–236.

Kim, J. (1978). Supervenience and Nomological Incommensurables. *American Philosophical Quarterly, 15,* 149–156.

Kim, J. (1979). Causality, Identity, and Supervenience in the Mind-Body Problem. In P. French, T. Uehling, & H. Wettstein (Eds.), *Midwest Studies in Philosophy, 4.* Minneapolis: University of Minnesota Press.

Kim, J. (1982). Psychophysical Supervenience. *Philosophical Studies, 41,* 51–70.

Kim, J. (1984). Supervenience and Supervenient Causation. *Southern Journal of Philosophy, 22,* 45–56.

Kinsbourne, M. (1980). Brain-Based Limitations on Mind. In R. Rieber (Ed.), *Body and Mind: Past, Present and Future* (pp. 155–175). New York: Academic Press.

Kinsbourne, M. (1982). Hemisphere Specialization and the Growth of Human Understanding. *American Psychologist, 37,* 411–420.

Kintsch, W. (1974). *The Representation of Meaning in Memory.* Hillsdale, NJ: Lawrence Erlbaum Associates.

Kitcher, P. (1980). How to Reduce a Functional Psychology? *Philosophy of Science, 47,* 134–140.

Kitcher, P. (1982). Genes, Reduction, and Functional Psychology. *Philosophy of Science, 49,* 633–636.

Kitcher, P. (1984). In Defense of Intentional Psychology. *Journal of Philosophy, 81,* 89–106.

Kitcher, P. (1978). Theories, Theorists and Theoretical Change. *Philosophical Review, 87,* 519–547.

Kitcher, P. (1982). Genes. *British Journal for the Philosophy of Science, 33,* 337–359.

Kitcher, P. (1983). Implications of Incommensurability. In P. Asquith & T. Nickles (Eds.), *Proceedings of the 1982 Biennial Meeting of the Philosophy of Science Association, 2.* East Lansing, MI: Philosophy of Science Association.

Kitcher, P. (1984). 1953 and All That: A Tale of Two Sciences. *Philosophical Review, 93,* 335–373.

Klima, E., & Bellugi, U. (1979). *The Signs Of Language.* Cambridge, MA: Harvard University Press.

Koestler, A. (1959). *The Sleepwalkers.* New York: Grosset & Dunlap.

Kohonen, T., Oja, E., & Lehtio, P. (1981). Storage and Processing of Information in Distributed Associative Memory Systems. In Hinton & Anderson (1981), 105–143.

Kosslyn, S. M., & Hatfield, G. (1984). Representation without Symbol Systems. *Social Research, 51,* 1019–1054.

Krellenstein, M. (1987). A Reply to Parallel Computation and the Mind-Body Problem. *Cognitive Sciences, 11,* 155–157.

Kuhn, T. (1970). *The Structure of Scientific Revolutions* (2nd ed.). Chicago: University of Chicago Press.

Kuhn, T. (1983). Commensurability, Comparability, Communicability. In P. Asquith & T. Nickles (Eds.), *Proceedings of the 1982 Biennial Meeting of the Philosophy of Science Association, 2.* East Lansing, MI: Philosophy of Science Association.

Lachman, R., Lachman, J., & Butterfield, E. (1979). *Cognitive Psychology and Information Processing.* Hillsdale, NJ: Lawrence Erlbaum Associates.

Lakatos, I. (1974). Falsification and the Methodology of Scientific Research Programmes. In I. Lakatos & A. Musgrave (Eds.), *Criticism and the Growth of Knowledge.* Cambridge: Cambridge University Press.

Lakoff, G. (1987). *Women, Fire and Dangerous Things.* Chicago: University of Chicago Press.

Langley, P., Simon, H., Bradshaw, G., & Zytkow, J. (1987). *Scientific Discovery: Computational Explorations of the Creative Process.* Cambridge, MA: MIT Press.

Laudan, L. (1977). *Progress and Its Problems: Towards a Theory of Scientific Growth.* Berkeley: University of California Press.

Lawson, R. A., Trowbridge, D. E., & L. C. McDermott. (1979). Students' Conceptions of Dynamics. *American Association of Physics Teachers Announcer, 9.*

Lenat, D. (1977). The Ubiquity of Discovery. *Proceedings of the Fifth International Joint Conference on Artificial Intelligence, 2,* 1093–1105.

Lenat, D. (1983). Theory Formation by Heuristic Search. *Artificial Intelligence, 21,* 31–59.

LePore, E., & McLaughlin, B. (Eds.). (1985). *Actions and Events: Perspectives on the Philosophy of Donald Davidson.* New York: Basil Blackwell.

LePore, E. (Ed.). (1986). *Truth and Interpretation: Perspectives on the Philosophy of Donald Davidson.* New York: Basil Blackwell.

Levin, M. (1984). Why We Believe in Other Minds. *Philosophy and Phenomenological Research, 44,* 343–359.

Lewis, D. (1974). Radical Interpretation. *Synthese, 23,* 331–344.

Lewis, D. (1983a). New Work for a Theory of Universals. *Australasian Journal of Philosophy, 61,* 343–377.

Lewis, D. (1983b). *Philosophical Papers, I.* Oxford: Oxford University Press.

Lieberman, P. (1984). *The Biology and Evolution of Language.* Cambridge, MA: Harvard University Press.

Lindsay, P. H., & Norman, D. A. (1977). *Human Information Processing* (2nd ed.). New York: Academic Press.

Lipsey, M. W. (1974). Psychology: Preparadigmatic, Postparadigmatic, or Misparadigmatic? *Science Studies, 4,* 406–410.

Losee, J., & Drake, S. (1966). Galileo and the Law of Inertia. *American Journal of Physics, 34.*

Louch, A. (1966). *Explanation and Human Action.* Oxford: Basil Blackwell.

Lycan, W. G. (1973). Inverted Spectrum. *Ratio, 15,* 315–319.

Lycan, W. G. (1981). Form, Function and Feel. *Journal of Philosophy, 78,* 24–50.

Lycan, W. G. (1982). Toward a Homuncular Theory of Believing. *Cognition and Brain Theory, 4,* 139–159.

Lycan, W. G. (1987). *Consciousness.* Cambridge, MA: MIT Press.

Lycan, W. G. (1988). *Judgement and Justification.* Cambridge: Cambridge University Press.

Lycan, W. G. (1990). What is the Subjectivity of the Mental? In J. E. Tomberlin (Ed.), *Philosophical Perspectives, 4: Action Theory and Philosophy of Mind* (pp. 109–133). Atascadero, CA: Ridgeview.

Lycan, W. G. (in press). Tacit Belief. In R. Bogdan (Ed.), *Belief.* Oxford: Oxford University Press.

Lynch, G., McGaugh, J. L., & Weinberger, N. M. (Eds.). (1984). *Neurobiology of Learning and Memory.* New York: Guilford.

MacCorquodale, K., & Meehl, P. E. (1948). On a Distinction Between Hypothetical Constructs and Intervening Variables. *Psychological Review, 55,* 95–107.

MacKay, D. M. (1978). Selves and Brain. *Neuroscience, 3,* 599–606.

Madell, G. (1986). Neurophilosophy: A Principled Skeptic's Response. *Inquiry, 29,* 153–168.

Malcolm, N. (1984). Consciousness and Causality. In D. M. Armstrong & N. Malcolm, *Consciousness and Causality: A Debate on the Nature of Mind.* Oxford: Basil Blackwell.

Maloney, C. (1989). *The Mundane Matter of the Mental Language.* Cambridge: Cambridge University Press.

Mandler, G., & Kessen, W. (1959). *The Language of Psychology.* New York: New York Publishers.

Marcel, A., & Bisiach, E. (Eds.) (1988). *Consciousness in Contemporary Science.* New York: Oxford University Press.

Margolis, J. (1978). *Persons and Minds: The Prospects of Nonreductive Materialism.* Dordrecht, Holland: D. Reidel.

Margolis, J. (1991). The Autonomy of Folk Psychology. In Greenwood (1991a), 242–262.

Marr, D. (1977). Artificial Intelligence: A Personal View. In Haugeland (1981), 129–142.

Marr, D. (1982). *Vision.* New York: W. H. Freeman & Company.

Marr, D., & Poggio, T. (1976). Cooperative Computation of Stereo Disparity. *Science, 194,* 283–287.

Massaro, D. W. (1989). Testing Between the TRACE Model and the Fuzzy Logic Model of Speech Perception. *Cognitive Psychology, 21,* 398–421.

Massaro, D. W., & Cohen, M. M. (1991). Interactive Activation and the Joint Influence of Sensory Information and Context in Perception. *Cognitive Psychology, 23,* 558–614.

Matthews, R. (1984). Troubles with Representationalism. *Social Research, 51,* 1065–1097.

Maull, N. (1977). Unifying Science Without Reduction. *Studies in the History and Philosophy of Science, 8,* 143–162.

McCarthy, J. (1959). Programs with Common Sense. In *Mechanisation of Thought Processes, 1.* London: HMSO. Reprinted in Minsky (1968).

McCarthy, J. (1977). *First Order Theories of Individual Concepts.* Stanford Artificial Intelligence Laboratory.

McCarthy, J. (1980). Circumspection: A Form of Non-Monotonic Reasoning. *Artificial Intelligence, 13,* 27–39.

McCarthy, J. (1986). Applications of Circumspection to Formalizing Common Sense Knowledge. *Artificial Intelligence, 28,* 89–116.

McCarthy, J., & Hayes, P. (1969). Some Philosophical Problems From the Standpoint of Artificial Intelligence. In B. Meltzer & D. Michie (Eds.), *Machine Intelligence, 4* (pp. 463–502).

McCauley, R. N. (1981). Hypothetical Identities and Ontological Economizing: Comments on Causey's Program for the Unity of Science. *Philosophy of Science, 48,* 218–227.

McCauley, R. N. (1986). Problem Solving in Science and the Competence Approach to Theorizing in Linguistics. *Journal for the Theory of Social Behavior, 16,* 299–313.

McClelland, J. L. (1981). Retrieving General and Specific Knowledge From Stored Knowledge of Specifics. *Proceedings of the Third Annual Conference of The Cognitive Science Society* (pp. 170–172).

McClelland, J. L. (Unpublished). Models of Perception and Memory Based on Principles of Neural Organization. Carnegie-Mellon University, Pittsburgh.

McClelland, J. L. (1991). Stochastic Interactive Processes and the Effect of Context on Perception. *Cognitive Psychology, 23,* 1–44.

McClelland, J. L., & Kawamoto, A. (1986). Mechanisms of Sentence Processing: Assigning Roles to Constituents of Sentences. In McClelland, Rumelhart, & the PDP Research Group (1986), 216–271.

McClelland, J. L., & Rumelhart, D. E. (1981). An Interactive Activation Model of the Effect of Context in Letter Perception. Part I: An Account of Basic Findings. *Psychological Review, 88,* 375–407.

McClelland, J. L., & Rumelhart, D. E. (1985a). Distributed Memory and the Representation of General and Specific Information. *Journal of Experimental Psychology: General, 114,* 159-188.

McClelland, J. L., & Rumelhart, D. E. (1985b). Levels Indeed! A Response to Broadbent. *Journal of Experimental Psychology: General, 114,* 193-197.

McClelland, J. L., & Rumelhart, D. E. (1986). Amnesia and Distributed Memory. In McClelland, Rumelhart, & the PDP Research Group (1986), 503-529.

McClelland, J. L., Rumelhart, D. E., & Hinton, G. E. (1986). The Appeal of Parallel Distributed Processing. In Rumelhart, McClelland, & the PDP Research Group (1986), 3-44.

McClelland, J. L., Rumelhart, D. E., & the PDP Research Group. (1986). *Parallel Distributed Processing: Explorations in the Microstructure of Cognition.* Vol. 2. Cambridge, MA: MIT Press.

McClosky, M. (1983). Intuitive Physics. *Scientific American, 248,* 122-130.

McClosky, M., & Cohen, N. J. (1989). Catastrophic Interference in Connectionist Networks: The Sequential Learning Problem. In G. H. Bower (Ed.), *The Psychology of Learning and Motivation, 44,* (pp. 109-165). New York: Academic Press.

McCloskey, M., Caramazza, A., & Basili, A. (1987). Dissociations of Number System Processes. In G. Deloshe & X. Seron (Eds.), *Mathematical Disabilities: A Cognitive Neuropsychological Perspective.* Hillsdale, NJ: Lawrence Erlbaum Associates.

McCloskey, M., Caramazza, A., & Green, B. (1980). Curvilinear Motion in the Absence of External Forces: Naive Beliefs About the Motion of Objects. *Science, 210,* 1139-1141.

McCulloch, G. (1986). Scientism, Mind, and Meaning. In Pettit & McDowell (1986), 59-94.

McDermott, D. (1976). Artificial Intelligence Meets Natural Stupidity. In Haugeland (1981), 143-160.

McDonough, R. (1991). A Culturalist Account of Folk Psychology. In Greenwood (1991a), 263-288.

McGinn, C. (1982a). *The Character of Mind.* Oxford: Oxford University Press.

McGinn, C. (1982b). The Structure of Content. In Woodfield (1982), 207-259.

McGinn, C. (1989). Can We Really Solve the Mind-Body Problem? *Mind, 98,* 359-366.

McGinn, C. (1991). Consciousness and Content. In Bogdan (1991c), 71-92.

McLaughlin, B. (Ed.). (forthcoming). *The Philosophy of Fred Dretske.* Oxford: Basil Blackwell.

Medin, D. L. (1989). Concepts and Conceptual Structure. *American Psychologist, 44,* 1469-1481.

Menzel, E. W. (1974). A Group of Young Chimpanzees in a One-Acre Field. In A. M. Schrier & F. Stollnitz (Eds.), *Behavior of Nonhuman Primates, 5* (pp. 83-153). New York: Academic Press.

Menzel, E. W. (1983). Parlez-Vouz Baboon, Bwana Sherlock? (Commentary on Dennett 1983). *Behavioral and Brain Sciences, 3,* 371-372.

Michaels, C., & Carello, C. (1981). *Direct Perception.* Englewood Cliffs, NJ: Prentice-Hall.

Michie, D., & Johnston, R. (1984). *The Creative Computer.* Harmondsworth: Penguin.

Mill, J. S. (1862). *A System of Logic Ratiocinative and Inductive.* London: Longmans, Green and Co.

Miller, G. A. (1956). The Magical Number Seven, Plus or Minus Two: Some Limits on Our Capacity for Processing Information. *Psychological Review, 63,* 81-97.

Millikan, R. G. (1984). *Language, Thought and Other Biological Categories.* Cambridge, MA: MIT Press.

Millikan, R. G. (1986). Thoughts Without Laws, Cognitive Science With Content. *Philosophical Review, 95,* 47-80.

Minsky, M. (Ed.). (1968). *Semantic Information Processing.* Cambridge, MA: MIT Press.

Minsky, M. (1975). Frame-System Theory. In Johnson-Laird & Wason (1977).

Minsky, M. (1980). K-Lines: A Theory of Memory. *Cognitive Science, 4,* 117–133. Reprinted in Norman (1981).

Minsky, M. (1981). A Framework for Representing Knowledge. In Haugeland (1981), 95–128.

Minsky, M., & Papert, S. (1969). *Perceptrons: An Introduction to Computational Geometry.* Cambridge, MA: MIT Press.

Moore, G. E. (1953). *Some Main Problems of Philosophy.* London: Allen & Unwin.

Morgan, L. (1896). *Habit and Instinct.* London: Edward Arnold.

Morick, H. (Ed.) (1972). *Challenges to Empiricism.* Belmont, CA: Wadsworth.

Morris, R. G. M. (Ed.). (1989). *Parallel Distributed Processing: Implications for Psychology and Neurobiology.* Oxford: Oxford University Press.

Morton, A. (1980). *Frames of Mind.* Oxford: Oxford University Press.

Morton, A. (1991). The Inevitability of Folk Psychology. In Bogdan (1991c), 93–122.

Nagel, E. (1961). *The Structure of Science.* New York: Harcourt, Brace & World.

Nagel, T. (1974). What Is It Like to Be A Bat? *Philosophical Review, 83,* 435–450. Reprinted in Block (1980).

Nagel, T. (1986). *The View from Nowhere.* New York: Oxford University Press.

Needham, R. (1972). *Belief, Language and Experience.* Chicago: Chicago University Press.

Neisser, U. (1967). *Cognitive Psychology.* New York: Appleton-Century-Crofts.

Neisser, U. (1975). *Cognition and Reality.* San Francisco: W. H. Freeman.

Nestle, J. (1982). Understanding Psychological Man. *Psychology Today, 16,* 40–59.

Newell, A. (1973). Production Systems: Models of Control Structures. In W. Chase (Ed.), *Visual Information Processing.* New York: Academic Press.

Newell, A. (1980). Physical Symbol Systems. *Cognitive Science, 4,* 135–183.

Newell, A. (1989). *Unified Theories of Cognition.* Cambridge, MA: Harvard University Press.

Newell, A., & Simon, H. (1972). *Human Problem Solving.* Englewood Cliffs, NJ: Prentice Hall.

Newell, A., & Simon, H. (1976). Computer Science as Empirical Inquiry. In Haugeland (1981), 35–66.

Newell, A., Rosenbloom, P. S., & Laird, J. E. (1989). Symbolic Architectures for Cognition. In Posner (1989), 93–132.

Newell, A., Shaw, J. C., & Simon, H. A. (1958). Elements in a Theory of Problem Solving. *Psychological Review, 65,* 151–166.

Newton-Smith, W. H. (1981). *The Rationality of Science.* London: Routledge & Kegan Paul.

Nickles, T. (1973). Two Concepts of Inter-theoretic Reduction. *Journal of Philosophy, 70,* 181–201.

Nisbett, R. E., & Ross, L. (1980). *Human Inference: Strategies and Shortcomings of Social Judgement.* Englewood Cliffs, NJ: Prentice-Hall.

Nisbett, R. E., & Wilson, D. D. (1977). Telling More Than We Can Know: Verbal Reports on Mental Processes. *Psychological Review, 84,* 231–259.

Norman, D. A. (1969). *Memory and Attention: An Introduction to Human Information Processing.* New York: Wiley.

Norman, D. A. (1973). Memory, Knowledge, and the Answering of Questions. In R. Solso (Ed.), *The Loyola Symposium on Cognitive Psychology.* Washington, DC: Winston.

Norman, D. A. (Ed.). (1981). *Perspectives on Cognitive Science.* Norwood, NJ: Ablex.

Norman, D. A. (1986). Reflections on Cognition and Parallel Distributed Processing. In McClelland, Rumelhart, & the PDP Research Group (1986), 110–146.

Norman, D. A., & Rumelhart, D. E. (1970). A System For Perception and Memory. In D. A. Norman (Ed.), *Models of Human Memory.* New York: Academic Press.

Norman, D. A., & Rumelhart, D. E. (1975). Memory and Knowledge. In D. A. Norman, D. E. Rumelhart, and the LNR Research Group (Eds.), *Explorations in Cognition.* San Francisco: Freeman.

Novak, G. S., & Araya, A. A. (1980). Research On Expert Problem Solving In *Proceedings of the First Annual National Conference On Artificial Intelligence.*

Nozick, R. (1981). *Philosophical Explanations.* Cambridge, MA: Harvard University Press.

Oakley, D. A. (Ed.). (1985). *Brain and Mind.* London: Methuen.

O'Brien, G. J. (1991). Is Connectionism Common Sense? *Philosophical Psychology, 4,* 165–178.

O'Brien, G. J. (Forthcoming). Connectionism and Analogicity.

Oppenheim, P., & Putnam, H. (1958). Unity of Science as a Working Hypothesis. In H. Feigl, M. Scriven, & G. Maxwell (Eds.), *Concepts, Theories, and the Mind-Body Problem: Minnesota Studies in the Philosophy of Science, 2* (pp. 3–36). Minneapolis: University of Minnesota Press.

Palm, G. (1982). *Neural Assemblies: An Alternative Approach to Artificial Intelligence.* Berlin: Springer-Verlag.

Peacocke, C. (1983). *Sense and Content.* Oxford: Clarendon Press.

Pellionisz, A. (1983). Brain Theory: Connecting Neurobiology to Robotics Tensor Analysis Coordinates to Describe, Understand and Engineer Functional Geometries of Intelligent Organisms. *Journal of Theoretical Neurobiology, 2,* 185–211.

Peters, R. S. (1958). *The Concept of Motivation.* London: Routledge & Kegan Paul.

Pettit, P., & McDowell, J. (Eds.). (1986). *Subject, Thought, and Context.* Oxford: Oxford University Press.

Piaget, J. (1971). *Insights and Illusions of Philosophy.* Trans. by Wolfe Mays. New York: World Publishing Company.

Pinker, S. (1984). *Language, Learnability and Language Development.* Cambridge, MA: Harvard University Press.

Pinker, S., & Prince, A. (1988). On Language and Connectionism: Analysis of a Parallel Distributed Processing Model of Language Acquisition. *Cognition, 28,* 73–193.

Popper, K. R. (1965a). *Conjectures and Refutations: The Growth of Scientific Knowledge* (2nd ed.). New York: Harper & Row.

Popper, K. R. (1965b). *The Logic of Scientific Discovery.* London: Hutchison.

Popper, K. R. (1972). *Objective Knowledge.* Oxford: Clarendon Press.

Popper, K. R., & Eccles, J. C. (1977). *The Self and Its Brain.* Berlin: Springer-International.

Posner, M. I. (1978). *Chronometric Explorations of the Mind.* Hillsdale, NJ: Lawrence Erlbaum Associates.

Posner, M. I. (Ed.). (1989). *Foundations of Cognitive Science.* Cambridge, MA: MIT Press.

Posner, M. I., Pea, R., & Volpe, B. (1982). Cognitive-Neuroscience: Developments Toward a Science of Synthesis. In J. Mehler, E. Walker, & M. Garrett (Eds.), *Perspectives On Mental Representation* (pp. 69–85). Hillsdale, NJ: Lawrence Erlbaum Associates.

Premack, D., & Woodruff, G. (1978). Does the Chimpanzee Have a Theory of Mind? *Behavioral and Brain Science, 4,* 515–526.

Presley, C. F. (Ed.). (1967). *The Identity Theory of Mind.* Brisbane: University of Queensland Press.

Preston, J. (1989). Folk Psychology as Theory or Practice? *Inquiry, 32,* 277–303.

Pucetti, R. (1981). The Case For Mental Duality: Evidence From Split-Brain Data and Other Considerations. *Behavioral and Brain Sciences, 4,* 93–99.

Putnam, H. (1960). Minds and Machines. In Hook (1961).

Putnam, H. (1962). The Analytic and the Synthetic. In H. Feigl & G. Maxwell (Eds.), *Scientific Explanation, Space and Time: Minnesota Studies in the Philosophy of Science, 3* (pp. 358–397). Minneapolis: University of Minnesota Press.

Putnam, H. (1965). Brains and Behavior. In Butler (1965).

Putnam, H. (1967a). The Nature of Mental States. In W. H. Capitan & D. D. Merrill (Eds.), *Art, Mind, and Religion* (pp. 37–48). Pittsburgh: University of Pittsburgh Press. Reprinted in Rosenthal (1971), 150–161.

Putnam, H. (1967b). Psychological Predicates. In W. Capitan & D. Merill (Eds.), *Art, Mind, and Religion* (pp. 37–48). Pittsburgh: University of Pittsburgh Press.

Putnam, H. (1970). Is Semantics Possible? In Keifer & Munitz (1970). Reprinted in Putnam (1975b).

Putnam, H. (1975a). The Meaning of 'Meaning'. In K. Gunderson (Ed.), *Language, Mind, and Knowledge: Minnesota Studies in the Philosophy of Science, 7.* Minneapolis: University of Minnesota Press. Reprinted in Putnam (1975b).

Putnam, H. (1975b). *Mind, Language and Reality.* Cambridge: Cambridge University Press.

Putnam, H. (1975c). Philosophy and Our Mental Life. In Putnam (1975b).

Putnam, H. (1981). Reductionism and the Nature of Psychology. In Haugeland (1981), 205–219.

Putnam, H. (1988). *Representation and Realism.* Cambridge, MA: MIT Press.

Pylyshyn, Z. (1980). Computation and Cognition: Issues in the Foundation of Cognitive Science. *Behavioral and Brain Sciences, 3,* 111–134.

Pylyshyn, Z. (1984). *Computation and Cognition: Toward a Foundation for Cognitive Science.* Cambridge, MA: MIT Press.

Quillian, M. (1966). *Semantic Memory.* Cambridge, MA: Bolt, Branak & Newman.

Quine, W. V. O. (1948). On What There Is. *Review of Metaphysics, 2,* 21–38. Reprinted in Quine (1953), 1–19.

Quine, W. V. O. (1953). Two Dogmas of Empiricism. In Quine (1953), 20–46.

Quine, W. V. O. (1953). *From a Logical Point of View.* Cambridge, MA: Harvard University Press.

Quine, W. V. O. (1960). *Word and Object.* Cambridge, MA: MIT Press.

Quine, W. V. O. (1969). Epistemology Naturalized. In Quine (1969).

Quine, W. V. O. (1969). *Ontological Relativity and Other Essays.* New York: Columbia University Press.

Quine, W. V. O. (1970). *Philosophy of Logic.* Englewood Cliffs, NJ: Prentice-Hall.

Quine, W. V. O. (1976). *The Ways of Paradox.* Cambridge, MA: Harvard University Press.

Ramsey, W. (1989). Parallelism and Functionalism. *Cognitive Science, 13,* 139–144.

Ramsey, W., Stich, S. P., & Rumelhart, D. E. (Eds.). (1991). *Philosophy and Connectionist Theory.* Hillsdale, NJ: Lawrence Erlbaum Associates.

Reichenbach, H. (1938). *Experience and Prediction.* Chicago: University of Chicago Press.

Reingold, E. M., & Merikle, P. M. (1990). On the Interrelatedness of Theory and Measurement in the Study of Unconscious Processes. *Mind and Language, 5,* 9–28.

Rescher, N. (Ed.). (1969). *Essays in Honor of Carl G. Hempel.* Dordrecht, Holland: D. Reidel.

Rescher, N. (1970). *Scientific Explanation.* New York: Free Press.

Richardson, R. C. (1979). Functionalism and Reductionism. *Philosophy of Science, 46,* 533–558.

Robinson, H. (1982). *Matter and Sense: A Critique of Contemporary Materialism.* Cambridge: Cambridge University Press.

Robinson, J. (1982). The Sodium Pump and its Rivals: An Example of Conflict Resolution in Science. *Perspectives in Biology and Medicine, 25,* 486–495.

Rock, I. (1983). *The Logic of Perception.* Cambridge, MA: MIT Press.

Romanes, G. (1884). *Mental Evolution in Animals.* New York: Appleton.

Romanes, G. (1888). *Mental Evolution in Animals.* London: Kegan Paul.

Rorty, R. (1970). In Defense of Eliminative Materialism. *Review of Metaphysics, 24,* 112–121.

Rorty, R. (1970). Incorrigibility as a Mark of the Mental. *Journal of Philosophy, 67,* 399–424.

Rorty, R. (1979). *Philosophy and the Mirror of Nature.* Princeton: Princeton University Press.

Rorty, R. (1982). *Consequences of Pragmatism.* Minneapolis: University of Minnesota Press.

Rorty, R. (1989). *Contingency, Irony, and Solidarity.* Cambridge: Cambridge University Press.

Rosch, E. (1981). Prototype Classification and Logical Classification: The Two Systems. In Scholnick (1981).

Rosch, E. (1973). On the Internal Structure of Perceptual and Semantic Categories. In T. Moore (Ed.), *Cognitive Development and the Acquisition of Language* (pp. 111-144). New York: Academic Press.

Rosch, E., & Lloyd, B. B. (Eds.). (1978). *Cognition and Categorization.* Hillsdale, NJ: Lawrence Erlbaum Associates.

Rosch, E., & Mervis, C. (1975). Family Resemblances: Studies in the Internal Structure of Categories. *Cognitive Psychology, 7,* 573-605.

Rose, C. F., & Bynum, W. F. (1982). *Historical Aspects of the Neurosciences.* New York: Raven.

Rosenberg, A. (1981). *Sociobiology and the Preemption of Social Science.* Baltimore: Johns Hopkins University Press.

Rosenberg, A. (1986a). Intentional Psychology and Evolutionary Biology Part I: The Uneasy Analogy. *Behaviorism, 14,* 15-27.

Rosenberg, A. (1986b). Intentional Psychology and Evolutionary Biology Part II: The Crucial Disanalogy. *Behaviorism, 14,* 125-138.

Rosenberg, A. (1991). How is Eliminative Materialism Possible? In Bogdan (1991c), 123-143.

Rosenberg, C. R., & Sejnowski, T. J. (1987). Parallel Networks That Learn To Pronounce English Text. *Complex Systems, 1.*

Rosenberg, J. (1974). *Linguistic Representation.* Dordrecht, Holland: D. Reidel.

Rosenberg, J. (1991). "Tractarian States" and Folk-Psychological Explanation. In Greenwood (1991a), 226-241.

Rosenthal, D. M. (Ed.). (1971). *Materialism and the Mind-Body Problem.* Englewood Cliffs, NJ: Prentice-Hall.

Rumelhart, D. E. (1984). The Emergence of Cognitive Phenomena From Sub-Symbolic Processes. *Proceedings of the Sixth Annual Conference of the Cognitive Science Society* (pp. 59-62). Hillsdale, NJ: Lawrence Erlbaum Associates.

Rumelhart, D. E., & McClelland, J. L. (1985). Level's Indeed! A Response to Broadbent. *Journal of Experimental Psychology: General, 114,* 159-188.

Rumelhart, D. E., & McClelland, J. L. (1986a). On Learning the Past Tense of English Verbs. In McClelland, Rumelhart, & the PDP Research Group (1986), 216-271.

Rumelhart, D. E., & McClelland, J. L. (1986b). PDP Models and General Issues in Cognitive Science. In Rumelhart, McClelland, & the PDP Research Group (1986), 110-146.

Rumelhart, D. E., & Norman, D. A. (1982). Simulating a Skilled Typist: A Study of Skilled Cognitive-Motor Performance. *Cognitive Science, 6,* 1-36.

Rumelhart, D. E., & Zipser, D. (1987). Feature Discovery By Competitive Learning. *Cognitive Science, 9,* 75-112.

Rumelhart, D. E., Hinton, G. E., & Williams, R. J. (1986). Learning Internal Representations by Error Propagation. In Rumelhart, McClelland, & the PDP Research Group (1986), 318-362.

Rumelhart, D. E., Lindsay, P., & Norman, D. (1972). A Process Model for Long Term Memory. In E. Tulving & W. Donaldson (Eds.), *Organization of Memory.* New York: Academic Press.

Rumelhart, D. E., McClelland, J. L., & the PDP Research Group. (Eds.). (1986). *Parallel Distributed Processing: Explorations in the Microstructure of Cognition.* Vol. 1. Cambridge, MA: MIT Press.

Rumelhart, D. E., Smolensky, P., McClelland, J. L., & Hinton, G. E. (1986a). Schemata and Sequential Thought Processes in PDP Models. In McClelland, Rumelhart, & the PDP Research Group (1986), 7-58.

Russell, B. (1940). *An Inquiry into Meaning and Truth.* London: George Allen & Unwin.

Rutkowska, J. (1986). Developmental Psychology's Contribution to Cognitive Science. In K. S. Gill (Ed.), *Artificial Intelligence for Society* (pp. 79-97). Chichester, Sussex: John Wiley.

Ryle, G. (1949). *The Concept of Mind.* London: Hutchison.

Sagan, C. (1977). *Dragons of Eden.* New York: Random House.

Salmon, W. (1971). *Statistical Explanation and Statistical Relevance.* Pittsburgh: University of Pittsburgh Press.

Salmon, W. (1984). *Scientific Explanation and the Causal Structure of the World.* Princeton: Princeton University Press.

Schaffner, K. (1967). Approaches to Reduction. *Philosophy of Science, 34,* 137–147.

Schank, R. (1981). Language and Memory. In Norman (1981).

Schank, R., & Abelson, R. (1977). *Scripts, Plans, Goals, and Understanding.* New Jersey: John Wiley & Sons.

Scheffler, I. (1963). *The Anatomy of Inquiry: Philosophical Studies in the Theory of Science.* New York: Knopf.

Schiffer, S. (1972). *Meaning.* Oxford: Oxford University Press.

Schilcher, C., & Tennant, N. (1984). *Philosophy, Evolution, and Human Nature.* London: Routledge & Kegan Paul.

Schmitt, F. O., & Worden, F. G. (Eds.). (1974). *The Neurosciences: Third Study Program.* Cambridge, MA: MIT Press.

Schmitt, F. O., & Worden, F. G. (Eds.). (1979). *The Neurosciences: Fourth Study Program.* Cambridge, MA: MIT Press.

Schmitt, F. O., Worden, F. G., Adelman, G., & Dennis, S. G. (Eds.). (1981). *The Organization of the Cebral Cortex.* Cambridge, MA: MIT Press.

Scholnick, E. (Ed.). (1981). *New Trends in Cognitive Representations: Challenges to Piaget's Theory.* Hillsdale, NJ: Lawrence Erlbaum Associates.

Searle, J. R. (1969). *Speech Acts: An Essay in the Philosophy of Language.* Cambridge: Cambridge University Press.

Searle, J. R. (1980). Minds, Brains, and Programs. *Behavioral and Brain Sciences, 3,* 417–457. Reprinted in Haugeland (1981), 282–307.

Searle, J. R. (1983). *Intentionality: An Essay in the Philosophy of Mind.* Cambridge: Cambridge University Press.

Searle, J. R. (1984). Intentionality and Its Place in Nature. *Synthese, 61,* 3–16.

Searle, J. R. (1986). *Minds, Brains, and Science.* Cambridge, MA: Harvard University Press.

Searle, J. R. (1990). Is the Brain's Mind a Computer Program? *Scientific American, 262,* 26–31.

Sejnowski, T. J. (1981). Skeleton Filters in the Brain. In Hinton & Anderson (1981), 189–212.

Sejnowski, T. J., & Hinton, G. E. (forthcoming). Separating Figure From Ground With a Boltzmann Machine. In M. Arbib & A. R. Hanson (Eds.), *Vision, Brain, and Cooperative Computation.* Cambridge, MA: MIT Press.

Seligman, M. E. P. (1975). *Helplessness.* San Francisco: W. H. Freeman & Co.

Sellars, W. (1956). Empiricism and the Philosophy of Mind. In H. Feigl & M. Scriven (Eds.), *Minnesota Studies in the Philosophy of Science, 1.* Minneapolis: University of Minnesota Press. Reprinted in Sellars (1963).

Sellars, W. (1963). *Science, Perception, and Reality.* London: Routledge & Kegan Paul.

Sellars, W. (1965). The Identity Approach to the Mind-Body Problem. *Review of Metaphysics, 18,* 430–451.

Sellars, W. (1968). Some Problems About Belief. *Synthese, 19,* 158–177.

Sellars, W. (1969). Language as Thought and as Communication. *Philosophy and Phenomenological Research, 29,* 506–527.

Servan-Schreiber, D., Cleeremans, A., & McClelland, J. L. (1988). Encoding Sequential Structure in Simple Recurrent Networks. Technical Report CMU-CS-99-183, Computer Science Department, Carnegie Mellon University, Pittsburgh, PA.

Shaffer, J. (1961). Could Mental States Be Brain Processes? *Journal of Philosophy, 58,* 812–822.

Shaffer, J. (1963). Mental Events and the Brain. *Journal of Philosophy, 60,* 160–166.

Sharpe, R. A. (1987). The Very Idea of a Folk Psychology. *Inquiry, 30,* 381–393.

Shoemaker, S. (1981). Functionalism, Qualia, and Intentionality. *Philosophical Topics, 12,* 93–118. Reprinted in Biro & Shahan (1982).

Simon, H. A. (Ed.). (1969). *The Sciences of the Artificial.* Cambridge: Cambridge University Press.

Simon, H. A. (1979). Artificial Intelligence Research Strategies in the Light of AI Models of Scientific Discovery. *Proceedings of the Sixth International Joint Conference on Artificial Intelligence, 2,* 1086–1094.

Simon, H. A. (1980). Cognitive Science: The Newest Science of the Artificial. *Cognitive Science, 4,* 33–46.

Simon, H. A., & Kaplan, C. A. (1989). Foundations of Cognitive Science. In Posner (1989), 1–47.

Skinner, B. F. (1953). *Science and Human Behavior.* New York: Macmillan.

Skinner, B. F. (1971). *Beyond Freedom and Dignity.* New York: Knopf.

Sloman, A. (1984). The Structure of the Space of Possible Minds. In Torrance (1984).

Smart, J. J. C. (1959). Sensations and Brain Processes. *Philosophical Review, 68,* 141–156. Reprinted in Chappell (1962).

Smart, J. J. C. (1962). Brain Processes and Incorrigibility. *Australasian Journal of Philosophy, 40,* 68–70.

Smart, J. J. C. (1963). *Philosophy and Scientific Realism.* New York: Humanities Press.

Smith, E. E., & Medin, D. L. (1981). *Concepts and Categories.* Cambridge, MA: Harvard University Press.

Smith, M. (1984). The Evolution of Animal Intelligence. In C. Hookway (Ed.), *Minds, Machines and Evolution.* Cambridge: Cambridge University Press.

Smolensky, P. (1986). Information Processing in Dynamical Systems: Foundations of Harmony Theory. In Rumelhart, McClelland, & the PDP Research Group (1986), 194–281.

Smolensky, P. (1987). Connectionist AI, and the Brain. *Artificial Intelligence Review, 1,* 95–109.

Smolensky, P. (1988). On the Proper Treatment of Connectionism. *Behavioral and Brain Sciences, 11,* 1–74.

Smythies, J. R. (Ed.). (1965). *Brain and Mind.* New York: Humanities Press.

Sober, E. (1981). The Evolution of Rationality. *Synthese, 46,* 95–120.

Sober, E. (Ed.). (1984). *Conceptual Issues in Evolutionary Biology.* Cambridge: MIT Press.

Spencer, H. (1855). *The Principles of Psychology.* London: Longman, Brown, Green & Longman.

Sperry, R. W. (1976). Mental Phenomena as Causal Determinants in Brain Function. In G. Globus, G. Maxwell, & I. Savodnik (Eds.), *Consciousness and the Brain* (pp. 163–177). New York: Plenum.

Sperry, R. W. (1980). Mind-Brain Interaction: Mentalism, Yes; Dualism, No. *Neuroscience, 5,* 195–206.

Stabler, E. (1983). How are Grammars Represented? *Behavioral and Brain Sciences, 3,* 391–421.

Staddon, J. E. R. (1983). *Adaptive Behavior and Learning.* New York: Cambridge University Press.

Sterelny, K. (1985). Review of Stich *From Folk Psychology to Cognitive Science. Australasian Journal of Philosophy, 63,* 510–520.

Stich, S. P. (1971). What Every Speaker Knows. *Philosophical Review, 80,* 476–496.

Stich, S. P. (1972). Grammar, Psychology, and Indeterminacy. Reprinted in Block (1981), 208–222.

Stich, S. P. (1976). Davidson's Semantic Program. *Canadian Journal of Philosophy, 4,* 201–227.

Stich, S. P. (1978a). Autonomous Psychology and The Belief-Desire Thesis. *The Monist, 61,* 573–591.

Stich, S. P. (1978b). Beliefs and Subdoxastic States. *Philosophy of Science, 45,* 499–518.

Stich, S. P. (1979). Do Animals Have Beliefs? *Australasian Journal of Philosophy, 57,* 15–28.

Stich, S. P. (1980a). Headaches. *Philosophical Books, 21.*

Stich, S. P. (1980b). Paying the Price for Methodological Solipsism. *Behavioral and Brain Sciences, 3,* 152–153.

Stich, S. P. (1981). Dennett on Intentional Systems. *Philosophical Topics, 12,* 39–62. Reprinted in Biro & Shahan (1982).

Stich, S. P. (1982). On the Ascription of Content. In Woodfield (1982), 153–206.

Stich, S. P. (1983a). *From Folk Psychology to Cognitive Science: The Case Against Belief.* Cambridge, MA: MIT Press.

Stich, S. P. (1983b). Armstrong on Belief. In R. J. Bogdan (Ed.), *Profile: David Armstrong.* Dordrecht, Holland: D. Reidel.

Stich, S. P. (1985). Could Man be an Irrational Animal? *Synthese, 64,* 115–135.

Stich, S. P., & Nisbett, R. E. (1980). Justification and the Psychology of Human Reasoning. *Philosophy of Science, 47,* 188–202.

Stone, J. (1983). *Parallel Processing in the Visual System.* New York: Plenum.

Stone, J., & Bogdan, D. (1982). Parallel Processing of Information in the Visual Pathways. *Trends in Neurosciences, 5,* 441–446.

Storms, M., & Nisbett, R. (1970). Insomnia and the Attribution Process. *Journal of Personality and Social Psychology, 16,* 319–328.

Strawson, P. F. (1959). *Individuals.* London: Methuen & Co.

Suppe, F. (1977). The Search For Philosophic Understanding of Scientific Theories. In F. Suppe (Ed.), *The Structure of Scientific Theories* (pp. 3–232). Urbana, IL: University of Illinois Press.

Suppes, P. (Ed.). (1973). *Logic, Methodology, and the Philosophy of Science, 4.* New York: American Elsevier Publishing Co.

Sutherland, N. S. (1970). Is the Brain a Physical System? In Borger & Cioffi (1970).

Swinburne, R. (1980). Review of Scientific Realism and Plasticity of Mind. *Philosophy, 55,* 273–275.

Swinburne, R. (1981). *Faith and Reason.* Oxford: Oxford University Press.

Taylor, C. (1964). *The Explanation of Behavior.* London: Routledge & Kegan Paul.

Taylor, C. (1971). Interpretation and the Sciences of Man. *Review of Metaphysics, 25,* 1–32, 35–45. Reprinted in Taylor (1985).

Taylor, C. (1985). *Philosophy and the Human Sciences: Philosophical Papers.* Cambridge: Cambridge University Press.

Tennant, N. (1984). Intentionality, Syntactic Structure, and the Evolution of Language. In Hookway (1984).

Tennant, N. (1987). Philosophy and Biology: Mutual Enrichment or One-Sided Encroachment. *La Nuova Critica, 1–2,* 39–55.

Thagard, P. (1986). Parallel Computation and the Mind-Body Problem. *Cognitive Science, 10,* 301–318.

Thompson, R. F. (1967). *Foundations of Physiological Psychology.* New York: Harper & Row.

Thompson, R. F. (1975). *Introduction to Physiological Psychology.* New York: Harper & Row.

Thomson, J. J. (1977). *Acts and Other Events.* Ithaca, NY: Cornell University Press.

Torrance, S. (Ed.). (1984). *The Mind and The Machine.* Sussex: Ellis Horwood.

Touretzky, D., & Hinton, G. E. (1988). A Distributed Connectionist Production System. *Cognitive Science, 12,* 423–466.

Trowbridge, D., & McDermott, L. (1980). An Investigation of Student Understanding of the

Concept of Velocity in One Dimension. *American Journal of Physics, 49.*

Turing, A. M. (1937a). On Computable Numbers, With an Application to the Entscheidungsproblem. *Proceedings of the London Mathematical Society, 42,* 230–265.

Turing, A. M. (1937b). Computability and Lambda-Definalilty. *Journal of Symbolic Logic, 2,* 153–163.

Turing, A. M. (1950). Computing Machinery and Intelligence. *Mind, 59,* 433–460.

Tye, M. (1986). The Subjective Qualities of Experience. *Mind, 95,* 1–17.

Van Fraassen, B. C. (1970). On the Extension of Beth's Semantics of Physical Theories. *Philosophy of Science, 37,* 325–338.

Van Fraassen, B. C. (1972). A Formal Approach to the Philosophy of Science. In R. Colodny (Ed.), *Paradigms and Paradoxes* (pp. 303–366). Pittsburgh: University of Pittsburgh.

Van Fraassen, B. C. (1980). *The Scientific Image.* Oxford: Oxford University Press.

Van Fraassen, B. C., & Hooker, C. A. (1976). A Semantic Analysis of Niels Bohr's Philosophy of Quantum Theory. In W. L. Harper & C. A. Hooker (Eds.), *Foundations of Probability Theory, Statistical Inference and Statistical Theories of Science, 3* (pp. 221–241). Dordrecht, Holland: D. Reidel.

VanLehn, K., & Brown, J. S. (1979). Planning Nets: A Representation for Formalizing Analogies and Semantic Models of Procedural Skills. In R. Snow, P. Frederico & W. Montague (Eds.), *Aptitude Learning and Instruction: Cognitive Process Analyses.* Hillsdale, NJ: Lawrence Erlbaum Associates.

Vendler, Z. (1984). *The Matter of Minds.* Oxford: Clarendon Press.

Von Neumann, J. (1958). *The Computer and the Brain.* New Haven: Yale University Press.

Walker, S. (1983). *Animal Thought.* London: Routledge & Kegan Paul.

Warrington, C., & McCarthy, R. (1987). Categories of Knowledge: Further Fractionations and an Attempted Integration. *Brain, 110,* 1273–1296.

Wason, P., & Evans, J. (1975). Dual Processes in Reasonong, *Cognition, 3.*

Wason, P., & Johnson-Laird, P. (1972). *Psychology of Reasoning: Structure and Content.* London: B. T. Batsford.

Watson, R. I. (1973). Psychology: A Prescriptive Science. In M. Henle, J. Jaynes, & J. J. Sullivan (Eds.), *Historical Conceptions of Psychology.* New York: Springer Publishing Co., Inc.

Wilkes, K. V. (1978). *Physicalism.* London: Routledge & Kegan Paul.

Wilkes, K. V. (1981). Functionalism, Psychology, and the Philosophy of Mind. *Philosophical Topics, 12,* 147–168.

Wilkes, K. V. (1983). Realizam i Antirealizam u Psihologiji. *Filozofska Istrazinvanja, 7,* 101–116.

Wilkes, K. V. (1984). Is Consciousness Important? *British Journal for the Philosophy of Science, 35,* 223–243.

Wilkes, K. V. (1984). Pragmatics in Science and Theory in Common Sense. *Inquiry, 27,* 339–361.

Wilkes, K. V. (1986). Nemo Psychologus nisi Physiologus. *Inquiry, 29,* 165–185.

Wilkes, K. V. (1988). *Real People: Personal Identity without Thought Experiments.* Oxford: Oxford University Press.

Wilkes, K. V. (1991). The Long Past and the Short History. In Bogdan (1991c), 144–160.

Wilson, T. (1985). Strangers to Ourselves: The Origins and Accuracy of Beliefs About One's Own Mental States. In J. H. Harvey & G. Weary (Eds.), *Attribution in Contemporary Psychology.* New York: Academic Press.

Wilson, T., Hull, J., & Johnson, J. (1981). Awareness and Self-Perception: Verbal Reports on Internal States. *Journal of Personality and Social Psychology, 40,* 53–71.

Wimsatt, W. (1976a). Reductionism, Levels of Organization, and the Mind-Body Problem. In Globus, Maxwell, & Savodnik (1976).

Wimsatt, W. (1976b). Reductive Explanation: A Functional Account. In R. Cohen, C. Hooker, A. Nicholas, & J. van Evra (Eds.), *PSA 1974.* Dordrecht, Holland: D. Reidel.

Winograd, T. (1972). Understanding Natural Language. *Cognitive Psychology, 1,* 1–191.

Winograd, T. (1981). What Does it Mean to Understand a Language? In Norman (1981).

Winograd, T., & Flores, F. (1986). *Understanding Computers and Cognition: A New Foundation for Design.* New York: Addison-Wesley.

Winston, P. (1975). *The Psychology of Computer Vision.* New York: McGraw Hill.

Wittgenstein, L. (1953). *Philosophical Investigations.* Oxford: Basil Blackwell.

Wittgenstein, L. (1958). *The Blue and Brown Books: Preliminary Studies for the "Philosophical Investigations."* New York: Harper & Row.

Woodfield, A. (Ed.). (1982). *Thought and Object.* Oxford: Oxford University Press.

Wright, L. (1989). *Practical Reasoning.* New York: Harcourt Brace Jovanovich.

Zimbardo, P., Cohen, A., Weisenberg, M., Dworkin, L., & Firestone, I. (1969). The Control of Experimental Pain. In P. Zimbardo (Ed.), *The Cognitive Control of Motivation.* Glenview, IL: Scott Foresman.

Author Index

Subject Index